Dance in America

Dance in America

A READER'S ANTHOLOGY

Mindy Aloff, EDITOR

Foreword by Robert Gottlieb

THE LIBRARY OF AMERICA

Interior design and composition by Gopa & Ted2, Inc.

Distributed to the trade in the United States by
Penguin Random House Inc.
and in Canada by Penguin Random House Canada Ltd.

Library of Congress Control Number: 2018935010
ISBN 978–1–59853–584–6

1 3 5 7 9 10 8 6 4 2

Printed in the United States of America

Dance in America: A Reader's Anthology
is published with support from

BRIAN J. HEIDTKE

and other friends of Library of America

Contents

List of Illustrations
(following page 150)

Isadora Duncan at the Theater of Dionysus, 1903

Bill "Bojangles" Robinson, 1935

Ginger Rogers and Fred Astaire in *Swing Time*, 1936

Merce Cunningham and Carolyn Brown rehearsing
Cunningham's *Suite*, with John Cage at the piano, 1972

Martha Graham, Matt Turney, and Stuart Hodes
in Graham's *Appalachian Spring*

Members of the Artistic Committee of Ballet Theatre, 1947.
Jerome Robbins, Agnes de Mille, Oliver Smith, and Aaron
Copland surrounding Lucia Chase, in Chase's apartment

George Balanchine and Lincoln Kirstein, in Kirstein's home,
c. early 1960s

Alvin Ailey in Ailey's *Hermit Songs*, 1961

Paul Taylor in his *Option*, 1962

Twyla Tharp, 1992

Suzanne Farrell in George Balanchine's *Vienna Waltzes*, 1978

Michael Jackson, 1989

Foreword

by Robert Gottlieb

EDITING ANTHOLOGIES is a fascination, an adventure, a drudgery, a responsibility. It can be thrilling, when you stumble on something totally unexpected and exciting, or deflating, when you realize, too late, that you've missed something terrific or couldn't get the rights (or afford them) for something you love. It's a rollercoaster ride—today you think what you've amassed is wonderful and original; tomorrow you think it's the same old stuff warmed over. Then the problems: How do you structure it? How do you balance the absolute essentials with the surprises? How do you balance your own predilections with your assumptions about what the presumed readership has a right to expect? Since an anthology is just as much about good writing as about touching all bases, what do you do when a piece of writing doesn't do justice to a subject that demands attention? And what about length—not what the reader will tolerate, but what the publisher will tolerate?

Putting an anthology together is a slow process, a process of accretion, and one with no natural cutting-off point. You may hope you've covered the waterfront, but you know that your subject is inexhaustible. You may be desperate to put the book to bed after three, five, ten years of either concentrated or sporadic reading, of judging, comparing, contrasting. But you also want to go on forever—because you love the subject to begin with (or you wouldn't be doing this book), and you're learning more and more as you proceed; and because you *know* that you'll find gold around the corner if you just don't flag. I know all this from experience, having produced several monstersized anthologies myself, one of them on dance writing (very different from this volume, which, since it comes from Library of *America*, is by definition devoted to American writing and American subjects).

I came to this project late, although I'd been talking about it occasionally with my friend Mindy Aloff almost from the moment she took on the job of editing it, since what could be more fun than sharing notions and opinions with someone whose taste and judgment you're greatly in sympathy with on a subject you both love? My practical involvement began with my masochistically volunteering to help out with the most gnarly aspect of any anthology: permissions. (I have all too much experience dealing with them, having worked on anthologies from my earliest days in publishing—*The Ladies Home Journal Treasury*, God help me—through my own books. It's hell, but I was eager to be useful to this book in particular as well as to Library of America, which I revere.) Then, of course, I couldn't resist making some editorial suggestions to Mindy, but only to complement and fill out her already heroic groundwork. Amazingly, our two dance anthologies barely coincide: There can't be more than two or three overlaps. (There would have been more if I'd been able to read her table of contents before completing mine!)

What you'll find here are the bedrock writers: America's two magisterial dance critics, Edwin Denby and Arlene Croce, without whom such a volume would be a travesty, and other writers whose work is beyond question essential: the prodigious Lincoln Kirstein; Agnes de Mille, whom many of us value more as a writer than as a choreographer. But also complete surprises, like John Updike (on Gene Kelly), Edmund Wilson (on The Follies), Black Elk on the Horse Dance, Yehuda Hyman on "Three Hasidic Dances"—how did Mindy come up with *that* one?—a fascinating smorgasbord of texts by George Balanchine (including a letter to Lincoln Kirstein on the death of his mother); Ralph Waldo Emerson on Fanny Elssler; Léonide Massine on working at the Roxy; W. H. Auden on *The Nutcracker*; and on and on. And then there's material simply unavailable elsewhere: Claudia Roth Pierpont's superb analysis of *The Four Temperaments* and Christopher Caines's anatomy of Antony Tudor, both written for this volume; a long, probing letter by Jerome Robbins to a friend, dictated and probably never mailed, on choreography; and a garland of scintillating pieces by Joan Acocella written for the New York magazine *7 Days*, which lasted two years in the late 1980s—and which have never been reprinted. That's an editorial coup.

The final result, as Mindy will discover, will be that she won't have (couldn't have) pleased everyone. Why include *this*? Why not *that*? Why poems? Why not more poems? Why not fiction? Why not more on postmodern dance? Why *anything* on postmodern dance? This book, as it had to be and should be, is a reflection of her own very wide interests and knowledge, not mine or yours. I've done my own book—now you can project, if not publish, your own.

Participating in this venture has been a pleasure and an education, and I'm grateful to Mindy and to Library of America for allowing me to do so.

Introduction

BY MINDY ALOFF

A NTHOLOGY, an English term that goes back some four centuries, is
derived from a much older Greek word (*anthologia*), which
means "a collection of flowers." The reference is to a legendary early
example of the genre whose title, in English, is *The Garland*. In this
lost, first-century BCE gathering of lyrics or epigrams, by a constel-
lation of Greek poets, each contributor was assigned an individual
flower, herb, or plant, creating not a bouquet but rather a crafted,
circular headpiece or wreath worked into a figure of appreciation or
praise.

Although, in our own era, the subjects of anthologies range much
further afield than the short poem or epigram, the traditional association of anthologies and poetry, organized according to an alphabetical
arrangement, informs our book. You'll find in it as well some of the
mad-scientist epiphanies crucial to the daunting effort of conducting
the experience of dance—visceral, occasionally transcendental—from
inchoate sensations into the exacting and somewhat idiosyncratic
English language.

Of course, here in the twenty-first century, even a grouping of
dance writings in English—one of the more narrowly specialized subjects for a literary anthology—has had predecessors. Out of respect
and affection, I've refrained insofar as I could from stepping on the
remarkable work of previous dance anthologists. Outstanding in
this group is Robert Gottlieb, whom I've known for over thirty years
and whose massive anthology *Reading Dance* is the sine qua non of
anthologies on the subject. As a writer, he was on my earliest list of
contributors—a wish list, incidentally, that resulted in some 2,000
pages by nearly 200 authors for a book that was expected to cover
four centuries of writing in 550 pages. Bob's two entries made cut
after cut long before he was in any way involved as advisor to this

project. He has provided significant help in two areas: One was editorial (his suggestions ranged from the adagio team of the De Marcos to Stuart Hodes's fraught and loving account of Martha Graham to the hilarious Johnny Mercer lyric about learning to dance at Arthur Murray's). And then Bob flung himself "masochistically," as he says, into the whole quagmire of permissions, for both the text and the picture section that ornaments the book.

Our anthology certainly includes work by writers of enduring renown, but it was not intended as a book of greatest hits by hall of famers. Nor was it meant to serve as a surrogate history of American dance or even of "important" or controversial American dance writing. At best, a book this size can only begin to approach its vast subject, if, by "American dance," one means more than dance traditions that were invented and developed here—like tap—but also at least several of the many that, transplanted from elsewhere, have thrived here. In the years I worked on it, I evolved a table of contents by repeatedly asking myself the same set of questions. What is a "Library of America" writer? What does "America" mean in this context? Must an example of "dance writing" reanimate a specific dance or performance? What kind of negotiations have to take place between focusing on writers and focusing on subjects? To what extent does one let practical considerations impinge on pure meritocracy? Wonderful writings on Balanchine were far more numerous than on any other figure in American dance: Is it okay to represent this lopsided proportion in the table of contents?

Professional dance critics per se in America didn't really emerge until John Martin was appointed the Dance Critic of *The New York Times*, in 1927. Yet, well back into the nineteenth century, freelance writers and New York correspondents for newspapers around the country contributed theatrical articles and reviews with an emphasis on dance. They can be found in the periodicals of Boston and Philadelphia, where there was (to me, anyway) a surprising amount of ballet along with tap and other vernacular dancing. *The Brooklyn Daily Eagle*, *The Oshkosh Daily Northwestern* (Wisconsin), and the *Advertiser* (Mobile, Tennessee) are just a representative trio of the many periodicals that published reports on the 1866 Niblo's Garden ballet-vaudeville spectacle, *The Black Crook*, in Manhattan, and on the regional versions of the show performed by touring groups and local productions into the 1880s. They also covered the copycat musical spectacles with dancing (*The White Faun, La Barbe-bleue*). Long before World War I, the young Carl Van Vechten was filing occasional dance reviews as an assistant music critic for the *Times*. Farther north, the drama and music critic H. T. Parker was offering readers of *The Boston Evening Transcript* indelible reviews of ballet and modern dancers from the first decade of the twentieth century up to the threshold of the Great Depression. Furthermore, individuals who didn't think of themselves as arts writers at all, such as the painter George Catlin in the early nineteenth century, were exercising their keen perceptions and vivid descriptive powers in chronicling ritual and dance movement, patching these skills into writings intended as travelogues or diaries or anthropological reports.

When I considered Catlin's article, I did stop to wonder whether, say, an anthology of writing on drama in America would reach out to Edwin Denby's landmark 1936 review of the epic preparations for a village marriage in "Nijinska's *Noces*" or whether an anthology of art in America would adopt Stark Young's 1932 appreciation of the abstract patterns in the choreography of Martha Graham. That is, could a widely embracing anthology of dance prove too unconventional for its own good? I decided that it's both interesting and fun to represent a writer—John Updike, for instance—most widely known for his fiction, with a profile of Gene Kelly. Yet, what happens if much admired dance artists aren't accounted for? Or entire dance genres? Will I be sentenced to solitary if I can't find an affordable, lucid article on an "all-American" tradition like square dancing? The last question brings up the issue of editorial subjectivity: one of my rules for myself was that I'm a reader like everyone else, and that, although the book represents more than my own taste, each entry not only had to satisfy external criteria—it had to attract me to it as well.

A huge question, as you might suppose, was: What should this anthology mean by "America"? The entire hemisphere, half the hemisphere, or the United States? If the last, suppose that American dancers were brilliantly written of by non-Americans, such as the British authors Charles Dickens, Clive Barnes, and Alastair Macaulay? (Of course, I include them—along with their compatriots W. H. Auden and David Vaughan and the Russian-born George Balanchine, who became American citizens.)

Yet what does an anthologist of dance writing in America (meaning the U.S.) do with the fact that, prior to 1776, there *was* no United States? In roaming through the catalogs of the Library of Congress and the New York Public Library for the Performing Arts at Lincoln Center, I learned that, with world enough and time, I might be able to find some arresting observations of Native American dancers in the journals and reports from seventeenth- and possibly sixteenth-century expeditions by European explorers and missionaries to the New World. The late folklorist Roger D. Abrahams, whose research on African American cultural practices and expressions I particularly admired, sent me his notes about slave drivers' practice, going back to the origins of the slave trade, of forcing parched, starving, half-suffocated Africans to dance on deck in the sea air, in order to bring at least some of them to U.S. ports alive. However, his notes were not yet writings. From the eighteenth century, I did find cameos of ballroom dancing, some featuring those dancing Revolutionaries President and Mrs. George Washington, though they were too brief to anthologize. I also consulted how-to manuals of social dancing written by French dancing masters who had emigrated to North America, many of them fleeing the Reign of Terror in France. But, though historically significant, examples from this pre- and early post-Revolutionary period don't make for illuminating or enjoyable reading unless you're a dance historian. The oldest entry in this anthology by virtue of its composition, then, is from the plainspoken, appealingly uninflated memoir of Philadelphia theatrical dancer (self-taught in folk dance and ballet), dancemaker, puppeteer, all-around thespian, and theater entrepreneur John Durang—a document hand-written (and delightfully hand-illustrated in watercolors) by him around 1821 from daybooks and papers drafted between the end of the eighteenth century and the early part of the nineteenth, yet published for the first time only in 1966.

In terms of flower garlands, the most important dance writing published in the colonies and early years of the United States would arguably be correlated with deadly nightshade and Venus flytraps: that is, publications railing against the practice of dance as a channel to corruption, especially the corruption of women, followed by a one-way express chute to Hell. The New England Mathers, Increase and his son Cotton, are the most notorious of the early anti-dance

polemicists, and, given their legalistic penchant for piling up eviden-
tiary quotations from Scripture, they are among the most unreadable.
An excellent account of why dancing—social and theatrical—has had
an uphill battle for recognition, much less encouragement, as an art
and worthy amateur practice in this country is authoritatively and
engagingly told by Ann Wagner in *Adversaries of Dance: From the
Puritans to the Present* (1997), a book much too long and seamlessly
written to excerpt, yet a candidate for my informal award of best social
history of dancing in America.

For a variety of reasons, I reluctantly let go of essays I value concerning dance history, dance anthropology, dance aesthetics, dance
technique, and dance notation. With the exception of Zora Neale
Hurston's vivid tale of dancing as a kind of spell, I put aside works
of fiction that contain carefully researched scenes of dancing. And
I reluctantly excluded many more examples of dance criticism and
reviewing. Retained were a number of poems, letters, excerpts from
journals, ephemera, transcripts of oral statements, a couple of translations into English (Nicholas Black Elk's memoir and Balanchine's
interview on what he thought makes American dance American—
given in French!), and essay-reviews written directly for the Internet, such as Tobi Tobias's on Trisha Brown and Nancy Dalva's almost
dreamlike column on Eiko and Koma. As the twentieth century was
not only an abundant period of theatrical dancing but also the century
of film, I was thrilled to discover almost-forgotten profiles of Fred
Astaire and Gene Kelly and the fine review by Walter Terry of Walt
Disney's 1940 *Fantasia* and to be able to include the clarifying story
of dance and the camera by Arlene Croce, herself a peerless writer on
Astaire and Ginger Rogers and, at points in her career, a film critic.
Balanchine's own interwar essay on dance fantasy and film is, with
Croce's, a writing that has enchanted me for several decades; like most
of Mr. B's expressions in any medium, it is full of surprises.

It is sometimes said that America has not produced much dance
literature of consequence. I hope that this anthology demonstrates
that this isn't true.

This anthology is dedicated to the New York Public Library for the
Performing Arts at Lincoln Center, a palace of learning, whose vast
and, in many cases, irreplaceable holdings constitute a celebration

and a defense of our need for music, dance, pantomime, and theater. The Library is open to all, for free. And yet the democracy of its public access is inseparable from the uncommon ideals its materials embody. The Library offers the best to the most, and it makes everyone who uses it an elite cadet in service of civilization.

Dance in America

Joan Acocella (1945–)

Joan Acocella has been the dance critic of *The New Yorker* for almost twenty years now—earlier she wrote on dance for *The Village Voice*, *Dance Magazine* (where she was also the reviews editor), *The Financial Times*, and *7 Days*, a weekly news and culture periodical—but her wide range of interests has led her to write deeply as well on such non-dance topics as multiple personality disorder and agenda-ridden criticism of Willa Cather. Among her books are a ground-breaking biography of Mark Morris, a rich collection of her pieces (*Twenty-Eight Artists and Two Saints*—the two saints are Mary Magdalene and Joan of Arc), and the unexpurgated edition of Nijinsky's diary. Like so many dance writers, she fell in love with ballet when she began watching New York City Ballet, but unlike most dance writers, she also learned a good deal about how ballet works backstage during the period when she was a dance mother, her son a School of American Ballet student who did duty in Balanchine's *Nutcracker*.

Acocella has been the recipient of a Guggenheim fellowship, currently appears in *The New York Review of Books*, and has twice been honored by the American Academy of Arts and Letters. She is represented below by four brilliant pieces from the sadly defunct journal *7 Days*.

800 Yards of Shiny Stuff

CLAUDIO SEGOVIA and Hector Orezzoli are less like directors than like men in love. First with *Tango Argentino*, then with *Flamenco Puro*, and now with *Black and Blue*, a tribute to black jazz and blues, these two Argentinean set designers have taken a music-and-dance tradition they love and created a setting for it, a way to show it off.

More than that, they have looked hard at it, studied it, asked *it* what it needed. The tango dancers don't want a choreographer? Fine, let them make their own numbers. The flamenco women all weigh 200 pounds? No problem—let out the dresses. Half the great tap dancers in the world are over 70? No sweat, just get a hotel close to the theater.

Consequently, these cabaret traditions that you would imagine could never be torn from their original contexts without losing their souls actually make it to Broadway intact. The performers look a little surprised, perhaps, to be wearing such gorgeous clothes, but what is amazing is how natural everyone acts. Like a loved creature, the tradition shines and expands, plump and happy, and shows you what it's got—all its beauties.

Like *Tango* and *Flamenco*, *Black and Blue* is a revue. There are five groups of performers: the 14-piece orchestra, featuring Sir Roland Hanna; the three rhythm-and-blues singers, Ruth Brown, Linda Hopkins, and Carrie Smith; the five "hoofers," or old-time tappers—Ralph Brown and Lon Chaney together with the bebop kings Bunny Briggs and Jimmy Slyde, and also Dianne Walker (who's not old, just accomplished); the "younger generation," consisting of three child tappers—Savion Glover, age 15, of *Tap Dance Kid* fame, and two little girls, Cyd Glover (no relation) and Dormeshia Sumbry, both 13; and, finally, the 16 corps dancers.

In various combinations, these people follow one another, routine after routine. In comes Carrie Smith, singing "I Want a Big Butter and Egg Man." To her side are her musicians—Sir Roland plinkety-plink on the piano, Jake Porter tootly-toot on his silver trumpet—and soon there arrive three cute guys in plaid trousers, doing one of those gentle, flickety-flick, stay-up-in-the-air tap numbers. The composition is like a perfect bouquet: Smith is all mellow bigness, gleaming in her orange velvet, sliding luxuriantly into her low notes, while the men are all light, playful sweetness—everything she could ever want from a butter-and-egg man.

In another number, another composition altogether. The curtain rises on a backdrop pierced by a thousand stars—the audience gasps—and, in front of it, Ruth Brown in a tiara and a vast, cascading gown. What will she sing? "Fly Me to the Moon"? "Vissi d'Arte"? She opens her mouth and out comes "If I Can't Sell It, I'll Keep Sittin' on

It" (". . . ain't no need to give it away"), a thrillingly dirty song that is ostensibly about the chair that the singer is sitting on but is really about you-know-what. This grand joke was the hit of the night.

With every roll of the dice, out shakes some new wonder. In his solo, Bunny Briggs knocks off maybe 60 or 70 taps before he'll re-acknowledge the beat. (You again? he seems to say. You still here?) A dancer named Kyme, a Josephine Baker look-alike, comes out in silver shorts and a total-body boa and demurely sings—"Ahm confessin' that ah love you"—while doing an unforgettable dance: her beautiful strong torso digs into the musical phrase like a surfer riding a wave, while her arms waft like palm trees overhead. Understandably, God sends her four men to choose from.

In a vernacular tradition such as this, dependent on improvisation, there is a great deal of heroism attached to the act of performance. People don't become jazz singers or jazz dancers for the money; this is *la forza del destino*. Without any *Chorus Line*-type homiletics, Segovia and Orezzoli pay tribute to this fact. Everything in the show seems to be a solo, even the group numbers. Everyone is allowed to shine in a personal and individual way. When the orchestra first appears, up they stand, one by one—the first trumpet, then the second, then the clarinet, then the trombone—to say by their songs who they are. When Carrie Smith's three butter-and-egg-men aspirants come jiving in, each one gets a moment to show his special stuff.

I know this is part of the tradition of jazz—solos, riffs—but Segovia and Orezzoli seem to understand better than most other people how to *present* something. All the scenography serves this goal. The decor has no realism; there is no "place" where this show happens. The set, lush though it is, is basically all just curtains and colored backdrops and various shapes—planes and discs and such—the purpose of which is to frame the artists as handsomely as possible. A special scenographic fuss is made over the three singers. They are always appearing and disappearing into and out of the floorboards. Carrie Smith sings "Am I Blue" while perched on a swing 18 feet in the air. (Her train, consisting of about 800 yards of white fluff, is held by four obliging guys in tuxedos.) Earlier, she sings "I've Got a Right to Sing the Blues" while reclining backward on a huge disk. This last bit didn't come off well—she looked like a big anchovy on a pizza—

but for the most part the sets made the singers look like queens. The costumes too. I think everyone in the audience loved this parade of glorious gowns, all feathers and gold, tassels and sparkles, and it is nice to know that you don't have to have a figure like Diana Ross to get a pretty dress.

Because everything is set off like a jewel, the show has a look of huge abundance, huge bounty and variety: a whole Macy's, a whole Museum of Natural History of jazz—everything you could ask for. There are dancers who are flickery-light (the elegant Bernard Manners), and others who are low-down, pelvic. And the contrasts between the singers! Ruth Brown is all ferocity and wit and eyeball-rolling; she looks like Charles Ludlam, only shorter. Linda Hopkins, whatever she is singing, always seems still to be a gospel singer, her voice breaking in ecstasy and her face turning up to heaven. Carrie Smith's voice is big, luxuriant, warm—very feminine. You want to crawl into it and go to sleep. The only things in the show that lacked variety were Henry LeTang's ensemble dances; they always seemed to be the same number.

More than variety, the show gives an impression of unity. As with *Tango* and *Flamenco*, what is so moving about *Black and Blue* is that it seems to sum up a whole tradition. All the great central themes of black music—the playfulness, the sexiness, the religiosity, the great tidal wave of sorrow—are all there. And as you look at the show, number after number, it seems that all the history of jazz music and jazz dance is there. In the elegant (and immensely difficult) slow tap number "Memories of You" you feel the presence of Honi Coles and Cholly Atkins, the grand masters of slow tap. (Not for nothing do you feel this; Cholly Atkins choreographed the number.) In Savion Glover's elongated rhythmic line—he too plays catch-me-if-you-can with the beat—you can see the tradition of musical heterodoxy handed down to him by the be-boppers, by Baby Laurence, who is dead, and by Jimmy Slyde and Bunny Briggs, who are up there on the stage patting Savion on the head. You look at the staircase that Savion dances on and you remember Bill Robinson's stair dance and the Nicholas Brothers' famous jump-down-the-stairs-in-splits routine (Fayard Nicholas worked on the show; it was he who made that adorable "Butter and Egg Man" dance). You look at the pelvic miracles that constitute the lindy number and in your brain you see again Mura Dehn's immortal films of the Savoy Ballroom lindy hoppers. And indeed, one of those lindy hoppers, Frankie Manning, choreographed this number.

You look, finally, at little Dormeshia Sumbry, and you can't believe your eyes, because here on a 13-year-old girl is the class and musical know-how—and the beautiful upper body, riding easy and cool over the pelvis—of the great old male tappers. And one thing more. When she finishes a step, Dormeshia's face scrunches up into a sudden little private smile, as if, oooh, she's so happy to be doing this and, oooh, didn't that come out just right. John Bubbles, the creator of rhythm tap, who died almost three years ago, had that same little squinty smile, that same sweet self-enjoyment. And so when you look at Dormeshia you feel that everyone is there, all the jazz artists, the living and the dead, and that the dead smile down on the living.

February 8, 1989

Patty McBride's Last Bow

LAST MONTH Patricia McBride took her final bow with New York City Ballet, and we lost one of our great artists to Bloomington, Ind. There, as she tells it, she will garden, look after the children (Christopher, 7, and Melanie, 10), and, together with her husband, Jean-Pierre Bonnefoux, another ex-NYCB principal, teach in the dance department of Indiana University. ("I even have tenure," she says wonderingly.) What she won't do is perform for New York City Ballet. After 30 years with the company—she joined in 1959, became a principal dancer in 1961, became an actual star in the late '60s— McBride has retired, age 46.

For a ballet dancer this is not too early, as witness the late careers of Rudolf Nureyev and Alicia Alonso. (Alonso, now over 70 and nearly blind, this year took the role of Aphrodite in a new work for the National Ballet of Cuba, of which she is, needless to say, the director.) So it's not wrong, just sad, that McBride has left us.

She didn't have a natural ballet body. She was short (5-feet-3) and bony, with an S-curve to her spine, and her feet had too much arch and too little turnout. But she had a wonderful stage face—American-pretty, with big, shiny eyes—and pale white skin that looked terrific in a pink tutu. She had a sweet easiness in ordinary steps—she was famous for her skips—and she carried her breastbone high, which gave her the look of a noble little animal.

She worked like a devil, but unlike most extra-hard workers, she had no grimness about her. She was gay and humorous and warm. When partnered, she always looked at the man. Whoever it was, that's who she was in love with, or at least happy to be on this date with. When not looking at him she looked at us, glad that we had come, pleased to see us. I have never known a dancer who had a more natural rapport with the audience. Children adored her. (Her picture still hangs over my son's desk.) So did everyone else. This or that person might have a different favorite, but no one didn't love Patty McBride.

And how, given these qualities, did she not become a tiresome little yum-yum, a cloying little ballerina doll? Especially since, given these qualities, she was so often cast as a doll (*Steadfast Tin Soldier*, *Harlequinade*) or the spunky girl next door (*Tarantella*, *Coppélia*, *Rubies*)? As with most problems on the highest level of ballet style, the answer has to do with a moral quality, translated into some special effort in dancing. This may consist of nothing more than the dancer's willingness, for those 20 or 30 minutes on the stage, to go on unceasingly, from one minute to the next, *imagining* the role—hearing the music newly, pouncing on it freshly—rather than letting it imagine her, and thus falling into formula. McBride was a soubrette, but with so little of the dead crust of cliché normally attached to that type—the freckle-faced pertness, the panty-peek erotics—that you hesitate to use the term in her presence. Better to say that she often got roles that glorified woman not as the Virgin Mary or The Love That Kills but as, for example, Claudette Colbert—wit, sparkle, common sense—and that she made each one of them different and new.

She felt, though, that she was typecast as a soubrette, and she longed occasionally to be something else: more romantic, more tragic—"You know, *flowy*," as she puts it. Balanchine made a few such roles for her—in *Who Cares?*, in *Divertimento from "Le Baiser de la Fée,"* in *Brahms-Schoenberg Quartet*—and to see her in them was a special heartbreak. For being in a flowy role did not change her personality. She remained the same: spiky and quick, "normal" and fresh—like us, if we were better. And this made her seem both noble and particularly vulnerable in the face of tragedy. That *she*, with no barge of Cleopatra, no armor of Brunhilde, should get caught in this big wave of love and sorrow seemed unbearable. It was as if a little American girl had gotten caught in a European fate.

And how nakedly she gave herself to it! In the *Brahms-Schoenberg* she appeared in a darkened ballroom, with her man. Her gown was pink and black, night and fire. Again and again the man lifted her, facing him, up into the air and then, on her descent, clasped her to his chest. As she hung there momentarily in the air, that beautiful breastbone of hers pressed to his, she made a double image. She was a high flier, triumphant, the Winged Victory. And she was caught, a butterfly pinned alive to the specimen board.

That's passion, right? Victory and surrender—we've seen it before. But to see it on McBride, to see her little bones gathered into that sweeping onrush and her sweet, open face tilt back in grave acknowledgment ("This is the most important thing that will ever happen in my life"), was to feel it in a new way. In that moment she embodied a great democratic fantasy: that an ordinary girl can have a big romance. And that in turn is a metaphor for our belief that to each of us something really big can happen.

All ballerinas, I imagine, tap into that belief, but at different angles. With Suzanne Farrell, for example, she is the thing that happens to us. With McBride, she is the us to whom it happens, and so we watch her with a special, unresisting love.

August 30, 1989

Rattled Bones

L AST WEEK, when Ennosuke Ichikawa III arrived here from Tokyo with his 60-man Kabuki troupe, he was heralded by all the sort of publicity that, with tiresome inevitability, accompanies every person identified as a reformer in a traditional field. Ennosuke has "shocked conservatives," said the press release, enlisting our liberal sentiments. Likewise *New York* magazine: once this "maverick" broke loose, it said, "the sushi hit the fan." "Ennosuke Rattles Kabuki's Venerable Bones," ran the headline on the *Times*' Sunday piece. Fogies beware.

The irony is that nobody around here really *wants* to see Kabuki's bones rattled. Whatever the situation in Japan—presumably it is comparable to the push for opera reform here—the Westerners I know who like Kabuki do so precisely because it is old-style, high-style ritualistic theater. They love its gorgeous clothes and slow pace. They love the *onnagata*, the male actors who specialize in women's roles, and out-female the female. (There are no women performers in Kabuki.) They love the dark deeds—lethal amours, enthusiastic suicides—and the great, sprawling plots: how everyone's mother had a complicated life, with the result that the hero invariably has a slew of jealous half-brothers, at least one of whom he is destined unwittingly to kill in battle. They love the *mie*, those freeze-frame poses where the performers stand stock still and stare out at us with a grisly cross-eyed stare: an action that, in the hands of certain Kabuki masters, is said to protect audience members from illness for up to a year.

They love all this—certainly I do—and when confronted with reform are not likely to shout hooray or throw their sushi into the fan but simply to ask whether the reform will make Kabuki more interesting.

In the case of Ennosuke's reforms, the answer is: not really. The company presented two plays, an abridged version of *Yoshitsune Senbonzakura* ("Yoshitsune and the Thousand Cherry Trees"), from 1747, about a brave hero caught in the grips of dynastic warfare, and *Kurozuka* ("The Black Mound"), which was adapted to Kabuki in 1939 from the more staid Noh theater and concerns a mild-mannered old lady who is also a man-eating demon. The plots are everything you could wish for. Yoshitsune has the half-brother problem, which has forced him to flee to a mountain retreat with his retainers. One of these, however, turns out to be a 400-year-old fox, who is following Yoshitsune around in the morbid hope of obtaining a certain drum, made from the skin of his parents, that Yoshitsune owns. Eventually the fox gets the drum, and the half-brother his comeuppance, but not until there has been a big fight, with evil priests leaping off buildings and dying upside down in midair. As for the old lady/monster play, how can it fail? At one point a character checks out her back parlor and emerges to report that it is full of bones with gobbets of flesh still hanging off them and bleeding onto the floor.

The pleasure here is not just of the Brian DePalma sort. Kabuki is profound. As men turn into foxes and foxes into gods, we feel the relatedness of all things—the animal, human, and spirit worlds—and as the half-brothers and forgotten sins turn up on the heroes' doorsteps, we have the sense, no different from in Dickens or the *Oresteia*, of how the past is never past, how we go on living it. Looking at Kabuki, we see the whole world knit together, bound by forces—loyalty, hatred, old loves—that we surely recognize. These monsters are real.

And Ennosuke's troupe serves it all up with the full, gaudy splendor for which Kabuki is famous. The men wear golden trousers that trail 10 feet behind them. The ladies in waiting wear purple kimonos hemmed in scarlet and pull them forward in front so that their rear ends are demurely outlined. Whole palaces rise up out of the floor and scoot in and out of the wings. The half-brother wears a hairdo that looks like a fire in a grain silo.

But what is scarce in these proceedings is the kind of delicate, subtle dancing that we know from the Grand Kabuki. Ennosuke's reforms are several. He has jacked up the stagecraft. He has employed women in artistic capacities (but not onstage). But his most comprehensive and striking reform has been the revival of the old tradition of *keren*, or physical clowning—animal impersonations, trap-door disappearances, blink-of-an-eye costume changes. Playing the fox in *Yoshitsune*, Ennosuke materialized on a staircase so suddenly that I had to ask the person next to me what had happened. Soon thereafter he vanished into the floor of a porch, reappeared in front of the house two seconds later in a totally different costume, then disappeared through a hole in the wall, reappeared immediately on the other side of the stage in a costume from ten minutes before, then dematerialized and a minute later—shazam!—tumbled out from under the roof of the house, again recostumed. Roadrunner could not have done better. At the end of the play, he took off into the sky on wires in a storm of cherry blossoms.

All this is fun, but when I think of what it takes the place of, it's a little less fun. I remember, when the Grand Kabuki was here four years ago, a scene in which two lovers (it was Kataoka Takao and the famous *onnagata* Bando Tamasaburo V) stood on a moonlit riverbank and did a love duet whose elegant fittings and knittings—archings and dippings, foldings and unfoldings, all pivoting on the sure central axis of the Kabuki dancer—were unforgettable. (Once it was over, he ax-murdered her, but that's another story.) No falling down a hole, however deft, can compete with something like this. Furthermore,

Ennosuke's tricks did not extend beyond the mere getting the thing done. He may have flown, but not like Mary Martin. Worse, he tended to save his energy for the tricks, so that when he was not disappearing or reappearing he seemed to go a little slack. The program says he has performed this fox role more than 700 times, and you can tell. Finally, it was not just Ennosuke's energy that was organized around his *keren*; it was the whole troupe's. Ennosuke is apparently the star of all his shows, and everything is focused on what he is doing. If he's not dancing, nobody is.

There are exceptions. In *Kurozuka* a little servant got to do a wonderful comic dance as he escaped from the demon. (He was played by Ennosuke's brother, so maybe he got a special favor.) And before that, the demon herself did a long, delicate dance as she considered the thought, just put into her mind by a priest, that despite her sins she might still achieve salvation. But since she was, of course, Ennosuke, and since he is just shy of 50 years old, the dance could have been a lot more delicate.

This de-emphasis of dance is a big shame. Just as Kabuki dancing swivels on a central axis, so Kabuki cosmology seems to me to revolve around the dancing. The dancing is the spine of the world's meaning. The way the dancers show their strength and their lovely manners, the way they answer one another's movements and the way the parts of their bodies answer one another: this seems to me, beyond character and story—or *within* them—the concrete pledge that everything in the world is connected, and therefore beautiful.

September 20, 1989

Tutu Much

IN the production of the *Don Quixote* pas de deux now being performed by the all-male Ballets Trockadero de Monte Carlo at City Center, the cavalier, as he comes onstage to perform his solo, does a long, slow walk that is probably the funniest thing to be seen in New York right now. How to describe this walk? How to say all the things that it is? It is a big, unhurried strut, going the full circle of the stage. It is imperious, it is portentous, it seems to move on pneumatic tubing.

JOAN ACOCELLA } 13

It is faintly lubricious. "Look at these haunches," it says. (In fact, the haunches of Alexis Ivanovitch Lermontov, the performer in question, are rather large and soft and look, how to say, as if they have been through a great deal.) "Wait till you see what I'm about to do," it says. And what Lermontov then does is the most inept, most hopelessly maladroit variation ever unleashed on a ballet stage. Having finished it, he looks out between the two flaps of his flaxen wig and says to us with his eyes, "I am dance."

It is an absolutely heavenly routine—stupider than anything you have ever seen in your life—and really, it is only Fernando Bujones, just pushed a little bit further.

This is the Trockadero's forte, to take the inherent absurdities of ballet and hold them up to view. Things that go on too long, things that are always done wrong and then have to be covered up, things that look funny—all these things they show us. My favorite is their lesson in pirouettes. Now, in a pirouette, a dancer doesn't just have to turn; she has to finish the turn pointing in a certain direction. Otherwise, the step she's going to do next will come out wrong. Many tense moments in ballet are related to this fact. You can see cavaliers working the Sugar Plum Fairy's waist as if she were a drain pipe they were trying to screw into place, and you can see Sugar Plum Fairies waiting with ill-concealed wrath until the idiot ("Why did they have to give me stupid Ricardo? Why can't I have Pavka? Why does Valentina always get Pavka?") gets them pointing the right way so that they can then melt—here is my heart!—into a ravished backbend.

You also see situations where the man just stops the woman in the wrong place, so that when she then goes into her arabesque, the leg she sticks out goes not into the air but into his abdomen, unless he quickly gets out of the way. And you can see situations where the man looks at the woman right as she's coming 'round the bend and says to her with his eyes, "Do we stop now, or do we go for another one?" And they hesitate, deciding, not knowing that having hesitated, they are already lost.

All these things the Trocks (the group's nickname) know well. The company was founded by three ballet fanatics—Peter Anastos, now director of Garden State Ballet; Antony Bassae, now dead of AIDS; Natch Taylor (a.k.a. Alexis Ivanovitch Lermontov), present director of the troupe—and the *danse d'école* has no secrets from them. The grand pas de deux of their *Swan Lake*, danced by Lermontov with Ludmilla Bolshoya (Rusty Curcio), the troupe's hamhocked little virtuosa, is a veritable decathlon of pirouette challenges: Bolshoya's leg swinging out in *à la seconde* like a piece of loose timber (Lermontov ducks), Lermontov stopping Bolshoya too soon in pirouette and she, enterprising girl that she is, finishing the job by sticking her hand smack against his chest and just pushing herself the rest of the way. Elsewhere, all the dancers do is just make something a little more emphatic—in the *Swan Lake* and *Don Quixote* they are dancing the traditional choreography—and it becomes funny.

For ballet is inherently extreme, elaborate, too much. And like most satirists, the Trocks get their laughs, or some of them, by taking the side of common sense. Against ballet's ideality—the moonglow, the dream-death, the *perfectness* of everything—they hold up reality: a prince who's a wimp, a swan queen who counts the roses in her curtain-call bouquet. Instead of ease, they show us effort. Instead of women, they show us men, with chest hair creeping out over their satin bodices like absurdity peeping out from behind beauty.

But then, like a trick box, the mechanism springs, and absurdity gives way again to beauty. I remember when I first saw this. In the *Swan Lake* there is a corps of six swans, each awful in her own way: one grimacing, one built like a fireplug, one who looks like Gracie Allen. But at the end of their ensemble dance they fall to the floor in a six-petaled flower formation, and suddenly—maybe it's the tulle— they look pretty. Likewise, in Peter Anastos' *École de Ballet*, there's a perfectly stupid little dance recital, but it's so exquisitely done that it starts to look like a Degas, each girl a humble vessel of ballerina dreams. And the fact that these big hairy boys could do this, could put flowers in their hair and charm us, makes life itself take on a sort of moonglow, a giddy instability: under every toadstool, a firefly.

What I love about the Trocks besides this is that they truly teach us what ballet is. Looking at their feet, we see, by its absence, what an arch is. Looking at the dauntless Ludmilla knock off her 32 fouettés with, however, her foot sticking off the end of her working leg as if it had been tacked on at the last minute, we understand what a stretched foot is and what this means to ballet. Likewise, turnout, a stretched knee, a waistline, a woman: we seem to see these things for the first time because they're not there.

The Trocks are best in their renditions of the classics—the *Don Quixote*, the *Swan Lake*, the *Black Swan*—and in the minutely observed ballet parodies that Peter Anastos made for them, including *Go for Barocco* (after Balanchine) and *Yes, Virginia, Another Piano Ballet* (Jerome Robbins) as well as the lovable *École de Ballet*. In the slow movement of *Go for Barocco* the men actually become beautiful dancers, pointe work and all. The troupe's new Paul Taylor send-up, *Gambol*, is too much a string of gags, and it seems to be as much about Robbins as Taylor. The Martha Graham piece, *Anarchic Heart*, is also a little gag-heavy, though it sports an onstage parturition that is not to be missed.

And throughout the repertory, from piece to piece, the Trocks show off their ballerina personalities, which are an art in themselves: glamorous Natasha Notgoudenoff (Mike Gonzales), glaring at the others through hooded eyes; Konstantina Kvetchskaya (Ronald Soucy), who looks as though she just wandered in from the stock-car races; Valentina Poshlust, huge, inert, like a sanitation truck; batty, blond Babushkina (James O'Connor-Taylor); and high-strung little Nina Enimenimynimova (Victor Trevino). Enimenimynimova's my favorite—with her hair down, she looks like Farukh Ruzimatov—but after a while, it's like the seven dwarfs: you love them all.

February 21, 1990

Jack Anderson (1935–)

In 1978, Jack Anderson joined Anna Kisselgoff and Jennifer Dunning as one of the three dance critics of *The New York Times*, a position he held until 2005. (He is still affiliated with the paper.) Before that, he had written for *Ballet Today* and *Dance Magazine*, whose staff he joined in 1964, when he first came to New York via his hometown, Milwaukee; his university, Northwestern; and his first job as a journalist, for the *Oakland Tribune*. Since then, he has written prolifically for publications in America and Great Britain as well as published a number of books on dance, of which perhaps the most important are *The One and Only: The Ballet Russe de Monte Carlo*, which won the 1981 José de la Torre Prize for the best English-language book on dance, and *Art Without Boundaries: The World of Modern Dance*. He is also an admired poet, having published eleven collections of his work over a period of forty years. For more than half a century his partner has been another distinguished writer on dance, George Dorris, whom Anderson married in Toronto, in 2006. The two men together made a significant contribution to dance scholarship by founding the journal *Dance Chronicle: Studies in Dance and the Related Arts*.

Anderson's essay, below, concerns the crucial issue of how to go about preserving the spirit and/or the literal text of a dance once the choreographer is gone.

Idealists, Materialists, and the Thirty-Two Fouettés

"If in the Black Swan pas de deux the ballerina cannot adequately perform all thirty-two fouettés, may she replace them with other brilliant steps?"

Balletgoers occasionally ponder this question after performances and, for practical reasons, dancers must ponder it, too. A scholarly friend once observed that more than practicality is involved here, for behind the question lies the whole problem of the identity of a dance.

Like a poem, a dance is something everyone can recognize, but no one can define. The definitions advanced often seem commonplace, even banal: thus, almost everyone would agree that a dance is an art work involving movement through space and time. From all the possible movements of which persons are capable, someone selects the limited number of movements that comprise a particular dance. But having summarized the obvious, difficulties still arise, since one can regard the movements in any dance in two distinct—and, at their extremes, nearly irreconcilable—ways. For convenience, I shall call these positions the Idealist and the Materialist, and I use the terms solely in the sense I define here, without reference to other meanings they may possess in philosophy or theology.

Idealist dancegoers regard a dance as the incarnation in movement of ideas or effects; typically, Idealists may not mind that in different productions of what is ostensibly the same ballet steps are changed, provided that the alterations express the same idea, produce the same effect, or illumine the work's central concept. The Materialist, in contrast, regards a dance as an assemblage of specific steps (or, in the case of improvisatory or indeterminate pieces, specific instructions for deliberately unforeseeable steps) from which ideas or effects may be derived. Therefore the Materialist can maintain that it is possible for two productions of the same work to employ identical steps and yet be different in effect—a familiar example being the way in which some ballerinas offer a birdlike Odette, while others emphasize her humanity. To cite a more recent example, there is Emilia in Limón's "The Moor's Pavane." In conversation, Pauline Koner, the role's creator, said that she deplores those dancers who stress what one critic admiringly calls Emilia's "evil abandon," for both she and Limón wanted Emilia to be a warm-hearted confidante. But a Materialist spectator might countenance such an interpretation, provided that steps remain unaltered, for the interpretation would suggest that the steps are capable of many emotional colorations, just as in the theater Hamlets have ranged from pale neurasthenics to stalwart men of action.

In the past, choreographers and balletmasters were frequently Idealists in practice, staging for local companies their own versions of ballets which other choreographers successfully mounted elsewhere. Necessity may have been partly responsible: before the age of air travel, choreographers could not whiz from city to city. Nor did there exist any compact record of a ballet comparable to a score or a playscript. So Bournonville staged his own "La Sylphide" in Copenhagen, while early "Giselle"s were produced in Italy and America, which apparently did not employ the Paris choreography.

However, following the rise of the Diaghilev Ballet and modern dance came emphasis upon the Materialist position. A dance was increasingly regarded as a sequence of specific steps chosen by a specific choreographer. Fokine might tinker with his steps from season to season, modernist exponents of "self-expression" might alter their choreography nightly, but all would rage if they caught someone else trying to do his unauthorized version of "their" dances. Conscientious balletmasters started sorting out their memories with the result that, despite emendations, several older works came to be viewed in Materialist terms—among them the Bournonville "La Sylphide," the Coralli-Perrot-Petipa "Giselle," the Ivanov-Petipa "Swan Lake," and the Petipa "The Sleeping Beauty." Interest developed in notation—and in the copyright laws.

Nevertheless, Idealism again flourishes. As before, expediency may be partly responsible. There exist many fine companies and star performers. What we lack are fine choreographers. We do, though, possess adroit second-rank choreographers, while several top stars also interest themselves in stage production. Consequently, companies find it convenient to produce ballets derived from existing sources, which may attract audiences because of the familiarity of their theme or score and which contain big leading roles that can be performed by the local stars and can also be learned by any guest stars who come to town. While the results may be pleasant, the practice may conceivably threaten the integrity of choreographic works.

Before indulging in dire speculations it might be useful to examine how works exist in repertoires. Most contemporary ballets are regarded in Materialist terms. Who would think of doing "his own" version of, say, "Undertow" or "Ballet Imperial"? Tudor and Balanchine themselves may constantly fuss with their ballets: Tudor may assign one ballerina a double role in "Undertow," while Balanchine may redo the mime and scrap the décor and even the very title of

"Ballet Imperial." But, as the authors of the works, their changes are comparable to a poet's revisions. No one else, though, would dream of touching these ballets.

In total contrast are works that exist not as carefully preserved choreography but as scenarios or generalized production notions. The most familiar example of this sort of ballet is "La Fille Mal Gardée." Dauberval's choreography was forgotten long ago. What survives is the idea of a certain kind of ballet in which certain kinds of things happen, and, in our time, the Ashton, Balachova, and Mordkin-Nijinska-Romanoff versions have fleshed out that idea in different ways. Yet even when the accompanying music varies, the results are identifiable as "Fille."

More common are works that exist because of an idea that is coupled with a musical score, particularly when no single treatment of these ballets has managed to supersede previous versions (as the Ivanov-Petipa "Swan Lake" superseded Reisinger and Hansen) or to intimidate other choreographers from attempting their own versions. Examples include "Sylvia," "Daphnis and Chloë," "The Rite of Spring," "Romeo and Juliet," "Cinderella," "The Miraculous Mandarin," "Don Juan," and "The Prince of the Pagodas." Related to this type of production are hypothetical reconstructions of older ballets (such as anyone's "Pas de Quatre" and the Gsovsky and Lacotte restorations of Taglioni's "La Sylphide"), as well as "Coppélia" and "The Nutcracker," for which, in effect, no standard choreography now exists, although it should be theoretically possible to find people who could produce older versions of both.

Significantly, most examples of Idealist principles in dance are narrative or thematic, since these works can be summarized in verbal concepts, which any choreographer can ponder. Yet, even though abstract dance is almost inevitably the product of Materialist thinking, there have been instances of an Idealist approach to abstraction: after the success of Balanchine's "Agon" several European choreographers did their own "Agon"s, using Stravinsky's music and the general concept of a contest, and certain basic categories of abstraction seem to be dominant from season to season. Presently, the ballet of dreamy-lovers-and-Romantic-music has largely replaced the neat-geometries-to-Baroque-concerti that flourished a few seasons back.

Judging from European critics and the few works shown here, it would seem that among current choreographers John Neumeier is emphatically Idealist. His ballets often employ existing scenarios, or Neumeier will take a familiar scenario and twist it to emphasize fresh, but thematically related, ideas, as when (according to reports) in his "Daphnis and Chloë" schoolchildren visit the archaeological site where the events of the legend may have occurred and then become involved in a reenactment of the legend. Neumeier's speculations sometimes presuppose considerable audience sophistication. His "Baiser de la Fée" virtually assumes familiarity with the sensibilities of Tchaikovsky and H. C. Andersen, the scenario of Balanchine's "Baiser," and the characteristics of Balanchine's choreographic style. It is refreshing when a choreographer assumes that an audience is intelligent. But what we have seen of Neumeier's works are more interesting for their ideological superstructure than for their actual choreography.

Whatever one thinks of them, their existence poses no threat. But Idealist principles can menace works which have heretofore occupied an honored place in a repertoire. The classics—first "Swan Lake" and "The Sleeping Beauty," and now "Giselle"—are gradually eroding. The influence of Soviet ballet may be partly responsible, for the Russians since Gorsky have stressed ideas for dancing and remain fond of separating the functions of scenarist and choreographer. Such modern ballets as "Spartacus" and "The Stone Flower" have been repeatedly rechoreographed, each time by someone who tries to reveal more clearly than his predecessors the essence of the scenario and score. Similarly, the Soviets use the classics as though they were the dance equivalents of Greek myths, the stories of "Swan Lake" and "The Sleeping Beauty" serving each new choreographer in the same way that the Electra myth has served playwrights from Aeschylus to O'Neill.

A few non-Soviet modern ballets have also been so regarded. Some years ago when Festival Ballet revived Fokine's "Schéhérazade" with moderate success, a critic wrote that he thought greater success might have been possible if the ballet had been rechoreographed, the critic apparently considering "Schéhérazade" not as steps by Fokine, but as an idea for a ballet. For several years the Royal Danish Ballet tried to get Ashton to rehearse his "Romeo and Juliet." When attempts failed, the company this season presented a totally new "Romeo" by Neumeier. My point has nothing to do with the strengths or weaknesses of Neumeier's ballet (several Danish critics admire it): what does fascinate me here is that the company seems to treat "Romeo and Juliet" not as a specific ballet by Ashton (or by Neumeier either, for that matter) but as an idea for a certain kind of ballet (by any appropriate choreographer), which the Danes ought to produce.

Idealists often accuse Materialists of pedantry for their concern with the establishment of a choreographic text. They like to remind Materialists that choreographers change their ballets and that many old ballets are works by several choreographers (or by a choreographer and his assistants), and they will argue that since certain variations were designed to feature the specialties of particular dancers, it should therefore be permissible for other dancers to introduce their own specialties into these passages.

Idealists are correct in claiming that in watching dance we do not always notice steps as detachable entities. As a dancegoer, I confess that I cannot supply the technical names for most of the steps I see, and I can describe few passages of choreography from memory in elaborate detail. Nor can I recall many passages from Shakespeare by memory. But if substantial changes were made during a performance of Shakespeare's language or someone's choreography, I might feel uneasy. For the changes would suggest that, for whatever reason, a particular work was being remade.

Several Idealist arguments appear less weighty when one examines how the other arts deal with comparable issues. Certain poets have constantly rewritten poems, and their revisions are often included by publishers in variorum editions. Choreographers have likewise changed their dances; frequently, these changes are small, but they can also be extensive. Which version is the "true" version? Since all are by the same choreographer, they might all be called "true." A greater problem is that of determining which is "best," especially since dance companies (and theatrical and musical organizations) cannot publish alternate readings in a variorum. If the choreographer is also the company director, he will probably declare that, despite possible protests to the contrary, his latest version is best. But if the choreographer is not in charge of the company—or, more drastically, if he happens to be dead—then the artistic director, like a scholar studying quartos and folios, must pick and choose among alternates.

That some variations were designed to display their original performers should not deter anyone else from preserving their steps. Artists are inevitably inspired, or limited, by the interpreters they have at hand and tailor their works accordingly. Some passages in Shakespeare are probably phrased as they are because of Burbage's abilities, while the operatic repertoire contains several roles for decidedly odd voices: in "The Magic Flute" alone are such curiosities as the Queen of the Night and Sarastro. But if the creative artist happens to be talented, he does more than devise stunts: from the idiosyncrasies of his performers he invents steps which are both appropriate and beautiful. It is, after all, Odile, not Odette, who does the fouettés. Therefore the choreography's very peculiarities may constitute a genuine artistic challenge to succeeding interpreters.

As for multiple authorship, only obdurate upholders of the purist view that an art work is necessarily the product of a single genius should find it troublesome that ballets may have passages by several choreographers. Many old master paintings contain the brushstrokes of both the master and his students, and successful theatrical collaborations extend from Beaumont and Fletcher to Kaufman and Hart.

However, the performing arts must resolve problems related to a particular kind of multiple authorship. During some, but by no means all, past periods, performers could add ornaments to the music they played or the choreography they danced. Should performers today add comparable ornaments? If so, how many? And of what kind? In dealing with these questions one should remember that the personal touches were only ornaments: decorations added to an existing structure, not a substitution for that structure—an extra trill in the music or turn in the choreography, but no wholesale rewriting. The story is told of the soprano who auditioned for Rossini by singing a heavily ornamented version of one of his own arias. "Very nice," the composer remarked. "Who wrote it?" Rossini later explained that, while he expected his music to be embroidered, he did not want it distorted out of recognition.

At least, since that soprano was Rossini's contemporary, her ornamentations probably contained no gross anachronisms. Adding ornaments becomes more difficult today when one has to make sure that they harmonize with the original. Among the peculiarities of Cranko's "Swan Lake" was the fact that the new choreography did not always blend with the bits retained from Ivanov-Petipa. To avoid comparable discrepancies, musicians study tables of ornamentation and sometimes, instead of inventing their own ornaments or cadenzas, play the conjectural ones suggested by scholars. Therefore, perhaps dancers today ought to be chary about embroidering steps, even where dancers of an earlier generation might have embroidered freely.

A related problem of authorship is peculiar to dance. Since dances are passed down by memory and memories are faulty, gaps exist in some ballets which have to be filled. Thus parts of our Bournonville stagings derive from Hans Beck and Harald Lander. If Beck and Lander, why not Nureyev or MacMillan? The question admits of no conclusive reply, but several factors may be taken into account. Obviously, if gaps exist, they must be filled—preferably with style and taste. In some circumstances, totally new dances may be added to expand a ballet, but they should not displace old choreography. The Royal Ballet was reprehensible when it supplanted Petipa's "Swan Lake" pas de trois with an Ashton pas de quatre (attractive though it was); it is no longer reprehensible now that it dances both divertissements.

Yet even when old choreography is retained, too many interpolations may destroy the character of a work; and the more time that elapses between the date of the original and the date of the interpolations, the greater danger there is of this occurring, since gaps in time also imply gaps in sensibility. Take Bournonville's "La Sylphide," for example. Modern producers wonder whether there should be a solo for Effie. Adding one probably does no mischief, since it can never take more than a few minutes. But what about a full-scale duet for James and the Sylph? A *Dance Magazine* critic writes that "La Sylphide" is "unsatisfactory" because it lacks "a proper pas de deux." But is what would be proper for Petipa or Balanchine also proper for Bournonville? The very lack—indeed, the impossibility—of physical contact between the principals is part of Bournonville's conception and contributes to the individuality of his ballet. To add a pas de deux might blunt that individuality: when Lander added such a duet for his Ballet Theatre production, some viewers thought the results, though tasteful, made the ballet ponderous. In the same way, despite the arguments that heroes in classical ballets should get chances to dance, the melancholy solos which recently have been devised for the princes in the Tchaikovsky classics not only look disquietingly alike, they usually look uninteresting. Curiously, cutting scenes entirely often produces less artistic trouble than replacing old choreography with new or adding extra choreography to an existing scene: almost nobody pines for the restoration of "Giselle"'s happy ending, while the supposedly complete Russian "La Bayadère" lacks the fifth act which Petipa originally choreographed.

Staging ballets might be less vexing if dance possessed a universally accepted system of notation. Yet there are dancegoers who may secretly rejoice that such a system does not exist. These fans insist that, rather than consisting of steps which may produce effects, a dance consists primarily of effects embodied in steps. Therefore steps may be altered if comparable effects are gained. According to this theory, one might contend that while Camargo, in her time, astounded audiences with entrechat quatre, any revival of a Camargo ballet (granting, for purposes of argument, the possibility of such a thing) should contain not entrechat quatre, which no longer astounds, but some other flashy step. This would then be called preserving the ballet's spirit, if not its letter.

But would it be? For who today can view the eighteenth century so unaffected by the artistic and social upheavals which have transpired since then that he can create choreography which would in all ways be equivalent to genuine choreography of the period? And just what shall our modern Camargo do, if not entrechat quatre? Thirty-two fouettés, perhaps? An obvious anachronism! Yet what step would not be? However, in our Camargo revival, if all the steps were preserved as they existed in her time, then the entrechat quatre—simply for being unlike the others—might still possess theatrical potency of a kind.

It is dangerous to believe that we know for sure what the "real" effects of a dance are supposed to be, for the kinds of effects we treasure may be partially determined by the taste of our age. Not long ago, sincere commentators argued that because Bach was hampered by the provincial musical forces he had at hand, the best way to achieve the true effects of the Bach cantatas was to utilize symphony orchestras and huge mixed choirs. Today, the vogue is for chamber orchestras, ancient instruments, and small all-male choirs, as we now consider sweet radiance more important than massive solemnity. Who knows what we shall feel a decade hence?

Similarly, in dance we have at different times prized different effects. At one time Odette's mimed account of her tribulations was dropped from the second act of "Swan Lake," perhaps because producers considered it stilted. Now it is back, possibly because the sheer multiplicity of Odette's gestures (even if one cannot literally "read" them all) conveys a sense of dramatic urgency. To achieve another effect, Benno no longer participates in the "Swan Lake" adagio. This traditional bit was changed only recently—but the change is well-nigh universal. Presumably the reason for dropping Benno is that it seems odd for a third person to intrude upon a love scene; besides, Benno was only put there in the first place to assist the aging Pavel Gerdt in handling the ballerina. Yet Ivanov, being a genius, made Benno's presence part of the beauty of that scene, for Odette was then able to swoon in a more ecstatic manner than she has been able to do now that a single man must hold her, let her go, and then also catch her.

Perhaps, someday, someone will want to rehabilitate Benno. (He has already turned up in the Ballets Trockadero de Monte Carlo travestie production.) But will people remember the choreography? At least, despite vagaries of taste and textual corruptions, scores exist for Bach. Still, some Idealists would regret the development of dance notation, since they fear that notation might stunt the organic growth of dance by making dance become cut and dried and, finally, mummified.

Arid choreography is always deplorable, but notation need not bring it about. Notation might even encourage individuality. With the standard repertoire notated, producers could feel free to stage that traditional choreography as they pleased—setting "Swan Lake," for instance, in any historical period or in outer space—for the Materialist approach to production implies that at various times the same choreography can be used to produce quite different effects, just as Shakespeare's words have been subjected to Christian, Freudian, Marxist, and existentialist interpretations. Moreover, with standard choreography notated, a choreographer might be emboldened to create a totally new and different ballet based upon a classic story, just as a playwright might reinterpret a classic myth. One trouble with even our most radical revisions of the classics is that they seldom are radical enough. Thus every "Swan Lake" contains a semblance of Ivanov's second act as an obeisance to tradition. But with Ivanov notated an innovator could choreograph a "Swan Lake" which in no way resembled Ivanov stylistically, just as O'Neill's conception of Electra is stylistically different from that of Sophocles.

Our present willingness to tolerate extensive changes in extant works may be a hangover from the old attitude that dance is not really an important art—that, finally, it does not matter what is danced, provided the results are diverting. Yet in our century dance has gained enormous artistic significance, and so what is dance surely matters as much as how it is danced. If no two productions of any work in the performing arts can ever be exactly the same, the work itself should possess some sort of solid identity and integrity.

Until the time when dance acquires a sense of its own identity, we are left with our original question about the Black Swan: To fouetté or not to fouetté?

Idealists will not hesitate to permit the ballerina to substitute steps, while Materialists would caution against the substitution. Conceivably, the ballerina, reluctant to look less than dazzling, might go ahead and change the steps anyway. Even so, her artistic conscience ought to be reminding her that she still remains at least thirty-two fouettés short of perfection.

1975–76

W. H. AUDEN (1907–1973)

THE GREAT English American poet W. H. Auden (born near Birmingham in England, he moved to America in 1939, becoming an American citizen in 1946) was also a brilliant critic who published at least four hundred essays in America, writing most frequently for *The New Yorker* and *The New York Review of Books*. After studying at Oxford he taught and traveled (frequently with his friend and lover Christopher Isherwood). His first collection of poems was published in 1930, and from the start he was recognized as a large talent, and soon he was identified as being, with Eliot and Yeats, one of Britain's three finest poets. Auden had a particular love of collaboration and worked frequently with Isherwood and Benjamin Britten, and co-wrote, with his lover Chester Kallman, the libretto for Stravinsky's opera *The Rake's Progress*. And he had a passion for friendship. One of his New York friends was Lincoln Kirstein, who persuaded him to write (for a New York City Ballet souvenir program book) the article below about Balanchine's poetic imagination as seen in his *Nutcracker*. Another of Auden's New York friends, Joseph Brodsky, once said that he had "the greatest mind of the twentieth century."

Ballet's Present Eden—Example of *The Nutcracker*

EVERY artistic medium has its peculiar nature, which allows it to express some things better than any rival medium and prohibits it from expressing other things altogether. The medium of ballet is the human body moving in rhythmical balance within a limited area of space. What it can express is whatever is immediately intelligible in terms of variety of motion—fast-or-slow, to-and-fro, round-and-round, up-and-down; and variety of spatial relations—absent-or-present, face-to-face, back-to-back, side-by-side, above-below, at-the-center, on-the-outside, far-or-near, approaching or receding, etc.

Ballet time, that is, is a continuous present; every experience which depends on historical time lies outside its capacities. It cannot express memory, the recollection of that which is absent, for either the recollected body is onstage and immediate or it is off and nonexistent. Memory distinguishes between the object and its invoked image; ballet deals only in the object. No character in a ballet can grow or change in the way that a character in a novel changes; he can only undergo instantaneous transformations from one kind of being to another. Ballet can show A protecting and comforting B, but it cannot tell us whether A is the mother, the aunt, or the fairy godmother of B. These observations, it should be said, refer to the forming principles of ballet; as with the other media, tension and excitement come from pushing against the form. A choreographer may take this risk again and again, but he will watch closely, being careful to make himself clear. And he will return in good time to safe ground.

In its dazzling display of physical energy, on the other hand, the ballet expresses, as no other medium can, the joy of being alive. Death is omnipresent as the force of gravity over which the dancers triumph; everything at rest is either a thing, or it is asleep, enchanted, or dead. If it moves, it comes to life, and its kind of life—man, bird, or animated toy—is a minor matter, to be indicated by slight details of costume, compared to the fact of life itself which dancing expresses. The more energy implied by an emotion, the more danceable it is. Thus defiance can be danced but despair is impossible, and joy is the most danceable of all. Since suffering, as human beings understand it, depends on memory and anticipation, which are alien to the medium, it may be said that nobody suffers in ballet: if they did, their movement would become unbalanced and ugly.

When ballet portrays funeral rites for the death of a hero, the glory and the pleasure in the rite itself are what it conveys. In other words, all real ballets take place in Eden, in that world of pure being without becoming and the suffering implied by becoming, a world where things, beasts, and men are equally alive, a world without history and without seriousness. The ballet character who becomes serious must either come to rest and die or he must exit. One could turn *Pickwick Papers* into a ballet up to the point where Mr. Pickwick enters the Fleet

Prison (The Fallen World), but neither the Fleet, nor Mr. Pickwick after he has been in it and tasted of the fruit of the knowledge of good and evil, are ballet subjects. It is not an accident that so many of the most successful ballets are based on fairy tales.

E.T.A. Hoffmann, who wrote the original story (in 1816) on which *The Nutcracker* is based, was haunted by nostalgic visions of a childhood Eden with its magical wonder. At the same time he was haunted by terrors and visions of evil. Black magic was as real to him as white. His Drosselmeyer is a much more complex and sinister character than Drosselmeyer in the ballet; the horrid things that happen to Princess Perribou [Pirlipat] and to Nutcracker, or to Drosselmeyer Jr., have quite rightly been kept off the stage, and the ballet battle is not the sadistic thing it is in the story.

Dumas turned Hoffmann's often fierce German tale into *Casse-Noisette*, a story for French children. Since children's stories also take place in a present Eden, he thus tended to preserve the incidents that Petipa and Ivanov could use for their scenario. What comes down to us now in dance are most of the ceremonial scenes like the Christmas party and the festivities in Confectionland. All the history of Nutcracker and Clara is telescoped into one ballet and a transformation scene; the long romantic journeys of the story are represented by the lovers in a snowstorm. Certain charming scenes had to be left out, not only on account of length, but also because they are too literary. For example, the sausage feast in which the King rushes from a Privy Council meeting to see how things are going in the kitchen:

> "Gentlemen!" he cried, rising from the throne, "will you excuse me? I will return in a minute."
>
> Then, hardly able to prevent himself from running to the door, he rushed to the kitchen, where, after embracing the Queen many times, he began to stir the contents of the cauldron with his sceptre. Afterwards he put it in his mouth, and, in a calmer state of mind, returned to his Privy Council, where, though still a little absent-minded, he succeeded in taking up the question of foreign policy where he had left it.

Some of this, e.g., "hardly able to prevent himself from running," is mimeable though not danceable, but not even mime can take up foreign policy; that requires words, as do Hoffmann's philosophic reflections on the difference between the ideal and the real. In ballet only the ideal remains.

In order of composition, *The Nutcracker* is the last of three full-length ballets which Tschaikovsky wrote. There is beautiful ballet music in the operas of classical composers like Gluck and Mozart, there are mid-nineteenth century ballet scores of great charm like those of Adam and Delibes, but Tschaikovsky was the first to raise ballet music to its present status as a serious orchestral form equal to that of the symphony. Before Tschaikovsky the choreographer and the composer had little to do with each other: the former told the latter what kind of dances he wanted and how many bars long they should be, and the composer went off and wrote them without bothering to find out what actions were to accompany his music. Tschaikovsky wrote to Petipa's orders, but he also wrote to sense, and in his ballet scores the music is always apposite to the scenario. The very difficulties which Tschaikovsky found in training his musical imagination to the traditional sonata and symphony forms may well have been an advantage when he came to write ballet music, which makes such different formal demands. Today, many of us find his compositions in this form his best music, the closest in spirit (though completely original) to the work of Mozart, who was his confessed idol.

Outside Russia, where it has become popular, the ballet has hardly been seen, and only the orchestra suite Tschaikovsky made out of some of the music is well known. After seeing the Vic-Wells 1934 revival, Cyril Beaumont complained in his *Complete Book of Ballets* that the first scene was suitable only to a juvenile audience and that the character dances in the last scene were ridiculous, but praised highly the solo numbers.

Apart from the fact that it requires a number of professionally trained children, which most ballet companies do not possess, *The Nutcracker* is not suitable for a company built, like the majority, around a few star soloists and with a corps de ballet capable of little more than calisthenics. George Balanchine has always set his face against such a structure. The ideal he has worked for is a company in which every member is technically capable of dancing a solo *rôle*: in his choreography, instead of the conventional corps de ballet acting in unison, every one has his unique part to play. Balanchine sees *The*

Nutcracker as a festival of joy, a sort of Christmas pantomime, and only those who have lost their sense of joy and for whom, consequently, ballet is a meaningless art will find it juvenile.

1954

JOSEPHINE BAKER (1906–1975)

THE SUBLIME musical star of stage and screen Josephine Baker (née Freda Josephine McDonald)—for whom the dread word "iconic" might have been invented—is indelibly associated with Paris of the 1920s, where and when she became a star, initially as a dancer. But before she arrived there as a teenager, she had experienced more of the world than one would wish on any child. Born in East St. Louis, where she learned both racism and poverty, she dropped out of school in the fifth grade and was married twice by the time she was fifteen (she retained her second husband's surname for the rest of her life).

However, intuitively rhythmical and entirely self-taught as a dancer, she successfully performed for coins on street corners (as Edith Piaf would). Her gift for rhythmic expression; her high-waisted and long-stemmed physique; her self-mocking, comic persona; and her genius for making the right gesture at the right moment catapulted her first into a vaudeville show in St. Louis and then, in New York, into the chorus lines of the Plantation Club and two swank, Harlem Renaissance–era Broadway shows: Eubie Blake and Noble Sissle's *Shuffle Along* (1921) and *Chocolate Dandies* (1924).

But her future lay elsewhere. At nineteen, Baker proved an overnight sensation in Paris as a member of the visiting 1925 Harlem show *La Revue Nègre*, in a jungly number known as her "Danse Sauvage," where the stimulating polyrhythms of her dancing (and of the responding pulses in the circlet of artificial bananas that, with a few strands of beads, comprised her entire costume) inspired the band. (Could her pet cheetah, Chiquita, have been named for this celebrated costume?) She triumphed at the Folies-Bergère, and then, with a new-found elegance in feathers and jewels, in her act at the Casino de Paris, for which, it seems, George Balanchine put her on pointe, in 1932. A couple of years later, he would choreograph a ballet for her and four male "shadows," *5 A.M.*, as well as a conga, in the 1936 edition of the

Broadway revue *Ziegfeld Follies: A National Institution Glorifying the American Girl.*

Baker sustained a lifelong career as an entertainer, albeit with inter-missions, and a huge offstage life that encompassed working for the Resistance during World War II (for which she was awarded the Croix de guerre and made a member of the Légion d'honneur) and the adoption of a dozen orphans from a variety of ethnic origins (a group she called "The Rainbow Tribe"). During the 1930s, when she mar-ried her third husband, a Jewish industrialist and a Frenchman, she renounced her American citizenship. Among her four husbands and stream of male and female lovers was her longtime manager Giuseppe Pepito Abatino, who (with Chiquita) figures in the delightful passage below excerpted from Baker's memoir, written with her fourth hus-band, bandleader Jo Bouillon.

The Casino de Paris (and Chiquita)

I COULD LISTEN to Pepito by the hour.
He had a convincing explanation for my success in post-war Paris.

"You were just what people needed after the restrictions of war. They craved something wild, natural, extravagant—you!" I gazed through the bay window at the handsome oaks that gave our property, Beau Chêne, its name. Perhaps it had been foolish to buy this peaceful haven in the Paris suburb of Le Vésinet, but we adored our new home.

"You also represented freedom," Pepito continued. "The right to cut your hair, to walk around stark naked, to kick over the traces, includ-ing corsets!" I smiled. Here was Pepito telling me what I had done for Frenchwomen when I was much more concerned with all that he had done for me. He had taught me the mysteries of fish knives and forks, how to dress discreetly, how to speak and stand and act like a lady.

"It helped that the time was ripe," Pepito reflected. "People were beginning to collect *art nègre*, the public was discovering jazz. Five years earlier you'd have been booed off the stage. Five years later—*now*—you've got to come up with something new, Josephine, if you want to stay in the public eye." "I'm sure you're right, Pepito, but *what?*" "You mustn't change *too* much or you'll disappoint your audience. They count on your earthiness and abandon." "Does that mean more bananas?" "No, *chérie*, they've served their purpose. It's time for feathers and charm, sensitivity, songs, wit, feeling. It's time to use everything you've picked up in the twenty-five countries we've visited in the last two years. . . . I think you're ready to do it. Monsieur Varna agrees." "*What?*" "It's all arranged, Josephine. All we have to do is sign."

Henri Varna? *The Casino de Paris?* I couldn't believe my ears. The Casino was famous as the domain of la Miss—the legendary Mistinguett. Only last year she had triumphed there in *Paris-Miss*, Henri Varna's first show. And now it was *me* he wanted! "He's come up with a marvelous title for your show: *Paris qui Remue*." "Bustling Paris" . . . Thirteen letters. How could we miss?

Things began moving at a breakneck pace. I could barely find a minute to play with my animals, stroll through my grounds, inspect my truck garden, talk to my hothouse flowers. . . . I was forced to leave my green oasis daily and hurry to the Rue de Clichy and Monsieur Varna's colorful, hectic world.

Henri Varna impressed me on sight. A slender, lively man with piercing yet gentle eyes, he was constantly on the move, experimenting, reworking, improvising: a creative power crackling with ideas.

"Josephine, here's what you'll be wearing." Monsieur Varna handed me a sketch of the costume for my first number, "L'Oiseau des Îles." It consisted mainly of two enormous white wings! How would I be able to move? "And here's a drawing of the set." I gazed at what appeared to be a virgin forest. Into it descended something reminiscent of our Reverend's description of Jacob's Ladder. "What in the world is that coming out of the sky?" "The ramp." "I'll never get down it wearing these wings." "She's right, Henri," a voice agreed dryly. It was Earl Leslie, Mistinguett's official dancer-choreographer, co-author of the show. I had heard rumors of bad feelings on the part of la Miss—it had taken all Monsieur Varna's tact and charm to persuade her to lend us "her" Earl—and Leslie showed signs of strain. I looked at him coldly. How little he knew me! Precisely because he had said I couldn't navigate the steps, I would! Once I was safely on the forest floor, I was pursued by a stageful of dancers. As I desperately tried to ward off the hunters, hopping and flapping, they surrounded me, tore off my wings, stripped me of my plumage and left me writhing on the ground. The dance was a cry for help, a protest against cruelty. "It's beautiful," murmured Pepito, "and very moving."

The atmosphere at the Casino grew tenser daily. The show was sold out for opening night; the demand for seats had been such that the theater could have been filled three times over. Again and again we rehearsed a flamboyant number about the French colonies, which included Algerian drums, Indian bells, tom-toms from Madagascar, coconuts from the Congo, cha-chas from Guadeloupe, a number laid in Martinique during which I distributed sugar cane to the audience, Indochinese gongs, Arab dances, camels and finally my appearance as the Empress of Jazz. It was hard to believe that Monsieur Varna was looking for something *more* spectacular for the second act!

One of the numbers I particularly liked watching in rehearsal involved a lake fairy. The chorus was charmingly dressed as irises, water lilies, dragonflies and nymphs. The fairy herself wore a diamond G-string from Van Cleef and Arpels. Two bodyguards followed her every move! It reminded Monsieur Varna, who loved to laugh and knew hundreds of theater stories, of an actress who owned a fabulous diamond necklace which streamed down to her thighs. Where else? After all, streams return to their source! Without being jealous of the lake fairy's finery, I *did* wonder what kind of special effect Monsieur Varna might have in mind for *me*.

Shortly before opening night, Monsieur Henri called me into his office. "Meet your new partner, Josephine." I couldn't believe my eyes. A sleek, golden-eyed leopard sat calmly on the rug, quietly switching its tail. "We ordered him from Hamburg." I remembered visiting the marvelous Hagenbeck menagerie during our German tour. "What's his name, monsieur?" "Chiquita." I knelt beside the big cat; he didn't stir. "You're not afraid?" "No, monsieur. Animals don't hide their feelings the way people do. That's what I like about them! Look what a beautiful creature he is." I gently stroked the leopard's cheek. Chiquita purred contentedly. "See, he likes me." I slowly reached for Chiquita's leash and gave a little tug. The leopard got to his feet and stretched. "You can take him everyplace with you. It'll be marvelous publicity." There was no doubt about that! I could forget about the lake fairy. She couldn't make it as far as the stage door in her G-string. The minute she left the stage, her diamonds were put away in the safe.

Chiquita turned out to be an excellent trouper. He appeared with me in a number called "Ounawa," which Monsieur Varna considered the high spot of the second half of the show. The plot revolved around a native girl who falls in love with a white man and wants to follow him back to civilization. A charming sequence, but something seemed to be lacking. Our composer, Vincent Scotto, saved the day when he arrived on stage waving a slip of paper excitedly. On the way to the theater he had ducked into an entranceway and scribbled down a tune. Hurrying to the rehearsal piano, he began to sing: "J'ai Deux Amours . . ." Monsieur Varna beamed. "Marvelous!" Leaning over the piano, I joined in: "Two loves have I: my country and Paris . . ." Monsieur Varna was right. The song was perfect. It expressed my feelings completely. Yet . . . I felt a sudden lump in my throat. I would never be able to sing it.

"Of course you will," Pepito insisted as we headed home in our Delage. (He had arranged a profitable advertising scheme in which I stated: "The secret of my hair style is Bakerfix [a hair oil marketed under my name], I buy my shoes at Perugia, I enjoy music from around the world on my Bitus portable radio and of course I drive a Delage.") "Listen, Josephine, if you really believe what you're singing, if the words truly come from your heart, you won't have any trouble with your throat." He was right. I laid my head on his shoulder. "The song should really go: 'Three loves have I: my country, Paris and Pepito.'"

A striking poster had been designed to promote the show. I appeared all over Paris emerging from a cloud of green feathers, nude except for ropes of pearls reaching below my loins, bracelets twisting from wrist to shoulders, sparkling shoe buckles and dangling earrings. Chiquita, seated on his haunches, a bow around his supple neck, was offering me an enormous bunch of flowers. In spite of its charm and humor, the poster was, of course, exaggerated. Chiquita was not one to offer posies, although I had supplied him with a collar to match each of my outfits.

Dress rehearsal was a disaster. One of the chorus girls sprained an ankle, a costume in the "Electricity" number short-circuited, Chiquita, unnerved by the general tension, chewed a hole in a dancer's trousers and the wind machine broke down. I had taken the precaution of stowing my good-luck penny and entire stock of rabbits' feet in my dressing table drawer. It looked as though I would need them.

September 26, 1930. Opening night. I tried to relax, but I knew that the fashionable audience was packed with journalists armed for the kill. The "savage" would receive no quarter. Pens sharp as arrows were poised to strike at Josephine and the Casino's new management. I recognized Mistinguett in one of the boxes!

When the crowd broke into wild applause, I was so moved that I walked to the front of the stage, placed my hand on my pounding heart and murmured, "Thank you, thank you so much, ladies and gentlemen." Monsieur Varna pounced on me in the wings. "Stop that, Josephine. None of this 'Thank you, ladies and gents!' You're not a street singer. You're the star of the Casino. Just nod from time to time like a queen." And he pushed me back onto the stage. After the curtain was lowered, the clapping continued. I turned to find the cast acclaiming me.

A few days later I woke up in my Louis Seize bedroom (the press insisted that I slept in Marie Antoinette's bed) and discovered Pepito covering me with newspapers. "You've done it, *chérie!* If Paris is bustling, it's you who put it on its toes. Listen to the reviews: 'She sings in French, dances, acts and lights up the stage with her exuberance and rhythm' . . . 'sensitive and sincere' . . . 'a smashing success' . . . 'a true artist.'" "Pepito, uncork the champagne."

During the following weeks Pepito busied himself making a scrapbook of the clippings that poured in from all over France and abroad. I was now being exposed to a new kind of criticism, that of the sharp-tongued music reviewers. My records had appeared on the market and were selling like hotcakes. Pepito assured me that the critics would eat out of my hand, just like Chiquita, and as usual he was right. "Josephine, we've won the prize for the best record of the year," he announced triumphantly one evening. I couldn't help smiling. Pepito always said "we." "We're" going to sing at the charity ball; "we" certainly caused a stir at the art show; "we" have a marvelous new song. Still, I was thrilled at his news. Imagine me, Josephine, at the top of the charts! Pepito was already negotiating next year's tour and Monsieur Varna was thinking ahead to 1932!

"Are you happy, Josephine?" Pepito frequently asked me. Of course I was. Our house was full of friends, animals and friends of friends who seemed to adore the ebony Venus. My dressing room was crowded with celebrities: Marcel Pagnol; Erich Maria Remarque, who said I brought "a whiff of jungle air and an elemental strength and beauty to the tired showplace of Western Civilization"; Le Corbusier, who was moved to tears by my performance; Luigi Pirandello, who wanted to write a play for me. I was also introduced to a Mr. Einstein, but had no idea who he was.

Chiquita and I went everywhere. "Here comes the panther and her leopard," the crowds would shout as flash bulbs popped. There were endless fittings—how I hated being trapped inside that latticework of pins; interviews during which I mouthed stock phrases unless the press answered their questions themselves, thereby simplifying matters for everyone; constant singing and dancing lessons. "You're at the top," Mr. Varna had said. And I didn't intend to forget it. But life is a series of summits and behind each crest looms another peak to be scaled. . . .

There were two Josephines now—the Josephine of Le Vésinet and the Josephine of the Casino de Paris. The latter posed at Monsieur Poiret's in fancy clothes and inaugurated the *Josephine Show*, an inspiration of Pepito's. He had collected portraits and caricatures of me made by a dozen or more well-known artists and hung them like a string of paper dolls of every shape and size, dancing, arms trailing on the ground, rump aloft, pinheaded, balloon-faced with an enormous grin; loins feathered, eyes crossed, breasts jutting. . . . The Josephine of the Casino rode horseback in the Bois de Boulogne, drove a roadster, took flying lessons.

The Josephine of Le Vésinet fed her ducks and rabbits, caressed her cats, exercised her dogs and napped with Chiquita. The Josephine of the Casino appeared at countless functions and gave endless autographs. ("Pepito, can't you find a photograph that doesn't show me *nude*?" "But this is the one they *like, chérie*.") The Josephine of Le Vésinet wore Peter Pan collars.

"Are you happy, Josephine?" "Of course, Pepito." At Beau Chêne my animals surrounded me with love. I drew strength and peace from their affection. It was a good life.

1977

George Balanchine (1904–1983)

GEORGE BALANCHINE did not leave behind an autobiography, a memoir, journals, a manual on technique, or an extensive correspondence. It is generally known that a good deal of what was published under his name, although reflecting his ideas, was actually written by Lincoln Kirstein, and that it was Francis Mason who did the actual writing of *Balanchine's Complete Stories of the Great Ballets*. Instead of writing, Balanchine left behind the greatest corpus of ballets the world possesses. Yet he was a highly verbal man (he was a lifelong reader of books in Russian) and was adept at conversational English. What's more, he could write in English when he chose to, or when Kirstein wasn't available. The indisputable proof is the personal and touching letter that he wrote to Kirstein when Kirstein's mother died. Again, the little notes he wrote to his wife Maria Tallchief, which she quotes in her autobiography, are loving and charmingly phrased. And when he chose to express his ideas on dance publicly and on his own, as in his comment on ballet in America, the results were lucid and sensible, if sometimes a touch quirky. The examples printed here, from a variety of somewhat arcane sources, add to our sense of him not only as a genius, but also as a man.

Ballet in Films

LAST SUMMER I had the opportunity to direct the ballet sequences in the United Artists production *The Goldwyn Follies*, which will open in February.

It was interesting to me that my work in the former Imperial Theatre of Leningrad, in the Diaghileff Ballet, the Paris Grand Opera, and the Metropolitan Opera of New York was not the main reason for my being called to Hollywood. The main reason was the work I did for two musical comedies on Broadway: *On Your Toes* and *Babes in Arms*. When I arrived in Los Angeles I was not considered a chore-ographer of classic ballet, but a musical comedy director, from whom one expected "comedy routines," which of course I did not know how to do and did not want to do.

The reason for this was that my work in the musical comedy field was considered to have elements of humor which were new, but to a certain extent traditional in musical comedy. My idea, as always, was to give the public good Theatre. Musical comedy, which I regard as seriously as classic ballet or classic drama, is simply one branch of the-atrical art. Actually, it was only because of my previous work in classic ballet that I was able to do the kind of work I did in musical comedy.

Musicals Need Imagination

Musical comedy is, first of all, theatre, and nowadays more than ever needs fantasy and imagination—but a fantasy and imagination based on solid craftsmanship. In recent years musical comedy, especially the dancing side of it, has become more and more standardized. Group movements became rigid and obviously unimaginative. There was little of the freshness and spirit of an Offenbach operetta or a Gilbert and Sullivan musical comedy. I felt that I had to introduce a new life into the musical comedy by applying to it some of the achievements of classic ballet and thus create new formulas for the benefit of American musical comedy audiences.

I frequently hear people say: "We give the public what it wants." This is generally only an excuse for productions built on the same old unimaginative pattern.

The public wants new things, even if it does not know what they are. It is only the artist, and sometimes the producer, who senses this and is therefore able to lead the way. One thing is sure. The public does not want the same old thing. I believe that it is much more open to new experiments than producers, directors, managers and especially box office officials are willing to admit. My own work in musical comedy has proved this to me.

If new ideas are needed for musical comedy, as I believe, they are absolutely imperative for the screen.

Larger Scope

It is absurd to regard movies as only a relaxation and pastime. One should have the same attitude toward motion pictures as one has toward any other form of theatrical art. Films should be a product of greater imagination and fantasy than the theatre because of the larger scope which elements of space and time have in a motion picture.

I also think that the responsibility of anyone working in motion pictures, whether he is producer, director or actor, is greater than in the theatre because he is addressing not only a selected group of people, not only a city public, but large masses of people all over the world. This is why I think a serious, artistic, creative, inventive and imaginative approach to the films is an absolute necessity.

By including a ballet sequence in *The Goldwyn Follies*, Samuel Goldwyn, a producer who is acutely interested in new ideas, opened completely new possibilities both for films and the classic ballet.

Pure Fantasy

The importance of ballet for motion pictures is the element of pure fantasy.

Although motion pictures have known quite a lot of fantasy, it has been limited to the field of comedy as exemplified by the Chaplin and Marx Brothers films. The average picture seldom deals with free fantasy, but is tied up closely with real life. The fairy tale type of unreality has up to now been employed in the field of animated cartoons. This field, through the medium of the technical tricks of the camera and the freedom it has over imaginative conceptions, is most suitable to the motion picture and, as yet, remains completely unexplored.

People have gotten into the habit of going to the movies to see reenacted their own lives or the lives of people they envy, but the world of make-believe and of pure fantasy is still only a by-product of present day production. Naturalistic theatre has always bored me, as I think that essentially theatre art is based on the audience's desire to escape rather than to relive reality.

Artificial Quality

It is mainly because of its purely imaginative—I would even say artificial—quality that ballet is important for motion pictures. It introduces a completely imaginative world whose form is of a plastic nature—a visual perfection of an imaginative life. This, for me, is the realm of complete fantasy. It has its own laws, its own meaning and cannot be explained by the usual criterions of logic.

On the other hand, the possibilities opened by motion pictures for the classic ballet are of even a greater importance and interest.

First of all, the frame of the screen is a far more movable thing than the frame of the theatre; it does not bind the ballet to the visual square of thirty or forty feet. The same applies to the space and movability of the settings. It is far easier to create a complete space fantasy on the screen than on the stage. Natural elements like wind, light, and sound can be more freely applied to the screen than to the stage and thus become by far more important additions to classic ballet than they are on the stage.

Same Angle, Same Distance

Another very important point is that the spectator sees a stage ballet always from the same angle and from the same distance. On the screen, however, the spectator moves with the camera and thus can see the ballet not only from a wide range of angles but also from a wide range of distances. He may even feel himself amidst the ballet performance.

This imposes completely new problems on the choreographer. It renders his task far more intricate and difficult, gives him new riddles to solve and a wide range of possibilities for his invention in the domain of fantasy.

It is also quite important to point out the fact that in the film, ballet is visually equally complete, no matter from what seat in the auditorium one looks at it. The camera does the work. In the theatre a person sitting high in the balcony generally sees only wigs and heads and thus has only an incomplete view of the ballet performance. It appears distorted and obviously he cannot enjoy and appreciate it. The movies correct this error of the theatre and render it possible for every member of the audience to enjoy ballet fully.

A Prediction Fulfilled

The picture *Goldwyn Follies* will soon be released and the audience will then be able to join me in admiring not only the artistic grace of Vera Zorina but also to witness the birth of an unquestionably great screen personality. She is the perfect combination of dancer, actress and artist.

As to my work with the American Ballet, I will leave that to the response of what I hope will be a kindly public.

1937/1944

The Crystal Palace

The two surprising and mysterious documents below, containing fairytale elements—some of which are cued to specific passages of Balanchine's story-less 1947 *Palais de cristal* in Paris—were included among his personal papers given to The Harvard Theatre Collection by The George Balanchine Trust, in 1992. Mr. B's longtime associate, Barbara Horgan, verifies that the ideas are Balanchine's.

LIBRETTO, CHOREOGRAPHY AND PRODUCTION
BY GEORGE BALANCHINE (1947)
MUSIC: *SYMPHONY IN C*, BY GEORGES BIZET (1855)

Score mark	Scenario
Part	Part I—The House of Rubies
1st mvt.: Allegro vivo	Tableau. Lights brighten slowly upon the façade of an Indian Temple, encrusted with rubies, set in heavy gold.
10 bars after /1/	Dancers appear, in short tutus, bearing gifts to the Ruby Priestess.
12 bars after /5/	Each lays her present on a low table in front of the center of the doorway.
/7/	The Ruby Priestess appears and greets dancers bearing gifts.
/9/	Ruby Priestess exits. Dancers bearing gifts are delighted to have pleased her.

/11/	Ruby Priestess reappears, describing an episode from the Ramayana. Pas de deux with Ruby Priest.
7 bars after /15/	Gift bearers express amazement at her beauty and pay homage.
/18/	Priestess chooses most beautiful stone and exits.
/20/	Recapitulation. Priestess reappears, wearing the chosen stone and leads celebration. ALL EXIT—BLACKOUT—CHANGE OF SCENE
	Part II—The Sapphire Gate
2nd mvt.: Adagio	The Sapphire Spirit, imprisoned in a cage guarded by enormous birds.
/3/	She tries in vain to open the gate.
/5/	The birds lull her to sleep.
7 bars after /7/	In a dream the Sapphire Sultan seems to open the gate and in a languorous dance they celebrate their passion.
/9/	At the end, the cage vanishes and the birds turn into beautiful girls and handsome men.

1947

Second Take

Part 1. The House of Rubies

The façade of an Indian Temple, encrusted with rubies, set in heavy gold. Dancers appear, in short tutus, bearing gifts to the Ruby Priestess. Each lays her present on a low table in front of the center of the doorway. The Ruby Priestess appears. She executes a brilliant dance and choses the most beautiful stone.

Part 2. The Emerald Pavilion

Part 3. The Sapphire Gate

Part 4. The Crystal Palace

A glorious palace of diamonds, lit from the interior. Through its colonnades, enter the procession of the Ruby, Emerald and Sapphire spirits. When all have taken their places, the Spirit of Crystal, in diamonds, appears with her retinue. Grand pas d'action. The spirits offer her their respective crowns, which she, in turn, accepts and restores to them. Then the Crystal Knight appears to crown her with her own diamonds. Tableau.

1947

Letter to Lincoln Kirstein

Dear Lincoln: *London, 4 August 1952*
I am very sorry to hear about your mother's death. I am so touched that she remembered me. She was always so nice to me. If it wouldn't be for her I don't think we would have a company now. But I believe that she's going to help us still, because I believe in that.

I don't think you should make any decisions now. And certainly don't put more money into the City Center. It is a bottomless pit. About your taking Baum's place, I am not very much in favor of it. It is not your nature to be involved in money and commercial things. You could be an official adviser or something like that.

It would be better to think about my idea of free performances for children. Not only ballet, but drama (maybe *Midsummer Night's Dream*) and opera. It's the only thing for the future and the only reason for keeping a theater in New York. I would say that if we eventually get people to help us financially it will be through this idea. There could be a committee of rich people to raise money for free performances for children. There is no progress in just inventing new small ballets every season just to exist. Until now, somehow we have created new ideas and we were progressive and now the company is established and can perform as well as the other famous companies. But that is not enough. If we continue in the same way we will become standardized, just like the others. We shouldn't do millions of little hors d'oeuvres. It is no longer progressive. And it is impossible to do new things so fast. It must be a process of evolution. But if we create a purpose for the company and for the theater, we can afford to fill in with little things now and then, but really have time to do something interesting. The new generation which would come to the performances will be the future citizens of the United States, some poets, some musicians. We have to do something for their souls and minds. Nobody is doing anything at all except the police department.

It's true that in the beginning there will be a loss. But we would have a loss anyway, and this idea eventually will help us. The nation that develops from this public will be the reason for asking people for money. Then people will give with pleasure. Maybe the Mayor will be interested, and all the rich people. But they are not interested in giving us money to pay [so-and-so's] salary.

We would still have one matinee a week to sell tickets for, and it will probably bring in as much money as two would. Please, Lincoln, think about this. It's not as stupid as it sounds at first. . . .

Don't worry about anything, Lincoln. Everything is all right.

Love

George

Some Thoughts on Ballet in America*

LINCOLN KIRSTEIN, writing about ballet in America, said: "In the last fifteen years there has been an enormous development of interest for traditional theatrical dancing in the Western classic idiom throughout the United States. Not only have many foreign companies enjoyed repeated success, but America supports at least three major local troupes, a huge number of ballet schools, a rising generation of dancers first appearing since the last war, and an enthusiastic and growing audience."

The question usually asked is: How has America influenced the classic dance? To my mind, this is not an essential question. Since ballet was invented, it has been influenced by all the countries where it developed, from Italy, to France, to Scandinavia, and it has adapted itself to the physical abilities of the different countries. It is not for me to state the historical development of the art, or to trace its evolution. The fact remains that there is a fully developed art form, which has now become universal, with a body of classified and organized techniques which will remain the basis of the vocabulary of classical dance until such time as ballet is replaced by some other form of theatrical entertainment.

I think that if there is such a thing as American ballet it is reflected not in style but in subject matter. For example, a ballet about cowboys might be called American, as a ballet about Sherlock Holmes might be called English, or the cancan might be called French. In the latter case, however, it is a question of national rather than classical dance.

*Original statement given in French. Translator unknown.

As for style in dancing, there are naturally some small differences in execution, but they are mainly differences of personality. For example, there may be ten different interpretations of *Swan Lake* or *Giselle*, all equally valid. Some people, whose taste is inclined towards the obvious, have come to expect certain stylistic clichés from dancers, as for example, that the dancer should be warm and passionate, but a dancer does not necessarily have to be warm or passionate. Some people are readily inclined to look for the obvious on stage. There are two types of personalities, for example, which seem to be universally pleasing to audiences. One is the vampire, almost like a female Mephistopheles. The other personality is the lyrical or the poetic one, often almost lethargic. Yet some very good dancers that I have seen in my life were beautifully cold, like birds with no warmth at all. Others were like Oriental queens, others again were like pure crystal. The technique of classical dance necessarily creates a certain uniformity in dancers, which has little or nothing to do with nationality, but which is certainly modified by the personality of the dancer. I am, of course, talking about dancers with talent. Talent is God-given; it is not given by a nation or by a passport. A dancer must certainly have this gift, but this gift can manifest itself in forms as various as the universe. One can not say that sunshine is better than shade, or that a glass of cold water is worse than a flaming chimney.

There are many so-called connoisseurs who try to dictate a certain style of ballet dancing, and they talk about a tradition that they never knew. Fortunately, this does not endanger the progress or development of ballet, because the real public, the people who sit in galleries, at a small admission price which most of them can ill afford, can distinguish good dancing from an inferior imitation of a style which was interesting a hundred years ago. Every performance demonstrates that this is the true ballet public, without prejudice or fake balletomanism.

I was brought up in St. Petersburg. The style of dancing there was very strict and precise. At the same time, in Moscow, 600 kilometers away, the style of dancing was close to that of a circus performance. The Moscovites accused us in St. Petersburg of being cold, and we accused them of bad taste. History shows that the dancers and choreographers who later influenced ballet as a whole came mainly from St. Petersburg.

The future of ballet in America, as well as in other countries, depends on the rise of new choreographers capable of furthering its development. A school of dancing is not enough. A school naturally perpetuates the technique, but it cannot lead to a new style in the ballet, nor can a new style of ballet be invented. Progress in any art is a slow and complex process, and therefore it cannot be generated by one person only. Many people are necessarily involved. In the field of ballet, it is not only the personality of the dancer and the art of the choreographer which achieve or create a style; one should not forget the composers. Delibes and Tchaïkowsky are, I believe, as responsible for what is now traditionally known as classic ballet as its choreographers and dancers.

Any good company needs a professional choreographer, just as any good restaurant needs a good chef. If a ballet company does not develop successfully the blame must be laid at the feet of its choreographer. If he were given all possibilities of choosing the best dancers, and if he were given the liberty to do what he wants, he should not have failed in his task of achieving adequate results.

Finally I must say that I do not like to write about ballet. More than that, I do not like to talk about ballet. I think the best thing is to see it.

1952

If I Were President

IF I were president, I would devote at least one speech to a very large section of our population which is not usually thought of or addressed as a separate unit by people in the government—I refer to the intellectuals and artists of the United States and to people who are interested in the intellectual and artistic life of our country, in other words in the spiritual and not just the material values of our existence.

There are a great many of us: writers, painters, sculptors, actors, composers, instrumentalists, and dancers. And there are uncounted millions of those for whom their interest in our creative efforts is as important and sometimes more important than all the other ordinary details of their lives. That is why we would like the president to show an interest in and speak to us about that other half of our life—the nonmaterialistic part of life, which we represent. Actually this very large group of citizens of whom I am speaking has never made any very great demands. None of us is especially interested in money or power, but all of us want to be recognized and given the possibility to create and to enjoy art. Certain forms of art have received wonderful support from the public itself; from private citizens and groups of interested people, who have created libraries and museums and supported symphony orchestras, and we owe them a great debt of gratitude. But writers and artists have never been accorded full recognition by a government body or official—and the person who first gives us this recognition will earn our wholehearted gratitude and support.

I firmly believe that woman is appointed by destiny to inspire and bring beauty to our existence. Woman herself is the reason for life to be beautiful, and men should be busy serving her.

That is why I feel that if the woman will take into her hands the task of restoring the true purpose and values of life, then the man, who in our civilization is caught like a squirrel in the wheel of fortune, will find the strength to escape out of it and bring all his highest qualities to this purpose.

This brings us to the important problem of our children who are our future. Their taste for art should be developed from early childhood. They should learn to love the beautiful and impractical as well as the useful and practical. One should give them fairy tales, music, dance, theater. This is real magic for children, and it is strong enough to overcome many dangers that threaten them, mainly because their minds are unoccupied and their imaginations unfed. Developing these qualities in our children is the first step to promoting peace in the world—by giving them true standards of what is most important in human life. Inner nobility will safeguard them from the cynicism of utilitarianism. Some twenty thousand young children saw special performances given for them by New York City Ballet. It was absolutely extraordinary to see how avidly they devoured those performances. The children must be reached before they are corrupted by life.

In conclusion I would like to say a few words about my special field of art—the ballet. American people have a special affinity to movement in general and to ballet in particular. They are superb dancers, and their interest in this art deserves to be encouraged and channeled in the right way.

In ballet, woman is all-important. She is the queen of the performance, and the men surround her like courtiers. This is perhaps why I have thought so much about the woman's role and enormous possibilities in real life as well as on the stage.

1961

Whitney Balliett (1926–2007)

Tapped by William Shawn to write a jazz column for *The New Yorker*, Whitney Balliett—himself a New Yorker—remained an ornament to the magazine for just under fifty years, universally admired for his superb ear, elegant prose, and utterly convincing reportages. Working from notes only (no recording devices), he managed to reproduce the sound and substance—the life—of his subjects, fueled by his love of the art and of the artists. Mostly he let them tell their own stories, playing them back, as the *Times* put it in its obituary, "as long, extravagant solos." Like, in fact, a jazz artist.

In person he was diffident, urbane, and humorous—a devoted family man whose work kept him up late at night in Manhattan's boîtes and jazz clubs. He had been to Phillips Exeter Academy, Cornell, the Army, and *The Saturday Review* before *The New Yorker* claimed him. And he published seventeen books—mostly collections of his reviews, profiles, portraits. Baby Laurence, about whom Balliett writes below, had danced with the bands of Duke Ellington, Count Basie, and Woody Herman, and with such masters as Art Tatum and Charlie Mingus, and has been credited with having transformed tap dancing into jazz dancing—a perfect jazz subject for a perfect jazz writer. Among his greatest admirers have been such unalike jazz aficionados as Philip Larkin and Nicholson Baker.

New York Notes

April 6th: A great drummer dances sitting down. A great tap-dancer drums standing up. Both make rhythm three-dimensional. But the only instrument a tap-dancer has is himself, so he is a special—and fragile—breed. Such was Baby Laurence, who died earlier this week in New York, at the age of fifty-three. Laurence was born (in Baltimore, as Laurence Donald Jackson) twenty years too late. Tap-dancing, which evolved in this country over the course of a hundred years from the ring shout, jigs and clogs, the soft-shoe, and the buck-and-wing, reached its apogee in the twenties and thirties, and went out of fashion when vaudeville was overrun by the movies. Laurence nonetheless patched together a career. He started at twelve, as a singer, when such child stars as Buddy Rich and Jackie Coogan were international darlings, but by his late teens he had turned formidably to dancing. He came to the fore on Fifty-second Street, around 1940, with a singing-and-dancing act that sang Jimmy Lunceford arrangements in six-part harmony, and then he went out as a single, hoofing mainly in the Midwest. In the forties and fifties, he danced with Duke Ellington, Count Basie, and Woody Herman, and occasionally surfaced at small clubs in Harlem. After a long illness, he materialized again, at the Showplace, on West Fourth Street, in the winter of 1960, and then for a time he seemed to be everywhere. He danced at the small Max Roach–Charlie Mingus rump festival in Newport that summer, and in 1962 he graced an abortive jazz festival sponsored by the government in Washington. A few months later, he appeared with sensational effect at the Newport Jazz Festival, along with such dancers as Pete Nugent, Honi Coles, and Bunny Briggs. (The first time Briggs watched Laurence dance, in the thirties, he paid him the tap-dancer's highest compliment: "I saw a fellow dance," he told his mother, "and his feet never touched the floor.") Then he drifted into an oblivion that finally ended in 1969, when word came that he was back in Baltimore, had a day job, and was dancing weekends in a restaurant in a shopping center in Gaithersburg, Maryland. It was a rending gig. Laurence, backed by an excellent trio led by the drummer Eddie Phyfe, who was also, willy-nilly, Laurence's guardian-manager-employer, danced a couple of times a night on a swaying plywood platform set up in the center of a big, dark room. He was in raw shape, and his steps were heavy and uncertain. The stolid Maryland burghers, sawing at their New York Cut sirloins, paid him little heed. But Laurence finished strong: early in 1973 he suddenly reappeared in New York, and during the year he headed up a successful series of Sunday-afternoon tap-dancing sessions at the Jazz Museum, took in students, danced at the Palace with Josephine Baker, did some television, and gave a triumphant performance at the Newport–New York Jazz Festival.

He was a strange little man. His arms and legs were pipes, his face was scarred, and he had hooded eyes. In the wrong light, he looked sinister, and, indeed, orphaned at thirteen and later hemmed in by drugs and alcohol and financial troubles, he tended to be devious and self-pitying. Yet his dancing belied all that. In many ways, he was more a drummer than a dancer. He did little with the top half of his torso; holding his head upright, he either let his arms flap at his sides or crooked them as if he were a begging dog. But his legs and feet were speed and thunder and surprise. Unlike many tap-dancers, who rely on certain changeless patterns, Laurence constantly improvised. His sound was not the serene clickety-tick-tick of Bill Robinson or Chuck Green; it was a succession of explosions, machine-gun rattles, and jarring thumps. There were no frills to his dancing. He seemed, in his fervent way, to try to sculpt out palpable rhythms. He would start a thirty-two-bar chorus with light heel-and-toe figures, drop in a heavy, off-beat heel accent with one foot and echo it with the other, go up on his toes and then release a double-time splatter of heel beats, resume the heel-and-toe steps, breaking them frequently with ominous flat-footed offbeats, spin completely around, and start crossing and recrossing his feet, letting off sprays of rapid toe beats each time his feet touched wood. Laurence tended to work in a small area (Briggs often skitters thirty or forty feet across a stage, like a stone skipping over water), but next he might move in a large circle, each toe stuttering alternately on the floor as he moved, and, the circle complete, abruptly sail into violent knee-pumping, followed by toe-to-heel explosions that might last ten seconds before giving way to a terrific double-time burst, a leap into the air, and a deep bow.

June 3, 1974

Clive Barnes (1927–2008)

Born in London, Clive Barnes gained his Honours degree at Oxford. On returning to London, he soon found himself as one of a small group of dance critics who broke with the generally uninformed and outdated views of the establishment critics, most of whom were music critics moonlighting. Referring to himself as "your typical working-class overachiever," Barnes fairly quickly established himself as the first purely dance reviewer of the *London Sunday Times*. He was a great admirer of Frederick Ashton, about whom he wrote a book, but, equally important, he was an early British champion (Richard Buckle was another) of George Balanchine and Martha Graham.

In 1965, partly through the influence of Lincoln Kirstein, Barnes was named chief dance critic of *The New York Times*, and, a few years later, he became its leading theater critic as well, wielding immense authority and power in both roles. In 1978, he left the *Times* for *The New York Post*, where he reigned as dance, theater, and opera critic until his death thirty years later. His obituary in the *Times* put it this way: "His erudition, distilled into shrewdly pithy analysis, prompted not just readers but also choreographers and dancers to sit up and learn something new." Among his many publications are *Ballet Here and Now*, *Inside American Ballet Theatre*, and a biography of Rudolf Nureyev.

The Clive Barnes Foundation, created by his wife, the former Royal Ballet soloist Valerie Taylor-Barnes, presents annual awards to two young artists in the fields of theater and dance, thus continuing his constant support and encouragement of young performers in their chosen field.

Paul Taylor

PAUL TAYLOR is a choreographer. Paul Taylor is a dance company, one of the select dance companies of our time, just as Taylor himself is one of our greatest choreographers. But Paul Taylor is also a way of looking at dance, and a way of looking at life. It is a way with very much a personal slant. That slant, that highly individualized and attitudinized attitude, colors the work and infuses the dances. In dance terms Taylor is recognizable four studios off. Today, following the death of Jerome Robbins, the 74-year-old Taylor and the 85-year-old Merce Cunningham are the sole survivors of the universally recognized great 20th-century choreographers. They are as different as chalk is to cheese—well, to be more accurate say as Stilton is to Camembert—but they stand alone. Taylor wears his eminence as lightly as ever, but that lightness has its own profundity, as his apparent ease is forever skating over depths mostly hidden, occasionally shatteringly revealed.

I first met Paul before I ever saw him dance, or for that matter, choreograph. It was in 1963—more than 40 years ago now, and two years before I left my native London for New York—and I was introduced to him by either Lincoln Kirstein or Edwin Denby. He looked, oddly enough, rather as he does now; younger, of course, but still like an Alex Katz painting of himself, bland but incisive, a doe-eyed Superman on his way to artistic posterity. His company wasn't performing at the time but he invited me to his studio, then on Sixth Avenue, where he and his dancers gave me a special rehearsal plus demonstration. I was fascinated by what I saw.

They were dancing Stravinsky's *The Rite of Spring*. But they weren't. Or rather they were, but Paul with a casual apology (which was not so much an apology as a kind of definition) that they were only rehearsing—just rehearsing—to the Stravinsky because he happened to have a recording handy, and new music would soon be written. I must have looked puzzled, for he assured me encouragingly that everything would be fine because the rhythms of the commissioned score would be the same as the Stravinsky. Right, I said. Anyway it looked great to me—it turned out to be a now seemingly lost work, *Scudorama*, one of Paul's more cynical satires on the State of the Union and its current address—and I thanked everyone, and the dancers smiled sweetly at me in the way dancers always smile at visiting firemen when there is no very clear fire-alarm in earshot.

For myself I said I would write about him when I got back to London, and once there I sat for some time in front of a blank-faced typewriter (it was in the days when we still used typewriters if quill pens and parchment were unavailable) doing my best to write about Taylor, but never could quite get type to writer. It was my first indication that Paul Taylor—whether a dancer or later solely as a choreographer—was going to be enormously difficult to write about. Enormously gratifying but enormously difficult. I had an awesome fear that I was never going to be able to write about him and his work to anything like my satisfaction.

The next time I saw him and his company was in Italy the following year at Gian Carlo Menotti's then wondrous annual Spoleto Festival, which in those days I regularly attended. This time I saw the company actually perform in a theater and I was enchanted. The work, not unexpectedly, seemed even better on stage than in the studio. Then I knew my enthusiasm was right in the first place. Unfortunately I also knew I was right in the second place. I was never going to be able to really write about him.

I recall seeing Paul at a street-side café, so I reintroduced myself and sat down and we drank coffee. He had just premiered a work called *The Red Room*. What did you think of it, he asked. Or did he say nothing, and I felt embarrassed and had to tell him; anyway I told him. It's a thing, unfortunately, critics do. We have big mouths—often smaller minds, but big mouths. What I told him was some interpretation, full of dust and symbolism. When it had flamboyantly trickled to its halting end, the hitherto silent Paul drained his coffee cup, gave one of those beatific smiles of his, and said, yes, it probably was like that. He himself had never considered, at least not considered in so much detail, what it meant. No, well . . . it brought home to me the fact (and I say this after watching dance for more than 60 years and writing about it for more than 50) that the only real criticism of a dance can be another dance. I recall composer/diarist Ned Rorem once saying: "Critics of words use words; critics of music use words." And, of course, so do critics of dance.

So what is one to say about Taylor? First, which Taylor are we talking about? Is it the dancer, now long lost, except indelible in our memory, loping his way through the undergrowths of theatricality like an indolent antelope, with a jump and a twist, a muscular awareness of kinetic fact so that one was never sure which came first, the impulse or the move. A natural dancer if ever Eden saw one. Then of course, and now so much more importantly, there is Taylor the choreographer, a profession he once shyly disavowed but has now embraced with cuddly arms of steel. How did he get started?

He was born Paul Belville Taylor, Jr., on July 29, 1930 in Edgewood, near Pittsburgh, PA. And went to school where he trained as a swimmer, obtaining a swimming scholarship to Syracuse University, where he first studied art, until a burgeoning interest in dance took over. In 1952 he moved to New York to further his dance interests, and studied with no one but the best: modern dance with Martha Graham, Doris Humphrey, José Limón and Merce Cunningham, and ballet—rather more desultorily—with Antony Tudor and Margaret Craske. The big influence was Graham. In a letter he once wrote to me: "Once, when I was a student, Martha let me get dressed all in black so nobody could see me and help push set pieces from the wings into the legs so the dancers could get at them. I was in heaven."

There is a story, possibly apocryphal, although it has no right to be, concerning the time Taylor made what you might call his public debut with Mary Martin in *Peter Pan*. And not so much with Mary Martin at that. Jerome Robbins had done the choreography and needed a boy who could do a back flip-flop. At auditions he asked: "Is there anyone who can do a back flip-flop." "Yes," said Paul out loud, adding *sotto voce* to someone standing by, "What's a back flip-flop?" He was told and straightway faked it. He didn't quite fake it on the first night though. He went straightway into the proscenium arch and broke his nose. That was his debut in the gentle art of show business.

He danced with various companies: Cunningham in 1954, Pearl Lang in 1955 and the late '50s found him with Graham. She created major roles for him in *Clytemnestra* in 1958, *Alcestis* in 1960 and *Phaedra* in 1962. He also took part in that singular, in every sense, 1959 Graham collaboration with George Balanchine, *Episodes*, to the music of Anton Webern, for which, in the New York City Ballet part, Balanchine created a solo for Taylor to the *Variations for Orchestra* (Op. 30).

However, to move back a little, he had formed his own—tentative—company by 1954, first appearing in concerts organized by James Waring's Dance Associates. At this period he was much influenced by his long-time collaborator, the painter Robert Rauschenberg (who was also Cunningham's friend, influence and collaborator) and was exploring, perhaps a little naively, the concepts of minimalism and "found" art. It was during this hopefully radicalized period in 1957 that Taylor gave that notorious concert at the 92nd Street Y called *Seven New Dances*.

One of these seven "dances" had Taylor standing stock-still, prompting a still celebrated review by Louis Horst in his magazine *Dance Observer*, consisting of nothing but four inches of blank space signed Louis Horst. This was Taylor at his most earnestly provocative—but remember he had a year earlier created the remarkable dance, still in the repertory, *3 Epitaphs*, to a recording of a New Orleans walking band, which contained the seed of much of his later work. It was original. It was genius.

By the beginning of the '60s Taylor's company, Taylor's dancing and, most importantly, Taylor's choreography were settling down nicely. In 1961 he produced *Insects and Heroes*, like *3 Epitaphs* a seminal work, and then in 1962 came his great white thought in a white shade, *Aureole*, which took its Handel score and revealed dancing of a new grace and simplicity. By this time Taylor had reached full maturity as a choreographer; it was the turning point in his career. From then on the Paul Taylor Dance Company was a dance force in the world. Taylor was now dancer, choreographer and—very much—company director.

I often think running a dance company would provide an excellent training ground for running for public office—so much of it is concerned with raising money. Art in the theatre is always partly business. However, there is also the hardly minor matter of creativity. He is arguably the most inventive and the most versatile choreographer alive today. Nor is that the most remarkable thing about him. Actually the most remarkable aspect of all this Taylor-made choreography is simply its consistency. We all know that the admirable Ralph Waldo Emerson termed "a foolish consistency the hobgoblin of little minds," but Emerson never met Paul Taylor. Or if he had he would doubtless have claimed that Taylor's consistency, turning out ballet after ballet, two a year, with exquisitely accurate quality control, is scarcely foolish.

George Balanchine liked to note that his muse had to arrive on union time—and indeed one of the characteristics of major choreographers of dance companies is timely consistency. They not only have to be prodigiously prolific, but they have to meet the virtually contractual needs of their respective companies. With Paul Taylor that has, for years, meant that come rain, come shine, come blizzard, come earthquake, he has through thick and thin delivered both for his dancers and for the never satiated appetite of his loyal audience, two brand new works a year.

Even if they were pretty bad ballets that would still be a logistical achievement and a triumph of will, but the enviable thing about Taylor is that almost all of them are pretty good, with the absolute dud being almost rare enough for a collector's item. Taylor's choreography remains neat, contained, imaginative and, yes, often funny. What is so remarkable about Taylor is the man's amazing versatility and fecundity. In this way he's like Mozart. Some new works admittedly are expendable and fairly soon expended. But others show a wonderful resilience suggesting that Taylor is building a whole storehouse of future dance classics.

For a painter, who can create a gallery-full of paintings, for a composer, who can maintain a shelf of scores, for a wordsmith, either novelist or playwright, who can offer a library of texts, fecundity is no problem. Sheer quantity can even be its own reward. But for a choreographer, the more works you make the more difficult it is to keep them alive and in repertory. Dance notation (still relatively primitive compared with its musical cousin) and video can help, but ballets can only really exist on stage. And there's the problem. Since he first hung up his choreographer's shingle in 1954, Taylor has created many more than 100 works. But how many survive as anything more substantial than memories, photographs and press clips? Comparatively few.

The gift to be simple is far rarer than it should be. In the world of dance it is one of the most special gifts that Paul Taylor has to offer. He is quite simply the most dazzlingly inventive choreographer alive. Steps flow from him and ideas bubble. The text of every dance is subtly provided with a sub-text, the rhythm and image of every step are locked loosely into the music, and his dancers are given the space to express wonder. One of Taylor's special skills is the manner in which he can thread dances together in some oddly satisfying chain of movement, and this is the dominant force of his choreography.

The French playwright Jean Anouilh liked to categorize his plays as "pink" or "black," and it is a characterization that might be well applied to Taylor. When he's at his best Taylor is almost inevitably disconcerting. There are two Paul Taylors out there. At least. But just for the sake of argument let's concentrate on two. Let's call them Paul Taylor the Good and Paul Taylor the Silly. Of course, Paul Taylor the Good often has a touch of divine silliness woven in, while Paul Taylor the Silly is more often than not very, very good. He delights in the prettiness of the rainbow film of oil on water, but insists on revealing the grime of the muddy puddle beneath.

His impeccably musical choreography is, apart from anything else, a perfect environment for dancers, but luckily for audiences it is an environment of an ever-variable emotional climate and poetic atmosphere, so even in a comedy, while giggling at the nostalgic belly-laughs, keep an eye and heart open for those overtones and undertones. The sweetly untroubled performers, as charming and playful as kittens, may bounce and cavort through a dance with the blithe assurance of a cloudless summer day where even dusk is just a rumor. Yet the work, quite stealthily, is hardly ever as helter-skelter cheerful as it might at first seem. There is usually either danger ahead or danger below.

It is the cool distancing of an often ironic, sometimes cynical artistic sensibility. But what is unexpected perhaps about Taylor is how brilliant he has become in compiling such exceptionally well-balanced programs. No other contemporary dancemaker has his range and ability to put a constant stylistic idiom to so many different theatrical purposes.

Cunning diversity is the heart and soul of a dance repertory. Taylor's works all bear the signature imprint of his genius, a profile as recognizable yet as indefinable as that of, say, Picasso's paintings, yet beyond this, also like Picasso, they are a blissfully varied bunch. You can take any program at will and get a great sampler of the Taylor method. A sampler that is illuminated not only by the superbly idiosyncratic dancing of the young company, much of it apparently always recently recruited, but also by the masterly designs of Santo Loquasto and the lighting by Jennifer Tipton, who have worked with him for many years.

His basic artistic method can perhaps be best demonstrated by pinpointing some of his most or at least more typical works. But which? Possibly the gentle yet suggestively tragic *Sunset*, an evocation to softly imperial Elgar, of soldiers and their girls on the eve of battle; or *Airs*, set to Handel, with Taylor in his cheery transcendental baroque mood; or *Cloven Kingdom*, that urbane picture of silk-gloved savagery and a dance satire of the satyr beneath the skin, a cutting comment on man's bestial nature.

The ballets are often so wonderfully different, from that steamy salute to the tango full of stylized sins of the flesh and spurts of the spirit, *Piazzolla Caldera*, to *Offenbach Overtures*, a frothy and satirical glance at all the frou-frou-and-chandeliers ballets you've ever seen, offering a semi-affectionate but wickedly clever and hilarious send-up of France, *La Gloire* and all things Gallic, particularly French operetta and French militarism.

Or if you like, take *Oh, You Kid!*, a wonderful ragtime romp with sinister overtones placed in a kind of time-locked Coney Island of the mind, which with its sardonic yet affectionate humors of the Age of Ragtime and the pop culture that flowed around it, runs the gamut of what made America shimmy, shake and occasionally dance during the second decade of the past century. Pop ballroom dance, vaudeville, silent movies—and because we are dealing with Taylor here and his darker side of midnight—carnival grotesqueries and even a bitterly absurdist sidelong glance at the Ku Klux Klan, run riot in a pastiche collage of period dance and period attitude. And with Loquasto's Keystone-style, bathing-beauty costumes and Tipton's warm, enveloping lighting, the entire ballet takes on the look of a sepia-toned seaside photograph of the era, but one long tucked away in some forgotten drawer.

Then you might cite the idiosyncratic and breezily whimsical *A Field of Grass*, with the easy, shuffling dexterity of its humor, or the very different, and sensuously beautiful, Wagnerian love-duets in the rhapsodic *Roses*. Then there are such black works as that dark tale of evil among repressed schoolboys, *The Word*, or Taylor's piece of 19th-Century Gothic, *Nightshade*, a nightmarish, surrealistic comedy set to Scriabin music, featuring twisted souls chased by something horrible from the woodshed. And how about that grim excursion into a lunatic snake pit, the horrifying *Last Look*, a sort of amorphous nightmare of untrammeled madness set in a house of mirrors, and powerfully enough envisaged to send you screaming out into the night.

But then there is the ever-popular *Company B*, danced to recordings by the Andrews Sisters, a paean to the times and attitudes of World War II, or that great runabout, freestyle, go-for-baroque ballet *Esplanade*, a dazzling piece of dance architectonics choreographed to Bach. But, talking of Bach, there is also *Cascade*, a ballet recalling the gentle classic gravity of Balanchine's *Concerto Barocco* as an essay in symmetry and form, with 12 dancers caught in mirror images and repetitions of patterns that both follow the intricacies of the music and comment on them, a jigsaw construction clicking into dance space and time. The work possesses a timeless classic assurance. Despite its architectonic formality it also has an unusually strong organic quality, making every dance episode seem the natural consequence of the last, thus managing to suggest a three-dimensional extension of Bach's bright-toned yet meditative music, providing a mysterious journey, almost a guided tour, through Bach formality and perfect dance etiquette.

Consider *Lost, Found and Lost*, a witty commentary, both acute and cute, on fashion and boredom, set to Golden Oldies of the '40s, or the beautiful *Eventide*, seemingly a picture of Edwardian youth before the slaughter of World War I, contrasted with the manic cartoon madness and epic stupidity of *Funny Papers* (a work he edited from suggestions from his dancers), and *Speaking in Tongues*, Taylor's dark study of Pentecostal old-time religion and small town hypocrisy.

Probably this darker side of Taylor's moon found its earliest expression in *Big Bertha*, a study in ambiguous horror that more than 30 years after its creation still proves as corrosively frightening as ever. And when he did finally get to choreographing *Le Sacre du Printemps* (*The Rehearsal*) he typically made it into a melodrama cum detective story, as mysterious as *Fiends Angelical*, a dark jewel, a black opal of a ballet. Here is a formalized ceremony of good and evil, complete with a ritual couple and a high priestess, the chaotic formations of the celebrants only resolved by the Priestess pulling a red cord from the group, which is instantly twisted into a star-shape, all offering an impression of some atavistic black ritual, decorative but unholy.

Paul the Dark is often banished by Paul the Light with works such as the blissfully nutty, humorously effervescent *Dandelion Wine*. Set to baroque music by the 18th-Century violin virtuoso Pietro Locatelli, it's a round-robin of pleasure and merrymaking. One of Taylor's special choreographic skills is the manner in which he can thread dances together in some oddly satisfying chain of movement, and this is the dominant force of these dances. They start out as a solo promenade by one dancer dressed in a shocking yellow jumpsuit, who is soon joined by three men and four women all contrasted in white with various pastel-colored trimmings. The general lightness of touch and dance is interspersed with anarchic moments of wry, inconsequential humor, and the whole ballet reaches its climax when all the dancers are joined up in a writhing mass on the floor, from which, like eight determined Houdinis, they finally extricate themselves, still holding daisy-chained hands.

As I have suggested, Bach has a special resonance for Taylor, enabling him to capture the precise complexities of the composer's *A Musical Offering*, with tribal-like dances said to be inspired by primitive Polynesian art. And then there is *Promethean Fire*. Walt Disney can have inspired comparatively few ballets, yet his movie *Fantasia*, in association with the great Anglo-American conductor Leopold Stokowski, helped a whole generation—Taylor's and my own—to an appreciation of classical music. Even now I can never encounter Bach's great *Toccata and Fugue in D Minor* without hearing and seeing in my heart Stokowski's grandiose orchestration and Disney's inspired squiggles and strokes—like a Kandinsky abstract painting come to life—that accompanied it in *Fantasia*. I suspect Taylor had the same reaction, only he transported that reaction to genius. Now, the fascinatingly "wrong" thing about Stokowski's Bach was that it gave the composer's baroque austerity a romantic voice. And in this *Promethean Fire* Taylor precisely encapsulates the ornate grandeur of Bach/Stokowski, presenting a complex yet pellucid view of the music. The choreography doubles in and back, twists inside itself, only to reform in great gushing segments of pounding movement—relentless, heroic and perfect.

Paul is a sorcerer with music; he hears with his eyes and transforms the result into dance. His eclectic musical tastes seem to embrace the whole world of civilized sound—but consider in detail his approach to just two totally different composers, the 19th-Century impressionist Claude Debussy and the 20th-Century modernist John Adams, and Taylor's ballets *Arabesque* and *Fiddler's Green*.

Arabesque glistening through the tonal images of Debussy's music is a perfectly crafted work of art. The music itself—taken from various scores, notably the scherzo from the Quartet and *Pan and Syrinx*—works perfectly for Taylor's swift and shifting choreography. Although the very term *arabesque* is hallowed in classic ballet, Taylor in his fluent, ballet-tinctured modern-dance idiom studiously avoids the step in this atmospheric evocation of Middle Eastern exoticism. It is basically a plotless work, although in the rhapsodic central role there is perhaps a slightest literary hint of love and particularly love's blindness. It's a hint, no more. For the rest, the work, effortlessly assisted by Santo Loquasto's sexy Eastern-style costumes and the rich chiaroscuro of Jennifer Tipton's lighting, is a stunning demonstration of Taylor's total command of both musical structure and musical texture.

Now for Adams, the structure and texture are completely, and naturally, different. There is no story to *Fiddler's Green*, for unlike *Arabesque* there is not even so much as a subtext to this sunny, pure dance piece set to selections from John Adams's *John's Book of Alleged Dances*. I suppose the music, like most Adams, could be lumped as "minimalist," but also like so many of the composer's scores it combines cheery harmonies with an ongoing rhythmic flow, here loosely structured as dances. Taylor has used the score to provide the groundwork for a series of bucolic episodes that suggest a hoe-down in a country barn, as envisaged by children; it's games and square-dances, circular rounds with hands held in childlike innocence, with the occasional touch of playground hurts and playtime rivalries. The title seems oddly literal, the sound of the Adams suggested fiddles and fiddlers, while Santo Loquasto has placed his white smock-like costumes against the background of a paint-box green so emerald it could make you dream of St. Patrick.

I have already mentioned Taylor's musical eclecticism not only in such classic fields as Bach, Debussy and Adams, but equally in pop music, for he seems attracted inevitably to the inherent nostalgia of its prescribed shelf-life of immediacy. Because by its nature, pop music implies a particularized time and place, and Taylor can draw on those period charms like a succubus. There are many examples here, but one

I particularly love is his superbly structured and layered ballet of the Great Depression, *Black Tuesday*, set to evocative, mostly poignantly upbeat Tin Pan Alley songs of the period. Although set on Taylor's own company it was first given by American Ballet Theatre, and with Loquasto's sardonically evocative costumes and lighting by Jennifer Tipton, it strikes me as a great ballet, one of Taylor's finest achievements, bouncing off the stage with sheer exuberance.

Fascinatingly, no music is a trifle unconsidered by Taylor, not even the corn-huskiness and melodic sentimentality of the Barbershop Quartet music recorded by The Buffalo Bills, for *Dream Girls*. This is a hilarious spoof of Western guys and the gals they left home for, conjuring up a goofy cartoonish sense of nutty fun. It starts with four cowpokes lounging around to the strains of *Wait Till the Sun Shines, Nellie*, and then we are off to the races. Throughout it is pure, crazy delight, but perhaps the highlight comes with a male solo deliciously describing unavailing attempts to handle the world's longest trouser-leg while the music laments, *Sam, You Made the Pants Too Long*.

It is too early to suggest what will be Taylor's lasting choreographic legacy. Probably, but sadly, some of the satiric pieces (especially those not backed by a resilient classic score) such as *Scudorama* and *From Sea to Shining Sea*, and even his breakthrough full-evening ballet to Beethoven quartets, the fascinating *Orbs*, will pass by the wayside. Yet it will certainly include many of the pure dance works—which, by the way, have shown that they can be easily transposed, albeit with perhaps some loss, to classic ballet companies—such as that early masterpiece, the ever-luminous *Aureole*, harbinger of so many of Taylor's later achievements; the explosive and lovely *Esplanade*, nowadays a signature piece for Taylor dancers; the airy *Airs*; and the delightfully fantasticated *Arden Court*.

The future, as ever, lies partly with ever-fickle chance. Taylor's creativity seems unabated, and his ability to train, select and nurture superb dancers is, if anything, stronger and firmer than ever. So, to return to our point of departure, Paul Taylor is a choreographer. Paul Taylor is a dance company, one of the select dance companies of the century, just as Taylor himself is one of its greatest choreographers. But mortality, and even its humbler henchman, retirement, insists that time must have a stop.

Will the Paul Taylor Dance Company be able to continue without

Paul Taylor? I should hope so, especially if the world is careful. As for Taylor's works, many of these should and will survive, if not in one repertory then in another. He has created a living library of dance, and it will find its own librarian custodians.

Here and now—on the 50th Anniversary of the company's beginnings—we can simply feel gratitude. For me it has been one of the privileges of my life for a chance to have pigeonholed my time-span alongside quite a few great artists, but there has been none that I have been more grateful to have shared my years with than Paul Taylor. His sensibility as much as his artistry has unerringly spot-lit the past half-century in the fashion of a dance, sometimes a dance of death, always a dance of life, and always with a disquieting genius to display the dog beneath the skin. Thank you, Paul.

2004

Lincoln Barnett (1909–1979)

Lincoln Barnett, who was born in New York and went to the Horace Mann school before attending Princeton, was for many years a leading editor at both *Life* magazine and Time-Life Books. He was also a highly successful writer—his *The Universe and Dr. Einstein* (1948) sold over a million copies and was translated into twenty-eight languages, and his *The Treasure of Our Tongue* (1964), a history of the English language, did almost as well.

He also wrote many fluent, entertaining profiles for *Life*, of which the August 1941 piece on Fred Astaire (below) is a prime example. According to *The New York Times*, "Mr. Astaire was impressed by Mr. Barnett when he discovered that he was an accomplished tap dancer who had developed his soft-shoe routines as a member of the Princeton Triangle Club." Could Henry Luce, who hired Barnett for *Life*, have been aware of this extracurricular talent?

Fred Astaire

It is a precept of American journalism that a good reporter should, like Sir Francis Bacon, take all knowledge for his province and refuse to recognize any area of human affairs as the exclusive preserve of a specialist. Most city editors operate on this principle; they will assign the same reporter to cover a convention of pigeon fanciers one day and an epigraphers' symposium the next. Where specialists are set apart, as in the sports and financial sections, their segregation is primarily a timesaving measure—they have come to know where their news sources lie and can approach them directly without reconnaissance. So although some reporters have regular beats, few will concede that their beats are the *only* ones they could cover. Even among the neatly geometrized news magazines, departmental assignments are seldom permanent, and a man who writes science in December is likely to find himself reporting night clubs in May.

The theory underlying this practice—which is certainly the antithesis of the trend in other professions—rests on the fact that journalism is first of all a process of getting information. There is one way to get information and that is by asking questions (of either a person or a reference library). The reporter's methods differ from those of the historian and the research scholar quantitatively—in the matter of time at his disposal; but his primary talent, like theirs, is his ability to know what to ask—*Prudens quaestio dimidium scientiae*: the sensible question is half of knowing. The reporter who is inquisitive and not proud, unwilling to set any sphere of knowledge outside his interest, unhappily aware of the great clamorous voids of his ignorance, and tormented by the fact that he seldom has time to do more than scratch the surface of any domain he invades—this reporter usually knows what to ask.

Such, at any rate, is the theory; and it explains in part why, as an individual product of the theory—encountered both on a newspaper and on a magazine—I have never become a specialist in anything. It also helps account for the presumptuous range of this book,* which takes off in Hollywood and lands ultimately at the Institute for Advanced Study in Princeton. And it relates directly to the fact that its first subject is Fred Astaire. For although I have never, as I say, acquired a real specialty, there is one small cheerful field which I plowed rather persistently at college and for a few years thereafter. Out of this avocation the present volume grew.

Some people may recall that in *Life*'s formative years as a picture magazine it contained no long articles, no editorials, no by-lines. Its textual substance was composed entirely of picture captions and short expository blocks of type seldom more than a few hundred words in length. These were (and are) lovingly wrought and hewn to exacting space requirements, and those of us who wrote them took as much pride in our efforts as though we were writing sonnets. (And indeed, apart from rhythm and rhyme, the spatial strait jacket to which they conform is scarcely less rigid.) Yet we sometimes wondered if anyone

*Writing on Life: Sixteen Close-ups, 1951.

read them, for time and again strangers would infuriatingly ask, "You say you write for *Life*? What do you mean, *write*? Oh, those little things under the pictures. . . ." I am convinced that most people outside the profession believe all such small and half-perceived typographical entities as subheads, captions, and italic notes simply sprout full-blown from linotype machines without authorship. It never seems to occur to them that *everything* has to be written by *somebody*.

For one reason or another the editors decided after a few years of growing success to enlarge *Life*'s text content by running at least one sustained, signed article each week. Having wanted for some time to write something long enough to be noticed, I went one day to the editor in charge of this new department of reading matter and asked for an assignment.

"What do you want to write about?" he asked tolerantly. "I mean, what do you know about mostly? Have you got any specialty?"

I thought back over my five years on the city staff of the New York *Herald Tribune*—general assignments, no regular beats, no two days alike; then back to my four years at Princeton—liberal arts course, mostly English, no original scholarship. Then I thought of the Triangle Club.

"Well," I said, "tap dancing, I guess—if you want to call that a specialty."

Somehow or other when I was small I had picked up a few tap steps—I think by watching hoofers in musical revues and vaudeville—and I had continued to add to them ever since. When I was about fourteen I went to a boys' camp on Lake Champlain, named Camp Dudley, and one night I won a dramatics contest by putting on a song-and-dance act with another boy of my own age. His name was Burgess Meredith and he taught me a good many tap steps that summer. Later on I took some formal lessons and at Princeton I danced in a couple of Triangle shows; in my senior year I did a violent acrobatic number combining tap steps and tumbling. It nearly destroyed me at every performance, but I remember feeling sure at the time that *that* would be my calling. Although a number of factors combined to lead me into newspaper work instead, I never worked up quite the same enthusiasm for Horace Greeley, Joseph Pulitzer, and Richard Harding Davis that I felt for Bill Robinson, Ray Bolger, and Fred Astaire. Even after I started reporting for the *Herald Tribune* I didn't give up completely—I still took occasional tap lessons whenever I could afford them, and earned a little extra money in spare time by dancing at parties and teaching children. I even appeared briefly in a Broadway show. This episode grew out of a slow afternoon when I was assigned to do a feature story for the drama page on a musical called *Shoot the Works*, an informal revue put on by Heywood Broun. The choreographer and star dancer happened to be Johnny Boyle from whom I had learned the acrobatic dance I did in the Triangle show. When I arrived backstage just before the matinee, Boyle introduced me to Broun and added that I was a former pupil. Broun at once declared that in return for my story I would have to do a spot in the show— then and there. "Go home and get your shoes," he ordered. I took a cab and was back at the theater half an hour later. Near the end of the second act Broun, who acted as master of ceremonies, announced to the audience that a newspaper reporter would be guest performer that afternoon, and explained the circumstances. "If you like his dance," he said, "we'll give him his story." The number went fine, and after the show I had no trouble picking up material for my piece, a routine feature which ran inconspicuously in the Sunday drama section that weekend. The account of my impromptu performance, however, was relayed by Broun to several of the Broadway columns, and as a consequence I enjoyed an ephemeral but immensely satisfying moment of fame in the *Herald Tribune* city room that fooled me for a few days into believing I had become a star reporter.

In the course of all those years of hanging around dancing schools and talking to old-time hoofers like Johnny Boyle, Jack Donahue, Ned Wayburn, and others, I had acquired a good deal of information about the etiology of tap dancing, its origins and primitive forms, and its gradual refinement by successive generations of minstrels, clog dancers, pedestal dancers, and soft-shoe specialists into the higher syntheses of Gene Kelly and Fred Astaire. I had also noticed that nothing serious had ever been written about what seemed to me an authentic and indigenous American folk-art form.

It was not, therefore, entirely a gag when I told the editor my specialty was tap dancing. Still I was surprised when he showed interest and asked me if I wanted to try a piece about it. After I had outlined my main ideas we agreed that for journalistic reasons the article should be integrated around the personality of an individual—i. e., that it should be a close-up rather than an essay. This was probably the first time I realized that a character sketch might originate out of an editor's or a writer's interest in a general subject rather than in the specific individual who plays the title role in the finished article. For every occasion when an editor announces flatly, "We ought to have a piece about Dr. Blank, the helminthologist," there will be another time when he says, "We ought to have a piece about helminthology. Whom shall we hang it on?" This explains why readers will often find themselves deeply interested by a sketch of a man whose name is completely unfamiliar to them; for every good close-up reveals its protagonist in the perspective of his calling and offers a store of wider information that transcends the pivotal facts of his life and personality. The real effectiveness of the close-up as a journalistic form derives from the fundamental fact (well known to Voltaire, Swift, and Aristotle, among others) that the best way to convey ideas is by dramatizing them through the lives of men.

So when the editor decided to let me try a piece on tap dancing he asked, "Who's the best tap dancer in the world?"

"I'd take Fred Astaire," I said. And the assignment was made.

This first story, then, is the only one for which I was previously equipped by any specialized knowledge or "laboratory" experience; the sections dealing with the history and evolution of tap dancing are based on original research. (Shortly after its publication I was told it had been dignified by inclusion in the dance archives of New York's Museum of Modern Art, and so far as I know it is still there.) Although it was my first close-up, the intervening years do not appear to have revised any of its details. At the time it was written, Fred Astaire was one of Hollywood's top stars, and unquestionably the most popular dancer alive; and a good case may be made for the statement that from the simple numerical standpoint of his total fans he is the most popular dancer of all time. Today his position is virtually unchanged. There was one brief interlude a few years back when he announced his retirement from the movies and opened a number of opulent dance studios in big cities across the country. But his "retirement" was short-lived. He soon returned to Hollywood, and since then his films have appeared with gratifying regularity and evoked the usual happy response. Anyone who has seen them knows that at fifty-two Fred Astaire is as good as he ever was. Although other dancers have come up, some of whom execute more turbulent or intricate steps and some of whom combine, as Astaire does, the visual patterns of ballet with the rhythms of tap dancing, the idiom is uniquely his and no one has ever employed it with greater elegance or grace.

In 1906 prohibitionists were making great headway in the state of Nebraska. Several years were to pass before they could convert their curious hobby into a national policy. But an immediate dry achievement of greater ultimate benefit to the American people was the closing of the Storz brewery in Omaha. For the extinction of this luckless concern cost Beer Salesman Frederick Austerlitz his job, and pushed his small son, Fred, then seven years old, into vaudeville as junior member of a sister-and-brother team. "Adele is a born dancer," said Mrs. Austerlitz to Mr. Austerlitz hopefully, "and Fred might not be too bad. Why not give them a chance to develop their talents?" The children were already well known in the school and parish halls of Omaha. Adele's dancing instruction had begun several years before. Fred, eighteen months younger, took lessons because he was too small to stay home by himself.

Today Fred Astaire—born Austerlitz—is unquestionably the best-known and best-paid dancer in the world. More people have seen and applauded his exceptional, light-footed, lighthearted grace than ever heard the word "Nijinsky." During the late twenties, with Adele as his partner, he was the foremost dancer on the American stage. Since the early thirties, teamed with Ginger Rogers, Rita Hayworth, Judy Garland, and others, he has been the foremost dancer of the American screen.

The perfect synthesis of music and movement evident in every Astaire team number is the result, most fans know, of arduous rehearsal. But few realize that every toe tap is as carefully planned as each quarter-note in a first violinist's score. Creating an original dance routine is roughly equivalent in mental exertion to composing a sestina, orchestrating an overture, or writing a one-act play. Astaire's genius as a dancer rests no less on creative talent than on the fluid perfection of his performance. He is his own dance originator. In 1936, when he disagreed with RKO, newspapers reported that the falling-out, as usual, involved money. Actually it concerned his producers' contractual demand that he make four pictures a year—a stiff stint for any performer but an overwhelming burden for Astaire, who ordinarily requires seven or eight weeks to compose and perfect the dance numbers for any picture before shooting begins.

During those weeks he shuts himself in a rehearsal room eight hours a day. A pianist incessantly hammers out the score. To make sure he doesn't repeat himself he runs off reels of his dances from previous pictures. He paces the floor, broods, chews gum, occasionally breaks into a cascade of taps, studying himself in a façade of mirrors. Since no one has ever devised a practicable system for recording a dance on paper, an assistant is constantly on hand to remember any of Astaire's extemporaneous evolutions that seem fresh and apt. Sometimes entire days pass without production of a single usable measure.

When at length the steps of a routine are set, Astaire devotes his attention to refinements of body movement, gesture, and expression. Satisfied with these, he gets rid of the mirror, lest he rely on it too much, and continues practicing until the routine is fixed in his mind. Final processes are to teach the number to his partner and make the difficult change from rehearsal clothes to tails—or whatever costume the script requires. When the finished number is finally ready for screening, Astaire and his partner walk through their steps for director, photographers, and technicians. Camera lines are marked and foregrounds designated. The lacquered presswood floor, which sound experts have found best for recording taps, is rosined and rubbed down. And shooting begins.

As a creative performer Astaire has notably influenced the American dance. He is an exponent—probably the No. 1 exponent—of this country's only native and original dance form. Curiously little has been written about the tap dance, though it is as distinctive a species of U.S. folk art as the cowboy ballad, the Negro spiritual, or jazz. Modern ballroom dancing is purely derivative. Its origins lie in the aristocratic pavane and passacaglia of Renaissance Europe. Square dances are unamended importations from the British Isles. But tap dancing sprang from U.S. soil. It is as indigenous as poison ivy, as popular as the ice-cream soda.

The first tap dancers, like the first "hot" musicians, were Negro slaves. Their footwork was simple—scarcely more complex than the heel thumping of their tribal ancestors in the jungle—but their rhythms were the basic rhythms of American jazz. Their body movements were loose, shambling, amorphous. Sometimes they wore shoes, sometimes they shuffled in bare feet. Plantation owners called their curious performances "levee" dancing. Though blackface minstrels became popular in U.S. music halls around 1800, it was not till the late thirties that levee dancing was introduced to the professional stage by two Negro impersonators, Zip Coon and the renowned "Jim Crow" Rice, whose names put the terms "coon" and "Jim Crow" into vulgar usage.

About this same time, clog dancing was developing in England and Ireland as a popular competitive and theatrical form. In 1840 Barney Williams, the first great Irish clogger, came to the United States. In footwork the Irish and Lancashire clog was more complicated and stylized than the levee dance of the American Negro. But its unsyncopated six-eight rhythms were far less subtle. A good idea of Lancashire cadence can be obtained by reciting very rapidly, without taking a breath, Byron's anapaestic lines:

> The Assyrian came down like the wolf on the fold,
> And his cohorts were gleaming in purple and gold;
> And the sheen of their spears was like stars on the sea,
> When the blue wave rolls nightly on deep Galilee.

The Negro levee dancer beat his feet in two-four or four-four time. His rhythms, the broken, restless rhythms of modern jazz and modern tap dancing, are set down with an unerring ear for accent and stress in Vachel Lindsay's "The Congo." Swing it:

> Fat black bucks in a wine-barrel room,
> Barrel-house kings, with feet unstable,
> Sagged and reeled and pounded on the table,
> Pounded on the table,
> Beat an empty barrel with the handle of a broom,
> Hard as they were able,
> Boom, boom, Boom,
> With a silk umbrella and the handle of a broom.

Visually the Negro "buck dance" was amusing, vainglorious, paradoxical in its contrasts of strut and relaxation. The clogger danced from the knees down. His art was purely auditory. In clog-dancing contests, which became popular in rural America in the latter nineteenth century, judges frequently sat behind screens or underneath the sanded dancing platform to eliminate the extraneous factor of appearance from their appraisal of the competitors' speed and pedal precision.

For several decades these two dance forms flourished concurrently. In 1866 *The Black Crook*, generally considered the first musical extravaganza, featured both clog and minstrel dancers. Cloggers wore tights and heavy shoes with thick wooden soles, and danced in stiff military attitudes, chests out, arms held rigidly at their sides, hands pressed against their thighs. The *reductio ad absurdum* of the clog was the so-called "pedestal" dance. Its practitioners, to demonstrate the miniature niceties of their art, climbed on marble or gilded shafts and went through their routines on a surface never more than twenty-four inches square. Most famous of the pedestal dancers was Henry E. Dixey, who used to whitewash himself and disclose his glistening musculature, as the curtains parted, in the attitude of Discobolus or Apollo of the Belvedere.

By the end of the century the old-fashioned static clog had virtually disappeared from the U.S. stage. A good deal of its heel-and-toe technique was appropriated by minstrel dancers and adapted to native American rhythms. It is probable, however, that in time all the complicated tricks of the clog dance would have evolved independently out of the Negro tradition. For it was to the Negro—though he did not appear on the professional stage until recently—that great minstrels like Sheridan & Mack and George H. Primrose ("The Adonis of the Step Dance") looked for inspiration. Year by year rhythms and routines became more interesting and more varied. Terminology changed. References to "levee dancing" disappeared and the terms "step dance" and "buck and wing" were heard. The misleading phrase "soft shoe" was applied to an increasingly popular form of mobile, eccentric step dance in rolling four-four time. (Actually, performers wore all kinds of shoes for soft-shoe routines.) The distinguishing characteristics of soft shoe were humor, a certain delicacy and lightness of touch, and a smooth but leisurely cadence that sounded like:

> I went to the animal fair,
> The birds and the beasts were there;
> The little raccoon
> By the light of the moon
> Was combing her auburn hair.

Blackface hoofers were exclusively masculine, though female clog dancers like Kitty O'Neil had appeared, snugly incased in acrobatic tights, in many a U.S. music hall. But in the winter of 1902–03 theatergoers flocked to the New York Theater Roof to see a novelty called "Ned Wayburn's Minstrel Misses." Then producer for Klaw & Erlanger, Ned Wayburn had blacked the faces of his chorus and taught them typical minstrel dances but, significantly, varied by the addition of graceful feminine gestures. To describe this new hybrid form, Wayburn coined the phrase "tap and step dancing." This was the first time the term "tap dancing" had been publicly and professionally employed. Wayburn's Minstrel Misses wore light clogs with split wooden soles. Aluminum toe and heel taps did not appear until about a decade later.

It was in the years from 1900–1920 that the modern tap dance evolved as we know it today. Great Negro dancers like Bill Robinson appeared on the Keith Circuit and the Broadway stage. Minstrels gradually vanished, but the dances they did were taken over and embellished by whiteface performers. Comedians like Jack Donahue and Jim Barton executed superbly difficult numbers with wry, sophisticated humor. Pat Rooney made his name synonymous with neat little rhythms in three-four (waltz) time that seemed to chant:

> Pussy's in the well,
> Pussy's in the well,
> Ding Dong Bell.
> Ding Dong Bell.

Pretty ingénues like Marilyn Miller and Ann Pennington tapped as ably as any men. Soon college boys, socialites, debutantes, and fat ladies who wished to reduce were chipping the floors of Ned Wayburn's elegant dance studios in New York and Chicago. Ability to tap had become a social asset.

The performer who brought the U.S. tap dance to its highest

pinnacle of virtuosity and refinement was Fred Astaire. Noël Coward once told him: "Freddy, when I see you dance it makes me want to cry." Even in more phlegmatic observers Astaire's agility and charm induce an emotional reaction, though it is usually one of exhilaration rather than tears. His numbers are more than mere metatarsal obbligatos set to sixty-four bars of music. They are always carefully integrated with the melodic theme and often interpretive in effect. Commenting on Bill Robinson's dancing, Astaire once observed: "He plays tunes with his feet as effortlessly and as accurately as a fine drummer plays a snare drum." But Astaire, whose footwork is impeccable, dances with his entire body. "I like to get my feet in the air and move around," he says. Wayburn contended that Astaire was the first American tap dancer consciously to employ the full resources of his arms, hands, and torso for visual ornamentation. He decorates his tap steps with tours jetés, pirouettes, entrechats, and other maneuvers of the classic ballet, but all fitted to American rhythms and executed with an air of gay spontaneity that consummately reflects the folk origins of his art. Debonair, exultant, amused, he has imparted to the tap dance an elegance and mobility of which the cloggers and minstrels of the last century never dreamed. As the Astaire technique evolved, the American dance washed off its black pigmentation and put on white tie and tails.

Not long ago Astaire was seriously mentioned for the post of soloist with the Metropolitan Opera ballet. It was ballet, as a matter of fact, that formed the groundwork of Astaire's dancing education. When he arrived in New York at the age of eight with his sister and mother (who for twenty-five years served as her children's promoter, manager, and chaperon), young Fred could already dance expertly on the tips of his toes. He had not yet, however, learned to make noise with them. Mrs. Austerlitz entered her children at Ned Wayburn's booming new Dancing, Singing and Dramatic School off Times Square, and Wayburn at once decided that it would be to Fred's advantage to discontinue his study of the effete ballet and learn the manly art of tap. He did not require many lessons.

Before the Astaires reached Broadway they worked the vaudeville circuits for nine years. There was an interlude of one season during which they attended school at Highwood, New Jersey. This academic adventure sprang not from a desire for conventional education but from the fact that Adele had grown so rapidly that Fred looked ludi-crous dancing by her side. Of school Astaire recalls that he entered the fourth grade, was soon promoted to the fifth (his mother had tutored her children conscientiously), and that he distinguished him-self in mathematics. He believes now he might have turned into a quite capable scholar had his schooling continued. Astaire is rather self-conscious about his lack of formal education. Perhaps as a con-sequence of this hiatus his intellectual interests are not far-ranging. What reading he does consists for the most part of newspapers, mag-azines, detective stories, and the *Racing Form*.

When brother and sister had leveled off again they returned to vaudeville in a revised act entitled "Fred and Adele Astaire in New Songs and Smart Dances"—a smash billing which Astaire had proudly composed—and toured the circuit for several years more before Shu-bert scouts spotted them and gave them their first show contract in *Over the Top* with Ed Wynn. Fred was then seventeen years old, Adele eighteen and a half. They never went back to vaudeville. *Over the Top* was followed by jobs in the Winter Garden *Passing Show of 1918* and the Fritz Kreisler operetta *Apple Blossoms*. Though in these produc-tions they had no speaking parts, their adroit rhythmic comedy and liquid but precise teamwork made a profound impression on New York. Drama reporters, puzzled by the etymology of their adopted name, decided they were French and applauded "the Parisian chic of the young Astaires." Today, because of his London-tailored clothes and pleasing, accentless speech, Astaire is mistaken by many of his fans for an Englishman.

Speaking roles and stardom came to the Astaires in 1922, when Pro-ducer Alex A. Aarons decided that a show should be written especially for them. The result, *For Goodness Sake*, and its sequels, the Gershwin-scored *Lady Be Good* and *Funny Face*, established Fred and Adele as international celebrities. They were embraced by reviewers and rushed by stage-struck socialites on both sides of the Atlantic. One transported English writer called Fred "an impish soul in an Every-man's body." Even the London *Times* was moved to gush: "Columbus may have danced with joy at discovering America, but how he would have cavorted had he also discovered Fred and Adele Astaire!"

The social attention granted Adele by wealthy young peers in Lon-don and tycoons' sons in New York often brought her into professional conflict with her brother. A habitual and painstaking worrier, Astaire rarely was satisfied with either her performance or his own. He thought nothing of arriving at the theater two hours before curtain time to limber up. Adele generally arrived only a few minutes before her initial entrance. Aarons recalls that Fred never trusted a property man to rosin the stage for him before a performance. He invariably attended to it himself, just as he attended to every minute business detail. During the difficult labors of composition and rehearsal, Adele would co-operate. But once a routine was set and a show on view, Adele wanted liberty. She found it difficult to turn down the flower-laden young men at the stage door just because her young brother had disliked the evening's work and called a midnight rehearsal. Astaire was and is an almost masochistic perfectionist.

When Adele married Lord Charles Cavendish and retired from the stage in 1932, her action was dictated partly by this conflict between Fred's conscience and her own predilection for fun. She made no bones about the fact that the theatrical tradition was not inbred in her. "It was an acquired taste," she said, "like olives." Another factor was the realization that Fred had at last stepped out of her professional shadow. As a boy people had dismissed him as "that talented Austerlitz girl's little brother." As choreographer he devised dances that made Adele appear the virtuoso of the team. Astaire never appeared to resent his role of serious-minded brother. One night Adele sang over the radio with Rudy Vallee's orchestra and received an uncomplimentary notice from a Broadway columnist. A few days later the same columnist called at the theater where the Astaires were appearing and reported that Fred had begged him, "Please, if you ever take a rap at us, direct it at me instead of Adele, will you?"

It was *The Band Wagon* that first proved to the Astaires and the public that Fred was separable from Adele. In the interest of economy the producers of *The Band Wagon* hired only a small cast and relied on Fred and Adele to do a great many things besides dance. Skits were varied, and with some misgivings the producers handed Fred a fantastic assortment of character parts. The morning after the opening, reviews offered the usual words of praise for the Astaires' incomparable dancing. But there was also an unexpected chorus of astonishment and delight at Fred Astaire's newly revealed talents as a comedian. When Astaire walked into the Lambs Club that evening he was greeted with "Boy, I hear you're an actor!" At the conclusion of *The Band Wagon*'s run, Adele married and went abroad, and Fred stepped out by himself.

Though many film executives had seen *The Band Wagon*, they made no rush to draft him for the screen. For one thing, Hollywood was still groping for a satisfactory musical-comedy frame of reference. Cinema musicals were, for the most part, vast stylized extravaganzas without any place for the intimate grace of Astaire footwork. Astaire's appeal, moreover, was rated as a "class" appeal. New York debutantes liked him, but there were grave doubts concerning his ability to charm shopgirls and stenographers. It was not until *Gay Divorce* proved him good enough to play Broadway for thirty-two weeks without Adele by his side that RKO doubtfully invited him to the West Coast.

If Fred Astaire made a great dancer out of Ginger Rogers, it is equally true that Ginger made a successful romantic lead out of Astaire. He had been handicapped on Broadway by the simple fact that Adele was his sister, which required librettists to devise tortuous plot complications in order to introduce love interest without suggestion of incest. But he was free to court Ginger Rogers, as well as dance with her, with perfect propriety. She had an alert, friendly, distinctively American charm that perfectly complemented his jaunty screen personality. She was, moreover, industrious and energetic. Astaire never had to bully or beg her to work as he did Adele. Her assiduity and competitiveness were as keen as his own.

Within twelve months of their initial collaboration Astaire and Rogers had become the greatest money-making team in Hollywood history. But for him those first months were filled with dire forebodings. He disliked his face and feared his fast footwork would blur hopelessly on film. He was depressed by the report of his first screen test on which some ignorant underling had written: "Can't act. Slightly bald. Can dance a little." Hollywood's huge sets unnerved him. Dancing on them, he said, was like performing in a circus tent. On seeing the rushes from *Flying Down to Rio*, his first major effort, he was convinced his career was over. To his gloomy eyes his dancing looked ponderous, his angular midwestern countenance grotesque. He told Ginger, and she agreed with him, that dancing in pictures would never be popular. He implored RKO either to remake or delete his numbers. When Producer Pandro Berman refused, Astaire went around Hollywood thanking people for being nice to him and saying goodbye.

He then took off for London to appear in the English company of *Gay Divorce*. London always welcomed him ecstatically and Lady Cavendish cried when she saw him dancing for the first time without her. He had almost forgotten Hollywood when a cable arrived from Mr. Berman. It said: "I told you so." *Flying Down to Rio* was a success and fans were writing in asking for more Astaire. He returned to the United States when *Gay Divorce* closed and went to work with Ginger on *The Gay Divorcee* (renamed by the Hays office on the assumption that a divorcée *might* be gay but a divorce shouldn't). It was the first of their great series of smash hits. When all reports were in, RKO gave him a five-year contract and insured his legs for a million dollars.

Today, by rights, Astaire should possess a reasonable quota of professional self-assurance. He rates seventeen agate lines in Who's Who. He gets around $150,000 for each picture he makes. Through his influence movie musicals have been transformed from dull, fourth-dimensional spectacles into a sprightly and comprehensible cinematic form. And he has seen his style of dancing become the national ideal.

Yet Astaire is probably Hollywood's foremost self-deprecator. The youthful bounce that characterizes his walking gait, off and on the screen, masks a tormented soul. He worries incessantly. He worries about his work, about his clothes, about Adele, his mother, and the state of the world. His No. 1 worry is that he will run out of dance concepts, and more than once he has interrupted golf matches and weekend trips and hurried to his studio because he sensed the approach of an incipient idea. Previews cause him immense anguish. Two of his films he has never seen at all. Yet Hollywood associates find him easy and agreeable to work with, a shy and sensitive gentleman whose temperament is completely introverted. He sometimes rages in rehearsal, but his anger is never directed at anyone but himself.

Though it is well established by now that feminine fans find him glamorous and men consider him altogether likable, Astaire is morbidly sensitive about his physical aspect. One day early in his screen career, on being told of a development in color processing, he groaned wretchedly, "Can you imagine how I'll look in Technicolor?" Since then he has made a number of Technicolor films, and he looks fine. He has been known to try on a suit as many as ten times before making up his mind to accept it, and mornings he will tie and untie a dozen of his 150-odd cravats before settling on one for the day. He has killed dozens of publicity stills because of some near-invisible wrinkle in trousers or coat. He wears his toupee, however, only before the camera.

Astaire's dancing shoes are specially made for him at $16 to $20 a pair. They are light, very snug, and generally last no longer than six shooting sessions. As a rule Astaire keeps up to a hundred pairs on hand, and he trusts no one but himself to hammer their aluminum taps to toes and heels. His only sartorial superstition is a red-and-green plaid bathrobe he bought in Bridgeport, Connecticut, in 1922. For some reason the Astaire act stopped the show the night of its purchase and he could think of no explanation save the new robe. Since then he has worn it religiously on opening nights and on the first days of screening each new film.

Astaire's wife is the former Phyllis Livingston Potter, Boston society girl and heiress. They were married July 12, 1933, in Brooklyn Supreme Court a few moments after Mrs. Potter had won a settlement on custody of her son, Eliphalet Nott ("Peter") Potter, Jr. Besides his stepson Astaire has a son, Fred, Jr., who is his special worry and delight. He has taught him quite a few steps and now, according to Astaire, whenever Freddy hears music "he rattles around a bit."*

It was no accident that Adele married an English lord and Fred a Back Bay aristocrat. Their mother never let them forget that they sprang from one of Omaha's best families and as a consequence they never formed an attachment for theatrical society. In New York they lived on Park Avenue and moved in Park Avenue circles. In London they were adopted by Mayfair and the fun-loving peer age. In Hollywood the Astaires have slid naturally into the so-called "conservative set." Astaire is one of the few theatrical people admitted to New York's Racquet and Tennis Club and the Turf and Field Club at Belmont Park, Long Island. The Astaire house is quietly furnished, wood paneled, and looks more like Westchester than California.

During their years of collaboration, Astaire and Ginger Rogers rarely saw each other outside the studio. Some fans complained because their pictures invariably ended with a dance routine instead of a clinch. Off the screen their relationship has been no less detached.

*A year after this was published in *Life*, the Astaires had a daughter, Ava.

Astaire is devoted to his wife and in all their years in Hollywood has seldom been seen in public without her. He corresponds regularly with Adele. In his letters he describes proposed numbers in considerable detail. She in return criticizes them and sends him ideas and sisterly advice. She still calls him "Babe" or "Sap." He calls her "Funny Face," a childhood nickname that suggested the title of the 1927 Gershwin hit.

Astaire has no thought at present of returning to Broadway. He prefers the Hollywood technique of perfecting a number and doing it once to the theatrical exigencies of nightly repetition. Moreover, he has always feared and disliked visible audiences. As a movie star, however, he has to cope with another problem: his shyness in the presence of fans and autograph hounds. Nothing disturbs him more than to have a perfect stranger shout "Hi, Fred," and then break into a dance. He always feels uncomfortably that he is expected to dance back. For this reason he dislikes going to night clubs. On the dance floor he appears subdued and indolent. For the most part he prefers to sit quietly in a corner and listen to the orchestra. He knows instrumentation and is himself an accomplished pianist, accordionist, and clarinetist. A persistent ambition of his is to score one of his own pictures. He has had five songs published, of which three—"Just Like Taking Candy from a Baby," "No Time Like the Present," and "Building Up to an Awful Letdown"—were comparative hits.

There has been no suggestion that Astaire, like Ginger Rogers, has planned to devote himself henceforth to straight roles. He is in perfect physical shape, and until he feels either his legs or his box office slowing he sees no reason to readjust his professional ways. He still finds himself able to dance a full working day, day after day, without misery in his feet. Between pictures he keeps in training with golf, which he shoots in the low eighties, tennis, fishing, and skiing. He eats lightly, smokes little, seldom drinks. For him one cocktail before a dinner party is par; two highballs afterward is a binge. Evenings he likes to play gin rummy or bridge and go to bed early. He still looks about thirty-two with his hat on. Only one tiny symptom reveals that he has conscientiously and uninterruptedly danced and worried, worried and danced, for four decades: his toes wiggle in his sleep.

August 25, 1941

MIKHAIL BARYSHNIKOV (1948–)

BORN IN Riga, Latvia, the son of a Russian military family, Mikhail
Baryshnikov entered the Vaganova Choreographic Institute in Leningrad (now St. Petersburg) in 1964, where he was trained by the great
pedagogue Alexander Pushkin, who had already trained Rudolf Nureyev. It was immediately apparent what a tremendous talent Baryshnikov had, and after a triumphant career in the Kirov Ballet company,
beginning when he was nineteen, he defected to the West, in 1974.
Almost immediately he was hailed by critics and audiences as the
world's leading dancer, his classical technique incomparable and his
dramatic genius already manifesting itself. Baryshnikov danced with
American Ballet Theatre, then for a short while with Balanchine at
New York City Ballet before returning to ABT as artistic director, a job
he held for almost a decade. He also danced for Martha Graham and
The Royal Ballet. Ballets created on him during this period include
Twyla Tharp's *Push Comes to Shove*, Jerome Robbins's *Opus 19* (*The
Dreamer*) and *Other Dances*, and Frederick Ashton's *Rhapsody*. He
then cofounded, with Mark Morris, the modern dance group White
Oak Project—from the start he has consistently sought to broaden
his artistic reach. Over the years, we have seen him prevail in modern dance, in movies (*The Turning Point*, *White Nights*), in theater,
on television (opposite Sarah Jessica Parker in *Sex and the City*). His
book *Baryshnikov at Work* reflects the high seriousness with which
he approaches his art, as does his tribute to Balanchine (below). The
Baryshnikov Arts Center, which he established in 2005, has extended
the possibilities for dance and multidisciplinary arts in New York City.
(In 2016, he appeared there in *Brodsky/Baryshnikov*, a one-man theater performance in tribute to his late close friend, Joseph Brodsky.)
"Misha," who became an American citizen in 1986, is married to
dancer Lisa Rinehart, with whom he has three children. He is also the
father of an older daughter, whose mother is the actress Jessica Lange.

Tribute to Balanchine

BALANCHINE always talked about his ballets as if they were some-thing only for the moment, for *now*—his familiar word. He never built a shrine to his work, or even to the profession of choreography. I remember when I was a dancer at New York City Ballet, he asked me several times if I wanted to choreograph. No, I told him, I was there to work on his ballets, not to make ballets of my own. "Dear," he said, "it's not so hard. Simpler than you think. Nothing much, really. Just go and do, and don't think so much about it." That's easy for you to say, I thought. But no, he said, "Just, if you like some piece of music, go and do. Just make something interesting."

That was his criterion: interesting. He really, seriously, thought of dance as entertainment. In his mind he was the ballet-master-in-chief-of-entertainment. More than anything, he hated whatever was boring . . . in music, in dance, and in films, too. He looked for inter-esting taste in food, interesting smell in perfume, interesting hairdo on a young woman, interesting way to twist the human body. He was a man who was interested, period. That's the way New York City Ballet was constituted, as he was. His ballets and his dancers were supposed to be interesting, and this was all he cared about. He claimed he had no thought for the future of his ballets. He was fond of the phrase "*Après moi, le déluge.*"

I wonder about this. It seems to me, actually, that he built New York City Ballet in very deliberate relation both to the future and to the past—that he *knew* he was creating what we now call neoclassical ballet, the modernist extension of Marius Petipa's work in Russia, and that he meant to give this to the people who came after him. I remem-ber asking him which choreographers, besides Petipa, he had admired when he was young, and the only confession I was able to wring out of him was that he was impressed by Bronislava Nijinska's early ballets. This was fitting. He and Nijinska, together with her brother, Vaslav Nijinsky, by whom she was so much influenced, formed a kind of troika, the first three neoclassical choreographers. All three, when they came to the West, could have done very well as traditional classi-cal choreographers. They could have staged Petipa's ballets. They were perfect ballet masters, all of them. They could have survived easily—

more easily than they did—setting *Giselle* and *Raymonda* and *The Sleeping Beauty* in England, Germany, France, or Italy. But they chose a much harder, more daring path: a quest for new forms, new musical collaborations, new ways of moving, based on the old way, Petipa. For different reasons Nijinsky and Nijinska fell away, and because they did, Balanchine has lost his context. He seems unique. But he was part of something larger, the birth of neoclassical ballet.

Balanchine's school, the system of dance he inculcated, was also a continuation of Petipa's practice. As many people have said, the Russian Imperial Ballet was a marriage of the French, Italian, and Scandinavian schools. The Scandinavian precision was provided by the old Swedish teacher Christian Johansson, with his cold, academic eye. The French lyricism came from Petipa and his predecessors at the Imperial Ballet, Didelot, Perrot, and Saint-Léon. Then came the Italian contribution—strength, attack—through the influx of Italian virtuoso ballerinas and above all through Enrico Cecchetti, who arrived at the Imperial Ballet School in 1892. Petipa clearly knew that his dancers needed more sparkle and fire, so he brought in Cecchetti. He *built* his school, combining the elements he wanted. Then, after him, a series of great teachers, from Pavel Gerdt to Alexander Pushkin, passed down the tradition he created.

Balanchine did the same as Petipa. When he founded the School of American Ballet in New York, he brought in his Russians, Pierre Vladimiroff, Felia Doubrovska, and Anatole Oboukhoff. Later he added others, such as Alexandra Danilova, Antonina Tumkovsky, and Helene Dudin. So the Russian school was the backbone. But he also engaged Muriel Stuart, with her modern dance training, and in the 1960s he brought in Stanley Williams of the Royal Danish Ballet. Balanchine had worked at the Danish company in the early 1930s, before he came to America, and he must have admired it very much. With its stylistic range from classical dance to character dance to mime, and the common practice of having young ballet students participate in professional performances, it would have reminded him of the Imperial Ballet. But especially, being a traditionalist, he would have admired the discipline, the *method* of Danish ballet, and he gave this to his own dancers in the person of Stanley Williams. So, like Petipa, he combined elements in order to build his school. And, like any well thought-out school, it became integrated and flexible, changing so as to accommodate the extraordinary gallop of his imagination. Balanchine may have constructed this style for "now," but clearly he had the future in mind. In any case, it was strong enough to bear fruit in the future. As in Russia after Petipa, the great dancers produced by Balanchine's unique methods have carried on as teachers after him.

There is also the matter of the help that Balanchine gave to other companies. Time and again, for little or no compensation, he allowed other troupes to present his ballets, asking only that the person staging the piece be paid for his or her time. Of course, his liberality on this score was related to his idea of his ballets, his belief that the piece was all there in the choreography, so that if the dancer would just listen to the music and do the steps, the ballet would be there. Still, he was exceedingly generous, and this was probably part of his building for the future. In many small companies, those Balanchine ballets became mainstays of the repertory—the reason many people in Pittsburgh and Philadelphia and Cincinnati went to the ballet.

It was not just other companies that he helped. He took an interest in other artists, inviting Martha Graham and Antony Tudor and Frederick Ashton to take part in his enterprise. Balanchine was so productive that he did not need collaborators, yet he knew enough to make Jerome Robbins a ballet master of the company, with the result that this other extraordinary career unfolded alongside his own. He nourished dance beyond himself, as he nourished music. He sent out waves of vitality into American art.

Looking over the history and prehistory of New York City Ballet, one can see it as a series of glittering moments. There is Balanchine's creation of *La Chatte* and *Apollo* and *Prodigal Son* for Diaghilev. Then, in 1930, we have Lincoln Kirstein in his very first essay on dance, writing prophetically that with these works Balanchine is leading ballet to "a revivified, purer, clearer classicism." Three years later, Kirstein finally meets Balanchine—and makes him the offer that could not be refused: basically, "You make the ballets, I'll do the rest." Then we have Balanchine's arrival in America and the opening of the School of American Ballet. Then Ballet Caravan, with its lineup of American talent: Lew Christensen, Eugene Loring, Elliott Carter, Aaron Copland. Then the South American tour of 1941, which gave us *Concerto Barocco* and *Ballet Imperial*, and Ballet Society, with *The Four Temperaments*. Soon after, the founding of New York City Ballet, with Maria

Tallchief, as the Firebird, flashing in red feathers across the stage—an annunciation. And then, all that came after, for the next fifty years.

But every one of those moments was prepared for, years before, and each was a preparation for the next. Though he asked for what he wanted in the moment, Balanchine knew how to wait. I heard a story once that Melissa Hayden told. One day when she was a new dancer at New York City Ballet, Balanchine was trying to teach her a certain kind of turn. He wanted it done in a special way. She attempted it again and again and couldn't quite get it. "Just keep trying, dear," he said to her. "You will do." "How long do I have?" she asked. "Oh, ten years," he said. He was a patient man.

1998

Black Elk (1863–1950) and
John Gneisenau Neihardt (1881–1973)

On April 27, 1971, the millions of viewers who tuned in to the late-night episode of *The Dick Cavett Show* on national television were presented with the idea that dancing is not only a form of entertainment but, in some circumstances, a prayer or record of divine revelation. Cavett, a native of Nebraska, was interviewing Nebraska's poet laureate and self-taught ethnologist John G. Neihardt, who spoke about his oral history project, beginning in 1931, with interviews of Black Elk, a holy man of the Sioux Plains clan the Oglala Lakota. Black Elk, fearful that his religious visions might die when he did, delivered his memories to Neihardt in the Lakota language, which was then translated into English by Black Elk's son, and crafted by the poet into piercing literary prose for a book called *Black Elk Speaks* (1932).

Crucial to the world of Black Elk and his tribe was dancing. It was a profound part of their cultural identity and of the legacy of their forebears, as well as of their daily spiritual reconnection with the natural world. The chapter below speaks of the Horse Dance that Black Elk was required to produce for his entire clan—and their painted steeds—when he was just seventeen. It was a confirmation of his terrifying Great Vision, which, his people hoped, would lead him to be their savior.

The Horse Dance

THERE WAS a man by the name of Bear Sings, and he was very old and wise. So Black Road asked him to help, and he did.

First they sent a crier around in the morning who told the people to camp in a circle at a certain place a little way up the Tongue from where the soldiers were. They did this, and in the middle of the circle

Bear Sings and Black Road set up a sacred tepee of bison hide, and on it they painted pictures from my vision. On the west side they painted a bow and a cup of water; on the north, white geese and the herb; on the east, the daybreak star and the pipe; on the south, the flowering stick and the nation's hoop. Also, they painted horses, elk, and bison. Then over the door of the sacred tepee, they painted the flaming rainbow. It took them all day to do this, and it was beautiful.

They told me I must not eat anything until the horse dance was over, and I had to purify myself in a sweat lodge with sage spread on the floor of it, and afterwards I had to wipe myself dry with sage.[1]

That evening Black Road and Bear Sings told me to come to the painted tepee. We were in there alone, and nobody dared come near us to listen. They asked me if I had heard any songs in my vision, and if I had I must teach the songs to them. So I sang to them all the songs that I had heard in my vision, and it took most of the night to teach these songs to them. While we were in there singing, we could hear low thunder rumbling all over the village outside, and we knew the thunder beings were glad and had come to help us.

My father and mother had been helping too by hunting up all that we should need in the dance. The next morning they had everything ready. There were four black horses to represent the west; four white horses for the north; four sorrels for the east; four buckskins for the south. For all of these, young riders had been chosen. Also there was a bay horse for me to ride, as in my vision. Four of the most beautiful maidens in the village were ready to take their part, and there were six very old men for the Grandfathers.

Now it was time to paint and dress for the dance. The four maidens and the sixteen horses all faced the sacred tepee. Black Road and Bear Sings then sang a song, and all the others sang along with them, like this:

> Father, paint the earth on me.
> Father, paint the earth on me.

---

[1] *Sage* (*Artemisia*), called pheží ňóta 'gray grass' in Lakota, was extensively used in rituals. Black Elk explained that sage, because it is the most fragrant of plants, was used as medicine and was burned ritually, using the smoke to purify persons and things. Its odor was said to drive away evil spirits.

Father, paint the earth on me.
A nation I will make over.
A two-legged nation I will make holy.[2]
Father, paint the earth on me.

After that the painting was done.

The four black horse riders were painted all black with blue lightning stripes down their legs and arms and white hail spots on their hips, and there were blue streaks of lightning on the horses' legs.

The white-horse riders were painted all white with red streaks of lightning on their arms and legs, and on the legs of the horses there were streaks of red lightning, and all the white riders wore plumes of white horse hair on their heads to look like geese.

The riders of the sorrels of the east were painted all red with straight black lines of lightning on their limbs and across their breasts, and there was straight black lightning on the limbs and breasts of the horses too.

The riders of the buckskins of the south were painted all yellow and streaked with black lightning. The horses were black from the knees down, and black lightning streaks were on their upper legs and breasts.

My bay horse had bright red streaks of lightning on his limbs, and on his back a spotted eagle, outstretching, was painted where I sat. I was painted red all over with black lightning on my limbs.[3] I wore a black mask, and across my forehead a single eagle feather hung.

When the horses and the men were painted they looked beautiful; but they looked fearful too.

The men were naked, except for a breech-clout; but the four maidens wore buckskin dresses dyed scarlet, and their faces were scarlet too. Their hair was braided, and they had wreaths of the sweet and

---

[2]Hunú pa oyáte "two-legged nation" here clearly refers to humans; in ritual language, it may also refer to bears. In the transcript, rather than "make holy," the penultimate line reads, "I will make over," i.e., heal. "Paint the earth on me" refers to painting the participants with makhá (earth; clay) paints.
[3]Black Elk mentioned that his forearms were also painted black.

cleansing sage, the sacred sage, around their heads, and from the wreath of each in front a single eagle feather hung. They were very beautiful to see.[4]

All this time I was in the sacred tepee with the Six Grandfathers, and the four sacred virgins were in there too. No one outside was to see me until the dance began.

Right in the middle of the tepee the Grandfathers made a circle in the ground with a little trench, and across this they painted two roads—the red one running north and south, the black one, east and west. On the west side of this they placed a cup of water with a little bow and arrow laid across it; and on the east they painted the day-break star. Then to the maiden who would represent the north they gave the healing herb to carry and a white goose wing, the cleansing wind. To her of the east they gave the holy pipe. To her of the south they gave the flowering stick, and to her who would represent the west they gave the nation's hoop. Thus the four maidens, good and beautiful, held in their hands the life of the nation.

All I carried was a red stick to represent the sacred arrow, the power of the thunder beings of the west.

We were now ready to begin the dance. The Six Grandfathers began to sing, announcing the riders of the different quarters. First they sang of the black horse riders, like this:

> They will appear—may you behold them!
> They will appear—may you behold them!
> A horse nation will appear.
> A thunder-being nation will appear.
> They will appear, behold!
> They will appear, behold!

Then the black riders mounted their horses and stood four abreast facing the place where the sun goes down.

---

[4]According to the transcript, all of the riders, including Black Elk, wore black masks; they each wore two feathers in the hair, "like horns." See Standing Bear's drawing, which depicts the mask and shows curved feathers, probably eagle pinion feathers. In the drawings, however, only one of the riders—presumably Black Elk—wears a mask.

Next the Six Grandfathers sang:

> They will appear, may you behold them!
> A horse nation will appear, behold!
> A geese nation will appear, may you behold!

Then the four white horsemen mounted and stood four abreast, facing the place where the White Giant lives.

Next the Six Grandfathers sang:

> Where the sun shines continually, they will appear!
> A buffalo nation, they will appear, behold!
> A horse nation, they will appear, may you behold!

Then the red horsemen mounted and stood four abreast facing the east.

Next the Grandfathers sang:

> Where you are always facing, an elk nation will appear!
> May you behold!
> A horse nation will appear,
> Behold!

The four yellow riders mounted their buckskins and stood four abreast facing the south.

Now it was time for me to go forth from the sacred tepee, but before I went forth I sang this song to the drums of the Grandfathers:

> He will appear, may you behold him!
> An eagle for the eagle nation will appear.
> May you behold!

While I was singing thus in the sacred tepee I could hear my horse snorting and prancing outside. The virgins went forth four abreast and I followed them, mounting my horse and standing behind them facing the west.

Next the Six Grandfathers came forth and stood abreast behind my bay, and they began to sing a rapid, lively song to the drums, like this:

They are dancing.
They are coming to behold you.
The horse nation of the west[5] is dancing.
They are coming to behold!

Then they sang the same of the horses of the north and of the east and of the south. And as they sang of each troop in turn, it wheeled and came and took its place behind the Grandfathers—the blacks, the whites, the sorrels and the buckskins, standing four abreast and facing the west. They came prancing to the lively air of the Grandfathers' song, and they pranced as they stood in line. And all the while my bay was rearing too and prancing to the music of the sacred song.

Now when we were all in line, facing the west, I looked up into a dark cloud that was coming there and the people all became quiet and the horses quit prancing. And when there was silence but for low thunder yonder, I sent a voice to the spirits of the cloud, holding forth my right hand, thus, palm outward, as I cried four times:

"Hey-a-a-hey! hey-a-a-hey! hey-a-a-hey! hey-a-a-hey!"

Then the Grandfathers behind me sang another sacred song from my vision, the one that goes like this:

At the center of the earth, behold a four-legged.[6]
They have said this to me!

And as they sang, a strange thing happened. My bay pricked up his ears and raised his tail and pawed the earth, neighing long and loud to where the sun goes down. And the four black horses raised their voices, neighing long and loud, and the whites and the sorrels and the buckskins did the same; and all the other horses in the village neighed, and even those out grazing in the valley and on the hill slopes raised their heads and neighed together. Then suddenly, as I sat there looking at the cloud, I saw my vision yonder once again—the tepee built of cloud and sewed with lightning, the flaming rainbow door and, underneath, the Six Grandfathers sitting, and all the horses

---

[5]The transcript starts with the north: "To the north the horse nation is dancing, They are coming to behold them. (This song was repeated to the different sides.)"
[6]Referring to the bay horse that Black Elk rides.

thronging in their quarters; and also there was I myself upon my bay before the tepee. I looked about me and could see that what we then were doing was like a shadow cast upon the earth from yonder vision in the heavens, so bright it was and clear. I knew the real was yonder and the darkened dream of it was here.

And as I looked, the Six Grandfathers yonder in the cloud and all the riders of the horses, and even I myself upon the bay up there, all held their hands palms outward toward me, and when they did this, I had to pray, and so I cried:

> Grandfathers, you behold me!
> Spirits of the World, you behold!
> What you have said to me, I am now performing!
> Hear me and help me![7]

Then the vision went out, and the thunder cloud was coming on with lightning on its front and many voices in it, and the split-tail swallows swooped above us in a swarm.[8]

The people of the village ran to fasten down their tepees, while the black horse riders sang to the drums that rolled like thunder, and this is what they sang:

> I myself made them fear.
> Myself, I wore an eagle relic.[9]
> I myself made them fear.
> Myself, a lightning power I wore.
> I myself made them fear,
> Made them fear.
> The power of the hail I wore,
> I myself made them fear,
> Made them fear!
> Behold me!

---

[7]The song as given in the transcript is simpler: "Grandfathers, behold me. / What you have said unto me, I have thus performed. / Hear me."
[8]The swallows come as akíchita of the Thunder-beings.
[9]The word "relic" designates a symbolic ornament, generally of rawhide, a bird skin or feathers, or cloth.

And as they sang, the hail and rain were falling yonder just a little way from us, and we could see it, but the cloud stood there and flashed and thundered, and only a little sprinkle fell on us. The thunder beings were glad and had come in a great crowd to see the dance.

Now the four virgins held high the sacred relics that they carried, the herb and the white wing, the sacred pipe, the flowering stick, the nation's hoop, offering these to the spirits of the west. Then people who were sick or sad came to the virgins, making scarlet offerings[10] to them, and after they had done this, they all felt better and some were cured of sickness and began to dance for joy.

Now the Grandfathers beat their drums again and the dance began. The four black horsemen, who had stood behind the Grandfathers, went ahead of the virgins, riding toward the west side of the circled village, and all the others followed in their order while the horses pranced and reared.

When the black horse troop had reached the western side, it wheeled around and fell to the rear behind the buckskins, and the white horse band came up and led until it reached the north side of the village. Then these fell back and took the rear behind the blacks, and the sorrels led until they reached the east. Then these fell back behind the whites, and the buckskins led until they reached the south. Then they fell back and took the rear, so that the blacks were leading as before toward the western quarter that was theirs. Each time the leading horse troop reached its quarter, the Six Grandfathers sang of the powers of that quarter, and there my bay faced, pricking up his ears and neighing loud, till all the other horses raised their voices neighing. When I thus faced the north, I sent a voice again and said: "Grandfather, behold me! What you gave me I have given to the people—the power of the healing herb and the cleansing wind. Thus my nation is made over. Hear and help me!"

And when we reached the east, and after the Grandfathers had sung, I sent a voice: "Grandfather, behold me! My people, with difficulty they walk. Give them wisdom and guide them. Hear and help me!"

Between each quarter, as we marched and danced, we all sang together:

[10]Small bundles of chąšáša or tobacco wrapped in red cloth, a traditional offering in ritual contexts.

A horse nation all over the universe,
Neighing, they come!
Prancing, they come!
May you behold them.

When we had reached the south and the Grandfathers had sung of the power of growing, my horse faced yonder and neighed again, and all the horses raised their voices as before. And then I prayed with hand upraised: "Grandfather, the flowering stick you gave me and the nation's sacred hoop I have given to the people. Hear me, you who have the power to make grow! Guide the people that they may be as blossoms on your holy tree, and make it flourish deep in Mother Earth and make it full of leaves and singing birds."

Then once more the blacks were leading, and as we marched and sang and danced toward the quarter of the west, the black hail cloud, still standing yonder watching, filled with voices crying: "Hey-hey! hey-hey!" They were cheering and rejoicing that my work was being done. And all the people now were happy and rejoicing, sending voices back, "hey-hey, hey-hey"; and all the horses neighed, rejoicing with the spirits and the people. Four times we marched and danced around the circle of the village, singing as we went, the leaders changing at the quarters, the Six Grandfathers singing to the power of each quarter, and to each I sent a voice. And at each quarter, as we stood, somebody who was sick or sad would come with offerings to the virgins—little scarlet bags of the chacun sha sha, the red willow bark. And when the offering was made, the giver would feel better and begin to dance with joy.

And on the second time around, many of the people who had horses joined the dance with them, milling round and round the Six Grand-fathers and the virgins as we danced ahead. And more and more got on their horses, milling round us as we went, until there was a whirl of prancing horses all about us at the end, and all the others danced afoot behind us, and everybody sang what we were singing.

When we reached the quarter of the west the fourth time, we stopped in new formation, facing inward toward the sacred tepee in the center of the village. First stood the virgins, next I stood upon the bay; then came the Six Grandfathers with eight riders on either side of them—the sorrels and the buckskins on their right hand, the blacks and whites upon their left. And when we stood so, the oldest of the Grandfathers, he who was the Spirit of the Sky, cried out: "Let all the people be ready. He shall send a voice four times, and at the last voice you shall go forth and coup the sacred tepee, and who shall coup it first shall have new power!"[11]

All the riders were eager for the charge, and even the horses seemed to understand and were rearing and trying to get away. Then I raised my hand and cried hey-hey four times, and at the fourth the riders all yelled "hoka hey," and charged upon the tepee. My horse plunged inward along with all the others, but many were ahead of me and many couped the tepee before I did.

Then the horses were all rubbed down with sacred sage and led away, and we began going into the tepee to see what might have happened there while we were dancing. The Grandfathers had sprinkled fresh soil on the nation's hoop that they had made in there with the red and black roads across it, and all around this little circle of the nation's hoop we saw the prints of tiny pony hoofs as though the spirit horses had been dancing while we danced.[12]

Now Black Road, who had helped me to perform the dance, took the sacred pipe from the virgin of the east. After filling it with chacun sha sha, the bark of the red willow, he lit and offered it to the Powers of the World, sending a voice thus:

"Grandfathers, you where the sun goes down, you of the sacred wind where the white giant lives, you where the day comes forth and the morning star, you where lives the power to grow, you of the sky and you of the earth, wings of the air and four-leggeds of the world, behold! I, myself, with my horse nation have done what I was to do on earth. To all of you I offer this pipe that my people may live!"

Then he smoked and passed the pipe. It went all over the village until every one had smoked at least a puff.

After the horse dance was over, it seemed that I was above the ground and did not touch it when I walked. I felt very happy, for I could see that my people were all happier. Many crowded around me

[11]In rituals, as in war, men rushed on the "enemy" and counted coup. Compare, for example, counting coup on the sacred tree before it was cut down and on the spot where it would stand in the Sun Dance enclosure.
[12]Black Elk's wording was more definitive: "The spirit horses had been dancing around the circle of the tipi."

and said that they or their relatives who had been feeling sick were well again, and these gave me many gifts. Even the horses seemed to be healthier and happier after the dance.

The fear that was on me so long was gone, and when thunder clouds appeared I was always glad to see them, for they came as relatives now to visit me. Everything seemed good and beautiful now, and kind.

Before this, the medicine men would not talk to me, but now they would come to me to talk about my vision.

From that time on, I always got up very early to see the rising of the daybreak star. People knew that I did this, and many would get up to see it with me, and when it came we said: "Behold the star of understanding!"

1932

Ruthanna Boris (1917–2007)

Born in Brooklyn, Ruthanna Boris trained at the Metropolitan Opera School of Ballet with Giuseppe Bonfiglio, Margaret Curtis, and Rosina Galli. She also studied modern dance in the studios of Martha Graham, Humphrey–Weidman, and Hanya Holm and was one of the first students at the School of American Ballet, under the all-seeing eye of George Balanchine. She danced with his American Ballet and with Lincoln Kirstein's Ballet Caravan; became a principal dancer with the Ballet Russe de Monte Carlo, where she began to choreograph; became a prima ballerina with the Metropolitan Opera; and served as a choreographer with the young New York City Ballet, where her works included her most popular ballet, *Cakewalk*, which had a second life a decade or so later with the Joffrey Ballet.

Boris's performing career was cut short by arthritis in the late 1950s, when she became a pioneer in undergoing what would be the first of three double hip replacements. She became interested in dance as a therapeutic endeavor, studying with and writing about Marian Chace, the founder of the American Dance Therapy Association, and studying psychology and therapy at the University of Washington, in Seattle. At UW, as an adjunct professor, Boris taught dance in the 1980s.

Even so, her early commitment to Balanchine as teacher, creator of genius, and intuitive psychologist permeated her conversations with colleagues up to the last months of her life. Her unpublished memoir, which includes extensive sections on Balanchine and Chace, is in the collection of the Performing Arts Library at Lincoln Center.

I Remember Balanchine

I was in the original *Serenade* in 1934; years later, for Toumanova, Balanchine made one big role out of all the smaller parts. Toumanova did the first and second entrance. There was only another person when the adagio began, when the Angel came in. Ballet Russe got that version, too, and Danilova danced it that way. When I joined Ballet Russe I wanted to dance that role because I identified with *Serenade*. And when I did finally dance it, I felt more and more strongly that it showed a pattern in Balanchine's life: a figure comes in and all the configurations change. That figure initiates the change but does not participate in it. Then, finally, she does the finale looking for her place, and the whole group turns away. In the end she's the one that goes to heaven. I knew by then that Balanchine had had tuberculosis. He said to me once, "You know, I am really a dead man. I was supposed to die and I didn't, and so now everything I do is second chance. That is why I enjoy every day. I don't look back. I don't look forward. Only now."

He started *Serenade* on a nice sunny day. There were seventeen girls in class. "Today I think I'll make a little something," he announced. He excused the gentlemen and started putting girls in place and standing back to see what it looked like. Annabelle Lyon and I were the two smallest, and we already knew that he liked tall ballerinas. He took forever to arrange everyone; he wanted all his girls to show. He placed Kathryn Mullowny, Heidi Vosseler, Holly Howard, until finally Annabelle and I were the only two left, standing across from each other. Her face told me what I felt: "Oh, God, we're too small; we're going to be the understudies." But then he jumped up on the bench and summoned us: "Ruthanna, Bella." We came running and he put her in front on stage left and me on stage right. "Like hungry birds in the nest," he told me later. We were starving for steps.

He was looking for a way to begin. He started talking about Germany. "I was there with Diaghilev. There is an awful man there [Hitler]. He looks like me but he has mustache. The people know him, they love him. When they see him, all people do like that for him." I still didn't know who Mr. Hitler was. "I am not such an awful man," Balanchine continued, "and I don't have mustache. So maybe for me you put together this. Your hand is high, and then falls down and thrusts forward."

I adored Balanchine. I waltzed up to him when I was fifteen and said, "Mr. Balanchine, I want to be a choreographer like you. How do you do it?" He replied, "I can't tell you how you will do it because

I am not you and I don't know how I do it. I don't think I am even yet choreographer. I make some steps for my friends. They are nice. Sometimes it's all right. But I will tell you what you have to do. You have to be very good dancer yourself. I didn't say famous, I said good. You have to know how dancers feel. You will never know unless you have done it. Then you have to know music very well." He went on and on about that. "Then you have to look everywhere, everything, all the time. Look at the grass in the concrete when it's broken, children and little dogs, and the ceiling and the roof. Your eyes is camera and your brain is a file cabinet."

When he was choreographing one ballet, he put us all on our knees a long time. "Well, you know, when I began I was dry," he explained. "I didn't have idea. And I had twelve pages of awful music. I didn't know what to do. I go in studio and I sit. I watch dancers. They put leg on barre and I get idea. But I look and I think of that awful music, what will I do, and I have to put them off. And mind open and picture come suddenly of that man on Broadway, with wheels, with pencils." He was referring to a World War I veteran who had no legs, who used to sit on a skateboard on Broadway. "He was one of the first people I meet in America," Balanchine told us. "When I saw this man without legs, I put all on your knees and I can begin."

I never knew anybody who trusted his unconscious and was able to follow it through as much as he. I had millions of little examples of how that happened, one when he made *Le Bourgeois Gentilhomme*. It was done in a great hurry. Balanchine kept saying, "I have a nice little pas de trois for you and Danielian and Nikita Talin." Berman designed a Columbine costume, with curls and a hat, but Balanchine hadn't yet made any choreography. I kept saying, "But Mr. B!" He reassured me. "You learn very fast. I will do for you." About a day and a half before the premiere, he finally got around to it after a performance one night. Nikita was Pierrot and Leon was Harlequin. We came in with three little screens and put them down and danced. The idea was they both wanted me and he made a big promenade where Leon had my hand and Nikita was pulling my foot. Balanchine put it together very fast; finally he came to the end. It was about two o'clock in the morning by then. "I have to make finale. But I am so tired I could kill myself." And so he had us set up our little screens. I was in the middle and Leon came up from behind his screen and approached me. I said, "No," and he killed himself and disappeared. Nikita came up and I told him, "No," too. He went down behind his screen. I ran around, they were both dead, so I killed myself too, and that's the way it ended.

After class one day Balanchine said, "I want to talk to you. I think you have to start to teach." "Oh, no," I protested. "I will never be a dancing teacher. I'm going to do *Swan Lake* and then I'm going to die." "You have gift," he said. "You will be good teacher. I will give you the most easy class." He gave me the advanced professional class, which was comprised of all my friends. For a week I came wearing a different chiffon every day and carried on like an idiot. Balanchine sat on the bench and wiggled his nose and batted his eyebrows and eyelashes. He didn't say a word, however, until after class on Friday. "You don't get salary this week because you didn't teach one class. You performed for them. You make nice choreography. I will steal your steps, a little bit. But you didn't teach." He pointed to the bench. "Until you can sit there and let them find, you are not teaching. You have to look, not do yourself, or they will only copy you. They are good dancers. They know everything. What would you like to see them do different than they do?" "Number one," I said, "I cannot stand the way they look in the mirror. They spend the whole class there." "What else?" he prompted me. "They don't run very well, particularly the women in their toe shoes. They make too much noise and they don't move." "Well, then you have something to teach. Do."

The next lesson I turned everyone away from the mirror and started them running, everywhere and every possible way and configuration. While I was doing that Mr. Vladimiroff arrived on the balcony to watch. Eugenie Ouroussow came in next. Then Mr. Oboukhoff. When I came out, Miss Ouroussow said, "Come into the office. I need to talk to you. Mr. Vladimiroff has complained that you are breaking tradition. The class is only running. They are not doing *enchaînement*." She told me Mr. Balanchine was waiting for me. He asked how it went and I told him, "We're beginning to break some ground. I'd like to do it again tomorrow." "Good," he said and walked out. As I walked out Mr. Oboukhoff hit me on the back and congratulated me. It was only Vladimiroff who made the scandal, but to keep him happy they called me into the office with Balanchine congratulating me in private. Balanchine told me, "You know, when I am dry I go to Oboukhoff's class and take it with my eyes. And I am full. He is such a choreographer."

Balanchine used to ask him to do a ballet, but he never would. "No, too sad, too sad."

After I retired from dancing, I was sitting on the bench with Balanchine at the School of American Ballet while he rehearsed. As they were working, he said to me, "You know, those men in Tibet up in the mountains. They sit nude in the cave and they drink only water through straw and they think very pure thoughts." I said, "Yes, the Tibetan monks. The lamas." He said, "Yes. You know, that is what I should become. I would be with them." And then he looked around and said, "But unfortunately, I like butterflies."

1991

CAROLYN BROWN (1927–)

CAROLYN BROWN'S mother, Marion Rice, was a Denishawn dancer and a respected dance teacher, so Carolyn, growing up in Fitchburg, Massachusetts, got an early start on her lifework. Even so, she studied philosophy at Wheaton and took some time before making the decision to dance. In 1951 she was in New York, married to the composer Earle Brown, and taking classes with Merce Cunningham and at Juilliard, part of a downtown art world that included Robert Rauschenberg and Jasper Johns. Two years later she became one of the founding members of Merce's company in its first season at Black Mountain College, in North Carolina, and she danced for him and with him for twenty years—his finest dancer and a star in her own right.

She has choreographed, taught, and written—her superb autobiography, *Chance and Circumstance*, was published in 2007, after decades of work on it. Why did it take so long? Perhaps because she hesitated to express a certain ambivalence she felt toward Merce (as a person, never as an artist). Her personal hero was Merce's lifelong partner, the composer John Cage, whose ebullience, warmth, and humanity were in clear contrast with Merce's more taciturn, even withholding, nature. She does, however, quote in her book what Merce remembered saying to her the night of her final performance: "'So beautiful,' I said to her, 'I never told you enough.'"

Brown, winner of countless awards and grants, was for years an adviser to the Cunningham Dance Foundation's board of directors and has staged Cunningham works for his own company and for others around the world. For a great deal of her life her companion was the photographer James Klosty, whose pictures of Cunningham and Cage (see portfolio of photographs) are our finest pictorial representation of them.

The VW Years

For SEVENTY dollars a week (fifty-seven take-home), new members of the corps de ballet danced four shows a day, seven days a week, three weeks out of four, and along with that performance schedule, they rehearsed up to an additional six hours when preparing for a new show, plus attending the obligatory costume, shoe, and wig fittings! Working at Radio City Music Hall pretty much meant living there. For many of the old-timers who'd persevered ten, fifteen, even twenty years, it was more like being part of an institution than holding down a job, and they suffered the conflicting feelings of passionate loyalty and carping disgruntlement that such situations spawn. The loyalty was from pride in the place itself: who isn't impressed by the Music Hall, that Art Deco marvel? Not only the auditorium, but the lobbies, the restrooms, and the staircases that connect them are astonishing. The auditorium—6,200 seats!—is awe-inspiring, with vast, gilded arches framing the stage and the boxes. In the theater's heyday, a heroic organ materialized out of the wall, and the orchestra seemed to levitate by magic as it floated into view on an elevator platform. This was everything a movie theater ought to be. It made moviegoing a real event, embodying the Hollywood world of luxury, elegance, and glamour that people could only read or dream about. At the Music Hall it was all theirs for three hours. "The 1950's were a golden age for the Music Hall," declared the *New York Times* (January 6, 1968), when "the stage was filled with dazzling pageants produced by Leon Leonidoff."

Backstage at the Music Hall was pretty amazing, too. Everything was provided: cafeteria, infirmary, lounges, smoking rooms, an auditorium just for the personnel to view the latest movies, a roof deck for sunning (although it was absolutely verboten for the dancers to get a tan), a dormitory for sleepovers or catnaps, administrative offices, scene shops, costume shops, music and dance rehearsal rooms, even places for live animals to be housed. The stage was a vast expanse 144 feet wide and 60 feet high. But the stage floor, at least from a dancer's point of view, was terrible—a cruel infliction of cement, sectioned off (with treacherous metal edges) so that each section could be raised or lowered at any time. Running along the entire front edge of the stage was a double metal rail that provided a wall of steam—a "steam curtain"—at the flick of a switch. Looking up into the flies, out to the wings, or into the auditorium at the thousands of lighting instruments was like trying to count the stars in the Milky Way. Had the Music Hall given Merce every light he might *ever* have needed, I'm sure no one would have missed even one of them. I couldn't stop wondering what Merce and John might have done with only a fraction of those fabulous resources. And hardly a day went by that summer that I didn't question the inequity represented by those two organizations: the one a lavish monument to popular culture, and the other a little modern-dance company struggling to exist on the most meager of terms. Obviously, I had no crystal ball to tell me that by the eighties the Music Hall's golden age would be over and the former marvel would become a white elephant fighting to survive while the little modern-dance company, grown a little larger, would be thriving, operating with a budget in the millions of dollars, its creator nationally recognized at the 1985 Kennedy Center Honors as "an individual who throughout his lifetime has made a significant contribution to American culture through the performing arts."

* * *

Although it was the crème de la crème of first-run Hollywood movies that kept the Music Hall so popular for so long, the stage shows were what gave it its unique prestige, enticing thousands of people to line up around the block for several hours to gain entrance. Along with the Statue of Liberty and the Empire State Building, Radio City Music Hall was a tourist "must." The main attraction, unquestionably, was the Rockettes—all-American, tap-dancing women, all 5´5″ to 5´8″, most of them pretty, whose thirty-six pairs of shapely legs were trained to execute routines beyond any military drill-sergeant's wildest dreams. The dancers in the ballet couldn't help feeling like second-class citizens, knowing full well that it wasn't the corps de ballet that the audience lined up to see. Even so, the ballet added a certain cachet to the extravaganza of each pageant, a cut above the jugglers and acrobats, dog acts, barbershop quartets, and bareback riders.

Backstage, the hierarchy was absolute: at the very top (*and how well they knew it*) were the Rockettes. Somewhere close to the bottom was the corps de ballet. Even the animals (via their trainers) had more clout. After my very first show, I was chagrined to receive a note from the corps de ballet dance captain, who'd received a note from the Rockettes' dance captain to the effect that one of the senior members of the Rockettes (fifty if she was a day, but—despite a haggard face and too many inches around the middle—still the possessor of a gorgeous pair of legs) had complained bitterly that I had put too much pressure on her shoulder in the "figure-eight bourrée section." My god. She couldn't turn around and tell me so herself? Ah! I had to remember, queens do not speak directly to parlor maids! The distance between us was that great; not imagined, terribly real.

I had the rotten misfortune of going into the current show one week before the new one was to open. So, having barely assimilated the material and the spacing for the show that I was performing four times a day, I had also to learn the material for the upcoming show. This meant starting rehearsals at eight in the morning and rehearsing constantly between shows, except during the dinner break. There were moments during that first week when I didn't think I'd make it. I wasn't used to doing that much pointe work, and especially not on such an immense bone-crushing cement floor, the hardest surface I can remember working on. It was a week of exquisite torture. My left leg, knee, calf, foot, and groin felt nearly paralyzed with pain. I had to spend every free second I had in the hospital-infirmary soaking my muscles, joints, and tendons and fighting back tears. There might have been some consolation (I felt none) in knowing that several other new girls and even a couple of the old-timers were in similar straits. If a dancer had made it through the audition, it was assumed that she could dance sufficiently well to do the choreography correctly. I never received a single note about my dancing, only about being on my mark. The vast reaches of stage and auditorium meant that for most of the 6,200 people in the audience the things clearly visible were pattern and spacing, not steps, not facial expression, and, heaven forbid, not quality. Being in the right place at the right time—i.e., "on your mark"—was *all*. For that amazingly streamlined race of beings called the Rockettes, the unforgivable breach of conduct was getting even the faintest blush of a sunburn, a sin punishable by a fine, and if it happened very often, it could mean getting sacked. The same rule applied to us in the ballet, but, since we were second-class citizens, the rule was less zealously enforced.

Within the well-appointed dressing room there was also a pecking order. We were ranked according to unwritten laws established by the senior members. Where one sat, which row and beside whom, was dictated to and accepted by the newest of us without question. There were always twenty-eight dancers working in the corps at any one time. We were a crazy mix: from sixteen to thirty years old, from the most eager, fresh, and starry-eyed would-be ballerinas to the most cynical, tough, lazy and disillusioned regulars who aspired to nothing beyond the weekly paycheck that came with the job. Those of us who looked upon the job as a training ground and a road to something better worked hard and took advantage of the available studio space to give ourselves class, practice, even choreograph a little. The cynical members never bothered even to warm up. What amazed me was that they rarely seemed to hurt themselves. There were also a dozen or so very talented, hardworking young dancers in both the Rockettes and the ballet who honestly believed they'd reached the zenith of their careers. They'd come from little dance studios in tiny provincial towns in far-off states where, in the fifties, dancing in the stage show at Radio City Music Hall meant one had gone as far as one could go, one had attained the very pinnacle of success.

I worked at the Music Hall for nine weeks, and in that time I did three different stage shows. The first, which I performed for only one week, had a rather sappy romantic ballet, set to Chopin. We wore long tutus, rhinestones around wrists and neck, and wigs with coronets of artificial flowers. The guest ballerina was New York City Ballet's Melissa Hayden, who, thirteen years earlier, had been a member of the corps there. That gave a number of us hope. But otherwise Melissa Hayden was more dismaying than she was impressive—at least for me. After having witnessed the regal courtesy of Margot Fonteyn, watching Hayden strut around like a little tough off the streets of Brooklyn and curse in language that might make a longshoreman shudder was a shocker. When we went on to the next show and Conrad Ludlow (then a soloist with the San Francisco Ballet, later a principal dancer with NYCB) replaced her as the main attraction, his manner couldn't have been more different. He was shy, soft-spoken, self-effacing, and very much a gentleman.

The stage show ran only as long as the motion picture it accompanied drew a house. As soon as audience attendance began to dwindle, a new film and a totally new show went on. The changeover happened on Thursdays, but we never knew which Thursday, and no one backstage ever seemed quite prepared for it. The week before each show opened was known as "Hell Week." As I've said, my first "hell week" was also my first week on the job, which made it hell and purgatory all rolled into one. The new show, "Blue Yonder," was one of those "dazzling pageants produced by Leon Leonidoff." It was advertised as "a gloriously exciting celebration of the golden anniversary of the United States Air Force." The Rockettes appeared as dancing WAFs. The corps danced in a "unique 'Space' spectacle." There were comedy acts, the Radio City Music Hall Glee Club singing patriotic Air Force songs, the full Radio City Music Hall Symphony Orchestra and "Special Added Attraction—the thrilling Air Force Drum and Bugle Corps and crack precision Air Force Ceremonial Drill Team." At the end, *everyone* appeared onstage in a humongous flag-waving finale, with huge projections of planes flashing across a giant screen. Posed a bit like the Statue of Liberty in a lipstick-red, sequined, strapless gown, I and two of my compatriots from the corps (one in silver, the other in blue) ascended out of the orchestra pit. The whole glee club, in Air Force uniforms, singing "Off we go, into the wild blue yonder" ascended with us—a stirring scene in which I felt utterly ridiculous. On the opening day of "Blue Yonder," we were up at 5:15 a.m., in makeup and onstage at 7 a.m. for a lighting rehearsal, which was followed by a studio rehearsal of the ballet, which was followed by the first performance of the usual four per day. At every rehearsal, including final dress, the dance was changed. Except when dancing for Antony Tudor (at his most quixotic) I'd never worked this way, certainly not with Merce, who rarely changed anything once he'd set a sequence of movement. The first performance was a mess. In the second, I came close to breaking a leg when someone let go of her wooden-paddle-with-two-yard-streamer-attached (all twenty-eight of us had them!) and the streamer wound twice around my leg while the paddle banged noisily on the floor behind me. I had to hobble off the stage to avert catastrophe.

But these trifling discomforts were nothing compared to my last Hell Week, which was rated by corps de ballet regulars who had been employed at the Music Hall six years or more as the very worst Hell Week in memory. On opening morning, after two weeks of rehearsals that had begun at seven or eight in the morning and gone on between performances, we still had no ballet. Poor Margaret Sande. We'd been told that she was unable to work well unless under pressure. Instead of creating a new ballet during the run of the current show, it was tradition for her to wait until the very last hours and hope for a heaven-sent ray of inspiration. But on this occasion, heaven—apparently—withheld its beneficence. The ballet was "The Dance of the Hours" from Ponchielli's opera *La Gioconda*. The previous April I'd been suddenly thrown into two performances of Zachary Solov's choreography for *La Gioconda* at the Met, replacing a badly injured company member who'd been shoved into an oncoming subway train at rush hour. At the time, I'd thought his choreography quite nice; four months later it seemed a work of genius! Running out of time, backed into a corner and desperate for inspiration that never came, Miss Sande got it into her head to have all twenty-eight of her dancers execute thirty-two *fouettés, in unison*! Now, it is rare to see even the most technically accomplished dancer perform thirty-two *fouettés en place*, without moving some slight degree to the side or forward. To expect twenty-eight Music Hall dancers to stay on their marks throughout thirty-two *fouettés* was lunacy. Of course she knew this, but, obviously desperate, she was adamant and kept us practicing them until our toes were bruised and bloody; only after the disastrous dress rehearsal, when it was abundantly clear that we would never get it right, were those accursed *fouettés* scrapped. We continued to rehearse between shows even after the opening, and *still* the steps were changed and we were threatened with still *more* rehearsals (into the wee hours of the morning, if necessary) if we didn't do well.

To add to our distress, Russell Markert, the founder of the Rockettes, had made an additional tap number just for the corps de ballet. Actually, most of us were thrilled to be working with him. My tap experience consisted of not-very-serious lessons in my mother's studio (not taught by my mother) when I was about ten years old. All I'd retained from those lessons was the basic time step, and that was exceedingly rusty. But working for Mr. Markert was really fun, even though his choreography seemed to me a bit tacky. He taught us our whole routine in three hours and never changed a step of it. We all wanted to do well for him, and on our own we practiced his routine assiduously right up until showtime. To our huge disappointment, the number was cut after the dress rehearsal. Mr. Markert assured us that he hadn't been displeased with our efforts; quite the contrary, but the whole show was too long, and our tap number was the only thing that could be cut. Rumor circulated that we'd shown up the Rockettes (if not in clarity, certainly in enthusiasm), and of course we wanted to believe it. We still had a short tap sequence with the Rockettes in the finale—vulgar, corny stuff standing on a staircase, Busby Berkeley style, costumed in tiny black velveteen bathing suits, cut low in the bust and high in the leg, a blue sequined strip from crotch to bust, and a black velveteen, blue-sequined tail attached to our bottoms and one wrist, black elastic mesh hose, and blue feathers in our hair. We did a series of bumps and grinds, high leg-kicks, plus a couple of rudimentary tap steps. In the front row center on opening morning were Jimmy Waring (who made almost a fetish of attending *every* Music Hall Thursday-morning opening) and Remy Charlip. I fully expected them to hoot with laughter, but Remy told me afterward that when he saw me in the finale, bumping and grinding and flicking my sequined tail, he cried. Backstage, I cried, too. And a couple of motherly corps senior members embraced me, patted me sympathetically on the back, and then proceeded to scold me for caring so much. "It's just a job, honey! It's not art. It's not worth crying about!" I knew they were right, but nevertheless, I wrote to my parents, "I don't think I'll ever forget the sense of frustration and shame of that week."

In any case, my days at Radio City Music Hall were numbered. On September 3, Merce—back from California—was to come after the show to take me to dinner. By this time, the choreography had finally been set, and I was beginning to relax and enjoy it, at least to enjoy dancing to Ponchielli's music played by the huge Music Hall orchestra. Perhaps I was enjoying it too much, because while executing my favorite step in the ballet (it was straight out of Cecchetti's manual) I tripped on one of the warped boards on the apron in front of the steam curtain's metal rail and fell sprawling. As I tripped I heard a terrible, ominous crunch. Fortunately I was close to the wings and could hop offstage quickly. Once off, I collapsed on the floor and wept. All I could think about was Merce witnessing my clumsy fall. Within seconds, stagehands and stage managers surrounded me, gently placed me in a wheelchair, and whisked me by elevator to the in-house hospital, where a flustered nurse put ice on my ankle and tried to give me a glass of Bromo-Seltzer; I suppose the bromo was to quiet my seemingly inconsolable weeping. I felt like an idiot and even more so when a lovely bouquet of miniature roses arrived for me. They'd been sent up from Merce, who was waiting for me at the stage door. Oh, God! He *had* seen my ignominious fall! I began to laugh and cry at once. Later on, he said he hadn't seen the performance. But if not, why the roses? I didn't dare ask him that. Still, I've never been quite sure whether he told me the truth or whether he was simply sparing me further embarrassment. Later I learned that I wasn't the only casualty from that Hell Week—there were at least a half-dozen others.

How wonderful Merce was. He took me in a cab to Roosevelt Hospital for X-rays (no broken bones; a severe sprain, that was all); then in another cab back to the Music Hall so I could collect my belongings; yet another cab to meet Remy at a favorite Italian restaurant in the East Village, and still another cab to take me home. So ended my Radio City Music Hall "career"—a month earlier than planned, but not a moment too soon as far as I was concerned. I had earned enough money to pay off my entire debt at the Metropolitan Opera Ballet School—a year's worth of classes!—and, thanks to my sprained ankle, I collected enough money through workman's compensation to be ahead of the game for the next year, and maybe, just maybe, if the opportunity ever presented itself, to go to Europe someday. I had no regrets about working at the Music Hall. There had been one lesson worth learning: be in the right space at the right time—be On Your Mark! And one lesson I never wanted to learn: "Don't care so much. It's not worth it." I knew for certain that I wanted to do something I cared about profoundly; then, whatever the difficulties, it *would* be worth it.

2007

Holly Brubach (1953–)

Holly Brubach is a journalist and the former style editor of *The New York Times* (1993–98), a staff writer at *The New Yorker* (1988–93) and *The Atlantic Monthly* (1982–88), and a contributing editor at *Vogue* (1980–86). In 1982, three of her essays about dance published in *The Atlantic* won the National Magazine Award. Specializing in design, architecture, dance, music, sports, and food, she has written for *Vanity Fair, Ballet News, House & Garden, Departures, Gourmet, Mirabella*, and *Golf Digest*. She continues to write for the *Times, W, The Gentlewoman*, and other publications. Brubach is the author of three books: *Choura: The Memoirs of Alexandra Danilova*, which won the De La Torre Bueno Prize for best dance book of 1983; *Girlfriend*, a meditation on drag queens and clichés of femininity in eight different cultures; and *A Dedicated Follower of Fashion*, a collection of essays. She has also written extensively for film and television, including "Balanchine," a two-hour documentary on the choreographer's life and work; "The Byron Janis Story"; and over twenty shows for WNET's *Dance in America* series.

Brubach is currently at work on a biography of Tanaquil Le Clercq, the New York City Ballet ballerina who was the fifth and last wife of George Balanchine. In support of this project, in the spring of 2017, she was awarded a Guggenheim fellowship.

A Classic "Beauty"

Tchaikovsky's score for *The Sleeping Beauty* is like a miracle waiting to happen, and occasionally—not nearly often enough—the miracle is brought into being on the stage. Always dance-worthy, the music describes the characters and the course of events, in detail.

When the staging keeps to this musical blueprint, as it does in the best productions of *Beauty*, this nineteenth-century storybook ballet manages to capture more of human nature than the most modern psychological dance-dramas.

The most recent *Sleeping Beauty* I've witnessed was brought by England's Royal Ballet to the U.S. this past summer. Though a few other companies, here and elsewhere, maintain their own productions, the Royal's undisputed claim to this ballet makes perfect sense: it rests partly with Margot Fonteyn, who remains the definitive Princess Aurora in many people's memories, and partly with the English national character, which takes hierarchy for granted (American ballet companies identify in the program every last dancer in a performance; the Royal lists only those dancers in featured roles and accounts for all the rest collectively, as "Artists of the Royal Ballet"). Anyone who ever doubted the plausibility of this ballet's fuss over a princess had only to consult his television screen in July to see the pomp and circumstance surrounding Aurora's wedding confirmed in real life, in the marriage of Prince Charles and Lady Diana Spencer.

The Sleeping Beauty culminates in a wedding, but its subject isn't love, or even marriage—this is a ballet about manners, about moral issues of the most everyday sort. The plot is a tug-of-war, declared in the music, between good and evil. From the first four bars of the Introduction, we learn that an entire kingdom is in peril: the fairy Carabosse's motif hovers around E minor, with a witchlike cackle built on an augmented-sixth chord. Tchaikovsky's marking is *fff* at the outset; only two measures later, a lightning-fast arpeggio that builds to a thunderclap demands a crescendo. There is something stingy and abrupt about Carabosse's rhythms: an eighth note, an eighth rest, an eighth note, an eighth rest, and then—a little fit of pique—four sixteenth notes. When Carabosse laughs, the harmony alternates between two dissonant chords; otherwise, it tends to move stealthily, chromatically. Nowhere in this twenty-seven-bar-long introductory passage is there a musical line continuous enough to constitute a melody. Carabosse extends her hand and snatches it right back again, in music that is furious and menacing. The curtain stays down. With nothing to look at onstage, nowhere to run for cover, the audience is caught in the storm. Then, suddenly, the weather changes.

The key changes, from E minor to E major, and we hear the Lilac

Fairy waft in on a harp glissando, hushed pianissimo. She sets our fears to rest, with a calm and expansive melody, four breathless measures long. The tempo is andantino (compared with Carabosse's allegro vivo), the rhythm is even and soothing. When, finally, the Lilac Fairy raises her voice to triple forte, it's to announce glorious news: the brass adopts her theme and brings it to full flower.

Throughout the ballet, Carabosse and the Lilac Fairy are pitted harmonically against each other, and their antagonism in the music is truly ingenious. A major key and its relative minor, which is lower by a third (the relative minor of E major is C#), are coexistent—they share the same scale. A major key and its parallel minor, however, do battle over the same territory: in both E major and E minor, the tonic is E, but the minor scale must lower the third tone by half a step. Parallel keys disagree; one or the other must win. So the Lilac Fairy and Carabosse come to blows in the key of E, major versus minor.

The Lilac Fairy's decree in the Introduction gives way to eleven bars of a march, off in the distance, and with that the music comes down to earth. The curtain rises on the ballet's prologue; we hear the procession coming closer. The next music, titled No. 1, March, in the score, echoes the tag end of the Introduction. Like most marches, this one sounds important, but, with its dotted eighth notes on the offbeats, it's too graceful and lilting to be mistaken for a military drill. This music heralds the arrival of noblemen, who walk tall, and women wearing wide skirts, stepping lightly. They are making their way to the palace, part of which we see onstage, for the christening of the newborn Princess Aurora. The time is the seventeenth century. Though we never learn the location of this king's realm, his palace and the fashions of his court look remarkably like those of Louis XIV, the king of France who founded the first official academy for ballet.

Presiding over the festivities onstage is Cattalabutte, the emcee, a self-important civil servant who wears his authority like a well-polished badge. The Royal Ballet's Leslie Edwards plays Cattalabutte in the tradition of Eric Blore's hotel managers and waiters in Astaire-Rogers movies—servile, slightly rotund, swaggering, fussy, easily befuddled. The ladies and gentlemen, who enter by twos, ask Cattalabutte's permission to go look at the baby in her cradle, upstage. Permission granted. Cattalabutte stalks the stage as if he owns it, until a footman hurries on to announce the King's arrival.

The King and Queen wear velvet cloaks lined in ermine; two atten-
dants follow along behind and carry their trains. The Royal's finery
(costumes for this production by David Walker) strikes a believable
balance between antique and lived-in: these cloaks, for example, don't
look as if they've spent the past few centuries hanging in a museum,
nor do they look like costumes—brand-new. The king asks Cattalabutte if he's sure the guest list is complete. Cattalabutte shakes his
head, as if to say, "You can place your faith in me." Not to worry.

In this ballet, mime becomes dancing; every gesture is positioned precisely on the music. Long speeches are designated in the
score ("*Récit de Cattalabutte*" is specified twice in this march alone).
Classical-ballet mime is, of course, stated according to French grammar: "I love you" becomes "I you love," or "*je t'aime*." But the music
underlying the words in this ballet makes them more lyrical and eloquent than any spoken language.

On the final chord of the march, everyone onstage pays his respects
to the King and Queen in *révérence*. Then the guests of honor arrive
(No. 2, Scène Dansante). In this kingdom, apparently, no one questions
the existence of fairies; they're invited as a matter of course for state
occasions like this one. They live in peaceful harmony with the people,
though their powers are clearly superhuman. Five fairies appear, each
with a cavalier and a footman bearing her gift to the baby Princess.
Then come eight girls—junior fairies, presumably—who pave the way
for the Lilac Fairy. In some productions, she is simply the last of the
fairies to arrive. But the Royal Ballet, which makes no apologies for
differences in rank, sets the Lilac Fairy apart from the rest. So, when
Carabosse arrives to deliver her curse, it is logically only the Lilac
Fairy who can countermand it.

To a waltz marked grazioso, the eight girls in the Lilac Fairy's retinue dance in canon—two lines of four, with one line taking up the
steps of the other. The music, with a big crescendo to fortissimo and
the addition of the brass, shoos the girls off and brings on the fairies' six cavaliers, who execute a fairly standard jumping combination,
impressive in unison, then *pirouette* and exit in time for the reprise of
the first theme and the girls' return. The six fairies finish out the waltz
in front of the Lilac Fairy's corps.

The King and Queen descend from their thrones; the Queen invites
the fairies to dance. The Lilac Fairy accepts for them all: Thank you.

The six fairies convene—*bourrées* in a circle—then sit on their cavaliers' knees, in a line at the foot of the stage, for the harp glissandi that open the Adagio (No. 3, Pas de Six). The fairies' six footmen—little boys—return with the gifts, each presented on a tasseled velvet cushion. Then, one by one, from left to right, the fairies turn two *pirouettes* and finish balanced in *attitude*, supported by their cavaliers.

All together, the fairies do *développé à la seconde*, and at the height of the extension their partners lift them, so that they seem to soar. They land in *arabesque*, and each of them dips one hand to the ground, as if rippling the surface of a pool, or consecrating the center of the stage. But the musical climax of this scene goes to the baby, brought down by her nurse from the crib to that hallowed spot where the fairies converged. The music swells from *ff* to *fff* to *ffff*, as the fairies gather round and the Lilac Fairy is lifted high overhead; then—more glissandi—they give their blessings with sensuous, rippling arm motions, working their magic. The tempo picks up, the adagio theme heard a few moments earlier returns, allegro vivo, and along with it come the eight girls. The stage is now set for the fairies to bestow their gifts individually, each with her own variation.

Our modern-day notion of fairies and who they might be is a rather insipid one, but, fortunately, Tchaikovsky and Marius Petipa, who choreographed the first *Beauty* in 1890 (based on the fairy tale by Charles Perrault), had a broader range of personalities in mind. No two of these six variations are alike.

The first occurs in B♭ major, the same key as the preceding adagio, with a sweet, sustained oboe melody over a clarinet walking up and down stairs. This is, in the Royal's version, the Fairy of the Crystal Fountain, and her dancing is gentle, with precious footwork—*bourrées, piqués*, soft *pliés* on point—and frequent changes of facing. Slowly, languorously, she extends one arm, then the other, like a woman admiring her long evening gloves. Midway through, a bassoon takes over the theme from the oboe. Harmonically, this variation makes quick little forays into G minor (the relative minor of B♭ major), and so prefigures the second fairy, of the Enchanted Garden, whose variation is set in G minor. Her music and her dance—mischievous *piqués* back and *bourrées* forward, little runs and quick double *ronds de jambe* on point, all set to fidgety, staccato woodwinds over galloping strings—set her apart from the first fairy. But, as if by some reciprocal arrangement, she too declares their kinship harmonically, by reverting to B♭ major for the middle eight bars. Though none of the remaining four variations in this suite makes reference to any other, the major/minor link between the first two fairies, with each briefly in the other's key, hints at some larger scheme: we understand by ear, right off, that these are not star turns for competing ballerinas but are six compatible solo variations in which each of the godmothers bestows her own charms on the baby Princess.

The third fairy is calm, enchanting. Her tiny walking steps, *emboîtés*, and hops in *attitude*—all on point—underscore the music's upper line, pizzicato strings that sprinkle a little trail of eighth notes. Then the dancing shifts our focus from the strings to the shorter, more melodic figure that began on the trombone and was taken over by the piccolo, an octave higher: the little hops and dainty pointwork give way to a larger, more sustained step—a slow *développé* from front to back, through *passé* into *arabesque*.

The fourth variation, set, like the one before, in D major, belongs to the Fairy of the Songbirds; a piccolo descant tweets along with the melody on the glockenspiel. This fairy scurries on point, with her hands fluttering. The music and the choreography together characterize her as vivacious. She raises the pitch of energy onstage, and it's in that new, higher register that the fifth fairy, of the Golden Vine, enters, shooting sparks. Hers is the famous "finger" variation, in which she points with both hands at once to one corner, then to another, up, down—her gestures seem designed to cast a kind spell on the Princess and, at the same time, to bewitch the audiences, onstage and in the theater. Twice she leaps out of a string of fast *châiné* turns, right on the top note of an octave-long chromatic scale, then runs back, as if to retract the outburst.

The last to take her turn is the Lilac Fairy, whose variation is the only waltz of the six, and everything about it is expansive—large and clear. The choreography also draws a subtle distinction between her and the rest of the fairies, not with steps we haven't yet seen but with many familiar steps on a grander scale than we've seen them so far. Like two of the others' variations, the Lilac Fairy's includes double *ronds de jambe*, but whereas theirs were low and quick, hers are leisurely, with a last-minute lift into a high *développé à la seconde*. The music builds until the melody's final round, fortissimo, when the

Lilac Fairy swings into *fouettés* in *arabesque*—her leg swooping down and up again into a well-held second position, her torso twisting into *arabesque*. The cavaliers return—to the strong, square music of the coda—with air turns, *cabrioles, assemblés battus*; the girls in the Lilac Fairy's retinue come back, then the fairies, two at a time, crossing the stage. The Lilac Fairy herself brings this finale to a close, wending her way downstage with a few steps, then an *arabesque*, as the orchestra peals the same note, bell-like. As soon as she arrives at the footlights, the fairies and their company all take their places in the tableau that concluded the preceding Scène Dansante.

The King and Queen come forward to thank the fairies; the fairies' footmen surround them and offer the gifts. Suddenly, the sky darkens. "*Bruit dans le vestibule*," the score says—a commotion just offstage. A page hurries on: Sire . . . But the warning comes too late. Carabosse has already arrived in the wings and will be onstage any minute. The King and Queen hastily review with consternation the scroll that is the guest list—Carabosse, also a fairy, has been forgotten. The menacing theme that began the Introduction, we now know, was an omen of this: hurling thunderbolts in E minor, Carabosse rides right into the midst of the festivities in a carriage driven by her pack of rats. Two rats run on ahead, paving the way, and point back to her: Here she comes! She descends from her coach and, about to explode but restraining her anger for the moment, walks forward and curtsies to the King and Queen. Then she unleashes her fury: You didn't invite me—why? The King fumbles for an excuse: I—I, uh . . . , it wasn't me, it was (pointing to Cattalabutte) him! This King, passing the buck, is only human. Cattalabutte cowers in fear. As the rats dance a little agitated jig, Carabosse slowly walks a circle around him, sizing up her prey. In some productions, she snatches his wig, as the score directs. But in the Royal Ballet, Carabosse has only to snap her fingers in his ear—Boo!—and Cattalabutte jumps. It's his own cowardice, not her cruelty, that finally makes him look ridiculous, and Carabosse is so shrewd a judge of character that she instantly perceives how easily Cattalabutte can be humiliated. Her rats take an imbecilic delight in this little scene. The score tells us, "*Les pages rient d'un air caustique*."
Traditionally, Carabosse is something of a witch: she comes wearing a long black gown, her mime gestures exaggerate the length of

her fingers, and she rubs her hands together the way witches do when they're concocting their brews. But Monica Mason, who now performs the role at the Royal, conceives the character on her own brilliant terms. Though there's no doubting her mean streak, Mason's Carabosse is beautiful where others are ugly, evil to the core (the role is sometimes played by a man, in travesty). It seems clear enough in her portrayal that Carabosse was once a nice fairy—a little touchy, perhaps, and jealous—whose feelings have been hurt. She isn't wicked, she's vindictive. While all the other fairies have come wearing their Sunday-best tutus, in jewel-like colors, with filigreed bodices, Carabosse intends her funereal attire as an affront: worse than wearing black to a wedding is wearing black to a christening.

The King and Queen beg Carabosse's pardon—there is alarm in the brass—and the other fairies, surrounding her in a deep *révérence*, recommend forgiveness. But Carabosse will have none of it: she laughs back at them; she mocks the Fairy of the Crystal Fountain to her face, mimicking the arm movements from her variation. She sneers at the Songbird Fairy: And you, *you* with your fluttery little hands . . . Carabosse will not be turned away from her purpose. She has come to deliver a curse.

She points to the crib. The baby Princess will grow up to be beautiful, Carabosse says. The crowd hangs on her every gesture. She milks the suspense and pauses, kicking the rats at her feet. Continuing, she points again to the crib, holds up a spindle, and, with long, graceful hand motions, spins an imaginary thread. The music runs along, fortissimo, until suddenly, gleefully, she pricks her finger: "She will fall asleep and her sleep will be eternal," the score says here, and the music fades to pianissimo. But Carabosse doesn't break the news so gently: she raises her arms overhead and, with one emphatic gesture, brings them crashing down in a death sentence—wrists crossed, her hands in fists. The court recoils in horror; the King and Queen, on their knees now, implore Carabosse to rescind the curse. She stands like a washerwoman, her hands on her hips, and laughs. She spreads her arms in front of her and makes waves; the music scurries, staccato, and the rats at her feet scramble back and forth on their bellies. Their exultation at last screeches to a halt when the music shifts to E major and the Lilac Fairy, in hiding all this time, steps forward.

She bows to Carabosse; then: Why do you want to harm the Princess? I heard what you said—and she reiterates Carabosse's mime speech, gesture for gesture, right down to the final grim prediction of Aurora's death. But then she breaks the spell: from that same awful, intractable gesture—wrists crossed, hands in fists—she opens her hands and smoothes the air in front of her, as much as to say, "But no," or "It doesn't matter." For—there's more—Aurora will not die but will fall asleep; the Lilac Fairy makes a pillow of her arms and rests her head on it. Aurora will sleep until a Prince comes and awakens her with a kiss. Unlike Carabosse's terse prophecy, the Lilac Fairy's is lyrical and unbroken; the contrast in their deliveries is as dramatic as if Gertrude Stein and Marcel Proust had been their speechwriters.

The music builds to a climax, reached when the Lilac Fairy predicts Aurora's awakening, and, rising from a deep *plié*, raises her arms in triumph. Carabosse crumbles before her. The coach stands ready; Carabosse, who has lost the battle but isn't about to concede the war, clambers back in and, drawn by her rats in harness, drives off in a huff. She rises to her feet, shakes her fist, points to her forehead—Mark my words!—and vanishes in a cloud of smoke: pouf. The crowd at court watches her go, raising an arm in salute, or perhaps in send-off: Be gone! Right away, the sun comes out and, as the people and fairies resume their processional and assemble for the prologue's final tableau around the cradle, the blue haze that is Carabosse's wake has lifted and hovers overhead.

From then on, the ballet unfolds exactly as predicted: the first act, a birthday party for the sixteen-year-old Princess Aurora, during which she pricks her finger on a spindle and falls into a dead faint, is according to Carabosse; the second, in which Prince Florimund awakens Aurora with a kiss, is according to the Lilac Fairy.

During Act I, it's the members of the audience who keep Carabosse's curse in mind, watching with trepidation. The members of the court seem to have forgotten it—sixteen years have passed, after all. Not even the King seems concerned. There is an awkward scene at the act's opening, when the King decrees that three women found knitting be hanged (the connection seems far-fetched—presumably knitting needles, or maybe all sharp objects, have been banned since Carabosse's prophecy). But the King's moment of recognition doesn't come until much later, when he sees an old hag, whose face is hidden by the hood of her cloak, present Aurora with a golden spindle. He puzzles for a moment—it's as if he has seen this before—and then recalls: this is the way Carabosse predicted that the Princess would come to her death. He tries to get the spindle away from her, growing impatient as she refuses to hand it over: Give it here, he pleads. But, of course, the machinery is already in motion. Aurora pricks her finger, embarks on a "*Danse-vertige*," as it's labeled in the score, and swoons, in arabesque. "*Aurore tombe morte*": the score's stage direction assumes the worst.

But the audience's first clue that Carabosse's hex is about to take effect comes much earlier than the King's. With the music for Aurora's entrance—frisky, shadowed with faintly minor harmonies—the Princess seems already under Carabosse's sway. Our first glimpse of Aurora, poised in the colonnade upstage before she runs into the midst of her party, confirms our fears: she is, as Carabosse foretold, beautiful. That sense of dread grows keener during the Rose Adagio, in which we see the fruits of the other fairies' blessings: this Princess is ingenuous, graceful, good-hearted, spirited, loving, undeserving of what's about to happen to her.

But no sooner has Carabosse carried out her threat than the Lilac Fairy returns to keep her promise. She organizes a cortège to transport the Princess to her bed, then dances a lullaby to put the rest of the court to sleep. She coaxes the palace's landscaped garden to grow into a wild forest, so that the people's sleep will go undisturbed, their presence undiscovered, for a hundred years.

When, a few minutes later, the curtain rises on Act II, we find ourselves in the eighteenth century: the clothes are different in style and in their deeper, more saturated colors. Prince Florimund's hunting party is picnicking in the woods, engaging in a round of social dances—a Colin-Maillard, a minuet, a gavotte, a farandole, a mazurka. The Prince, though, is distracted, not in the mood for dancing, and he stays behind when the party continues on. The Lilac Fairy shows him a vision of the Princess Aurora and then, at his request, takes him to the palace in her mother-of-pearl boat, which looks as fragile and seaworthy as a Fabergé egg. This is the Panorama (No. 17), and in the music we can hear the waves lapping against the side of the boat.

The Awakening in itself is brief, but before it can take place, the Lilac Fairy must drive out Carabosse, who has made one last, desperate but feeble attempt to hold the fort and see that the Princess sleeps on forever. Without much of a struggle, Carabosse surrenders and then skulks off into the overgrown woods. The Prince's kiss resurrects Aurora and, stretching and yawning, the rest of the court comes back to life.

Act III, in which Aurora and Florimund are married, is another state occasion for character-dance divertissements and more variations. Invitations have gone out to representatives of other Perrault fairy tales: Beauty and the Beast, Red Ridinghood and a lusty Wolf attend. A Bluebird arrives with a Princess in tow: she is charmed by his song and follows him; he flies around her. Three other guests, Florestan and his sisters, dance a *pas de trois*. The bride and groom take their vows in a *pas de deux*, and the ceremonies conclude with a mazurka. The only fairy in attendance is the Lilac Fairy, and the others are sadly conspicuous in their absence. But, despite his nearly fatal oversight in the prologue, Cattalabutte's services have been retained, and he patrols the stage, puff-chested, with new and deepened pride.

Like most ballets, *The Sleeping Beauty* is only as good as its cast, and in the five performances I saw, no single cast seemed quite complete. Only two Lilac Fairies—Pippa Wylde and Bryony Brind—had authority enough to command the stage, and the Royal lacks a great Aurora. Lesley Collier makes a pugnacious Princess; Jennifer Penney, who looks the part, seems slightly bored by life at court. Merle Park in the role is intelligent above all, which is not unappealing but not especially appropriate, either—it's not the Princess's mind we are out to admire.

But even without a true ballerina in the title role, and without strong dancers in the leads, the Royal Ballet understands *The Sleeping Beauty* and never for a moment betrays the ballet's spirit. The dancing is distinctly British: slightly chauvinistic, always proper; the girls see that they don't spread their legs too far in turned-out positions, or open their hips too much in *arabesque*. No step is ever made too large or too fast—nothing urgent. The girls' insteps are ravishing, delicately curved to the point. Their arms make cameo-frames for their faces. Positions are always correct, decorum prevails—as befits royalty.

The marriage of this particular company to this ballet was made in heaven, and each has served the other well over the years. When, in 1939, Nicholas Sergeyev restaged Petipa's version (or so he claimed;

we'll never know how accurately he had preserved the original in his notebooks) for the company that later became the Royal Ballet, he set English dancing on its feet. *Beauty*, in one production or another, has been the repertory's staple ever since, the bread and butter by which the company survived hard times. The ballet's style has become the code by which the Royal conducts all its dancing. Now the hard times are over, but the Royal Ballet, in its fiftieth anniversary season, dances with *Beauty* in its soul.

December 1981

George Washington Cable (1844–1925)

OFTEN REFERRED to as the most important writer of the nineteenth-century South, George Washington Cable was born in New Orleans, served in his youth in the Confederate army, and lived in his native city until his outspoken writings on racism stirred up so much resentment that, in 1885, he moved himself and his family to Northampton, Massachusetts. His first and best-known books were *Old Creole Days* (1879) and the highly influential novel *The Grandissimes: A Story of Creole Life* (1880), and his many other novels and collections of stories and essays were also much admired—north of the Mason-Dixon line. His subjects, both in fiction and nonfiction, included racial injustice and miscegenation, yet his novels were seen as romances as well as important revelations of the sociology of Creole life. Among his close friends and admirers was Mark Twain, with whom he went on extended lecture expeditions known (and billed) as the "Twins of Genius" tours. The piece below first appeared in *The Century Magazine.*

The Dance in Place Congo

Congo Square.

WHOEVER has been to New Orleans with eyes not totally abandoned to buying and selling will, of course, remember St. Louis Cathedral, looking south-eastward—riverward—across quaint Jackson Square, the old Place d'Armes. And if he has any feeling for flowers, he has not forgotten the little garden behind the cathedral, so antique and unexpected, named for the beloved old priest Père Antoine.

The old Rue Royale lies across the sleeping garden's foot. On the street's farther side another street lets away at right angles, north-westward, straight, and imperceptibly downward from the cathedral

and garden toward the rear of the city. It is lined mostly with humble ground-floor-and-garret houses of stuccoed brick, their wooden
doorsteps on the brick sidewalks. This is Orleans street, so named
when the city was founded.

Its rugged round-stone pavement is at times nearly as sunny and
silent as the landward side of a coral reef. Thus for about half a mile;
and then Rampart street, where the palisade wall of the town used to
run in Spanish days, crosses it, and a public square just beyond draws
a grateful canopy of oak and sycamore boughs. That is the place. One
may shut his buff umbrella there, wipe the beading sweat from the
brow, and fan himself with his hat. Many's the bull-fight has taken
place on that spot Sunday afternoons of the old time. That is Congo
Square.

The trees are modern. So are the buildings about the four sides,
for all their aged looks. So are all the grounds' adornments. Trémé
market, off, beyond, toward the swamp, is not so very old, and the
scowling, ill-smelling prison on the right, so Spanish-looking and
dilapidated, is not a third the age it seems; not fifty-five. In that climate every year of a building's age counts for ten. Before any of these
M. Cayetano's circus and menagerie were here. Cayetane the negroes
called him. He was the Barnum of that region and day. That is, "who
came from Havana with his horses and baboons."

Up at the other end of Orleans street, hid only by the old padre's
garden and the cathedral, glistens the ancient Place d'Armes. In the
early days it stood for all that was best; the place for political rallying, the retail quarter of all fine goods and wares, and at sunset and
by moonlight the promenade of good society and the haunt of true
lovers; not only in the military, but also in the most unwarlike sense
the place of arms, and of hearts and hands, and of words tender as
well as words noble.

The Place Congo, at the opposite end of the street, was at the opposite end of everything. One was on the highest ground; the other on
the lowest. The one was the rendezvous of the rich man, the master,
the military officer—of all that went to make up the ruling class; the
other of the butcher and baker, the raftsman, the sailor, the quadroon,
the painted girl, and the negro slave. No meaner name could be given
the spot. The negro was the most despised of human creatures and the
Congo the plebeian among negroes. The white man's plaza had the

army and navy on its right and left, the court-house, the council-hall and the church at its back, and the world before it. The black man's was outside the rear gate, the poisonous wilderness on three sides and the proud man's contumely on its front.

Before the city overgrew its flimsy palisade walls, and closing in about this old stamping-ground gave it set bounds, it was known as Congo Plains. There was wide room for much field sport, and the Indian villagers of the town's outskirts and the lower class of white Creoles made it the ground of their wild ball game of *raquette*. Sunday afternoons were the time for it. Hence, beside these diversions there was, notably, another.

The hour was the slave's term of momentary liberty, and his simple, savage, musical and superstitious nature dedicated it to amatory song and dance tinctured with his rude notions of supernatural influences.

* * *

And yet there was entertaining variety. Where? In the dance! There was constant, exhilarating novelty—endless invention—in the turning, bowing, arm-swinging, posturing and leaping of the dancers. Moreover, the music of Congo Plains was not tamed to mere monotone. Monotone became subordinate to many striking qualities. The strain was wild. Its contact with French taste gave it often great tenderness of sentiment. It grew in fervor, and rose and sank, and rose again, with the play of emotion in the singers and dancers.

The Gathering.

It was a weird one. The negro of colonial Louisiana was a most grotesque figure. He was nearly naked. Often his neck and arms, thighs, shanks, and splay feet were shrunken, tough, sinewy like a monkey's. Sometimes it was scant diet and cruel labor that had made them so. Even the requirement of law was only that he should have not less than a barrel of corn—nothing else,—a month, nor get more than thirty lashes to the twenty-four hours. The whole world was crueler those times than now; we must not judge them by our own.

Often the slave's attire was only a cotton shirt, or a pair of pantaloons hanging in indecent tatters to his naked waist. The bondwoman was well clad who had on as much as a coarse chemise and petticoat.

To add a *tignon*—a Madras handkerchief twisted into a turban—was high gentility, and the number of kerchiefs beyond that one was the measure of absolute wealth. Some were rich in *tignons*; especially those who served within the house, and pleased the mistress, or even the master—there were Hagars in those days. However, Congo Plains did not gather the house-servants so much as the "field-hands."

These came in troops. See them; wilder than gypsies; wilder than the Moors and Arabs whose strong blood and features one sees at a glance in so many of them; gangs—as they were called—gangs and gangs of them, from this and that and yonder direction; tall, well-knit Senegalese from Cape Verde, black as ebony, with intelligent, kindly eyes and long, straight, shapely noses; Mandingoes, from the Gambia River, lighter of color, of cruder form, and a cunning that shows in the countenance, whose enslavement seems specially a shame, their nation the "merchants of Africa," dwelling in towns, industrious, thrifty, skilled in commerce and husbandry, and expert in the working of metals, even to silver and gold; and Foulahs, playfully miscalled "*Poulards*,"—fat chickens,—of goodly stature, and with a perceptible rose tint in the cheeks; and Sosos, famous warriors, dexterous with the African targe; and in contrast to these, with small ears, thick eyebrows, bright eyes, flat, upturned noses, shining skin, wide mouths and white teeth, the negroes of Guinea, true and unmixed, from the Gold Coast, the Slave Coast, and the Cape of Palms—not from the Grain Coast; the English had that trade. See them come! Popoes, Cotocolies, Fidas, Socoes, Agwas, short, copper-colored Mines—what havoc the slavers did make!—and from interior Africa others equally proud and warlike: fierce Nagoes and Fonds; tawny Awassas; Iboes, so light-colored that one could not tell them from mulattoes but for their national tattooing; and the half-civilized and quick-witted but ferocious Arada, the original Voudou worshiper. And how many more! For here come, also, men and women from all that great Congo coast,—Angola, Malimbe, Ambrice, etc.,—small, good-natured, sprightly "boys," and gay, garrulous "gals," thick-lipped but not tattooed; chattering, chaffering, singing, and guffawing as they come: these are they for whom the dance and the place are named, the most numerous sort of negro in the colonies, the Congoes and Franc-Congoes, and though serpent worshipers, yet the gentlest and kindliest natures that came from Africa. Such was the company. Among these *bossals*—that is, native Africans—there was, of course, an ever-growing number of negroes who proudly called themselves Creole negroes, that is, born in America;[1] and at the present time there is only here and there an old native African to be met with, vain of his singularity and trembling on his staff.

The Bamboula.

The gathering throng closed in around, leaving unoccupied the circle indicated by the crescent of musicians. The short, harsh turf was the dancing-floor. The crowd stood. Fancy the picture. The pack of dark, tattered figures touched off every here and there with the bright colors of a Madras *tignon*. The squatting, cross-legged musicians. The low-roofed, embowered town off in front, with here and there a spire lifting a finger of feeble remonstrance; the flat, grassy plain stretching around and behind, dotted with black stumps; in the distance the pale-green willow undergrowth, behind it the *cyprière*—the cypress swamp—and in the pale, seven-times-heated sky the sun, only a little declined to south and westward, pouring down its beams.

With what particular musical movements the occasion began does not now appear. May be with very slow and measured ones; they had such that were strange and typical. I have heard the negroes sing one—though it was not of the dance-ground but of the cane-field—that showed the emphatic barbarism of five bars to the line, and was confined to four notes of the open horn.[2]

But I can only say that with some such slow and quiet strain the dance may have been preluded. It suits the Ethiopian fancy for a beginning to be dull and repetitious; the bottom of the ladder must be on the ground.

The singers almost at the first note are many. At the end of the

---

[1]This broader use of the term is very common. The Creole "dialect" is the broken English *of the Creoles*, while the Creole *patois* is the corrupt French, not of the Creoles, but rather of the former slave race in the country of the Creoles. So of Creole negroes and Creole dances and songs.

[2]

An - no - qué, An - no - bia, Bia - ta - ia, Que - re - qué, Nal - lé - oua.

Au - mon - dé, Au - tap - o - té, Au - pé - to - té, Au - que - ré - qué, Bo.

first line every voice is lifted up. The strain is given the second time with growing spirit. Yonder glistening black Hercules, who plants one foot forward, lifts his head and bare, shining chest, and rolls out the song from a mouth and throat like a cavern, is a *candio*, a chief, or was before he was overthrown in battle and dragged away, his village burning behind him, from the mountains of High Soudan. That is an African amulet that hangs about his neck—a *greegree*. He is of the Bambaras, as you may know by his solemn visage and the long tattoo streaks running down from the temples to the neck, broadest in the middle, like knife-gashes. See his play of restrained enthusiasm catch from one bystander to another. They swing and bow to right and left, in slow time to the piercing treble of the Congo women. Some are responsive; others are competitive. Hear that bare foot slap the ground! one sudden stroke only, as it were the foot of a stag. The musicians warm up at the sound. A smiting of breasts with open hands begins very softly and becomes vigorous. The women's voices rise to a tremulous intensity. Among the chorus of Franc-Congo singing-girls is one of extra good voice, who thrusts in, now and again, an improvisation. This girl here, so tall and straight, is a Yaloff. You see it in her almost Hindoo features, and hear it in the plaintive melody of her voice. Now the chorus is more piercing than ever. The women clap their hands in time, or standing with arms akimbo receive with faint courtesies and head-liftings the low bows of the men, who deliver them swinging this way and that.

See! Yonder brisk and sinewy fellow has taken one short, nervy step into the ring, chanting with rising energy. Now he takes another, and stands and sings and looks here and there, rising upon his broad toes and sinking and rising again, with what wonderful lightness! How tall and lithe he is. Notice his brawn shining through his rags. He too, is a *candio*, and by the three long rays of tattooing on each side of his face, a Kiamba. The music has got into his feet. He moves off to the farther edge of the circle, still singing, takes the prompt hand of an unsmiling Congo girl, leads her into the ring, and leaving the chant to the throng, stands her before him for the dance.

Will they dance to that measure? Wait! A sudden frenzy seizes the musicians. The measure quickens, the swaying, attitudinizing crowd starts into extra activity, the female voices grow sharp and staccato, and suddenly the dance is the furious Bamboula.

Now for the frantic leaps! Now for frenzy! Another pair are in the ring! The man wears a belt of little bells, or, as a substitute, little tin vials of shot, "bram-bram sonnette!" And still another couple enter the circle. What wild—what terrible delight! The ecstasy rises to madness; one—two—three of the dancers fall—*bloucoutoum! boum!*—with foam on their lips and are dragged out by arms and legs from under the tumultuous feet of crowding new-comers. The musicians know no fatigue; still the dance rages on:

"Quand patate la cuite na va mangé li!"

And all to that one nonsense line meaning only,

"When that 'tater's cooked don't you eat it up!"

It was a frightful triumph of body over mind, even in those early days when the slave was still a genuine pagan; but as his moral education gave him some hint of its enormity, and it became a forbidden fruit monopolized by those of reprobate will, it grew everywhere more and more gross. No wonder the police stopped it in Congo Square. Only the music deserved to survive, and does survive—coin snatched out of the mire. The one just given, Gottschalk first drew from oblivion. I have never heard another to know it as a bamboula; but Mr. Charles P. Ware, in "Slave Songs of the United States," has printed one got from Louisiana, whose characteristics resemble the bamboula reclaimed by Gottschalk in so many points that here is the best place for it:[3] As much as to say, in English, "Look at that darky,"—we have

3

VOICE.

ARR. BY H. E. KREHBIEL.
Fine.

Vo - yez - ce, mu - let la, Mi - ché Bain - jo, comme il est in - so - lent. Cha - peau sur co -

PIANO—*Sempre staccato.*

té, Mi-ché Bain-jo, La canne a la main, Miché Bain - jo, Bottes qui fé crio, crio, Miché Bain - jo.

D. C.

to lose the saucy double meaning between *mulet* (mule) and *mulâtre* (mulatto)—

> Look at that darky there, Mr. Banjo,
> Doesn't he put on airs!
> Hat cocked on one side, Mr. Banjo,
> Walking-stick in hand, Mr. Banjo,
> Boots that go "crank, crank," Mr. Banjo,—
> *Look* at that darky there, Mr. Banjo,
> *Doesn't* he put on airs!

It is odd that such fantastical comicality of words should have been mated to such fierce and frantic dancing, but so it was. The reeking faces of the dancers, moreover, always solemnly grave. So we must picture it now if we still fancy ourselves spectators on Congo Plains. The bamboula still roars and rattles, twangs, contorts, and tumbles in terrible earnest, while we stand and talk. So, on and on. Will they dance nothing else? Ah!—the music changes. The rhythm stretches out heathenish and ragged. The quick contagion is caught by a few in the crowd, who take it up with spirited smitings of the bare sole upon the ground, and of open hands upon the thighs. From a spot near the musicians a single male voice, heavy and sonorous, rises in improvisation,—the Mandingoes brought that art from Africa,—and in a moment many others have joined in refrain, male voices in rolling, bellowing resonance, female responding in high, piercing unison. Partners are stepping into the ring. How strangely the French language is corrupted on the thick negro tongue, as with waving arms they suit gesture to word and chant (the translation is free, but so is the singing and posturing):

The Counjaille.

Suddenly the song changes. The rhythm sweeps away long and smooth like a river escaped from its rapids, and in new spirit, with louder drum-beat and more jocund rattle, the voices roll up into the sky and the dancers are at it. Aye, ya, yi![4]

I could give four verses, but let one suffice; it is from a manuscript copy of the words, probably a hundred years old, that fell into my hands through the courtesy of a Creole lady some two years ago. It is one of the best known of all the old Counjaille songs. The four verses would not complete it. The Counjaille was never complete, and found its end, for the time being, only in the caprice of the improvisator, whose rich, stentorian voice sounded alone between the refrains.

But while we discourse other couples have stepped into the grassy arena, the instrumental din has risen to a fresh height of inspiration, the posing and thigh-beating and breast-patting and chanting and swinging and writhing has risen with it, and the song is changed.

But the dance is not changed, and love is still the theme. Sweat streams from the black brows, down the shining black necks and throats, upon the men's bared chests, and into dark, unstayed bosoms. Time wears, shadows lengthen; but the movement is brisker than ever, and the big feet and bent shanks are as light as thistles on the air. Let one flag, another has his place, and a new song gives new vehemence, new inventions in steps, turns, and attitudes.

More stanzas could be added in the original *patois*, but here is a translation into African English as spoken by the Creole negro:

CHORUS. I done been 'roun' to evvy spot
         Don't foun' nair match fo' sweet Layotte. } *Bis.*

SOLO. I done hunt all dis settle*ment*
      All de way 'roun' fum Pierre Soniat';
      Never see yalla gal w'at kin
      'Gin to lay 'longside sweet Layotte.
            I done been, etc.

SOLO. I yeh dey talk 'bout 'Loïse gal—
      Loïse, w'at b'long to Pierre Soniat';
      I see her, but she can't biggin
      Stan' up 'longside my sweet Layotte.
            I done been, etc.

SOLO. I been meet up wid John Bayou,
      Say to him, "John Bayou, my son,
      Yalla gal nevva meet yo' view
      Got a face lak dat chahmin' one!"
            I done been, etc.

The fair Layotte appears not only in other versions of this *counjaille* but in other songs.

Or in English:

    Well I know, young men, I must die,
        Yes, crazy, I must die.
    Well I know, young men, I must crazy die,
        Yes, crazy, I must die. Eh-h-h-h!
    For the fair Layotte, I must crazy die,—Yes, etc.
    Well I know, young men, I must die,—Yes, etc.
    Well I know, young men, I must crazy die,
        I must die for the fair Layotte.

February 1886

Christopher Caines (1963–)

BORN AND raised in Halifax, Nova Scotia, Christopher Caines took his first dance class at age eighteen as a freshman at Harvard. He fell into dancing with passion. After he had earned an A.B. in literature, he moved to New York, where he studied on scholarship at the Merce Cunningham school, danced with many contemporary companies, and worked as a writer, a translator from French and German, and a book editor. In 2000, he founded his own chamber-dance ensemble, for which he has created more than thirty-five works; he has also received commissions to create for other dance, opera, and theater companies; universities; ballet competitions; public artworks; and films and videos. Caines has worked as a choreographer, dancer, director, composer for dance and theater, actor, singer, percussionist, lighting designer, and every kind of stage technician; his musicality has been frequently praised by critics, and, in 2006, he was awarded a Guggenheim fellowship. He has long been absorbed by the ballets of Antony Tudor, the subject of his essay below.

The Sylph Inside Us

ANTONY TUDOR died in 1987, more than a quarter century ago. An artist's death frequently enables shortly thereafter a synoptic overview of his career that results in significant reevaluation. Yet because Tudor composed almost all his important ballets before 1950, informed opinion of his career congealed long ago. For nearly four decades, Tudor simply did not make new ballets that challenged the critical and audience consensus regarding his work. Today, our view of Tudor is darkly overshadowed by conventional wisdom so continually repeated that we have long since ceased to question it.

Tudor and his partisans have often, for example, credited him with being the first choreographer to make ballets about real, ordinary people: "people like us," "people we know from life." The choreographer himself made this claim most memorably in an obviously scripted interview with Martha Myers in "Modern Ballet," an episode in the television series *A Time to Dance*, broadcast on WGBH Boston in 1958. "It would seem to me," Tudor says, "that a very important change is the decision to enlarge the range of characters to represent. Instead of always using princes and enchanted princesses, gypsies, forlorn little dryads and sylphs, we could come to grips with people and types that are familiar to us in everyday life. We didn't have to make ballets about royalty and exotic people, but could choose characters from the middle classes if we wanted to. We could even make a ballet about the girl living next door. We were able to present people with the same feelings as ourselves, and to see them in straightforward dramatic terms as human beings."

However, Tudor was not really the first ballet choreographer to create story ballets about "everyday" people. The canon of extant classical ballets, small though it is, does in fact include works focused on more or less real, ordinary characters: *La Fille Mal Gardée* (1789), the oldest of the full-length classics still danced (albeit with none of its original choreography), presents no exotic or fairy-tale characters, and its story concerns real people—if we allow that at least the romantic leads in a such a comic pastorale must be danced, in some sense, as *real* if we are to care about them.

Indeed, as Cyril Beaumont writes in *The Ballet Called Giselle* (self-published in 1944 and slightly revised in 1945), Jean Dauberval, the original choreographer of *Fille*, based several ballets on "scenes of village life, not the artificial life of Marie Antoinette's dairy at Versailles, but the workaday existence of the peasantry." Dauberval is in a sense Tudor's spiritual great-grandfather, and the anti-Baroque revolution that Dauberval instigated set the precedent for the reformist impulse that motivated Tudor's early work in the period between the two world wars. Within two decades, Dauberval's democratic idiom had given rise to a whole genre of ballets at the Paris Opera (all now lost), as Beaumont says, "concerned with the life, grave or gay, of the common people." These common folk—the ballet peasants who have survived in works such as *Giselle* or *La Sylphide*—surely look stylized to our eyes now, but then so do Tudor's characters. The process through which themes and people borrowed from life come to belong wholly to the theater—and must therefore be refreshed by contact with the world outside it—is an unending cycle.

Closely linked to this notion of Tudor's originality as a naturalistic storyteller, and perhaps the most distracting of all the received ideas about his work, is the proverb anointing him "the father of the psychological ballet," an inexact and inadequate formula, lazily repeated for seventy years, and a fatigued cliché that has long obscured much more than it has illuminated Tudor's idiosyncratic achievements. Arlene Croce is right to note in her 1987 *New Yorker* review-essay "Zeitgeist" that Tudor "became famous as the choreographer of a new type of dramatic ballet (*Pillar of Fire, Undertow*), which could be discussed in the clinical language of pop psychology"—right, that is, to point away from the ballets themselves and toward the cultural context of their initial reception. *Pillar* (1942) and *Undertow* (1945) are indeed the two works that most nearly justify the label *psychological ballet*.

Yet despite his influence—which in the 1940s was sufficiently extensive that his works constituted a standard against which other new dramatic ballets were sometimes judged—Tudor never had enough epigones or imitators to found a school and no such genre as "the psychological ballet" has ever really existed. Tudor's only real legacy, I would contend, is the *Tudor* ballet, which must in truth be defined above all by his movement style and musical sensibility, since each of the few extant ballets from his relatively small output is in some sense sui generis.

Critics and historians (to say nothing of publicists) have tended to recycle the term *psychological ballet* without defining what they mean by it. This label has hovered over Tudor's work at least since his American debut. The first writer to use the phrase (if somewhat hesitantly) appears to have been Walter Terry, who, according to David Vaughan in his entry on Tudor in the *International Encyclopedia of Dance* (1998), called *Lilac Garden* "almost a psychological ballet" around the time of its 1940 American premiere, at Ballet Theatre. *Almost.* Yet what does this phrase really mean?

In the theater, the word *psychological* must refer to a performer who, impersonating a character, somehow externalizes, makes visible (for a dancer, by bodily means alone) that character's imagined inner life: thoughts, feelings, emotions, desires, motivations, objectives, illusions, fantasies. In this sense, Tudor in no way invented psychology in dance. None of the extant nineteenth-century classic story ballets can be lucidly performed without at least all the dancers in leading roles having a view of their characters' interior lives and giving us access to them. Ballet psychology was invented long before Tudor, as the emblematic, allegorical personifications (Music, Discord, Glory, Sleep), classical divinities, and other mythological characters that dominated French Baroque ballet and opera gradually yielded to the human characters populating classical and Romantic works (together with a number of supernatural creatures, of course)—the revolutionary process epitomized by Dauberval's *Fille*.

I find it suggestive that Tudor, who hardly ever staged ballets other than his own, of all the full-length classics staged only *Giselle*, for the Royal Swedish Ballet in 1949, and again in 1963. I would yield my heart's blood to travel back through time to view Tudor's *Giselle*, which the Swedish dance scholar Bengt Häger remembered as Tudor's "most important gift" to Sweden during the choreographer's first professional sojourn there—meaning, more important even than *Lilac Garden*. Given the mixed technical abilities of the Swedish dancers in 1949, Tudor did not, could not, try to teach them the traditional choreography that traces its lineage back to the original 1841 production by Jean Coralli and Jules Perrot. Tudor's was, said Häger, in a 1998 interview with Tudor biographer Muriel Topaz, "Not really an authentic *Giselle*, it was very 'interpreted.' But it had all the fine points of *Giselle*, all the sensitive things. . . . He gave us a really, really wonderful *Giselle* that the audience understood and loved. It gave us a new appreciation of ballet."

It is likewise suggestive that among Tudor's most formative early experiences was witnessing Olga Spessivtzeva's Giselle in 1932. According to Topaz, Tudor was so overwhelmed that he spent his very last penny to present the ballerina with a wreath of orchids backstage. The enduring influence of a choreographer's first encounter with the quintessence of dancing in female form cannot be overestimated: Ashton throughout his career honored his memories of Isadora Duncan and Anna Pavlova, whom he had seen in his youth, by repeatedly choreographing their afterimages into his ballets. Not until Tudor saw Gelsey Kirkland's legendary Giselle at ABT in the 1970s, he said, could he finally forget Spessivtzeva.

Alone of the core repertory, *Giselle* takes as its ultimate theme forgiveness, just as compassion—longed for, given, denied, offered, accepted, refused—is the silver thread that connects Tudor's finest ballets one to another. (Compassion is also, of course, a spiritual ideal of Zen, which Tudor embraced in the late 1950s, as it is of all Buddhist traditions.) Tudor's masterworks could, I believe, trace their line of descent back to *Giselle*, whose heroine is faced with a very Tudoresque predicament. Like Caroline and Hagar in different ways, Giselle is an ordinary, "real" woman pinioned between two men. With her famous mad scene, Giselle is moreover surely the most "psychological" of the classic ballerina roles; the acting decisions that confront the dancing actress preparing to play Giselle are not unlike those Tudor ballerinas face (although the technical challenges are quite dissimilar). Caroline and Hagar have Giselle's genes in their DNA—both her human genes and, so to speak, her Wili genes, for Tudor in his heroines transmutes the Romantic obsession with the supernatural into a fascination with the uncanny otherness of real human beings deeply known. In Tudor's ballets, the forlorn little sylph is inside us. Of course, *Giselle* is very different from Tudor's works in many significant ways—scale (duration and size of cast), musical and movement idioms, narrative structure, conventions of visual design—but not because it is essentially any less "psychological." Tudor's originality lies not, as the received idea suggests, in his choosing to represent his characters' interior lives through movement but in *how* he sought to do so.

The classic story ballets deploy three largely separate modes of expression: pantomime, which in ballet means a special coded dialect of arm and hand gestures (ideally supported by the entire body) that conveys dialogue and narration; the pas d'action, a dance in which story and character are continuously revealed; and the divertissement, a pure dance episode in which storytelling is suspended for the sake of the lyrical expansion of a theme or mood or moment in the story. *Giselle*'s first act is essentially an extended pas d'action with episodes of miming and a brief (I think superfluous and better omitted) divertissement, the peasant pas de deux; the second act mainly alternates and sometimes ingeniously marries divertissement with pas d'action.

His admirers (including his two biographers, Donna Perlmutter and Muriel Topaz) often claim that Tudor never "resorted to pantomime," and it is true that even echoes of the traditional ballet gesture language occur hardly ever in his extant work, and that representational miming (performing actions without their objects, such as smoking an invisible cigarette) occurs not at all. Yet Denby nonetheless asserts that Tudor "gives to the whole classic ballet system of movement a pantomime bias" while "the traditional ballet (whether of 1890 or 1940) tries for a radically different kind of meaning than that of pantomime description; it appeals to a different manner of seeing dancing and requires a different technical approach in the dancer."

Denby struggled—to the degree that this most gracious of prose stylists may be said ever to struggle—to define the distinctive way in which Tudor creates meaning in two short essays published back-to-back in July 1943 in the *New York Herald Tribune*: "Tudor and Pantomime" and "On Meaning in Ballet." Denby further addresses this pantomime aspect of Tudor's work in many of his reviews of Ballet Theatre's early seasons as well; the problem would not let him go. As always, Denby dug at the very roots of a problem.

Pantomime describes, the pas d'action presents, dance *is*. Ashton and Balanchine, in their story ballets, always respected the utility of this tripartite division of expressive labor. Tudor sought to fuse these three modes together, striving to refashion even the most purely academic dance step into a gesture, to make it *mean* in the language-like way that miming does (this is, I think, what Denby is striving to say) yet simultaneously to infuse this mime-dance amalgam with the divertissement's access to lyric exaltation and sustained poetic mystery. Tudor wants his movements to *express* the character's emotions (*Ah! My heart is breaking!*), to *describe* them (*See how she suffers!*), and somehow to *be* them, all at once. This means that, ideally, each step and gesture simultaneously represents a subjective truth (the character's conscious or unconscious expression of her feelings), a quasi-objective truth (her behavior as observed by other characters), and what might be called a supra-objective, theatrical truth (Tudor's—and our—view of her).

While the rhetoric of Tudor's mimesis—the means by which he persuades us of the truth of his representation of reality—is not wholly without precedent in the Romantic ballet, Tudor is unique in ballet in seeking a synthesis of expressive impulses that before him were conventionally kept separate. In Tudor's work this fusion results in a highly unstable alloy that coheres only under enormous pressure and tends not to hold together for long. Without ever intending to, Tudor set himself a nearly impossible task. That is one reason why *Lilac Garden* (1936), at only sixteen minutes, is perfection, while *Pillar of Fire* (1942), twice as long, even while it affirms and extends the manner and means of the earlier ballet, is not. *Pillar* is less economical, has less momentum, and includes passages diffuse or excessively oblique in intent. In its stress on frustrated sexual, rather than more inclusively romantic, desire, and its heavier emphasis on the surreal and symbolic elements of Tudor's dramaturgy, Hagar's ballet skews the delicate balance that Caroline's improbably sustains.

Tudor was not entirely alone in his project: Central European expressionist dance and American modern dance in the 1930s and 1940s, both of which Tudor certainly knew, espoused parallel or convergent expressive ideals, although from a drastically different technical point of departure. As Croce points out, Tudor's "closest American contemporary" is not any other ballet choreographer, but Martha Graham. And in one of Tudor's masterpieces, the points of departure are not so different. As David Vaughan has written more than once, *Dark Elegies* (1937) is in its movement idiom and costuming essentially a modern dance work (it has even been staged for the Limón Dance Company, in 1999, with its pointe work, which is restricted to the soloists, omitted). However, although both Tudor and many of his admirers consider *Elegies* his greatest achievement, the epitome of his style, I believe, remains *Lilac Garden*. In that ballet, the dancing represents, by turns and sometimes even simultaneously, the characters' social behavior, whispered dialogue, layers of conscious and unconscious emotion and intent—and perhaps even, as in Virginia Woolf's novels, their mingling streams of consciousness.

All Tudor's work embodies his resolute faith in the expressive power of movement, and of the academic vocabulary, the *danse d'école*, in particular—a language that Tudor sought to pronounce with his own unique accent, as Ashton said he himself hoped to do. Yet dancing in most of Tudor's ballets is seldom to be read directly *as dancing*. Exceptions occur in his comic ballets, such as *Gala Performance, Judgment of Paris* (both 1938), and *Offenbach in the Underworld* (1954)—set, respectively, onstage before and during a performance; in a sleazy cabaret-cum-brothel; and in a vast and elegant *belle époque café dansant*—works in which dancing occurs as an event embedded naturally, inevitably, in the setting and the story. It is telling that Tudor tended to dismiss *Gala Performance*, and other ballets in which he felt his powers of movement invention were least evident, as mere "dance arrangements."

In the tragic works—his real choreography, in Tudor's view—the dancing, weirdly, never represents *dancing* itself of any kind. Caroline's engagement party, the occasion presented in *Lilac Garden*, includes no social dances, as I imagine it might have if Balanchine or Ashton had addressed Tudor's scenario. When the score, Ernest Chausson's *Poème* (opus 25, 1896), a brooding and mercurial single-movement, concerto-like work for orchestra and solo violin, glides into an urgent, hypnotic waltz rhythm late in the ballet, the entire ensemble passes through a circling formation of couples, but no one waltzes. The passage evokes social dance only vestigially; it appears to represent party conversation—and perhaps a troubled form of what Woolf so charmingly called "party consciousness"—while functioning as an image of emotions churning beneath the surface of a confining social order. Likewise, if Hagar's world includes social dances—which, since the ballet is set in a small town around 1900, it well might—the choreographer chooses not to show them to us, as Agnes de Mille does, for example, in her 1942 *Rodeo*. None of Tudor's tragic heroines are dancers, and dancing in itself does not appear as a motif in their stories.

By contrast, whether she appears to us as a living girl or a ghost, we are always meant to perceive Giselle's dancing *as dancing*. She expresses her emotional states not so much through her steps themselves as through *how* she dances them. While all Giselle's steps can, and do, occur in many other ballets, each Tudor character would ideally have a movement idiolect unique to her or him (even if that would be, in practice, impossible). *Giselle* proves that a tragic work may successfully take dancing itself as its leitmotif, even though to dance is a fundamentally exuberant, even joyful act, by the choice of dancing as the crucial plot device throughout. In the first act, Giselle loves and lives to dance, yet her mother forbids her to do so because her heart is weak; betrayed, heartbroken, stricken with sudden madness, she dances, and dies. In the second act, the Wilis, the restless nocturnal spirits of girls who have died before their wedding day, wreak their vengeance by forcing the men they capture in the forest to dance themselves to exhaustion, then drowning them. Or as Beaumont insists so sweetly, "The theme of *Giselle* is unique and ideal because its mainspring is *the dance*. The many strange and varied incidents which make up the story of the ballet are all the outcome of Giselle's passion for *the dance*."

Pillar and *Undertow* responded to and, in ballet, largely defined the cultural climate of the "psychoanalytic forties," the period in which Freudianism was domesticated and vulgarized in the United States, infusing the "applied psychology" and self-help fashions of the 1920s and 1930s (whose roots reach back down into the nineteenth-century "mind power" fads) with an emphasis on sexuality and a glib pseudo-clinical vocabulary that besets us still today. In truth, critical discussion of the "psychological" aspect of Tudor's ballets has seldom reached beyond the readymade terms of pop psych, as Croce pointed out. Certainly, *Pillar* can validly be interpreted as a drama of so-called repression (even if that phenomenon may not in fact really exist at all as Freud imagined it); the text of the ballet itself, not only the nimbus of discourse that surrounds it, licenses that view, because Tudor makes the theme of sexual desire explicit (whereas in the classics, such as *Giselle*, sex largely remains implicit, metaphorical). While Caroline is heartsick and helpless, the ostracized Hagar, with her fraught isolation and meticulously phrased self-accusing tics, has always read as "neurotic."

But *Pillar* does not *have* to be seen that way. Hagar, one could say, is a woman who longs to give the love of which she feels herself capable—both romantic and erotic—and to be loved truly in return. Yet she has no experience of love or sex, and fears them. In those terms, a dancer, or a viewer, would need a heart of stone, or perhaps titanium, to be incapable of "relating" to Hagar's story. There are lonely Hagars (male ones too) of many ethnicities, ages, and sexualities in communities everywhere; her predicament is by no means categorically inaccessible. Furthermore, our whole reason for going to the theater is at least as much to enlarge our souls by experiencing stories of those different from ourselves as to see ourselves incarnated or mirrored onstage. The ballet does not need to be revived as an artifact in a theatrical museum display. In any case, dance never works that way. As Croce once memorably wrote, all dances, no matter how old, inevitably are and must be contemporary or else they are simply not alive—they do not really even exist—onstage.

Piety, however sincere and well intended, serves no artist well, and Tudor worse than most, since in his lifetime he so often encouraged, even extorted it. In truth, no mere reevaluation of Tudor (including this essay) could suffice. What we need now—in how we stage Tudor, how we dance him, how we watch and listen to him, how we talk and think about him—is a revolution.

2014

GEORGE CATLIN (1796–1872)

BORN AND raised in Pennsylvania, George Catlin was from childhood focused on the life and customs of Native Americans, avidly collecting local artifacts—apparently his mother as a child out West had at one point been held captive by a tribe, and she encouraged his precocious interest. By 1830 he was off on his first travels up the Mississippi, visiting at least thirty tribes; a few years later, he would go up the Missouri, visiting at least eighteen more. He was both writing and painting nonstop, creating at least 500 works of art depicting the various tribes at work and play and making superb portraits of the people.

Since dance was such a crucial aspect of Native American day-to-day experience, Catlin painted dozens of highly specific pictures of tribal dances—the War dance, the Buffalo dance, the Pipe dance, the Eagle dance, the Snow-shoe dance—with convincing verbal descriptions to complement them. For years he worked in Central and South America, too, and he lectured and toured his gallery through the major eastern cities and Europe, always hoping, but failing, to sell his oeuvre to the United States government for display in the Smithsonian. (It was not until the mid-twentieth century that his accomplishments were properly acknowledged.) Meanwhile he was turning out book after book narrating his adventures, not necessarily with total accuracy. Along the way he found time to marry and father four children. Mrs. Catlin accompanied him on his adventures only once, and there has been talk of a second, Native American, family. We'll never know. Among his books was a self-help manual called *Shut Your Mouth*, asserting that "there is no person in society but who will find . . . improvement in health and enjoyment from keeping his or her mouth shut." It went into at least eight printings.

Mandan Village, Upper Missouri

THE MANDANS, like all other tribes, lead lives of idleness and leisure; and of course, devote a great deal of time to their sports and
amusements, of which they have a great variety. Of these, dancing is
one of the principal, and may be seen in a variety of forms: such as the
buffalo dance, the boasting dance, the begging dance, the scalp dance,
and a dozen other kinds of dances, all of which have their peculiar
characters and meanings or objects.

These exercises are exceedingly grotesque in their appearance, and
to the eye of a traveller who knows not their meaning or importance,
they are an uncouth and frightful display of starts, and jumps, and
yelps, and jarring gutturals, which are sometimes truly terrifying. But
when one gives them a little attention, and has been lucky enough to
be initiated into their mysterious meaning, they become a subject of
the most intense and exciting interest. Every dance has its peculiar
step, and every step has its meaning; every dance also has its peculiar song, and that is so intricate and mysterious oftentimes, that not
one in ten of the young men who are dancing and singing it, know
the meaning of the song which they are chanting over. None but the
medicine-men are allowed to understand them; and even they are
generally only initiated into these secret arcana, on the payment of a
liberal stipend for their tuition, which requires much application and
study. There is evidently a set song and sentiment for every dance, for
the songs are perfectly measured, and sung in exact time with the beat
of the drum; and always with an uniform and invariable set of sounds
and expressions, which clearly indicate certain sentiments, which are
expressed by the voice, though sometimes not given in any known
language whatever.

They have other dances and songs which are not so mystified, but
which are sung and understood by every person in the tribe, being
sung in their own language, with much poetry in them, and perfectly
metred, but without rhyme. On these subjects I shall take another
occasion to say more; and will for the present turn your attention to
the style and modes in which some of these curious transactions are
conducted.

My ears have been almost continually ringing since I came here, with the din of yelping and beating of the drums; but I have for several days past been peculiarly engrossed, and my senses almost confounded with the stamping, and grunting, and bellowing of the *buffalo dance*, which closed a few days since at sunrise (thank Heaven), and which I must needs describe to you.

Buffaloes, it is known, are a sort of roaming creature, congregating occasionally in huge masses, and strolling away about the country from east to west, or from north to south, or just where their whims or strange fancies may lead them; and the Mandans are sometimes, by this means, most unceremoniously left without any thing to eat; and being a small tribe, and unwilling to risk their lives by going far from home in the face of their more powerful enemies, are oftentimes left almost in a state of starvation. In any emergency of this kind, every man musters and brings out of his lodge his mask (the skin of a buffalo's head with the horns on), which he is obliged to keep in readiness for this occasion; and then commences the buffalo dance, of which I have above spoken, which is held for the purpose of making "buffalo come" (as they term it), of inducing the buffalo herds to change the direction of their wanderings, and bend their course towards the Mandan village, and graze about on the beautiful hills and bluffs in its vicinity, where the Mandans can shoot them down and cook them as they want them for food.

For the most part of the year, the young warriors and hunters, by riding out a mile or two from the village, can kill meat in abundance; and sometimes large herds of these animals may be seen grazing in full view of the village. There are other seasons also when the young men have ranged about the country as far as they are willing to risk their lives, on account of their enemies, without finding meat. This sad intelligence is brought back to the chiefs and doctors, who sit in solemn council, and consult on the most expedient measures to be taken, until they are sure to decide upon the old and only expedient which "never has failed."

The chief issues his order to his runners or criers, who proclaim it through the village—and in a few minutes the dance begins. The place where this strange operation is carried on is in the public area in the centre of the village, and in front of the great medicine or mystery lodge. About ten or fifteen Mandans at a time join in the dance, each one with the skin of the buffalo's head (or mask) with the horns on, placed over his head, and in his hand his favourite bow or lance, with which he is used to slay the buffalo.

I mentioned that this dance always had the desired effect, that it never fails, nor can it, for it cannot be stopped (but is going incessantly day and night) until "buffalo come." Drums are beating and rattles are shaken, and songs and yells incessantly are shouted, and lookers-on stand ready with masks on their heads, and weapons in hand, to take the place of each one as he becomes fatigued, and jumps out of the ring.

During this time of general excitement, spies or "*lookers*" are kept on the hills in the neighbourhood of the village, who, when they discover buffaloes in sight, give the appropriate signal, by "throwing their robes," which is instantly seen in the village, and understood by the whole tribe. At this joyful intelligence there is a shout of thanks to the Great Spirit, and more especially to the mystery-man, and the dancers, who *have been the immediate cause of their success*! There is then a brisk preparation for the chase—a grand hunt takes place. The choicest pieces of the victims are sacrificed to the Great Spirit, and then a surfeit and a carouse.

These dances have sometimes been continued in this village two and three weeks without stopping an instant, until the joyful moment when buffaloes made their appearance. So they *never fail*; and they think they have been the means of bringing them in.

Every man in the Mandan village (as I have before said) is obliged by a village regulation, to keep the mask of the buffalo, hanging on a post at the head of his bed, which he can use on his head whenever he is called upon by the chiefs, to dance for the coming of buffaloes. The mask is put over the head, and generally has a strip of the skin hanging to it, of the whole length of the animal, with the tail attached to it, which, passing down over the back of the dancer, is dragging on the ground. When one becomes fatigued of the exercise, he signifies it by bending quite forward, and sinking his body towards the ground; when another draws a bow upon him and hits him with a blunt arrow, and he falls like a buffalo—is seized by the bye-standers, who drag him out of the ring by the heels, brandishing their knives about him; and having gone through the motions of skinning and cutting him up, they let him off, and his place is at once supplied by another, who dances into the ring with his mask on; and by this taking of places, the scene is easily kept up night and day, until the desired effect has been produced, that of "making buffalo come."

* * *

Dancing is one of the principal and most frequent amusements of all the tribes of Indians in America; and, in all of these, both vocal and instrumental music are introduced. These dances consist in about four different steps, which constitute all the different varieties: but the figures and forms of these scenes are very numerous, and produced by the most violent jumps and contortions, accompanied with the song and beats of the drum, which are given in exact time with their motions. It has been said by some travellers, that the Indian has neither harmony or melody in his music, but I am unwilling to subscribe to such an assertion; although I grant, that for the most part of their vocal exercises, there is a total absence of what the musical world would call melody; their songs being made up chiefly of a sort of violent chaunt of harsh and jarring gutturals, of yelps and barks, and screams, which are given out in perfect time, not only with "method (but with harmony) in their madness." There are times too, as every traveller of the Indian country will attest, if he will recall them to his recollection, when the Indian lays down by his fire-side with his drum in his hand, which he lightly and almost imperceptibly touches over, as he accompanies it with his stifled voice of dulcet sounds that might come from the most tender and delicate female.

These quiet and tender songs are very different from those which are sung at their dances, in full chorus and violent gesticulation; and many of them seem to be quite rich in plaintive expression and melody, though barren of change and variety.

Dancing, I have before said, is one of the principal and most valued amusements of the Indians, and much more frequently practised by them than by any civilized society; inasmuch as it enters into their forms of worship, and is often their mode of appealing to the Great Spirit—of paying their usual devotions to their *medicine*—and of honouring and entertaining strangers of distinction in their country.

Instead of the "giddy maze" of the quadrille or the country dance, enlivened by the cheering smiles and graces of silkened beauty, the Indian performs his rounds with jumps, and starts, and yells, much to the satisfaction of his own exclusive self, and infinite amusement of the gentler sex, who are always lookers on, but seldom allowed so great a pleasure, or so signal an honour, as that of joining with their lords in this or any other entertainment. Whilst staying with these people on my way up the river, I was repeatedly honoured with the dance, and I as often hired them to give them, or went to overlook where they were performing them at their own pleasure, in pursuance of their peculiar customs, or for their own amusement, that I might study and correctly herald them to future ages. I saw so many of their different varieties of dances amongst the Sioux, that I should almost be disposed to denominate them the "*dancing Indians.*" It would actually seem as if they had dances for every thing. And in so large a village, there was scarcely an hour in any day or night, but what the beat of the drum could somewhere be heard. These dances are almost as various and different in their character as they are numerous— some of them so exceedingly grotesque and laughable, as to keep the bystanders in an irresistible roar of laughter—others are calculated to excite his pity, and forcibly appeal to his sympathies, whilst others disgust, and yet others terrify and alarm him with their frightful threats and contortions.

1841

Isadora Duncan at the Theater of Dionysus, 1903. Photograph by her brother, Raymond Duncan.

Bill "Bojangles" Robinson, 1935. Photograph by George Hurrell.

Ginger Rogers and Fred Astaire in *Swing Time*, 1936.

Merce Cunningham and Carolyn Brown rehearsing Cunningham's *Suite*, with John Cage at the piano, 1972. Photograph by James Klosty.

Martha Graham, Matt Turney, and Stuart Hodes in Graham's *Appalachian Spring*. Photograph by Serge Lido.

Members of the Artistic Committee of Ballet Theatre, 1947. Jerome Robbins, Agnes de Mille, Oliver Smith, and Aaron Copland surrounding Lucia Chase, in Chase's apartment. Photograph by Cecil Beaton.

George Balanchine and Lincoln Kirstein, in Kirstein's home, early 1960s.
Photograph by Tanaquil Le Clercq.

Alvin Ailey in his *Hermit Songs*, 1961. Photograph by Jack Mitchell.

Paul Taylor in his *Option*, 1962. Photograph by Jack Mitchell.

Twyla Tharp. Photograph by Greg Gorman, 1992.

Suzanne Farrell in George Balanchine's *Vienna Waltzes*, 1978.
Photograph by Kenn Duncan.

Michael Jackson, 1989. Photograph by Annie Leibovitz.

Janet Collins (1917–2003)

PIONEER African American dancer Janet Collins, born in New Orleans, grew up and attended college as an arts major in Los Angeles. But she had always wanted to study classical dancing, and for several years, African American teacher Louise Beverly taught the child ballet and "toe dancing." When she was fifteen, she joined an acrobatic adagio vaudeville act called "Three Shades of Brown." She performed as many as five shows a day with them, but she still wanted "real ballet," and at sixteen, she was encouraged by her family to audition for the Ballet Russe de Monte Carlo despite her color—an ugly experience that did not derail her. When she was twenty or so, she was approached by modern dance choreographer Lester Horton to appear in his *Rite of Spring* and she studied modern dance with him. Still, it was not until she was in her late twenties that she was able to study ballet with a number of important white L.A. teachers: Carmelita Maracci, Mia Slavenska, and Adolph Bolm.

As strong-minded as she was talented, beautiful, and intelligent, Collins went on to fashion an illustrious career for herself, appearing in the Cole Porter musical *Out of This World* (for which, in 1951, she won the Donaldson Award as the year's best dancer on Broadway); performing with Katherine Dunham; and becoming the leading ballerina in the Metropolitan Opera's ballet company—the company's first full-time African American artist. She appeared on TV, she taught, and, most importantly, she toured the country extensively, presenting her highly original and effective choreography. In 1965, she premiered her most ambitious work, *Genesis*, reflecting her increasing absorption in religion, and, in 1974, she premiered *Canticle for the Elements*, for the Alvin Ailey Company. She made her final work of choreography in 1994.

At her death this formidable figure left behind portions of an autobiography, from which the selection below was taken. Her book, happily for us, was eventually completed by the dance historian, editor, and choreographer Yaël Tamar Lewin and Janet Collins.

Léonide Massine

I WAS terrified—awestruck and daring, but terrified! I was all of about sixteen years of age, awaiting my turn to audition before the great Léonide Massine of the world-famous Ballet Russe on the stage of the Los Angeles Philharmonic Auditorium, where they were performing. The picture is now in reverse—instead of my being in the audience inspired and delighted by the brilliant performances of the artists and swept into the magic of the ballets . . . the dark house, the stage lit, the story, music, costumes all to embellish the movements of the dancers . . . no, this was not so now. I was *on* the Philharmonic stage! That huge house was empty—it was like looking into the face of some giant with his mouth wide open to devour me! Whatever ran through my mind I cannot fully remember at this time, but my surroundings I remember vividly as though they are sealed in my memory forever.

Léonide Massine, dancer, choreographer, and director of the company, was sitting with his back to the audience on the apron of the stage with another gentleman seated to his left. The stage was lit—all of the work lights were on—so that he could clearly view the auditioning dancers. I did not bring pointe shoes—I was to dance in ballet slippers "Anitra's Dance," by Edvard Grieg, which my teacher, Charlotte Tamon, had taught me.

Among the auditioners I remember one who had come with her teacher, and she was warming up on pointe before her turn came. Her teacher was coaching her. I recall vividly he was carrying the ballet rod or stick and beating time for her and correcting and approving some of her movements. I remember thinking that she must be his prize pupil or protégée. The rest of us were alone at the audition. I was especially very much alone—neither teacher, friend, nor anyone of my large family was there with me. I was *alone*. Not only that, but as I looked about me, everyone was *white*. How in the name of Heaven did I get in here!

The audition was about to begin—Massine indicated to the person in charge of the auditioners that he was ready to see the first dancer. There was almost a reverent silence. I looked upward slightly behind me and there, on a spiral staircase, which must have led to upper dressing rooms, stood members of the Ballet Russe—some were dressed in street clothes—to watch the auditioners. I remember distinctly seeing one ballerina in high-heeled red shoes, which I thought looked very beautiful on her exquisite feet and showed off her lovely legs. Dancers watching dancers, I remembered from past vaudeville experience, can sometimes be cruel, very ready to criticize the least fault.

My eyes went back to the first auditioner. My heart was pounding. Several dancers auditioned, then came the turn of the dancer with her teacher. She performed on pointe. I remember being disappointed—I was not impressed. Her warm-up was better than her performance. Several other dancers performed, then I was called. I remember a hush in the theater—a silence you could have cut with a knife when I stepped forward with a little hand phonograph and carrying the Grieg recording in my other hand (for I did not have an accompanist) and in my practice clothes.

As I came forward to approach Mr. Massine, the gentleman on his left leaned over and spoke to him privately. Whatever he said, Massine violently shook his head and indicated a definite *no* with his hand. I stood before him—I remember his large, beautiful dark eyes and a gentle sadness about his face, just like I had seen him in his photographs. I explained that I did not have an accompanist—and he said that was all right—and he indicated to a stagehand to attach my phonograph to an electrical outlet onstage.

Charlotte Tamon had choreographed this dance for me. It began with the hands of Anitra bound in chains in front of her, below her waist. She finally breaks the chains (imaginary, of course), and with her hands free, she abandons herself to the wonderful freedom of the dance! I forgot everything but the dance. I danced with all my heart. I remember the burst of applause when I finished. I was so happy—I was stunned! I looked up and there were those ballerinas on the spiral staircase applauding and smiling down at me! I was overwhelmed! I smiled happily up at them.

Massine beckoned to me as I came back to earth. I came forward to the front of the stage where he sat and knelt down, sitting back on my feet in front of him—and he smiled down upon me. He said in his

Russian accent, "You are a very fine dancer." I said, "I don't think I am very strong yet for pointe, so I performed for you in ballet shoes." "No, no," he said. "You *are* strong. You will make a fine character dancer. I could train you." I knew what he meant because character dancing was his forté in ballet. He stopped, thought very seriously—then, looking into my upturned waiting eyes, he stated in both a kindly and realistic manner, "In order to train you and take you into the company, I would have to put you onstage with the ballet corps first in performances— and I would have to paint you white." He paused. "You wouldn't want that, would you?" I looked directly at him and said "No." We both understood. I arose, thanked him sincerely, and left. I went to the dressing rooms and put my street clothes on, after first collecting my phonograph and recording. I only remember a very numb feeling in my heart and head—I was in a state of sleepwalking.

When I finally got into the open air again, I walked up the hill, past the Biltmore Theater, crossed the street, and sat down on the entrance steps leading to the Los Angeles Public Library, and I cried, and cried, and cried. I could not stop crying. It was all I could do. When the tears were all gone—I had cried myself dry—I caught a streetcar and went home.

I remember none of my family's reactions to this affair but Auntie Adele's. She was the one who had put me up to this in the first place! I remember how she came to our house one day and said, "Janet, I see the Ballet Russe is in town performing, and they are holding auditions to take dancers with their company. Why don't you go and audition?" "Auntie, I am not good enough for that, I couldn't possibly do that!" She answered, "How will you know if you don't try? How do you know how good you are? Let them tell you. We know how talented you are, but let them tell you. That is what counts." These were not necessarily her exact words, but this was the thought and meaning. I felt excited and encouraged. I knew she was telling me the truth. So I did it.

"Well, how did the audition go?" I told her everything and in detail. "Now, that is marvelous and this is only the beginning. You must not strive to be as good as they are—you have the talent to be better! Now, you get right back to the barre on Monday and keep right on working at your dancing! You see, the best recognized your gift!" She was right, and Monday, back to the barre I went!

Several days later I had to go downtown and I happened to be passing in front of the Philharmonic Auditorium—and to my surprise, I saw Léonide Massine approaching in the opposite direction! He recognized me, smiled, and tipped his hat to my great surprise—it was probably a European custom of courteous acknowledgment. I smiled, returning his courtesy with a bow of my head as we passed each other and went our separate ways. These are my most cherished memories of Léonide Massine. He will always have a very special place in my heart.

c. 1990

Hart Crane (1899–1932)

THE POETRY Cleveland native Hart Crane wrote during his brief and tumultuous life—the magic of his incantatory lyrics—continues to lure. It astonished twentieth-century American writers of the first rank, such as Robert Lowell, John Berryman, and Tennessee Williams, and outstanding critics, such as Harold Bloom—not to speak of choreographer Martha Graham, who gleaned the title of her 1944 masterpiece, *Appalachian Spring*, from an exclamation in Crane's canto "The Dance" in his ambitious and influential long poem, *The Bridge*. Crane's interest in dance went beyond metaphor to attendance at the theater and fascination with dancers as personalities, as the poem and letter below demonstrate.

"To Portapovitch"

(*du Ballet Russe*)

> Vault on the opal carpet of the sun,
> Barbaric Prince Igor:—or, blind Pierrot,
> Despair until the moon by tears be won:—
> Or, Daphnis, move among the bees with Chloe.
>
> Release,—dismiss the passion from your arms.
> More real than life, the gestures you have spun
> Haunt the blank stage with lingering alarms,
> Though silent as your sandals, danced undone.

1919

Letter to Gorham Munson

Dear Gorham:

Tuesday, December 12

You, as well as some of my local friends must share in my excitement at seeing Isadora Duncan dance on Sunday night. She gave the same program (All Tschaikowsky) that she gave in Moscow for the Soviet celebration and, I think, you saw it in New York recently. It was glorious beyond words, and sad beyond words, too, from the rude and careless reception she got here. It was like a wave of life, a flaming gale that passed over the heads of the nine thousand in the audience without evoking response other than silence and some maddening catcalls. After the first movement of the "Pathétique" she came to the fore of the stage, her hands extended. Silence,—the most awful silence! I started clapping furiously until she disappeared behind the draperies. At least one tiny sound should follow her from all that audience. She continued through the performance with utter indifference for the audience and with such intensity of posture and such plastique grace as I have never seen, although the music was sometimes almost drowned out by the noises from the hall. I felt like rushing to the stage, but I was stimulated almost beyond the power to walk straight. When it was all over she came to the fore-stage again in the little red dress that had so shocked Boston, as she stated, and among other things, told the people to go home and take from the bookshelf the works of Walt Whitman, and turn to the section called, "Calamus". Ninety-nine percent of them had never heard of Whitman, of course, but that was part of the beauty of her gesture. Glorious to see her there with her right breast and nipple quite exposed, telling the audience that the truth was not pretty, that it was really indecent and telling them (boobs!) about Beethoven, Tschaikowsky and Scriabine! She is now on her way back to Moscow, so I understand, where someone will give her some roses for her pains.

I am in great ferment, and have been staying at a hotel for several days until I talk to my mother about some things that will determine whether or not I shall continue to live out at the house any more. They are little things, mostly, but such little things accumulate almost into a

complex that is too much for me to work under. There is no use in discussing them here, but just the constant restraint necessary in living
with others, you may appreciate, is a deadening thing. Unless something happens to release me from such annoyances I give up hope of
doing any satisfactory writing. This isn't a letter, it is a "state of mind".
I await news from you in order to have something decent to say.

Yours as ever, Hart

Write me at 1709—

1922

Arlene Croce (1934–)

Arlene Louise Croce grew up in Providence, Rhode Island, and Asheville, North Carolina. Although she didn't study dancing formally as a child, she learned about it from studying dancers who modelled for the figure-drawing classes she took at the Rhode Island School of Design. She spent her first two years of college at the University of North Carolina, Greensboro, and the last two at Barnard, where, in 1955, she was the first winner of the Elizabeth Janeway Prize for Prose Writing. Although she began writing criticism about film, she soon discovered the ballets of George Balanchine at the New York City Ballet, including the Balanchine–Stravinsky *Agon*, whose world premiere she attended, and found her life's work.

During the 1960s, Croce was an editor of William Buckley's magazine, *The National Review*, and she wrote articles on various cultural subjects for other publications as well. In 1965, she founded the widely admired and influential quarterly *Ballet Review*, editing it, writing for it, and producing it by herself on her Brooklyn kitchen table until turning it over to others in 1978. Meanwhile she contributed a New York Letter to *The Dancing Times*, of London. Her first book—*The Fred Astaire & Ginger Rogers Book*—sharpened the perceptions of audiences for both dance and film and brought Croce into public view in the United States. The book was reviewed in *The New Yorker* by Pauline Kael, and in 1973 the magazine's editor, William Shawn, launched the "Dancing" column, which he created expressly for Croce. She continued to write "Dancing" until 1998, bringing her formidable intellect, acuity, refined taste, and brilliant command of the declarative sentence to the most knowledgeable and most passionate readership for dance enjoyed by any American writer. Whether one agreed with her or not, she wrote with a seriousness and magnetism that put a large cultural spotlight on dancing of all kinds. She occasionally contributes to *The New York Review of Books* and remains at work on an avidly awaited study of Balanchine.

Dance in Film

Dance in film is a subject that has taken on a semblance of controversy owing to the insistence of some writers that a conflict between dance and film exists. Many dances designed for the stage are not suited to film presentation, but to assume that dancing is exclusively a theatrical medium is to take a needlessly restricted view of it. People danced long before theatres were built, and people dancing in the movies are demonstrating one kind of human activity the camera can capture as well as any other. Movies can also invent dances that cannot be done anywhere except on film; this method isn't necessarily preferable, because "purer," to photographing dances that have already been choreographed and may just as easily be seen on a stage, in a ballroom, or on the street. Most successful screen dances lie somewhere between total cinematic illusion and passive recording. But it is also true that movie dance has offered the most excitement when it is operating at, or close to, the polar extremes of its range (possibly because here the risks are greater). Partisan debate provides for such extremes by telling us that one or the other medium is being "violated," but it may be a violation that has consistency, purpose, and style. Whether a filmmaker creates a dance out of an array of mechanical effects or whether he photographs a staged routine has no bearing on the validity of the sensation he is trying to produce. A cleanly photographed dance can be pretentious and boring; a complex cinematic extravaganza can be utterly devoid of kinetic charm. We can only look at the results and judge whether we have had a dance experience and a true one.

Though dancing could not achieve full expression on the screen until the coming of sound, the silent film immediately set about developing the two major approaches to dance in the work of a single man, Georges Méliès (1861–1938). Dancers were among Méliès's favorite subjects; he was in love not only with the new medium of film but with theatre, ballet, and the music hall. He photographed dance pantomimes and routines in simple box sets, and he also created optical effects to heighten their appeal for the camera. Sudden transformations, tricks of scale and continuity, things popping out of nowhere, people whose body parts become separated and dance off on their own were the stuff of Méliès's illusions. His films are excellent visual records—though fragmentary ones—of the dance theatre of his day. At the same time, they indicate nearly every possibility that has since been developed in the field of "camera" choreography. Also, with their subtly hand-tinted frames, they are mysteriously beautiful to look at. In one of the most bewitching trick shots, Mme. Méliès (who with her husband often appears as a kind of onscreen conjuror) produces tiny pierrots who dance on point in the palm of her hand. (There is a curious repeat of this effect much later in the history of movies when, with the arrival of sound, movie directors reverted for a brief moment to Méliès's neglected box of tricks. In *The Hollywood Revue of 1929*, Jack Benny as the m.c. pulls Bessie Love out of his pocket.)

At about the same time, Edison, Pathé, and Biograph (among other companies) were busy filming dancers. Theatrical, social, and folk dances were recorded at the turn of the century in the thousands, and a considerable fraction of this footage is extant in paper or film prints. Leading dancers of the day are to be glimpsed in their specialties: Pierina Legnani in *Cinderella* can be seen, if not comprehended, in one of the earliest fragments, and, in one of the most famous ones Pathé recorded Loïe Fuller, who enchanted Rodin and Mallarmé, in her *Fire Dance* in 1906. (A cross-eyed woman flailing in huge draperies, she has an impact on the modern viewer as bewildering as the sight of Sarah Bernhardt keeling over in *Camille*.) Primitive film techniques, which often distorted even the simplest dances, did not keep dancers from recording themselves, less for posterity than for extra money. Stars of the ballet tended to stay away from the camera—they could afford to—but probably it was Diaghilev's intransigence that kept Karsavina and Nijinsky from being filmed. Diaghilev was not opposed to film; he was to use film projections in *Ode* (1928), one of the first mixed-media ballets. But it was a fact that motion-picture film could not capture the clarity of developed ballet technique or preserve the sense of its continuity in space. Diaghilev knew, too—who knew it better than he?—that it was enough to dance in the present without taking risks in the future. Tastes change, styles fade, and what is novel and exciting to one generation may prove incomprehensible and even ludicrous to the next. Both Diaghilev and Nijinsky had ideas about the expressive potential of films. However, Nijinsky, who visited Chaplin on the set of *Easy Street* in 1916, wrote in his diary, "I will leave filming to those who love to do it." No record of him in action has been turned up. Pavlova starred in *La Muette de Portici* in 1916; a straight acting role with passages of dancing, it is her most vivid performance on film. When she was filmed in her stage repertory in 1924, she was past her prime. Still, the test shots taken of her in famous solos (including *The Dying Swan*) on the set of Fairbanks's *Thief of Baghdad*, together with another series of excerpts compiled in 1935 (*The Immortal Swan*), are remarkable and invaluable with all their imperfections. There is a marvellous record of the legendary Spessivtseva in portions of *Giselle* Act I, crudely yet tenaciously filmed from a box during a rehearsal in London in 1932. This fragment has been incorporated into a documentary about Spessivtseva, *The Sleeping Ballerina* (1964), where it is combined with a piano accompaniment and an affecting narration by Marie Rambert. Those who have seen it have had a glimpse of a great dancer still at her peak.

Despite the hazards of filming and the egregious omissions (no extended footage of Isadora Duncan dancing is known to exist), the catalogue of dance films dating from the silent era is an impressive one. It was a period, too, of unusually close harmony between dance and film. Dance trends of the day injected their vigor into an essentially wordless medium. In America, where large ballet academies were just beginning to be established, dancing meant vaudeville, ballroom, or various forms of "aesthetic" theatrical dance. All had their reflection in commercial film production. Probably the most successful dance film of the period was The *Whirl of Life*, which starred Vernon and Irene Castle. The most popular ballroom dancers of the age—indeed, the team that had done the most to spread the craze for ballroom dancing in the years before World War I—the Castles made only one feature film, but it is almost a complete summation of the era in which they danced. *The Whirl of Life* (1914) was loosely biographical, with a few melodramatic incidents (a kidnapping, a chase on horseback) thrown in to excite their fans. The best part is the exhibition dance sequence filmed in their ballroom at Castles by the Sea on Long Island. Here, as rarely in dance films, we can see what made these dancers great. Their ability to embody and at the same time exalt the spirit of an era was to have no equal until the emergence of Astaire and Rogers as a team in the thirties.

In 1915, the year of the release of *The Birth of a Nation*, Denishawn opened in Los Angeles. To this school, attached to the dance company of Ruth St. Denis and Ted Shawn, came many film actresses, including most of those working for D. W. Griffith. The Denishawn influence is evident in the fluid physical style these actresses used in their film performances. Dancers from the Denishawn school appear in the Babylonian section of *Intolerance*, and Carol Dempster, a Denishawn dancer and later a Griffith star, danced frequently in her films. St. Denis had been filmed as a teen-ager performing a "skirt dance" with bouncing Pickford curls. Shawn started collaborating with Edison in 1913, amassing an extensive library of films which incorporates an important segment of American dance history.

The great dance influences on Griffith's films were not all Denishawn. The greatest was D. W. Griffith himself. Quite apart from actual dancing, of which he appears to have been very fond, Griffith's films contain more dance elements than many of the movie musicals that came later. Films eliminated declamation from classical acting and the declamatory aspects—studied poses—of mime as well. Griffith cultivated this new style by stressing the dance impulse in characterization; he wanted actors who were like live wires. The stress is related to his gift for overall architectural rhythm in the making of a film. *Broken Blossoms* appears seamless to the eye, one tragic gesture. The three principals—Lillian Gish's waif, Barthelmess's Chinese drug addict, and Crisp's slum bully—are each characterized by choreographed attitudes reminiscent of Fokine's *Petrouchka*. Barthelmess's angularities derive from nothing naturalistic; their twisted introversion contrasts powerfully with the exaggerated spread stance of Crisp (cf. ballet turnout) and with the helpless slow creeping and curling of Gish's body, which in the closet scene accelerates in a whirl of terror. Such physicality of characterization has been absent so long from the performing tradition that one has to search for it today even on the ballet stage.

"Chaplin has always been at his greatest when he approached ballet," wrote John Grierson. The fine line between acrobatics and dance is crossed repeatedly in silent film comedy. Chaplin loved to parody serious dance—the dance in *Sunnyside* is an extended burlesque of Nijinsky's *Faune*—and Denishawn's nymphs—but his own dance exploits, such as the globe dance in *The Great Dictator*, the dance of the rolls in *The Gold Rush*, and the roller-skating sequences in *The*

Rink and *Modern Times*, are almost too beautiful to be funny. Douglas Fairbanks's athletic feats were designed frankly for their beauty; Buster Keaton's concealed their aesthetic purpose in an elaborate rationale of functionalism. Flying from the handlebars of a speeding motorcycle to land exactly where he has to land to knock the villain off his feet (in *Sherlock Jr.*), Keaton is like a fateful bullet fired from a cosmic gun. He does not conquer space or time, but passes through both in an orderly if unseemly fashion, and his own motion is graceful because it *works* along with everything else. The whole universe dances.

Laurel and Hardy, greatest of the soft-shoe comedians, continued well into the sound era along with W. C. Fields, who never danced. Laurel and Hardy were the opposite of the high-style comedians—the reverse of brilliance and grace; they flourished through their *lack* of expertise. They could dance and sing without making a production number out of it, whereas the Marx Brothers never could. Sound and the Marx Brothers were made for each other, Harpo's silence notwithstanding. Interestingly, it is Groucho, the most verbal of the brothers, who is also the most devoted dancer.

The freedom of expressive movement achieved by the silent screen suffered an initial setback with the coming of sound. The musical gave dancing a place it had never enjoyed before in movies, but in the beginning there was hardly any dancing of note to be seen in feature films. Dull choreography and substandard execution were the norm. Good dancers appeared most frequently in two-reelers and were easier to appreciate away from the interminable dialogue scenes and rigid production numbers that dominated feature-length films. The musical as a new form of movie underwent a severe trial-and-error process during the Stone Age of sound, and what began in the excitement of novelty ended, all too quickly, by driving audiences away because producers hadn't grasped that the musical *was* a new form of movie. Musicals renewed the careers of such stars as Clara Bow, Nancy Carroll, and Bebe Daniels, but these newfound careers were short-lived. Sound posed key problems of expression to which producers remained indifferent or insensible even after they had conquered the technological difficulties. It meant a whole new way of coming to grips with the attention of the audience. Overhead shots of dance sequences, for example, rapidly became a commonplace, but the position of the camera mattered less than the pace of the action and the variety of moods and situations. The first wave of movie musicals (c. 1929–31) inundated the public with static adaptations of Broadway shows. Apart from some exterior shots, though, these usually didn't pretend to be movies. Some of the better adaptations (e.g., *The Cocoanuts, Rio Rita*), stage-bound though they may have been, were in fact far more shrewdly paced, amusing, and stylish than the "original" movie musicals that were being made at the same time.

Hollywood quickly invented three main types of musical: the stage show at one remove, or "backstage" musical (*The Broadway Melody, On with the Show*); the all-star movie revue (*The Hollywood Revue of 1929, The Show of Shows, Paramount on Parade*); and the modified-operetta movie (*Monte Carlo, Hallelujah*) in which musical numbers were inserted straight into the dramatic action without the usual device of framing them as performances for a theatre audience. These were all versions of theatrical stereotypes and there was nothing intrinsically wrong with any of them. The backstage musical came to be especially despised by purists, but this was because the work of Ernst Lubitsch, René Clair, and King Vidor in the unconfined lyric form made it seem much sillier than it was. It was not the formulas that were faulty, it was the lack of sophistication with which they were applied.

And the cheap ingredients. The technique of the playback had been mastered early, freeing sound stages from the perils of direct recording (the mike in the flower pot, satirized in *Singin' in the Rain*, had been a common resort), but this brought new perils in the cutting room. Film editors were totally unfamiliar with the task of cutting a dance sequence to a prerecorded musical track and would frequently unite dance accents with the wrong beats. Dances that were simple in their relation to music made postsynchronization a good deal easier. However, you didn't need good dancers to perform mickey-mouse choreography, and until the advent of music cutters in the studios you didn't get them. Many more singing stars (Jeanette MacDonald, Maurice Chevalier, Al Jolson, John Boles, Helen Morgan, Dennis King, Grace Moore, Lawrence Tibbett) than dancing stars were launched in movie careers during this period.

Choreographers, however, were considered indispensable. From Broadway came Sammy Lee, Seymour Felix, Larry Ceballos, Busby Berkeley, and Albertina Rasch, all of whom survived when the bottom dropped out of the musical market sometime in 1930. The ubiquitous Mme. Rasch, a Viennese dancing teacher with a strong background in opera ballet, became the queen of the operetta films (*The Cat and the Fiddle, The Merry Widow, The Firefly, Rosalie, The Great Waltz*). Her specialty was toe-dancers doing relevés in strict time and strict formation or fluttering in mothlike droves while the camera peered down from the flies. In England, Gaumont attempted a few dance talkies with ballet star Anton Dolin, but in Hollywood the tradition of ballet was ersatz ballet and was to remain such until the fifties. Busby Berkeley, who became the king of the backstage musicals, was brought to Hollywood to stage the dances for the film version of the Ziegfeld show *Whoopee* (1930), which he did with such finesse that, measured against the prevailing standard, they almost seem too *short*. In that film, he also began the practice of bringing each of his chorus girls into a closeup, a variation on the *Follies* showgirl parade that remained a feature of his style throughout the thirties.

Berkeley's girls were not conspicuously well-trained dancers, and he seldom presented them as such. Ruby Keeler, his dancing lead, tapped with such vehemence that she made up for the bevy that not only didn't dance but often disappeared into kaleidoscopic spectacles choreographed entirely by the camera as it roved through space. By 1933, when *Forty-Second Street* (a remake of *On with the Show*) made musicals box-office again, sound technique had been so perfected that directors could now explore what they formerly only exploited. The title number unleashed Berkeley in the format that was to become his trademark, a kind of visual orchestration of motifs inspired by the lyrics of a song rather than the mechanics of a plot. "Naughty, gaudy, bawdy, sporty Forty-Second Street" was seen in all or most of those aspects, Ruby Keeler pounded away on top of a taxi, and there was a parade of dancing skyscrapers. "The Shadow Waltz" (in *Gold Diggers of 1933*) had a hundred chorines dressed in china-silk lampshades and playing a hundred illuminated violins which then assembled in the shape of one monster violin. In *Footlight Parade* (1933), Berkeley created a series of aquatic images for "By a Waterfall." Photographed from above, his mermaids melted into water lilies or undulating water snakes. From below water level, they suggested the wheel of a paddleboat. And in the title number of *Dames* (1934), he played not only with human geometry but with optical mazes and illogical transitions in scale, reaching the Nirvana of sheer abstraction. The end of the number is a pull-back from a giant scaffold on the several levels of which girls recline. When the screen becomes a grid filled with tiny figures, Dick Powell's head bursts through it in closeup.

Berkeley was still choreographing on a massive scale in 1962 (*Jumbo*) when his thirties period was revived as a precursor of the Pop Art movement in America. Since then, Berkeley has moved from being a semi-fatuous enthusiasm of the avant-garde to being a staple of the thirties-memorabilia addicts and the subject of something like a popular cult. His prestige has never been higher than it is today, and it no longer seems necessary to defend him against the literal-minded ("But it isn't *theatre*! It isn't *dance*!"). Too many television viewings may have taken the edge off the supreme joke of Berkeleyan spectacle, which was that his numbers characteristically are framed by the rise and fall of a curtain, as if the theatre audience in the film could see what we see. A film like *Footlight Parade*, which ends with two of the most colossal numbers played back to back to a cheering audience, loses much of its delicious absurdity when it is fragmented by commercial interruptions and seen alongside TV sit-coms with their canned laughter and variety shows in which we aren't certain which parts the studio audience is seeing live and which parts are on film. As a choreographer, Berkeley can be reduced to his simplest routines (the chorus of marching girls in "All's Fair in Love and War" from *Gold Diggers of 1937*) and still come out in the front rank, but he was probably the greatest choreographer who has ever worked directly with the processed effects possible only in the movies. Walt Disney, whose Silly Symphonies very likely gave Berkeley ideas (and whose reputation inexplicably declines as Berkeley's rises), was not controversial in the sense that Berkeley was as long as he drew his dance material before photographing it. Berkeley, on the other hand, manipulated live people. The only ground on which Berkeley can be attacked is taste, and, strangely, it is Disney's weakness, too. When Berkeley manipulates people, it is much more likely to be in the interests of prurience than of lyrical fantasy. But vulgarity is in some ways essential to the imaginative exuberance that drives these mad productions on. Less primitive taste possibly would not have supported such extremes of invention.

In 1933, the man who was Berkeley's opposite—the man whose screen choreography could consist merely of himself dancing alone in a living room—made his first appearance in a feature film. "Either the camera will dance or I will," said Fred Astaire. "But both of us at the same time—that won't work." When the curtain went up on an Astaire dance (and often there was no curtain—Astaire just danced), it was usually the kind of dance that one could imagine seeing on a real stage, but the experience was so dazzling that the only sane response was gratitude to film for having brought it into existence. Astaire was the first dancer to establish himself on the screen, and the greatest. He raised technical standards in every department—camerawork, cutting, synchronization, scoring. He inspired the best efforts of the best song writers, and his personal style set a criterion for masculine elegance that has persisted through two generations. He did more than anyone else to develop the dance musical. Yet in the forties, when his career was faltering, there were critics who suggested that he wasn't able to get as much out of the film medium as Gene Kelly was. The point about Astaire, though, is that he could always give more to the film medium than he could get out of it. He gave himself as a superb virtuoso whose every gesture was penetratingly clear to the camera. And when he experimented with the capacities of film, it was usually in order to give more of himself by multiplying his image, as in "Bojangles of Harlem" (*Swing Time*, 1936) or "Puttin' On the Ritz" (*Blue Skies*, 1946). In 1938, he used slow motion for the first time; later, he used animation. He danced on the ceiling. None of these things would have been possible on the stage, and none of them improved on the perfection of his dancing. They merely provided new ways for it to show itself.

In any Astaire film, the high spot is his solo. Only in the period 1933–39, when his partner was Ginger Rogers, were the duets on the same level. Later, there were other girls whose technical abilities were more developed than Ginger Rogers's—Eleanor Powell, Rita Hayworth, or Cyd Charisse—but with none of them was Astaire able to achieve the romantic intensity of his dances with Rogers. There have never been wittier flirtatious duets than "I'll Be Hard to Handle" (*Roberta*, 1935) or "Isn't This a Lovely Day?" (*Top Hat*, 1935), or more nobly passionate ones than "Night and Day" (*The Gay Divorcee*, 1934) or "Let's Face the Music and Dance" (*Follow the Fleet*, 1936). Passion—the missing element in just about every "sexy" duet that has been attempted since—is usually confused with emoting or going primitive. With Astaire and

Rogers, it's a matter of total professional dedication; they do not give us emotions, they give us dances, and the more beautifully they dance, the more powerful the spell that seems to bind them together.

Astaire and Rogers made nine films for RKO, beginning with *Flying Down to Rio*, in which they introduced "The Carioca," and ending with *The Story of Vernon and Irene Castle*, in which they saluted the great dance team of another era. Astaire and Rogers were never surpassed as dancing idols. The mood they projected in their great romantic duets has become part of the mythology of the 1930's—so much so that, to young audiences especially, the whole decade seems romantic in retrospect. Certainly by 1949, when MGM's *The Barkleys of Broadway* reunited an Astaire who had just come out of retirement (for *Easter Parade*) with a Rogers who had given up musicals, the climate had changed. At MGM, the new vogue in musicals tended toward Broadway parasitism and hardhearted chic. The studio's big musical that year was *On the Town* with Gene Kelly and Vera-Ellen, adapted by Betty Comden and Adolph Green from their stage hit. Comden's and Green's script for *The Barkleys of Broadway*, like their scripts for *Singin' in the Rain* and *The Band Wagon*, was big on satire, wisecracks, and production *ideas*. Astaire, with his light informality, his classical emphasis on steps rather than ideas in choreography, seemed less suited to these ambitious new musicals than dancer-manager Gene Kelly, who, besides choreographing his films, was already codirecting them (with Stanley Donen). Astaire never wanted to direct whole films or even whole production numbers. Working with an assistant, usually Hermes Pan, he would choreograph and direct the filming of his own dances; the ensembles he would leave to Pan. But where Astaire achieved dance films with stories, Kelly made story films with dances. In Kelly's best film, *Singin' in the Rain* (1952), the brightest performance is given by a nondancer, Jean Hagen. It could never have happened in an Astaire film.

This distinction between Astaire and Kelly is more important than the fact that Astaire stuck mostly to tap-dancing while Kelly went in for the large-scale effects of Broadway's latest export, ballet. In terms of dance content, *Yolanda and the Thief* (1945), in which Astaire collaborated with ballet choreographer Eugene Loring, is loaded, whereas it's the big ballets that are the least diverting features of *On the Town, Singin' in the Rain*, and *An American in Paris* (1951). Movie critics pressed for their favorite musicals will generally name one of Kelly's or, if it's an Astaire film, *The Band Wagon* (1953)—MGM's magic is hard to resist. It's the nondance values in these films that make them entertaining—the pace and tunes and color and locale, the "literate" scripts and funny performances. Even when the big empty ballets are replaced by a good one—Michael Kidd's "Girl Hunt" in *The Band Wagon* (which isn't all that good, just less pretentious)—the result still isn't a dance film, it's a story film told by dancers and a dance-minded director (Astaire, Jack Buchanan, Nanette Fabray, and Cyd Charisse, directed by Vincente Minnelli). Astaire is an outsider in this film, just as he is in the plot. Times had indeed changed, and Astaire's lack of ease in the new "art" musical is one point the film gains by exploiting. It's fun watching him trying to adjust and seeing how well his style holds through all the nonsense of the "Girl Hunt" ballet, but no dance fan *prefers* a film in which Astaire works this far from his true center.

A dance film is one in which the dance values are more lucid and exciting to the mind than any other kind; it is not necessarily a film in which we see nothing but dance. There has never been a satisfactory all-dance feature film. *Tales of Beatrix Potter* (1971), with choreography by Frederick Ashton, has some delightful dances, but after the first half-hour it has delighted us long enough. The tales never get onto the screen; they're blocked by choreography. This business of eliminating every expressive resource of movies in the conviction that dance will take their place is founded on a mistaken notion of pure expression. Purity of expression is achieved by cutting away excess; poverty results from the cutting away of essentials. In the Potter film, nothing takes the place of Potter's text. The dances are charming but dramatically inconsequential—and would seem so on the stage, too. So we have neither filmed ballet nor a ballet film. In *Invitation to the Dance* (1957), Gene Kelly attempts three ballets which can scarcely be said to fail because he has limited himself to the one form of expression. His material is so routine that the fact that it is mimed and danced rather than spoken or sung makes no difference. Nor is the material enhanced by the "cinematic resources" that Kelly employs: the long animation sequence is a long *bad* animation sequence. It would be a great pity if Kelly's contributions as a choreographer (or "choreo-cinema maker," as the dance profession designates him) should take precedence in our minds over his much more solid contributions as a performer. He came along at a time when the wartime boom in ballet was making everyone conscious of dance as a high art. He was supposed to do great artistic things with dance in the movies and is thought by many to have done them. But Kelly the artist is Kelly the performer, and his best choreography consists of the brilliant solos he invented for himself—the alter-ego dance in *Cover Girl* (1944), the statue dance in *Living in a Big Way* (1947), the newspaper dance in *Summer Stock* (1950), the title number in *Singin' in the Rain*.

For a long time, it was generally agreed that ballet was not expressive in the movies, and in fact (as the Jeremy Fisher sequences in *Tales of Beatrix Potter* show) camera speeds are still registering fanlike impressions of big jumps and rapid steps in the air. In the 1938 *Goldwyn Follies*, Balanchine arranged his American Ballet dancers in a highly effective series of still poses with wind streaming through the shot. Vera Zorina "rode" a statue of a horse. The movement sequences were less interesting. It was the first time, however, that a trained classical corps de ballet had appeared in a Hollywood film. *Goldwyn Follies* was a terrible movie and Balanchine's part of it caused no great stir. Nor did his later film dances for Zorina (*I Was an Adventuress*, 1940, and "That Old Black Magic" in *Star Spangled Rhythm*, 1943), in which he continued to try things that couldn't be done on a stage. It is doubtful that movie audiences unfamiliar with ballet could appreciate Balanchine's effects, and today they appear rather academic. Balanchine's ideas about film choreography at that time were negative in principle—or he was never given screen time to work out dances that were more than negations of stage conventions. In 1948, *The Red Shoes* dramatized many of Balanchine's fancies to sensational effect. In the climactic ballet in that film, optical printing went wild, with seas beating against the footlights, the stage dissolving into a desert or a ballroom, and a slow-motion fall through space. There were not many more times this sort of thing could happen, and even *The Red Shoes* didn't get completely away with the pretense that it was all happening in the ballerina's mind. But it worked because nothing was attempted in dance that could not be seen clearly, or improved upon, by the camera. Robert Helpmann's choreography was thin to the point of misty suggestion. The lovely young classical dancer Moira Shearer was given runs, arrowy arabesques, dartlike passages on toe. She remained in the eye like the point of a flame (an image—life's candle—that actually appears to the audience as the film ends).

What was special about the *Red Shoes* ballet was not so much its free use of movie devices—audiences had seen lurid visual tone poems before—as its assimilation of those devices in a picture of the ballet's stage world. The things that could have happened on the stage were almost as strange as the things that couldn't. The taste of the moviemakers was so consistent—so consistently outrageous—that they made the imaginary happenings seem like plausible (though not, of course, literal) extensions of the behavior of classical ballet. The fetishistic emphasis on toeshoes, red like the color of Moira Shearer's hair, was the most brilliant touch of all. But Powell and Pressburger went even further than this. They enclosed the ballet in a story about a dancer's life and loaded it with a specialized atmosphere that was more suggestive than the fictions it was intended to support—such forties-movie themes as mad genius, the culture-sadism link, the career-marriage conflict. Their dancers looked real, their ballets (gems from the classic repertory, unerringly selected and photographed) looked real, even their fabrications looked real. *The Red Shoes* was a horror story told in the form of a dance musical with dance supplying the main thrills, and it aroused tremendous popular interest in ballet. It had a direct influence on the success of the Sadler's Wells (now Royal) Ballet on its first American tour, and it brought a new and young audience to the support of the crucial first seasons of the New York City Ballet. The whole surge was extraordinary and has never been repeated in just that way. The fans it created realized soon enough that the film was shallow, but they did not feel cheated. The kind of excitement it offered was the excitement of good caricature, of certain presumptions about ballet technique and the ballet *Gestalt* carried to a point of ecstatic involvement. *The Red Shoes* is witty rather than moving, and its wit is distinctly *outré*, as in the point it makes about "spotting" by having the camera do flash pans, seeing what Moira Shearer sees when she does pirouettes. (Hitchcock makes the joke again in *Torn Curtain* when he has Toumanova spot off Paul Newman, sitting in the audience.) Although the kind of power it gets from its subject is not the best that subject has to offer, and although it launched the ballet trend in all the musicals that won honors in the fifties, there really is no other ballet film.

As a *horror* film, it summed up and externalized all the things that had kept ballet off the screen or just barely, cringingly, on it. Before *The Red Shoes*, ignorance and intuition had combined to create a minor movie tradition where ballet was concerned. The movie producers were no more interested in ballet than they had to be. It was just starting to become popular in the thirties, and they used it then because (a) it symbolized culture and (b) it seemed to exercise a malign fascination. Everyone had heard of the mad Nijinsky. John Barrymore had played Diaghilev (and Donald Cook, Nijinsky!) in a film actually called *The Mad Genius* in 1931. Shakespearean adaptations had to have ballets, which were generally scissored to ribbons in the release prints: a Nijinska one in Max Reinhardt's *A Midsummer Night's Dream* (1935) and an Agnes de Mille one in Thalberg's *Romeo and Juliet* (1936). When producers wished to show respect for art, they invariably created a lavish number around some performing freak who would knock the public's eye out. Even Astaire and Rogers in *Shall We Dance* (1937) had to make way for a ballet starring Ziegfeld's ballerina Harriet Hoctor. During this period, in England, Jessie Matthews had forged a lightly idiosyncratic and highly appealing dance style out of ballet steps done in jazz rhythm. There was nothing gloomy or perverse about Jessie Matthews, and her musicals were charming, but she had no American counterpart. In America, you were either Tap or Toe, and Toe was art. Hoctor, who was a contortionist specializing in backbends on point, and Vivian Fay, who was a toe dancer specializing in whiplash turns, made numerous film appearances as stand-ins for Ballet. In 1938, arthouse audiences saw European classical dancers in *Ballerina (La Mort du Cygne)*, a backstage ballet drama in which a trapdoor is opened under Mia Slavenska. Though it contained scarcely any dancing, the Vivien Leigh–Robert Taylor *Waterloo Bridge* (1940) reworked Robert E. Sherwood's play to make the doomed heroine a dancer and her story identical to that of Odette-Odile in *Swan Lake*. (It was remade in the fifties as a vehicle for dancer-actress Leslie Caron.)

The morbid tradition continued into the forties with the Hollywood remake of *Ballerina* (*The Unfinished Dance*, 1947) and *Specter of the Rose*, starring a dancer named Ivan Kirov as a Bronx Nijinsky who did beats with turned-in legs and leaped to his death through the plate glass of a window high over Manhattan. Written, produced, and co-directed by Ben Hecht in 1946, *Specter* is one of the most richly naïve movies ever made, constantly plastering sticky tributes to ballet over the alarming gaps in its author's knowledge. The dialogue is justly famous ("Hug me with your eyes." "I am." "Harder . . .") and the dancing is justly forgotten. Hecht should be given points for the characters, though, if not for their speeches. There are ineffectual people like this in the ballet world, particularly on its fringes, where Hecht must have run into them and assumed they were doing something important.

Like the rest of these movies, *The Red Shoes* said that ballet dancers were crazy and/or doomed. It capped the tradition of morbidity and raised the status of ballet in the movies at the same time. After that, things got healthier but duller. Goldwyn spent a fortune capitalizing on *The Red Shoes* with *Hans Christian Andersen* (1952), featuring Jeanmaire in uninteresting choreography by Roland Petit. (Originally, it was to have had Shearer dancing Balanchine.) The next film by Powell and Pressburger, *Tales of Hoffmann* (1952), was an overstuffed culture sandwich with one indigestible ruse: it tried substituting dancers for singers, and there was a lot of frantic lip-syncing on the hoof. Chaplin made a ballet film with undistinguished dances (*Limelight*, 1952). Dance sequences by Petit, Loring, Kidd, Helen Tamiris, Valerie Bettis, Jack Cole, James Mitchell, or Herbert Ross turned up in nearly every major musical. The find of the fifties was Bob Fosse (*The Pajama Game*, 1957); like Ross, he turned to directing. The ballet binge produced no stars. Stars of the ballet appeared in special spots, but their appearances were only newsworthy; they were rarely given a chance to do the kind of dancing that made them famous. There was a general attempt to make ballet winsome and cute or cold and jazzy. Leslie Caron, introduced in *An American in Paris*, had a hit in the minor *Lili* (1953), but eventually withdrew to straight roles. Because ballet was still thought of as a woman's art, there were no opportunities for male dancers; and a danseuse without a male co-star was hard to cast. It was not only the fear of effeteness that kept male classical dancers off the screen. The technique is too hard to photograph. (Rudolf Nureyev, whose style is measured and emphatic, is more photogenic than the equally brilliant but mercurial Edward Villella.) The wide screen brought two notable attempts to make large-scale masculine movement appealing to audiences. *Seven Brides for Seven Brothers* (1954) had some roughhouse clowning in an innocently gymnastic style, but *West Side Story* (1961) was not so innocent. Perhaps the most overpraised dance film yet made, it tried so hard to generate art from the violence of street warfare that it became bombastic kitsch.

Filmed ballet, a minor category of dance film, is just what it is and no more: a chance to see something of what goes on in the theatre. Unobtrusive camera work and editing can heighten the illusion of a performance (and are rarer than one would think), but they cannot redeem discrepancies between stage and film time. The screen can go dead while dancers labor to build an effect that has power in the theatre. Studio treatments of stage choreography should work, but don't; compromise shows as falsity. The look of a real stage becoming gradually stained with sweat is preferable to the cosmetic smoothness of a performance that is obviously not being filmed in one piece. We can understand more of an event and have more patience with it if we can discount in advance the effects it is *not* going to give us. A *Giselle* or a *Romeo* that is played to a camera still doesn't look like a movie; and what is the point of asking stage performers to modulate their technique for the camera if that technique is what we have paid to see? The films that Paul Czinner has made of the Bolshoi and the Royal Ballet in performance are good examples of the risks and virtues of straight, unpretentious filming, and there have been some enthralling fragments from Russia. (Warning signs should be posted against Jean Negulesco's filming of two Massine pieces, *Gaîté Parisienne* and *Capriccio Espagnol*, for Warner Brothers in 1941. Negulesco competes with Massine in bravura and cancels every choreographic effect. The films are still shown because of the star casts, but *Gaîté* excludes the great Danilova from one of her most famous roles—Warners' thought she wasn't pretty.)

Art films on the dance, from the rhythm-and-motion studies of the twenties down to Maya Deren's experiments in the forties and fifties and the contemporary camera choreography of Norman McLaren, Ed Emshwiller, and Hilary Harris, have traditionally concentrated on abstract, impersonal expression rather than on dancers in performance. The dancers in most of these films have no personalities; they are exactly what one of Hilary Harris's titles suggests they are: themes for variations by the camera. These films are often pleasant and even sensual experiences in their own terms. They would be more exciting, though, if they hadn't lost the point of their tradition—if they'd continued to present a contrast rather than a correlative to general

tendencies in commercial moviemaking. Front-of-the-camera performing is now so rare that the starring role in a film biography of one
of the world's great dancers, *Isadora*, can be taken by a nondancer with
little or no protest from the dance press. With the decline of the movie
musical, there seems to have arisen a vague impulse to transplant
dance values to other forms of screen entertainment, in extended
motion sequences—bike-riding, car-driving, running through woods
(in slow motion)—that have no point other than to beguile us with
their abstract beauty. The screen is said to be dancing when often it is
only temporizing. When musicals of the past are revived, the choices
reflect the current taste for impersonal sensation: Berkeley in quantity, the Disney of *Fantasia*. In order to see dancing by dancers, more
people are going to the ballet than ever went before. Dance as an experience for the spectator has just about ceased to exist any place else.

The personality of the dancer comes through in the two documentaries that are really performances for the camera by Martha Graham.
In *A Dancer's World* (1957), she sits at a dressing table making up for
performance, and as she talks to us, with the camera cutting away to
her company in a classroom demonstration, we get caught up in her
personality and theatrical style as we have no chance to do in the dim
and musty films that were made of her stage works about the same
time. In a 1943 film study of her famous solo *Lamentation*, which she
performed seated, Graham becomes living sculpture examined by the
camera from different angles. The camera's explorations don't wipe
out Graham. Because of their modesty of scale, these Graham films
are among the few dance films of their kind that can be shown successfully on television.[1]

Abstraction need not mean depersonalization. There probably
should be a special category for *Olympia*. Although it is not a dance
film, it is unsurpassed as a study of physical motion. Although it was
made in Nazi Germany, it is not propaganda. It is abstract and yet
it does not leave out the personalities of its subjects. Produced and

1. Postscript 1977: Since this encyclopedia article was written in 1971, there has been
one first-rate dance movie—the version of *Eight Jelly Rolls* made by Twyla Tharp with
London Weekend Television, which used a full range of optical effects to orchestrate
the dances. But videotape choreography (Merce Cunningham has also made some
fascinating examples) is an area of experimentation different from choreography on,
or for, film.

edited by Leni Riefenstahl, a former dancer, and accompanied by a fine musical score composed by Herbert Windt, *Olympia* transcends its obligations as a documentary of the 1936 Olympic Games to become a ritual celebration of beautiful bodies and heroic movement. But it is always moving on two planes: journalism and poetry. It is the most *sensuous* of documentaries. The editing is so lyrical and so exactly timed to the differently charged proportions of regular or slowed motion that we are often displaced before we know it from one plane to the other—from stadium to "theatre." The javelin-thrower dances into his takeoff, the gymnast lifting himself on parallel rings (a slow movement slowed further by the camera) is seen to rise with a massive strength, and each collapse across the finish line of the twenty-six-mile Marathon is an individual aria of pain. The effect has been widely imitated, but no other film of this type has quite succeeded in enhancing the event without blurring or falsifying the record, and certainly none has enhanced it to the extent that *Olympia* does, with its classical nudes, its radiant morning mists, and its high divers falling out of the sun.

The current emphasis on a directors' cinema makes most movie musicals look very bad indeed—and some bad directors look good. Not all directors who have been interested in movement as a film subject have been great. The directors who were concerned with what most audiences wanted to see—great performing in great routines—made musicals that, on the whole, were not up to the routines that were in them. It is the performers whom we remember in these movies; the directors' names may matter less than the choreographers', and some of the greatest moments may occur in movies we wouldn't want to see again—Hermes Pan's dances for *Moon Over Miami* (1941) and *Coney Island* (1943); Robert Alton's "The Lady Dances" in *Strike Me Pink* (1936); LeRoy Prinz's Charleston in *Tea for Two* (1950); the Nicholas Brothers in *Kid Millions* (1934) and *Orchestra Wives* (1942); the astounding Merriel Abbott Dancers in *Man About Town* (1939), *Buck Benny Rides Again* (1940), and *Sensations of 1945*. There are performers—Bill Robinson, Ray Bolger—who always seem halfway out of the movies they appear in, as if on loan from another and better movie that really belonged to them. For these reasons, film students who are interested in the musical are less interested in it as a showcase for performers than as a showcase for direction. But very few musicals that really work all the way through—e.g., *Good News* (1947, with Charles Walters's direction and Robert Alton's production numbers)—can be attributed exclusively to good direction—or to good writing or good performing. Musicals combine too many forms of expression to be analyzed in this way; they're the ultimate fantasy movie.

Not all directors who have been interested in movement were great, but few have been great who were not. Griffith, Murnau, Lubitsch, Eisenstein, Dovzhenko, Ford, Flaherty, Riefenstahl, Disney, Clair, Cocteau, Ophuls, Kurosawa, Satyajit Ray—all have different ways of making films move; each is the way of a virtuoso. Not only do their films move; their dance scenes—scenes of actual dance or dancelike movement—are among the greatest ever recorded. With the death of the musical, the dance-lover's film repertory has almost stopped growing. Now it will expand only when the best of today's directors become good choreographers, too.

1971/1977

Adagio and Allegro

IN *Ballo della Regina*, the new ballet that Balanchine has made for Merrill Ashley, she carries bravura allegro dancing to a peak it may never have reached before. The adagio, partnered by Robert Weiss, requires the singing line that Ashley doesn't have and is dispatched with typical efficiency, but her polka variation, whirling to a close with hops in fifth on pointe, cuts like flying glass. Balanchine seems to have taken Ashley's role in last year's *Bournonville Divertissements* as a sketch for the brilliant new material he has given her, and he has orchestrated the Ashley "theme"—her strangely characteristic ability to move her tall, straight body through rapid and complete changes of shape. Ashley doesn't combine different shapes in the same movement, but she can achieve counterpoint through juxtaposition, and she's so fast she can even appear to be in two places at once. The dances for an all-girl corps (four demi-soloists and an ensemble of twelve) are as spontaneous and fresh as the dances for Ashley. Balanchine has designed them for contrast—her fleet footwork against their wide striding and turning, their plasticity against her square-cut, erect style. All this is allegro in range, although as Balanchine allegro it is unfamiliar. Those high, sailing jumps, for example—where did they come from? The ballet makes the audience very happy, especially at the end, when, to slamming final chords, Ashley takes three or four flash poses on the way down from a supported position in second to a kneel: it sums up her phenomenal high-speed accuracy.

In spite of the show put on by Ashley, Bonita Borne, Sheryl Ware, Debra Austin, Stephanie Saland, and the ensemble, *Ballo della Regina* doesn't add up to much. It lacks conviction as a ballet. Weiss's role is trumped up; musically there doesn't seem to be a real place for him, and he gets wedged into corners. (Flat and stiff as he looks, it's still unfair treatment.) The music is the seldom-performed ballet from Verdi's *Don Carlos*, written to a libretto that Balanchine has disregarded. Musical echoes of that libretto remain, nevertheless, in passages (*azione mimica*) that don't easily support the straight dancing that Balanchine has choreographed to them. In another ballet to music by an opera composer, *Donizetti Variations*, Balanchine has drawn a sharp, and sharply satirical, picture of Donizetti. But he doesn't appear to have had Verdi's qualities much in mind, perhaps because the music has no particular Verdian savor. (It was one of the composer's attempts to satisfy Parisian taste.) Balanchine's *Ballo della Regina* remains a quarter-hour discourse about the qualities of Merrill Ashley.

When Suzanne Farrell dances an allegro role and brings to it an adagio feeling, as she did this season in *Allegro Brillante*, she creates a complex and interesting event. Farrell wouldn't be interesting in *Ballo della Regina*, since for the most part the role completely blocks out any adagio quality. The prima role in *Divertimento No. 15* doesn't need her, either, as one none too successful fling with it last year showed. For Farrell to captivate in allegro, the role has to be porous. For Ashley, it has to be airtight. *Allegro Brillante* isn't, and she probably wouldn't be terribly exciting in it. It took the enormous range of Farrell to show me that *Allegro Brillante* could be danced, with no loss of allegro values, as an adagio part. (I mean all the way through, not just in sections.) But the big Farrell occasion of the season so far has been her dancing in *Chaconne* the night of the *Ballo* première. To watch Farrell stretching a Farrell part is a frontline experience; dancing just does not go further. On this night, there were quantitative embellishments of all sorts: quadruple pirouettes, sixes instead of quatres in the entrechats, even triple soutenu turns. But quantity is not the end of virtuosity. What Farrell achieved was a heightening of all those fluid transactions between extreme ends of her range—between allegro and adagio— which Balanchine wrote into her role. And though she advanced to the very limit of the ballet's style, she never toppled into distortion.

1978/2000

Edwin Denby

1

MY INTRODUCTION to Edwin Denby was his great essay on the Nijinsky photographs, which I first encountered in Paul Magriel's book. *Nijinsky: An Illustrated Monograph* (Holt, 1946) had been long out of print, but it was the only thing of its kind at the time, and I remember the mild stun it produced in my consciousness, like being hit on the head with a soft mallet. The Denby commentary, its centerpiece, was unique in giving us the mind of the critic together with the object it is fixed upon, and to read it with a selection of the photographs at hand (something one could not do again until years later, when Lincoln Kirstein reprinted the piece in his *Nijinsky Dancing*) was to be guided with an unerring precision toward a knowledge not only of Nijinsky's art but of all the beauty that dancing has to offer. It is not enough to say that Denby sees more than you do, or even that his eye acts like a corrective lens to your own, helping you to see more, too. He sees what you had not dreamed was there, as when he speaks of the thighs in a supporting pose with Karsavina in *Spectre*: "as full of tenderness as another dancer's face." He notices a "poignant duplicity of emotion" in the poses from *Faune* and *Jeux*. He looks at "the savage force of the arms and legs" in *Narcissus* and from this makes the thrilling deduction that "the hero's narcissism was not vanity, but an instinct that killed him, like an act of God."

On first reading Denby, I don't think I was moved as much by his perceptions as by the emotion that lay behind them. It certainly never occurred to me that this was the greatest essay on dancing I had ever read; Heaven knows I had read little enough about dancing. So little, in fact, that the wonders of Denby's prose impressed me as only natural and proper—the only way to talk, if one is going to talk at all, about the ballet. But the more closely I read, the more the words seemed to create their own drama in relation to the pictures. Who but Denby, after all, would have imagined what lay concealed there—those thighs, for example, or the hands in *Jeux*, "as mysterious as breathing in sleep"?

Then I found and devoured *Looking at the Dance*. I remember it was on the Second Avenue bus that I opened the book for the first time—"Second Avenue," as Denby was to write in a later volume, "where herds of vehicles go charging one way all day long disappearing into the sky at the end like on a prairie"—and read about *Apollo*:

> *Apollo* is about poetry, poetry in the sense of a brilliant, sensuous, daring and powerful activity of our nature.

Denby was himself a poet, and it was as a poet that he wrote about dancing. *Looking at the Dance* may be the most universally admired book of dance criticism in American publishing history. As one who has spent years combing Denbyisms out of her prose, I can testify that it's also the most infectious. ("Wonderful, this dignity," I once wrote of Nureyev. "Wonderful and sad, too. . . ." Dear Edwin!) But those images of his that stick in the mind are quite beyond imitation. Who can forget "Miss Toumanova, with her large, handsome, and deadly face" or the "trees in the wind" passage in the review of *Concerto Barocco*? Nor can one escape the casual force of Denby the aesthetician. The idea that seems to me central to all his criticism, that "art takes what in life is an accidental pleasure and tries to repeat and prolong it," is so indirectly proposed *as an idea* that the exact wording has just taken me a half hour to look up in a book I thought I knew well. (You will find it in the essay "Against Meaning in Ballet.")

When *Dancers, Buildings and People in the Streets* was about to come out, I was invited to a party for Edwin by our mutual friend Bob Cornfield. By that time, I had launched *Ballet Review* very much under the sign of Denby. But Edwin didn't seem to take much interest in *Ballet Review* until one day he agreed to let himself be interviewed for our Fall issue in 1969. Alex Katz contributed a portrait for the cover.

My happy discovery on meeting Edwin was that he talked almost exactly as he wrote, so the fact that he'd more or less officially stopped writing dance criticism didn't mean that there could be no more Denby in print. But when I worked with him on the transcripts of our interviews, I began to see what had stopped his pen. He worried incessantly over every point he'd made in his recorded remarks, modifying, qualifying, refining his meaning until sometimes the point would start to get lost, whereupon I would try to coax him back to the original wording. Then he would demand a footnote. The tape recorder, he said, backed him into corners. But he rewrote and re-rewrote and still wasn't satisfied. I remember sitting in Edwin's loft into the early hours, snow whirling outside, while he delicately tore apart pages of incomparable commentary, asking himself, "Is this really true? Do I really mean that?" It was Edwin's great gift to illuminate the experience of subjectivity in watching dance, but he agonized lest he be even fractionally misunderstood.

Edwin never relinquished his interest in what was going on. To the very end his reactions were the keenest of anyone I knew and his need to ventilate them quite heartbreakingly apparent—the communicator in him never did die. (He once said that to write about dance one has to be interested in communication almost for its own sake.) I was often struck by how long he could remain at his post—by not only the hours he put in attending performances but also the weeks of meditation. Long after I'd filed a piece (filed and, as usually happened, forgotten it), there would come a call from Edwin, who'd been thinking. And he'd have worked the event I'd written about so deeply into the fabric of his consciousness that it was available to me whole and fresh once more. No one else could do this, and no one else would have been so patient with my reluctance to respond when the moment of his call found me tired or past caring. Edwin did me the exquisite courtesy of treating me like a colleague, but I don't think his comments were designed for me personally—I think he spoke that way to everyone.

Once, about the time of our *BR* interview, he analyzed a new ballet by a young choreographer in terms I'd never heard before. I knew he was talking "in the abstract" as only he could, and I was doubly alert, and I didn't understand a word he said. Edwin must have known this because he kept on and on, becoming, for Edwin, quite vehement. He was saying that this choreographer had no sense of how shapes changed their proportions in dancing; he was describing one of the elemental powers of ballet, as yet invisible to me. "You see, it's the thing of getting bigger or smaller," he would say, as if I were only momentarily failing to recognize something I knew quite well. A state of blank incomprehension is difficult to remember. If I knew that dancing could do this thing, I didn't know that choreographers could control it. And even after Edwin told me, I still didn't know. What I remember about this moment is my utter misery. It was during an intermission at the Brooklyn Academy. We stood at the back of the orchestra, getting bumped on all sides. It took me years to get what he was driving at that evening, and I got it at last only because he had insisted: it was important.

How many other dance critics must have a story like this to tell! Edwin spoke—and wrote—as if everyone saw things the way he did. His genius made us believe it was true.

November 4, 1983

2

"THE BEST dance critic living." That is what Edwin Denby, in 1940, called Serge Lifar. He thought Lifar, who had just published a book on Diaghilev, was good "because, first, he has the professional experience which turns dancing from a thing you buy readymade into a thing you make yourself. And second, he sees dancing with the eyes of intelligence, as an ordinary person sometimes sees a friend or sees the weather; sees and believes at the same time. 'The eyes of a poet,' people say who know what poetry is about."

If today those words sound more generous than exact as applied to Lifar, it is because they strike us as a good description of Denby himself. He, too, had been a professional dancer (in Germany before Hitler), and he saw with the eyes of a poet—so much so that "people who know what poetry is about" were more than likely to have noticed the resemblance between the dance critic of the bimonthly *Modern Music* and the image he drew of Lifar. Denby by then had been at the craft of dance criticism for four years. He had already written, in *Modern Music*, the pieces on *Noces* and *Faune*, on ballet music, on Balanchine's *Poker Game* and *Baiser*, and on Ashton's *Devil's Holiday* which would become immortalized in *Looking at the Dance*. He had addressed central issues in the work of Graham and

Massine, identifying the qualities of pictorial tension which he found differently disturbing in each; and on Massine he had written one of the most luminous passages he would ever write: "As a pictorial arranger Massine is inexhaustible. But dancing is less pictorial than plastic, and pictures in dancing leave a void in the imagination. They arrest the drama of dancing which the imagination craves to continue, stimulated by all the kinetic senses of the body that demand a new movement to answer the one just past. Until a kind of secret satisfaction and a kind of secret weariness coincide."

This is the writing not only of a poet who sees but of a poet who feels, and who feels what we all feel. Denby gained from having been a dancer an incalculable advantage, but it is Denby the spectator who is the true artist of criticism. *Looking at the Dance*, the book that established his reputation as a critic, is very precisely named. Looking—perceiving with all his senses—is what Denby did. It is sometimes erroneously said that a School of Denby exists in American dance criticism. Schools are based on ideas and theories, and Denby's critical insight was a gift—his alone. The only idea he ever proposed (and it was more an article of faith than an idea) was that each of us should develop the critical insight he was born with. When he says that Lifar (read Denby) sees as an ordinary person "sees and believes," he is saying that the experience of dancing is a normal and subjective one—no special knowledge is needed in order to understand it—but also that this subjective experience is heightened by belief, by an unconditional acceptance of the truth of what one sees. Another way of saying it is that dancing appeals to the poet in us. But that still isn't all there is to it. Dancing is physical, a spectacle of grace in movement. The "kinetic senses of the body," more than the optic nerve, are what stimulate the imagination. I believe that Denby discovered these kinetic senses in his role as a critic, sitting there in the dark, and that the more he thought about it the more it seemed that kinetic excitement was what made viewing dancing a normal and subjective but by no means universal pleasure. Three years later, writing for the readers of the *New York Herald Tribune*, he arrived at a formulation both generous and strict: "To recognize poetic suggestion through dancing one must be susceptible to poetic values and susceptible to dance values as well."

This statement forms the cornerstone of *Looking at the Dance*, yet, because of the way that book was edited (it came out in 1949), it is

extremely difficult to see how—by what cognitive process—the statement might have crystallized in Denby's mind. Not, in fact, until the
publication, earlier this year, of a complete edition of the criticism was
it possible to follow Denby's thinking as it evolved from one piece to
another. The articles and reviews in *Looking at the Dance* were selected
by the music and dance critic B. H. Haggin, who had championed
Denby's work for years. Pieces written years apart were united under
single headings—"Dancers in Performance," "Modern Dancers,"
"Dancers in Exotic Styles," and so on—and the entries within each
category were not always reprinted in their original sequence. The
internal logic of the book (devised, I take it, by Haggin) is admirable.
In the opening section, "Meaning in Ballet," an amalgam of various
magazine articles and what appear to have been Sunday columns from
the *Herald Tribune* actually creates the impression that Denby had
composed a primer in dance technique and dance aesthetics for the
popular audience. (Of course, he had done just that, but not system-
atically.) Grouping scattered reviews on specific topics also points up
the variety of the dance scene in New York in the forties and the variety of Denby's response to it. But though *Looking at the Dance* remains
a classic, it gives us an Olympian Denby, whose most decisive utter-
ances are as casual and unpremeditated as bolts from the blue. *Dance
Writings* (Knopf), edited by Robert Cornfield and William MacKay,
collects all but the most marginal critical work that Denby published,
including the reviews and portions of reviews that were excluded from
Looking at the Dance, adds some unpublished material, and presents
the lot chronologically except where chronology would destroy some
more significant order. Thus, although the *Modern Music* series (1936–
43) overlapped for seven months the *Herald Tribune* series (1942–45),
it does not do so here; all the pieces on Balanchine and New York City
Ballet from 1946 onward appear in one section; and essays on matters
unrelated to topical events appear in another.

The consequence of this new and complete presentation is the
emergence of a Denby who is a more complex, more vividly real
character than the deity of *Looking at the Dance*. We see him as a
working critic and, when he joins the staff of the *Herald Tribune*, as
a most improbably robust *hard*working critic. The dance calendar
in those days was blank for long periods and insanely congested for
brief ones; Denby filled out the year with ice shows, night-club acts,

and Broadway musicals. He went to modern-dance recitals in hellish places; he reviewed the Rockettes. Constitutionally a frail man, he seemed to thrive under the pressure. During the fall ballet season of 1943, he filed fifteen pieces in October alone, and among these were two major essays and six reviews of collectible caliber. It is the opinion of Minna Lederman, the editor of *Modern Music*, that Denby's newspaper pieces, written to tight deadlines, are better than the articles he labored over for her; I agree with this—no finer body of dance journalism exists. But except for a few places here and there the *Modern Music* series doesn't seem labored, and there is no break in style when Denby takes up his newspaper job. If anything, he grows more precise, his tone becomes more intimate still, and his communicative zeal is palpable. Even in the most crushingly routine assignment he is a good reporter. The conscientiousness with which he reviews cast changes, program fillers, conductors, costumes, and scenery comes as a revelation to those of us who were bred on *Looking at the Dance*. (I remember thinking that these things couldn't have mattered to Denby, because he never discussed them. Well, he did.) In matters of opinion, too, there are some surprises. Ballets trounced in *Looking at the Dance* bob up restored by second or third viewings; a few personal reputations are sealed or unsealed. Normally the most benign of critics, Denby could be dangerous when provoked. Of Baronova's antics he writes, "She seems to want the title of 'Miss Ironpants.'" On the whole, though, fewer dancers than one might expect enter or leave the winner's circle. The famous portrait, verging on caricature, of "Miss Toumanova with her large, handsome, and deadly face," her "blocklike torso, limp arms, and predatory head positions" isn't radically altered by the addition of a few favorable comments, one of which—"When she dances it is a matter of life and death"—is reminiscent of a remark he'd made about Carmen Amaya: "She can dance as if nothing else existed in the world but dancing and death."

But Denby's Lifar turns out to have been a very different creature from what we had thought him up to now—chiefly an object of satire: "Poor Lifar. He looks older onstage than Dolin or Massine," and so on, in a vein of malicious sympathy that becomes openly derisive with a description of Lifar's pomposities in *Giselle*. But this was in 1950. In 1940, not only was Lifar the best living critic; he was also, of all the dancers of the prewar period, the one closest to Denby's heart. The

passages on Lifar the dancer and Lifar the critic (both omitted from
Looking at the Dance) are cast in the same terms. Lifar in performance
has a naturalness

> that goes beyond the gestures required, as though the char-
> acter were as much alive as anybody living. As though on the
> stage, he seems to believe in the life that is going on outside
> of the theater in the present. He seems to believe, that his part
> makes sense anywhere, that his part (in the words of Cum-
> mings) is competing with elephants and skyscrapers and the
> individual watching him. They all seem real at the same time,
> part of the same imagination, as they are really. There is some-
> thing unprofessional about carrying reality around with you
> in public that goes straight to my heart.

Denby seems to be in love. He is, as we never again see him, at a loss,
fumbling for words. And he realizes how he must sound; his very next
sentence is "This is the kind of criticism it is hard to prove the justice
of; I wish we could see Lifar more often so I could try." The echo of
Lifar the dancer in Lifar the critic is, I think, brilliantly illuminating, but it tells us more about Denby—about the qualities he loved
and valued—than about Lifar. The echo of Amaya in Toumanova is
also illuminating, but there Denby is talking about something he saw
rather than thought he saw or hoped to see. He doesn't draw a parallel,
and, indeed, none should be inferred. But he didn't strike that chord
twice by accident.

Nor is "pictorial tension" coincidentally a problem in the work of
both Graham and Massine. From *Looking at the Dance* you might be
able to tell that this business of visual and kinetic suggestion was on
Denby's mind in 1937 and 1938—the Graham and Massine articles are
both from that period. But they're placed under different headings,
and the Graham piece, in which Denby *first* brings up the matter,
comes ninety pages after the Massine. In *Dance Writings*, it comes
eleven pages before. Again, I don't wish to suggest a parallel, still less
an "influence." But photographs from the past reveal conventions of
the era that were invisible at the time, and dances of past eras may do
the same, even though they were composed and staged under very
different auspices. Nothing is harder to spot than the unconscious

patterns that connect the work of contemporaries. Yet Denby's eye saw something—probably the only thing—in Graham's work that was like Massine's. That he didn't make a critical point of the similarity is immaterial. He may not have had the chance. Companies didn't perform, and critics didn't write, often enough in those days for such tight connections to be made. Or he may not, so early in his critical career, have completely understood the implications of what he saw, or may have thought them self-evident—who knows? And who cares? The test of a critic is not how many points he can clinch but how transparent he is; unless we can see through him to the way it was, it won't help to know what he thinks it means. As Denby says, "It is not the critic's historic function to have the right opinions but to have interesting ones. He talks but he has nothing to sell." For Denby, a critic is functioning properly when his readers feel free enough to have interesting opinions of their own.

Denby expressed these views on the job of the critic in 1949 (in an essay twice as long as it appeared in *Looking at the Dance*); he was by then the polished professional craftsman, the poet who became a journalist without losing his personal voice. It must have been with some misgiving that he forsook his privacy as a little-magazine critic for the public glare of a newspaper post. Newspapering is the most difficult work imaginable for a dance critic, and it was more so in Denby's day than in our own. The mood you were in when the curtain fell on *Pillar of Fire* was not the mood you had to be in to race to a typewriter and rap out a smart lead for the bulldog edition. Denby was exactly one year into the job, right in the middle of that congested 1943 season, when he had a mishap. He mistook Nora Kaye for Markova and wrote a glowing notice of the wrong ballerina. His apology was a characteristically elegant tribute to both ladies, but the episode embarrassed him profoundly; thirty years later, he still spoke of it. Denby, who'd had no journalistic training, was proud of his professionalism. Then, too, as a proponent of ballet at a time when most intellectuals preferred modern dance, he had an evangelical mission. Denby's supporters formed up against the modern-dance legions behind John Martin, of the *Times*. But it was more than ballet versus modern dance. Virgil Thomson, in his autobiography, speaks of the appeal of the city's two leading newspapers to "the educated middle class," saying that the *Times* "has regularly in its critical columns followed a little belatedly the tastes of this group; the *Herald Tribune* under Ogden Reid aspired to lead them. It did not therefore, as the *Times* has so often done, shy away from novelty or elegance." With Denby on dance (and he certainly did not neglect modern dance) and Thomson on music, the *Trib* was a juggernaut of opinion. Martin and Olin Downes, on music, were no match for it. One can imagine how Denby's enemies used his mistake against him.

Denby was a professional, but he loved Richard Buckle's monthly *Ballet*, because, as he put it when the magazine folded, it didn't make him feel like "a harried fellow-professional." After 1945, he never wrote for a newspaper again. He relinquished his *Herald Tribune* post to Walter Terry, who reclaimed it after the war, and for the next two decades he concentrated on his poetry, writing dance pieces more or less when the spirit moved him. Some of the critical writing from that period appears to have been motivated more by a wish to satisfy friends and editors who were friends than by a need to get things said. Still, the publication, in 1965, of a second collection, *Dancers, Buildings and People in the Streets*, revealed a Denby whose pertinacity of thought was undiminished. Only the sporadic nature of the pieces keeps us from making cognitive connections among them. Connections are anyway more a matter of tone. The title essay and its companion, "Forms in Motion and in Thought," were originally prepared as lectures to dance students, and it is to dance students rather than to the general public that one feels Denby is speaking in the fifties and sixties. Though the writing has a new, Jamesian density, the tone becomes more frankly confiding; he sounds like a man among friends and often writes as one, casting his reviews in epistolary form. It is a fair guess that the epistles were all addressed to Buckle, who published them. (It would have been nicer to be told who the "you" is, and where the "here" is in his letters from abroad.) But though Denby invoked the privileges of the form, he didn't abuse them. Far from writing for a coterie, as he was sometimes accused of doing, he was working to broaden access to the subject on its deepest levels, both for the reader and for himself. By the intensity of one's interest in dance one is made to feel a part of Denby's circle.

The editors tell us who some of Denby's actual friends were, and an imposing list it is: the poets Frank O'Hara, Kenneth Koch, James Schuyler, John Ashbery, Ron Padgett, Anne Waldman, Alice Notley,

Ted Berrigan; the painters Willem and Elaine de Kooning, Franz Kline, Alex Katz, Red Grooms, Larry Rivers; the composers Virgil Thomson, Aaron Copland, Roger Sessions, John Cage; the photographer and filmmaker Rudolph Burckhardt; the choreographers Merce Cunningham, Paul Taylor, Jerome Robbins. This is the true School of Denby—his fellow-artists, with whom, as the generations passed, he had more in common than with the pack of inattentive children who were trying to become dance critics. Gentlest of men, he bore our presumption with angelic patience and never presumed, in return, to educate us. Rather, he just talked and listened as if we were his equals. The only piece of practical advice he ever gave me was when, at the end of a long ballet summer in the city, he found me staggering: "Get a beach vacation." (He also said that he used to prepare for Tudor's premieres by downing a steak at Gallagher's, then going home and sleeping for two hours.) But Edwin by then was part of the intellectual history of New York; he belonged to that artistic community which had made New York in the decades after the Second World War what Paris was in the decades before the first one. He was the chronicler of the great New York dance renaissance of the forties and fifties. He witnessed Graham's peak, Cunningham's and Taylor's emergence; he saw Balanchine (whose work had first impressed him in Paris, in the season of Les Ballets 1933) consolidate his powers on his New York power base.

Looking back on years we never knew, it's easy to think "Bliss was it in that dawn," and yet the reality of life as Denby lived it was not magnificent. It was a life of cafeterias, cigarettes, and stale coffee, of dancers, buildings, and people in the streets. (And the dancers were starving.) Denby took all this as part of his subject. If, as Cornfield says in his introduction, he changed the way we talk and think about dance, it was a change that could not have come about in any other city in the world. The artificial character of life in New York turns the natural world into an abstraction, something for the mind to contemplate. That is why abstract art is so intensely true an expression of New York—it is nature lived as a value. When Cunningham revived his 1953 piece *Septet* this season, he brought back those long-ago New York summers, with their mental weather, their intent street-corner conversations about painting and dance. Denby muses on a Markova performance in 1952: "Her dancing was queerer than anyone had remembered it. A few days later, meeting a balletomane usually far stricter than I on the street, I asked him what he thought of her this season. 'More wonderful than ever,' he cried aggressively." Once, Denby runs into Cunningham; they talk about Markova, naturally, and Denby goes home and writes. In *Septet*, it is possible to see traces of Markova, also Graham, also Balanchine, and to sense the spiritual presence of Denby. The young Paul Taylor was a member of the original cast. Later, it was Denby who introduced Taylor to Lincoln Kirstein and then to Alex Katz.

On the night of July 12, 1983, at the age of eighty, Edwin Denby killed himself with sleeping pills. The notes he left were clearheaded, but his faculties were failing, and he was miserable in his dependency on others. His last published remarks are sad. They concern Balanchine, who had died two months before. Denby begins, ominously enough, with the revival of *Symphonie Concertante* by American Ballet Theatre, which had upset him. Then, as he had done so often in the past, he concentrates on what makes Balanchine different from other choreographers, but having to go through it all again (he is being interviewed for *Dance Magazine*) seems to dishearten him. You feel him near to desperation in the effort to be clear, as if it were a once-and-for-all-time effort, and he keeps underlining his remarks with "This is a rare gift," or "Few choreographers have known how to do that." He wishes that the ballets—"Balanchine's butterflies"—could be preserved, but he seems to think they won't be.

Dance Writings does not end on this note of anguish. The last piece in the book is the great analytical essay "Forms in Motion and in Thought," in the concluding pages of which Denby comes closer to capturing the dance experience than any other writer ever has, even his beloved Mallarmé. The dance is in his mind, a replay of something he's seen (undoubtedly by Balanchine), or perhaps something he's made up, and it is conveyed to us—such is his virtuosity—in three distinctly different phases of activity. First comes a description of how a classical ballet works, in writing that is entirely sensory, with no steps and no images, but so lucidly composed as to evoke continuous gestural force:

> But the action of a step determines the ramifications, the rise
> and fall of the continuous momentum. You begin to see the

active impetus of the dancers creating the impetus moment by moment. They step out of one shape and into another, they change direction or speed, they erect and dissolve a configuration, and their secure and steady impetus keeps coming. The situations that dissolve as one watches are created and swept along by the ease and the fun and the positive lightness of it. They dance and, as they do, create in their wake an architectural momentum of imaginary weights and transported presences. Their activity does not leave behind any material object, only an imaginary one.

One of Denby's cherished beliefs about dancing had to do with the persistence of images as a key to comprehension. Dancing leaves behind "an imaginary object," "a classical shape," "a visual moment of climax," that goes on gathering force in the mind. From ballet in the theatre, then, he turns to ballet recollected in tranquillity:

> As you lie on the hot deserted beach far from town and with closed eyes recall the visual moment of climax, and scarcely hear the hoarse breathing of the small surf, a memory of the music it rose on returns, and you remember the prolonged melodious momentum of the score as if the musical phrase the step rose on had arrived from so far, so deep in the piece it appears to have been.

Finally, after all this so-to-speak disembodied language, he gives us an actual ballet in choreographic script and pictures, danced by cats and dogs on city streets. Every bit of it is wonderful. Here is one excerpt:

> And while cats one meets on different nights all like to follow the same adagio form, one cat will vary it by hunching her back or rolling seductively just out of reach, another, another night, by standing high on her toes as you pat her, and making little sous-sus on her front paws; a third by grand Petersburg-style tail wavings; a fourth, if you are down close enough, by rising on her hind paws, resting her front ones weightlessly on you, raising her wide ballerina eyes to yours, and then—

delicate as a single finger pirouette—giving the tip of your nose a tender nip.

Only Denby's eye, only Denby's sweetness of wit, his deep understanding of the collusion of art and nature could have produced this incomparable fun. He left us a little too soon for friendship's sake. Still, his timing told us what we had known and feared to admit—that an era was really over. He had said his farewell years before, in the last poem in *Mediterranean Cities* (incidentally one of the few poems of his with a reference to dance):

> For with regret I leave the lovely world men made
> Despite their bad character, their art is mild

The seasons roll on. The music starts, the dancers appear on the vast stage and begin to dance, "creating the impetus moment by moment." And, moment by moment, it is as if nothing had changed since the days when we would see him there, gazing pensively out at what he helped to establish and would not have abandoned without cause.

April 13, 1987

Merce Cunningham (1919–2009)

GROWING UP in Centralia, Washington, Merce Cunningham learned to love the natural world. However, as one of three brothers born to a family whose other men went into law or business, Cunningham referred to himself as a "changeling" (and made a challenging early solo for himself with that title). His boyhood performances in a small company with former vaudevillian Maude Barrett, whose programs were a mix of tap, ballroom, and eccentric dancing, gave the young Merce a joy in performing that he retained for the rest of his life. Several years later, as a student at the Cornish School, in Seattle, his first interest was in acting; however, while at Cornish, he shifted his focus to dance. After leaving the school, he performed for six years (1939 to 1945) as a soloist with Martha Graham's company, where his gift for dramatic suggestion and his spectacular jump can be glimpsed in the fire-and-brimstone solo for the Preacher of *Appalachian Spring*, which Cunningham choreographed at Graham's behest. He then founded his own company, in 1953, with the composer John Cage, his partner in art and life. Soon, Cunningham adopted "chance procedures," often painstakingly employed, to structure his dances, as Cage used them to structure sound.

The entire Cunningham–Cage enterprise required tremendous discipline in every way, which may help to account for Cunningham's paean to technique, below, as the dancer's route to spiritual release and to the re-creation of an edenic naturalness. Written around the time he was studying and teaching at the School of American Ballet, the essay suggests the opposite of his popular legacy as a pillar of the avant-garde. A sentence such as the following one, in which Cunningham—the changeling and consummate jumper—seems to reach beyond his personal gifts for an enduring ideal, is as good a definition of classicism in the art of dancing as one can find anywhere and could as well have been authored by George Balanchine or Fred Astaire: "To walk magnificently and thereby evoke the spirit of a god seems surpassingly more marvelous than to leap and squirm in the air in some incredible fashion, and leave only the image of oneself."

The Function of a Technique for Dance

SINCE he works with the body—the strongest and, at the same instant, the most fragile of instruments—the necessity to organize and understand its way of moving is of great urgency for the dancer.

Technique is the disciplining of one's energies through physical action in order to free that energy at any desired instant in its highest possible physical and spiritual form. For the disciplined energy of a dancer is the life-energy magnified and focused for whatever brief fraction of time it lasts.

In other words, the technical equipment of a dancer is only a means, a way to the spirit. The muscles used in exercises every day are validly used only if it is understood that they lead the way, sustain the action. But it is upon the length and breadth and span of a body sustained in muscular action (and *sustaining* immobility is an action) that dance evokes its image.

The most essential thing in dance discipline is devotion, the steadfast and willing devotion to the labor that makes the classwork, not a gymnastic hour and a half, or at the lowest level, a daily drudgery, but a devotion that allows the classroom discipline to be moments of dancing too. And not in any sense the feeling that each class gives an eager opportunity for willful and rhapsodic self-expression, but that each class allows in itself, and furthers the dancer towards, the synthesis of the physical and spiritual energies.

The final and wished-for transparency of the body as an instrument and as a channel to the source of energy becomes possible under the discipline the dancer sets for himself—the rigid limitations he works within, in order to arrive at freedom.

An art process is not essentially a natural process; it is an invented one. It can take actions of organization from the way nature functions, but essentially man invents the process. And from or for that process he derives a discipline to make and keep the process functioning. That

discipline too is not a natural process. The daily discipline, the continued keeping of the elasticity of the muscles, the continued control of
the mind over the body's actions, the constant hoped-for flow of the
spirit into physical movement, both new and renewed, is not a natural
way. It is unnatural in its demands on all the sources of energy. But
the final synthesis can be a natural result, natural in the sense that
the mind, body and spirit function as one. The technical aim is not
to do a few or many things spectacularly, but to do whatever is done
well, whether a smaller or greater amount of actual physical skill is
required, and approaching as a goal, the flawless. To walk magnificently and thereby evoke the spirit of a god seems surpassingly more
marvelous than to leap and squirm in the air in some incredible fashion, and leave only the image of oneself. And for that very reason, the
dancer strives for complete and tempered body-skill, for complete
identification with the movement in as devastatingly impersonal a
fashion as possible. Not to show off, but to show; not to exhibit, but
to transmit the tenderness of the human spirit through the disciplined
action of a human body.

The dancer spends his life learning, because he finds the process of
dance to be, like life, continually in process. That is, the effort of controlling the body is not learned and then ignored as something safely
learned, but must and does go on, as breathing does, renewing daily
the old experiences, and daily finding new ones. Each new movement
experience, engendered by a previous one, or an initial impress of
the action of the body upon time, must be discovered, felt and made
meaningful to its fullest in order to enrich the dance memory.

The possibilities of movement are enormous and limitless, obviously, but the understanding of organization of movement is the high
point of the dancer's craft. If the spine is taken as the center of radius,
much as the animal makes it his physical conscience, then the action
proceeds from that center outwards, and also can reverse the process
and proceed from outward back to the center. The legs and arms are
only a revelation of the back, the spine's extensions. Sitting, standing,
extending a leg or arm, or leaping through air, one is conscious that
it is to and from the spine that the appendages relate and that they
manifest themselves only so far as the spine manifests itself. Speed,
for instance, is not a case of the feet or arms twiddling at some fantas-

tic tempo, but speed comes from the diligence with which the spine allows the legs and arms to go. At the same time, the spine can allow rapid action in the legs and feet, and by the control centered in it, allow serenity in the arms—seemingly still and suspended in the air. The reverse too is possible.

The spine, moreover, acts not just as a source for the arms and legs, but itself can coil and explode like a spring, can grow taut or loose, can turn on its own axis or project into space directions. It is interesting, and even extraordinary, to see the improvised physical reaction to most of the music of the nineteenth century, and then that to the folk form we know as jazz. The first is usually immediately apparent in the arms and legs, the second happens in the torso, or there is a definite visual indication that the movement impetus, however small or large in circumference, starts from an action in the torso. It is not really extraordinary, because of what lies at the root, but it is interesting to see.

Certainly everybody including dancers can leap, sit down and get up again, but the dancer makes it apparent that the going into the air is what establishes the relationship to the air, the process of sitting down, not the position upon being down, is what gives the iridescent and life-quality to dancing.

The technical equipment for a dancer involves many things. There must be an understanding of the correct vertical position of the body, and how it is obtained and held. This involves the problem of balance of the body, and the sustaining of one part against another part. If one uses the torso as the center of balance and as the vertical axis at all times, then the question of balance is always related to that central part, the arms and legs balancing each other on either side and in various ways, and moving against each other. If one uses the torso as the moving force itself, allowing the spine to be the motivating force in a visual shift of balance, the problem is to sense how far the shift of balance can go in any direction and in any time arrangement, and then move instantaneously towards any other direction and in other time arrangements, without having to break the flow of movement by a catching of the weight whether by an actual shift of weight, or a break in time, or other means. The dynamics of the torso are thus sustained and distilled, and not lost in moving from one direction to another.

Paul Weiss says in *Nature and Man*:

> The will is employed to discipline the body by making it the locus of techniques—means for acting well habitually so as to reach objectives mentally envisaged. There is little pleasure in setting about to master a technique. One must first concentrate on its different component movements and steps. Then one must firmly relate them by going over them in sequence, again and again. But there are compensations. While the technique is being willingly mastered, the body and the mind are in accord, for a willing mastery of a technique requires that one keep in mind what one is doing and keep one's body from disturbing the intent of the mind. And so far as nothing arises which provokes the mind or body to work in opposition to the acquired technique, the technique promises a fairly enduring resolution of the conflict of mind and body. Though techniques enable a mind and body to work together for a considerable time, they tend to force the one or the other into a groove. The more a technique is mastered, the greater the risk that one will be too inflexible to overcome those oppositions between the mind and the body which are inevitable when the differently structured mind and body confront a novel situation.

One of the things that Western dance, and principally here in America, has not explored in any formal or technical sense, is the disciplined use of the face. The place we know of primarily that has made a continuous disciplined use of the face for definite expressive purpose—that is, a particular facial image for wrath, another for the hero, etc.—is the Hindu classical dance. But here in the United States where there has been an extraordinary amount of technical exploration into kinds of expressive movement, there has been little or no formal cognizance taken of the face. Every other part of the body has been subjected to many kinds of motion, the face left to its own devices.

The element that underlies both music and dance is time, which, when present in component parts, is rhythm. As an element coordinating the two arts, it is more useful when the phrase and parts longer than the phrase are considered, rather than the small particularities of accent and even of individual quantity. The concentration on the minutiae of rhythm in the music-dance relationship leads to the "boom-with-boom" device, giving nothing to either and robbing both of freedom. Working, however, from the phrase leads to a related independence, or to an interdependence of the two time arts. Accents, even and uneven beats, then appear, if they do, where the music continuity or the dance continuity allows them to. (That is, an accent in the music is an incident in the music continuity which does not necessarily appear in the dance, and vice versa.)

In coordinating dance and music the one should not be submerged into the other, as that would tend to make one dependent upon the other, and not independent as they naturally are. The dance and music can be brought together by time, by a particular rhythmic structure of time involving phrases, which indicate the meeting points convenient for use, thereby giving to each a freedom to expressively play with and against a common structural idea.

Plato, in the *Timaeus*, says, "Time is the moving image of eternity." Time, the very essence of our daily lives, can give to dancing one of the qualities that make it, at its most beautiful, a moving image of life at its highest.

1951

NANCY DALVA (1950–)

NANCY DALVA is a writer, interviewer, and documentary filmmaker in New York City. She has been a Critic Fellow of the Eugene O'Neill Theater Center and the American Dance Festival and a panelist and grantee of the National Endowment for the Arts. Her broadcasts have been heard on National Public Radio, WNYC-FM, and the British Broadcasting Corporation. Her writing has appeared in publications including *The New Yorker*, *The Brooklyn Rail*, *The Atlantic Monthly*, *Texas Monthly*, *artforum*, *The New York Times*, and *The New York Observer*, and she is the senior writer for *2wice* and *Dance Ink* magazines. She currently serves as the Merce Cunningham Trust Scholar in Residence, reflecting her lifelong passion for his art.

Letter from Manhattan

A RT WORKS change over time—not because they alter, but because we do. This is most clear with paintings, which—with the exception of time-based art made with materials that decay and morph—stay the same. You go to a museum to visit a beloved painting, and lo! You see something unexpected, you understand the scene differently, and it's not because the painting has changed. You have. With music you can encounter this experience with a recording—or when you yourself play a piece of music over time, hearing and bringing out different elements. In the theater, you can have this relationship with a text. At the movies, or in the sculpture garden, you're in the same situation. But with dance! You have the dance, and you have the people in it at any given moment, and then you have, even with the same people, their own variability from performance to performance.

And yet. Somehow, over time, seeing the same work with successive generations of dancers, its architecture becomes clear to you, and its tone, its character, its world. A platonic notion of the work separate from its passing inhabitants takes up residence. You think you know it, and indeed you do have a sense of it apart from any idiosyncrasies of individual interpretation. But still, you can go to the theater one night after decades of seeing it, and can find yourself not so much seeing as understanding in a whole new way. Yet this metamorphosis can also happen quickly, with the same work with the same cast in the same week: from one night to the next, something changes. The dance is the same, but you are not.

Another spring. March, 2011. City Center, The Paul Taylor Dance Company. *Esplanade.* Paul Taylor is himself in the house (in his usual back row seat), and so, on opening night, are many of his former dancers. (Carolyn Adams can be seen in the original *Esplanade* on You-Tube, enchanting in her skittering yet gracious flurry of small gestures and quick steps, and here she is in the audience. David Grenke, with the company from 1989–96, sits down next to me.) The place is a time machine. There they are all around me, and there they are, in my mind's eye, still on stage, dancing beneath the current company. Casts in palimpsest, but the dance stays young. It's still the harbinger of spring.

Two things stay with me in the weeks that follow the season. First, the surprise of the newly revived *Orbs*, which dates from 1966, especially the surprise of the section called "Spring." It is so clearly a reading of Graham's *Appalachian Spring*, so clear a reminder of where Paul Taylor came from—he's the son of Martha. As was of course Merce Cunningham, his older sibling, if you will, on that branch of modern dance's family tree. Paul came after Merce in the Graham company, and went on to dance with Cunningham's troupe in 1953–4. Now, half a century and more later, Taylor's company is presenting a Graham parody of sorts—or at any rate a commentary. So, too, is the Merce Cunningham Dance Company, later that month, in their newly revived version of *Antic Meet*, which Cunningham made in 1958.

Back then, Merce wore a many-armed sweater he himself sewed together from pieces knit by his then-apprentice Valda Setterfield, pulling it up over his head like some kind of bizarre Thurberesque hat. Out danced four women in dresses fashioned from actual parachutes, making Grahamesque gestures of heel-of-hand-to-forehead, tilting forward in a Graham-y way, with a Graham-y flexed foot extending behind. What have we? Odd vestments, strange hat, a small tribe of female followers? *Antic Meet* is a series of references to various dance styles—and this passage is clearly a recension of sorts of Merce's preacher role in *Appalachian Spring*. He's a very reluctant Revivalist, trying to escape his little flock.

What's going on now, here, in *Orbs* in the "Spring" section? There is a wedding scene, repeated twice. The first time, the groom refuses to kiss his blonde dumpling of a bride at the altar, and kisses the preacher instead. Then the bride's mother does an angsty little Graham number downstage to our left. (The preacher and the groom essentially elope.) Then there is a second wedding. This time the groom kisses the bride, and they seem set on a course of connubial bliss. There you have it: subtext and text. What the groom desired and what was expected of him. Let us remember that Martha danced the bride in *Appalachian Spring*, and Erick Hawkins—whom she was to marry—was her Husbandman, and Merce Cunningham was the preacher. So, Taylor is slyly suggesting, Erick was more interested in Merce than in Martha. This, at least, Martha's boys had in common: a wicked sense of humor.

The second thing that stayed with me from the Taylor season was my new, wholly unwelcome reading of the central, slow section of *Esplanade*, the one that has everyone crawling around in a pool of light. One recurrent trope in this movement (you find it again in Taylor's *Dust*) is not seeing, but "unseeing." A dancer—originally Bettie de Jong, tall, slim, the only woman in trousers—walks across the stage. Another smaller woman—a girl, really—repeatedly scurries around her to fling herself down at her feet, as if to stop her.

I've seen this many ways before, but never the way I saw it this year: I saw the tall figure walking towards the wings slowly, inexorably, in measured pace, with the other trying so very hard to stop her, hurling herself in her path to keep her from leaving. Not to get her attention, as I'd seen it before—like a child with a parent—but to stop her. From dying. From leaving forever. I'll never see it any way again, and I doubt I'll ever see it without crying, as I did that night. But if you spent the spring, as I did, watching someone progress into the wings, into death, into beyond what can be seen, what else could it mean, and what else can it mean, next year, or the year after that? *Don't leave me*, I thought.

And thought it again, when Paul Taylor came out, frailer than last year, still so handsome, still so present. Don't leave me. (Merce left.) You stay, please.

April, Baryshnikov Arts Center, Eiko and Koma's *Naked: An Installation*. There they are, bony, Butoh-white, slender to the point of emaciation, curled in a bed of black feathers and leaves, in a dim stuffy room curtained in scorched, feather-encrusted muslin. The only light is from above, and from above water drips. They move incrementally, so slowly you can look away and look back and think about something else and not miss a thing, hour after hour. You can come, you can go, you can come back; you can move to a different vantage point. No right way to experience, no wrong way to experience. You might see what I saw: creatures left for eagles to eat for dinner later, dropped into their nest to keep for a midnight feast. Refugees from disaster, manmade or natural. (It happened to be just at the time of the tsunami in Japan, though the piece was made earlier, and had been shown at the Walker Art Center, in Minneapolis.) That couple in Pompeii, buried alive by lava, their infant cradled between them.

Later in the week, I went back. I took my husband. We went into the room separately—I sat on a bench near the left wall, he stood in back, at the right. Again I watched, and saw strangeness. And then my husband came and sat beside me and I saw sameness. As my body relaxed into his, I saw Eiko and Koma sleeping, apart, yet together, touching from time to time as if in reassurance, and echoing each other's shapes. In separate dreams, in separate hollows of pillows. Long married themselves, they sleep, they breathe. Apart, together, warm, paralyzed by dreams, waking enough to stir, birds of a feather in their feather marriage bed, the water ticking down, marking time.

June 3, 2011

Agnes de Mille (1905–1993)

THE WORD for Agnes dc Mille is "indefatigable"—unless you prefer "driven." She certainly was talented—as dancer (though neither classical nor strictly modern), as choreographer, and, perhaps most of all, as writer.

She wasn't pretty, she was informed when young, but she was smart. And she was connected: her father, William de Mille, was a successful playwright, screenwriter, and movie director; her uncle was the redoubtable Cecil B. DeMille (note the grander spelling); her mother was the daughter of the world-famous radical economist Henry George and an impassioned lifelong advocate of his ideas. Agnes was born in New York but raised in Los Angeles, attending the Hollywood School for Girls and then UCLA as an English major. Believing that she couldn't be an actress because she wasn't pretty enough, she determined to be a dancer, despite family discouragement. She persevered—she *always* persevered—and started presenting herself in little dance sketches that she created for herself.

In London she began to make her way, choreographing Cole Porter's *Nymph Errant*, appearing in the premiere of Antony Tudor's *Dark Elegies*, growing close to Tudor himself and Frederick Ashton while they all slaved away for Marie ("Mim") Rambert's school and company. (This part of her life is wonderfully told in her third memoir, *Speak to Me, Dance with Me*.) Back home, having failed to satisfy her Uncle Cecil with her work on his film of *Cleopatra*, she failed to satisfy herself with her work on the Norma Shearer–Leslie Howard *Romeo and Juliet*. Her first substantial success came in 1942 with the ballet *Rodeo* (to an Aaron Copland score) for the Ballet Russe de Monte Carlo—a folksy, barn-dancey piece of Americana that is still in the repertory. *Rodeo* led to *Oklahoma!*—and theater history.

Now she was famous, and later musicals confirmed her fame: *One Touch of Venus, Carousel, Brigadoon, Gentlemen Prefer Blondes*. But her string of hits ran out, and of the many ballets that followed *Rodeo*, only the comic *Three Virgins and a Devil* and *Fall River Legend* (Lizzie Borden) have lasted. She was central, however, to the early Ballet Theatre. And she went on and on (of course), surviving even a severe stroke that incapacitated her for a long time. She lectured, she coached, but most important, she wrote: a brilliant narrator, a superb portraitist, a total charmer. And she was happily married, and happy as a mother. No doubt she would have liked to be remembered first and foremost as a dancer and choreographer, but it seems likely that her most lasting contribution will prove to be the magnificent legacy of her many books.

La Argentina (1890–1936)

I MANAGED TO procure a seat at the top of Carnegie and saw a lone woman take the stage accompanied by a single female pianist and dance a whole evening. It was a gallant spectacle. And ordinary people, three thousand of them, laughed and clapped and sighed with delight.

Every detail of her program was effective. Callot had done her clothes. The program was beautifully planned and professional all the way. After the experimental, unevenly attended local entertainments, after the tarnished shabbiness of my recent adventures, this was a great comfort to see. It could happen. Beautiful, magnetic and superbly dressed, she danced as a star is supposed to dance, with fervor and excitement. And, oh, the sound of her castanets and the swing of her body! She released us. She carried us through the rhythms and they were enough. The gestures were enough. There was no part of us pent up, unexpressed to be taken home to ferment. Dancing was an honorable profession when it worked, which it so very seldom did. It was worth a lifetime of pain and sacrifice. In the middle of the third dance as I saw and heard the rhythms resolving and changing and merging so satisfactorily, so rich, so altogether lovely, I felt the blood rush back to my breast. How many young artists the world over took heart of grace from this single enchanting figure? She was a sign and a vindication.

What made her supreme?

First, her sense of rhythm, which has never been approached, not only in the castanets, but in the feet and arms and swinging skirts and the relation of all to the music. Second, in her classic, her architectural sense of composition. (Curiously Argentina could not compose for a group—something most choreographers find easier.) But above all, it was the utter womanliness of her presence. Behind her towered a tradition older than ballet dancing and she was schooled in the last etiquette of the tradition. Behind her loomed generation on generation of anonymous lovely women who had lived out their lives in obscurity and died decently and left no trace except in the innuendo of a fan or the turn of a flounce. She was what the northern European has always dreamed about, the Romantic, the Southern, the distant anonymous lady. She never for one moment seemed like a professional. She had the magic of great evocation and summoned up brilliant women, darling and unregenerate. There never was such a parade of ladies. When she lifted an arm, one felt like standing in recognition. And oh—her smile—the flashing of her dazzling teeth, sudden, free and audacious! She was utterly and completely bewitching, as easy as gardens, or wasted time, or skies. And this is a rare quality these days. Female dancers try too hard—their charm has all run to their tendons.

Bear in mind she came to town at a period when women were flattening their bosoms, shaving their heads, sheathing their trunks in tubes to reveal only the insect legs of the overmuscled athlete and you can imagine the effect of those perfumed skirts and antique veils. But the mystery and suavity of her technique, the lordliness of her creations you cannot imagine—and although sound film had been perfected before she dropped dead of a heart attack in 1936, not one foot of film was ever exposed of her dancing. The Rose of Spain! The irreplaceable lovely lady!

I was profoundly impressed and also no little disturbed by her. Here was lyric movement, nondramatic, without story or particularized character, in unbroken flowing design. The design moved the audience, as the design in music moves and compels, the phrasing, the choice and arrangement of gesture. The grave limitations of my own composition became by contrast shockingly apparent. I could not compose thirty-two bars of continuous dance without using character acting to give it interest. Argentina's creations were as intricately formed as a sonnet. All were delightful and several overwhelming. And although, I noted smugly, she was unbearably coy in her comedy, she was nevertheless a master in handling movement, and movement is the stuff of great communication. "We are interested in you," my theater friends used to say, "because you are more than a dancer. You are an actress." But I knew one could not be more than a dancer— being an actress was less. Of the two media of expression, except in the hands of the very great, dancing is the higher, and more evocative and powerful. I do not think this point can be argued. When Argentina crossed the stage, tears filled my eyes.

1952

Rhythm in My Blood

THE ENDING of *Tally-Ho*, or the lack of it, haunted me then as it still does; I intend one day to put it right.

I find it hard to make up my mind about endings; beginnings are, for me, somehow easier come by, as they are for everybody. Fokine, I believe, began frequently at the end and worked backward. Doris Humphrey always composes the end long before she gets to it, about the middle of the work or shortly thereafter. An ending has to be a summing up, the logical total of all that precedes, the final statement; in other words, the point of view. And this was seemingly so difficult for me to achieve I thought it wise to pause at this moment and consider why. And so I set about reviewing my work, its characteristics, patterns and methods, as another choreographer might.

Every worker recognizes his own devices. I can name mine easily. I cannot always control them, but I can name them: I have an affinity for diagonal movements on the stage, with figures entering at one corner and leaving at the opposite, and unless I watch myself, this pattern recurs tiresomely. Why in one corner and out the other? I am not such a fool that I don't recognize the tendency, nor so starved for invention that I cannot think of other geometric directions. But this particular arrangement moves me and releases ideas. Could it be because the first fine choreographic design I ever saw was the *Sylphides* mazurka danced by Lydia Sokolova with the Diaghilev ballet? And when I think of her great leap and the lines of still and waiting women leaning in a kind of architectural wonder for the next cross flight, I understand. That was the path of the first comet and it blazed a mark on my brain. That track spells ecstasy. But behind this reason, there must be more.

I use a still figure, usually female, waiting on the stage, side or center, with modifying groups revolving about, always somehow suggesting the passing of time and life experience. Why does the woman waiting seem to me so emotionally pregnant? One woman standing alone on the stage while people pass until a man enters upstage behind her. Why upstage and why always behind and why the long wait? I cannot be sure, but I remember waiting for years, seemingly, shut away in my mother's garden. My father was absent most of that time and I longed for him to come home to release me from the spell. Possibly the answer is somewhere here.

Why is my use of circles, open or closed, a constant? The avoidance of symmetrical design, with the exception of the circle, my acute difficulty with all symmetrical design, even including square-dance pattern, which one might think was my native language? My repeated use of three female figures, a trilogy which because of plurality takes on symbolic force? And the falling patterns—the falling to earth, the swooning back, the resurrection, the running away always to return to a focal point—seem also to be insistent; and more important, more gross and unbearable, the breaking of all lyric line with a joke, as though I could not trust emotional development but must escape with a wisecrack.

It must be obvious even to people not familiar with dancing that these relations are individual, that they are to some degree sexual, and that they reflect a special personality pattern. I speak of my own work because I have a right to, but these observations apply to everyone. Consider, for instance, some of the recurring idioms of Balanchine: the single male figure embroiled with two to six females, one of whom either blinds or strangles him; the entanglement of either male or female bodies in endless ropes or chains (the lines are seldom made up of both men and women); the repetitive use of the grand reverence, or imperial court bow, as part of the texture of movement; the immaculate discipline of traditional gesture; the metrical, machine-like arrangement of school positions as unadorned as the use of unmodified scales in a musical composition; the insistence on two-dimensional symmetrical design; the superb but classic relation to music. One might build an interesting picture of Balanchine, the man, from these points of style. They are as natural to him as his sniff.

The characteristics of Jerome Robbins are very different. There is above all his free-limbed and virile use of the body, a complete spontaneous release as in sports, an exuberance, a total employment of all energies. Whether the gesture is gay or anguished, all resources are put into play and the strength and vigor of the movement communicates with the gusto of an athlete's. This in part may explain his enormous popularity with all audiences. The gesture is manly, it is keen and bold, and it is complete. Briefly, it is exhilarating, and it brings to the spirit the satisfaction that a yawn or a stretch brings to the muscles. Women choreographers are less released, their movement often blocked or broken, or modified by reticences, not shyness of content but carefulness in physical effort. The difference is equivalent to that between a man and a woman throwing or jumping. Her gesture may be exact and serviceable; his will be total. Robbins enhances this quality by quoting literally from acrobatics and stunts.

His skill in rhythmic invention is the greatest in the business, according to Trude Rittmann, who has worked with all of us. Robbins is besot by rhythm, visual and bodily rhythms as well as auditory, and when he gets hold of a gesture he continues inventing out of the core of the matter until he has built an entire design and must wait for the composer to catch up. His rhythms will then work in counterpoint to the musical pattern. It is thought that if he had turned his attention to music, he might have been a first-class composer. Whereas Balanchine's rhythmic sense is spatial and linked to the music, Robbins's is independent. I, on the other hand, am totally derivative and lean and grow on melody. I cannot move without melody. May there not here be revealed a subtle sexual distinction? The men work free and on their own; the woman must wait for the lead.

But Robbins's most easily recognized trait is, praise heaven, his humor. In its grossest aspects, it takes the form of straight gags—very good ones, but bald and outrageous. In its more sophisticated manifestations, he introduces surprising and impertinent conclusions into his pattern, deliberately leading one on to expect a certain resolution and then insolently offering another, untraditional and slightly rude, though always logical because he is never foolish. He jokes with rhythms, with space, with relations of bodies, with light, with silence, with sound. These are all elements of style.

The grosser emotional fixtures of theme and content are plainly manifest—fixtures such as, in the case of Robbins, a preoccupation with childhood and games, with the bewilderment of growing up, with the anguish of choice. The unexpected, the joke, in this field seems to turn back on the choreographer and sit hard; each love story splits into three or more people; each romance spells destruction or transience; all repeats over and over. There is no resolution. In short, life turns out not to be a joke.

For my part, I seem to be obsessed by an almost Henry Jamesian inability for hero and heroine to come together happily, and by that other bedeviling theme, the woman as hunter. These are easily read. But the impregnation of abstract pattern with personality adjustments is, I find, far more subtle and more interesting. A great deal has been written about the kinesthetic transference between audience and dancer in the actual muscular technique; the field of spatial aesthetics remains, however, almost unexplored.

We know much about emotional symbols. They have a history and a science, iconography. Those used by the medieval and Renaissance painters were understood by the scholars and artists of the time—but, more wonderful, they mean to us today spontaneously just what they meant then; they seem to be permanent. We dream, Jung tells us, in the terms and symbols of classic mythology. Moreover, primitives shut away from classic learning dream in the same terms. Is it not also likely, then, that certain space relations, rhythms and stresses have psychological significance, that some of these patterns are universal and the key to emotional response, that their deviations and modifications can be meaningful to the artist in terms of his own life experience and that these overtones are grasped by the spectator without conscious analysis?

Doctors are aware of this and utilize the knowledge in diagnosis. The significance of children's manipulation of space in writing and drawing is carefully studied, and the insane are observed for their relation to and use of walls, floor, doorways, heights, and so forth.

Obviously these matters are basic to our well-being as land and air [are to] animals. And as plants will turn to sunlight or rocks or moisture according to their nature, so we bend toward or escape from spatial arrangements according to our emotional needs. In the diseased mind, the reactions are overwhelmingly overt. But look around any restaurant and see how few sane people will sit at a center table unless the sides are filled up. Yet formerly the king always dined dead center and many times in public.

The individual as a personality, then, has his own code in space and rhythm. It is evolved from his life history and from his race memory or, as Jung calls it, the collective unconscious. It is just the manipulation of these suggestions through time-space that is the material of choreography.

Take, for example, a simple daily gesture like walking forward and shaking hands. There are in this, first, the use of a separate limb common to most vertebrates, the upright position of the spine and head characteristic of man, the instinctively recognized expression of friendliness shared by all species as opposed to the instinctive expressions of fear and distrust. With animals, when approaching a friend, the hair lies flat, the ears are relaxed though alert, and all enlargements and ferocious distentions subside; breathing is normal. So with man. Heart, pulse and lungs are easy, the eyes alert but neither distended to see danger nor contracted to pinpoint a target; the mouth is closed or smiling because no unusual demands will be made on hearing (to hear extraordinarily in times of acute danger, the mouth is opened and breathing suspends). And since no unusual effort will be necessary, the muscles neither brace nor tremble. The sum total of all this will be spelled out in the rhythm and position of the reaching hand.

But let there occur the slightest rebuff and see now what happens; hackles rise, hair bristles, lips curl to bare incisors, hearts pound, lungs fill, and on the instant all muscles prepare for attack. In ordinary intercourse, this naturally is not visible on full scale. But it needs only the slight widening of the pupil or nostril, the barest flicker of fingertip, to give the signal; the enemy has been recognized and addressed. Further subtle and meaningful modifications take over when the passage alters by the tension of a specific situation—when, for instance, someone who is often frightened of encounter meets a friend, or one who is never frightened meets someone not to be trusted, or two trusting friends meet under dreadful conditions, and so ad infinitum. Within each of these circumstances the body becomes a totally different chemical organization and yet retains the stamp of its own life habits. (A primary school teacher told me that she knew that children were beginning to trust her when they touched her with the palms of their hands; at first they only poked. It is only at moments of intimacy, possession or pity that an adult will touch with his palms.)

It is the actor's art to mimic exactly with a full awareness of all the overtones and significances. The dancer, on the other hand, explodes the gesture to its components and reassembles them into a symbol that has connotations of what lies around and behind the fact, while the implications of rhythm and spatial design add further comment. Of course the choreographer is no more troubled by all this than is the businessman by the enormous anthropological heritage he puts into play every time he casually tips his hat.

Coleridge says of portraiture: "A good artist must imitate that which is within the thing, that which is active through form and figure, and discourses to us by symbols . . . the universal in the individual or the individuality itself—the glance and the exponent of the indwelling power. . . . Hence a good portrait is the abstract of the personal; it is not the likeness for actual comparison, but for recollection." Every gesture is a portrait. Behind it lie the histories of the race and the individual as well as the comment of the artist.

When I, as an artist, am moved, I must respond in my own instinctive way; and because I am a choreographer, I respond through my instinctive gestures. I may come into the pattern with conviction and the excitement of fresh experience, but this must also reflect a personality habit. It cannot be otherwise. Somehow, as in the grooves in a gramophone record, the cutting edge of my emotion follows a track played deep into the subconscious.

There is a further personal identification in choreography because most choreographers compose on their own bodies. Certain recurring steps can be explained simply by the fact that the choreographer performs these steps well and has a tendency to use them when demonstrating. Martha Graham has a kick and a particular skip that have stood her in good stead for twenty years. The explanation is simply that her left leg kicks straight up in a split, 180 degrees—a very spectacular feat. The right does not; hence the single-legged pattern.

(It has been very interesting to observe over the years that Graham pupils who began by imitating her mannerisms have gradually eliminated the personal idiosyncrasies and maintained the great style unblemished. In *Diversion of Angels* and *Canticle for Innocent Comedians*, Graham's gesture has been purified of all subjective tricks and stands in the keeping of her disciples as abstract as the ballet code. It is overwhelmingly beautiful.) I am right-legged and right-footed, and most of the sustaining and balancing work in my choreography is done on the left leg; many of my dancers have complained bitterly. A dancer with short legs jumps in one manner, whereas a dancer with longer ones performs the same jump in quite another. So with composing. And identical pattern problems take on the modification of the composer's physique as well as his character adjustment, for it is always the choreographer who has to start the moving, and naturally he does it his way. If there were no instrument on which a song writer could work except his own voice, unquestionably his vocal restrictions would shape the melodic line.

The choreographer is also influenced by his performers. If I were to work, let us say, with a soloist whose arms and back were the strongest in the dance world and whose phrasing of legato lifts the most beautiful, but whose footwork, on the other hand, and allegro were weaker, quite obviously my composing style would adjust to his needs. Were I to compose with a man of enormous elevation and brilliant *batterie* but less dramatic force, my approach would then be necessarily different. And it must be noted that one works with the dancers at hand. One cannot summon from outer space a dream body capable of anything—or even exactly what one wishes. In the matter of one's own body one has obviously even less choice and must make do.

Furthermore, all artists, including choreographers, are influenced by their peers as by their antecedents. This is the way of organic development. Late Beethoven and early Schubert, for instance, are almost indistinguishable; while Brahms took certain themes, note for note, from Beethoven; and Shakespeare stole nearly all his plots—all the good ones certainly. Had they worked as contemporaries in the same studio, as do choreographers, with the same performers, the tie would have been closer yet. Furthermore, most choreographers, like the apprentice painters of the Renaissance, get their initial experience studying under the personal influence of a master, taking part in the actual creation of his works, and spending years—the formative years—under constant artistic domination. The wonder is that any individual expression develops at all.

But it does develop, and with it the deviations and mannerisms we call personal style. Usually the artist is unaware of the process, as he is unaware of his other spontaneous modes of expression. Few willingly believe the insistent repetition, the catch phrases, the special idioms we use in conversation. Who among us has recognized a first recording of his own voice? We prefer to think of ourselves in terms of universals shared by all mankind—by all the ways, in short, in which we resemble or possibly surpass others. Our neighbors, on the contrary, distinguish us by our oddities and crotchets, and it is just for this reason that a cartoon when effective strikes everyone but the subject as revealing.

If idiosyncrasies of expression constitute a key to others' understanding, they serve the artist in much the same way, as a means of self-revelation and a technique for reaching his emotional reservoir. They determine his work habits and of course the character of his expression. But whereas each worker will develop his own combination, his own formula, so to speak, he will have virtually nothing to do with its choosing and can use his critical faculties only to shape and correct. The emotional key, the kindling spark, lies beyond the reach of his mind deep in instinct. When we find these habitual patterns pleasing, we say the artist has developed style; when they appeal to our taste less, we say that he is repeating himself.

But the great repeated constantly. How do we, for instance, recognize Bach in any two measures of his music? Obviously because it sounds precisely like him and no one else. It is a question, I believe, of what is basically present and not how often the devices and tricks are employed. Indeed, if variety were all, one could compose with a slide rule. There is great style and lesser style, and style altogether to be condemned; but none of it has to do either with repetition or derivation.

It is difficult for the individual to evaluate his own strengths and characteristics, and the theater is strewn with lives ruined by unwarranted determinations to sing, or write, or act. No guarantee goes with desire, and there is unhappily just enough genuine talent neglected to confuse the issue. Nevertheless, granting a modicum of true ability, one must not be afraid to fail now and then. It all depends on the reason why.

One may, of course, fail because one has chosen the wrong kind of work.

One may fail because one has no discipline either in work or the handling of emotional problems.

One may fail because one wishes to fail—a hard tendency to detect, but a history of avoidable catastrophe indicates a need for medical help.

One may fail temporarily because of grief, harassment, or exhaustion and, in the theater, from lack of time.

And then one may fail in trying new and unknown ways of expression. A creative life without failure is unthinkable. All physical growth and emotional change involve discomfort and a good bit of highly unattractive transition. Consider any adolescent, for example, taken at face value and with no thought of what is to come.

This fear of defeat haunts the creative worker uncomfortably, and there are fat days when all of us long to be left alone. But the first moment we permit ourselves to feel safe, the first moment we save ourselves from exposure, we are in danger of retreating from the outposts. We can be quite sure that this particular job need not be done, for, in all probability, it will have been done before.

"One must risk one's career every six months," says Elia Kazan, "in order to stay alive and [be] effective in one's work."

But although work will never be safe, it may happily sometimes be easy and quick. Very frequently the best work is the easiest. But the rhapsodic release comes only infrequently and the professional must learn to compose at will—to employ aesthetic aphrodisiacs. For a young artist, this is perhaps the hardest task. Each person must learn his own path through the labyrinth of escape and idleness. Anne Lindbergh speaks of a technique of "acquiring grace": "Most people are aware of periods in their lives when they seem to be 'in grace' and other periods when they feel 'out of grace.' . . . In the first happy condition, one seems to carry all one's tasks before one lightly as if borne along on a great tide; and in the opposite state one can hardly tie a shoestring. It is true that a large part of life consists of tying the shoestring, whether one is in grace or not."

To translate this into terms of the working artist, the state of "grace," or inspiration, occurs when an idea is both clearly perceived and deeply felt, when circumstances do not block realization, and when technique waits ready and almost unconsciously available. The last is the controllable factor, a technique ready and available at the needed moment. Behind this lies a life's ordering.

For three weeks preceding any big job Jerome Robbins works himself into a lather of excitement on studies, all of which, he explains, may very well be discarded once the dancers are assembled, but without which he cannot begin. These preliminary exercises furnish him with momentum and conviction. They are a warming-up process. Hanya Holm, on the other hand, never prepares this way. She studies and thinks, but when she walks into the studio, no plan has been determined on. It is between her and the dancers and God, she says. But God, I have found, cannot be held to a schedule, and any kind of composition that involves a finishing time—and this is the essence of all theater—makes definite demands on inspiration. Inspiration has to be on tap as long as the components of design are living bodies paid by the hour.

But we may be grateful that very seldom are circumstances propitious and that the work fights through hard and slow. The moment one knows how, one begins to die a little. Living is a form of not being sure, of not knowing what next or how. And the artist before all others never entirely knows. He guesses. And he may be wrong. But then how does one know whom to befriend or, for that matter, to marry? One can't go through life on hands and knees. One leaps in the dark. For this reason creative technique reduces itself basically to a recognition and befriending of one's self. "Who am I?" the artist asks, and he devotes his entire career to answering.

There is one clue: what moves him is his. What amuses or frightens or pleases him becomes by virtue of his emotional participation a part of his personality and history; conversely what neither moves nor involves him, what brings him no joy, can be reckoned as spurious. An artist begins to go wrong exactly at the point where he begins to pretend. But it is difficult sometimes to accept the truth. He has to learn who he in fact is, not who he would like to be, nor even who it would be expedient or profitable to be.

He may think he cannot afford this risk, but it is equally evident he cannot afford hackneyed success. For this is no success. And everyone instantly recognizes what has happened. The breath of life has gone; the workshop has become a morgue.

The real failing, the killing off, is not in taking risks but in choosing some work beneath his capacities and in doing it in a slick and routine fashion purely for recompense. This hurts the whole field of work, dirties and dulls down the audience, and destroys the individual. In the disreputable suburbs of each art form flourish great fortunes made just this way. I do not for one moment wish to imply that first-class work does not also bring in money. God is good, and it frequently does. But let us be sure in our hearts, no first-class job was ever achieved without a good deal in view besides the check.

The folks who think only of money may cynically pretend they do not care, but their stomach ulcers and their alcoholism prove they do most dreadfully. It is not so much a matter of what work is done but how it is done. It is vital to everyone to know that work is necessary and done to the best of ability whether making soap operas or washing floors, and it is only when the dust is swept under the rug that the process of disintegration sets in.

Far better than succeeding regularly is a good tough falling-short of a challenge. All work—one's own and everyone else's—benefits from this effort, successful or not, just as all science benefits from each difficult experiment—even the ones that seem not directly to bring results.

Louis Horst said recently at a testimonial banquet tendered him by the dancers of New York that he wished to thank all the dedicated and devoted artists with whom he had had the privilege of achievement; and he wished also to thank those who had tried and failed, because without them, the great could not have gone so far.

It is not for the individual to demand a certificate of quality before starting. He cannot and he may not. He has to work on faith. And he must listen only to his conscience, which will be stern enough in truth. He must listen to no other voices. For to listen is to be lost—to listen to critic, or friend, or business interest. He can pray only that his tastes and passions will be common to many. But he must suit himself first, himself before everyone else. He must, in other words, marry the girl of his heart despite the family or he will bed down for life with a wench not of his choosing.

I know now how the *Frail Quarry* should end, as I know that this should be its rightful title, but it has taken a deal of living and shaking down to come to terms with my instincts. The ballet was essentially a wry piece and not at all the romantic comedy I had hoped. It had, however, an honorable enough life; poor maimed pretty little thing, it had six years of performing. But today it lies in limbo waiting for a great comedian and waiting for the finish that burns in my brain.

1956

Edwin Denby (1903–1983)

"Edwin Denby was born in Tientsin, China, in 1903. He received his early education in Europe, to which he returned after several years at Harvard. Since the early 1930s he has lived mostly in New York." This is the mini-bio that Denby approved late in life, since he shied away from personal publicity.

For further information, see Arlene Croce's essay on Denby on page 180 of this volume.

Flight of the Dancer

IF YOU travel all over the world and see every brilliant and flying dance that human beings do, you will maybe be surprised that it is only in our traditional classic ballet dancing that the dancer can leap through the air slowly. In other kinds of dancing there are leaps that thrill you by their impetuousness or accuracy; there are brilliant little ones, savage long ones, and powerful bouncing ones. But among all dance techniques only classic ballet has perfected leaps with that special slow-motion grace, that soaring rise and floating descent which looks weightless. It isn't that every ballet leap looks that way. Some are a tough thrust off the ground, some travel like a cat's, some quiver like a fish's, some scintillate like jig steps; but these ways of jumping you can find in other dancing too. The particular expression ballet technique has added to leaping is that of the dancer poised in mid-flight, as easy in the air as if she were suspended on wires. Describing the effect, people say one dancer took flight like a bird, another was not subject to the laws of gravity, and a third paused quietly in midair. And that is how it does look, when it happens.

To be honest, it doesn't happen very often. It is a way of leaping only a few rare dancers ever quite achieve. But it can be achieved. You can see it in the dancing of Alicia Markova, the English-born star of our present Ballet Theatre company; though no one else in this country—perhaps no one else in the world—can "fly" quite as perfectly as she does. No one else is so serenely calm with nothing underneath her. In *Pas de Quatre* she sits collectedly in the air, as if she were at a genteel tea party, a tea party where everyone naturally sat down in the air. There is something comic about it. That is because Miss Markova, who in the part of Giselle is a delicate tragic dancer, also has a keen sense of parody. *Pas de Quatre*, a parody ballet, represents the competition in virtuosity of four very great ballerinas at a command performance before Her Majesty Queen Victoria. (It actually happened in 1845.) In the ballet, Miss Markova takes the part of the greatest of the four, Marie Taglioni—Marie *pleine de grâce*, as she was called—who was a sallow little lady full of wrinkles, celebrated not only for her serene flight through the empty air, but also for the "decent voluptuousness" of her expression. Watching Miss Markova's performance, one feels that not even the eminently respectable British queen could have found any fault with the female modesty of such a look as hers. And that "refined" look is Miss Markova's joke on Victorian propriety, and a little too on the vanity of exhibiting technique just for its own sake.

Her expression is parody, but the leap itself is no parody of a leap. It is the real, incredibly difficult thing. Taglioni's leap couldn't have been any better. A leap is a whole story, with a beginning, a middle, and an end. If you want to try it, here are some of the simplest directions for this kind of soaring flight. It begins with a knee bend, knees turned out, feet turned out and heels pressed down, to get a surer grip and a smoother flow in the leg action. The bend goes down softly ("as if the body were being sucked to the floor") with a slight accelerando. The thrust upward, the stretch of the legs, is faster than the bend was.

The speed of the action must accelerate in a continuous gradation from the beginning of the bend into the final spring upward, so there will be no break in motion when the body leaves the ground. The leap may be jumped from two feet, hopped from one, or hopped from one with an extra swing in the other leg. But in any case the propulsive strain of the leap must be taken up by the muscles around the waist; the back must be straight and perpendicular, as if it had no part in the effort. Actually, the back muscles have to be kept under the strictest tension to keep the spine erect—the difficulty is to move the pelvis against the spine, instead of the other way around; and as the spine has no material support in the air, you can see that it's like pulling yourself up by your own bootstraps.

But that isn't all. The shoulders have to be held rigidly down by main force, so they won't bob upward in the jump. The arms and neck, the hands and the head have to look as comfortable and relaxed as if nothing were happening down below. Really there's as much going on down there as though the arms and head were picnicking on a volcano. Once in the air the legs may do all sorts of things, embellishments sometimes quite unconnected with what they did to spring up, or what they will have to do to land. And if there are such extra embellishments during the leap, there should be a definite pause in the air before they begin and after they are finished. No matter how little time there is for them, the ornaments must never be done precipitately.

But the most obvious test for the dancer comes in the descent from the air, in the recovery from the leap. She has to catch herself in a knee bend that begins with the speed she falls at, and progressively diminishes so evenly that you don't notice the transition from the air to the ground. This knee bend slows down as it deepens to what feels like a final rest, though it is only a fraction of a second long, so short a movie camera will miss it. This is the "divine moment" that makes her look as if she alighted like a feather. It doesn't happen when she lands, you see; it happens later. After that, straightening up from the bend must have the feeling of a new start; it is no part of the jump, it is a new breath, a preparation for the next thing she means to do.

In other words, the action of a leap increases in speed till the dancer leaves the ground. Then it diminishes till it reaches the leap's highest point up in the air. From then on it increases again till the feet hit the ground, when it must be slowed down by the knee bend to a rest; and all these changes must be continuously flowing. But most important of all is the highest point reached in the air. Here, if the dancer is to give the feeling of soaring, she must be completely still. She must express the calm of that still moment. Some dancers hold their breath. Nijinsky used to say he just stopped at that point. But however he does it, the dancer must project that hair's-breadth moment as a climax of repose. The dancer must not be thinking of either how she got up or how she is going to get down. She must find time just then to meditate.

When Nijinsky exited through the window in the *Spectre de la Rose* thirty years ago it was the greatest leap of the century. He seemed to the audience to float slowly up like a happy spirit. He seemed to radiate a power of mysterious assurance as calmly as the bloom of a summer rose does. Such enthusiastic comments sound like complete nonsense nowadays, when you go to the ballet and see a young man thumping about the stage self-consciously. But the comments were made by sensible people, and they are still convinced they were right. You begin to see what they mean when you realize that for Nijinsky in this ballet the leaps and the dance were all one single flowing line of movement, faster or slower, heavier or lighter, a way of moving that could rise up off the ground as easily as not, with no break and no effort. It isn't a question of how high he jumped one jump, but how smoothly he danced the whole ballet. You can see the same quality of technique today in Miss Markova's dancing.

In one respect, though, Nijinsky's way of leaping differed from hers: in his style the knee bend that starts the leap up and the other one that catches it coming down were often almost unnoticeable. This is a difference of appearance, of expression, but not really of technique. Nijinsky could make the transitions in speed I spoke of above with an exceptionally slight bending of the knees—a very unusual accomplishment indeed. When a dancer can do this it gives an expression of greater spontaneity to the leap; but several modern ballet dancers who try to do it aren't able really to land "light as a sylph or a snowflake," as Nijinsky could. The slight jolt when they land breaks the smooth flow and attracts more attention than the stillness of the climax in the air. And so the leap fails to concentrate on a soaring expression. The correct soaring leap is a technical trick any ballet dancer can learn in ten or fifteen years if he or she happens to be a genius. The point of learning it is that it enables the dancer to make a particular emotional effect, which enlarges the range of expression in dancing. The effect as we watch Markova's pure flight can only be described as supernatural, as a strangely beneficent magic. It is an approach to those mysterious hints of gentleness that occasionally absorb the human mind. It is a spiritual emotion; so Nijinsky's contemporaries described it, when he danced that way, and so did the Parisian poet Théophile Gautier when he saw first Taglioni and then Grisi take flight a hundred years ago.

It was a hundred years ago, most likely, that the trick was first perfected, together with that other trick so related to it in expression, the moment of airy repose on one toe. (Toe dancing, like leaping, has many kinds of expression, but the suggestion of weightless, poised near-flight is one of its most striking.) Toe dancing, like the technique of aerial flight, took a long series of dance geniuses to develop. The great Mlle Camargo two centuries ago, in Paris and in London, was already "dancing like a bird." But it seems likely that she fluttered enchantingly, rather than soared calm and slow. Certainly Camargo's costumes didn't allow some technical resources that are related to our technique of flight; they allowed no horizontal lift of the leg, no deep knee bends, no spring and stretch of foot in a heelless slipper.

In the next century, soaring of a different kind was being perfected. They literally hung the dancer on wires, and hoisted him or her through the air. Theaters had machinery called "flight paths," one of them fifty-nine feet long—quite a fine swoop it must have made. Maybe these mechanical effects gradually gave dancers the idea of trying to do the same thing without machinery. In an 1830 ballet, girls dressed as woodland spirits bent down the lower boughs of trees and let themselves be carried upward into the air on the rebound, which sounds like some wire effect. And in 1841 the great dancer Carlotta Grisi—Taglioni's young rival—opened in the ballet *Giselle*, in the second act of which there was one passage at least where her leaps were "amplified" by wiring. (She was supposed to be a ghost in it, and it was meant to look spooky.) In the little engraving of her in this part she certainly floats over her grave in a way no ballet star ever could; but probably the pose is only an imaginary invention by the artist. The same *Giselle* is still being danced today both in America and Europe, and, according to report, in Paris, in London, and in Leningrad, at least, this particular hundred-year-old wire trick is still being pulled.

October 1943

A Briefing in American Ballet

TOWARD the end of the war, during several seasons, ballet in the United States had a bright moment of eagerness and glory. A number of strikingly original choreographies appeared, and with them a burst of dance talent, new stars, a new atmosphere onstage,

and a lovely freshness in classic dancing. The choreographic innovations were ballets by George Balanchine in a dazzling new classicism; absorbing dance-pantomime-dramas of protracted anguish by
Antony Tudor; and lively American local-color comedies by Agnes de
Mille and Jerome Robbins. The two touring companies of the period,
Ballet Theatre and the Ballet Russe de Monte Carlo, were largely
composed of Americans, young, exact, strong, and charming. It was
their new dance impetus that triumphed. They won their first decisive
victory in 1942 in Tudor's *Pillar of Fire* at Ballet Theatre. Two years
later, the Monte Carlo, its style suddenly transformed by Balanchine,
presented his *Danses Concertantes*. From then on all over the country
the vitality of both companies delighted a great new ballet audience
night after night.

The difference between the two companies added to the pleasure.
Ballet Theatre's aesthetics, under its English choreographer Tudor,
tended to dramatic pantomime; the Monte Carlo's under Balanchine,
toward a classic dance grace. They had different repertories, though
both included nineteenth-century classics, Diaghilev, and prewar
pieces. Ballet Theatre was the larger, stronger but somewhat heavier
and harder company. Both companies had a few remarkable foreign-
born principals. And each had a very great artist as its star ballerina.
The Monte Carlo's was the witty warmhearted Alexandra Danilova.
Delighted by the fresh stimulus around her, she reached in 1944–45 a
new magnificence in strict classicism. Ballet Theatre's ballerina, on the
other hand, was the frail English classicist Alicia Markova; but Ballet
Theatre's tendency toward pantomime developed her latent genius as
an actress. For several seasons she showed us a shyly dazzling spirituality of expression, the secret force of which captivated alike war
workers, housewives, and intellectuals. Her *Giselle* became New York's
big ballet night.

Wartime, here as abroad, made everyone more eager for the civilized and peaceful excitement of ballet. More people could also afford
tickets. And in wartime the fact that no word was spoken on the stage
was in itself a relief. Suddenly the theaters all over the country were
packed whenever the two companies appeared. They sold 1,500,000
tickets a year. The new public fell in love with the stars, with the dancers, and with ballet in general. It liked everything. It applauded a glaring variety effect and twenty minutes later applauded as eagerly a quiet

poetic one. When the critics praised a piece, the public rushed to the theater and loved it; when they damned a piece, it rushed to the theater and loved it too. It was not so much a failure of taste as an abundance of stimulation. Thanks to the unconsciously American air the ensembles had in everything they danced, the new public found an unexpected contact with the brilliant strangeness of what they saw. As they watched any ballet, an indefinable something in the atmosphere, in the quality of movement and youthful manners, was unconsciously familiar and immediately touching.

The older balletgoers, familiar with prewar performances, had expected nothing like what they now saw. What they expected of ballet was the prewar Ballet Russe. When the war began in Europe, both of the prewar Ballet Russe companies, the de Basil Original and the Massine Monte Carlo, managed to reach New York intact. With the composers and painters of the School of Paris who were here, these extraordinary ensembles intended to continue a brilliant Ballet-Russe-in-exile in peace and comfort. But nothing of the sort happened. Within a few years hardly a trace of Paris-Russian atmosphere or dance style or choreographic fashions remained. Instead ballet had adapted itself to the American dance climate, as it had a few years before in England to the English, and more than a century earlier to the Russian.

The acclimatization of ballet in the United States had begun a decade earlier. It began with local semistudent companies in New York, Chicago, Philadelphia, San Francisco. (Europeans saw Miss Littlefield's Philadelphians tour in '37.) All these groups commissioned local choreographers, composers, and painters. The most interesting of them was Lincoln Kirstein's American Ballet in New York, of which George Balanchine was artistic director. About half of our current best talent seems once to have been in this group. On its first program in '34 it produced Balanchine's *Serenade*, which when he presented it in '47 at the Paris Opéra astonished the audience by the abundance of its invention and the novelty of its style. But none of these groups was strong enough to compete with the Ballet Russe in scale, stars, or repertory. Finally in 1940 Lucia Chase's Ballet Theatre opened in New York, with the intention of becoming an American repertory company of as high a quality as the Paris-Russian ones.

Ballet Theatre, however, compromised on its chauvinism. It sought assistance from Fokine; Baronova joined it; it soon came under the guidance of its British artists Tudor, Dolin, and Markova. For a season it enlisted Nijinska, and it achieved the celebrity it aimed for as Massine and other Ballet Russe stars joined it. And it was Massine who awakened in Ballet Theatre's Americans the dance verve and drive that characterized the company ever after. During these same years, however, the Monte Carlo, as anxious to remain Paris-Russian as Ballet Theatre was to remain American, found itself forced to compromise too. Its ensemble atmosphere became more and more diluted. Its American contingent had grown too large to be assimilated. In '42 it even presented the first well-made ballet that had a real American tone and flavor, Agnes de Mille's *Rodeo*, and the "Russians" danced it convincingly. This double direction of ballet in the United States made the situation confusing as late as '42.

But until '42 for the public the prestige of the prewar Ballet Russe still concealed the changes that were taking place. What first-nighters still expected was the prewar fashion, its odd elegance and its nervous glamour. There was to be sure a sort of malaise in the air. One group—the Original—had disappeared. Some prewar stars had vanished, others grown lax; the ensemble style was no longer so vivid and the novelties had less and less point. No doubt the glorious Ballet Russe was a little out of order, but the spell of its prewar prestige covered everything.

The spell was broken by the overwhelming triumph of Ballet Theatre at the premiere of Tudor's *Pillar of Fire*. Neither in its style nor in its cast of dancers did it show any traces of Paris-Russianism. And by contrast it suddenly made apparent to everyone how devitalized the prewar formula had become. Now Tudor's earlier works already in the repertory became popular. Even the most effective of the prewar-style ballets created here during the war, Massine's *Aleko*, done by Ballet Theatre a few months later, could not change the current; though it had far more dance verve than Tudor, its melodrama could not compete with his real anguish. Now that the prestige of prewar ballet had collapsed, the old Monte Carlo was doomed; poor and desperate, it lost its prewar stars, all but Danilova and Franklin. Youskevitch joined the Navy. But when in the fall of '44 Balanchine took over the crumbling company and at a stroke rejuvenated it, the triumph of the American-style company, the new Monte Carlo, proved to have ended any interest in the resurrection of a Paris-Russian atmosphere. Indeed no one danced that way convincingly anymore; the old stars who remained had now assimilated themselves to the new style. Twice, however, an exhumation of the past was attempted—by Ballet International in '44 (its single season is said to have cost the Marquis de Cuevas $600,000), and by the de Basil Original brought back from South America in '46; both attempts failed.

The decay of the Paris-Russian ballet style in the United States was due to the isolation of the Ballet Russe from its natural sources of vitality in Paris. It affected the prewar Ballet Russe choreographers disastrously. Massine, for instance, created a dozen or so pieces in this country (including three with grandiose décor by Dalí). But of Massine's work only *Aleko*—magnificently decorated by Marc Chagall—was at all comparable to his European work. Large in scale, hollow in sentiment, it had an ingenuity, a sweep, and a hectic activity reminiscent of his "symphonic" style. None of his other pieces were remarkable and some were appallingly shoddy. Fokine produced two ballets of no interest. Lichine created three or four, some pretending to great spiritual conflicts, but only one fine scene among them—one of exuberant South Russian folk dances. His 1940 *Graduation Ball*, a harmless comedy to Johann Strauss music, remained his best work. Nijinska created several ballets but none as attractive as her prewar *Chopin Concerto*. The new ones of the forties were highly ingenious, false in sentiment, willfully odd in musicality, and crabbed in their arbitrary construction of the dancer's actions; she retained, however, a greater force of style than any of the other choreographers of this group. It was sad to see how inexpressive they all became in the dance climate in which they found themselves.

These celebrities did not respond to the human medium which the more and more American ensembles offered to choreographers. A few of the stars sometimes developed interestingly in the choreographies in exile, but the effect failed because even then there was no resonance between star and ensemble, no coherent dance atmosphere to create a coherent poetic illusion. The fact was that several fine qualities the Paris-Russians had had by temperament and tradition, qualities their choreographers presupposed in a company, were foreign to the American dancers. Correct and clear the new dancers were, stricter in these matters than the Europeans; but the Americans, most of them

too young ever to have lived abroad, did not understand those overtones of European local color, both geographical and historical, which
the prewar Ballet Russe often suggested so imaginatively. Ballets pre-
supposing such overtones (from *Petrouchka* to *Gaîté Parisienne*) lost
in consequence most of their savor and point. The Americans were
unimaginative too in suggesting nuances of social differentiation,
or of sexual experience. The foreign choreographers for their part,
even after living here, found no inspiration in local manners. But the
American dancers had neither an instinct for imaginative characterization through liberties of rhythm and accent in classic variations,
nor an ensemble instinct for the kind of rhythmic liberty the Ballet
Russe had used for a sweeping collective climax. A European who
sees ballet only in such terms may wonder if anything is left without these effects—if all that is left is not merely a machine, hard and
monotonous.

The excitement and freshness of our ballet toward the end of the
war, after the Ballet Russe impetus had disintegrated, proves the contrary. The American steadiness and exactitude of rhythm, its reticence
of phrasing, have not the same but a different clarity and sweep. They
do not underline the pathos of a scene by taking sides, but its tragedy by not taking any. They can show largeness of scope and power
and they avoid greasiness of detail. The bold decision, the easy calm,
and the large openness which Americans derive from the tradition of
sports that permeates the country can give their dancing in complex
dance figurations a noble clarity. Their sober friendliness of manner
can have, as Balanchine once wrote, an expression such as one imag-
ines angels would have, who can take part in tragic events without
becoming themselves miserable. When one watches attractive young
Americans in a ballroom or in a dance hall, one notes instinctive traits
of dance style not unlike those I have mentioned; their dancing looks
different from that of Europeans—it has a different style and expression—but style and expression it clearly has.

Of all the foreign-born choreographers who have worked in the
United States, Balanchine has responded most to the stimulus of
this country's natural dance gifts. Since he came here in 1933 he has
worked successfully in all our forms of ballet, in musical comedy, in
opera, in the films (where he was the first to compose dance phrases
directly to suit the camera field and camera angle), in student perfor-

mances (down to the age of six), and with both ballet companies. He can use Americanisms of rhythm or nuance in classic ballets without a trace of self-consciousness. Long before the war he lost interest in the Ballet Russe style of the period; and ever since he has been here he has worked by preference with American dancers. He is more than anyone else the real founder of the American classic style. He has shown our dancers how to be natural in classicism, and he has shown them how to become unaffectedly brilliant in their own natural terms. He has shown the public how effective they are with their charming long-limbed figures, their simple carriage, strong legs, their dazzling speed and their clean grace of line; how animated in the variety of their impetus, in their technical exactness and the exactness of their musicality; how touching in their unselfconscious delight in dancing, their cooperativeness, in the sobriety of their appeal, in the strength of their grace. And when he has come across a dramatic gift, he has placed it where it made its full effect without straining for emotional miming or for a verbal meaning.

Balanchine's choreography, whether during the Diaghilev period or the present one, has always suited the unconscious atmosphere of his ensembles and the innate gifts of grace of his principals. They have always looked both free and brilliant. His recent style differs from his European one in that it no longer shows his former lovely erotic interruptions. Since 1940 it has become strictly classical; the dancer's figure is a clear unit, the dance impetus is unbroken, sustained, and clear. Balanchine has inherited the empire of Petipa and Ivanov. You recognize their purity of idiom, their harmony of motion, and their power of rhythm. But the effervescence of invention, the exquisite musicality, the variety of momentum, the complexity of structure are new. The startling details are often, technically speaking, novelties in the timing, the size, the transposition, or the reversal of classic dance elements or of the phases of a step. Since they remain logical according to the classic technique of balance and impulse, the dancer in them keeps her free impetus. The expression she gives these inventions is merely her graceful freedom, her sovereign assurance; the drama of their happy surprise, of their startling development, of the poignant relations between dancing figures they suggest is resolved by the dazzle and sweep of the ballet's dance rhythm. Balanchine's classicism and his musicality give the dancers the spring in dancing that modern ballets don't have when they try for "meaning." And yet each piece of his touches the imagination with a mysterious expressive message.

The animating subject matter of these new classic ballets is no more explicit than that of *Swan Lake*. Their announced subject is occasionally a plot as unreal as that; more often it is merely the musical structure of the score. But each of Balanchine's ballets has a quality of motion in its development of impetus that is different and specific. One senses that at the core of this dazzling, joyous grace there is, as its source of energy, a specific human gesture, a real image, a slip of fate. Isolated in the imaginary rise and fall of musical time, it offers its transfigured drama in silence. It has become a game for dancers. And as one watches their rapid figures, happy in their animation, caught in their buoyant rhythm, the plastic emphasis of a dance gesture, defining for an instant the impetus, looks poignantly beautiful. Beautiful in its proportion, in its freshness. Beautiful in the innocent dignity of the dancer as she darts past. The echoes the instant awakens are worthy of her. The secret of the movement, its human characteristic, reverberates in memory as it does fantastically in the brilliant surprises of the dancing one is watching and of the music one hears. Neither the dancers nor the audience is required to justify the apparition of these evanescent dance images. They strike as lightly as the sound of a heartbreaking word. And the frightful truth of them remains suspended in an innocent and harmonious world of fantasy.

Of Balanchine's eight creations here since 1940 the most astonishing are three dance ballets of the purest classicism whose subjects are their scores: *Concerto Barocco* (1941) to Bach's Concerto for Two Violins; *Danses Concertantes* (1944) to Stravinsky's score of that name—a ballet brilliantly decorated by Eugene Berman; and *The Four Temperaments* (1946) to Hindemith's composition, danced in a décor by Kurt Seligmann. *The Four Temperaments*, formally a set of themes and elegant variations, is a long fantasy of incredible violence and amplitude, savage speed, and packed weight. *Danses Concertantes*, formally a comedy-style pas de deux with playful entrées by the chorus, is glittering in sharpness, in jets of power and tenuous resilient articulations, in witty grace, in the mystery of a menace withheld all one's life. *Concerto Barocco*, a long supported adagio framed by allegro chorus entrées, has the effect of an ample grace and a cheerful freshness accompanying like a landscape the savage wound of an individual, its untouched force persisting before and after the private event. At times the sweetness of its plastic harmonies is heavenly. It is a pity it is given in the most meager of décors. The Monte Carlo has had seven ballets of Balanchine in recent repertory, Ballet Theatre two, and Ballet Society, a new organization that presents four evenings a year in New York, also has two. For Ballet Society, Balanchine is now preparing Stravinsky's as yet unplayed *Orpheus*, a Rieti ballet, one to a Haieff score, and one to Mozart; for Ballet Theatre, Tchaikovsky's *Theme and Variations*.

In a completely different aesthetic as well as choreographic style is the work of Antony Tudor, artistic director and a principal mime of Ballet Theatre, who is the other ballet choreographer of genius working in the United States. Tudor's three major creations have all been very long pieces. *Pillar of Fire* (set to Schoenberg's *Verklärte Nacht*), half dream, half reality, tells the story of a love-starved English girl tortured by the fear that the young man who frequently comes to call loves not her but her younger sister; it turns out that she has no reason to, and at the end she becomes engaged. Full of self-humiliation, of gnawing envy, sex-frenzied orgiastic images, striking shifts of dance style, fragments of middle-class gesture, full of dance impulses suddenly released and suddenly frozen, it overwhelmed the audience at its first performance. It also established the young American Nora Kaye as a real dramatic ballerina, and the young English dancer Hugh Laing as an intensely imaginative dramatic star. Kaye has since won herself recognition as a classic ballerina as well and had a real success in London a summer ago, when Ballet Theatre danced there. A second major work of Tudor's was *Romeo and Juliet* (to several Delius pieces). Its effect is that of a reverie on Shakespeare's text that transmutes his fire into a Tennysonian pathos. It is a reverie luxuriously embroidered with quattrocento pictorial devices, as carefully cut as an Eisenstein film, and its rhythmic weight steeps the story deeper and deeper in a protracted and absorbing High Church gloom. *Romeo and Juliet* opened with a décor by Eugene Berman, which in its opulence, its wealth of invention and complex grace is itself an event in ballet annals. And Alicia Markova, slight, intensely still, intensely musical, was the most luminous of Juliets. Unfortunately the present state of the production is abominable. The third (1945) and least successful of Tudor's major long works was *Undertow* (to a score by William Schuman). It tells the case history of a sex murder, beginning with the hero's birth (breach presentation) and his infantile frustrations; later, grown into a repressed and gentle adolescent in the slums—which are full of sex—he strangles the girl who seduces him, and suffers remorse. There are dull stretches and a long evasively symbolic ending; but there are also brilliant passages, notably the rape of a horrid little girl by four little boys.

Tudor's ballets have obvious weaknesses. Their shock value, thrilling at first, does not last; their shaping force is discontinuous; they have a weak and fragmentary dance impetus; they peter out at the end. They can find no repose and no spring because balance is no element of structure in them. Their sentiment, acutely envious, acutely humiliated, weakens into self-pity. But they also have exceptional virtues. They are perfectly serious. Their sentiment is real till toward the end; they are full of passion, of originality, of dramatic strokes, of observation, of brilliant pantomime ideas and fastidiously polished detail. Tudor discovers dramatic gifts in his dancers and shows them off to striking advantage. There is no vulgarity in his obscene images. His ballets are not primarily dance conceptions, but their sustained expressive intensity is clearly large-scale.

On a much smaller scale than Tudor, derived from pantomime and novel character-dance elements, is the American local-color ballet. Its first great success was Miss de Mille's *Rodeo*, in which she dance-mimed the star role. It has an excellent scene suggesting cowboys rodeo riding and another of Saturday-night ranch-house dances. The dance steps are lively and the rhythmic sequences well contrasted. Its emotion is humorous-sentimental. It has a lively score by Aaron Copland, who had already written another "Western" ballet score, a beautiful and tragic one, for an interesting but now vanished pre-war American piece, *Billy the Kid* (choreography by Eugene Loring). *Fancy Free*, by Jerome Robbins (score by Leonard Bernstein, décor by Oliver Smith), is about three sailors in town for an evening, and by far the best of the Americana to date. Its local color is sharply observed, its wry pathos is honest, and its jokes sound. The flow of movement, the rhythmic tautness, the concise storytelling are admirable, and it proved as successful in London as in New York. It is still a fresh piece to see after many repetitions. Robbins, a remarkable dramatic dancer himself, has since made two small ballets that show a great advance in construction but a sentiment more confused. Though his experience in classicism is not large, formally his choreographic genius is of the highest order. He understands by instinct the formal unity of a ballet in stage space and musical time, a unity created and filled by a coherent dance impetus. He also conceives every dance action in terms of a drama of real characters. In point of expression he has difficulty as yet in the complete transformation of specific pantomime images into the larger and sweeping rhythm and images of direct dancing. But there is no doubt that he is the most gifted of American-born ballet choreographers. At the moment unfortunately he is about to direct plays and films.

A remarkable choreographic talent appeared in the spring of '47 when Ballet Society presented *The Seasons*, the first ballet by Merce Cunningham (score by John Cage, décor by Isamu Noguchi). Cunningham, a pupil of Martha Graham and a prodigiously gifted dancer, is not a ballet dancer but a modern-dance or expressionist one. His piece, though not in classic idiom, was danced cleanly by dancers classically trained. Its subject was phases of weather and subjective states induced thereby, a subject in the tradition of Thoreau. The phrases were brief but clear, the plastic instinct forceful and imaginative. Though the emotion was tremulous and delicate, the piece showed strength as a dance structure. Cunningham may prove to be a choreographer as soundly gifted as Robbins, though in a style as hermetic as Robbins's is plain-spoken.

Though my subject is ballet and not modern dancing, I cannot omit mentioning Martha Graham, the greatest dance celebrity in the United States. Now past fifty, she is an actress of magnificent power, a dancer of astonishing skill; her choreographies abound in extraordinary plastic images of great originality. They are expressionist in rhetoric, violent, distorted, oppressive, and obscure; there is rarely a perceptible rhythmic unit or any dance architecture. But the ardor of her imagination, the scope of her conceptions, the intensity of her presence make her a dance artist of the first rank.

I have tried to give an impression of the character and of the resources of our new ballet. Among its greatest resources are the young American ballerinas now developing. The most interesting now are Alicia Alonso, Nora Kaye, Mary Ellen Moylan, Maria Tallchief; and

Ruthanna Boris, Rosella Hightower, and Nana Gollner are in the same category. Kaye I have already mentioned; Alonso, Ballet Theatre's Cuban-born classic ballerina, with greater natural gifts than Kaye for a rapid and delicate grace, lacks Kaye's large-scale dramatic force. Moylan, with all the facility of a lovely virtuoso and its greatest gift of plasticity in motion, has a verve that suggests a genius for lively characterization; Tallchief has a tragic beauty and a distinction that set her apart. Among the students, Tanaquil Le Clercq looks like a ballerina to come and a great one. (Brilliant Tamara Toumanova, Ballet Russe ballerina, appears less and less.) Men of similar quality are rarer—John Kriza and, as a dramatic dancer, Francisco Moncion are the most remarkable; Leon Danielian has great gifts too; the most promising among developing dancers is Dick Beard. Our best male stars during the period have been Eglevsky, Franklin, Laing, and Youskevitch—all European trained.

Though the resources exist, though the public is still eager for ballet, since the war the two companies have not kept the high standards they had reached. Managerial disputes and rising costs have reduced both of them to less than forty dancers apiece; and a number of their best dancers have left them. Ballet Theatre's greatest loss was that of Markova some seasons back; unfortunately Markova herself, now touring with Dolin and their small group, has weakened noticeably as an artist. The Monte Carlo's greatest loss was that of Balanchine. It now has no master choreographer to inspire it and it is doubtful if it can long survive without one. Last season, however, the artistic energy which the big companies lacked was shown by Ballet Society, organized by Kirstein and Balanchine. In its first experimental season, together with its eight new ballets, it presented four one-act operas, and also gave us a glimpse of the lovely Javanese dancing of Ratna Mohini. After a remarkable second season—notable for the Stravinsky-Balanchine-Noguchi *Orpheus*—Ballet Society has now become the resident ballet company of New York's City Center.

I have suggested the elements of strength in American ballet style. Its chief weakness seems to be in the art of imaginative characterization. The Tudor ballets, with their many personages, give our dancers experience in the field. But his stylized gesture does not pose the question quite distinctly either. A dance character cannot be explained or justified; and he must remain himself in repose, where there is no distortion of mimicry possible. This is a problem of amplitude in style. Another problem of our style is that of differentiation from musical comedy. Our choreographers and many ballet dancers work in musical comedy and this tends to confuse and banalize their approach to ballet. These are not problems to be solved by verbal argument. They are questions the imagination of our dancers can answer only by dancing in ballets of imaginative force. American ballet is well paid, but its working conditions are the most exhausting in the world. The only thing that can refresh its spirit and enrich its style is the sense of artistic integrity, of imaginative abundance that the managements must supply by encouraging our best choreographers to create for them. This is the main problem ahead of our ballet. Contact with the work of artists from other countries with different resources of style will be stimulating too.

1948

Against Meaning in Ballet

SOME of my friends who go to ballet and like the entertainment it gives are sorry to have it classed among the fine arts and discussed, as the other fine arts are, intellectually. Though I do not agree with them I have a great deal of sympathy for their anti-intellectual point of view. The dazzle of a ballet performance is quite reason enough to go; you see handsome young people—girls and boys with a bounding or delicate animal grace—dancing among the sensual luxuries of orchestral music and shining stage decoration and in the glamour of an audience's delight. To watch their lightness and harmonious ease, their clarity and boldness of motion, is a pleasure. And ballet dancers' specialties are their elastic tautness, their openness of gesture, their gaiety of leaping, beating, and whirling, their slow soaring flights. Your senses enjoy directly how they come forward and closer to you, or recede upstage, turning smaller and more fragile; how the boys and girls approach one another or draw apart, how they pass close without touching or entwine their bodies in stars of legs and arms—all the many ways they have of dancing together. You see a single dancer alone showing her figure from all sides deployed in many positions, or you see a troop of them dancing in happy unison. They are graceful, well mannered, and they preserve at best a personal dignity, a civilized modesty of deportment that keeps the sensual stimulus from being foolishly cute or commercially sexy. The beauty of young women's and young men's bodies, in motion or in momentary repose, is exhibited in an extraordinarily friendly manner.

When you enjoy ballet this way—and it is one of the ways everybody does enjoy it who likes to go—you don't find any prodigious difference between one piece and another, except that one will have enough dancing to satisfy and another not enough, one will show the dancers to their best advantage and another will tend to make them look a little more awkward and unfree. Such a happy ballet lover is puzzled by the severities of critics. He wonders why they seem to find immense differences between one piece and another, or between one short number and another, or between the proficiency of two striking dancers. The reasons the critics give, the relation of the steps to the music, the sequence of the effects, the sharply differentiated intellectual meaning they ascribe to dances, all this he will find either fanciful or plainly absurd.

Has ballet an intellectual content? The ballet lover with the point of view I am describing will concede that occasionally a soloist gives the sense of characterizing a part, that a few ballets even suggest a story with a psychological interest, a dramatic suspense, or a reference to real life. In such a case, he grants, ballet may be said to have an intellectual content. But these ballets generally turn out to be less satisfying to watch because the dancers do less ballet dancing in them; so, he concludes, one may as well affirm broadly that ballet does not properly offer a "serious" comment on life and that it is foolish to look for one.

I do not share these conclusions, and I find that my interest in the kind of meaning a ballet has leads me to an interest in choreography and dance technique. But I have a great deal of sympathy for the general attitude I have described. It is the general attitude that underlies the brilliant reviews of Théophile Gautier, the French poet of a hundred years ago, who is by common consent the greatest of ballet critics. He said of himself that he was a man who believed in the visible world. And his reviews are the image of what an intelligent man of the world saw happening on the stage. They are perfectly open; there is no private malignity in them; he is neither pontifical nor "popular"; there is no jargon and no ulterior motive. He watches not as a specialist in ballet, but as a responsive Parisian. The easy flow of his sentences is as much a tribute to the social occasion as it is to the accurate and elegant ease of ballet dancers in action. His warmth of response to personal varieties of grace and to the charming limits of a gift, his amusement at the pretensions of a libretto or the pretensions of a star, his sensual interest in the line of a shoulder and bosom, in the elasticity of an ankle, in the cut of a dress place the ballet he watches in a perspective of civilized good sense.

Ballet for him is an entertainment—a particularly agreeable way of spending an evening in town; and ballet is an art, it is a sensual refinement that delights the spirit. Art for him is not a temple of humanity one enters with a reverent exaltation. Art is a familiar pleasure and Gautier assumes that one strolls through the world of art as familiarly as one strolls through Paris, looking about in good weather or bad, meeting congenial friends or remarkable strangers, and one's enemies, too. Whether in art or in Paris, a civilized person appreciates seeing a gift and is refreshed by a graceful impulse; there is a general agreement about what constitutes good workmanship; and one takes one's neighbors' opinions less seriously than their behavior. Gautier differentiates keenly between good and bad ballet; but he differentiates as a matter of personal taste. He illustrates the advantages the sensual approach to ballet can have for an intelligence of exceptional sensual susceptibility and for a man of large sensual complacency.

Gautier assumes that all that people need do to enjoy art is to look and listen with ready attention and trust their own sensual impressions. He is right. But when they hear that ballet is an elaborate art with a complicated technique and tradition, many modest people are intimidated and are afraid to trust their own spontaneous impressions. They may have been to a few performances, they may have liked it when they saw it, but now they wonder if maybe they liked the wrong things and missed the right ones. Before going again, they want it explained, they want to know what to watch for and exactly what to feel. If it is really real art and fine great art, it must be studied before it is enjoyed; that is what they remember from school. In school the art of poetry is approached by a strictly rational method, which teaches you what to enjoy and how to discriminate. You are taught to analyze the technique and the relation of form to content; you are taught to identify and "evaluate" stylistic, biographical, economic, and anthropological influences, and told what is great and what is minor so you can prepare yourself for a great reaction or for a minor one. The effect of these conscientious labors on the pupils is distressing. For the rest of their lives they can't face a page of verse without experiencing a complete mental blackout. They don't enjoy, they don't discriminate, they don't even take the printed words at face value. For the rest of their lives they go prying for hidden motives back of literature, for psychological, economic, or stylistic explanations, and it never occurs to them to read the words and respond to them as they do to the nonsense of current songs or the nonsense of billboards by the roadside. Poetry is the same thing—it's words, only more interesting, more directly and richly sensual.

The first taste of art is spontaneously sensual, it is the discovery of an absorbing entertainment, an absorbing pleasure. If you ask anyone who enjoys ballet or any other art how he started, he will tell you that he enjoyed it long before he knew what it meant or how it worked. I remember the intense pleasure reading Shelley's *Adonais* gave me as a boy—long before I followed accurately the sense of the words; and once, twenty years later, I had two kittens who would purr in unison and watch me bright-eyed when I read them Shakespeare's *Sonnets*, clearly pleased by the compliment and by the sounds they heard. Would they have enjoyed them better if they had understood them? The answer is, they enjoyed them very much. Many a college graduate might have envied them.

I don't mean that so orderly and respectable an entertainment as that of art is made for the susceptibilities of kittens or children. But consider how the enormous orderly and respectable symphonic public enjoys its listening, enjoys it without recognizing themes, harmonies, or timbres, without evaluating the style historically or even knowing if the piece is being played as the composer intended. What do they hear when they hear a symphony? Why, they hear the music, the interesting noises it makes. They follow the form and the character of it by following their direct acoustic impressions.

Susceptibility to ballet is a way of being susceptible to animal grace of movement. Many people are highly susceptible to the pleasure of seeing grace of movement who have never thought of going to ballet to look for it. They find it instead in watching graceful animals, animals of many species at play, flying, swimming, racing, and leaping and making gestures of affection toward one another, or watchful in harmonious repose. And they find it too in seeing graceful young people on the street or in a game or at the beach or in a dance hall, boys and girls in exuberant health who are doing pretty much what the charming animals do, and are as unconscious of their grace as they. Unconscious grace of movement is a natural and impermanent gift, like grace of features or of voice or of character, a lucky accident you keep meeting with all your life wherever you are. To be watching grace puts people into a particularly amiable frame of mind. It is an especially attractive form of feeling social consciousness.

But if ballet is a way of entertaining the audience by showing them animal grace, why is its way of moving so very unanimal-like and artificial? For the same reason that music has evolved so very artificial a way of organizing its pleasing noises. Art takes what in life is an accidental pleasure and tries to repeat and prolong it. It organizes, diversifies, characterizes, through an artifice that men evolve by trial and error. Ballet nowadays is as different from an accidental product as a symphony at Carnegie Hall is different from the noises Junior makes on his trumpet upstairs or Mary Ann with comb and tissue paper, sitting on the roof, the little monkey.

You don't have to know about ballet to enjoy it; all you have to do is look at it. If you are susceptible to it, and a good many people evidently are, you will like spontaneously some things you see and dislike others, and quite violently too. You may be so dazzled at first by a star or by the general atmosphere, you don't really know what happened; you may on the other hand find the performance absurdly stiff and affected except for a few unreasonable moments of intense pleasure; but if you are susceptible you will find you want to go again. When you go repeatedly, you begin to recognize what it is you like, and watch for it the next time. That way you get to know about ballet, you know a device of ballet because you have responded to it, you know that much at least about it. Even if nobody agrees with you, you still know it for yourself.

That the composite effect of ballet is a complex one is clear enough. Its devices make a long list, wherever you start. These devices are useful to give a particular moment of a dance a particular expression. The dancers in action give it at that moment a direct sensual reality. But if you watch often and watch attentively, the expressive power of some ballets and dancers will fascinate, perturb, and delight far more than that of others, and will keep alive in your imagination much more intensely long after you have left the theater. It is this aftereffect that dancers and ballets are judged by, by their audience.

To some of my friends the images ballet leaves in the imagination suggest, as poetry does, an aspect of the drama of human behavior. For others such ballet images keep their sensual mysteriousness, "abstract," unrationalized, and magical. Anyone who cannot bear to contemplate human behavior except from a rationalistic point of view had better not try to "understand" the exhilarating excitement of ballet; its finest images of our fate are no easier to face than those of poetry itself, though they are no less beautiful.

March 1949

Charles Dickens (1812–1870)

CHARLES DICKENS—"Boz" to his legion of admirers—liked to dance and certainly saw a good deal of professional dancing, given his passion for the theater, both in London and abroad. He also wrote about it, not only in his early journalism but in his novels—consider Prince Turveydrop, the sympathetic dancing master in *Bleak House*. His interest is underscored by this celebrated passage from his *American Notes for General Circulation*, written after his first American tour, in 1842. It's a report on Five Points, New York's most violent slum district, located in lower Manhattan, and on the dancing he observed and relished there during a guided walk for well-heeled tourists. The young African American whose bravura crossings and shuffle steps Dickens describes so vividly is thought by dance historians to have been the legendary "Juba," whom P. T. Barnum would disguise as a white minstrel and who, six years after the publication of *American Notes*, was billing himself in London as "Boz's Juba."

Dancing at Five Points

WHAT PLACE is this, to which the squalid street conducts us? A kind of square of leprous houses, some of which are attainable only by crazy wooden stairs without. What lies beyond this tottering flight of steps, that creak beneath our tread? a miserable room, lighted by one dim candle, and destitute of all comfort, save that which may be hidden in a wretched bed. Beside it, sits a man: his elbows on his knees: his forehead hidden in his hands. 'What ails that man!' asks the foremost officer. 'Fever,' he sullenly replies, without looking up. Conceive the fancies of a fevered brain, in such a place as this!

Ascend these pitch-dark stairs, heedful of a false footing on the trembling boards, and grope your way with me into this wolfish den, where neither ray of light nor breath of air, appears to come. A negro lad, startled from his sleep by the officer's voice—he knows it well— but comforted by his assurance that he has not come on business, officiously bestirs himself to light a candle. The match flickers for a moment, and shows great mounds of dusky rags upon the ground; then dies away and leaves a denser darkness than before, if there can be degrees in such extremes. He stumbles down the stairs and presently comes back, shading a flaring taper with his hand. Then the mounds of rags are seen to be astir, and rise slowly up, and the floor is covered with heaps of negro women, waking from their sleep: their white teeth chattering, and their bright eyes glistening and winking on all sides with surprise and fear, like the countless repetition of one astonished African face in some strange mirror.

Mount up these other stairs with no less caution (there are traps and pitfalls here, for those who are not so well escorted as ourselves) into the housetop; where the bare beams and rafters meet over-head, and calm night looks down through the crevices in the roof. Open the door of one of these cramped hutches full of sleeping negroes. Pah! They have a charcoal fire within; there is a smell of singeing clothes, or flesh, so close they gather round the brazier; and vapours issue forth that blind and suffocate. From every corner, as you glance about you in these dark retreats, some figure crawls half-awakened, as if the judgment-hour were near at hand, and every obscene grave were giving up its dead. Where dogs would howl to lie, women, and men, and boys slink off to sleep, forcing the dislodged rats to move away in quest of better lodgings.

Here too are lanes and alleys, paved with mud knee-deep: underground chambers, where they dance and game; the walls bedecked with rough designs of ships, and forts, and flags, and American Eagles out of number: ruined houses, open to the street, whence, through wide gaps in the walls, other ruins loom upon the eye, as though the world of vice and misery had nothing else to show: hideous tenements which take their name from robbery and murder: all that is loathsome, drooping, and decayed is here.

Our leader has his hand upon the latch of 'Almack's,' and calls to us from the bottom of the steps; for the assembly-room of the Five-Point fashionables is approached by a descent. Shall we go in? It is but a moment.

Heyday! the landlady of Almack's thrives! A buxom fat mulatto woman, with sparkling eyes, whose head is daintily ornamented with a handkerchief of many colours. Nor is the landlord much behind her in his finery, being attired in a smart blue jacket, like a ship's steward, with a thick gold ring upon his little finger, and round his neck a gleaming golden watch-guard. How glad he is to see us! What will we please to call for? A dance? It shall be done directly, sir: 'a regular break-down.'

The corpulent black fiddler, and his friend who plays the tambourine, stamp upon the boarding of the small raised orchestra in which they sit, and play a lively measure. Five or six couples come upon the floor, marshalled by a lively young negro, who is the wit of the assembly, and the greatest dancer known. He never leaves off making queer faces, and is the delight of all the rest, who grin from ear to ear incessantly. Among the dancers are two young mulatto girls, with large, black, drooping eyes, and head-gear after the fashion of the hostess, who are as shy or feign to be, as though they never danced before, and so look down before the visitors, that their partners can see nothing but the long fringed lashes.

But the dance commences. Every gentleman sets as long as he likes to the opposite lady, and the opposite lady to him, and all are so long about it that the sport begins to languish, when suddenly the lively hero dashes in to the rescue. Instantly the fiddler grins, and goes at it tooth and nail; there is new energy in the tambourine; new laughter in the dancers; new smiles in the landlady; new confidence in the landlord; new brightness in the very candles. Single shuffle, double shuffle, cut and cross-cut: snapping his fingers, rolling his eyes, turning in his knees, presenting the backs of his legs in front, spinning about on his toes and heels like nothing but the man's fingers on the tambourine; dancing with two left legs, two right legs, two wooden legs, two wire legs, two spring legs—all sorts of legs and no legs—what is this to him? And in what walk of life, or dance of life, does man ever get such stimulating applause as thunders about him, when, having danced his partner off her feet, and himself too, he finishes by leaping gloriously on the bar-counter, and calling for something to drink, with the chuckle of a million of counterfeit Jim Crows, in one inimitable sound!

The air, even in these distempered parts, is fresh after the stifling atmosphere of the houses; and now, as we emerge into a broader street, it blows upon us with a purer breath, and the stars look bright again. Here are The Tombs once more. The city watch-house is a part of the building. It follows naturally on the sights we have just left. Let us see that, and then to bed.

What! do you thrust your common offenders against the police discipline of the town, into such holes as these? Do men and women, against whom no crime is proved, lie here all night in perfect darkness, surrounded by the noisome vapours which encircle that flagging lamp you light us with, and breathing this filthy and offensive stench! Why, such indecent and disgusting dungeons as these cells, would bring disgrace upon the most despotic empire in the world! Look at them, man—you, who see them every night, and keep the keys. Do you see what they are? Do you know how drains are made below the streets, and wherein these human sewers differ, except in being always stagnant?

Well, he don't know. He has had five-and-twenty young women locked up in this very cell at one time, and you'd hardly realise what handsome faces there were among 'em.

In God's name! shut the door upon the wretched creature who is in it now, and put its screen before a place, quite unsurpassed in all the vice, neglect, and devilry, of the worst old town in Europe.

Are people really left all night, untried, in those black sties?—Every night. The watch is set at seven in the evening. The magistrate opens his court at five in the morning. That is the earliest hour at which the first prisoner can be released; and if an officer appear against him, he is not taken out till nine o'clock or ten.—But if any one among them die in the interval, as one man did, not long ago? Then he is half-eaten by the rats in an hour's time; as that man was; and there an end.

What is this intolerable tolling of great bells, and crashing of wheels, and shouting in the distance? A fire. And what that deep red light in the opposite direction? Another fire. And what these charred and blackened walls we stand before? A dwelling where a fire has been. It was more than hinted, in an official report, not long ago, that some of these conflagrations were not wholly accidental, and that speculation and enterprise found a field of exertion, even in flames: but be this as it may, there was a fire last night, there are two to-night, and you may lay an even wager there will be at least one, to-morrow. So, carrying that with us for our comfort, let us say, Good night, and climb up stairs to bed.

1842

EMILY DICKINSON (1830–1886)

A NUMBER of Emily Dickinson's poems touch on imagery associated with dance, but the poem "I cannot dance opon my Toes" can be recognizably specific to anyone familiar with the ballet *Giselle*. Following its premiere in Paris, in 1841, the ballet was soon performed across Europe and in American theaters in Boston, New York, and Philadelphia. Dickinson scholar Joanne Barclay Skoller notes that in 1846 and 1847 in Boston alone, *Giselle* was performed thirty to fifty times.

Dickinson's poem, from 1862, animates particular moments from *Giselle*, the quintessential Romantic ballet: Giselle's descent into madness before the horrified onlookers; the supernatural Wilis pumping from wing to wing in opposing lines by way of small, chugging hops, their figures arranged in arabesque; a variation in which Giselle's spirit seems to toss herself into the air in a series of entrechats quatres. But there is no evidence that Dickinson actually attended a performance of the ballet in Boston, New York, or Philadelphia or perhaps learned about its particulars from reviews or illustrations or from friends or family members who saw it. Alas, it's unlikely that we'll ever be able to settle this matter with tangible proof.

> I cannot dance opon my Toes -
> No Man instructed me -
> But oftentimes, among my mind,
> A Glee possesseth me,
>
> That had I Ballet Knowledge -
> Would put itself abroad
> In Pirouette to blanch a Troupe -
> Or lay a Prima, mad,

And though I had no Gown of Gauze -
No Ringlet, to my Hair,
Nor hopped for Audiences - like Birds -
One Claw opon the air -

Nor tossed my shape in Eider Balls,
Nor rolled on wheels of snow
Till I was out of sight, in sound,
The House encore me so -

Nor any know I know the Art
I mention - easy - Here -
Nor any Placard boast me -
It's full as Opera -

                                    c. 1862

Isadora Duncan (1877–1927)

No LIFE in dance has been more celebrated—and debated—than that of Isadora Duncan, whose modest beginnings in San Francisco could hardly have suggested that she would become the glorious, tragic, and scandalous Mother of Modern Dance. She was driven to move east to Chicago and New York, then on to London, Paris, and the world, proclaiming her belief in a new kind of dancing—free, natural, unrestrained, defying the mannerisms and strictures of classical ballet. She danced barefoot—running, skipping, leaping—generally dressed in Grecian robes that revealed her legs and arms, shocking traditionalists by performing to symphonic music: Beethoven, Brahms. Isadora became not only one of the most applauded (and highly rewarded) artists of her time, admired by Rodin and Stanislavsky among legions of others, but one of the world's most notorious celebrities, her private life all too public. Among her amours were the famous theater designer Gordon Craig, the Singer sewing machine heir Paris Singer, and her only husband, the Russian revolutionary poet Sergei Essenin, eighteen years her junior. (They had no language in common, nor anything else, except a taste for extreme behavior.) She was obsessed by what she saw as her mission, establishing dance schools wherever possible and proclaiming her vision in passionate speeches and writings.

Isadora never really recovered from the horrifying death by drowning of her two young children when she was thirty-five, and her later years were spent in a downward spiral of promiscuity, desperate lack of funds, and alcoholism. She died at fifty in a bizarre car accident in Nice. That same year, 1927, her memoir, *My Life*, was published, causing yet another sensation. It could hardly be called anchored to mere data, but it's bursting with energy and life. As Dorothy Parker wrote in *The New Yorker*, it was "abominably written," but it revealed Isadora to be "a great woman; a magnificent, generous, gallant, reckless, fated fool of a woman. There was never a place for her in the ranks of the terrible, slow army of the cautious. She ran ahead, where there were no paths." She left behind a new art form.

The Dance of the Future

I AM ASKED to speak upon the "Dance of the future,"—yet how is it possible? In fifty years I may have something to say. Besides, I have always found it indiscreet for me to speak on my dance. The people who are in sympathy with me understand what I am trying to do better than myself, the people who are not in sympathy, understand better than I why they are not.

A woman once asked me why I dance with bare feet and I replied, "Madam, I believe in the religion of the beauty of the human foot"— and the lady replied, "But I do not" and I said, "Yet you must, Madam, for the expression and intelligence of the human foot is one of the greatest triumphs of the evolution of man." "But," said the lady, "I do not believe in the evolution of man"; At this said I "My task is at an end. I refer you to my most revered teachers Mr. Charles Darwin and Mr. Ernest Haeckel"—"But," said the lady, "I do not believe in Darwin and Haeckel"—. At this point I could think of nothing more to say. So you see, that to convince people, I am of little value and ought not to speak.

But, I am brought from the seclusion of my study trembling and stammering before a public and told to lecture on the dance of the future.

If we seek the real source of the dance, if we go to nature, we find that the dance of the future is the dance of the past, the dance of eternity and has been and will always be the same.

The movement of waves, of winds, of the earth is ever in the same lasting harmony. We do not stand on the beach and inquire of the ocean what was its movement of the past and what will be its movement in the future. We realize that the movement peculiar to its nature is eternal to its nature. The movement of the free animals and birds remains always in correspondence to their nature, the necessities and wants of that nature and its correspondence to the earth nature. It is only when you put free animals under false restrictions that they lose the power of moving in harmony with nature and adopt a movement expressive of the restrictions placed about them. So it has been with civilized man. The movements of the Savage, who lived in freedom in constant touch with Nature were unrestricted, natural and beautiful. Only the movements of the naked body can be perfectly natural. Man, arrived at the end of civilization, will have to return to nakedness, not to the unconscious nakedness of the savage, but to the conscious and acknowledged nakedness of the mature Man, whose body will be the harmonious expression of his spiritual being.

And the movements of this Man will be natural and beautiful like those of the free animals.

The movement of the universe concentrating in an individual becomes what is termed the will; for example, the movement of the earth, being the concentration of surrounding forces, gives to the earth its individuality, its will of movement; as creatures of the earth receiving in turn these concentrating forces in their different relations, as transmitted to them through their ancestors and to those by the earth, in themselves evolve the movement of individuals which is termed the will.

The dance should simply be then the natural-gravitation of this will of the individual, which in the end is no more nor less than a human translation of the gravitation of the universe.

—It is noticed that I speak in the terms and views of Schopenhauer. His terms are more convenient for what I intend to express.—

The school of the ballet of to-day vainly striving against the natural laws of gravitation or the natural will of the individual, and working in discord in its form and movement with the form and movement of nature, produces a sterile movement which gives no birth to future movements but dies as it is made.

The expression of the modern school of ballet wherein each action is an end, and no movement, pose, or rhythm is successive or can be made to evolve succeeding action, is an expression of degeneration, of living death. All the movements of our modern ballet school are sterile movements because they are unnatural, their purpose is, to create the delusion that the law of gravitation does not exist for them.

The primary or fundamental movements of the new school of the dance must have within them the seeds from which will evolve all other movements, each in turn to give birth to other in unending sequence of still higher and greater expressions, thoughts and ideas.

To those who nevertheless still enjoy the movements from historical or choreographic or whatever other reasons, to those I answer: They see no farther than the skirts and tricots. But look—under the skirts, under the tricots are dancing deformed muscles.—Look still farther—underneath the muscles are deformed bones: a deformed skeleton is dancing before you. This deformation through incorrect dress and incorrect movement is the result of the training necessary to the ballet.

The ballet condemns itself by enforcing the deformation of the beautiful woman's body! No historical, no choreographic reasons can prevail against that!

It is the mission of all art to express the highest and most beautiful ideals of man. What ideal does the ballet express?

No—the dance was once the most noble of all arts—and it shall be again. From the great depth to which it has fallen it shall be raised. The dancer of the future shall attain so great a height that all other arts shall be helped thereby.

To express what is the most moral, healthful and beautiful in art—this is the mission of the dancer, and to this I dedicate my life.

These flowers before me contain the dream of a dance; it could be named: "The light falling on white flowers." A dance that would be a subtle translation of the light and the whiteness. So pure, so strong, that people would say: it is a soul we see moving, a soul that has reached the light and found the whiteness. We are glad it should move so. Through its human medium we have a satisfying sense of the movement of light and glad things. Through this human medium, the movement of all nature runs also through us, is transmitted to us from the dancer. We feel the movement of light intermingled with the thought of whiteness. It is a prayer, this dance, each movement reaches in long undulations to the heavens and becomes a part of the eternal rhythm of the spheres.

To find those primary movements for the human body from which shall evolve the movements of the future dance in ever variating natural unending sequences, that is the duty of the new dancer of to-day.

To give an example of this, we might take the pose of the Hermes of the Greeks. He is represented as flying on the wind. If the artist had pleased to pose his foot in a vertical position he might have done so, as the god, flying on the wind, is not touching the earth; but realizing that no movement is true unless suggesting sequence of movements the sculptor placed the Hermes with the ball of his foot resting on the wind, giving the movement an eternal quality.

In the same way I might make examples of each pose and gesture in the thousands of figures we have left to us on the Greek vases and bas reliefs; there is not one which in its movement does not presuppose another movement.

This is because the Greeks were the greatest students of the laws of nature, wherein all is the expression of unending ever increasing evolution, wherein are no ends and no stops.

Such movements will always have to depend on and correspond to the form that is moving. The movements of a beetle correspond to its form. So do those of the horse. Even so the movements of the human body must correspond to its form. They should even correspond to its individual form. The dance of no two persons should be alike.

People have thought that so long as one danced in rhythm, the form and design did not matter; but no . . . one must perfectly correspond to the other. The Greeks understood this very well. One of our illustrations shows a dancing Cupid. It is a child's dance. The movements of the plump little feet and arms are perfectly suited to its form. The sole of the foot rests flat on the ground, a position which might be ugly in a more developed person, but is natural in a child trying to keep its balance. One of the legs is half raised: if it were outstretched it would irritate us, because the movement would be unnatural. The satyr in the next illustration shows a dance that is quite different from that of the Cupid. His movements are those of a ripe and muscular man. They are in perfect harmony with the structure of his body.

The Greeks in all their painting, sculpture, architecture, literature, dance and tragedy evolved their movements from the movement of nature, as we plainly see expressed in all representations of the Greek gods, who, being no other than the representatives of natural forces, are always designed in a pose expressing the concentration and evolution of these forces. This is why the art of the Greeks is not a national or characteristic art but has been and will be the art of all humanity for all time.

Therefore dancing naked upon the earth I naturally fall into Greek positions, for Greek positions are only earth positions.

The noblest in art is the nude. This truth is recognized by all, and followed by painters, sculptors and poets; only the dancer has forgotten it, who should most remember it as the instrument of her art is the human body itself.

Man's first conception of beauty is gained from the form and symmetry of the human body. The new school of the dance should be that movement which is in harmony with and will develop the highest form of the human body.

I intend to work for this dance of the future. I do not know whether I have the necessary qualities: I may have neither genius, nor talent, nor temperament, but I know, that I have a Will; and will and energy is sometimes greater than either, genius or talent or temperament.

Let me anticipate all that can be said against my qualification for my work in the following little fable:

The Gods looked down through the glass roof of my studio and Athena said: "She is not wise, she is not wise, in fact, she is remarkably stupid."

And Demeter looked and said,—"She is a weakling small thing—not like my deep-breasted daughters who play in the fields of Eleusis; one can see each rib, she is not worthy to dance on my broad-wayed Earth." And Iris looked down and said: "See how heavily she moves—does she guess nothing of the swift and gracious movement of a winged being?" And Pan looked and said "What, does she think she knows aught of the movements of my satyrs, splendid twyhorned fellows who have within them all the fragrant life of the woods and waters." And then Terpsichore gave one scornful glance: "And—she calls that dancing! Why, her feet move more like the lazy steps of a deranged turtle."

And all the Gods laughed; but I looked bravely up through the glass roof and said:

"O, ye immortal Gods who dwell in high Olympus and live on Ambrosia and Honey-Cakes and pay no studio rent nor bakers bills thereof, do not judge me so scornfully. It is true O, Athena that I am not wise, and my head is a rattled institution; but I do occasionally read the word of those who have gazed into the infinite blue of thine eyes and I bow my empty gourd head very humbly before thine altars. And, O, Demeter of the Holy Garland," I continued, "it is true that the beautiful maidens of your broad-wayed earth would not admit me of their company: still I have thrown aside my sandals that my feet may touch your life-giving earth more reverently and I have had your sacred Hymn sung before the present day Barbarians and I have made them to listen and to find it good.

"And, O, Iris of the golden wings, it is true that mine is but a sluggish movement;—others of my profession have luted more violently against the laws of gravitation, from which laws, O, glorious one you are alone exempt. Yet the wind from your wings has swept through my poor earthy spirit and I have often brought prayers to your courage-inspiring image.

"And, O, Pan, you who were pitful and gentle to simple Psyche in her wanderings, think more kindly of my little attempts to dance in your woody places.

"And you most exquisite one, Terpsichore, send to me a little comfort and strength that I may proclaim your power on Earth during my life; and afterwards, in the shadowy Hades my wistful spirit shall dance dances better yet in thine honour—." Then came the voice of Zeus the thunderer:

"Continue your way and rely upon the eternal justice of the immortal Gods: if you work well they shall know of it and be pleased thereof."

In this sense then I intend to work and if I could find in my dance a few or even one single position that the sculptor could transfer into marble so that it might be preserved, my work would not have been in vain; this one form would be a gain; it would be a first step for the future. My intention is, in due time, to found a school, to build a theatre where a hundred little girls shall be trained in my art, which they in their turn will better. In this school I shall not teach the children to imitate my movements, but to make their own. I shall not force them to study certain definite movements, I shall help them to develop those movements which are natural to them. Whosoever sees the movements of an untaught little child cannot deny that its movements are beautiful. They are beautiful because they are natural to the child. Even so the movements of the human body may be beautiful in every stage of development so long as they are in harmony with that stage and degree of maturity which the body has attained. There will always be movements which are the perfect expression of that individual body and that individual soul: so we must not force it to make movements which are not natural to it but which belong to a school. An intelligent child must be astonished to find that in the ballet school it is taught movements contrary to all those movements which it would make of its own accord.

This may seem a question of little importance, a question of differing opinions on the ballet and the new dance. But it is a great question. It is not only a question of true art, it is a question of race, of the development of the female sex to beauty and health, of the return to the original strength and to natural movements of woman's body. It is a question of the development of perfect mothers and the birth of healthy and beautiful children. The dancing school of the future is to develop and to show the ideal form of woman. It will be as it were a museum of the living beauty of the period.

Travellers coming into a country and seeing the dancers should find in them that country's ideal of the beauty of form and movement. But strangers who to-day come to any country and there see the dancers of the ballet school would get a strange notion indeed of the ideal of beauty in this country. More than that, dancing like any art of any time should reflect the highest point the spirit of mankind has reached in that special period. Does anybody think that the present day ballet school expresses this?

Why are its positions in such a contrast to the beautiful positions of the antique sculptures which we preserve in our museums and which are constantly represented to us as perfect models of ideal beauty? Or have our museums only been founded out of historical and archeological interest and not for the sake of the beauty of the objects which they contain?

The ideal of beauty of the human body cannot change with fashion but only with evolution. Remember the story of the beautiful sculpture of a Roman girl which was discovered under the reign of pope Innocent VIII and which by its beauty created such a sensation that the men thronged to see it and made pilgrimages to it as to a holy shrine, so that the pope, troubled by the movement which it originated, finally had it buried again.

And here I want to avoid a misunderstanding that might easily arise. From what I have said you might conclude that my intention is to return to the dances of the old Greeks or that I think that the dance of the future will be a revival of the antique dances or even of those of the primitive tribes. No, the dance of the future will be a new movement, a consequence of the entire evolution which mankind has passed through. To return to the dances of the Greeks would be as impossible as it is unnecessary. We are not Greeks and cannot therefore dance Greek dances.

But the dance of the future will have to become again a high religious art as it was with the Greeks. For art which is not religious is not art, is mere merchandise.

The dancer of the future will be one whose body and soul have grown so harmoniously together that the natural language of that soul will have become the movement of the body. The dancer will not belong to a nation but to all humanity. She will dance not in the form of nymph, nor fairy, nor coquette but in the form of woman in its greatest and purest expression. She will realize the mission of woman's body and the holiness of all its parts. She will dance the changing life of nature, showing how each part is transformed into the other. From all parts of her body shall shine radiant intelligence, bringing to the world the message of the thoughts and aspirations of thousands of women. She shall dance the freedom of woman. O, what a field is here awaiting her! Do you not feel that she is near, that she is coming, this dancer of the future! She will help womankind to a new knowledge of the possible strength and beauty of their bodies and the relation of their bodies to the earth nature and to the children of the future. She will dance the body emerging again from centuries of civilized forgetfulness, emerging not in the nudity of primitive man, but in a new nakedness, no longer at war with spirituality and intelligence, but joining itself forever with this intelligence in a glorious harmony.

This is the mission of the dancer of the future. O, do you not feel that she is near, do you not long for her coming as I do? Let us prepare the place for her. I would build for her a temple to await her. Perhaps she is yet unborn, perhaps she is now a little child, perhaps O, blissful—it may be my holy mission to guide her first steps, to watch the progress of her movements day by day until, far outgrowing my poor teaching, her movements will become godlike, mirroring in themselves the waves, the winds, the movements of growing things, the flight of birds, the passing of clouds and finally the thought of man in his relation to the universe. O, she is coming, the dancer of the future: the free spirit, who will inhabit the body of new women; more glorious than any woman that has yet been; more beautiful than the Egyptian, than the Greek, the early Italian, than all women in past centuries: The highest intelligence in the freest body!

1903

KATHERINE DUNHAM (1909–2006)

WHAT a life! Katherine Dunham was a formidable dancer, an irre-pressible choreographer, a driven social activist, a groundbreaking ethnologist and anthropologist, a serial autobiographer, an interna-tional star, an inspiration, a scandal (banned in Boston!), and a model for generations of African American performers. It's surprising that she found time to die, even if it was at the age of ninety-six. She starred as Georgia Brown in George Balanchine's Broadway musical *Cabin in the Sky*, the show that Ethel Waters stopped with "Taking a Chance on Love." (Lena Horne played Georgia in the movie.) She went on a forty-seven-day hunger strike to protest American policies toward Haitian refugees. (Speaking of Haiti, she became a priestess of the Vaudon reli-gion there.) She choreographed a new production of *Aïda* at the Met, featuring Leontyne Price. For decades, she toured the world with her Katherine Dunham Dance Company, mostly performing revues she created with names like *Bal Nègre* and *Caribbean Rhapsody*. (Danc-ers affiliated with Dunham's company include Eartha Kitt, Janet Col-lins, and Talley Beatty.) She married the artist and scenic designer John Pratt, her collaborator on her shows as well, and they adopted a French baby. Occasionally she approached bankruptcy, though she hardly noticed. She was awarded the Presidential Medal of the Arts and received the Kennedy Honors. "Judging from reactions," she said, "the dancing in my group is called anthropology in New Haven, sex in Boston, and in Rome—art!"

Thesis Turned Broadway

IN THE great raft of publicity which, in the past few months, has appeared in connection with my role in the Broadway show *Cabin in the Sky*, I find myself referred to, and on the very same day, both as "the hottest thing on Broadway" and "an intelligent, sensitive young woman . . . an anthropologist of note." Personally, I do not think of myself as either one of these extreme phenomena. But eager reporters, confronted by the simultaneous presence of two such diverse elements, have often failed to grasp the synthesis between them; they have chosen, instead, to account for effectiveness by an exaggerated emphasis upon either one or the other. Then there is always the fact that the attempt to relate the dignified and somewhat awesome science of anthropology with the popular art of Broadway dancing and theater works the interviewer back to the question of which came first. Actually, that consideration is as unimportant as the chicken-egg controversy. Now that I look back over the long period of sometimes alternating, sometimes simultaneous interest in both subjects, it seems inevitable that they should have eventually fused completely.

Every person who has a germ of artistry seeks to recreate and present an impression of universal human experience—to fulfill either human needs or wants. The instrument is the specific art form which may have been chosen; the effectiveness depends upon skill in handling the form and upon the originality of the individual imagination. But the experience which is given expression cannot be either too individual or too specific; it must be universal. In the Greek theater, for example, the importance of the universals was so great that an entire system of formal absolutes was worked out of their expression. Consequently, any effective artistic communication is impossible if the artist's understanding of human experience is limited by inadequate knowledge. Anthropology is the study of man. It is a study not of a prescribed portion of man's activity or history, but a study (through some one of the five fields of anthropological specialization—ethnology, archaeology, social anthropology, linguistics, physical anthropology) of his entire state of being throughout his entire history. In such a survey, the student of anthropology gradually comes to recognize universal emotional experiences, common alike to both the primitive Bushman and the sophisticated cosmopolitan; he notes patterns of expression which have been repeatedly effective throughout the ages and which, though modified by many material circumstances, persist in their essential form; and finally, he acquires an historical perspective which enables him, in the confusion of changing maps and two world wars within a single generation, to discern the developing motifs and consistent trends.

As nearly as I can remember, I have been dancing since I was eight years old and it has been my growing interest to know not only how people dance but, even more importantly, why they dance as they do. By the time I was studying at the University of Chicago, I had come to feel that if I could discover this, not only as it applied to one group of people but to diverse groups, with their diverse cultural, psychological, and racial backgrounds, I would have arrived at some of the fundamentals, not only of choreographic technique, but of theater artistry and function. I applied myself to acquiring this knowledge and eventually, as a "Julius Rosenwald fellow, student of anthropology and the dance," spent a year and a half traveling through the West Indies in pursuit of this understanding.

In the beginning, I had great hopes of turning out a thesis for the University of Chicago which would take care of the entire field of primitive dance. It was to be entitled "A Comparative Analysis of Primitive Dance." I ended up by limiting my thesis to "A Comparative Analysis of the Dances of Haiti: Their Form, Function, Social Organization, and the Interrelation of Form and Function." (Still too much for one sitting!) In the West Indies the peasant natives (primarily Negroes of Koromantee, Ibo, Congo, Dahomey, Mandingo, and other west coast derivation, mixed perhaps with a little Carib Indian and varying degrees of European stock) think very much and behave basically very much as did their African forebears. Consequently they dance very much in the same fashion. Differences there are, of course, due to the shift from tribal to folk culture, to miscegenation, cultural contact, and other items making for social change. But the elements of the dance are still what, in my analysis, would be termed "primitive." Almost all social activity is dancing or some type of rhythmic motion (it may be the unified movement of the *combite* or work society of Haiti in cutting sugar cane, or a similar activity in the work societies of the Jamaican Maroons, or the cross-country trek of a Carnival band). Out of a maze of material from the concentrated fields of study—Jamaica, Haiti, Martinique, and Trinidad—one important fact stood out: in these societies the theater of the people ("theater" being practically synonymous with dance activity) served a well-integrated, well-defined function in the community; in the case of the Carnival dances of social integration and sexual stimulus and release; in the funeral dance the externalization of grief; the social dances, exhibitionism and sexual selection along with social cohesion; in the ceremonial dances, group "ethos" solidarity in an established mechanism of worship, whether through hypnosis, hysteria, or ecstasy. And so on through the several categories of dances arrived at.

It was one thing to write a thesis and have it approved for a master's degree. It was another thing to begin earning a living on Broadway. In making use of field training to choreograph for my group, I found persistently recurring in the back of my mind, in some form or another, "function." It never seemed important to portray, as such, the behavior of other peoples as exotics. But the cultural and psychological framework, the "why" became increasingly important. It became a matter of course to attack a stage or production situation in the same way in which I would approach a new primitive community or work to analyze a dance category. As in the primitive community certain movement patterns, which I cannot go into here, were always related to certain functions, so in the modern theater there would be a correlation between a dance movement and the function of that dance within the theater framework. And certainly a broad and general knowledge of cultures and cultural patterns can be advantageously brought to bear upon the problems of relating form and function in the modern theater. Or so has been my theory and so my practice in my own theater experience.

What would be the connection between the Carnival dance, whose function is sexual stimulus and release, and almost any similar situation in a Broadway musical—for example, the temptation scene on the River Nile in *Cabin in the Sky*? It would be the similarity in function, and through this similarity in function the transference of certain elements of form would be legitimate.

August 1941

John Durang (1768–1822)

Born in Lancaster, Pennsylvania, to a family of immigrants from Alsace, the eldest child of eight, John Durang was, as Lillian Moore phrased it, "the first native American to win widespread recognition as a dancer," including public admiration from George Washington, who, himself, was known to cut a mean minuet. Durang's memoir, despite its sprinkling of misspellings and misremembered years, is wonderfully clear and filled with theatrical detail, as well as being the first dancer's memoir in English from the New World; and it calls attention to the fact that, prior to the twentieth century, it was Philadelphia, rather than New York or Boston, that was the dance center of the United States. (The unique manuscript of the memoir—written from journals kept in the last third or so of Durang's life, and richly ornamented with his own watercolor paintings of himself in various ballet and folk-dancing roles—resides in the York City History Center. Its first publication was not until 1966.) Durang originally performed his famous Sailor's Hornpipe dance in the late 1700s with the Lewis Hallam company. The dance has survived for two-and-a-half centuries thanks to the satisfying swing and fit of the choreography to the music and to the foresight of one of Durang's dancer-sons, who published the sequence of steps. As Durang's biographer Lynn Matluck Brooks observes in *John Durang: Man of the American Stage*, John was also the first native-born American to sire a theatrical dynasty into our own time. (The playwright Christopher Durang is his descendant.) Most of all, though, his career is marked by an overwhelming appetite to dance and participate in all the roles available to him in the theater: dancer, ballet master, actor, set builder and painter, pantomime master, puppeteer, stage manager. The excerpt below describes Durang's early encounter with a hornpipe and his first independent tour as a professional dancer.

The Greatest Dancer in America

THE FIRST wire dancer I ever saw was one Templeman who was most compleat in the art. He performed in the old Theatre South Street; the house was crowded every night. The next was a dramatic performance by Wall and Ryan and Company; they had among them a Mr. Rusell [*Roussel*], a dancer. I saw him dance a hornpipe which charmed my mind. I thought I could dance as well as any body but his stile set it off, with his dress. I practised at home and I soon could do all his steps besides many more better hornpipe steps. He was a Frenchman and the French seldom do many real ground steps. The pigeon wing I never saw done by any other person, and I could not make that out from the front of the house. I contrived to get Mr. Rusell to board at my father's house that I might have the opportunity to dance more correct then I had been used to. I learned the correct stile of dancing a hornpipe in the French stile, an allemande, and steps for a country dance. Except the pigeon was the only difficulty I had to encounter: he could not show me the principle and the anatomy of the figure of the step, nor I never met with a dancer since that could show it me. The mystery of the figure occured to me in bed, for my thoughts where constant on that object. I dream'd that I was at a ball and did the pigeon wing to admiration to the whole company; in the morning, I rose in the confidence of doing the step. By this strange circumstance on trial I was master of the step, and could explain the anatomy of the figure, and by a certain rule and method, I never failed in teaching it and make my pupils master of it.

There was a woman in Ryans company celibrated for singing, "Tally ho." She was known by the name of Miss Hyde. She sung on the South St. stage when the British officers performed in the same theatre at the time the British where winter quartered in Philad'a. A scene still remained in the old theatre within late years which was painted by Major Andre. I have been told they where all good actors.

Music and dancing was my attraction; I was noticed for my dancing. A man whose performance I would sometimes go and see exhibited in a house the corner of the little street runing from South, to Shippen St., between Front and Second St. This house is part of the oldest and the first theatre that was build in Philad'a by old Hallam and Douglass; it is a large old red frame building at the corner of South and the little street, and stands there yet to this day occupy'd in tenements. This man whose name I forgot, his performance consisted of a miscellaneous collection: transparencies, the magic lantern, sea fights in machinary, singing—all bad enough, but anything was thought great in those days. As I had a mechanical genious, and a turn for music (I could play on several instruments of music), by his flattering and promises, I consented to go with him from this to Boston, on the conditions he was to pay my whole expense while I chuse to stay with him, and to give me one night's performance to my profit, and not publish my name, and pay my journey home. A desire for travelling, and in the hope of improveing myself, and gain a better knowledge of the world, I consented to go with him. This was the first and the only thing I ever done without the consent and knowledge of my father, in obedience to his will while under his command.

And now the ups and downs of my life begin. I was just in the age of 15, active, industrious, full of health and cheerfulness. I was preparing to make my first tour, to leave my father's house and mingle with the multitude of the world. My confidence in God was the security and hope in my chance of fortune; my aversion to vice, couplet with prudence, was my guide thro' life. My association was confined to partial select company; I could allways pass my time better in my chamber than in company; I was doing while some only talk of it. Idleness, resorts to taverns, low company, drinking, smokeing, gaming &c., was always my detestation. With a clear, independent spirit, I set out with this man in the stage by way of New York to Boston. In our passage we pass'd thro' (Jersey) Bristol, Trenton, Princeton (with a stately college), New Brunswick, Woodbridge, Bridgetown, Elizabethtown. From Elizabethtown point we took passage in an open boat to New York, distance 11 miles. We stop'd one day in New York; next day took passage in a packet and sailed up the East River to New Haven, took passage from there in the land stage thro' Connecticut, by way of Middletown and Harford, then thro' Massachusetts, Springfield, Worcester, and Camebridge; cross'd a flat bridge upwards of a mile long over a low water and marshy ground into Boston.

For a bout two months this man perform'd with success. He gave me a night's profit, which I saved, except a few little articles I stood in need for I bought. I also got my passage money home from him. At intervals I would be in company with a genteel young man who lived with his parents next door to my lodgings. He was a pupil of Mr. Turnner, dancing master. He introducet me in to the school, where I would often go as a spectator or visiter. Mr. Turnner had a great number of scholars of both sexes and would sometimes practice them all together when I would make sure to attend. I learned at once his method and the dances then in vogue. I saw the master's boast lay principally in hornpipes, for he would have his best hornpipe dancer dress'd in a neat sailor's dress. At a practice in the daytime my young friend was one of the hornpipe dancers. In return of friendship I taught him many steps and soon made him the best dancer in the school, by private lessons.

* * *

I took a parting glass of red wine with my young friend in the wine celler of under Dr. Cooper's church (the bell of this church is too heavy to ring, but is sounded by strikeing it with a large hammer). The citizens frequent this celler and drink the wine at eighteen pence the bottle. I took leave of my young friend and set out on my journey to return home. I took the rout that leads out of Boston thro' the neck, reaching to a small town inhabited by shoemakers and weavers. From this town, I think is called Rocksberry, our cities are furnished and supply'd with what is call'd Yankey or New England shoes and whare. I bought a pair of fairtop good new boots for three dollars. I journey'd on to Providence; from this I took passage in a packet to New Haven. There I took the land stage again thro' the state of Connecticut, and towns of Stradford, Fairfield, Norwalk, Stamford; (state of New York) Kingsbridge, passed the White Plains, Fort Washington, and Fort Lee, arrived at New York, cross'd the Powlus Hook ferry, took the land stage thro' New Jersey by way of Newark and [. . .] arrived safe in Philadelphia. As I step'd out of the stage with my small parcel in my hand, I met with an old school fellow who was rejoiced to see me. He revived my spirits by insisting to carry my baggage tho' but small and accompany me to my father's house. I approached the house with timorous steps and fluttering heart. Like the Prodigal Son returned, I entered the house, and with submissive reverence approch'd my father, who stretch'd forth his hands and with transport embraced me in his arms with a parental affection. Our tears where our substitute for words; they express'd at once a welcome and reconciliation with my father.

At this time, 1785, Lewis Hallam, Mr. Allen and wife, and Mr. Moore, where performing in the old Theatre, South St., under the head of "Lectures on Heads." Mrs. Allen sung; they gave scenes of plays and scraps of pantomimes.

I had an invitation to a ball. I dress'd in costume of the times, a blue coat cut in the French stile, a white tissue vestcoat, white casemere small clothes, white silk stockings, French shoes, stitch'd heels, with small sett buckles in the knee and shoes, ruffle on the wrist and bosom; the hair full dressed with the toupee, the hair tied in a fantail club with a black rose, two curls each side well powdered; a cock'd hat, gloves, and small cane, a gold watch with gold trinkets on the chain. I attended the ball. On entering the hall, I saw a large assemblage of ladies and gentlemen, many of my acquaintance, and here it was, the only time I ever could be prevaild on to dance a hornpipe in a private company. The next day commendation where bestow'd on my dancing thro' the city. The report reach'd Mr. Hallam's ear, who waited on my father to negotiate on liberal terms for me to dance on the stage, which with my father's consent I excepted.

Mr. Hallam wish'd me to rehearse my hornpipe in the morning on the stage, to get used to it—I expect a desire on his part to see a specimen of my talents. When I came on the stage, Mr. Hallam introduced me to Mr. and Mrs. Allen. The presence of them setting in the front of the stage to see me rehearse rob'd me of my best powers. A kind of fright seized me and weaken'd my better strength, which will allways be the situation of a novice on his first examination, especially when before such sterling old actors; you dread the criticism of their judgment. Mr. Hallam play'd the "Collage Hornpipe" on the violin. I dancet a few steps and made an apology, and hoped he would be satisfy'd, with my dancing at night. He encouraged me by assurance that he was already satisfied with the certainty that I would please. Mrs. Allen gave me a compleat discription of the suitable dress, with the advise to finish every step beating time.

The interest of the theatre principally belong'd to Hallam. Mr. Allen had a property in town, the house he lived in.

My dress was in the caracter of a sailor, a dark blue round about full of plated buttons, paticoat trousers made with 6 yeard of fine linnen, black satin small clothes underneath, white silk stockings, a light shoe with a hansome set buckle, a red westcoat, a blue silk handkerchief; my hair curled and black, a small round hat gold laced with a blue ribband, a small rattan.

With anxiety I waited the result of the night. The theatre on this occasion was crowded to see a fellow townsman make his first appearance on any stage. I had contrived a trample behind the wing to enable me to gain the centre of the stage in one spring. When the curtain rose, the cry was, "Sit down, hats off!" With the swiftness of Mercury I stood before them, with a general huzza, and dancet in busts of applause. When I went off the stage, I was encored. They made such a noise, throwing a bottle in orchestre, apple, &c. on the stage, at last the curtain was raised again and I dancet a second time to the general satisfaction of the audience and managers, and gained my point.

c. 1821/1966

Ralph Waldo Emerson (1803–1882)

It's hard to imagine the revered Ralph Waldo Emerson—transcendentalist, abolitionist, the most influential intellectual of nineteenth-century America, the "Sage of Concord"—as a ballet (or ballerina) lover, but here we are. He was far from the only man to be dazzled by the sensual allure and flashing technique of the brilliant Viennese ballerina Fanny Elssler during her immensely successful American tour of the early 1840s. But then the great transcendentalist had always had an eye for an attractive woman. Most famous for his lectures (1,500 of them) and his essays—"Self-Reliance," "Nature," etc.—he also won considerable popularity for his poetry, especially for the first stanza of his 1836 "Hymn to Concord"—

> By the rude bridge that arched the flood,
> Their flag to April's breeze unfurled,
> Here once the embattled farmers stood,
> And fired the shot heard round the world.

—as romantic in its way as Elssler's most popular dance, *La Cachucha*.

On Fanny Elssler

Oct. 16. I saw in Boston Fanny Elssler in the ballet of Nathalie. She must show, I suppose, the whole compass of her instrument and add to her softest graces of motion or "the wisdom of her feet,"—the feats of the rope dancer & tumbler: and perhaps on the whole the beauty of the exhibition is enhanced by this that is strong & strange, as when she stands erect on the extremities of her toes, or on one toe, or "performs the impossible" in attitude, but the chief beauty is in the extreme grace of her movement, the variety & nature of her attitude, the winning fun & spirit of all her little coquetries, the beautiful erectness of her body & the freedom & determination which she can so easily assume, and what struck me much the air of perfect sympathy with the house and that mixture of deference and conscious superiority which puts her in perfect spirits & equality to her part. When she courtesies, her sweet & slow & prolonged Salam which descends & still descends whilst the curtain falls, until she seems to have invented new depths of grace & condescension, she earns well the profusion of bouquets of flowers which are hurled on to the stage.

As to the morals, as it is called, of this exhibition, that lies wholly with the spectator. The basis of this exhibition like that of every human talent is moral, is the sport & triumph of health or the virtue of organization. Her charm for the house is that she dances for them or they dance in her not being (fault of some defect in their forms & educations) able to dance themselves. We must be expressed. Hence all the cheer & exhilaration which the spectacle imparts and the intimate property which each beholder feels in the dancer, & the joy with which he hears good anecdotes of her spirit & her benevolence. They know that such surpassing grace must rest on some occult foundations of inward harmony.

But over & above her genius for dancing are the incidental vices of this individual, her own false taste or her meretricious arts to please the groundlings & which must displease the judicious. The immorality the immoral will see, the very immoral will see that only, the pure will not heed it, for it is not obtrusive, perhaps will not see it at all. I should not think of danger to young women stepping with their father or brother out of happy & guarded parlors into this theatre to return in a few hours to the same; but I can easily suppose that it is not the safest resort for college boys who have left Metaphysics, Conic Sections, or Tacitus to see these tripping satin slippers and they may not forget this graceful silvery swimmer when they have retreated again to their baccalaureate cells.

It is a great satisfaction to see the best in each kind, and as a good student of the world, I desire to let pass nothing that is excellent in its own kind unseen, unheard.

1841

Barbara Milberg Fisher (1931–)

Ballet soloist, professor of English literature, pianist, mother of three: Barbara Milberg Fisher has led many lives. A student of classical piano from early childhood in her native Brooklyn, she also studied ballet. In 1946, at the age of fourteen, while a student at the School of American Ballet, she was invited by George Balanchine to join Ballet Society and immediately began performing in Balanchine ballets. She was a charter member of New York City Ballet, where she performed from 1948 to 1958, rising to the rank of soloist, choreographing a section of *Jeux d'Enfants* at Balanchine's behest and, when needed, serving as the page-turner for Balanchine's rehearsal pianist, Nicholas Kopeikine. The last ballet she performed at NYCB was the 1957 Balanchine–Stravinsky collaboration *Agon*, in which Fisher danced the Galliard duet as part of the original cast. In 1958, Jerome Robbins—who had been casting her in his choreography since 1949—invited her to dance with his new company, Ballets: U.S.A., and she performed with it until 1962. During the 1970s, Fisher went back to school and, by 1980, she had earned her B.A., M.A., and Ph.D in English literature and had joined the faculty of City College, where she earned tenure. She has published scholarly books on Wallace Stevens and on mathematics in poetry. The chapter below was drawn from her memoir, *In Balanchine's Company*.

Nightmare in Copenhagen

Betty Cage, our business manager, was a striking woman. She had black hair, wide-set bottomless black eyes, a broad face with good bones, and a complexion that ranged from pale to tan. She appeared to have an admixture of Native American and African bloodlines along with the Caucasian, but could easily have passed as a gypsy. Surrounded by skinny people, Betty tended more toward plumpness; she wore comfortable black clothing and bore an uncanny resemblance to a large black pussycat—with the feline's built-in smile. And while she could be devious, also like the cat, it was hard not to like her.

With Barbara Horgan, and the help of Eddie Bigelow, Betty ran the office on the eighth floor of the City Center Building with placid assurance, calmly smoothing irritations and unknotting the problems that constantly arose. Bigelow was Balanchine's right-hand man and liaison with the staff. He was a laconic Yankee from Massachusetts who took care of just about anything that required doing. Eddie was the carpenter who crated Mr. B's Vespa in Florence; the dancer who appeared on stage as Von Rothbart, the Sorcerer in *Swan Lake*, the Mouse King in *Nutcracker*, and as Pluto, god of the Underworld, in *Orpheus*; Bigelow was the friend who took me home to Brooklyn in a cab when I severely sprained an ankle in class. And I will never forget that afternoon at the City Center when Eddie marched into dressing room #7—empty except for me—with the *Peloponnesian War* in his hand, parked himself at the next dressing table, and with a kind of grim relish read out Thucydides' celebrated description of the plague that devastated Athens. He was devoted to Mr. B and worked with Betty and Horgie in the office when needed.

Fortunately, Betty possessed a sense of humor as well as competence; she handled a myriad trivial and not-so-trivial concerns that would have driven lesser souls hysterical. I can still hear those amused, ironic tones repeating *"No good deed goes unpunished!"*—her mantra. In temperament, Betty was a combination of the sanguine and phlegmatic "humours." Each week, at home and on tour, she cheerfully handed us our paychecks; and so far as I know, she never lost patience with any of us. Whether it was a nervous Lincoln, a beset Mr. B, or a bewildered new member of the corps, she directed her attention to each individual with the same pragmatic serenity. Betty, we thought, was a witch—a good witch. *And* she was psychic.

Several times I'd attended informal séances at her walk-up on Third Avenue along with Eddie and Horgie and a few friends. Bigelow was more inclined to relax with a drink and talk to people than to investigate the paranormal. Horgie also enjoyed Betty's gatherings but didn't go in much for the séance stuff either, thought the whole thing "too intense." The rest of us sipped red wine, nibbled on hors d'oeuvres, consulted the Ouija board, and heard indistinct table-knockings. In between, we passed around tales of ghastly appearances, sudden drops in temperature, ghostly hand-prints in hot wax, and various other occult manifestations. Every so often a train on the "El" would rumble by. We gathered around the table with our palms down, fingers spread out, our hands touching in an unbroken circuit; in the flickering light of candles we asked questions of the Spirits. I remember gasps, one evening, when the table canted to one side at a sudden terrifying angle.

Betty's real gift was for reading the Tarot cards, although she didn't care to do it too often. She was very good at interpreting the configurations of the Higher Arcana—allegorical images of *Death, the Lovers, the Falling Tower, the Wheel of Fortune, the Hermit, the Jester,* and so forth—and analyzing the disposition of the numbered cards in the deck, Cups and Staves, Swords and Pentacles. Once she laid out the Tarot deck in a short version for me when I pressed her *please* to "tell my fortune." When she'd finished turning over the cards, we saw that the vertical axis at the center had the *Popess* at the apex of the column and the *Devil* at the base. I was mystified, but Betty said I had the choice to go either way—or could go both ways. A prescient reading.

Over a period of years Betty had grown more and more adept, not only in readings of character but in predicting changes, dangers, and the probable outcome of some tangled turn of events. Some people have twenty-twenty eyesight; Betty had twenty-twenty insight. That's why we called her "psychic." And that was why (as I heard soon after from people close to her, and learned from Betty herself many years later) she deliberately equivocated when, in Berlin, during the 1956 "German Tour," Tanaquil persuaded her to lay out the Tarot cards and read her fortune. The forecast was ominous. And painful for Betty. She could not tell Tanny [Le Clercq] she had seen catastrophe. She was desperately hoping she was wrong.

We'd been traveling north and toward winter at the same time. After closing in Berlin on the first of October, our itinerary took us to Munich, Frankfurt, Brussels, Antwerp, Paris, Cologne, and finally Scandinavia. We were scheduled to perform in Copenhagen during the last week of October, then go on to Stockholm for a week ending in mid-November. The days had grown shorter as we traveled. Every day the dark closed in a little sooner than the day before, and every day it grew colder.

We arrived in Copenhagen by train, settled into our hotels, received invitations to a royal party in our honor, and opened as planned on the twenty-sixth of October at the Kongelige Teater. There were the usual Company classes, and a couple of brief rehearsals to accommodate to the stage. The tour was nearly over. Some of us traveled to Elsinore, some miles north of Copenhagen, to visit the castle of Kronborg (the original of Shakespeare's "Elsinore") and I was disappointed to find that Hamlet's castle was not what I'd imagined—that is, a ghost-ridden Gothic stronghold perched on craggy cliffs at the edge of a wind-tormented North Sea—but a spare symmetrical structure of hewn rock housing a maritime museum. In Copenhagen, the famous Tivoli Gardens were closed for the winter, but we did find Hans Christian Andersen's Little Mermaid perched on a rock in the bay, her tail intact.

At the theater, after the first few days, there was a growing sense that something was wrong. Mr. Balanchine was missing a good deal of the time. Todd Bolender was teaching Company class. Eddie Bigelow went about his business and danced his usual parts but grew gloomier and more laconic as the days and hours passed. A general malaise began to spread through the Company. I don't remember exactly which night it was—was it opening night?—that an anxious Yvonne Mounsey stood in for Tanaquil in *Divertimento*. She was hastily replaced in *Swan Lake. Bourrée Fantasque*. Another ballet was substituted for *La Valse*. Tanny couldn't dance. Nobody could tell us exactly what was wrong with her but she was ill, very ill. Muscle cramps. Weakness. Headache. Fever.

News of her condition leaked out sporadically. Annie Inglis learned that Tanny had called out "George! I need to go to the bathroom and I can't get out of bed." Early on, I remember stopping a worried Mr. B who was moving quickly toward the back of the stage, just before the performance, to ask about Tanny and to let him know I had the phone number of a young doctor at the American Hospital. He'd been in the seat next to mine on the train to Copenhagen and given me the hospital number "just in case." Mr. B broke in, told me that a highly recommended massage therapist had been contacted. He was giving Tanny special massage treatments at their hotel. Her mother was with Tanny night and day. He raced off.

The next day the news was terrifying. Tanny was experiencing excruciating pains in the spine, the fever had mounted to an unbelievable 106 degrees, and a medical doctor had been called in. He thought she might have contracted spinal meningitis, a sure killer at the time, and immediately had Tanny removed to the hospital. Then there was silence. We waited. No more news leaked out. At least not to the company in general.

But when the diagnosis was final, some people had to be notified immediately. Vida Brown, our Ballet Mistress, was probably the first person—after her husband and her mother—to learn what disease Tanny had contracted. When Vida told me about it more than forty years later, I could sense the distress that was loaded into the remembrance. In Copenhagen, Vida said, she and Melissa Hayden were sharing a room in the same hotel as the Balanchine party. Every night after the performance they'd gone to Mr. B to ask how Tanny was doing. Toward the end of that week they were both fast asleep when Vida heard knocking and got up to open the door.

As she recalls it, an insistent knocking awakened Vida at 5:30 in the morning. When she opened the door Mr. B was there, standing in the hall. He looked drawn, pale, somehow shrunken. Come in, come in! No, he just stood there speechless in the doorway. "What is it? What's the matter?" Vida prompted with some urgency. And Balanchine finally was able to say the words: "It's Tanny. She has polio." I put my arms around him, said Vida, and he started to cry, we both started to cry. Then Millie flung her arms around them both, and all three were weeping. Vida asked if she could order some coffee, couldn't think what else to do, but the stricken Balanchine didn't respond. He retreated back into the hallway and leaned against the wall.

We left Denmark, bundled up against the cold, boarding the ferry from Copenhagen to Malmö in the south of Sweden, then the train to Stockholm in the north. Somebody, maybe Horgie, photographed me on the ferry; I had on earmuffs and was clutching a little Steiff leopard I'd acquired on the way. It was strange to be traveling without Tanny and Mr. B. At some point, either on the ferry or the train, each of us was handed a letter on U.S. Army letterhead, a bald notification that we could be vaccinated against poliomyelitis—if we wanted it—when we arrived in Hamburg, our take-off point for the United States and home.

Poliomyelitis was the highly contagious disease we knew as "infantile paralysis," the disease that had crippled President Roosevelt. With the exception of Barbara Walczak, who had contracted and recovered from polio as a child, everyone was pretty scared. Was the disease already incubating in some of us? How long before we'd know? Several decided to refuse the vaccination offer. Some of the younger members had already been vaccinated. It turned out the medics didn't have enough vaccine, in any case, to innoculate everyone in the company. But at least we knew now what had happened to Tanny. In Stockholm we learned that she was still alive. Barely.

She'd been admitted to the American Hospital in Copenhagen but the prognosis was uncertain; she might or might not recover. Her mother and Mr. Balanchine were staying with her. She was in an iron lung. A paralyzed dancer locked up in her own body. How many years would go by before fifty or sixty dancers would stop having nightmares?

In the United States polio had been rampant for years. Its first symptoms could be mistaken for flu; but then the virus attacked the central nervous system. It wasted muscles, caused paralysis, crippling, and often death. Children were particularly vulnerable. The organism that caused the disease had been isolated in 1913, but it was not until July 1952 that Jonas Salk perfected the vaccine that bears his name. By 1954 there was mass inoculation of schoolchildren. In that one year, according to government statistics, the disease had killed over 1,300 people in the United States alone, and crippled more than 18,000. In 1955, with rigorous standards in place, vaccination had reduced the known cases of polio in the States to approximately 29,000. By 1956, the number had decreased by more than half, and 1957 saw fewer than 6,000 cases. Looking back, it seems a devastating irony that the Salk vaccine was not one of the multiple inoculations we were *required* to have before we could leave the country and be allowed to return.

Tanaquil survived, although it was touch and go for a while. Two months after she was stricken, the School sent Natasha Molo (Natalie Molostwoff), one of the administrators and a dear friend of Tanny's, to Copenhagen as a Christmas present. "Tanny was just out of the iron lung," she told Francis Mason, "but she was in despair, in tears. She was white and slack as a piece of paper and scared to death." Mason, well-known dance critic, scholar, editor, ballet historian—and co-author with Mr. B of *Balanchine's Complete Stories of the Great Ballets* and *101 Stories of the Great Ballets*—was collecting interviews from dancers and associates intimate with Balanchine over his life-span, an invaluable collection that remains a prime source of information on the man, certainly the most varied. It was Natasha who revealed, at that time, what most of their intimate friends had long known. Tanny and Balanchine had been on the verge of breaking up and would have separated, she said, if Tanny had not become ill.

They brought her home and Mr. B took her to Warm Springs, Georgia, where Roosevelt had received regular therapy. Tanny was determined to recover as much as possible, and with hard work she gradually regained the use of one arm fully and the other in part. Balanchine continued to work with her, exercise her, but the legs did not recover. She would need a wheelchair to get about. But as we discovered over a period of years, her spirit was anything but crippled.

The woman was indomitable. Collaborating with Martha Swope, the dancer who became one of the great photographers of dance, she wrote a charming whimsical text for *Mourka: The Autobiography of a Cat* (1964), about the house pet Balanchine had trained himself. It was marvelously illustrated by Swope's photographs: Mourka, outdoing the dancers in class. Mourka, spread-eagled in a leap, jumping over Balanchine's crouching form. Mourka, lovingly held in his trainer's arms. A remarkable collaboration among four uniquely gifted individuals.

Jerry Robbins brought her to the theater, carried her when necessary. Eddie Bigelow and Diana Adams were constantly with her. Her friends stayed her friends and she made new ones. For a while, she taught classes from her wheelchair at Arthur Mitchell's ballet school in Harlem. She was the composer of several crossword puzzles published in the *New York Times*; at least one appeared in the magazine section of the Sunday *Times*. She developed into a fine photographer herself. She entertained. She read. She summered in Connecticut. In January of 1984, with willing helpers, she hosted the fiftieth anniversary of the founding of the School of American Ballet at her West 79th Street apartment.

Out of the blue she sent me a funny little book one Christmas, *Horoscopes for Pussycats*, inscribed on the last page in her own strong hand: "To Barbara—Merry Christmas, all my love—Tanny." How had she remembered—and combined!—my delight in pussycats and early fascination with the occult? A few months after my daughter was born, in 1961, Diana called to ask if I would like to bring the baby over to 79th Street so that Tanny could see her. I had not seen Tanny since before Copenhagen and didn't realize her hair had turned the color of her mother's. She held the infant Alexandra on her lap for a minute but Diana had to help support the weight. Maybe twelve pounds. When *Mourka* came out in 1964, she sent me a copy, this time inscribed on the copyright page to "the most beautiful feline-fancier," from "Mourka + Tanny." She had drawn whiskers, eyes and a mouth on the outsized "M" of "Mourka," and used the peaks of the M to provide ready-made ears.

The last time I saw Tanny was at the Fiftieth Anniversary of the New York City Ballet in 1998. The celebration took place in the State Theater at Lincoln Center and the performance was specially dedicated to Tanaquil Le Clercq. I sat in the balcony with my "generation" of NYCB dancers, and watched as that remarkable woman was greeted by a resounding ovation the moment she appeared in the aisle at the left of the orchestra. We joined the cheering audience as she waved, from her wheelchair, with royal aplomb.

2006

George Gelles (1942–)

From 1970 to 1976, George Gelles was the dance critic of *The Washington Star*, and, as we now discover by reading the recently published collection of his reviews, *A Beautiful Time for Dancers*, he was a knowledgeable, acute, and judicious one—and one who could actually *write*. Working at the height of the famous "dance boom," he was in a position to observe and anatomize the work of everyone from Balanchine, Graham, Taylor, and Tharp to Nureyev, Kirkland, and Baryshnikov, and his rich take on the period and its players constitutes a valuable and convincing report from the front. Gelles, however, thinks of himself basically as a musician—a horn player—who just happened not to play professionally for thirty-seven years. During this layoff period, he wrote about music and dance for *The New York Times*, the *New Grove Dictionary of Music and Musicians*, and *Musical America*, while lecturing on music and dance at the Smithsonian, George Washington University, and the San Francisco Conservatory of Music. And, from 1986 to 2000, he was the executive director of San Francisco's Philharmonia Baroque Orchestra. At least the world of dance criticism lost him to a host of other worthy endeavors.

Outside Time, Out-of-Date

WATERMILL would have thrilled an audience a dozen years ago. Its stylistic sources were fresher then, and what it says bore saying. But Jerome Robbins' theater piece, which was recently premiered by the New York City Ballet, has come too late and brought too little. Theatrically cunning and stylishly conceived, it is fundamentally an artificial, stagey work whose attitudes already have atrophied.

Robbins has written a Haiku in movement: a wispy, wistful lyric etched in gestures that are lean and spare. Two stylistic streams converge in *Watermill*. From Asia comes the atmosphere of Japanese theater, primarily Gagaku and Noh, which establishes the large-scale temporal framework through which the work inches its way. And from America comes self-consciously poetic posing, its mythic overtones echoing Martha Graham, and the actual language of the dance itself.

There is very little choreography, per se, in the piece, and none of it is in the formal grammar of classical ballet. Instead, the performers are active in the wide spectrum of today's modern movement, where theatrical touches are fully as important as kinetic technique.

The scenario is one man's meditation on his past, yet Robbins hasn't rested with a simple series of flashbacks but has overstructured the work and overburdened it with a heavy layer of symbolism. We see a lifetime lived within the phases of the moon. Boyhood, for instance, is recalled by the faintest of crescents, adolescence by a growing golden sliver, and manhood by the moon's ripest moment.

Each of man's seven ages is accounted for, and the entire cycle is coordinated not only with the flow of lunar time but also with the passage of the seasons. As our hero remembers it, a child sows the seed; a young man bands with comrades in common pursuits; and a mature man takes a woman, reaps his harvest, and later learns of death.

Throughout the story, however, Robbins has rubbed the edges off the dramatic details, introducing an element of uncertainty into an otherwise straightforward work. His hero is in a sense outside time, ruminating in solitude, and what we see is supposedly the life of his mind. But now and again Robbins has him cross the temporal divide, bringing him in contact with the objects of his reveries.

It seems to me that this has a double effect. First of all, it creates a state of dramatic entropy, a self-defeating standstill that robs *Watermill* of its impetus and force. Ambiguity is one thing, but it's something else again when the focus of a work slips out of sight when its forward thrust is blunted. In the mid-1930s Antony Tudor, of course, dealt similarly with the psychological perception of time, and in comparison with the creativity behind *Watermill*, how elegant his intelligence seems today, how sophisticated his understanding. Robbins, however, blurs the outlines of his work and avoids facing the issues—including the ultimate issue of life and death—head-on.

Second, indecisiveness sets Robbins at a tremendous distance from the heartbeat of the piece. Despite its aura of autobiography, the work feels impersonal. You get the feeling that he's not quite sure of his stylistic turf, that he's falling back on the platitudes implicit in his scenario, and because of this we're cheated of the warmth and openness of his choreography at its best.

The City Ballet's production is marvelous. Dominating the decor by Robbins and David Reppa are three outsized sheaves of wheat, in front of, around, and through which the action moves. At the back of the stage is a drop cloth that shimmers with silky ripples, and the front curtain has the gentle fragility of rice paper.

Teiji Ito's score, played on a variety of Orientalia, strikes me as so much sukiyaki. It is the ultimate refinement in mood music, full of reedy whooshes from bamboo flutes, microtonal swoops and glides, and suggestive, sensitive plunks and scratches on inscrutably delicate drums and gongs. There's even the background barking of dogs and the hollow squawking of gulls.

Edward Villella's intense performance as the protagonist is full of concentrated energy that suits the work admirably, and the rest of the cast is always adequate. Nevertheless, in spite of all the consideration and care it has been shown, *Watermill* doesn't equal its ambitions. For Robbins, it's an unfulfilling footnote to a remarkably distinguished career.

February 18, 1972

NANCY GOLDNER (1943–)

NANCY GOLDNER has written extensively for *The Nation*, *The Christian Science Monitor*, and *Dance News*, and was for many years the dance critic for *The Philadelphia Inquirer*. Her great subject has been the work of George Balanchine, about which she is uniquely qualified to write: she studied at his School of American Ballet and saw her first New York City Ballet performance when she was six and it was one.

Among her publications are *The Stravinsky Festival of the New York City Ballet* (with Lincoln Kirstein) and an accordion book about the Balanchine–Alexandra Danilova version of *Coppélia*. But her magnum opus is *Balanchine Variations* (2008) and its follow-up, *More Balanchine Variations* (2011)—titles as direct, modest, and revelatory as her work is universally acclaimed as being. In these two volumes, she anatomizes more than forty of Balanchine's ballets, almost all of them masterpieces, giving us our most comprehensive consideration of the individual major works that make up the oeuvre of our greatest choreographer. Her observations are deeply personal as well as tellingly analytical. They're the reactions—registered over decades of assiduous watching—of profound knowledge, clear perception, a brilliant eye, and superb talent as a writer.

Symphony in C

BALANCHINE was a master of the finale, and the finale of *Symphony in C* was his masterpiece. With an enormous cast of fifty-two, it was destined to be a winner, but what gives it the blue ribbon is one iconic moment: when the thirty-six women of the ensemble ring the perimeters of the stage and do a series of simple leg and arm movements, while the four principal women pirouette madly in stage center. While the strings of the Bizet score are whirring equally madly,

Balanchine gives us a panoramic view of controlled, organized activity. It's like looking into a beehive, except that Balanchine's bees wear white tutus.

It's fun to subject such a supreme moment to the what-if game. What if the ensemble were not grouped into pristine lines? Well, there's nothing as powerful as a line; you need only think of the procession of the shades in the dream scene of *La Bayadère*, or of the Rockettes in their *grand battement* routine. What if the corps and principals were dancing in unison? Well, that's always exciting, but what we do see—a contrast between the more simple steps of the ensemble and the intensity of the principals' pirouettes—is in exciting counterpoint to the music, which at the moment is "dancing" in unison. And then there's the matter of playing one's hand judiciously in what is the fourth movement's long finale. There will be unison dancing, but it will come later, toward the very end of the ballet.

As perfect as the setup is, however, it doesn't quite explain the brilliance of the moment. What if the ensemble did a simple series of *tendus* and corresponding arm movements? It would be splendid—with so many legs and arms moving, it couldn't be anything less—but Balanchine adds a few complications that give the visual and kinetic fabric of the choreography even more texture. The legs move front and side in *tendu* rather than in one direction, but they don't move absolutely front and side. That might end up being flat and heavy. Balanchine shades the direction by having the dancers stand at an angle to the audience. Thus, the foot moves forward in a *croisé*, or crossed, position and to the side in *écarté*, or on a diagonal. The arms, meanwhile, change every time the dancers switch from *croisé* to *écarté* and back again. Taking in the whole stage picture with one gulp, you notice (or eventually notice) that while the principals are galloping ahead in four beats to the measure, the ensemble is moving in three beats. Thus, the new dance measure for the ensemble begins just before the principals' next measure.

The *tendus* have their own complications. After much squinting at a videotape with the help of Sabrina Pillars, a former dancer with the New York City Ballet, and Victoria Simon, a ballet mistress for The George Balanchine Trust, I hereby present the recipe for those *tendus*. On count one the right foot moves forward. On count two it moves to the side and closes in fifth position behind the standing leg. On count three the leg moves to the side again, and closes in fifth position with the moving leg in front. This set is done two times on the same working leg. On the third set, however, the dancers do only two *tendus*, front and side. The dancers on the left side of the stage close front, and those on the right side close back, so that each side is a mirror image of the other. They do three more sets like the first two, except that the working leg changes each time and each side has the opposite working leg. At this point the ensemble stops dead in its tracks while the principals keep the momentum going by fairly pounding the floor with *bourrées*.

The moral is that there's more to the *tendu* story than meets the eye. Its pattern is asymmetrical, and its counts for the ensemble don't jibe with those for the principals. Finally, although the whole *tendu* section looks like unison dancing, only the first half truly is. It doesn't matter all that much whether you catch the irregularities right away, upon repeated viewings, or not at all. They are felt subliminally. Sensing them is sufficient to make the whole passage vibrant and light and unpredictable.

Of course, even at its most superficial level the mere sight of all those legs and arms moving together (more or less) makes the spirit soar no matter how many times you see the ballet. And the spectacle is always something of a surprise—despite the fact that Balanchine has been dropping clues along the way. The first thing the eight corps women do in the first movement is a sequence of *tendus*. In the fourth, last movement the women line up and *tendu* in counterpoint to the principal couple's more intricate steps. And the table is all but laid out before our eyes in the prelude to the big moment. This prelude—the second half of the fourth movement—is a recapitulation of the first three. Each of the casts rushes on and repeats (with some variation) signature moments of its choreography. At the end of their respective encores the principals exit, while the ensemble steps to the sides of the stage and poses. Slowly the perimeters of the stage fill in, so that by the time the principal women return to begin their pirouettes, the entire ensemble is assembled and ready to go.

This *tendu* extravaganza takes less than a minute, and there is much more finale derring-do to come. In typical Balanchine fashion, the excitement simmers down and then builds again as the four balle-rinas enter and repeat their turns and then join all the women in a jamboree of dancing. Just as the clock strikes midnight, all fifty-two dancers form a fabulous tableau: the corps poses on its toes, the eight female demi-soloists are lifted onto their partners' shoulders, and the ballerinas stand in *passé* and snap their torsos way, way over to the side. All of this contrasting movement happens in a flash, and the curtain drops. The audience feels that it has been splashing in the fountain of youth.

Georges Bizet was all of seventeen years old when he wrote *Symphony in C* in 1855. The score gathered dust for many years in the Conservatoire de Paris. Some musicologists believe that Bizet kept it hidden away because he felt it was too derivative. Not until 1935 was the symphony given a public performance. The wording in the New York City Ballet's program note for *Symphony in C* suggests that Balanchine was the first to choreograph to the score. This is not so. First honors goes to Andrée Howard. She set the music on the junior company of the Sadler's Wells, in London, where it premiered in April 1946 under the name *Assembly Ball*. Balanchine heard about the score not from London sources, but from Stravinsky. When he traveled to Paris in February 1947 to begin a six-month residency as ballet master at the opera house, he chose this French music as the vehicle for a new ballet for the Paris Opera. It premiered on July 28, 1947, under the name *Le Palais de Cristal*, reflecting the sumptuous decor and costumes by Leonor Fini. The tunics and tutus were in a different color for each of the four movements. When the ballet premiered in New York on March 22, 1948, as part of a Ballet Society bill, the crystal palace was replaced by a simple blue cyclorama; the tutus were all white and the men's tunics black.

Bizet composed his first symphony in five weeks. Balanchine choreographed to it in two. The speed with which Balanchine worked was typical. Whether Bizet was as nimble I do not know, but certainly both compositions have an exuberance and spontaneity suggesting that the Muse sat very near as both artists worked. As for the ballet, every step, every pattern, and every compositional device flows so naturally and effortlessly out of the music that the choreography hardly seems a translation from one medium into another. Undoubtedly the ballet underwent some translation as it crossed the ocean from Paris to New York, particularly if it enhanced the special talents of the dancers. Maria Tallchief, the lead in the first movement in New York, thinks that Balanchine added some pirouettes for her; she was a champion turner. My hunch is that in the adagio movement in Paris, Tamara Toumanova had a few more balances than her American counterpart, Tanaquil Le Clercq. I surmise this because Balanchine often told the story of how he gave Toumanova lots of balances because it was a specialty of hers. But what happened at the premiere? The great balancer kept falling off pointe. He told this story as a warning to young dancers rehearsing difficult pas de deux. Don't stop when you make a flub; flubs are inevitable, he would say. The point of rehearsals was to prepare for "disaster," as he called it.

I am not sure that Balanchine actually did alter the adagio to ward off disaster—or, indeed, that he significantly altered it at all. It so happens that there was a perfect opportunity to compare versions when in 1986 the Paris Opera Ballet performed *Le Palais de Cristal* at the Metropolitan Opera in New York. But the opportunity eluded me because I was so disoriented by the different-colored tutus that I could not focus on what the dancers were doing. The American *Symphony in C* nails the music so perfectly that it seems impossible, my ignorance notwithstanding, to imagine Balanchine doing it any other way.

Sometimes Balanchine captures the music with unusual literalness, especially in the third movement. When the main musical theme repeats itself, so does the choreography for the lead couple—step for step, from their brilliant leaps around the stage to the ballerina's fast pirouettes ending in a faster dip into an arabesque *penchée*. Balanchine cheerfully follows the music's command with no ifs, ands, or buts. My favorite example of this, also in the third movement, is when the violins are in a brief holding pattern before the main theme takes over. The dancers mimic the music's anticipatory feeling by quickly springing up onto pointe and down four times. Yes, Balanchine is Mickey-Mousing the music, but to wander from Bizet's irresistible beat would be perverse.

Mostly Balanchine captures the music's spirit with parallel constructs. Except for the second, adagio movement, the score is allegro. It contrasts bold, declarative statements, especially in the first, most developed movement, with melodies that sing; indeed, you can't help but sing them to yourself. The dancing, likewise, alternates between fast, emphatic footwork and broader, spacious movement. This dualism is seen right off the bat with the ensemble and two demi-soloist couples. The first motif is a little curtsy to the front leg, then a sharp hop onto pointe, then a fast, even sharper twist of the whole torso so that the dancers face to the back. That's a lot of robust dancing packed into three beats. Soon they take large steps sideways, ending with their bodies softly stretched sideways, picking up the music's singing quality. In some of the loveliest moments of the first movement the ensemble, split into two groups, volleys a phrase back and forth, which makes you hear the music's dialogue between the bold and the delicate.

This contrast is seen most concretely in the choreography for the ballerina in the first movement—in her elongated arabesques and loping canters with her partner versus the delicate but strong thrusts of her pointes into the floor. There are few roles that challenge the dancer to move so rapidly between almost percussive vigor and largesse. To my mind, the principal in the first movement is the ballet's heroine. But she is an unsung heroine, for two reasons. First, the ensemble fairly dominates the stage, so rich and ever-present is its dancing. Second, it's the adagio woman who has the glamour, as always.

The adagio ballerina in *Symphony in C* is perhaps the most prized role in the Balanchine repertory. To contemporary dancers she is what Odette used to signify to ballerinas of earlier generations. This Bizet ballerina is imperturbable. She moves in one long, sustained pulse unbroken by breathing (so it seems). Aided by her cavalier, she glides through the air without ever touching ground (so it seems). Balanchine likened her to "the moon gliding across the sky." Yet she does not dwell alone in her own universe. Following the example of the adagio in *Concerto Barocco*, Balanchine sets the dancers in interplay right from the beginning. As a prelude to the entrance of the ballerina and her partner, the demi-soloist couples make a bridge over the ensemble, who nod as the two couples walk by. As the ballerina does big arabesques soon after, the demi-soloists enclose her and her cavalier with their arms. And when she's lifted across the stage in an arabesque, her partner dips her into the middle of a circle the demi-soloists make with their arms, as if they were awaiting her arrival. You might say that these courtesies are recognition of rank, but they also bespeak tenderness, care, and intimacy—all the qualities we might wish for in our own communities.

In the *Barocco* adagio these niceties are continuous. In this adagio, however, they function as preliminaries for the main musical event, which is the introduction of Bizet's second theme for this movement. The six women of the ensemble *bourrée* toward the back of the stage under the arms of the demi-soloists. The men exit and the women recede to the back and sides, clearing the space for the ballerina and cavalier, who leads her forward. As the grand melody begins, she slowly lifts her leg in a *grand développé à la seconde*, a moment, which, as followers of Petipa's and Balanchine's ballets know, creates a special gravity, the coronation, if you will, of the ballerina. In the following passages—of difficult balances, hushed lifts, and deep arabesques *penchées*—she does indeed seem to exist in her own universe. Then the spell is broken with a fugue. The ensemble joins the ballerina again with the sharp movements befitting a fugue. The return of the oboe theme, which began the adagio, heralds the return of the ballerina as the gliding moon. At the end, her partner drapes her over his knee and slowly rotates her in a circle as she sinks closer and closer to the floor. As she is reaching her final resting place, the demi-soloists make a bridge over the ensemble and pass by in arabesques; the ensemble responds by lunging forward. Whereupon the audience takes its first breath in some nine minutes.

There was one occasion when the audience was literally breathless. On January 16, 1976, Suzanne Farrell marked her homecoming to the City Ballet in this adagio, after an absence of six years. Balanchine sets the stage for the ballerina's entrance with a relatively long introduction by the ensemble and demi-soloists. I don't think I've ever felt such stillness in the audience during this prelude; in retrospect I sometimes ask myself, What were we expecting? Was it the mere sight of Farrell after so many years that had us all on edge? When at long, long last, it seemed, she slowly *bourréed* onstage, her face was so rapt and her body so attuned to the sad strains of the oboe that you felt the years of her hiatus evaporate. She was paler and thinner than you remembered, but she was the artist she had always been.

Symphony in C has been the occasion for countless other debuts, though unheralded. By company tradition, City Ballet apprentices step onto the stage for the first time with the company in the fourth movement. I often think of the exhilaration these novices must feel when they participate in the festival of *tendus*. Something of that exhilaration could be felt when Mikhail Baryshnikov danced the lead in the third movement in 1978. He obviously had a great time soaring in circles around the stage, but it was in the finale that he seemed most happy. For once, he was a player in a grand show rather than the show himself. He looked more at home in *Symphony in C* than in any other ballet he performed during his year and a half with the City Ballet.

Symphony in C makes everyone happy—and more. Watching it is a rejuvenating experience. Since its New York premiere in March 1948 it has joined works like *Serenade, The Four Temperaments, Concerto Barocco*, and *Agon* as definitions of classical ballet at the City Ballet. But I don't think that any of them lifts the spirit in such an irresistibly straightforward way as the Bizet.

2011

A Midsummer Night's Dream

FIREFLY SEASON is in full swing as I write. In Central Park laughing children and their parents charge the beetles with glass jars and promises to release them from their captivity the next morning. Older folk sit on park benches and simply enjoy the spectacle. Everyone loves fireflies, including, apparently, George Balanchine, who as a child played an insect in a theatrical production of *A Midsummer Night's Dream*. For he begins his dance version of the play with a swarm of child insects and adult butterflies darting around the stage like fireflies. This being a ballet, however, the first bug to make an appearance is poised for flight appropriately in *tendu*.

Mendelssohn's music indicates the scurrying of nature's most fleet-footed creatures, but dancing insects aren't the only option for a choreographer. Ashton's *The Dream*, created in 1964, two years after the Balanchine version, sets dancing fairies to the same music and to marvelous effect. That Balanchine chose an insect corps de ballet tells one much about a central theme of *Midsummer*. It is an affectionate contemplation of nature in summertime, when the evening hours hum and buzz with particular intensity. Insects and butterflies fairly dominate the first act. (In his autobiography, *Prodigal Son*, Edward Villella complained that Balanchine barely had time to set his variation as Oberon, so preoccupied was he in working out the moves for the children.) One of the most moving moments in the ballet is when the baby insects, obeying the call of Mendelssohn, settle down for a night's sleep. They are followed by the butterflies, obedient to the silent call of Puck. Hark, he says, it is time to rest. At least the insect world is in harmony with nature. Nobody else is, of course, and that's the other theme of the first act of this two-act ballet, Balanchine's first original full-evening work.

Balanchine presents the cast of characters and their troubles in one breath. Within six minutes, a sorrowful Helena walks across the stage absent-mindedly plucking a leaf from Puck's invisible (to her) hand. Oberon and Titania fight over the changeling boy. Tipsy rustics galumph. Oberon and Titania have another fight. Then the scene switches from the forest to the court in Athens, where Theseus hears the complaints of Hermia, Lysander, Helena, and Demetrius. Demetrius lunges toward Hermia. Rudely stamping his foot, he demands, Why can't I have her? Theseus dismisses them all with a disgusted wave of the hand. Now back to the forest, where Helena resumes her sad, dazed walk. The insects try to comfort her, but to no avail, and so lulled by Mendelssohn's lullaby they go to sleep.

Whereas Ashton's *The Dream* progresses logically, Balanchine's ballet begins as a jumble of events. But then, Shakespeare's play is about jumbles. Although the scenes are staged in sequence, they could be happening simultaneously, particularly the arguments between Oberon and Titania and the dance of the rustics. (Does Balanchine mean to equate the rustics' antics with the dispute between the king and queen of the fairies? Likely so, I think.) Balanchine also takes us backward and forward in time with cinematic speed. First, Helena is in the forest, next in Athens, next in the forest again.

In preparing a libretto for *The Dream*, Ashton wanted to stick to the main points of the story. Conciseness was usually Balanchine's approach as well, but in *Midsummer* he cast his net wider than Ashton does by including the characters of Theseus and Hippolyta (who has a long dance of her own in the first act). I think he decided to bring them into the proceedings to show that disorder ruled not only the enchanted forest but civil life as well. Theseus is the Duke of Athens; the four lovers appearing before him at his palace care not a whit for his authority.

Throughout the first act, the problems among the mortal lovers are comically conceived with well-timed gesture, all in pantomime. Demetrius is a lout, and Lysander stupid. The women, however, are portrayed with more sympathy. Helena's solo of lament is rather generic, but one truly feels for the abandoned Hermia during her long solo, when, lost in the forest, she twists and turns as if losing her mind.

The discord between Oberon and Titania is harder to read, having a quality not of the rustics' nonsense but of mindlessness. The key here is the fact that they repeat their claims for the little boy with exactly the same gestures and affect. The repetition makes their argument a ritual exercise, habitual, ingrained. This is the kind of couple whose natural mode is disharmony. Their reconciliation, after Titania emerges from her dream, is perfunctory; that is, they walk off the stage together. They do not dance a pas de deux, as they do in Ashton's version.

The great moment in *The Dream* is the duet between Oberon and Titania, the subtlest evocation of erotic love in all ballet literature. In *Midsummer* the two, as I have written, have no pas de deux. To music swelling with grandeur (the Overture to *Athalie*), music that could well serve as a grand pas de deux for Titania and Oberon, she dances instead with an unnamed cavalier. Her other duet is with Bottom. Ironically, this pas de deux between an adoring Titania and an uncomprehending donkey is set to the same music Ashton uses for his Titania/Oberon tryst. This impassioned music (the Nocturne from the incidental music to the play) is perfectly attuned to the sexual complexities that the two fairies ultimately resolve—his need to contain her independence and her need to resist. The Nocturne music also brings out the comic nature of the Titania/Bottom story: all that musical urgency bestowed upon an animal!

The story is simple: Titania loves Bottom and Bottom loves grass. Their impasse is encapsulated in the moment when Titania, in a swoon, bares her bosom to the animal while he responds by staring blankly at the audience. I, for one, associate that stare with the Jack Benny look, and that's because Balanchine loved Jack Benny. I know this because I remember an interview in which he responded to a question about his reputation by saying something like, "I'm overrated. Shakespeare is overrated. Mozart. Stravinsky. Even Jack Benny is overrated." In any case, Bottom's steadfast dumbness in the face of amorous longing always draws a laugh from the audience. Their duet is comedy at its sweetest.

Oberon's solo, danced to the scherzo, is the dance climax of Act I. With its speed and space-devouring thrust, it is a technical marvel and is considered one of the most challenging roles in the City Ballet repertory. Villella, for whom Oberon was created, summed up the technical paradox of the variation by writing that in preparation for the jumps, the *plié* had to be fully articulated, which means that you have to dance slower to dance faster.

The curious aspect about this first act is that, although the mortals make up, the hero and heroine go their separate ways. Thus no love pas de deux, thus no revelatory moment for the ballerina, the figure through whom Balanchine typically expresses his most profound feeling. But there is Act II to set things right.

Ashton could wrap up the story in one act and within the boundaries of Mendelssohn's incidental music for Shakespeare's play. Balanchine needed a second act. Set at the court of Theseus in Athens, it is a wedding divertissement for the quartet of now-reconciled lovers, Theseus and Hippolyta, and a large ensemble. By choreographing a pure-dance final act Balanchine was following a time-honored convention from the nineteenth century. A second act also gave him the opportunity to use more and less familiar Mendelssohn, whom he much admired. By the time *Midsummer* is over, we have heard, in addition to the famous incidental music to the play, overtures to *Athalie*, *The Fair Melusine*, *The First Walpurgis Night*, and *Son and Stranger*, and the *Symphonia No. 9 for Strings*. But the main reason for Act II is to enable Balanchine to interpret the play in his own way.

For it is in the second act that we see the sublime pas de deux so markedly absent from the first. It is performed not by the fairy king and queen, as it would be in Shakespeare's play were it a ballet, but by an anonymous man and woman. In this duet the couple dance in slow whispers. He wafts her in low lifts forward and back. He slowly lifts her and places her down in quarter-turn rotations so that we can see her rest in always-changing perspectives, each of them utterly precious because of the deliberate softness with which the man carries her. He escorts her in a long diagonal of *bourrées*, her body quietly weaving left and right and so entwining us all in a spell. At the end, she falls backward into his arms, then way forward so that her chest almost touches the floor. From there he revolves her in a half-circle into the traditional swoon with which many romantic pas de deux conclude.

The partnering is tricky, but in this duet the mechanics are invisible. Act I is all push and pull, but here you don't know who is leading and who is following. When a hand is needed for support, it materializes out of thin air. It thus becomes a metaphor of trust and intimacy between two people. And compared to everything else that's come before, in Act II as well as Act I, it is so quiet and tender—so at home with itself. As one watches the duet, everything and everybody recedes into the distance. All that matters are these two dancers. Shakespeare said that the mortals are fools. Balanchine says that the whole lot of them are, except, of course, this one couple who dance the pas de deux. There is a streak of darkness in this comic ballet.

Obviously, it's crucial to Balanchine's game plan that the ballerina in the duet and Titania are not the same person, and in my experience they never have been. Once, though, at the end of a talk I had given on this ballet, the wife of the artistic director of the company I was visiting approached me with a twinkle in her eye. She told me that many years ago, when she was dancing with a troupe in Switzerland, Balanchine came for a few days to oversee the final rehearsals of the ballet. He was so taken with the dancer who performed Titania that he had her dance the pas de deux as well. He wanted to see her dance as much as possible in the short time he was there. Well, so much for my theory about the ballet's meaning. I guess the story shows that Balanchine was more interested in dancers than in ideas. Still, was it perverse of him to wreck the structure he had carefully built? Perhaps he was playing Puck.

It happens that Puck is the character who ends *Midsummer*. In *The Nutcracker* Balanchine chose to end the story in the Land of Sweets instead of returning to the reality of Marie's home. In *Midsummer*, though, he leaves the equivalent of the Land of Sweets to go back home to the forest. After the long divertissement—with its expansive (and sometimes dull) dancing and abundance of tutus—Mendelssohn's incidental music returns and so do the insects, who once again scurry about. Titania and Oberon join hands in a symbolic gesture of reconciliation, then parade off in opposite directions with their respective retinues. The lights grow darker, and Puck emerges from the shadows. The last we see of him, he's flying into a night sky sparkling with fireflies.

2011

Robert Gottlieb (1931–)

Robert Gottlieb, perhaps the most eminent editor in American publishing of the past sixty years, identifies so energetically with language on the page that he entitled his autobiography *Avid Reader*. However, as a high school student in his native New York City, his life was changed, in 1948, by his attendance at a performance of the Balanchine–Stravinsky ballet *Orpheus*, during the last season of Ballet Society. "My fate was sealed," he writes. "Dance liberated me from the bondage of language, and balanced my life." Esteemed for his achievements at his day jobs (editor-in-chief of Alfred A. Knopf and Simon & Schuster, editor of *The New Yorker*) and admired for his biographies of Sarah Bernhardt and of the children of Charles Dickens, and for his long, incisive essays for *The New York Review of Books* and *The New Yorker*, Gottlieb is known to the dance world for his editing of a marvelous group of books on ballet (by Lincoln Kirstein, Margot Fonteyn, Arlene Croce, Paul Taylor, Mikhail Baryshnikov, Natalia Makarova, and others); for his editing of *Reading Dance*, his doorstop of a dance anthology; for his decades of volunteer service to New York City Ballet and Miami City Ballet; for his curation of a landmark Fonteyn-in-America exhibition at the New York Public Library for the Performing Arts; for his bringing about musical support for silent films of Balanchine ballets; for his decades of reviewing dance for *The New York Observer*; and—all in a day's work!—for his biography of Balanchine. In 2015, he received the annual Award for Distinguished Service to the Arts from the American Academy of Arts and Letters.

Free Spirit

THE MOST famous woman of the first quarter of the twentieth century may have been Mary Pickford, but the most influential, and the most notorious, was Isadora Duncan. She was the progenitor and soul of a new art form, modern dance. She was the prototype of the uninhibited young American whose freshness and originality charmed jaded old Europe. And for decades she startled respectable society—even as she helped transform it—with her flouting of conventions, both onstage and off. You would have to go back to George Sand or Byron to find a comparably galvanizing figure. Early in 1927, in the fledgling *New Yorker*, Janet Flanner identified her as "the last of the trilogy of great female personalities our century produced," along with Duse and Bernhardt. But those two supreme actresses were dead ends; no one could follow in their footsteps. Isadora's accomplishments reverberate through the history of dance to this day.

Isadora Duncan was born in San Francisco in 1877, the youngest of four children. Her father regularly made and lost fortunes, and eventually was gone from the family (he was to die in a shipwreck—nothing the Duncans did was ordinary). The children and their mother lived from hand to mouth; there is more than a touch of Micawberism in the way they got by—high spirits in the midst of semi-penury. But already Isadora was demonstrating the vigorous independence that was to carry her to world fame.

From the start she was clearly the Chosen One within what the family called the Clan Duncan. At eighteen, with her mother in tow and $25 in her pocket, she started east and soon wangled a job with Augustin Daly's prestigious stage company, spending months in various demeaning (to her) roles and developing "a perfect nausea for the theater." She confronted Daly: "What's the good of having me here, with my genius, when you make no use of me?" By the time she was twenty-one, she was established in New York, appearing in concerts, dancing to Chopin at special matinees, providing entertainment in private salons (including Mrs. Astor's, in Newport). She was young, slender, very pretty with her vivid red hair and Irish button nose, and exceedingly charming—a Botticelli figurine. She was also highly respectable, with her formidable mother at the piano and her brothers and sister accompanying her dancing with recitations, often from "The Rubaiyat." Yet she was already shocking people with her "unobscured limbs." And she was already lecturing—hectoring?—her audiences about The Dance.

In May 1899, after a typical Duncan calamity (a near-fatal fire in their hotel), Isadora set out for the larger opportunities of Europe. Her reputation grew as she succeeded in London, then Paris, and was sealed in Budapest in 1902—twenty sold-out performances, ovations, roses thrown at her feet. She was also no longer a virgin. Oszkar Beregi, a handsome young actor, was performing Romeo, and very quickly she was his offstage Juliet, only without benefit of Friar Lawrence. She had waited a long while to discover sex—she was twenty-five—but she would make up for lost time.

Not for long with Beregi, however; soon he tactfully suggested that she proceed with her career, and, having fantasized about marriage, she felt as if she had "eaten bushels of broken glass." On she went, though, to Vienna and Munich, where she had an even greater triumph. It was there, her latest biographer Peter Kurth tells us,* that "the German 'cult of Isadora' was born, a national craze that took her beyond success and notoriety into the realms of literature, philosophy, feminism and even science . . . as the realization of Darwin's dream, the 'Dancer of the Future,' whose coming proclaimed the triumph of beauty and the liberation of women in the final perfection of the race." In *My Life*, her more readable than accurate autobiography, she recalls that it was in Berlin at this time that "on my return from performances where the audience had been delirious with joy, I would sit far into the night in my white tunic, with a glass of white milk beside me, poring over the pages of Kant's 'Critique of Pure Reason.'" Her blue-stocking earnestness had found its perfect match in Germanic high-seriousness. It was also in Berlin that she was invited by Cosima, the Widow Wagner, to perform in the bacchanal from "Tannhäuser" at Bayreuth. This experience proved to be a mixed blessing, but a passion for Cosima's son-in-law helped distract Isadora from the loss of Oszkar.

*In *Isadora: A Sensational Life.*

Through these years, she was constantly studying the sources of movement and refining her own liberating approach to dance, which she claimed to have discovered in the waves breaking on California shores, in the art of ancient Greece, in the ideas of Whitman, Nietzsche, and Wagner. Wherever she went, she proclaimed her aesthetic, both from the stage and in writing. Her costumes were scant, but she was shrouded in her lofty ideas: "Art which is not religious is not art, is mere merchandise." Within a short time she was being acclaimed everywhere as a profound revolutionary spirit.

But what was her dancing really *like*? She never allowed herself to be filmed, so all our evidence is secondhand. In a 1992 article, Anne Hollander, having studied the numberless photographs and artistic representations that constitute the massive Duncan iconography, reported that they "tell a fairly consistent story, showing the thrusting knee, the bowed or thrown-back head, the open arms, the whirling colored stuffs veining the torso. None show Duncan in midair. Along with running, she seems to have done a great deal of skipping and prancing, with her bare knees pushing up through slits in the drapery, but no high or broad leaping, no extended legs. Instead, she used the floor, kneeling and reclining, collapsing and rising. The face in the pictures is always blank—attention is riveted on those flashing naked legs and feet, those sweeping bare arms, that rounded exposed throat." In other words, throw in Isadora's radical insistence that movement must come from the solar plexus, and here is modern dance. We also know how musical she was, responding spontaneously rather than analytically to her beloved Chopin, her Gluck, her Beethoven, her Brahms, her Wagner. In this, too, she was radical—critics violently disapproved of her presumption in dancing to symphonic masterpieces.

In 1903 Isadora temporarily abandoned her career so that the Duncans could fulfill their dream of setting foot in Greece, which—in order to make the trip "as primitive as possible"—they approached in a little sailing boat, at dawn. On the beach, Isadora and her brother Raymond knelt down and kissed the soil, Raymond declaiming poetry. "The inhabitants all came down to the beach to greet us, and the first landing of Christopher Columbus in America could not have caused more astonishment among the natives." Soon the clan had rejected their already unusual garments to don "tunic and chlamys and peplum"; they had already substituted sandals for shoes. (Isadora was to dress this way for much of her life, and Raymond for all of his.) They bought land and started to erect a temple, but alas, the land they had acquired had no water within two and a half miles. Still, "we were living under the reign of Agamemnon, Menelaus, and Priam." (Priam, presumably, was on a visit from Troy.) After a year of the simple life, she was touring again, to the usual acclaim.

Soon Isadora met the man who was surely the great love of her life, the avantgarde stage designer Gordon Craig, who was the illegitimate son of England's most treasured actress, Ellen Terry. Craig was handsome, he was brilliant, and he was a ruthlessly selfish womanizer. (He was not only married but was the father of eight children, only four of them with his wife.) Craig brought Isadora the sexual and intellectual companionship she craved, the satisfaction of being linked with a great man (as she and he both saw him), and her first child, Deirdre. He also brought her anguish, as their passion and their competing obsessions with their work turned them into characters out of Strindberg. (The evidence is all there in Francis Steegmuller's invaluable edition of their correspondence, *Your Isadora*.) As usual, Isadora held nothing back: "O I tell you I have no caution or care," she wrote to him, "& if I don't see you soon I will pull myself up by the roots & throw myself in the Sea. . . . Come nice growly Tiger—Eat me up . . . Come Eat me—Put your lips to mine & begin that way." Her need to give too much had found its fatal counterpart in his bottomless need to take.

Late in 1904, in the flush of her early happiness with Craig, she arrived in St. Petersburg on her first trip to Russia—a crucial moment in ballet history, given the liberating influence her dancing was to have on the young Michel Fokine's experiments. There has been endless discussion as to exactly how great an influence this was, but according to Diaghilev, she dealt the Russian ballet "a shock from which it could never recover." Despite her animadversions against ballet—"an expression of degeneration, of living death"—she was warmly welcomed by the ballet establishment and, of course, by the public. And she made a powerful impression on Stanislavsky, who later wrote, "It became clear to me that we were looking for one and the same thing in different branches of art."

It was around this time that Isadora began her lifelong struggle to establish a school for children. The first one was in Berlin, and was run mainly by her sister, Elizabeth; there were to be others. Wherever she went, Isadora battled to convince not only rich patrons but governments to back her grandiose plans. These schools were Isadora's obsession, reflecting both her determination to spread her word—that to live was to dance—and her fierce need to mother. For years she spent the fortune in fees she was earning to support them.

In her endless pursuit of money for the Berlin school, Isadora often joked about acquiring a millionaire, and as usual she had her way. In 1909, she encountered the astonishingly rich Paris Singer, an imposing, well-educated, and generally amiable forty-year-old who was one of the heirs of the Singer Sewing Machine Company. She reports: "He entered, tall and blond, curling hair and beard. My first thought was: Lohengrin." A second thought: "I realized that this was my millionaire, for whom I had sent my brain waves seeking." Lohengrin was instantly smitten, and soon was providing jewels, yachts, a magnificent chateau in which she could start yet another school, and a second child, Patrick. She loved Singer, was grateful to him, and then perversely and repeatedly treated him so badly that he backed away. The last straw came in 1917 when he offered to buy her Madison Square Garden. "What do you think I am, a circus?" she snapped. "I suppose you want me to advertise prizefights with my dancing!" At that, he was finally gone.

But by then she was no longer the Isadora the world had celebrated. Four years earlier had come the great tragedy of her life. Deirdre and Patrick, five and three years old, were drowned when their car slid down a muddy embankment and into the Seine. It was a death blow to Isadora: "When real sorrow is encountered there is for the stricken no gesture, no expression. Like Niobe turned to stone, I sat and longed for annihilation in death." She fled to Greece with her brothers and sister; to Turkey, Italy, Switzerland, Paris, back to Italy, finding solace nowhere.

What eventually brought her back to life was, of course, dancing. Her most famous work during this period was "Marseillaise," which ended with "her left breast bared in evocation of Delacroix's 'Liberty Leading the People,'" and she was to bare her breast in Europe and across North and South America throughout World War I. Agnes de Mille, who saw her at this time, described her as a "prematurely aged and bloated woman," yet added, "Isadora wore a blood-red robe which she threw over her shoulder as she stamped to the footlights and raised her arms in the great Duncan salute. . . . This was heroic and I never forgot it. No one who saw Isadora ever forgot her."

After a period of relative calm, the final significant episode of Isadora's life began in 1921 with an extended stay in the Soviet Union, which had promised her an official school. (She now saw herself as a Communist, insisting to the startled Russians on being called "Comrade.") This was the trip that kindled her last full-blown romantic liaison, with the brilliant but dangerously unstable poet Sergei Esenin. She was forty-five when they met; he was twenty-six. It was another case of love at first sight, followed at once by every kind of trouble—yet, presumably to ensure Esenin safe passage to the West, she married him, after decades of proclaiming herself above marriage.

To call this relationship a fiasco is to fail to do it justice. Disaster? Debacle? Catastrophe? He was violent, alcoholic, and untrustworthy, but also extraordinarily talented and famous—essential for Isadora. Besides, with his baby face and golden hair, he reminded her of her poor dead little Patrick. (There's a recipe for marriage!) He loved her, needed her, sponged from her, abused her. They racketed around Europe and America creating bedlam wherever they went—drunken scenes, unpaid bills. (As one observer put it, "Every intelligent person, in Moscow and everywhere else they went, from Paris to Kansas City, knew that this blind union was a disaster to them both, as well as to the hotel furniture.") She got him back to Russia, where he dumped her; she saw him only twice more. A year later, he hanged himself in a hotel room, having first slit one of his wrists so that he could write a final poem in his blood.

By then she was back in France, and for the rest of her life she lived mainly in Nice and Paris. She was in a dire state. Friends loyally denied that she was a drunk, but she was one. And she was fat. The seventeen-year-old George Balanchine had watched her perform in Petrograd in the early twenties, and, with all the heartlessness of youth, saw her as "a drunken, fat woman who for hours was rolling around like a pig." (He did add, though, "She was probably a nice juicy girl when she was young.")

She was equally far gone emotionally. She had grown sexually rapacious and undiscriminating, and was living precariously, with occasional handouts from friends and a few francs earned from makeshift performances. There were pawnshops, dispossessions; always one step ahead of the sheriff. (On a train trip to Paris—the deluxe train, of course—the porter had to pay for her dinner.) Then, flings and extravagant generosity when money came through. Economy and moderation were, needless to say, alien to her nature. In 1927, desperate for cash, she finally settled down to write her memoirs. (Her publishers had insisted that she spice them up; well, maybe they were right—*My Life* is still in print.) Her last lover in residence was a young Russian musician, but she also became involved with the notorious Mercedes de Acosta, who later took up with Garbo and Dietrich, among others. The evidence points to a passionate affair. (Until then, Isadora had presumably been too busy with men, as she lurched from the great and the near-great—Picabia, Steichen, the pianist Harold Bauer, the war ace Roland Garros, to name a very few of her scores, even hundreds, of conquests—to just plain Joes, like the stoker, the boxer, and the gigolo she dallied with on the steamship that took her to South America in 1916.)

By the fall of 1927 she had little to look forward to; at fifty, and given her physical condition, she could not realistically count on a dance future. The famous death came swiftly. Flirting with a young garage mechanic from Nice, she demanded that he take her out in a racing car that she announced she was thinking of buying. (Isadora had always loved fast cars.) She stepped into the car, wearing a large shawl that her closest friend, Mary Desti, had designed for her. *"Adieu, mes amis, je vais à la gloire,"* she cried. The fringes of the shawl caught in the spokes of the left rear wheel, the car started forward, and within seconds Isadora's neck was broken and she was dead. It is certainly tempting to see her instantaneous and painless death as a merciful release.

How to make sense of this immense, complicated, beautiful, and grotesque life? Many have tried; the Isadora Duncan literature is a tidal wave of loving reminiscence, obfuscation, self-glorification, infighting, and supposition by those who knew her, followed by a series of generally worthy biographies and extended commentaries on her work. Yet we are left with questions. First, how good a dancer was she? There is so much testimony to her performing genius, her irresistible stage charisma, that they can hardly be doubted. Consider: Edith Wharton ("That first sight of Isadora's dancing was a white milestone to me. It shed a light on every kind of beauty"); Tamara

Karsavina ("She moved with those wonderful steps of hers with a simplicity and detachment that could only come through the intuition of genius itself"); Frederick Ashton ("I got an impression of enormous grace, and enormous power in her dancing—she was very serious, and held the audience and held them completely"); Sergei Koussevitsky ("She incarnated music in her dance"); Ruth St. Denis ("For Isadora, I would do battle. To reject her genius is unthinkable"); Rodin ("The greatest woman I have ever known. . . . Sometimes I think she is the greatest woman the world has ever known"). If we can't trust witnesses like these, whom can we trust?

It is her life that presents the unanswerable question. Why did this glorious girl, with the world at her feet, turn into the ghastly wreck who could say toward the end, "I don't dance anymore, I only move my weight around," and "There are only two things left, a drink and a boy"? The easiest explanation is that the death of the children permanently unhinged her. But the seeds of her destruction must always have been there, and two of her early New York friends suggest what they may have been.

Arnold Genthe, who took superb pictures of her, wrote in his memoirs: "Where her work was concerned she had integrity and patience, knowing no compromise with what she felt to be the truth about beauty. In her personal life she had charm and a naive wit. Of tact and self-control she had very little, nor did she wish to have. She was the complete and willing tool of her impulses."

And the socialist writer Max Eastman, who knew her intimately, confesses that "despite her beautiful and triumphant deeds," her "courage, kindness, wit and true-heartedness," he did not like her. "She had made a cult of impulse and impracticality, rapture and abandon. . . . She had confused caprice with independence, heroics with heroism, mutiny with revolution. . . . How embarrassed I always was by the admirable force of character with which Isadora insisted on being half-baked."

In other words, she demanded total, untrammeled freedom. "I am the spiritual daughter of Walt Whitman," she had declared, and indeed "Song of Myself" could stand as a motto for her entire life. She is an extreme example of the American spirit of self-reliance that believes only in itself and refuses all limits. For Isadora there were no rules, there was only the Song of Herself; she lacked the discipline, the emotional and moral resources, to keep liberty from collapsing into license.

It was this that Max Eastman grasped and deplored. Yet he could also say, "All who have escaped in any degree from the rigidity and prissiness of our once national religion of negation owe a debt to Isadora Duncan's dancing. She rode the wave of revolt against Puritanism; she rode it, and with her fame and Dionysian raptures drove it on. She was—perhaps it is simplest to say—the crest of the wave, an event not only in art but in the history of life."

December 30, 2001

Farrell's Revival of Don Q

GEORGE BALANCHINE'S *Don Quixote*—that ambitious, mysterious work that fascinated and confused us all back when it was made in 1965—has just been restaged, by Suzanne Farrell, for the first time since it disappeared from the repertory in 1978. When it was made, Balanchine was sixty-one, Farrell, his newest muse, was nineteen, and this extraordinary dance-drama was taken by everyone to be his unequivocal tribute to, and surrender to, her powers. Now forty years have gone by. Balanchine, of course, is dead. Farrell is approaching sixty. And an entire generation has never seen it. Once it was retired, not many people can have believed they'd ever see it again. (I certainly didn't.) But Farrell, for whom it naturally has profound significance and to whom Balanchine left it in his will, has against all odds resurrected it for us. Combining her own small company with dancers from the National Ballet of Canada, she's presented it at the Kennedy Center in Washington (it will later be performed in Canada), and she's done it superbly. With very little time to mount this elaborate production, and with dancers not many of whom approach the first rank, she's made the most plausible case possible for *Don Quixote*, as spectacle and as art.

From the start, *Don Quixote* was seen as a problem, most of all by Balanchine himself—he was always fiddling with it: adding music, moving sections around, creating new dances. Audiences were perplexed by its unique and unexpected combination of drama, pageantry,

religiosity, formal divertissement and the heightened passages he created for Farrell, as well as by the central character being a non-dancing
role. The music, by Balanchine's old friend Nicolas Nabokov (they
went back almost forty years, and had been discussing this ballet for
almost that long), took much of the blame for what was generally seen
as a flawed effort. And yet *Don Quixote* was compelling, especially
when on occasion Balanchine himself took the central role.

Act I is the weakest. The servant girl Dulcinea, who lovingly ministers to the Don, also appears to him in the guise of the Virgin Mary.
The hero, with his befuddled grasp of reality, sets off on his quest to
vanquish injustice, accompanied by the faithful Sancho Panza. There's
some generic peasant dancing in a town square, a juggler, a puppet
show with children, a horse, a donkey and a remarkable solo for Dulcinea, who at this point appears as a young girl accused of complicity
in a murder.

Act II takes place at the court of a duke and duchess who mali-
ciously welcome the mad Don as an honored guest only to encourage
their courtiers to torment him. Here we witness the bitter cruelty of
Cervantes' Spain, but also the Don's courtesy, innocence and generosity. His innate chivalry keeps him from grasping that he's being made
a fool of. There's an extended divertissement—a suite of ingenious
formal dances (flamenco, Mauresque, Sicilienne et al.)—and finally
an orchestrated assault on the Don by the masked courtiers, who
prod him with their rapiers, blindfold him, leap on his back, pum-
mel him, and leave him almost dead, after a surreally horrible final
moment when one of them smears his eyes with a gout of whipped
cream. During this powerful and deeply disturbing passage, Dulcinea
appears as a vision of tenderness and consolation.

It's the third act that explodes into brilliance. Surrounded by a
formal group of maidens led by two demi-soloists and their cavaliers, Dulcinea—now divorced from any direct responsibility to the
plot—performs one of the most intense and thrilling dances in all
Balanchine. At first she's grave, but soon she erupts in a galvanic outpouring of ardor and despair. And now it becomes almost impossible to speak about "Dulcinea" rather than about Farrell. Here was
Balanchine's first and most indelible presentation of her astounding
qualities; here, almost at the start of their unprecedented collaboration, she was fully and magnificently identified.

Fortunately, there's a murky film, available to the public, of the first performance of *Don Quixote*. It features Balanchine and Farrell, and to watch it is to experience the miracle of his total grasp of her potential genius. If this were the only documentation of Farrell, you could infer her entire artistic life from it—it's as valuable as the famous filmed passages from the first act of *Giselle* that give us our only glimpse of the legendary Olga Spessivtseva. Farrell's performance is heart-stopping—the amazing off-balance lunges, the ravishing back-bends, the absolute fearless abandon, the total commitment to the gesture and the moment. Yes, she's still a baby, but she's also, already, a peerless ballerina, in complete charge of her body, her role and Balanchine.

This dance is superbly constructed, the solos and the material for the corps effortlessly integrated, and for once Nabokov's music is appropriate—romantic and exciting in the right way. (At other times, it's pure movie music, and second-rate movie music at that.) The two dancers Farrell chose to portray Dulcinea carried things off with admirable aplomb and to good effect, despite the light-years disparity between their talent and Farrell's. Sonia Rodriguez is accurate and hard-working—she's an excellent executant—but she's essentially unexciting: a ballerina, but a provincial one. Heather Ogden, second-cast, is younger and freer—both more innocent and more involving. How odd that Farrell, of all people, cast her second. After all, if Balanchine had stopped to consider status or age, he wouldn't have made *Don Quixote* on her in the first place.

After the climactic third-act pas d'action, the ballet returns to its story—the final degrading assaults on Don Quixote; his famous delusional attack on the windmill; his grotesque journey home in a pig cage. His last fevered vision is of an ominous procession of church dignitaries, and then of Dulcinea, once again seen as the Virgin, welcoming the hero in his martyrdom. When he dies, she reappears as the simple peasant girl placing two wooden sticks in the shape of a cross on his body.

Balanchine, as seen in the film, keeps the ballet from veering into self-pity—his Don is vigorous in his old age, bewildered rather than distraught or loony, aristocratic without being proud. Farrell's Momchil Mladenov is tall and thin (Balanchine's preference for the role), but at the start his body and movement style give him away as inappropriately young. He recovers, though, through focus and intelligence, and creates a credible Don.

Farrell has handled the complicated stage business impeccably—scene flows into scene, the transformations and other special effects work easily, and the sets (by Zack Brown) are an improvement on the heavier aesthetic of Esteban Francés. The weakness in the production lies in the secondary performers. Although there are several pleasing dancers in the second-act divertissement and in the third act—Natalia Magnicaballi, Erin Mahoney, Shannon Parsley—they can't compare with Balanchine's 1965 company: dancers of the caliber of Patricia McBride, Suki Schorer, Mimi Paul, Patricia Neary, Marnee Morris, Gloria Govrin, Arthur Mitchell and on and on. It's a dazzling honor roll. That Farrell succeeded as well as she did with dancers considerably below this level of talent is a tribute to her teaching and coaching skills—no surprise to anyone who has watched her guide dancers over the past several years. One of the many things she learned from Balanchine is to cheerfully and honorably make the best of whatever resources are available, and her respect for her dancers has been repaid with their obvious devotion to her, and to him.

Just as it did forty years ago, *Don Quixote* leaves us fascinated, moved—and puzzled. Back in the '60s and '70s, it was less easy to see it as a link in a chain of related works—related not because they're all dance-dramas but because they all center on a certain kind of male figure. Yes, Balanchine has given us the male glorious—Apollo, Oberon, the "Rubies" boy—and the male humorous and the impersonal cavalier. But surely we sense a more direct connection between him and a parade of men in extremis which begins with the Prodigal Son, debased by the vicious Siren, and proceeds through the romantic Poet undone by the fatal dazzle of the Sonnambula, the tragic Orpheus destroyed by Eurydice's importunities, and the desperate Schumann, succumbing to madness. Don Quixote, despite the loyalty and solace offered by his fantasy Dulcinea, is humiliated like the Prodigal, maddened like Schumann, and driven to death like the Poet and Orpheus.

What sets *Don Quixote* apart from these other ballets is that there isn't a great deal of distance between Balanchine's own pain and the pain suffered by his hero: He's so personally affected by the buffetings life inflicts on the Don—so obviously identifying with him—that he seems to be saying, "I don't deserve this." And then he rewards himself with Heaven.

We're not used to a Balanchine so humanly exposed, and Farrell, at nineteen, could hardly have understood what *Don Quixote* was revealing. Her devoted reconstruction of it makes it clear that now she understands.

The important practical question raised by her production is whether such a large-scale, problematic work can become a permanent part of the Balanchine repertory. Certainly it will stay alive as long as Farrell has the opportunity to present it, and perhaps there are major companies—the Kirov, say—who might take it on. It's even possible, I suppose, that Farrell and New York City Ballet might eventually accommodate each other. But is *Don Quixote* worth preserving? After all, other important Balanchine works have vanished—*Cotillon*, the full-length *Le Baiser de la Fée*, the early versions of *Mozartiana*, *Balustrade*, *The Seven Deadly Sins*.

None of these works, however, was as meaningful to him, or as revealing. The lesson we just learned in Washington is that although we didn't know we've been missing it since it vanished almost thirty years ago, *Don Quixote* does still matter, both for its own sake and because of its unique place in the Balanchine canon. When you're dealing with a supreme master—a Shakespeare, a Mozart—you need to be able to revisit his entire corpus of work. You need *King Lear* all the time, but every decade or so you also need *Timon of Athens*. Otherwise your understanding of a genius like Shakespeare—or Balanchine—is diminished, and so are you.

July 11, 2005

Robert Greskovic (1944–)

Admired by his colleagues and by dancers of the caliber of Mikhail Baryshnikov, who wrote the foreword to Robert Greskovic's *Ballet 101: A Complete Guide to Learning and Loving the Ballet*, Greskovic has contributed reviews and articles on dance to *The Wall Street Journal* since 1998. He has also published essays, reviews, and features on dancing, art, and other cultural subjects in many other periodicals, including *Ballet Review*, in the United States and abroad.

Reared in Blakely, Pennsylvania, Greskovic graduated from Pratt Institute and taught art full-time for fifteen years in the New York City public schools. A 1983 recipient of a Guggenheim fellowship, he has been named to the 2017–2018 class of Dance Research Fellows at the Jerome Robbins Dance Division of the New York Public Library for the Performing Arts.

The essay below on the sculptural aspects of Merce Cunningham's choreography brings together the author's extensive background in visual art and his first-rate eye for dancing of all techniques and traditions.

Merce Cunningham as Sculptor

(N.B. This essay, written nearly thirty-five years before my revision here, should be read with the understanding that Cunningham, who continued to work and evolve his dancemaking until his death in 2009, was a slightly different artist by the 1980s than the one he became in the early twenty-first century. Or, as Agatha Christie once observed: *Plus c'est la même chose, plus ça change.* R. G., 2018)

As an artist, Merce Cunningham possesses expertise far beyond the confines usually identified with the art of choreography. A focus on any singular facet of Cunningham's art helps sort through its rich complexities and bring some particular element into considered view. So long as no one aspect is presented as a solitary or even dominant ingredient of Cunningham's artistry, such considerations can particularize our understanding of this man and his work, and provide vocabulary for our sometimes speechless admiration of him. By now Cunningham the dancemaker has been thoughtfully considered as a dancer, as a soloist, as a director, and as an actor. All these distinctions have been made in due course along the way of his formidable career, which, if we take his scrawly handwritten word for it—on one of the un-numbered topsy-turvy pages of his *Changes: Notes on Choreography*—began in 1944. This year, 1983, marks the 30th anniversary of his own company of dancers and the present company's two-week season made me decide to add sculptor to Cunningham's array of artistic sensibilities.

Dance values have been compared often to the values of sculpture, specifically figure sculpture. Though figure sculpture exists statically in three dimensions, the plastic command it has of spacial possibilities (up and down, side to side, front to back) is conveniently related to the individual moments of a dancer dancing. Certain archetypical arrangements that recur in sculpted figures for limbs, torso, and head correspond directly to basic positions in academic dance. The *attitude* derived from the celebrated Mercury of Bologna is, of course, the most obvious example. All the world's great classical choreographers refer us, at some point or other during phrases of their work, to the clear and full dimension that great statuary defines. There is an inherent awareness of all directions in space, simultaneously. True, such alertness is basic to sound dance technique, but the inspired choreographer makes the technically well-equipped dancer larger than life by designing original ways for him to exert his occupation of space. George Balanchine, for example, shaped the extant classical vocabulary with which his dancers were bred to achieve further heights of speed, shape and reach. He chose to show dancers with tighter closed positions and more expansive open ones. He intensified the basic shape of the dancer's vocabulary and made it clearer and theatrically more pure. Frederick Ashton, it seems to me, has created embellishments within the dance vocabulary's very bounds, devising sharper, more complex internal details to dancing. Varied and elaborate oppositional accents—épaulement, batterie, hip-to-shoulder oppositions—give Ashtonian steps and poses both their clarity and density. I find it appropriate that of the two basic ways for designing the figure in academic dance, Balanchine shows a decided preference for effacé; Ashton, for croisé: the former, enlarging and opening up the figure; the latter, elaborating and enriching the figure through added accents and details.

The distinctions and definitions with which Balanchine or Ashton designs dancing offer more-or-less keen views of the plasticity we have come to know from strict, classical dancing. The heroic, lyrical, or fanciful expression each gives to classical maneuvers and stances emanates directly from their true academic basis. With the work of Merce Cunningham, the base is often altered as well as heightened. These adjustments that I note make me see Cunningham's choreographic hand in terms of a sculptor's. Cunningham shows us dance views not only of unique scale and complexity but also of heightened definition. His dancers work *from* positions that we normally expect dancers to work *through*. These in-between positions—half-tones, if you like—get an emphasis in Cunningham's work that, in other choreographers' work, is usually reserved for fuller, more regular designs. Probably the most obvious parallel to be drawn with Cunningham's "other" positions is the twelve-tone scale in twentieth-century music. Like the twelve-tone composers, Cunningham has not sought "new" elements outside familiar academic vocabulary; rather, he has seen fit to expose and give full weight to positions that previously were subordinate to the established, regular ones.

Another related precedent, however, springs to mind, and with it Cunningham's sculptor's touch. Whenever I'm watching a Cunningham dance, the great or the good, I am struck by the evident personal care that the choreographer apparently gave to its making. For all the chance procedures, the alternatives, and the casual serenities of tone involved, *nothing* about these works is ever arbitrary. Even small-scale, light-touch details have the weight of definite intent. There is a sense ever-present in Cunningham's work, as in all inspired choreography, of the masterful hand that predetermined every increment of the dimension involved in it. An invisible insistence controls and animates the whole moving picture. Everywhere in the Cunningham repertory we sense the watchfulness of his vision. And it is in this light that I recall an image of a great ancestor of Cunningham's— Marius Petipa. It's a specific Petipa image that I think of, one given us by Nicolas Legat in his reminiscences of the past master of classical dance: "He worked on many of his groupings at home, where he used little figures like chess pawns to represent dancers, arranging them all over the table." Just as I can sense the elegant nineteenth-century ballet master determining his designs whenever I'm admiring the arrangements of a Petipa ballet, so can I imagine Cunningham at work when I'm enthralled by his dances. The Cunningham process I envision as I'm struck by the complexity of his dancers' plastique and of the ways in which he disposes each individual in space suggests not only unique arrangements among dancers in space but also uniquely posed individual dancers. It's as if Cunningham had inherited Petipa's figurines, all struck in various standard poses—croisé, effacé, épaulé, écarté—and, before setting about planning his choreography for them, he adjusted and altered their standard positions to suit his particularly enriched sense of their basic vocabulary. I can easily see Cunningham looking, through a characteristic twinkle of his eye, at a figure in a standard extension position, say, à la seconde, and nudging the raised leg forward or back, that is, repositioning the limb's direction in space to an alternate one that deepens the figure's three-dimensionality and offers a fresh angle on its usual positioning.

What keeps poses like these adjusted alternatives of Cunningham's from seeming uncommonly distorted or unnervingly imbalanced is the structural harmony they maintain. Along with the major adjustment of a regular dance design, Cunningham will make smaller, related alterations—a tip of the head, an accent of the shoulder, a tilt of the pelvis. Those revealing additional accents and positions beyond the traditional eight that make up classical ballet's set schooling are based on simple principles of balance and counterbalance. So, as we look at Cunningham's unusual configurations, we still see something of Petipa's usual geometry—a pleasant surprise that's never a jolting shock.

Though Cunningham always shows his sculptural sensitivity in his dances, one of his recent pieces appears actually to be "about" statuary. In their simplest sense, the travels and pauses that make up this particular dance remind us of the game called "Statues" we played as kids, where the leader kid set us all in helter-skelter motion and then without warning dared us to freeze and hold whatever askew pose we happened to be in. (It might be well here and now to state however that Cunningham's dances are never about something in any specific sense. Any time one notes, and uses, for purposes of discussion, a definite point of reference, suggesting that a certain Cunningham dance is about something in particular, say that the 1968 *RainForest* is about a wet woodland, it must be viewed as a momentary convenience rather than as a keystone concept.)

My example here is *Locale* (1979: I mean the stage version rather than the filmdance), and I use its particulars because they easily exemplify the sculptural authority of Cunningham's work. The dance involves two trios and four duos—a particularly rich choreographic compound. Not only does Cunningham show us his dancers in marvelously arranged plastic poses, he also arranges his richly torqued dancers in similarly rich combinations and configurations to an end that implies sculpting with sculpture. It's as if Cunningham had gathered round him various classical caryatids and atlantes, archaic korai and kouroi, and old-world sphinxes, and orchestrated them all into various activities, every now and then arresting them in statuesque poses of his own devising. In spite of the fact that the poses that make up this dance are filled with asymmetrical, unusual details of opposition and extension, there is a pervasive formality all through the work. Partly this formal air is due to the unstrained and lifted carriage that the dancers calmly maintain as they rearrange their torsos. Partly, too, there is, alongside the alert pleasures of the unpredictable poses, a sense of inevitability that comes from the calm control and precision with which the dancers interrelate their unique plastiques.

Always formal, constantly original, never static or distorted, the cast of fourteen in *Locale* is subdivided into sets by Charles Atlas's color-coded leotards, bodysuits and tights. The palette and textures are especially handsome: each of the six hues is matched by a neutral gray tone equal in value to the color it's coordinated with: lemon yellow is paired with the palest gray, lime with a slightly stronger gray, sky blue with the next gray up, rosy pink with its equal in gray, bittersweet orange with an even deeper gray, and a bright Prussian blue with an almost slate gray. The colors are in glossy Milliskin, which in this array looks like satin-candy coating, while all the grays are in matte plain jersey. As is sometimes the case with the designs in a

Cunningham dance, one layer of color is removed during the course of the dance—in this instance it's the men's gray tights that eventually are removed to reveal the one basic color that each is wearing. The middle of the dance has all the men wearing only their colored body-suits, they having taken off their tights. Subsequently, everyone has on gray again for the final groupings of the last pose. While the men are minus their gray legs, the schematic clusters of the piece open up, and larger groupings are created out of the multicolor combinations. But—typical of such Cunninghamian shifts in plan—this happens just as viewers find themselves following and admiring the color mixings, noting how alike the lemon and lime hues are, and pondering how the proverbial *change* has resulted in more *même chose*.

Perhaps because Cunningham initially played with the various visual possibilities of *Locale* on film, where the energetic use of Steadi-cam takes the viewer all around the work, his stage version remains fairly straightforward. Set off against the all-black side pieces and backdrop, *Locale* "live" aims neatly and plainly out from its prosce-nium setting. But *Trails*, made solely for the stage (in 1982), plays with more than one angle of view at once. And it's another kind of sculp-tural experience that we get here from Cunningham, one different in scale. As some dancers enter the piece and pick up the phrases and step sequences initiated by the other dancer(s) already on stage—and in this follow-through I think I detect the "trails" of the title—Cun-ningham is not content to set simple unison dancing. So, as we see the same steps executed, we do not see them facing the same direction. And as we note the side, back and/or three-quarter views of these same movements, we sense Cunningham compensating for the fact that we are unable to move around his dance: he offers us the views we would get if we were able to go around his work. The same sculp-tural sensitivity that designs moves and poses richly occupying their space is at work here, but at a distance. Besides working close-in to fix his dancers in space, Cunningham's eye also goes clearly outside and around his work to show how various it can look.

The persistent clarity of position—with which Cunningham's dancers pose and move in space, and to which Cunningham alerts us through varied views of their dancing—makes his basic way of working separate from that of his "modern" peers. Nowhere else in theatrical barefoot dancing do we see so full a use of the foot as from

314 \t DANCE IN AMERICA

Cunningham. The full definition of the foot is an understandably per-
tinent detail to someone whose formal concerns with dancing's physical dimensions are as considered as Cunningham's. As his dances got
performed alongside those offered by ballet companies, Cunningham's work was variously recognized as being based in ballet's ways
of working, and, with some regularity, as something that might be
dubbed ballet-manqué. I think such observations are generally aimed
at the overall lifted carriage of the Cunningham dancer's posture and
the keen readiness out of the center of that vertical axis to move in any
direction at any time. All this is of course true, but the lifted weight
and center would grant little more than decorative lightness to Cunningham's dancers were it not for their fully articulated footwork.
Cunningham's bifocal view of the foot—as a separate appendage to
the leg, and as a means of extending the length of the leg—makes his
barefoot technique unique. The other barefoot choreographer whose
technique has been called "balletic"—a facile word I'd gladly banish
from dance writing—is Paul Taylor. But could two ways of working be more dissimilar? Taylor's work, even in his most quicksilver
inventions, consistently uses and shows the foot, unapologetically,
as feet—i.e., as independent appendages of the leg. His dancers take
flight easily and fluently from quick-sprung feet, and their "landing
gear" remains ever ready for as simple and articulate a recovery. Taylor's use of the lower center of gravity keeps his dancers consistently
over or on their feet. The flexible facility of his dancers' footwork is
everywhere evident. There are next to no moments when the foot's
function completely disappears into the length of the leg.

Cunningham's footwork comes and goes through two extremes.
At one end, the full surface of the foot slides along the stage, through
glissade-like travels and into dégagé impetus for raised-leg moves; at
the other end, the full shape of the foot acts, through a fully stretched
ankle, to further the length of the leg. In between, Cunningham's hawk
eye for detail has seen fit to work with various demi-pointe positions,
including a consistent use of relevé that balances all the weight of the
dancer on the hinge joint at the ball of the foot. The only detail lacking
in Cunningham's footwork is the full pointe; but missing this position
in so rich a barefoot technique is a little like missing the sight of the
toes in an accomplished slipper technique.

My own focus on the rich footwork in Cunningham's canon arose while I was watching *Coast Zone*, one of his new works in 1983. Like *Locale* and *Channels/Inserts* (1981), *Coast Zone* is the stage version of a work made originally for film. Unlike my experience with these two predecessors, it was difficult for me to follow the structural coherence of *Coast Zone* as a piece. Perhaps that's why I ended up dwelling on its feet. In a subsequent article by Jennifer Dunning on the making of the film version of *Coast Zone*, I learned that Cunningham was motivated by the "possibility of close-ups" for this project. Since close-range scrutiny is not something we can get readily in a theater space, I feel I'll have to wait for the filmed version of *Coast Zone* to "see" it. (Though the film was planned and shot before the stage version was mounted, the finished video was still being produced when *Coast Zone*, the repertory work, had its premiere.)

The season's one other new work was *Quartet*, for Cunningham himself and four of his dancers. It follows the pattern that Cunningham has developed over the past few years for group pieces in which he casts himself. He remains separate from the group—not only by his movement vocabulary but also by his distance from the others. On the surface, of course, there is a definite dramatic edge to such a breakup, where the solitary older figure stands outside a group of younger figures.

Underneath this scenario of sorts I see evidence of Cunningham the sculptor. In the beginning, Cunningham's agile, articulate abilities as a dancer put him in the position of, if you will, his own artist's model. Now that his own limbs have ceased to be exceptionally supple or strong, he has transferred his exploration of what the fully equipped dancer can do from his own person to that of his various dancers. And now that Cunningham is working more and more "outside" his own capabilities, he is plumbing more and more choreographic possibilities. The extraordinary depth and concentration with which he was always able to intensify the design of his own performing may not be shared by all his company performers, but the all-over sensitivity that he eagerly brings to creating for others is reasonable compensation. His sculptural attention makes deliberate in others what was likely intrinsic in himself.

The sculptural concerns that I find in Cunningham's choreography—his unquenchable fascination for working the full of the dancer's figure into every conceivable angle in space—have become more and more pronounced. And the larger and more workable the ensemble he has available, the more he can invent. While I don't deny the importance of presence in a dancer or the desirability of great technical proficiency, I do sense a sympathy to Cunningham's aims in an ensemble that's not especially shot through with potent individual distinction. By doing exactly what Cunningham wants, his dancers are acting like panes of clear, colorless glass as they execute the moves they've been given. I suppose I'm trying to take some of the edge off the argument of those Cunningham watchers who, as a matter of course, will claim the company is in limbo because it lacks what they call personally distinctive artists. (I don't really mind the fact that many of the present company women have similar haircuts. Some feel it makes for monotony, but I feel it forces us to look at *how* the dancers do what they're doing even more closely. If we don't have immediately and easily distinguishable characteristics available to us, we have to find other, probably more organic, *dance* values to go on.) While I can't imagine Cunningham suppressing a dancer's individuality, it seems just possible to me that, as he chooses members for his larger and larger ensembles, he's drawn to the innocent and open ones, rather than to the idiosyncratic, in hopes of seeing what he designs as plainly and as clearly as possible. We know Balanchine was fond of saying, "Just do the steps"; perhaps Cunningham is fond of finding the dancers who will just do what they are asked to do.

One of the features of Cunningham's art, and of all great art, really, is how uncompromising it is—its integrity to itself. If we consider the area of design, especially costume design, for Cunningham's work, we find an amazing array of distinction and originality inside the narrowest of ranges. The only requirement that Cunningham gives (or simply implies) to his designers is a rather specific one: that the full shape of his dancers' figures be clearly shown. (2018: There would eventually be cases late in Cunningham's career that individuals would see as being costumed in shape-changing designs: Rei Kawakubo's designs for *Scenario* [1997] come to mind. Even here, however, arguably the most shape-changing of costumes in Cunningham's repertory, the added shapes—effected by lumpish pads that fit under the stretch gingham costuming, which the "deformations" created—came and went at odd moments, so that the part of the dancer's physique that was distorted by Kawakubo's designs was left free and clear at other moments when the lumps and bumps were rearranged.) What master figure sculptor would ask his models to pose in form-concealing garments? In the early days, the uniform for the Cunningham dancer was various colors and cuts of leotard and tights. Of late, the same has been true for bodysuits and, occasionally, sweat pants. Particularly where Cunningham himself was performing, this thicker, less form-fitting garment became a helpful aid to concealing the no-longer-youthful silhouette of the master's legs.

Certain artists have been Cunningham's design collaborators over the years, most notably in the past, Robert Rauschenberg and Jasper Johns, and, most recently, Mark Lancaster and Charles Atlas. The current phase under Lancaster and Atlas has been especially fine. They have maintained the sense that in Cunningham dances the dancers are more colored figures than clothed characters. Occasionally, each designer has chosen pieces of plain clothing for costuming in place of standard dancewear, as Atlas did for *Channels/Inserts* and Lancaster did for *Gallopade*. Even in these instances the dancer's limbs and joints remain free—able, without constriction, to achieve the full range of Cunningham's space-exploring designs. Reading the skirts, sweaters, or pants on Cunningham's dancers as clothing is a little like identifying the original function of the design elements in a Kurt Schwitters collage; you are reminded of another, former context, but you remain enthralled by their immediate, nonspecific existence in the new world. Still, these costumes' dualities are always subordinate to the dominant design ingredient in Cunningham's work: that of pure color. The red-and-gray palette of *Trails* (Lancaster) is at an intense pitch. Both hues are of equal, high-key value, and the opposition of one to the other zings where they meet. Intense chroma is not an element we usually associate with sculptural exploration, least of all in the look of the classical cool statuary suggested by Cunningham's bodysuited dancers; but Cunningham's designers give his dances, with their three-dimensional sensibilities, the separate dimension of color. Probably the only avenue of approach I had for watching the diffusions of *Coast Zone* was through Lancaster's designs; out of a palette limited to three colors (plum, orange, and turquoise) each dancer was colored (by leotard and tights) in two of these. No matter what combination of dancers performed out of this cast of twelve, there always seemed to be a common color denominator among them. These consistent color constants helped me find a bit of focus on what looked, from these initial viewings, like rather disconnected movements in space.

The plain but by no means simple ingredients of design and movement that make up Cunningham's dance theater may be independently conceived, but they both become part of the same visual experience. The audio part of this theater, based on the School of John Cage, has always been the most controversial of the disparate elements in the Cunningham experience. Except when a miked stage, accenting the sound of the dancers' feet, becomes part of the score (as in *10s with Shoes*, and if memory serves, *Canfield*), the sound component of Cunningham's dances remains largely separate from the rest of the work. It can be jarring by its volume and/or suddenness, or somewhat distracting by its specificity, such as when stories get told or phone calls are made, or it can be soothingly or dramatically atmospheric. What it rarely does is support the dancing the way traditional music supports traditional dancing—though this *can* happen, such as in the spluttering energies of David Tudor's "Toneburst" for *Sounddance* or in the pitter-pattering pulsations of Cage's "Improvisation III" for *Duets*. I have what I gather is a high tolerance level for high-decibel sound, so except for the start an unexpected burst of noise can give me, I find little in these sound scores disturbing. In general they seem to me incidental to the Cunningham experience. The striking and often stirring formality and pre-arranged physicality of Cunningham's dancemaking remains matter-of-factly separated from the soundwork produced by the individual composers of each dance. The interest the musicians regularly reveal in found material is pronounced and, for me, quite unrelated to any such focus from Cunningham, or, for that matter, from that of his designers. The naturalness and everyday-ness in Cunningham's moves and designs give contemporary texture to classical aesthetics; they give human accent to formal values. With Cage and the others, the found sounds retain their casual values. There is little transformation in these collages; we recognize all the bits in a linear way that ends up more strung out than strung together.

Cunningham's eyes and hand have artfully worked to mold his dancers and his theater throughout his career. He has shown an inexhaustible interest in shaping his dancers in countless directions, setting their limbs and torsos to extend, angle, and occupy their stage space with visual richness and notable clarity. It should be mentioned that for Cunningham the spine, from the small of the back up into the carriage of the neck, gives his dancers a plastique all his own: for starters his teachings—emulating perhaps ballet's set of five positions for the feet—include five positions for the back, i.e. upright, arch, twist, tilt, curve. Sometimes he has even shown his sculptor-like way of working right in the dance. Throughout his exploration of male-female double work in *Duets* (1980), he shows one dancer in each pair manipulating and placing his partner's limbs into some new arrangement. In his own duet with Catherine Kerr, there's a moment when she stands in relevé passé with one arm raised straight up out of her tilted torso. After steadying Kerr in her pose, Cunningham then focuses on that vertical arm. He alternately grabs, pats, and tags her arm from shoulder to wrist. It could be seen as a hand-over-hand climb to claim a baseball bat, but I prefer, for my purposes here, to see it as a sculptor patting the finishing touches onto the clay of a sculptured arm. There's an even more pointedly sculptorlike task in Cunningham's *Roadrunners* (1979)—more pointed and more witty, too. He goes up to one of his women (I recall Megan Walker) who's standing with one leg poised tautly in Cunninghamian seconde en l'air. He takes her extended leg in his two hands (one below the knee and one above) and bends it into an angled extension. And, you get a feeling, from moments like these, of how Cunningham gets much of his original design with a dancer's figure: he takes the possibilities in his hands and literally and figuratively plays with them.

There is something especially poignant in such moments. Even when they're part of a generally light, whimsical air (as in *Road-runners*), these manipulations remind us of the unbounded delight Cunningham takes in shaping his dancers into a dance. There is no sign on his face, as he performs his interested work in full view of his audience, that he's melancholy over the fact that his own body is not as easily articulated as it once was. Quite to the contrary, there is the sly sense of relish he takes in being able to stand back and create further new ways for dance to live in its spaces. And the extra sparkle that comes into Cunningham's eyes suggests that beyond the pleasure he takes in giving us some view of a dancer we've not quite had before, there is a more private thrill: the one Cunningham himself feels when his explorations show him something even he's never previously seen.

1984/2018

Margaret Case Harriman (1901–1971)

Margaret Case Harriman was the proud daughter of Frank M. Case, the owner of Manhattan's Algonquin Hotel, in which she was born and grew up. *The Vicious Circle*, her account of the wits and celebrities who congregated at the hotel's famous Round Table, and whose repartee she had grown up overhearing, was a best seller in 1951, by which time she had for decades been writing profiles of star performers and other famous personages for *The New Yorker* and the original *Vanity Fair*.

Harriman was married twice, divorced twice, and had one child, a son, Guion Case Morgan. Her insistence on privacy and independence were remarkable—her brother, Carroll, was quoted in 1953 as saying, "I haven't heard from her since 1946, but I know her son teaches at Princeton." And despite having published several well-received books as well as scores of nonfiction stories she seems to have left no obituaries in her wake. *New Yorker* files in the magazine's archives hold a few documents about the profile here of the ballroom team Tony and Renée De Marco, confirming that the couple eventually divorced and that Mrs. De Marco returned to California to teach dance privately.

Dance Team

It costs a team of ballroom dancers in the white-tie-and-tails class—such as Veloz and Yolanda, Medrano and Donna, Mario and Floria, or the De Marcos—about $10,000 to produce their act before the public ever sees it and approximately $30,000 a year to keep it going after that, if it is successful. These sums include the rent of a rehearsal studio, accompanists' wages, and money paid out for music, orchestral arrangements, publicity, and clothes. In addition to the financial investment there is the constant worry about "good will," which means, to the team, that night-club patrons must be pleased not only by the skill and appearance of the couple but by their exchange of tender glances, their effect of being soulfully one. This is especially true if the members of the team are married to each other. Something about the spectacle of a man and his wife dancing romantically together moves the customers to a mellowness which can put a pair of married dancers into a terrible state of nerves if things are not going well at home. Of all people in show business—notoriously an emotional calling—they are most rigidly forbidden the frown, the whispered battle cry, the slight kick on the instep that might relieve them. The spotlight is on them, the patrons are at their elbows, and all must seem harmonious. The team's profit on the money invested in the act, and on the hours of grim rehearsal, depends so much on the illusion of mutual enchantment the dancers create that one understands the married hoofer, maddened by domestic cares, who once worked out a routine with his wife to the tune of "Why Do I Love You?" "Two grand a week," he explained to her on opening night, just before they moved graciously onto the floor.

A year and a half ago the De Marcos separated professionally and matrimonially. They had been dancing partners for eight years and husband and wife for five. Shortly before their separation they appeared nightly at the Persian Room in the Plaza and were generally considered to be the best white-tie-and-tails team in the country, although some dissenters held out in favor of Veloz and Yolanda. The woes that parted the De Marcos had nothing to do with dancing; they were merely the familiar headaches that can threaten any marriage—trouble over money and trouble with in-laws. As a dance team they remained indestructible, even when they weren't dancing, and neither Tony nor Renée De Marco had any thought of taking on a new partner. Last November the Waldorf-Astoria announced the return of the De Marcos ("Together Again!") and hundreds of people crowded emotionally into the Sert Room to welcome them back. It was a sentimental occasion. Pub-crawlers, always mushy beneath the sable coat and the flowered lapel, like to look at happiness, and the De Marcos had always seemed to be more genuinely pleased about dancing with each other than most fashionable dancers; they were little and likable and full of affectionate tricks. On opening night in the Sert Room, one ringside matron stood up and kissed Renée De Marco impulsively as she passed the table, and exclaimed, "I'm so happy for you, dear child!" Another was seen to weep freely as she grasped Tony by the arm and murmured fiercely, "Now you be *good* to that darling girl!"

Demonstrations like these gratify the De Marcos and startle them, since their reunion is strictly a professional one. They are friendly to the extent that each of them states this fact emphatically to other people, but they live apart. Renée has her own apartment at the Delmonico these days, where she lives in a happy whirl of telephone calls, shopping trips, and friends dropping in. She is dark-haired, soft-spoken, beautifully dressed, and feminine to the point of looking fragile. Tony likes to think of his wife as helpless, as enchanted by her new freedom and by a full social life for which he has never had much time or energy. "Renée is only a kid," he says, "and she's crazy about society. *You* know—A. C. Blumenthal and those people."

Renée is in her late twenties, but Tony, some ten years older, is far jauntier. He has a flip way of pulling the brim of a soft hat down over his eyes, and he walks like a dancer, quickly and gracefully. Waiting for a green light at a street crossing, he is apt to go into a tap routine at the curb, and when he crosses against the light—as he would rather do—his progress among taxicabs and trucks is a dance number in itself. It is only when he sits down that he looks tired.

He lives alone in the apartment once occupied by the late Florenz Ziegfeld, in the Ziegfeld Theatre Building on Sixth Avenue. Tony has furnished the apartment with pieces from a house he and Renée once had at Rockville Centre, and the décor includes some rather massive furniture, several oil paintings, and a mink coverlet for the bed. The large living room contains almost nothing except a grand piano and a phonograph, and the De Marcos rehearse there before a mirror which covers one wall. The mirror is blue, so Tony and Renée see themselves with a kind of gloomy accuracy, unrelieved by any reflection of light from the windows opposite. Whatever personal conflict troubles the De Marcos is apparently forgotten as soon as they begin to work together. At rehearsals, Tony, in a white shirt, gray slacks, and gray suède shoes, shuffles thoughtfully around the floor at first, while Renée, barelegged, in sandals, and wearing print culottes and a backless, halter-neck sweater, sits expectantly on the piano. At the piano is a young man, earnest and spectacled, named Sam or Paul or Charlie. (The De Marcos change their rehearsal accompanists often, so as to surprise themselves into keeping things lively.)

Presently Tony puts a record on the phonograph and the accompanist listens attentively, his hands off the keys. Tony dances slowly across to the piano. "Do you get it?" he asks the accompanist. "Da da *dee-ee*, dada dum de um hm-m . . ." For a minute he stands over the boy at the piano, his arms and shoulders and feet moving, his hands conducting the music from the phonograph in the corner. "Pick it up from there," he says suddenly, shutting off the phonograph. "All right, Renée." Renée slides down from the piano and accurately meets him in the middle of the floor. Tony whistles the melody continuously as they dance, except for occasional directions thrown over his shoulder to the piano-player. "Wait. Right there, bring it *up*"—here he curves one hand, lifting it—"now, sh-h-h. . . . Retard. . . . Now! Bring it *up* again." Sometimes Leonard, the colored valet, plods through the room during rehearsal, laden with packages and bound for a storeroom in the rear. "Hello, Leonard," Renée says, her face upside down and whirling. "Hello, Leonard," says Tony, spinning madly, "did you get that suit from the cleaner?" Leonard replies briefly and goes on his way. Sometimes the end of a dance comes out wrong at rehearsal. "Why do you finish over there, sweetheart?" Tony asks mildly. "I'm over here." Renée explains that she thought he had said he wanted to finish nearer the middle of the floor, so there would be more room between themselves and the ringside tables in the Sert Room. The De Marcos like to keep the size and shape of the Sert dance floor in their minds when they practice, and Tony has counted the exact number of steps he can take from various points on the floor before his coat-tails begin brushing the customers' champagne glasses. "When in doubt," he tells Renée, "always take the first ending." This is part of the De Marco team language and it means that Tony and Renée dance away from each other for sixteen bars of music and back for another sixteen bars, to finish with Renée bent backward over Tony's arm; this gives him time to improvise or fill in if anything has gone wrong, or occasionally just for variety.

Sometimes Tony simply happens upon a good finish for a dance. Rehearsing a new number one day during one of their Persian Room engagements, he took out his handkerchief to mop his brow while he waited for Renée to dance across the floor to him and sink into the low curtsy he had planned. Feeling prankish, Tony bent down as his partner approached and lightly dusted off with his handkerchief the spot on the floor where she was to subside. When he caught this gesture in the mirror it seemed good enough to keep in the act, and it is still a popular finish with De Marco fans—the one in which Tony dances around the floor courteously dusting off one spot after another for Renée to sink onto.

Another number which patrons still call for came about in a haphazard way some four years ago. One night Tony learned that Jerome Kern was in the Persian Room; as a compliment, he had Eddy Duchin play one of Kern's current hits, "The Way You Look Tonight." It was a tune the De Marcos had never used, and they set about ad-libbing a dance to it. "You go out on the floor, take out your compact, and fuss with your face and hair," Tony said to Renée, "and I'll come out and dance around you, admiring you." The impromptu dance was a hit, and the De Marcos later worked it up into a waltz, abandoning Mr. Kern's music for Noël Coward's "I'll Follow My Secret Heart."

Generally they do not like to dance to the music of popular song hits unless, like "Tea for Two"—a standard De Marco number—they have become so popular as to be classics. A dance routine to a current time becomes quickly dated; also, it is easier for other dancers to copy than, say, a number danced to the music of Chopin or Debussy. The De Marcos are always as fiercely on the lookout for style pirates as any fashionable couturier.

Two of their new dances, introduced in the Sert Room last autumn, are traceable partly to such shrewd reasoning and partly to a more romantic origin. Last spring Tony was living in a Hollywood hotel, spending a good deal of time brooding over his separation from Renée. He had danced only once professionally in nearly two years—a number with Joan Crawford in "The Shining Hour," which sent him to a hospital for two weeks with a sprained shoulder and hip. "It was not Miss Crawford's fault," Tony explains earnestly in his high, husky voice; "she is a perfectly proportioned girl, but you can't get away from the truth. She weighs one hundred and twenty-eight pounds and I weigh one hundred and thirty-seven, with all my clothes on." When he got out of the hospital a friend in San Francisco sent him some phonograph records to cheer him up. Among them were Debussy's

"Clair de Lune" and Chopin's waltz in C sharp minor—an odd choice, perhaps, for jollying along a lonely man with sprained muscles, but, as it turned out, a fortunate one. Dancing alone around his hotel room to the music of those two records, Tony began, for the first time in over a year, to think up a couple of new routines.

Renée was in Hollywood too, impelled there by the flaming ambition which also flickered in her husband. Like most dancers, bandleaders, and other people in the voiceless branches of show business, the De Marcos want to act. As a dance team they have been offered contracts by several film companies, but, as a team and individually, they are still holding out for speaking parts in pictures, at least for a few lines to say.

When Tony is asked what actually brought about the reunion between himself and Renée, he points out the stubbornness of Hollywood producers in refusing to give either of them dramatic rôles, and thoughtfully adds, "There comes a time in anybody's life when the bank balance doesn't look so good." Another factor is perhaps even closer to his heart. "Renée is the best dancer in the world," Tony says simply; "she was born for it, her bones were made for it. I could never dance with anybody else." Renée's comment is equally artless. "It is good to dance with Tony again," she says; "he makes me dance better than I can." Tony likes to hear of his wife's saying things like that. "It helps the good will," he explains. The De Marcos' troubles with in-laws have quieted down now, and their financial troubles have been settled by a peaceful, if temporary, truce. The team receives $2,250 a week, which is paid to Tony; Renée is under contract to him for five years, at a guaranteed yearly income based on a fixed minimum. "What the minimum is, I would rather not divulge," Tony replies to questions concerning it, "but as far as the *maximum* goes, the sky is the limit." When the De Marcos are working Renée is paid forty rather than fifty per cent of the team's weekly salary, but Tony figures that this is just, since the remaining ten per cent covers about half of the team's publicity and other expenses.

Tony De Marco is Renée's first professional dancing partner; Renée, according to Tony, is his last. He is especially emphatic about this because she is also his eighth in the twenty-two years he has been dancing and the second to become Mrs. De Marco. The first Mrs.

De Marco was Mabel Scott, from whom Tony was divorced some fifteen years ago. The trouble that split the team that time began when the De Marcos—Tony and Mabel—were touring the Keith-Orpheum vaudeville circuit and Mabel was taken so sick that she had to leave the act. Tony wired the booking office to send another partner to fill in until Mabel got well, and the office sent a girl named Helen Kroner. Helen's dancing suited Tony so admirably that, when Mabel was well enough to stand a bit of news, Tony told her he had decided to engage Miss Kroner as his permanent partner. The battle that followed lasted for more than a year, off and on, until Mabel and Tony were divorced in Chicago, in 1924. Tony was dancing in George White's "Scandals" then, with Helen Kroner as the other half of the act, and he had already persuaded Miss Kroner to abandon any independent ambition she may have had, for the good of the team.

Helen Kroner had danced in a ballet company with Pavlowa and Tony respected her artistic training, but the De Marcos were beginning to be known to audiences and booking agents, and to change the billing would be bad for business. Tony rechristened Miss Kroner Nina De Marco, announced that she was his sister, and continued the act with the usual billing. All of his other partners—Peggy Hooper, Maxine Arnold, Albertina Vitak, Patricia Bowman, and Arline Langen—became De Marcos professionally, for the sake of the billing. Some of these girls were trained dancers (Miss Bowman and Miss Vitak were successful later under their own names), but they took instruction willingly from Tony, who has never had a dancing lesson. It takes several days, according to De Marco, just to get the established notions about ballroom dancing out of a new partner's head. For instance, the customary motion of the arm in a waltz is a wide, semicircular sweep in an unbroken line; Tony likes to scatter this gesture into two or maybe three smaller movements, accenting the rhythm of the music. In a fox trot, he likes to time his "breaks" vividly. A "break" in two-four time usually comes at the end of eight or sixteen bars, where the melody changes into another phrase. To take "Tea for Two" as an example:

> Picture you upon my knee
> With tea for two, and two for tea,

Me for you and you for me
Alone . . .

The break comes after the word "alone." One reason the De Marcos can do a considerable amount of ad-libbing around a dance floor is that they know when the breaks are coming. "I'll take it," Tony murmurs to Renée as a break approaches, and that means that he will improvise a dance around her; sometimes he says, "You take it," meaning that she must ad-lib a few steps around him.

Except for such casual inventions, between partners who are sure of each other, exhibition ballroom dancing is an exact business, carefully planned and timed. Tony has found that, training a new partner, he must restrict her to plain fox trots, waltzes, tangos, and rumbas for two or three days before he begins to teach her steps in groups—so many steps for the first sixteen bars, another group for the next sixteen. Generally the girls want to leap high in the air in his arms or to toss themselves onto his shoulders for a spin right away, but he discourages this kind of acrobatics—known in the profession as a "lift"—until his partner has perfected her other steps and has learned to hold her back straight and her hips in when dancing and to use her hands and arms as entertainingly as she uses her feet. A "lift" in ballroom dancing is accomplished by a method borrowed from the ballet. No dancer could raise his partner high off the floor or let her down again gracefully if his legs were stiffly poised or placed apart, so a lift begins with the *assemblé* (feet together at a slight angle) and ends with the *plié* (knees bent). One of De Marco's early partners was fond of food and Tony began to find it hard to get her off the floor, even with the *assemblé* and the *plié*, although she vowed that she had not altered from her original weight of one hundred and fifteen pounds. That partnership dissolved when, one day, Tony shoved her unexpectedly onto a drugstore scale. "It's a lie!" she cried as the needle trembled at one hundred and thirty. Renée weighs one hundred and ten, a nice weight for a De Marco. The tricks of whirling a partner on the shoulders or raising her high on one arm and spinning with her depend less, however, on physical strength than on timing and balance. Nearly all ballroom exhibition dancers wear rubber soles on their dancing shoes, to preserve their balance on waxed floors. The reason they can tap wearing rubber soles, as the De Marcos do, is that they put the full weight of each leg into every tap step, swinging the leg from the hip. Eccentric dancers and solo tap specialists use their feet more than their legs in dancing—Fred Astaire, for example, dances from the knees down, Bill Robinson from the ankles down; ballroom dancers dance from the hips down.

Tony De Marco began to be fairly well known in vaudeville about 1921, when he was presented to trustful audiences as "a native Argentinian dancer." The Valentino fever was approaching its height and people everywhere were sighing for Argentines. Tony's act with Mabel (who soon became Mabelle) was billed as "The De Marcos from the National Theatre, Buenos Aires, with Their Seven Musical Sheiks." Neither Tony nor Mabelle had ever seen the National Theatre or Buenos Aires, and the Seven Musical Sheiks were just seven Filipinos who played on Spanish guitars, but nobody seemed to mind, except possibly the Filipinos, who never got quite used to their long white robes and burnouses. When Nina De Marco (née Helen Kroner) replaced Mabelle in the act, ostensibly as Tony's sister, she added a further exotic tang by giving out arresting interviews about her childhood in South America with her brother, and about riding on muleback across the Andes one time to keep a dancing engagement. In San Francisco a feminine admirer wrote to Tony in Spanish, apologizing for her poor knowledge of the language he had inspired her to study. Tony got a stagehand who knew Spanish to read the letter to him and replied in perfect English, explaining that since the lady had made the flattering gesture of addressing him in his native tongue, he wished to return the compliment by responding in hers. When the National Theatre in Buenos Aires got wind of these goings-on and began writing protests to *La Prensa*, New York's Spanish newspaper, Tony sadly dropped the South American touch from his vaudeville billing. He continued to be known as an Argentinian, though, and to speak, when called upon to do so in the line of business, with a faint accent which he hoped was South American. It was not until a few years ago that he felt himself sufficiently established as a dancer to drop the accent and reveal the whole truth. "I was born in Buffalo," he told interviewers peacefully then.

Actually, Antonio De Marco was born in Fredonia, New York, fifty miles from Buffalo. His father, an Italian immigrant, operated a small truck farm there and hated all dancers because his own father, Carmelo di Marco, who owned a mill near Palermo, had lost it on account of an uncontrolled desire to leave his business and travel around the countryside dancing at *festas*. (The name di Marco was Gallicized by Tony's father.) It grieved and alarmed the elder De Marco to see his only son, Antonio, with his hair greased and his ears deaf to any sound but dance music, streaking off night after night to compete in one of the amateur dance contests regularly held at the Academy Theatre in Buffalo, and when Tony, at sixteen, demanded long trousers to dignify his social life, his father declined to give them to him. Tony bought them, and other fancy wearing apparel, by delivering meat for Valentine Brothers, a firm of butchers on Main Street, at $3 a week in winter (for deliveries made after school hours) and $8 for full time in summer. One warm payday the butcher's boy took his $8 to the race track at Fort Erie and won $160 on a horse named Jim L. With money in his pocket, he then departed without notice to anyone for New York, where he eventually got a job touring with a burlesque troupe called Jean Bedini's Mischief Makers. One night in Wheeling, West Virginia, Tony came off the stage after doing a tango and a maxixe with his partner, a large blonde, and found his father and the principal of the Fredonia High School waiting for him in the wings. Dragged home and slapped into school again, he remained an indifferent scholar and explained to his teachers that he couldn't think sitting down. Nowadays De Marco gets up and moves his feet around in a tentative dance step when he has anything important to say. Most of his thinking is concerned with dancing, and he talks about it better when his legs and feet are in motion.

De Marco *père* at last consented to let his son dance professionally, on condition that he change his name, and from 1918 to 1921 Tony and Mabel Scott appeared as The DeMarrs at the Cataract House in Niagara Falls, at the Café Frontenac in Detroit, and on the Pantages vaudeville circuit, where the team got $300 a week in "The Act Different." The following year Tony resumed his own name and his friendly relations with his father, and, first with Mabel and later with Nina as his partner, whirled through the Keith-Orpheum circuit to the Palace Theatre in New York. The De Marcos began appearing in fashionable night clubs and occasionally in musical comedies. Nina and Tony's partnership, begun in 1922, lasted seven years, although it was split by temperamental differences three times during that period. When they separated finally, in 1929, Nina put on a dancing act by herself. She is still dancing alone, here and there, under the name of Nina De Marco.

After the separation, Tony, temporarily without a partner, went to Hollywood to stage dances for a revue. In answer to a chorus call, a girl named Renée Leblanc applied. She was about eighteen and she was dressed in a sports dress, socks, and sandals. To this casual costume she had added, for the occasion, a brown moiré coat trimmed with ermine tails. Renée, born in Montreal, was the daughter of a French Canadian woman, née Leduc, and an Englishman named Nerny. One of Renée's uncles was George Primrose, the minstrel and soft-shoe dancer. She had had one lesson from Theodore Kosloff, the Russian ballet master, had danced with a Fanchon & Marco unit in vaude-ville, and had lately been doing a rather inconspicuous solo number at Montmartre, a Hollywood night club. She had tried Renée Leduc as a stage name, but because everybody pronounced her last name Leduck, she had changed it to Leblanc—not the happiest selection, since everybody, including Mr. De Marco, the dance director, pro-nounced *that* Leblank. Renée got a job in the revue, and when Tony had taken her out dancing several times after the show, he told her one night that he thought she could learn to dance if she worked at it, and asked her to be his partner. Renée agreed to try and to drop her troublesome French names for the name of De Marco.

The De Marcos rehearsed at odd hours during the run of the show, and when it closed they opened in vaudeville at the Hill Street Theatre in Los Angeles. Tony, who had acquired a sensitive taste in clothes, restrained Renée from a sudden, shouting desire for spangles and ordered for her a simple white chiffon dress with three wide ruffles at the hem. On opening night, Renée, anxious to please, danced so hard that she put her foot through the bottom ruffle and tore it to a bandage that clung around her ankles and locked them together throughout the first number, a waltz. Although she is now as accomplished a per-former as Tony, things like that still happen to her so often that Tony patiently carries two safety pins in his pocket whenever they dance. Besides being a practical precaution against the emergency of a bro-ken shoulder strap, or of an entire dress top's giving way under the strain of dancing, as it once did, the safety pins amuse the customers when they are brought into use. They are, in a way, typical of the airy inventiveness which distinguishes the De Marcos from other, sultrier ballroom dancers.

In 1934 the Plaza announced the opening of a new room for dinner and supper dancing, with Emil Coleman's orchestra and the De Marcos. Nobody in New York had heard much about the De Marcos. They had appeared briefly at the Central Park Casino and at the Empire Room in the Waldorf-Astoria, and they had been married to each other recently. The Plaza seemed, to expert night-clubbers, an unlikely place for a supper club anyway. It was a place for tea, for Sunday-morning breakfast, for dowagers and potted palms; any excitement it held belonged to the past, when Scott Fitzgerald débutantes danced in the Plaza Grill and the Rose Room was so famous a song was written about it. In 1934 the Grill was occupied mostly by middle-aged people from the suburbs, and the Rose Room had been turned into an automobile salesroom. At the risk of public indifference, the Plaza management moved the cars out of the salesroom, had the place decorated by Joseph Urban, and rather nervously gave out the news that the Persian Room was open for business. For almost three weeks after the opening night, which was principally an invitation affair, almost nobody came. Then business began to improve, partly by way of the Plaza's own elevators, when the calm and opulent residents of the hotel wandered in to see what was going on and later spread the word around town. Night-club explorers, bored by night-club dancers who seemed to be bored with each other, suddenly discovered that the De Marcos were different. The De Marcos were gay, they talked to each other, to Coleman, and to people at the tables while they danced, and they had a way of laughing together when a certain step pleased them, or when another went wrong. When Tony went into an intense tap solo and his partner, Renée, sitting aloof at a small table, said scornfully, "Ha! Six-seven-*eight*, I know *that* one!," and got up and did it, the customers were fascinated. The Persian Room took in an average weekly gross of $23,000 during the four years the De Marcos danced there, and it was a popular guess that without that income the Plaza might have had trouble financially. Tony likes to think of himself as the savior of the Plaza, and sometimes refers to his engagement there with a trace of melancholy. "We lived in a two-room apartment in the hotel, free, of course—that was in the contract," he says. "So one day Renée had a fitting, and the place was full of dressmakers and dogs and pins and people, and I had a pain in my back. So I telephoned downstairs and asked for a small room where my masseur could give me a rubdown. They gave me a very small room for an hour and charged me a full day's rate for it. It was unjust." Tony makes these remarks mildly, looking down at his feet and moving them around.

A good many things seem unjust to Tony, who has gone through a lot to achieve success. He cannot understand, for one thing, why Renée, who is supposed to pay for her clothes out of her percentage of the team's salary, is always broke when a bill comes around. Renée's explanation is that she must have a hundred dancing dresses and must keep at least thirty-five in rotation during a six-week engagement. Besides, there is the cost of shoes, stockings, cosmetics, and hairdressers. "It's the percentage trouble," Renée says softly, giving you a dark, puzzled look; "percentage is never enough."

Tony's wardrobe consists of twenty-three suits of dress clothes, ten dozen dress shirts, three hundred white ties, and eighty or ninety pairs of shoes in use. Like most dance teams, the De Marcos are sentimental about giving away their old clothes. They give them to friends who, they know, will go out dancing in them. They like to think of their discarded dancing dresses and tailcoats still whirling around somewhere, never limp and never still. Tony never gives away any of his old dancing shoes. When a pair loses its gleam or begins to crack, he pastes a strip of paper, bearing the date of retirement, inside one shoe and puts the pair away in one of the wooden packing cases he keeps for that purpose. He has some two hundred pairs of retired shoes now, and he was recently overtaken by a gracious idea about them. He would like to have each pair silver-plated, by a process he has heard of, and he would like then to send them as gifts to his friends, one pair to each pal. There are drawbacks to this plan. For one thing, the silvering process is expensive. "And besides," Tony says, "it's hard to think of two hundred people who would appreciate a present like that."

January 6, 1940

MARINA HARSS (1973–)

MARINA HARSS is a writer, journalist, and critic based in New York City, where she covers all aspects of dance and, occasionally, opera. Her features, profiles, and interviews have appeared in *The New York Times*, *The New Yorker*, and many other periodicals in the United States and Europe; she is also a frequent reviewer of dance for *Dancetabs.com* and a dance critic for WNYC. Harss is an accomplished translator from French, Spanish, and Italian, and, in 2012, she received the French American Foundation Prize for her translation of Elisabeth Gille's *Le Mirador: Mémoires Rêvés*, a biography of Irène Némirovsky.

For most of her life she has been a serious student of the piano. She is at work on a critical biography of the choreographer Alexei Ratmansky.

Plainspoken

"DANCE? Dance is pretty much just people dancing." The choreographer Mark Morris is responding to a question from one of fifty or so earnest music lovers gathered for a performance of his work. It is the second night of the Ojai Music Festival, held in the bucolic enclave of Ojai, California, about a two-hour drive northeast from LA. Morris is looking very pleased with himself, in rumpled cargo shorts, a red polo shirt, matching red socks and Franciscan-style sandals. With his broad chest and even broader belly, a scraggly beard, leonine head of graying hair and gleaming greenish eyes, he looks like a Welsh poet, a mischievous Buddha, a disheveled and possibly disreputable emperor. In his right hand he daintily clasps a tartan umbrella angled to protect his eyes from the waning sun. Something about the arrangement of his limbs as he perches on a stool—the extreme angle of his knees,

333

perhaps—reveals the uncanny flexibility of a former dancer. "I was a fabulously good dancer," he tells me later, and it's true, too. I've seen the tapes.

Every summer for the last sixty-seven years, Ojai's main street and outdoor amphitheater have been overrun by avid consumers of contemporary music, mostly of the experimental and avant-garde variety. A new music director is selected each year, though some have made repeated appearances. Pierre Boulez has been in charge on seven separate occasions, Stravinsky twice, as well as Esa-Pekka Salonen (twice) and John Adams (once). This time around, the baton was passed to Morris, the first choreographer to be invited. One wonders whether any of the previous musical eminences would have had the gumption to describe Samuel Barber's *Adagio for Strings* as "that sob-fest, boohoo" or to define tone clusters as "hitting the piano with your fist and calling it a day."

Morris's level of participation is astonishing. With the encouragement of Tom Morris (no relation), the festival's permanent artistic director and guardian angel, the choreographer has cooked up a dizzying assortment of events, up to ten a day, certainly more than is remotely possible to take in. He is everywhere, at just about every talk, every performance (even the early morning concerts at a meditation center in the hills) and every late night event. These include a karaoke night—accompanied by the jazz trio The Bad Plus—and social dancing with patrons and assorted guests. Morris's dancers, who perform on the second night of the festival, are nearly as ubiquitous. They sing at the karaoke night and at an afternoon concert of gamelan music by the West Coast composer Lou Harrison, and attend concerts—always as a group—when they're not rehearsing or teaching morning exercise classes. They look more like an appealing and youthful band of acolytes than a dance troupe; they bring their babies to rehearsals and appear perfectly content to tag along with their boss to most events rather than head off on their own to eat ice cream or read in the shade.

At the dance party, Morris whips up a series of rounds, one based on the polka, the other on the waltz. He exhorts the participants to hold hands with strangers and look into their eyes, frankly, *without irony*. The dances are fun to do, and not without their small complications—steps that go toward and away from the center, lines turning in opposite directions, a slap here, a slap there. Like the karaoke, they are accompanied by live music, an obsession of Morris's. His company performs exclusively to live accompaniment—anything from solo piano to full orchestra and chorus—and has done so for most of its thirty-three years. (In 1996, it officially made a commitment to have live music at every show and formed its own musical ensemble.) When dancers move to recorded music, steps can become fixed and stale; it is possible to perform without actively listening or responding to minute changes in tempo, accent, dynamics. Plus, recordings reduce the choreographer's options—what if he or she likes a certain passage a little faster or slower or louder or more staccato? Owing to the expense—musicians almost always make more money than dancers do—performing and rehearsing to live music is a rare luxury outside the world of ballet. That live music represents a significant expense (just under 10 percent of Morris's budget last year) is no excuse, in his opinion: "It's bullshit. You can afford it. You can get some darling student to play a synthesizer or a drum or singers or make the sound yourself, or use electronic music that's meant to be that way." On this point, and others, he is uncompromising.

From the beginning, life and work in Morris's company have amounted to almost the same thing. Back in the late 1970s, when he got his start in New York City—he moved there in 1976 to dance and put on his first show at the Merce Cunningham Studios four years later—Morris's friends used to take the train over to his loft in Hoboken to drink beer, watch television, eat food he had prepared, listen to records and do folk dances, devised by Morris. The group—centered around his interests, enthusiasms and imagination—is his natural habitat. (Paul Taylor, in contrast, spends long periods of the year on his own on Long Island.) He expects his company and trusted collaborators—people like Nancy Umanoff, his intimidatingly efficient and down-to-earth executive director—to be engaged, "interested in the world, in art, in books, food, Jeopardy, sex and everything else," in the words of Maile Okamura, a dancer with the company since 2001. He also draws ideas from the group dynamic. "He's very interested in behavior in a group," Okamura notes, and those interactions show up in his dances.

It is also a reflection of how he works. "I make up everything in the room with the dancers," he recently told an interviewer on NPR. "I don't work in the studio alone ever." First he gets a certain feeling, an itch triggered by a piece of music. That, of course, is a solitary experience, though he is famous for coercing everyone he knows into listening to the music he loves. Then there is the period of mulling, which may last years. He studies the musical score. ("He's a scrupulous analyst," says the musicologist Simon Morrison, who collaborated with him on a *Romeo and Juliet* based on Prokofiev's original version of the ballet score. "He reads all the technical literature.") But once he decides to make a dance the real work begins, in the studio, score in hand, with his dancers. (He is one of very few choreographers to use the musical score; another was Balanchine, who used to create his own piano reductions.) Which is not to say that the dancers improvise or help come up with steps. "There is this strange assumption that people make . . . where they wonder, are you a complete fascist/ tyrant/dictator or do the dancers improvise? Well, neither. I mean, it's more that I'm a fascist dictator, but the dancers dance. They contribute by dancing." The dancers are his instruments, the movement itself.

In addition to the modern dance works for his company, Morris has also made ballets, with *pointe* work, for various troupes, including American Ballet Theatre and the San Francisco Ballet. He also teaches a daily ballet class for his dancers at the Mark Morris Dance Center, the company's headquarters in Brooklyn. Unlike modern dance masters of previous generations, such as Martha Graham and José Limón (and to a certain extent Paul Taylor) who created their own technique, Morris is happy to teach ballet, which he considers a kind of lingua franca of dance, complete enough to prepare the body for all kinds of movement. In his own ballets, he tends to downplay the Balanchinean ideals of lightness, speed and hyper-flexibility. In *Drink to Me Only With Thine Eyes* (1988), a chamber work for ABT based on a series of limpid piano études by Virgil Thomson, the movements of the dancers have a pleasing weight and loose-limbed feel; they sink down into deep pliés, tip over until they are about to fall, and torque their upper bodies to give each position a lush three-dimensional quality. (You can watch passages from *Drink to Me* on YouTube.) Because of the way dancing on pointe accentuates gender specificity, ballet allows him to toy with the way men partner and lift women, though even here, his focus remains more on the ensemble and the individual than on the balletic ideal of the couple. His recent *Beaux*, for the San Francisco Ballet, is an ensemble work for nine men, with, in his words, "no fighting, no competition and no sexual predation."

In his own company, gender can seem almost irrelevant, pointedly so. (In the 1980s, when the company emerged on the dance scene, this stance was more of a statement than it is today.) Extended duets are not really Morris's thing, though he has made some beautiful ones, like the tender coming-of-age dance for Drosselmeier and his nephew in his version of *The Nutcracker* (*The Hard Nut*, 1991) and the brutal *Jenn and Spencer*—a kind of battle to the death he created earlier this year. There is also the disturbingly erotic pas de deux he made in 1985, *One Charming Night*, depicting a brief love affair between an adoring (and aroused) vampire (played by Morris) and a little girl (played by an adult, Teri Weksler). But for the most part, the individual and the group are the main subjects of his dances. Women lift and support men just as often as the opposite, and roles are often shared by dancers of both sexes. In the original cast of his *Dido and Aeneas* (1989), for example, Morris himself danced both the role of Dido and that of her nemesis, the Sorceress. (He was half-woman, half man, with long, curly hair and earrings, but also bulky muscles and a markedly heavy, strong way of moving.) In more recent casts, the roles have been assigned in many different ways: split between a man and a woman, both performed by a man or both by a woman—most memorably, by Amber Star Merkens, who has the profile of a Byzantine princess and the musculature of a young Greek wrestler.

Morris tells me that when he starts to make a dance, "I try to figure out something to do while they're all waiting there trying to pretend they're not bored." Sometimes he already has the germ of a movement idea. When he made *Falling Down Stairs* (1997), a dance inspired by Yo Yo Ma's execution of the Third Cello Suite by Bach, he told Ma that just before he started he'd dreamt of falling down stairs. The Prelude begins with a group of dancers arrayed on a wooden staircase opposite the cellist; as Ma plays the opening phrase—a descending scale and arpeggio—the dancers run down the steps and tumble to the ground in a fanlike pattern. Morris seems to love the effortfulness of falling and getting up.

A few years ago, when he began to work on the choreography for *Socrates* (2010), a spare, meditative work based on a pellucid song cycle by Satie, he started things off by asking the dancers to re-create poses from Jacques-Louis David's *Mort de Socrate*—the raised finger, the downturned face of the man in red holding a cup of hemlock. Most of the gestures and poses didn't end up in the piece, but a few did, and those became compositional elements, divorced, at least in part, from their literal meaning. They became the visual equivalent of a chord or motif in music. The odd thing about bodies in space is that in different contexts, their movements take on new meanings: "the audience doesn't know why that part is sad, it's just that she's facing away from you that time instead of toward you," is how Morris explains it. For this reason, he isn't afraid of repetition; each time the gesture or step seems a little bit different. Repetition and variation is one of the elements that lends his dances such emotional resonance. It also drives some people crazy. "It seems as if he uses about four steps," the critic Leigh Witchel complained of one piece, "a fifth would be nice."

If, as Morris claims, dancing is merely "walking and running and fall-ing" to music, how does he avoid making the same dance over and over? First, he imposes a series of rules for each dance, a different set of problems. How many groups will there be? Will they interact with each other? What sorts of floor patterns will he work with? In response to these self-imposed rules, he devises ingenious solutions. But he's not bound to his own systems. If he gets tired of a step, he throws it out and replaces it with another that makes more sense to him at the time: "it's like changing the color." Sometimes, in order to obtain unpredictable results—he likes to see what will happen—he asks for actions that cannot be fully controlled, like bending backward "until you fall over." If ten people do this at once, they will do it in ten slightly different ways, because there is no way to predict how you will fall over. Then there are all the tactics he uses to manipulate the mate-rial he invents. He might ask the dancers to do a phrase in reverse, or change direction, or do it while lying on the ground with their feet in the air, or as a canon or a fugue. He creates many variations on a theme, versions that contain some of the same material but also add or subtract from it, or shift the emphasis. One of the most brilliant examples is a solo he created for himself in 1984, *O Rangasayee*, set to a South Indian Carnatic song; for twenty minutes, he spun seemingly infinite loops, riffing on a series of crouches, lunges, Isadora Duncan–like leaps and rhythmic footwork that echoed the syllabic, accented scatting of the singer's voice. The principles that guided this morphing structure were indecipherable from the outside, but their relationship to the logic of the music was thrillingly palpable. His dancing allowed the audience to hear the music more clearly by providing a kind of memory palace of movements.

In a related vein, when he works with music that has an accompanying text, like Satie's *Socrate*, a scenario—or a phrase, or even a word—can become a point of departure. In *Dido and Aeneas*, when a sailor bellows the words "come away, fellow sailors, your anchors be weighing," the dancers mime pulling at ropes and raising the sails of a ship. In last year's *A Wooden Tree*, when the singer utters a series of blips and beeps imitating Morse code, the dancer (Mikhail Baryshnikov, in a guest appearance) taps out the rhythms precisely on a chair. Morris has even buried bits of American Sign Language in his choreography. The conjunction between words and gestures isn't always this obvious, but he has been accused more than once of "Mickey Mousing." It's true, in a sense, but at the same time, different forms of "word-painting" and "music visualization"—as these practices are called—are common to much of the classical and folk dance around the world.

He's also keen on rhythm. The patterns of the footwork he creates are more varied and more percussive than those of just about any other modern dance or ballet choreographer. (He likes to joke that the only dancers who can equal his in rhythmic acuity are in the Ballet National du Sénégal.) Sometimes they follow the beat, or double it, or to the contrary, slow things down to half-time, suspending a step to create tension and syncopation. "He understands subdivision," says Reid Anderson of The Bad Plus, the jazz trio that supplied Morris with the version of *The Rite of Spring* he used for his *Spring, Spring, Spring* earlier this year. (The title was borrowed from a musical number in the film *Seven Brides for Seven Brothers*, which Morris loves and will happily sing.) His understanding of the subdivision of the beat allows him to work within or against the rhythm, shifting the accents of the body to complement or play against those in the music. He loves hemiolas, rhythmic patterns that allow him to insert steps between the beats (three against two or two against three). He didn't invent this practice, of course; it's typical of many folk dance forms, in which he is well versed. Rhythmic variety is simply another tool he uses to mine the textures and layers of a musical work. But craft isn't everything. What makes the dances come alive are the surprises, the man dragging himself across the floor like a lowly beast in the opening of *Gloria* (1981) as the chorus bellows "Gloria! Gloria!"; the mad whoosh of dancers at the start of *L'Allegro, il Penseroso ed il Moderato* (1988); the almost unbearable stillness at the end of *Socrates* (2010). These are what stay with you when you leave the theater.

It helps that he seems to have an endless supply of ideas. "I make way too much stuff and then I edit," he says. In the video of *Falling Down Stairs*, we see him working in the studio; at one point, unsatisfied with something he has just made up, he says, "Never mind, fuck that," and does something new. The process may not be pretty—"He shouts a lot," says Isaac Mizrahi, who has designed several of his shows, and Morris himself admits "I'm daunting and bossy and I get my way"—but the dances he ends up creating are their own reward. "It's a joy to do them . . . there's nothing like it," Rob Besserer, who danced with Mark Morris on and off for twenty years, told me, a blissful smile spreading across his face.

Morris was born in Seattle in 1956. He began dancing after being taken to see a José Greco concert by his mother. Watching videos of Greco, one can see what might have excited the young Morris: the playfulness that could quickly veer into solemnity; the powerful, rhythmically exciting footwork, the crystalline movements and razor-sharp timing, as well as the hammy virility that alternated with touches of almost feminine sensuality (especially in the way Greco used his hips). Morris's mother took him to a local school directed by the open-minded and eclectic teacher Verla Flowers, a place where one could learn everything from ballet to acrobatics to belly dancing. He studied mainly Spanish dance and ballet. Then, as a teenager, he joined a Balkan group, the Koleda Folk Ensemble. With Koleda, Morris experienced, perhaps for the first time, the creative excitement generated by a group of people joining hands and shoulders and forming varied patterns across a stage, illustrating the complexities of folk rhythms with their stamping feet and bobbing knees. In this context, personal virtuosity—which Morris had in spades—faded away. Unlike ballet, it didn't really matter how high you could lift a leg or how much stage presence you had or how many times you could spin, so long as you could really hear the music and communicate its energy to your fellow dancers and the audience. As Joan Acocella, *The New Yorker*'s dance critic, has written in her excellent biography of Mark Morris, Koleda became "an image of the world," one that would serve as a perpetual reminder of what dancing really was.

The plainspokenness of folk dance has endured in Morris's work, even as it has grown more refined, more sophisticated. Somehow, he has managed to combine it with his analytical, meticulous approach to composition. Through his daily ballet classes, he eliminates the mannerisms and distortions that worm their way into the most advanced ballet training, in part as a result of technique being pushed to the limit so that dancers can raise their legs higher, turn more, exaggerate their lines, embellish their movements. Morris isn't interested in extremes. "He's interested in anatomy," says Okamura. "He's looking for each person's ideal form. He sees a beautiful body as one that is coordinated in a seemingly natural way. It's a more honest expression of the body." This may be why his dancers tend to look more like regular people than like creatures from another, perfect planet. When they perform, they exhibit the same frankness that Morris expects in social dance. "He teaches us to look directly out of our eyes, with our pupils going straight out of our face, to really look."

The theme at Ojai, selected by Morris, is American twentieth-century music, especially from the West, and even more specifically, from the circle of Lou Harrison. The company's performance on the second night of the festival, which includes dances set to music by Henry Cowell, Charles Ives, Samuel Barber and Harrison, is a highlight. Two days later, there is an unscheduled performance of the solo *Ten Suggestions* just before a concert of songs by Cowell and Ives. Morris originally made this solo for himself, but, now 57, he no longer dances, so here it is performed by Dallas McMurray, who looks a bit like an overgrown boy from a children's book. The 1981 work is a touchingly simple, almost hokey suite of solos set to Alexander Tcherepnin's evocative *Bagatelles* for piano (played with great panache by Colin Fowler, the music director of Morris's company). Though they lack titles, the pieces are like miniature musical mise-en-scènes, each evoking a clear mood and style. McMurray enters, wearing pink pajamas, and seems to improvise in an exploratory, almost naïve style. On a long suspended note, he revolves three times on one leg, then plunges into a squat, hitting the bottom of the drop squarely on a rich, low chord. Then, as Fowler plays a repeating series of rising and falling notes, McMurray rolls forward, twice, and then flicks one foot to mark an accent, then rolls again, this time to the right, then backward, then to the left. After this, the theme having reached its conclusion, he jogs back to the spot where he began. When the melody begins again, so does the dance. Before a new, dreamier melody is introduced, McMurray takes a few casual steps, as if to wipe away the mood. Then his torso loosens and hinges forward, riding the wave of a long accented note, vividly showing the effect of gravity pulling it downward. In this next section, his swinging arms, plunging torso and tilting head illustrate the outline of the melody. The pattern is repeated as often as it is heard on the piano. When Fowler stretches the music with a little rubato, McMurray takes a slight breath.

Nothing could be simpler, in a way. There is music, and one man's utterly personal response to it. It's obvious, but specific. No one else would have imagined that exact series of movements. The ideas are straightforward, easily legible, often repeated. Many of the elements of *Ten Suggestions*—the rhythmic incisiveness and playfulness, the casual affect, the literalness, the idiosyncrasy, the fanciful (but knowing) naïveté—are to be found in one Morris dance after another. Of course, he can also be dark. He has made dances about death and murder and sexual brutality and fear. Even seemingly gentle pieces like *Ten Suggestions* are laced with an underlying whiff of sadness, a recognition of human limitation and failure. The dancer in *Ten Suggestions* often falls to the ground; his quietly focused demeanor is contrasted by moments of discouragement. The piece ends with him standing on a chair, but also covering his face.

As often happens with audiences who are unfamiliar with Morris—the dance and music worlds overlap surprisingly little—the response at Ojai is extremely warm. Music lovers dig his work; so do musicians, which is curious, because musicians are, I've found, often slightly resistant to dance. They tend to feel that dance is superfluous, unmusical and distracting—the music is complete without it. Morris's dances come across as transparent, smart and surprising, even when they are provocative or deeply strange. More than that, his choreography has a symbiotic relationship with the music. It goes beyond understanding to a kind of empathy: "He finds the character of the piece of music," says Okamura, "and once it's choreographed, you can't imagine it any other way." Morris's reputation in the dance world is more divided. There are the enthusiasts—Joan Acocella, who published her 1994 book on Morris when he was only 37, is one, as well as her predecessor at *The New Yorker*, Arlene Croce, who was an early booster—but there are the skeptics, among them the late Clive Barnes and for a long time Anna Kisselgoff of *The New York Times*. Robert Gottlieb recently described Morris's *Choral Fantasy* as "run, run, run; leap, leap, leap; and, most persistently, march, march, march." Barnes once wrote that he found *L'Allegro, il Penseroso, ed il Moderato*—which was performed as part of the White Light Festival at Lincoln Center this fall—to be "commonplace and totally irrelevant," even though it is considered by many to be one of the great dance works of the last twenty-five years.

The superficial simplicity of the dances is a frequent bone of contention. In Europe, where there is an expectation that contemporary dance will be knotty and densely packed with ideas, Morris's work is less popular than here and in England. "We went to Holland a couple of years ago and we got some of the worst reviews ever, saying, 'This is nursery school kind of dancing,'" Nancy Umanoff told me this summer. Rather than bombard you with his erudition, Morris sometimes has a tendency to amuse himself with jokey references to popular culture: professional wrestling and comic strips and B movies like *3D House of Stewardesses*. This deliberately lowbrow esthetic can appear arch, even campy, and in a way it is (though he truly admires these things). But like them or not, the homey references and plainspokenness represent core elements of his style. For Morris, the complication should remain beneath the surface, in the construction of the dance, not in its cultural references. "That stuff is not important. Or if it is, you should just do the fifty pages of program notes explaining your ideas. Which some people do," he says.

Morris is branching out. His dance center in Brooklyn, which in many ways reflects his own experience with Verla Flowers, hums with community classes for children and adults and professional master classes, all accompanied by live music. The center also produces educational programs for schools based on his dances, and free classes for people suffering from Parkinson's, taught by former company members, which include barre work, dances in the round, partnering and, on the day I attended, a bit of flamenco. (Morris has said that he considers the center to be his true legacy.) In the last decade, he has begun working more directly with singers and musicians (especially at Juilliard and at the Tanglewood Summer Festival), directing opera, even conducting. A few years back, he began studying conducting with the baroque specialists Craig Smith and Jane Glover, as well as with Stefan Asbury, a champion of new music. He has found the experience "terrifying and very enlivening." Apparently he sweats so much that he prefers to conduct barefoot. Musicians seem to agree that he's a good conductor, with strong opinions about tempo and the quality of sound he wants and a firm but elastic sense of meter. "The main thing I've learned from him is that all music has to swing," the soprano Yulia Van Doren, who often collaborates with the company, told me. He also teaches graduate music courses at Princeton with the musicologist Simon Morrison. He directed a surprisingly drab production of Gluck's *Orfeo* at the Met (2007), but also a wonderfully irreverent staging of Purcell's *King Arthur* at City Opera (2008); the latter included one of the most rousing, imaginative maypole dances ever seen.

This summer, he directed the Tanglewood Fellows' staging of Benjamin Britten's chamber opera *Curlew River*. Most of his work with singers consists of clearing away habits that build up in vocal training and performance, distorted (to his ear) English diction and preconceptions about musical style. He also pushes singers to take chances with vocal color for dramatic effect—not to always worry about making a pretty sound—and to make clear choices about rhythm. He asks them to acknowledge the rests in the music and give them full value, but also to allow themselves certain liberties for a more natural, conversational delivery. He favors character and directness over sheer vocal beauty—like most Baroque enthusiasts, he's not especially fond of vibrato. As with dancers, he constantly reminds singers to look out at the audience and at each other rather than "at the inside of your own head," as Isaiah Bell, one of the Tanglewood Fellows, put it. His frankness can be jarring: "You have to be thick-skinned and you have to have a sense of humor," one singer who has collaborated with him

over the years told me. Even among musicians, his musical ear surprises: "At one point," Bell told me, "he said to someone in the band,
'There's an eighth-note tied over to a triplet, and you're coming off the
first eighth-note in that triplet too late,' and it was true." The minute
adjustment—usually the territory of a conductor, not a director—was
enough to clarify a shift in meter. The production had no conductor,
so Morris found ways for the singers and musicians (who were all
onstage) to give each other cues, without worrying about creating a
"perfect" sound or a seamless visual effect. If the audience noticed a
cue, so be it. This fluidity between performers is typical for him. In
his next big project, the Handel opera *Acis and Galatea*, which will
premiere at Cal Performances in April, the principal singers will be
onstage with the dancers throughout, as they were in *King Arthur*. In
this way, "Everyone occupies the same world," as he puts it.

Morris is beginning to transcend the boundaries of the dance world,
which may be one of the reasons some of the figures in that world
resent him a bit. It's understandable. He can sometimes seem hell-bent
on offending. At Ojai, he spoke of dance as being seen as the "pathetic
bottom drawer embarrassment of the arts." (At a pre-performance
talk, he scolded a lady on the bleachers for making noise: "Hey you,
keep your chips quiet!") But his love for the basic truths of the body is
unshaken. "Every gesture means something," he told me the first time
we spoke. When I reminded him of this later, he elaborated on what he
believes dance can do better than any other art: "There's a sympathetic
response to watching someone dance. It helps you stay alive. People
watching people dance have incredible undisclosed empathy. When
you see a great Indian dancer who suddenly has Krishna's revelation,
you get it, you feel it yourself. That's what I think."

December 23/30, 2013

Stuart Hodes (1924–)

Stuart Hodes began dancing when almost twenty-one after being discharged from the United States Army Air Corps, in which he served as a B-17 bomber pilot. In 1946, he returned to Brooklyn College but happened to take a class at the Martha Graham studio. It sealed his fate. Within months, Hodes (born Gescheidt) was in the Graham company and dancing in such works as *Errand into the Maze*, *Diversion of Angels*, and other masterpieces. He stayed in the company for eleven years, then continued to teach and coach, in 2000 becoming head of the Graham school. He was also, in the early years, married to another superb Graham dancer, Linda (Margolies) Hodes. *FLAK*, a solo from his early years as a choreographer, marries his two passions: dancing and flying. His dances have been performed by the Joffrey Ballet, Boston Ballet, San Francisco Ballet, and others. With his second wife, Elizabeth, he toured coast to coast in their own two-person company. He danced on Broadway in, among others, *Kismet*, *Annie Get Your Gun*, and *Once Upon a Mattress*. He was Graham's partner in the 1958 film version of *Appalachian Spring*. He has headed the Department of Dance at NYU Tisch School of the Arts, served as a dance panelist for the National Endowment for the Arts, and was president of the National Association of Schools of Dance. And he has written a wonderful, revelatory book, *Onstage with Martha Graham: A Dancer's Memoir*, whose pages on Graham (see below) are transporting and deeply moving. He appreciated her, loved her, served her, and fought her, and this unique account of his years with her is his final homage to her genius and her humanity.

(from) Onstage with Martha Graham

Martha's Technique Class, 1947

THE ADVANCED class met at 4:30 P.M. By 4:15, choice spots in the center and in front of the mirrors had been taken. Others picked their way to places near the back or at the sides. I sat with the soles of my feet together, letting the weight of my torso gently stretch the muscles of my lower back. The maple floor, clean as a cutting board, felt good beneath my bare thighs.

Ethel Winter, Martha's demonstrator, faced the class. A minute before 4:30, Ralph Gilbert entered, sat at the piano and arranged his newspaper. Martha entered, looked the class over, glanced toward Gilbert, who met her eye.

"And. . . ."

Gilbert's compressed chords marked each pulse as torsos dropped into opening bounces, sixteen with soles of the feet together, sixteen with legs outspread, sixteen extended to the front. The breathings followed, an expansion that filled the torso and lifted the gaze.

Then, contractions: Martha's signature torso modulations. From deep in my pelvis I drew my body into a concave arc from hips to head, relishing the feel of deep muscles working. A surge of energy gathered, curved my torso, extended into my arms and legs, and shot out of my flexed hands and feet. Release straightened me, like an uncoiling spring. As each contraction began, my face lifted, lengthening my throat.

"Open your eyes," Martha commanded. She hated seeing them closed, deeming it self-indulgent. "Present your gaze."

I presented mine to the vaulted ceiling, through the ceiling to the sky, to space, beyond space. My gaze felt weighted. I panned it like a searchlight, chopped it down like a cleaver, as my body turned with an accelerating sweep that articulated my spine and flowed through my torso into my mouth, where it burst into a second contraction that began the entire sequence again.

"Sit to the side, fourth position."

I was not comfortable in the sitting fourth, and studied Ethel Winter, trying to fathom her comfort and ease in this curious body posture. My tendons seemed long enough, but I was not quite relaxed and believed it to be some muscle group that hadn't learned not to resist. We changed sides on counts, each marked by a percussive piano chord. Gilbert's improvised music followed familiar patterns yet was always fresh.

My left hip lifted, to insinuate a rotating wave through my stomach, chest, and head. My left arm engaged, then the right, then both. Head and gaze swept through an arc and the room spun past my eyes, yet within I felt stillness. My torso arched up, back, and around until my weight hung over my right forearm, where I paused in a suspension until a contraction sucked me in and drew me into a ball where a release filled me once more. The move ended delicately, like silk settling. In the stillness that followed effort, I relished my quickened heartbeat, and presented my gaze to the mirror, where thirty others presented their gazes to me.

Martha moved about, giving corrections. She stopped over me. "Go to the count of five." I spiraled back, placing weight on my right forearm. She poked me lightly under the ribs. "Lift, there." I strove into my rib cage. "At least you're wet," she said. The floor was wet, too, as sweat ran off my thighs and dripped from my arms. Heavy sweating felt cleansing, a shower taken inside-out. The room was hot, comforting my muscles; the humid air felt nourishing, like broth.

"Over on your face." I stretched out face down, body parallel to the front wall. "Back on your knees. Exercise on Six." Martha's most dramatic floor sequence was named simply by the number of its counts.

I took the starting position, weight on my knees and insteps, torso horizontal, body shaped like a "Z." Martha looked us over. "Lengthen your torso. Keep your back parallel to the floor like a table." She pressed gently on the hips of a dancer, lowering her torso, lifted another's shoulders, traced her finger along the spine of one who wasn't in a full release, pressed down a pair of tensely lifted heels. She took her time. Simply holding the position demanded strength. I was uncomfortable with weight on my knees, actually the tops of my tibias, below the kneecaps. I felt my jaw tighten and tried to relax all muscles not engaged in holding the position.

"One." A powerful contraction lifted the center of my back as head and shoulders scooped toward the floor, coiled, then uncoiled into a steep backward tilt from knees to head.

"Two." The count caught the tilt and it held there, thighs pulled taut from within.

Years later, a student from Japan, Akiko Kanda, transformed herself in the Exercise on Six. She'd arrived with muscle-heavy thighs, giving her slender torso a grounded look. She took three classes a day and did the Exercise on Six relentlessly.

"She is samurai," said Martha approvingly. In a year, Akiko's thighs were slender as reeds. When she became a leading dancer in the Graham company, no one could believe she'd ever been anything but the steely sylph who appeared on stage. When she returned to Japan, she became a celebrated dancer, teacher, and "National Treasure."

"Three." From full-body contraction into release.

"Four." The release was sucked back into a second contraction, a steeper tilt, buttocks an inch from heels, the limit of my strength, held half a count.

"And, release, sit." Buttocks dropped onto heels, head flung back, gaze up, spine striving for length as the torso folded forward toward the floor then into an exaggerated "hyper-release."

"Five." The release reversed, becoming contraction.

"And, Six." Return to the cantilevered horizontal thrust of the opening.

We did it again. Exercise on Six was always done at least twice.

"Sit to the side." I settled gratefully off my knees. Martha nodded to Ethel. Ethel had done every movement along with the class; now she demonstrated the Exercise on Six, slowly, as Martha explained the impulse beneath each move. It looked effortless, her control rock steady in positions that had made my thigh muscles shudder. Then it was our turn again, four more times. It yielded, at last, exultation.

A dozen years later, when I was teaching, musician Reed Hansen, accompanying the class, played the dramatic opening of Richard Strauss's *Also Sprach Zarathustra*, surrounding the Exercise on Six with a shimmering musical aura. I began calling it "the Zarathustra." It didn't catch on.

"Rise from the floor." We stretched out full length, face down, then pushed back onto hands and knees.

"One." The left leg reached back.

"Two." Stepped through onto the left foot, straightened the right, made one line through heel, hip, head.

"Three." Rose on the left leg as the body swiveled toward the mirror and the right scissored in, meeting the left in first position.

Mini-break, fifteen seconds. Men tucked T-shirts into trunks and subtly adjusted dance belts. Women pulled leotard bottoms over exposed buttocks.

"Brushes." We began with the legs parallel, weight on one, the other beating like a bird's wing.

"Make arrows," said Martha. I was not happy with my feet, and I pointed them hard on each brush. The brushes broke free of the floor, rose parallel to the floor at a tempo faster than the pendulum swing of the leg, so that the body had to absorb the effort or, in weakness, reveal it.

Martha's voice softly into my ear: "You're gripping with your arms. Let go. Let light pass through your body." I responded with a shake of my torso as I tried to disconnect my arms from the force energizing my leg. I tried to feel transparent, to float above the commotion of my legs. I imagined that my pumping leg was not part of me and encouraged it in a friendly yet insistent way.

We did deep pliés, done by every dancer who ever lived. My body neared the floor, knee angle acute, as the bones lost mechanical advantage, spilling weight into thigh muscles, which had to support me with sheer strength.

"Lift. Lift," exhorted Martha, and I tried to imagine gravity flowing upward through my body, opposite to jumps where the thrust was down: resolution sought in opposites, hoping that with enough concentration, the look of effort would vanish.

"Slow Sits to the Floor."

We began in a wide second position, spilled weight onto the left leg, body curved like a filled sail, right foot passing behind and to the left of the left, sickling at the ankle, an unmitigated sin in classic ballet. In Bombay, 1956, a Bharatanatyam master demonstrated moves with a sickled foot. When I asked if it had a specific meaning, as do many Indian moves, he said, "No. We only do it because it is beautiful."

My instep caressed the floor and accepted my weight as I dropped my right buttock all the way to the floor, settling into the sit. Thirty dancers held it there, curving coils of muscle from shoulder to knee. Ralph held the pedal down, letting the chord ring as he turned the page of his newspaper and Martha counted: ". . . Six, seven, eight."

Then Ralph slammed his thick fingers down, hitting more than ten keys. Thirty backs snapped straight, flinging weight through thighs and curved-in feet into skin-polished floor. Thirty torsos cut upward, suspended, then settled carefully, like mountain birds landing. The music drained away.

Martha had Ethel demonstrate prances, and challenged us with a look that asked why we didn't dance like *her*. The first time I saw Ethel perform was in a rehearsal of *Letter To The World*, chaste as Diana, the virgin goddess. Then I saw her in jazz improvisations at a company party, and, after that, steamy routines in Broadway's *Ankles Aweigh*.

Daydreaming, I missed an explanation, felt woozy, bent to drain blood into my brain, then straightened up as we began prances, doing them as a rest step by letting the spring in my calves and feet carry me through the first set. We repeated, knees rising high, then with jumps ending on a double upbeat. Martha worked them into a turning jump combination with tricky syncopation, and I attacked with gusto, no longer tired.

A second mini-break while the class shuffled to the corner and lined up in pairs for traveling moves across the floor. Men crossed last. There were three other men, Sasha and Bob Cohan, both in the Graham troupe, and a smallish wiry newcomer in a white leotard whose horn-rimmed glasses were tied on with elastic. Cohan and the newcomer hung back, wanting to go last, so I paired up with Sasha.

We began with low walks, slow at first, then faster, keeping the body's weight centered between footfalls. After several crosses, Martha gave a ludicrous illustration, chest caved in, belly thrust out, head poked forward.

"This is how little babies walk. Selfish little babies." We started again. "No." She stopped us. "Watch Ethel."

Ethel moved in a seamless flow, toes touching the floor with the sensitivity of fingers, the heel following soundlessly to take the body's weight.

"Do it."

We did it again, and again, then faster, becoming low runs that swallowed the studio's sixty-five-foot diagonal in four seconds.

Triplets. One low step, two high. Martha added a wide turn, a traveling skip, and worked it into a dance combination that reversed and cut back in a semicircle to end with leaps the length of the studio.

Ralph hammered out the triplets on low notes, then switched to a four-beat for the leaps, buoying each with a slashing chord accented on "two" instead of the down-beat, giving us a musical lift at the crest.

"Stop." Martha clapped her hands together, halting music and dancers. "You're missing it. Push off on one, stay in the air on two, land on three. Listen to Ralph. He's trying his best to help you. Sasha and Stuart, will you please demonstrate?"

A bouquet. We leaped across, trying to outjump each other, followed by the eyes of Intermediates who crowded the doorway, waiting for our class to end. Then, everyone leapt continuously, a sustained crescendo until the clock said one minute after six.

"We've run over. That's all. Thank you."

We applauded as Intermediates dashed in to grab choice spots in front of the mirror.

Martha

Martha never spoke of religion, although she once told me that we are always surrounded by a great field of energy from which we can draw, if only we learn how. Once, she spoke of entering a cottage that belonged to a friend, instantly sensing a presence in it, to learn that a close friend of her friend had recently died there.

Martha regarded animals as sentient beings, if on a slightly different plane than her own. When I joined the company in 1946, she had no dog. Mark Ryder soon told me she had given her dachshund to Katherine Cornell as atonement for having thrown it at Louis Horst. In his memoir, José Limón described a scene with a dachshund, which I assume was the one she tossed:

"Late at night, during these middle years of the 1930s, coming home from performances of *As Thousands Cheer*, at the Music Box Theatre, I would sometimes encounter at Tenth Street between Fifth and Sixth Avenues, a lady walking a dachshund. The dog's name was Max, and he belonged to Louis Horst. The lady was Martha Graham."

Surely no dog was ever walked by a more distinguished personage. Even the high-bred borzois of that pampered darling of Tsar Nicholas II, the prima ballerina assoluta Mathilde Kchessinska, were probably attended by a groom or lackey. But here was the great Miss Graham, very primly attired in tweeds, with a small hat perched on top of a severe coiffure, attending to Max's canine necessities.

Martha doted on every dog that showed up at the studio, most often Cedric, Bertram Ross's cocker spaniel, and Roderick, her sister Georgia's big poodle. She could never resist stopping to talk to an appealing dog, like the sheepdog encountered on the sidewalk in London after a triumphant performance at Covent Garden, where a paparazzo snapped her picture.

Martha's fury when I told her I was taking more ballet than Graham classes, later explaining it was because she cared about me, had been instantly forgiven. Eventually I began to understand that Martha's wrath was a mix of jealousy, fear of desertion, drive for power, and one other, the sheer ecstasy of rage. How joyously she related having torn a telephone out of the wall after Ted Shawn called with a message she did not wish to hear! Eventually I realized that when I was overcome by temper, a strange sort of ecstasy commanded me, too.

Dancers spend their lives building the skills which give them exquisite control over their bodies, yet, however brilliant, it is never enough. They are the ultimate "control freaks," except that the control they seek is over themselves.

Martha was driven to dominate, and yet I never felt freer than when working with her. She explored her own creativity relentlessly and called upon her dancers to explore theirs. I have worked in places— the Harkness Ballet in New York; the Guangdong Modern Dance Company in China—where people worked secretively, closely guarding their ideas, which they might have stolen shamefully, no credit given the originator. Martha liked to say, "I am a thief but I only steal from the best," which is entirely different, a cross-fertilizing of ideas in the ageless process through which art evolves. Martha spurred me, as she did so many, to explore my own ideas, to make dances, and I did.

After a fight with Martha, one might feel intimidated, outraged, or deeply wronged, but never cheapened. She invested you with fearful strength when she cried, "You are trying to destroy me!" or to Louis Horst, "You are breaking my very soul."

I hardly ever heard her badmouth other choreographers, although she once compared my *Beggar's Dance* to one by another in her company. "Your dance? It is what it is. P's dance? I don't know what it is." I took it to mean that without commenting on its worth, my dance had an individual stamp.

Writing of her early days at Denishawn, she said of Doris Humphrey, "I really did not take much notice of her with the exception of wanting to be the seamless choreographer she was." As for Hanya Holm, I was pretty sure she didn't much like her, yet the only disparagement she ever uttered was of Holm's technique class.

Martha surrounded herself with trained, disciplined, hard-driving dancers, who put working with her before anything else in their lives. This led some to believe she wished to be surrounded by acolytes. If by acolytes is meant supinely adoring fans, judging by the number who left her to do their own work, she did not achieve it, and, in my opinion, it was not at all what she wanted. Anna Sokolow worked with her while holding powerful reservations: "I didn't relate to her . . . I think Martha realized I could never be her disciple. I wouldn't say anything, but I felt inside, 'What the hell. I don't want that.'"

Paul Taylor wrote of being drawn to her dancing, yet he always kept a personal distance. "Our devotion as dancers went beyond devotion to an individual. We all saw Martha's faults and flaws every day. Martha was human, if not more human than most people." Finally, "Martha's grandeur was a little too grand for me."

I'm convinced that, from the start, Martha saw through Paul's calculated simplicity to the profound genius beneath. But if he threatened her a little, the threat was not his genius, which she welcomed. It was simply that while she had Paul's admiration, even his love, she could never dominate him.

I shocked two young Graham adherents, dancer Jennifer Conley and musician Patrick Daugherty, when I said that, in my opinion, the greatest dance created in the twentieth century is Paul Taylor's *The Rite of Spring* (*The Rehearsal*).

"Are you serious?" cried Patrick.

I had to explain that the greatest dance does not mean that Taylor edges out Martha Graham as the century's most "important" choreographer. No one approaches Martha, who had discarded what she did not need, created her own kinetic language, a body of great dances, and a vision that the world has embraced.

Martha fulfilled the dream of all who joined her quest; she changed the world! Paul Taylor's dances, like Johann Sebastian Bach's music, bequeaths priceless treasures, yet can one claim that either changed his art form as Martha did?

Merce Cunningham changed dance, too, although in an entirely different way. He offered no story or human setting in which one can imagine one's self. Watching his dances is like tracing fractal patterns, staring at cloud formations, where one's thoughts coalesce and are rearranged. One emerges pondering the universe, which is surely why the French, with their passion for abstruse thought, go mad for Cunningham, and why others can be stymied or outraged.

Martha is compared to two twentieth-century giants who changed their arts, Pablo Picasso and Igor Stravinsky. She deserves to be, yet my personal ardor is not generated by her effect upon dance, but in her explorations of the human soul. I think Martha is better compared to William Shakespeare.

I experienced transcendence when I first soloed a plane, again when I flew one across the Atlantic Ocean, and, in a conflicted way, on every combat mission. In the U.S. Army of Occupation, I could "sign out" an airplane, fly to Rome, Pisa, Florence, Naples, gaining a feeling of power. But when I began to understand that all people have similar dreams and bewilderments, I lost the urge to fly hither and thither for brief stays.

Flying an airplane offers glimpses of a world not dreamed on the earth's surface. Dancing reveals the heart of a world of which non-dancers cannot even dream. During performance, as on a combat mission, thoughts are so tightly focused it feels like not thinking, but afterward one feels intensely alive. Dancing with Martha could be a kind of possession, each performance a reach toward unscaled heights.

No rational person would choose to live with demons that command every relationship, every act, every thought. Martha's life chose her, and some were compelled to choose Martha. Amid the laughter and groans, revelations and furies, it was life in the eye of a storm, at the epicenter of an earthquake. Having flown and fought as a 19-year-old, I could live with nothing less.

In *Moondust*, Andrew Smith's rhapsody on the still-living astronauts who walked on the moon, he describes their varying reactions to the oft-asked, "What did it feel like to walk on the moon?" Some tried to answer, others were irritated by the question. In show-biz terms, a moon-walk "is a hard act to follow." The first astronauts are my age, so I can't help but dream that if I'd stayed in the Air Corps after WWII, maybe I could have been one. And could anything top a walk on the moon? Whatever the answer, all returned with a new comprehension of Earth. Which still doesn't answer how it felt.

People still ask, "What was it like to dance with Martha Graham?" Some peaks came when making dances, an adventure of the intellect experienced physically. And because Martha invited her dancers into the process, it was an adventure of the imagination as well. In magical moments when Martha drew, focused, and shaped our creative energy, I felt excitement, elation, and joy. Less exalted feelings faded, but the moments of illumination blazed with a fire that compelled me to keep notes for some forty years, and a dozen more to put them into comprehensible form.

Martha was brilliant, irrational, flirting, rejecting, generous, vulnerable, impenetrable, isolated, surrounded, and, for me, impossible not to love. Looming over all and making all else trivial, were those fleeting, transcendent, eternal moments in her rehearsals and on her stage. Working with Martha was like going into battle, physically demanding, emotionally charged, and fraught with danger. Martha Graham was the adventure of a lifetime.

2011

Jennifer Homans (1960–)

A PROMINENT dance critic who began as a professional ballet dancer is a rarity—in our day, only Jennifer Homans fits the bill. Having trained at the North Carolina School of the Arts and the School of American Ballet, she performed with the San Francisco Ballet and Pacific Northwest Ballet before retiring at the age of twenty-six to further her education. After receiving her M.A. from Columbia and Ph.D. from NYU, she became the dance critic for *The New Republic*, writing as well for other publications such as *The New York Times* and *The New York Review of Books*. In 2010 she published her widely admired history of ballet, *Apollo's Angels,* and in 2014 established the NYU Center for Ballet and the Arts. Homans's husband, and the father of their two sons, was the intellectual historian Tony Judt, who died in 2010.

The Universalist

A LONZO KING is not a celebrity. He is virtually unknown outside the dance world, and even to insiders he is something of an outsider, a choreographer-monk working away with a small troupe of devoted dancers in San Francisco. It is not that his work has gone unrecognized: he has won dozens of awards and made ballets for companies as diverse as the Alvin Ailey Dance Theater and the Royal Swedish Ballet. But King doesn't head up a major dance company and you will not see him jet-setting between New York, London, Paris, and Moscow as the "hot" choreographers of the day are inclined to do. To know who Alonzo King is and what he is doing, you have to see his company, called LINES Ballet. You have to see his dancers.

I first encountered King in the early 1980s at a small dance studio in the once run-down Mission district of San Francisco. He was teaching ballet and I was a young dancer, dissatisfied and a bit bored by the kind of training I had been receiving at prestigious schools of dance in New York and San Francisco. King, I had been told, was different. And so he was. Classically trained at George Balanchine's School of American Ballet, among other places, he taught classes that were extremely tough and physically demanding but were never only about technique. He had a way of making everything personal, even spiritual, without ever resorting to New Age nonsense. This was California, but there was nothing "feel good" about King. He had a different tone and a different vocabulary, inspirational and almost religious in character.

Partly, this was owed to his past. King was born in 1952 into a prominent civil rights family in Georgia. His father, Slater King, was the son of C.W. King, who founded the Albany (Georgia) chapter of the NAACP. His uncles include the civil rights lawyer C.B. King and the philosopher Preston King, who was stripped of his citizenship for draft evasion in 1961 and lived in exile in Britain until he was later pardoned by President Clinton. Slater King, who was tragically killed in a car accident in 1969, managed real estate: he bought properties in all-white areas and sold them to African Americans, arranged housing for elderly African Americans, and was a pioneer in the development of low-income housing. His papers include correspondence with John F. Kennedy, Adam Clayton Powell Jr., and W.E.B. Du Bois, among others. The "Albany Movement," aimed at desegregation and non-violent protest, was founded in his living room in 1961, and Slater was arrested with Martin Luther King Jr. (no relation) in what became a national showdown between racist local authorities and the black community, led in part by the King family. And Alonzo King's mother is Valencia King Nelson, whose wide circle of artistic friends visited their home often, exposing King to music, dance, art, and culture from Guyana to Japan to Europe; she, too, was involved in civil rights and later founded AfriGeneas, dedicated to tracing African American ancestry.

King has brought all of this to ballet. He has the aspect of a minister pulling people up to their ideals and articulating a big vision, which in his case is artistic but also, as he likes to point out, implicitly political. You can hear it in his cadence and timing when he teaches and works with dancers, and in his sense of mission and commitment.

King has extraordinary dancers: beautifully trained, sensitive, intelligent, and physically elegant in ways that are rare in today's more acrobatic and athletically inclined dance world. He never went the path of so much contemporary choreography, which uses extreme physical distortion to "update" classicism, nor has he followed the trend to fuse ballet with a variety of modern dance idioms. Instead he has remained intent on, even obsessed with, classicism, not in a hollow adherence to "tradition" or modesty (his dances are a far cry from *Swan Lake* or *The Sleeping Beauty*) but out of his stubborn belief in the mathematical relationships and the sense of proportion in the human body, and in the space around it, which is finally what makes ballet classical. So while most of the dance world was looking outside ballet to find a way forward, King and his dancers were focusing ever more resolutely inward.

I always liked King's ballets because they looked so glorious to dance. Yet at times his beautiful and hyper-refined choreography seemed difficult to enter or to feel from across the footlights. There was clearly a soulful aspiration in the work, as there was in the teaching, but over the years I could not always discern the patterns and the structures of the dances—I could not see through the appealingly wrought movements to the larger picture of what he was doing or saying. All I could see was the details and the dancers: a kind of dance for dancers' sake.

Until now. A recent appearance by LINES at the Joyce Theater in New York suggests a clear and far more expansive ambition: King is redirecting ballet away from its centuries-old European orientation and establishing it on a new axis. This is not ballet that looks to Paris or St. Petersburg: it is ballet—rigorous classical ballet—that takes its lead instead from Morocco and Baghdad and Jerusalem. Not by borrowing or fusing, which is the conventional use of such exotic origins, but by finding a path to these older traditions within ballet itself.

How does King do this, and what does it look like? Consider the ballet *Resin*, which King created last year. At first glance, this dance seems to have no familiar reference points in the past: it is not "classical" in the sense of sylphs or swans or court dances, nor is it in the line of twentieth-century abstract works with their spare, exposed, and even machine-like imagery. *Resin* is plotless, but it has a lusher, more luxurious feel than almost any ballet I have ever seen, for two reasons: its movement and its sense of ritual. The ballet's long phrases and open-ended structure seem keyed more to the rhythms of day and night, or waking and sleeping, than to the more immediate time-frame of theater and entertainment.

Resin, the program notes tell us, is a substance that bleeds from a tree when its bark is slashed or wounded, a sap that then hardens into "tears." Myrrh gum and frankincense are resins. In King's ballet, these hard gem-like "tears" pour down on the stage at various points in cones or sheets of amber hail, which the dancers move through, shower in, are battered by. Resin is the color of gold but it has the sticky feel of grit—something every dancer knows because it is also the stuff of rosin, which dancers crush with their feet and rub onto their shoes to avoid slipping onstage. (Violinists apply it to their bows.) The "tears" that rain down, then, belong to a vaguely religious past but also to the rituals of a dancer's life, and anyone who has danced or been backstage will know the sound of its breaking under the dancers' feet. Now it is pouring down on them—as rosin but also as resin.

The music for *Resin* is a compilation of Sephardic music, past and present, from Turkey, Morocco, Israel (from the National Sound Archives of the National Library of Israel in Jerusalem), Spain, and other points Mediterranean, including several pieces performed by the Catalan artist Jordi Savall and his group, Hespèrion XXI. The movement is fluid and malleable, with isolations of the ribs, shoulders, chest, arms, hands, and elbows, all coordinated in contrapuntal sequences that echo without exactly reproducing movements typical of North African and Middle Eastern dance forms. Yet the dancers do not—this is crucial—appear African or Arab or Eastern, even if they are drawing on a wide range of sources.

King shares with Savall and many of the other musicians with whom he works an interest in the pre-classical and Eastern roots of Western art forms. Savall wants to draw our attention to a Mediterranean moment during the Renaissance when East and West discovered and drew freely from each other, before one became "the other" and a culture of difference and conflict arose. He does this by bringing the techniques and insights of the Early Music movement, which has brought new life to forgotten baroque scores, to bear on Sephardic music in an effort authentically to recreate the sounds of this past.

In impressive collections bearing titles such as *Mare Nostrum* and *Jerusalem*, Savall tries to make us hear that, in matters of culture at least, East and West, Arabs and Europeans, Arabs and Jews, were not always violently divided.

King is interested in this Mediterranean moment, and has suggested that ballet may have Arab as well as Western roots, and may share ideas and forms with Muslim cultures. The task, as he seems to see it, is to reveal the connections—to find them within the geometrical and anatomical structures of ballet itself, or to work them in so deeply that they appear to derive from the same anatomical sources. We never feel that his dancers are performing new or foreign moves; to the contrary, the dances seem to come out of a deep exploration of how these particular musical forms make these particular—and very balletically trained—dancers move. If there are connections to other traditions, which there are, they grow from the music and from what the dancers know and discover in their own bodies.

Unlike Savall, however, King is not really interested in historical authenticity. He is not attempting to take us back to, or to faithfully reproduce, any moment or movement in dance, be it Baroque or Romantic, European, Middle Eastern, Asian, or African. As if to make the point, the second ballet on the program at the Joyce was *Scheherazade*. This ballet, first performed in Paris by Diaghilev's Ballets Russes in 1910, to music by Rimsky-Korsakov with choreography by Mikhail Fokine, is still danced today by the Kirov Ballet and others—it is a kind of classic, even if it is also shameless kitsch and a deliberately exotic "Eastern" ballet made by Russians for Parisian consumption.

King does not reproduce the ballet in the usual ways. He does not even use the original score. Instead, he invited the tabla master Zakir Hussain to rewrite the score, "after" Rimsky-Korsakov. Hussain combined ancient Persian and Western instruments and turned the ballet back through an Eastern lens. We hear the old familiar rhythms and melodies weave hauntingly through driving rhythmic drum dances and the achingly lyrical sounds of the *duduk* (a double-reed instrument from Armenia and the Caucasus) and the *nay* (an end-blown flute featured in classical Arabic music).

Of course *Scheherazade* itself has this kind of history. The story has no known author and there was never a set text; it came out of Persia, medieval Baghdad, Egypt, and elsewhere with themes drawn more widely still. The core text may originally have been Syrian, although the version we know today probably came from a seventeenth-century French translation that was later "back-translated" into Arabic. So its history is one of breaks and gaps—of flux. What matters to King, however, is not the "messy" instability of the tradition, but the ways in which this music opens up something in him and his dancers.

The dances are only faintly balletic. Classical ballet traditionally divides the body at the waist, separating the upper from the lower body—feet and legs from shoulders and arms. In King's work, there is no such divide: the movement flows from the upper body through to the legs and feet such that the whole body is engaged in a mellifluous sensual style. The women are on pointe because this is the longest extension of their line, not because (as tradition would hold) they are elevated from the earth or using their points as rhythmic instruments that dig into the ground, mark time, propel them into space. Here the pointe is an extension; we hardly notice it.

Does the dance look Oriental or classical? Is it *really* ballet? Does it matter? The dances that people in the nineteenth century described as ballet would have been unrecognizable to people in the seventeenth century; and the dances that people described as ballet in the middle of the twentieth century would have been unrecognizable to them both. What makes a dance "ballet" is the linear and mathematically and geometrically proportioned organization of the human body. I don't see why it matters if the dancers are on pointe or off, on balance or off, in or out of sync, in the air or on the ground. It is ballet if it encompasses certain principles, and what it looks like after that is up to artists. Why *not* back-translate from French (and in this case Russian) to Arabic?

Resin and *Scheherazade* are not multicultural dances, and they are not "world dance," even though it is true that LINES is multicultural in ways that no other ballet company in the world has managed to become: the dancers come from the United States (white, African American, Hispanic), South Korea, Australia, Spain, and France, and the diversity of color, shape, and size makes the company look far more "normal" in today's world than the white-with-splashes-of-Latin ranks of most ballet troupes. This diversity no doubt also gives the company knowledge that other companies lack. But in the end it is of no consequence where the dancers are from, because it is their training and their approach, not their ethnic or national origins, that give them a common language. When they move, they are not self-consciously from anywhere.

Consider the pas de deux for two men in *Resin*. The couple, bare-chested, begin in a state of dependence, each pulling against the other, counterbalanced with arms flowing and undulating outward like seaweed. As they begin to dance, they separate and come together, kneading the steps and movements as they go, until we feel that they are made from the same clay, even when they are apart. The dance is not amoeba-like, not just physical forms: these are human beings who rest on each other, seek independence and solace and closeness, and finally, in the last moments of the dance, find themselves curled and bent, leaning and pulling on each other as they awkwardly but somehow gracefully exit the stage.

In this dance, weight is primary—these are muscular men, and they move into and against each other with alternating force and restraint, pushing through the sinews of their own musculatures; and as they move we feel them going inside the movement, inside their own bodies, and sensing the weight of each other's legs, arms, and bones, in ways that appear spontaneous and improvised, even though the dance is highly choreographed. The idea of using weight and improvisation between dancers to find new ways of moving is common enough in contemporary ballet, but in most dances this becomes an exercise in physical free association—I push, which makes your elbow bend, which pushes my arm back, which wraps around you, and so on. In this kind of experiment, a single initiating movement can unleash a chain reaction between two bodies, and this chain reaction, or some modified version of it, is then "set" as the dance. King's dance is different: one man gives his weight and the other absorbs it, but they do not necessarily let it follow through—they stop the chain reaction. Instead there is a suspension, a moment of uncertainty as the impulse finds its way through the body and the dancer feels its implications, feels where it might go, but then lets it return, eventually, or pass through to a position, or line, or some principle of classical form—not balletic looking, necessarily, but symmetrical or aligned or linear, even if it is also curved and spiraled.

The classical base in such a work is not always visible, but it is there:

the dancers have a known reference point, a set of principles that ground their movements—and them. And although there is a grammar and there are rules, the language is not rigid: there is plenty of space and time within the movement for the dancers' free will. Indeed, part of what makes the dance so riveting is that we are watching the dancers find their own way through this mellifluous movement. We are engaged because they are engaged.

Once we are inside the movement, any distinction between physical and emotional falls away: this is a story of dancing, but also a complicated relationship between two men. King has been asked if his choreography is homoerotic, and it is true that his best dances are for men. This may have to do with King, but it also may have to do with ballet, where the traditional pas de deux for a man and a woman has become so encrusted with clichés that it would take something drastic to make us see it anew. King's many pas de deux for men and women tend to be less distinctive and interesting. With men, by contrast, the way is more open.

This is not, at least directly, political. King's dances for men do not come across as "statements"—as male pas de deux so often and tiresomely do—about men dancing (or living or marrying or making love) with men. The dance looks natural—it *is* natural—because it starts and ends with movement. This, of course, makes the political point even more strongly. In King's lexicon, love dances between men are not a fight or even a right; they just are.

Everything in King's dances seems to lead back to the dancers. Thankfully, they don't go in for the false smiles, mugging, and "watch what I can do" egotism that is poisoning even some of the best dance companies today. There is no posturing or posing or showing off. King's dancers leave all these masks behind. They are just present and working, intensely focused on what they are doing. In a way—and this is the strength of the choreography—they have no choice: the dances are so difficult and involved that rote is not an option. The work, and the state of mind, it takes to achieve this kind of immediacy should not be underestimated. It requires a rare openness and honesty.

By honesty I do not mean that we know these dancers in the Twitter way we are lamentably coming to know many dancers today, as they rush to communicate their every mood in an effort to build a "fan base." King's dancers do not tell us if they have stage fright, or if they own a car or a cat or a dog, or if they like chocolate or vanilla. Instead they take a physical stance that is so open that we know, intuitively, confidently, based on the evidence of our senses in the theater, that they are telling us the truth about the dances they are performing. If they are lying, or dissembling, or putting on airs, we will know that, too.

To grasp how unusual this kind of dancing is, it is worth recalling how degrading most ballet training has become. Too many young dancers think that the way to get a job with a ballet company is to enroll in competitions that treat ballet as sport—see the movie *First Position* for details. Or there is the *Black Swan* image of what it means to dance: starvation, self-punishment, self-absorption, and an obsessive quest for "purity" and "perfection." And now we have the ballet TV shows, "Bunheads" and the reality show "Breaking Pointe," whose titles speak for themselves. The major schools and companies are not immune to any of this: too often their directors can be seen judging or scooping up dancers at competitions, and everyone knows how desperate ballet companies are today to attract young audiences (all that tweeting) whatever the artistic price.

King gives us another model. In San Francisco, the old studio where I first encountered him has relocated and grown into a busy, fully equipped center of dance, which houses LINES and a full professional dance program, along with classes open to the public. There is even an enrichment program for dancers who have completed their training but are not yet performing professionally: the idea is to enhance their physical skills, but above all to make them think. To this end, King has also developed a program in conjunction with the Dominican University of California, in which aspiring dancers study dance technique (with King and his dancers) but also take a range of liberal arts courses in the history of dance, art, philosophy, and religion. King wants dancers who are not afraid of cultivation, knowledge, and self-reflection.

If ballet is languishing today, it is not for want of funding, or a failure of dance companies to attract the social media crowd, or a polarization between high culture and popular culture. These are all problems, of course; but the real crisis is a crisis of ideas and imagination. Too much choreography today feels locked into mere steps and technical execution—those arid chain reactions. And this locks the dancers in, too. They are not free really to dance, to think their way into and through a dance.

Alonzo King is one of the few ballet choreographers working today who is genuinely thinking and asking his dancers to think, too. And if his choreography errs on their side—on the side of dance for dancers' sakes—we should remember what he is trying to achieve. Who would have thought that ballet—so historically Western, hierarchical, and white—could be renewed by an African American child of the civil rights movement whose aesthetic vision and inquiring mind are pushing it out of its provincial state and into the world? LINES is not just a ballet company; it is a laboratory, an artists' retreat, a school, a community, and a test of King's notion of what dance and dancers can be. Wherever this leads, one thing is clear: King's dancers are not just his dancers, they are his equals. In ballet today, that alone is a revolution.

August 2, 2012

RICHARD HOWARD (1929–)

BORN IN Cleveland and educated at Columbia, Richard Howard went on to an extraordinary four-faceted career. He has been an outstanding teacher, most recently as a professor at the Columbia School of the Arts. He has been a widely heralded poet, much of his work taking the form of dense yet brilliant dramatic monologues. (His 1969 collection *Untitled Subjects* won the Pulitzer Prize for Poetry.) He has been a highly influential critic and editor—his magisterial *Alone in America: Essays on the Art of Poetry in the United States Since 1950* (also 1969) was nominated for the National Book Award—and for many years he served as the poetry editor of *The Paris Review*. And he has been an amazingly prolific and successful translator from the French: his more than one hundred translations stretch from the Nouvelle Vague writers Alain Robbe-Grillet, Michel Butor, and Claude Simon to Charles de Gaulle and numerous books by Roland Barthes; from Baudelaire's *Les Fleurs du Mal* (1983 National Book Award) to a revelatory new version of *The Charterhouse of Parma*. He has been given a MacArthur Award and the French National Order of Merit. *And* he has been a lifelong lover of dance, going back to the earliest days of the New York City Ballet.

"Famed Dancer Dies of Phosphorus Poisoning"

. . . said to be the consequence of many years' exposure to costume paint.   LE FIGARO, 1928

> April 20, 1905
> Dear Professor—No, my dear Madame,
> English is my language, so I write
> in that, although I am no writer at all
> but a sort of daytime insomniac whose ink

has American notions of its own—but since
you have visited my country, I must hope
you make me out. . . . I write to *you*, Madame,

rather than to your husband (though you both
might be addressed as Dear Professor, no?)
for you and I, in Paris, I perceive
are equally outsiders, and I trust
this may, between us, prove a bond.
We foreigners learn a busy lesson here:
the cure for loneliness is solitude.
Perhaps because the two of us are each

inside a place which by no accident
is known to the world as the City of Light,
my plea will strike you as appropriate
(a little like my dancing: something alive
and flexible, not going on too long).
The silver card you find enclosed admits
you and your party, any night you like,
to my box at the Folies-Bergère. You may have heard

of my endeavors on the stage: the Dance
of Wings, of Wands, the Meteor of Fear,
the Flame, the Lily, and the Butterfly. . . .
But I am sure that if I were to bring
my efforts to your own inquiring gaze,
the chances of convincing you would be
far beyond what my uncertain words
might win—indeed beyond the wingèd ones

of Monsieur Anatole France himself, or those
of a greater master still, by some accounts,
Monsieur Auguste Rodin, who is my friend
and good enough to speak on my behalf:
I add their letters to my own appeal,
though I believe that what you see, yourself,
will work upon you more than *any* words,
even theirs. Let me persuade you by

all the liberal magic I have learned
to wield—another mode of creating life,
the poetry of an incarnate Now—
in order that *you* may capacitate my art
to cast a deeper spell. For once *you* see
I know you will help me to be better seen. . . .
My dancers have to move against a light
which cannot move: its source is fixed—

yet what if light itself could move—could dance?
The very darkness would be visible!
As I gather, you have found the way
our costumes and our limbs themselves might be
made luminous, without depending on
the placement of a lamp or two offstage. . . .
Endued with the substance I hear you have named
by a happy inspiration *radium*,

we'd have no further need of phosphorus
which blackens in no time on human skin.
They say your new-found, final element
generates a light within itself
and would inspire—were you to let me have
the merest feather-touch of such a thing—
a freedom unsuspected by the world
of illusion which we artists live within.

I do not ask for charity, Madame—
only your presence, which I know would make
the soul of kindness the body of kindness too.
Come see my dancers, come see me! and if
you judge my craving worthy of my craft,
I know you will be generous. . . . My warm
respects to your husband, and to you my hopes,
L. Fuller, or as they call me here, La LOIE

1987

Langston Hughes (1902–1967)

Jazz music is essential to much of the work of poet and novelist Langston Hughes, one of the writers at the forefront of the Harlem Renaissance. But images of dancing also wind through his writings. They flood his first collection of poetry, *The Weary Blues* (1926): "Negro Dancers," "Midnight Dancer (To a Black Dancer in the Little Savoy)," "Nude Young Dancer," "Song for a Banjo Dancer," "Danse Africaine," and—one of Hughes's most famous poems—"Dream Variation." Yet the dance figures continued long past the poet's first youth. In 2016, *The New Yorker* (where Hughes had often published poems and stories) brought out a previously unpublished story about race and sex, "Seven People Dancing," which Hughes biographer Arnold Rampersad, editor of the collected poems and coeditor of the selected letters, dates to around 1961.

However, little if anything else that Hughes wrote pays tribute to dancing with the specificity and historical detail of *Mister Jazz*, the one-act play below, written in the late 1950s to serve as half of a Broadway production (apparently never produced).

"Dream Variation"

> To fling my arms wide
> In some place of the sun,
> To whirl and to dance
> Till the white day is done.
> Then rest at cool evening
> Beneath a tall tree
> While night comes on gently,
> Dark like me,—

That is my dream!
To fling my arms wide
In the face of the sun,
Dance! whirl! whirl!
Till the quick day is done.
Rest at pale evening . . .
A tall, slim tree, . . .
Night coming tenderly,
Black like me.

July 1924

"Midnight Dancer"

(To a Black Dancer in the Little Savoy)

Wine-maiden
Of the jazz-tuned night
Lips
Sweet as purple dew,
Breasts
Like the pillows of all sweet dreams,
Who crushed
The grapes of joy
And dripped the juice
On you?

1926

Mister Jazz

A Panorama in Music and Motion
of the History of Negro Dancing

JAZZ DANCES in Historical Sequence for MISTER JAZZ by
Langston Hughes utilizing adaptations of the popular music of
each period

Pre–Civil War:	AFRICAN DANCES
	JUBA DANCE
	BUCK-AND-WING
	JIG (JUMP JIM CROW)
	STRUT
	CAKE WALK
	SAND
	SOFT SHOE
Post–Civil War:	MARCH (NEW ORLEANS)
	TAG ALONG (SECOND LINERS)
	SLOW DRAG (RAG TIME)
	EAGLE ROCK
	SHIMMY
	CAMEL WALK
	TEXAS TOMMY
Roaring Twenties:	SUZY-Q
	SNAKE HIPS
	BALLING-THE-JACK
	CHARLESTON
	BLACK BOTTOM
	SHIM SHAM
	LINDY HOP
Depression:	JITTERBUG
	TRUCKIN'
	PECKING
	SHAG
	BIG APPLE
Latin:	RUMBA—CONGA
	MAMBO—CHA CHA
Contemporary:	BOP
	SLOP
	ROCK AND ROLL
	COOL

MUSIC: *African drums—a long rumbling roll gradually developing into syncopation as the house lights dim.*

SETTING: *A cyclorama or scrim before which dancing shadows are seen as stage light comes up.*

ACTION: *In silhouette the figures of AFRICAN DANCERS in feathered headdresses move slowly to tribal rhythms.*

MR. JAZZ: Africa! .... Long ago Africa! .... Then across the Western Ocean came drums—and dancers.

(As the African shadows fade to merge into the figures of SLAVES in Congo Square in New Orleans dancing much the same movements, only faster, the drums grow loud in fervid syncopation)

Congo Square in New Orleans. . . . Sunday—the slaves' one day for fun and dancing—the juba dance in Congo Square. In those feet, those hands, those drums—the roots of jazz.

(Drum beats merge into hand clapping)

Where there were no drums, in the slave quarters of the cities, or on remote plantations, hands took over—just the clapping of hands.

(The CONGO DANCERS disappear and a single jiggling figure is seen)

The Juba Dance became a jig. . . . the jig the buck-and-wing . . . And sometimes after work in worn-out finery and hand-me-downs, the slaves would get together for their walk arounds.

(The DANCER dons a wide hat, picks up a cane and leads a procession of shadow figures across the screen, dancing and clapping hands)

And maybe on holidays when they didn't have to walk the chalk, they might celebrate with a big cake walk.

(The scrim rises and lights come up to reveal MR. JAZZ leading TIPPER and the DANCING SINGER in the cake walk as he calls out gaily)

Oh, walk your lady! .... Walk for the cake! .... Dance! Prance! .... Step to the music! ....

(As the DANCERS exit stepping lively, MR. JAZZ comes forward to sing)

That's how jazz was born—a long time ago. And the principal is still the same. You just:

SYNCOPATE THE RHYTHM
WITH A STEADY BEAT,
LET THAT RHYTHM TINGLE
RIGHT FROM HEAD TO FEET—
THAT'S JAZZ!

MIX IT WITH A BLUE NOTE
LIKE A LONESOME MOAN,
ADD A LOT OF LAUGHTER
PLUS A JIVING TONE—
THAT'S JAZZ!
PLENTY ROOM FOR SWINGING,
PLENTY ROOM FOR PLAY,
ROOM FOR EVERYBODY
TO JAZZ IN HIS OWN WAY—
KEEP IT FREE AND EASY
SO YOUR HEART WON'T BREAK
THAT'S THE WAY TO JAZZ
THE JAZZING JAZZ MEN MAKE—
THAT'S JAZZ!
(He dances, then puts his hand to his ear)

Cock your ear a little. Listen to the past. New Orleans again! Oh, my lands! Serenade wagons, marching bands! Famous for funerals—
(A typical old New Orleans marching band dirge is heard in slow tempo as Mr. Jazz continues to talk and TIPPER with bowed down head, as if following a casket, crosses to stage)

The living's got to live and the dying's got to die. Mourners got to mourn and criers got to cry—but when the dying is done and the last prayers have been said, I'm sorry—the living's got to live—though the dead is dead. On the way to the cemetery, sad and mournful is the beat—but it's a different story headed back to Rampart Street.
(Drum roll into syncopated tempo as both MR. JAZZ and the MOURNING FIGURE fall into rhythm and begin to dance in line behind the band as TAG ALONG enters to join them in rhythm)

MR. JAZZ: The Second Liners—jazzing with their feet!

TIPPER: Mr. Tipper!

TAG ALONG: Mr. Tag Along!

MR. JAZZ: Mister Jazz!
(Their half-prance half-dance gradually develops into a series of old jazz steps of former years as the music becomes a medley merging from the syncopated march into ragtime then into Dixieland and later jazz)

Where did these steps come from? Where were they born?

TAG ALONG: New Orleans marching bands, Buddy Bolden's horn.

MR. JAZZ: Jelly Roll's piano, Scott Joplin's ragtime beat.

TAG ALONG: That same old steady rhythm—

MR. JAZZ: Runs from head to feet.

ALL: That's jazz!

(As THEY dance, the GIRL SINGER enters to sing)

SINGER: TELL ME, BABY, WHERE DID
    ALL THIS SYNCOPATION START?

MR. JAZZ: IT MUST HAVE STARTED, BABY,
    IN THE HUMAN HEART.

TAG ALONG: ADAM'S JAZZ!

SINGER: EVE'S JAZZ!

MR. JAZZ: JUST JAZZ!

SINGER: TELL ME, TELL ME, DADDY,
    WHAT'S THAT NOTE I HEAR?

MR. JAZZ: BESSIE SMITH AND BILLIE
    WHISPERING IN MY EAR,
    OLD JOE TURNER
    WHO'S COME AND GONE.

SINGER: MA RAINEY, MAMA YANCEY—
    HOW LONG? HOW LONG?

MR. JAZZ: C. C. RIDER,
    SKINNY, TALL, AND BLACK—

SINGER: UP ON THE MOUNTAIN
    TRYING TO CALL HIS BABY BACK.

ALL: WHEN YOU LAUGH TO KEEP FROM CRYING
    'CAUSE THERE'S A SCREAM IN YOUR THROAT
    AND YOU CAN'T BREAK LOOSE AND HOLLER—
    IT'S A BLUE, BLUE NOTE—
    THAT'S THE BLUES! THAT'S THE BLUES!
    THE BLUES. . . . .

(MR. JAZZ steps aside, TAG ALONG and the SINGER dance
together a Slow Drag followed by each dance in succession as
named, the SINGER changing partners as required, sometimes
the men dancing alone)

MR. JAZZ: The Slow Drag.
    The Camel Walk.
    The Texas Tommy.

The Shimmy-Sha-Wobble.

The Eagle Rock.

And when the lights are low—

> (*A sudden wail of sirens. Cymbals crash. The music changes to the blatant blare of the twenties*)

The Roaring Twenties! Bootleg days!

Snake Hips.

Balling-The-Jack.

Suzy-Q.

Black Bottom.

Shim Sham.

And later came the Shag.

The Big Apple.

Trucking.

Pecking.

> (*Suddenly the music stops and only clapping hands are heard*)

And what do you know?

The Charleston, Joe!

> (*MR. JAZZ begins to Charleston as OTHERS take up the beat*)

Not long after the Charleston, a great event took place. A man all by himself went winging through space—and if you want the exact year to be given, it was when Lindbergh flew the ocean in 1927 that the Lindy Hop was born in joy at a dance hall in Harlem called the Savoy!

> (*A COUPLE burst onto stage in a mad Lindy Hop. When dance is over, as DANCERS take their bows, MR. JAZZ shoos them off stage*)

Move on! I say, move on! I'm making like a cop.

> (*As DANCERS exit, he turns to audience*)

Did anybody ever tell you to "Move on," when you want to stop?

TIPPER: What's that got to do with jazz?

MR. JAZZ: Did you ever get beat all over your head by a cop?

TIPPER: What's it got to do with jazz?

MR. JAZZ: Be-bop Mop! Mop! Mop! That's Be-bop.

TIPPER: What?

MR. JAZZ: Mop! Mop!

TIPPER: Be-bop Mop!

MR. JAZZ: Be-bop! Were you ever born dark with a very dark skin, and walked up to some café and couldn't get in?

TIPPER: All the tables are gone.

MR. JAZZ: But that's just what I want—a *gone* table.

BOTH: Be-bop Mop! Mop! Mop! Ooool-ya-koo! Bop!

> *(TIPPER and TAG ALONG do a brief bop dance as MR. JAZZ leans against side of stage. When DANCERS finish, he speaks)*

MR. JAZZ: From my looks, you might not know that I'm old John Henry, I'm Stackolee. And I could be John Lewis—if John Lewis was me.

> *(Music à la Modern Jazz Quartet is heard)*

TAG ALONG: Cool, fool, cool!

MR. JAZZ: I'm also Chico Hamilton. I'm Buddy Collette. I'm the bee in the bop of the Modern Jazz Quartet. Mister Jazz!

TAG ALONG: Cool, fool, cool!

MR. JAZZ: I'm Casey Jones. I'm a folk song lane. I'm the motorman on Duke's "A" train.

TAG ALONG: Cool, cat, cool!

> *(SINGER enters)*

SINGER: I'm the Countess Fontessa—and I'll have you know, I'll be cool when you're hot—down below.

TAG ALONG: Cool, girl, cool!

SINGER: I grew up at Juilliard, raised on ballet.

TAG ALONG: I got a beard on my—

MR. JAZZ: Come on, now, let's not play!

TAG ALONG: Cool, you-all, cool!

MR. JAZZ: I was beat before the beatniks.

TAG ALONG: Bopped before the bop.

SINGER: Progressed before progressive.

MR. JAZZ: And I don't intend to stop.

TAG ALONG: Cool, fools, cool!

MR. JAZZ: Jazz! Going to go right on!

ALL: Got to go right on!

MR. JAZZ: Yes! Just—

> *(He sings and ALL join in as a cool couple dances, followed by a burlesque of cool couples by TIPPER and TAG ALONG)*

MR. JAZZ: From marching bands to Dixieland to blues to bop—from hot to cool—put it all together and it's jazz!

> *(He sings)*

SYNCOPATE THE RHYTHM
WITH A STEADY BEAT.

LET THAT RHYTHM TINGLE
RIGHT FROM HEAD TO FEET.
ALL: THAT'S JAZZ.
MR. JAZZ: MIX IT WITH A BLUE NOTE
LIKE A LONESOME MOAN.
TAG ALONG: ADD A LOT OF LAUGHTER
PLUS A JIVING TONE.
ALL: THAT'S JAZZ.
MR. JAZZ: PLENTY ROOM FOR SWINGING
SINGER: PLENTY ROOM FOR PLAY
ALL: ROOM FOR EVERYBODY
TO JAZZ IN HIS OWN WAY
MR. JAZZ: KEEP IT FREE AND EASY—
SINGER: SO YOUR HEART WON'T BREAK
MR. JAZZ: THAT'S THE WAY TO JAZZ THE JAZZING
THAT JAZZ MEN MAKE.
ALL: THAT'S JAZZ.
TAG ALONG: YEAH, MAN! THAT'S JAZZ!
MR. JAZZ: OLD JAZZ! NEW JAZZ!
TAG ALONG: HOT JAZZ! COOL JAZZ!
SINGER: SWEET JAZZ! GOOD JAZZ!
MR. JAZZ: J—A—Z—Z—
ALL: JAZZ!

(ALL dance as the curtain falls)

1960

Zora Neale Hurston (1891–1960)

A prominent figure in the Harlem Renaissance, Zora Neale Hurston was a novelist (acclaimed for her 1937 *Their Eyes Were Watching God*), short story writer, and author of children's books. A trained anthropologist (having been a student of Franz Boas at Barnard and Columbia), she also published collections of folklore, material gathered on research trips through the American South and in Haiti. Although today Zora Neale Hurston is firmly positioned in the pantheon of twentieth-century African American writers, she died in penury and obscurity in Florida, her body committed to an unmarked pauper's grave. The rebirth of her reputation and the republication of her books are largely due to the novelist Alice Walker, who made a pilgrimage in order to discover what had happened to her. Walker published the widely influential and movingly immediate personal essay "Looking for Zora" in *Ms.* magazine, in 1975. She also wrote the foreword to Hurston's recently published *Barracoon: The Story of the Last "Black Cargo,"* an oral history that Hurston recorded in 1927 with Cudjo Lewis, the last living person to have been brought to the United States from Africa as a slave.

The story printed here about dancing as a prescription for ensuring a lover's fidelity is included in the anthology *Mules and Men*, comprising folktales that Hurston collected from African Americans in Florida.

Hoodoo

Kitty Brown is a well-known hoodoo doctor of New Orleans, and a Catholic. She liked to make marriages and put lovers together. She is squat, black and benign. Often when we had leisure, she told funny stories. Her herb garden was pretty full and we often supplied other doctors with plants. Very few raise things since the supply houses carry about everything that is needed. But sometimes a thing is wanted fresh from the ground. That's where Kitty's garden came in.

When the matter of my initiation came up she said, "In order for you to reach the spirit somebody has got to suffer. I'll suffer for you because I'm strong. It might be the death of you."

It was in October 1928, when I was a pupil of hers, that I shared in a hoodoo dance. This was not a pleasure dance, but ceremonial. In another generation African dances were held in Congo Square, now Beauregard Square. Those were held for social purposes and were of the same type as the fire dances and jumping dances of the present in the Bahamas. But the hoodoo dance is done for a specific purpose. It is always a case of death-to-the-enemy that calls forth a dance. They are very rare even in New Orleans now, even within the most inner circle, and no layman ever participates, nor has ever been allowed to witness such a ceremony.

This is how the dance came to be held. I sat with my teacher in her front room as the various cases were disposed of. It was my business to assist wherever possible, such as running errands for materials or verifying addresses; locating materials in the various drawers and cabinets, undressing and handling patients, writing out formulas as they were dictated, and finally making "hands".* At last, of course, I could do all of the work while she looked on and made corrections where necessary.

This particular day, a little before noon, came Rachael Roe. She was dry with anger, hate, outraged confidence and desire for revenge. John Doe had made violent love to her; had lain in her bed and bosom for the last three years; had received of Rachael everything material and emotional a woman can give. They had both worked and saved and had contributed to a joint savings account. Now, only the day before yesterday, he had married another. He had lured a young and pretty girl to his bed with Rachael's earnings; yes. Had set up housekeeping with Rachael's sweat and blood. She had gone to him and he had laughed at his former sweetheart, yes. The police could do nothing,

---

[1] Manufacturing certain luck charms.

no. The bank was sorry, but they could do nothing, no. So Rachael had come to Kitty.

Did she still love her John Doe? Perhaps; she didn't know. If he would return to her she should strive to forget, but she was certain he'd not return. How could he? But if he were dead she could smile again, yes—could go back to her work and save some more money, yes. Perhaps she might even meet a man who could restore her confidence in menfolk.

Kitty appraised her quickly. "A dance could be held for him that would carry him away right now, but they cost something."

"How much?"

"A whole lot. How much kin you bring me?"

"I got thirty-seven dollars."

"Dat ain't enough. Got to pay de dancers and set de table."

One hundred dollars was agreed upon. It was paid by seven o'clock that same night. We were kept very busy, for the dance was set from ten to one the next day, those being bad hours. I ran to certain addresses to assemble a sort of college of bishops to be present and participate. The table was set with cake, wine, roast duck and barbecued goat.

By nine-thirty the next morning the other five participants were there and had dressed for the dance. A dispute arose about me. Some felt I had not gone far enough to dance. I could wait upon the altar, but not take the floor. Finally I was allowed to dance, as a delegate for my master who had a troublesome case of neuritis. The food was being finished off in the kitchen.

Promptly on the stroke of ten Death mounted his black draped throne and assumed his regal crown, Death being represented by a rudely carved wooden statue, bust length. A box was draped in black sateen and Kitty placed him upon it and set his red crown on. She hobbled back to her seat. I had the petition and the name of the man written on seven slips of paper—one for each participant. I was told to stick them in Death's grinning mouth. I did so, so that the end of each slip protruded. At the command I up-ended nine black tapers that had been dressed by a bath in whiskey and bad vinegar, and bit off the butt end to light, calling upon Death to take notice. As I had been instructed, I said: "Spirit of Death, take notice I am fixing your candles for you. I want you to hear me." I said this three times and the assembly gave three snaps with the thumb and middle finger.

The candles were set upside down and lighted on the altar, three to the left of Death, three to the right, and three before him.

I resumed my seat, and everyone was silent until Kitty was possessed. The exaltation caught like fire. Then B. arose drunkenly and danced a few steps. The clapping began lightly. He circled the room, then prostrated himself before the altar, and, getting to his hands and knees, with his teeth pulled one of the slips from the jaws of Death. He turned a violent somersault and began the dance, not intricate, but violent and muscle-twitching.

We were to dance three hours, and the time was divided equally, so that the more participants the less time each was called upon to dance. There were six of us, since Kitty could not actively participate, so that we each had forty minutes to dance. Plenty of liquor was provided so that when one appeared exhausted the bottle was pressed to his lips and he danced on. But the fury of the rhythm more than the stimulant kept the dancers going. The heel-patting was a perfect drum rhythm, and the hand clapping had various stimulating breaks. At any rate no one fell from exhaustion, though I know that even I, the youngest, could not have danced continuously on an ordinary dance floor unsupported by a partner for that length of time.

Nearly all ended on the moment in a twitchy collapse, and the next most inspired prostrated himself and began his dance with the characteristic somersault. Death was being continuously besought to follow the footsteps of John Doe. There was no regular formula. They all "talked to him" in their own way, the others calling out to the dancer to "talk to him." Some of the postures were obscene in the extreme. Some were grotesque, limping steps of old men and women. Some were mere agile leapings. But the faces! That is where the dedication lay.

When the fourth dancer had finished and lay upon the floor retching in every muscle, Kitty was taken. The call had come for her. I could not get upon the floor quickly enough for the others and was hurled before the altar. It got me there and I danced, I don't know how, but at any rate, when we sat about the table later, all agreed that Mother Kitty had done well to take me.

I have neglected to say that one or two of the dancers remained upon the floor "in the spirit" after their dance and had to be lifted up and revived at the end.

Death had some of all the food placed before him. An uncorked pint of good whiskey was right under his nose. He was paid fifteen cents and remained on his throne until one o'clock that night. Then all of the food before him was taken up with the tablecloth on which it rested and was thrown into the Mississippi River.

The person danced upon is not supposed to live more than nine days after the dance. I was very eager to see what would happen in this case. But five days after the dance John Doe deserted his bride for the comforting arms of Rachael and she hurried to Mother Kitty to have the spell removed. She said he complained of breast pains and she was fearfully afraid for him. So I was sent to get the beef heart out of the cemetery (which had been put there as part of the routine), and John and Rachael made use of the new furniture bought for his bride. I think he feared that Rachael might have him fixed, so he probably fled to her as soon as the zest for a new wife had abated.

1935

Yehuda Hyman (1955–)

At the end of 2016, Yehuda Hyman—dancer, choreographer, dramatist, and teacher of dance in the New York City public schools—appeared in New York with his small dance-theater troupe, Mystical Feet Company, in his dance-play *The Mar Vista*, whose title commemorates the working-class West Los Angeles neighborhood in which Hyman was born and grew up, a child of Jewish immigrants (his father from Poland, in 1938, and his mother from Istanbul, c. 1949). Although *The Mar Vista* presented both of his parents as characters, his mother, a trained dancer in her youth, was the focus.

Hyman's memoir below spotlights his father, whose restored memories of quasi-ceremonial dancing, learned in boyhood from other male congregants in the synagogue, were absorbed by the author in his own childhood through his father's gentle demonstration of them. Many years later, the steps and gestures his father showed him come back to him as physical memories. Separating these mirror experiences of father and son is the author's memory of energetically dancing peers, whose bravura circle he longs to join.

"Three Hasidic Dances: A Personal Journey" was initially part of the widely ranging collection of essays, *Seeing Israeli and Jewish Dance*, edited by Judith Brin Ingber.

Three Hasidic Dances

WHEN I was 12 years old, my Hebrew school teacher taught us two dances for the Purim show. The first was an Israeli folk dance, the second was a dance she called Hasidic. I had never heard the word before. What did it mean? Our "Hasidic dance" consisted of a line of shoulder-linked 12-year-olds shuffling around the stage to some medium-tempo brassy music. Occasionally we would raise our arms and slowly wave them above our heads, side to side. The climax of the dance was a vigorous shoulder shimmy shake. Our costumes were black bathrobes and black cardboard hats with black crepe paper streamers attached to the sides with scotch tape ("like *peyos*," our teacher said). This "Hasidic dance" was something foreign to me, an American boy in an assimilated Jewish household of the late 1960s. I relished dancing it.

I was practicing my dance in the living room one night when my father, in his customary TV-watching position on the couch, asked what I was doing. I told him it was a "Hasidic dance." He sat up, interested. This was unusual. A retired tailor in bad health, he seemed to live on the other side of a gray void. His sunken-shouldered body carried the weight of being the only member of his large family to survive the ovens of Poland. But that night, he stood up with a slim suggestion of a smile on his face. "In mine town, Ratno," he said, "this was how they danced, the Hasidim." He cupped his left hand just behind his ear and began to move across the gray carpet, his torso leaning forward, one foot passing in front of the other in a slight to-and-fro, as if walking a tightrope. His right hand was held out in front of him, feeling the air like a blind man navigating his way—in fact, my father's eyes were closed. The dance seemed to transport him far beyond the walls of our West Los Angeles home. My father danced one full circle around the living room, then opened his eyes and said I should do what he did. I was an avid mimic, always imitating the rock 'n' roll dancers on my favorite TV show, *Hullabaloo*. Now I did my best to please my father. He corrected me, telling me to hold my hand against my ear, "like you listen to something." But what? He didn't say. "Raise the shoulders a little, make the hand not so hard, hold something." What? No answer. I tried to give him what he wanted, repeating the dance over and over until at last he said, "That's it," and went back to his couch. The lesson was over. That was the first time I saw my father dance. That was the only time.

It was to be another twenty years before I did another "Hasidic dance." This time I was in a rehearsal room facing a group of thirty-one disgruntled actors. I had been hired to choreograph the American premiere of the prominent Israeli writer Joshua Sobol's play *Ghetto* (the tragic story of the Jewish theater troupe of Vilna, Lithuania).

This was my first big job, and I had "choreographer's block." I was intimidated by the extremely opinionated actors and frozen by my desire to please the Tony Award–winning director Gordon David-son. I had been hired at the last minute with no time for research. I demonstrated a sort of jazz/balletic/generic folk dance combination. The actors grumbled. The director looked on with a "wait-and-see" attitude. Assistants whispered behind me. Then, horror of horrors, two of the actors refused outright to do what I had given them. "It just feels wrong," they said. I knew they were right. All I wanted at that moment was to flee the room. Then, out of the corner of my eye, I saw the half-blind man with the clarinet heading toward me.

Giora Feidman is an Argentinean-born clarinetist of Bessarabian stock. A renowned master musician, he travels the world spreading his message through what he calls soul music. I was a little afraid of him. He had an air of chutzpah, a touch of arrogance, and with a pen-etrating glare from his one working eye, he saw right through your skin. On the day he arrived, Maestro Feidman commanded the cast and musicians to sit and listen to him play "real klezmer." I could see that some were put off by his performance, but for me it was amaz-ing—and complicated. His music was as low as the gutter and as high as heaven, stirring conflicting emotions: Jewish pride and Jewish shame. Now, at this troubled moment in my rehearsal, Mr. Feidman put his pale delicate hand on my shoulder and whispered in my ear, "Close your eyes. I will play and you will dance. Do it." I was out of options. I closed my eyes.

First silence. Always silence first. Then, from Feidman's clarinet, a sound emerges, small, barely audible, just breath. He blows harder, breath into tone, a cry rising from some ancient well. Shrill and sweet, ugly and exquisite, this cry reaches into my chest until it grabs hold of my heart. I am shattered. Everything falls away. Nothing to hold on to and nothing to lose. All right, I say to myself, I will dance this dance. I touch my chest where the music lives inside me and coax it out, holding it like a ball of electricity between my hands. I pass it gently from palm to palm, moving it around my body. Feidman's music is lighter now, rhythmic. Eyes still closed, I follow his music as we glide around the room, then trotting. A *freylekh*. He slows the pace; I slow down. The tone goes softer and deeper; I lower myself to the floor. The music is on the ground; I am on my knees, bending my torso backward until my shoulders touch the floor, the music washing over me, only my arms still moving, moving, gathering and pouring music over my body, washing away any confusion of who I am and what this dance will be. Silence. I lower my arms and open my eyes, sit up. Feidman is smiling. The actors are staring at me, wide-eyed, alert, and ready to dance now.

In the fall of 1999 (thirteen years after that dance with Feidman), I was squeezed into a tight seat on a sold-out Air Ukraine flight, the only passenger not wearing Hasidic black. I was one of 6,000 men from all over the globe traveling to Uman, Ukraine, to spend Rosh Hashanah with Rebbe Nachman of Breslov.

I was doing research for my play *The Mad Dancers*, loosely adapted from Rabbi Nachman's tale *The Seven Beggars*. Rebbe Nachman died in 1810, but before he did, he promised that if a person came to his gravesite, recited the Tikkun Ha-Klali (ten specific psalms) and gave at least a shekel for charity, he would pull them out of hell by their *peyos*.

It was a difficult trip for me both physically and emotionally. I was an outsider here in almost every way: language, dress, religious observance, politics, sexuality, etc. Still, I was a Jew—I shared that with everyone else—and there were a few transcendent moments: an elderly Hasid gently adjusting my prayer shawl and offering me his seat at the overcrowded Rosh Hashanah service, the exuberant *niggunim* (wordless melodies) sung at the Shabbat table, a moment of communion with the spirit of the rebbe just as the sun was setting by his tomb.

As soon as Rosh Hashanah formally ended, I ran from the synagogue over the low hill to the armory where I was told the dancing would take place. Nachman was a legendary dancer who placed great importance on the spiritual power of dance. His custom was to end each prayer session with dancing. This remains a Breslov tradition to this day.

I was the first to arrive at the armory. I hadn't factored in HPT (Hasidic People's Time), so it would be several hours before the dancing actually started. Eventually, tables were piled high with sweet cakes and bottles of "L'chaim" (whiskey) and at last, a ramshackle klezmer band started up. Men joined hands and moved in a circle. The music got faster. Daring young Hasids broke off and formed a second circle inside and then the best dancers broke off and formed another circle inside that. The inner circle danced—no, ran so fast that anyone who dragged even the slightest was in danger of being trampled. In the middle circle were the more moderate dancers, trotting in rhythm. On the outside were the elderly and the fathers with the little boys clutching their hands, walking slowly in rhythm.

The inner circle of dancers broke off into subgroups of four or five, and things got wild. At first, their dancing seemed to draw from traditional Russian folk dance: scissor steps, rising high on the toes, hands behind the head, torso held still while the hips twisted to the right and then back. After a few minutes of this, they dropped the formal steps and began improvising, throwing themselves around, looking a bit like rave dancers in a mosh pit. They were dancing solo variations, yet each one was in close physical contact with the collective group. Eyes were closed or half-lidded, the dance partner an invisible force. The movements were deeply expressive—hands outstretched and yearning, tense with desire. The dancers seemed to draw inspiration from each other—a contest to see who could fling himself to the farthest point, balancing just above the abyss. They were electrifying to watch. The music got faster and faster, the men sweatier, and then suddenly, they broke into groups and began a circus show. I had observed this sort of thing at a Hasidic wedding in Tsfat, Israel. It is traditional for wedding guests to gladden the hearts of the bride and groom by doing outlandish acrobatic tricks. Now these Uman dancers became the Chinese acrobats of Taiwan. Standing on each other's shoulders, and on the shoulders of shoulders, they did the human pyramid, cartwheels, back flips, and more. It was funny and entertaining but also distancing—they were the dancers and I was a spectator. I longed for an invitation to enter the circle within the circle within the circle.

Then the music changed to a *doyne*, a slow, stately dance. The crowd parted for a man who seemed to be someone of great importance in the community. He was not old—he looked to be in his early 40s—blond, red-cheeked. He closed his eyes, stood quite still. He lifted his hands. Slowly, his hands painted abstract images in the air. Fingers together, then apart. Sometimes he used only one finger, pointing. Sometimes two fingers, the others folded in a kind of Hasidic mudra (a hand gesture of traditional dance of southern India). Now, his knees bent slowly as if submerging in water, then straightened. He repeated, bending lower and lower each time, until at last he reached the ground, standing on his knees. The hands continued to speak. The other dancers mirrored him: He rose, they rose. He turned, they turned. He pressed one hand to his ear, so did they. He put it behind his ear, listening to something, his other hand holding something. His eyes closed. I knew this dance. My body knew. A long-ago lesson from my father. I joined in now: Listening to the silence. Looking with eyes closed. Holding nothing.

2011

Jill Johnston (1929–2010)

Raised on Long Island and educated at Tufts and at Women's College in Greensboro, North Carolina, Jill Johnston became known as a radical feminist leader with her 1973 book, *Lesbian Nation*. She was an ultra-vivid writer and an ultra-vivid personality, who became a central character in the New York downtown life she wrote about with such exhilaration and intelligence. She was also a superb if unconventional dance critic, primarily for *The Village Voice*, whose 1971 collection of reviews, *Marmalade Me*, is an essential text for those who care what dance—and the culture—were like in the mid-twentieth century. Her writings on art were as provocative and influential as her writings on dance (much of her work appeared in the magazine *Art in America*), and her two volumes of memoirs, *Mother Bound* and *Paper Daughter*, were searing narratives that she described as "an autobiography in search of a father."

In 1963, Johnston was the subject of one of Andy Warhol's silent "portrait films," four and a half minutes long and aptly titled *Jill*. Johnston was outrageous, provocative, and funny—as she herself put it, an "east west flower child hip psychedelic paradise now love peace do your own thing approach revolutionary." Although her parents had never married, she would marry three times, her first (brief) marital adventure resulting in two children. In 1993, in Denmark, she married Ingrid Nyeboe and married her again in Connecticut, when same-sex marriage was made legal there, a year before Johnston's death.

Lucidly Defined

In 1953 I danced in a revival of Doris Humphrey's "Soaring" (1920). Five of us ran and frolicked with an enormous chiffon square. True to the latter style of a great organizer this simple dance was lucidly defined; yet it was close to the origins of a dance freed from shackling propriety. The veils of Loïe Fuller and the Greek gowns of Isadora were right behind it. In the Dance Collection of the New York Public Library you can see some photographs of Doris Humphrey posing naked. That was the real hey-day of the early modern dance, back in the '20s. Ted Shawn of course was famous for walking around like Adonis. Nijinsky himself created a furore in 1912 when he climaxed his premiere of "L'Après-Midi d'un Faune" by doing something "obscene" with a scarf between his legs. Both Nijinsky and Isadora suffered in their own ways for themselves and a world caught between the revelations of Freud and the bodices of Queen Victoria. In their example and others like them we find the clue to the misery and the quest of our time. "Soaring" was a beautiful dance. But by 1953 Miss Humphrey was close to death. She was very far from the early days of lying naked in a net that her teacher Ted Shawn lowered into the sea. She had struggled in her life with grandiose forms and new ways of transforming the body to fit the rigorous demands of the Puritan that she really was. Thus by 1953 she was rightly venerated as a successful inventor, but even "Soaring," in its revival, was no longer a naive expression of forbidden fruits; certain parts that its creator couldn't remember too well were touched up to suit the technical requirements of a later age.

Even before the ballet in America eclipsed the modern dance, in the '40s and '50s, the modern dancers succumbed to the aspirations of the Western tradition. The shapes were different but the stress remained. Martha Graham's breathing exercises in the form of contractions and releases became studies in painful contortion. Miss Humphrey's discoveries in respiration led from an easy-going "fall and recovery" syndrome to the dynamic pressures of studio "technique." All the new techniques entered the institutions of the country as taught vocabularies. Thus the new academies of modern dance flourished alongside the academies of ballet. The students were happy mannikins in a paradise of safety. Our colleges and universities are still laboring in this manner. And creative license is granted in composition courses, which are also institutionalized methods of choreography handed down from master to teacher.

If there is a crisis in dance at this time it is to be found in a black cloud hovering over the studios and the fields waiting to fall down in torrents of rain to refresh all bodies ready to leave the stuffy studios. Already of course this is happening, and I predict the country will be taken by storm. The crux of the crisis is the dawning revelation that it isn't necessary to be a dancer in order to be a choreographer. Anyhow, once the dancers leave the studios what are they going to do if they still want to do something? And behind the presumption that all the dancers would like to be choreographers is the deeper presumption that all the people would like to be choreographers too. In the new dance of action the people are being confronted by this idea. When the idea hits the colleges and universities a revolution of individuality will replace authoritarian restrictions. Robert Dunn's revolutionary course in composition in 1961 begat the New York movement that turned into the Judson Dance Theatre. On the West Coast Ann Halprin was taking the dancers outside and letting them take off their clothes inside. From what I know about it her ideas of teaching composition have been as open-ended as Robert Dunn's were. The idea is not to teach anything, since there is no longer anything to teach, but to encourage the dancers to do whatever they want to do. If they feel like standing on their heads and spitting out nickels they'll do that too. Methods of teaching are revealing. Methods are not guidelines to correct performance. Methods are like road signs at an intersection indicating the possibility of many directions. Dunn's method of presenting chance operations as a mode of departure was a study in the absurdity of method. The tremendous variety of approach in the early Judson concerts testified to the absence of method in Dunn's course.

Participation of artists, painters, and composers also constituted a celebration of freedom. Robert Morris, for one, demonstrated the absurdity of correct action. Morality is not in conformity but in the acceptance of diversity. How to win friends and influence people: make up your own rules and try to be charming about it. Luckily for the dancers the artists entered the picture to assist the proof that the choreography can be made inside and outside, standing up and lying down. The picture can be a falling Icarus by Breughel or a naked Olympia by Manet. Morris's naked lady after Manet's Olympia is a historical shakedown to illustrate the facts of naked ladies around the globe at all times. That Morris's choice was an idealized poetic image familiar in Western iconography is simply an irony of location, for the woman is "everywoman" no matter where she comes from. Being a sculptor Morris probably found it easier than most dancers to present a static image as one component in a piece of choreography. But the dancers have kept abreast with the artists, so much so as to give up their studio training if necessary, whenever it seemed right, and at the risk of appearing to forfeit the well-deserved prize of a super-functional body. Now it becomes clear the body can be super in its natural state, which brings me back to Isadora, who proclaimed the same thing at the turn of the century. The whole Theatre of Action has been rampant with strippers and other exhibitionists eager or willing to demonstrate the power of flesh. Most recently there were some excellent displays in the avant-garde series at Judson Hall: Charlotte Moorman playing her cello in plastic wrap and chased through the corridors after her performance by the police, who should stay on the streets to check the aberrations of people in clothes; the revival of Satie's "Relâche," which called for a stripper in the original score. The finale of "Relâche" as revived at Judson Hall beautifully exemplified the spirit of positive revolt born in the '50s and carried forward with dedicated persistence. Satie's stripper of '65 was Meredith Monk, who climaxed her performance by climbing into the audience and onto the laps of a couple of available men on the aisles; I think she was testing the power of "anyman" to respond, for the third man was her choice of the night and he followed her with pleasure as she led him to the stage to be seated as the man of honor, to watch Miss Monk and three other performers pay him simple homage in the form of looking at him and bowing a little, expressing a neat reversal of the performer-spectator relationship. Naturally the rest of the audience was delighted, for their man on the stage was a man from the people, and who does not want to be a performer in an age when the role of spectator is constantly in question?

October 14, 1965

Deborah Jowitt (1934–)

Deborah Jowitt began to dance professionally in 1953, to show her own choreography in 1962, and to write a regular dance column for *The Village Voice* in 1967. She has published two collections of reviews: *Dance Beat* (1977) and *The Dance in Mind* (1985). Her book of linked essays on aspects of dance history, *Time and the Dancing Image*, won the de la Torre Bueno Prize for 1988. She edited and wrote the introduction for *Meredith Monk* (1997) as well as the introductions for the revised edition of Jill Johnston's *Marmalade Me* and for José Limón's *An Unfinished Memoir*. Her most recent book is *Jerome Robbins: His Life, His Theater, His Dance* (2004).

Dance Theater Workshop honored Jowitt with a Bessie Award in 1985, and Dance/USA presented her with an Ernie Award in 1998. She has also received awards from the Congress on Research in Dance (1991) and the John Simon Guggenheim Memorial Foundation (2002). In 2016, Mark DeGarmo Dance honored her as an "Educational Visionary," and she received a Lifetime Achievement Award from the Martha Hill Dance Fund. From 1975 to 2016, she taught at New York University's Tisch School of the Arts.

On *Afternoon of a Faun*

For the New York City Ballet's 1953 spring season, Robbins prepared two works simultaneously. It's likely that one, *Fanfare*, was suggested by Balanchine and Kirstein. Princess Elizabeth was to be crowned Queen of England on June 2, and Balanchine, something of an Anglophile since his days there in the early 1930s staging numbers for Charles Cochran's Revue, wanted a new piece for that evening's celebratory program. The music for *Fanfare* was *The Young Person's Guide to the Orchestra*, op. 34, by British composer Benjamin Britten. Its mix of pomp, whimsy, and sweetness suited both the occasion and Robbins's gifts. The other new ballet was much more personal: a new version of *Afternoon of a Faun*, using the Debussy music that had inspired Nijinsky to choreograph his *L'Après-midi d'un Faune* in 1912. Robbins's nymph of choice was, naturally, Tanaquil Le Clercq, with Francisco Moncion as the "faun." He had wanted Buzz Miller to play the role, as a guest artist, but some miscommunication between Miller and Balanchine scotched that. (Miller later told Brian Meehan, "That is me. I am that boy.") Jerry also considered Louis Johnson, the gifted black dancer who had appeared in *Ballade*. A chance glimpse of Johnson had been crucial to his vision of the work: "I walked into a rehearsal studio and Louis Johnson was practicing a *Swan Lake* adagio with a student girl. They were watching themselves in a mirror. I was struck by the way they were watching that couple over there doing a love dance, and totally unaware of the proximity and possible sexuality of their physical encounters." Johnson had one rehearsal with Robbins and Le Clercq and heard no more; perhaps the New York City Ballet was not yet ready for a racially mixed pas de deux.

In April, Jerry wrote to Buzz, who was working out of town, with news of the house he planned to build in Fire Island Pines (he'd owned a lot there since the late 1940s, and Miller owned an adjoining one), the doings of their oversized puppy, Otis, whom he referred to as "our son," and the progress of his two ballets. About the Britten piece: "Yvonne Mounsey, the queen in 'The Cage,' is slightly marvelous as the harp. And the drum section looks like it will be very funny . . . a huge camp for Todd (only I do it better)." He had reworked the beginning of *Faun* for the ninth time "(actually!) and yesterday I seemed to break some of the ice around it. God I hope so. I had to address and be asked questions by the N.Y. Ballet Club on Sunday and boy were they curious about Faune. So is everyone. So am I." This season was an ambitious one, with new ballets by Bolender and Lew Christensen, as well as by Balanchine. Robbins noted that there were some financial worries about the season—he wasn't sure how serious—but was "going to put the bite on" about twenty-five people and ask for money.

In this letter, he returned yet again to his fatalist view of the ephemerality of talent and was delighted that his hadn't dried up yet.

You know talent is really a gift from nowhere, alighting on some poor slob in spite of himself; and anyone who thinks that he has something to do with it himself is nuts. Sure, if you've got it doesn't mean it will come out and be clear. That takes work, and effort and technique (and on my part hell of a lot of agony). But the nice thing with me is that the older I grow the more I appreciate what I manage to do and *that* gives me great happiness in this world.

Romola Nijinsky said that her husband had never read the poem by Stéphane Mallarmé that had inspired Claude Debussy's music (although Nijinsky's lover and mentor Serge Diaghilev knew it). It is certain that Robbins studied it in translation. And he had probably seen some rather distorted versions of Nijinsky's ballet that the Ballet Russe companies toured. In 1912, Nijinsky had embraced ideas that came to define early modernism in dance: economy of means, angularity, clarity of design. His nymphs in their handsome Greek draperies arrived to bathe in flat, two-dimensional processions, like those crossing a wall in friezes or running eternally around an archaic vase. Compressed into the same narrow, horizontal corridors of space, the faun roused himself from sensuous reverie and pursued them in a path that snaked across the stage. The ballet's stylized vocabulary stymied Parisians, used to seeing the world's greatest jumper show his skills, and many were shocked by the ending with its fairly obvious depiction of the onanism that's only hinted at in the poem. When the Chief Nymph fled the Faun's attentions, she dropped her scarf; he carried it back to his rock, arranged it in the semblance of a supine woman, lowered himself deliberately onto it, and arched upward in a silent orgasmic outcry.

Robbins deleted the attendant nymphs and recast the principals as young contemporary dancers meeting in a studio. His hero, bare-chested and wearing tights, is asleep on the floor when a young female dancer enters to practice some steps. Jean Rosenthal's set and lighting create an idyllic studio: white floor, transparent white fabric "walls," and beside the stage-right barre, a filmy curtain that stirs slightly in an unseen breeze. The scrim that initially veils the scene casts the audience as voyeurs, but as it rises and the man wakes and stretches to the music's opening notes, the audience understands the stage's "fourth wall" to be the studio mirror. (So mysteriously potent is this illusion that it's surprising to discover that Robbins originally considered placing the imagined mirror on one side of the "room.") While his choreography is fully three-dimensional, the dancers, continually appraising their movements in the mirror, stress the almost two-dimensional legibility that is crucial to ballet's presentation on a proscenium stage.

Robbins's vision was contemporary and natural. He had remembered the way one day in class a teenager (Edward Villella), standing next to him at the barre, "suddenly began to stretch his body in a very odd way, almost like he was trying to get something out of it. And I thought how animalistic it was . . . that sort of stuck in my head." After the woman has walked lightly on tiptoe behind the transparent wall to its doorway, she presses the points of her slippers into a resin box, adjusts the belt of her pale blue tunic, enters, and studies her pose in the "mirror" without seeing the sleeping man. Robbins imagined her, he said, having just washed her hair, and it hangs free. The two young people gradually begin to dance together, and, although the fact that their eyes remain fixed on the mirror has suggested narcissism to some viewers, their gaze doesn't really express self-love. They look into the glass to see what they *might* be, at how they transform themselves through the rituals of ballet. *We* see through the mirror into their desires.

Their pairing seems to happen naturally, from the moment he goes behind her where she is doing her quiet exercises at the barre, places his hands on her waist, and lifts her. Against the mood of sensual reverie that seeps from Debussy's music, they act no roles; they simply explore the steps as if discovering them—almost "marking" them the way dancers sometimes do in rehearsal (a look Robbins loved). Unlike Nijinsky, Robbins felt no need to invent a vocabulary. The ballerina's sudden spin, stopped by her partner's arm, her introspective attention on how a lift feels, build narrative onto classical steps and strategies. His dancers too occupy a drowsy sunlit space that is suddenly infused with a reticent but unmistakable sexual tension, but it is a place of safety for them, a room where their daily work occurs.

All the gestures but one allude to their lives as dancers. At the climax, as they kneel on the floor, the man leans gently forward and kisses the woman's cheek. She watches this in the mirror, turns to look at him, and then—gazing back at their reflections—touches the spot with her hand. It is a moment fraught with irony. So intent are these young people on their reflected otherness that even an intimate gesture must be studied for its effect. When the two are feeling out their pas de deux, he often grasps her body and presses it to him; yet at the moment "real life" enters the studio, the suddenly electric point of contact is very small—the size of two lightly pursed lips.

Robbins took only the basic structure from Nijinsky's scenario. His "faun" wakens to the presence of the solitary nymph, encounters her, and, after she has left, goes back to his place on the floor and stretches out. Perhaps he has only dreamed her. Some years after the ballet's premiere on May 14, Robbins added a gesture. Just before curling up, the man arches up from the floor, a chaste allusion to Nijinsky's climactic moment. Robbins did draw on imagery from Mallarmé's poem (as well, perhaps, as some ideas from Mikhail Fokine's *Narcisse*, a vehicle for Nijinsky based on the myth of a man doomed to fall in love with his own reflection in a pool). Moncion has spoken of gestures like "pushing through the reeds on a hot, humid afternoon." The lonely faun of the poem dwells beside a lake. At one moment, Robbins's nymph is seated on her partner's shoulder; as he gazes up at her and she down at him, very lightly paddling her feet in the air, they might be seeing each other as reflections of the ambition they share. Later, standing behind her, he frames her head almost awkwardly within his angled arms and, in the next instant, lowers and tilts that frame to catch her stretched body as she dives through it.

It is one of Robbins's greatest works.

There have been many fine interpretations of this small masterpiece, but the original cast can be said to embody most fully the choreographer's idea (a silent black-and-white film, shot slightly from the side, is the only record of Moncion's and Le Clercq's performance). Moncion conveys a restrained yet intense sensual interest in Le Clercq from the moment he awakens at the sound of her footsteps to the moment when she backs out of the room and he, kneeling, raises his head slightly, as if scenting the trail of her perfume. She can seem innocent, hastening away from him, but a minute before, she has slowly turned one bent leg in and out, watching him in the mirror watching her, very aware of her seductiveness. Interestingly, in another early film, made by the Canadian Broadcasting Corporation, Le Clercq danced with Jacques d'Amboise, who played the man as a young tough. He brought out the hoyden in her.

Mallarmé's faun dreamed of two nymphs—one chaste, one more knowing.

> Reflect . . .
>> whether these women you ponder
> might embody your fabulous senses' desire!
> Faun, illusion escapes the eyes of the first,
> Blue and cold as a weeping spring.
> But the other, all sighs, would you say she is different,
> Like a hot day's wind in your fleece!

It is possible to interpret these nymphs as two aspects of the eternal feminine. Whether or not Robbins and Le Clercq consciously followed this reading, they reembodied it as the play of conflicting feelings within one young woman. Le Clercq's father, a professor at Queens College and a Mallarmé expert, wrote Robbins, "What you have understood so well is that the two nymphs of the original are one and the same. The very text, obscure as it is, proves it. . . . You have reached the core of the meaning that poor sterile Mallarmé was unable to convey and that all his commentators have missed."

2004

Two New Ballets at NYCB Glance Backward with Trick Glasses

THE New York City Ballet hasn't collaborated extensively with an architect since the 1981 Tchaikovsky Festival, when Philip Johnson and John Burgee designed for George Balanchine something resembling a glass cathedral cum ice palace that, with modifications, would serve all the ballets. But this year, the company's New Choreography and Music Festival is billed as "Architecture of Dance," and Spanish architect Santiago Calatrava has designed settings for five of the seven choreographers who are contributing new ballets (four of them with commissioned scores). In the short film that preceded NYCB's opening gala, Calatrava expressed his delight at working with dance, and, indeed, some of his buildings, with their intersecting, wing-like curves, look ready to lift off.

His fan-shaped set for Benjamin Millepied's *Why am I not where you are* consists of two concentric white semi-circles set on edge—one tall and almost the width of the stage, the other the size of a very large curved doorway; the elastic cords that connect them like the teeth of a giant comb vibrate delicately with the motion of the dance and shimmer notably when Mark Stanley's lighting turns them to copper.

The splendid commissioned score by the French composer and organist Thierry Escaich is aptly titled *The Lost Dancer*, and the mutter of low piano notes, soft drum beats, and high-pitched shimmer that begins it sets us up for mystery. Millepied is, I think, trying to tell a story without exactly telling a story. That is, he wants us to interpret the events and steps of his very intriguing ballet as we will. Which is fine, most of the time, but occasionally makes me want to say things like, "Wait, didn't she just . . . ?"

The scenario of *Why am I not* seems to hinge on the notion of who may be included in a powerful clique and who excluded from it. The excluded, without the uniform attire that denotes acceptability, become virtually invisible. In the beginning, Sean Suozzi is clearly the outsider; he may swoop around the stage performing expansive leaps and pas de chat in his opening solo, but he also lurks at the edges, and he's unseen by a bevy of women in black net skirts with fuschia satin bodices, who waltz with men wearing green pants and somewhat bizarre jackets, irregularly patched in blue and purple (costumes by Marc Happel). Suozzi wears white, but although the woman he craves (Kathryn Morgan) doesn't see him, she senses his presence and, eventually, ceases to back away from his touch. Gradually her metaphoric vision improves.

Sara Mearns and Amar Ramasar are the devilish leaders of the sprightly pack, and bit by bit, as the ballet spins along, they contrive to slip articles of clothing on Suozzi until he's dressed like the other men. Several times, the way the ensemble crowds around him, hoists him, manhandles him a bit, and points him (at last Mearns and Ramasar do) in conflicting directions recalls Balanchine's Prodigal Son at the hands of the Siren's thuggishly mischievous servants. I'm not sure why, or at what moment, the hero's sweetheart becomes a pariah, but—this is admirably theatrical—people passing by swiftly strip off her over-skirts and her bodice; you can barely see the changes amid the tumult, but suddenly she's all in white. She rushes between two parallel lines of marching revelers, and no one sees her, not even her erstwhile lover. She's alone onstage as the curtain comes down.

The performers are dynamite. Mearns plays the voluptuous bitch with élan, and she and dagger-sharp Ramasar make a power couple you'd rather not know. Suozzi has been catching my eye for some time, even before he was promoted to the rank of soloist; whether in a classical role or rumbling with the Jets and Sharks in Jerome Robbins's *West Side Story Suite*, he has a gift for shaping a phrase and making the space around him alive. As for Morgan, she's a buoyant delight, and her legs look as if they begin at the waist—not because they're long but because of the expansive way she steps out with them.

Why I am not gives off whiffs of earlier Balanchine works—not just *Prodigal Son*, but the mad ballroom of *La Valse* and the seductively evil hosts of *La Somnambula*—as well as playing with such ballet tropes as the lone man seeking his beloved amid a flock of similarly clad beauties. Millepied has his own approach, however, to traditional steps and patterns, and it's heartening to see a young choreographer working in his own, often striking ways with the classical vocabulary, instead of accessing modernity through a virtuosic wrangling of legs, arms, and torsos, as do some contemporary ballet choreographers.

The second new piece shown at the premiere also alludes to earlier works. And how!

Alexei Ratmansky's extravagant new ballet *Namouna, A Grand Divertissement* has the air of a charmingly assembled crazy quilt—with patches cut from Petipa family remnants, Soviet ballet's grab bag, and personal mementoes stitched brightly together. It says in a festive undertone, "Don't think about plot. You want to see pirates? See pirates. You wonder how a ballerina in semi-disguise (a longer skirt in the same color) came to be addicted to cigarettes? Stop that!" After all, that's what a grand divertissement of the late 19th century was all about; the tale is told, enjoy the party.

The original two-act *Namouna* was created for the Paris Opera Ballet in 1882 by Lucien Petipa, a major ex-dancer, the great Marius Petipa's older brother, and a competent choreographer. One of the work's major plot ideas was that a beautiful elusive slave on a pirate ship anchored in Corfu manages to get enough money to buy the ship, free all the captives at an island slave market, and marry her love— mixups and scoundrelly interference notwithstanding. The music, originally in 23 sections, was commissioned from Edward Lalo. As I understand it, Ratmansky found 16 musical selections from *Namouna* on a CD made by the Monte Carlo Philharmonic Orchestra and used them in the same order, plus additional music from the composer's orchestral suites. One of the selections from *Namouna* is the "Pas des Cymbales," and at some inexplicable point, the 16 members of the female corps march in carrying pairs of smallish cymbals and stand clashing them together while the hero (Robert Fairchild) does some dazzling dancing.

These women open the ballet by running around the stage in a long line and into a formation. Like the swans from *Swan Lake*'s second act, they run with their heads up and their arms thrown slightly back. But they're wearing long, pleated, high-waisted yellow dresses and black wigs cut in a Louise Brooks bob (costumes by Marc Happel and Rustam Khamdamov). And right off the bat, Ratmansky cracks a joke that raises memories of Balanchine's *Serenade* and Robbins's "Mistake Waltz" from *The Concert*, along with Red-Army conformity, today's high-school cliques, and heaven knows how many ballet rehearsals. One woman stands up when the others are kneeling; with a concerted gesture, they evict her (a few seconds later, she's back in step).

Fairchild makes his entrance in pursuit of three women he can't keep up with. Like Suozzi in Millepied's ballet, he spends a lot of time looking on in bafflement. He wears what looks like a little boy's sailor suit (short pants). The women are garbed in cleverly cut modernist tutus (a short, stiff, translucent skirt, slit in front) and close-fitting white wigs that look like both 1920s bathing caps and the headgear that Aurora and her Prince used to wear in Soviet-era productions of *Sleeping Beauty* to denote 18th-century attire. These mysterious ladies are the ballet's female stars: Mearns (in navy blue), Jenifer Ringer (in powder blue), and Wendy Whelan (in white), and right away, each gets a turn to show off, backed by four-at-a-time yellow-garbed corps members. (Ratmansky doesn't use a Calatrava set piece, just creates his own architecture, abetted by Stanley's lighting.)

There are three other important dancers. Daniel Ulbricht enters with a cadre of eight men. They're in blue and he's wearing a copper-colored outfit, but they all have headgear that's part aviator helmet, part pirate do-rag. This gang is convivial, and it includes two first-class little women. Megan Fairchild and Abi Stafford execute a clever tongue-in-cheek trio with the ebullient, high-jumping Ulbricht. He lifts them and turns them one by one in such close quarters and in such rapid succession that you fear he'll make a mistake, but no, he exits triumphantly toting both of them.

This is a ballet in which the ends of numbers draw applause, and performers take bows. The applause is well-deserved. Ratmansky makes beautiful, fluent, intricate steps for his dancers. The trio is followed by a tricky solo for R. Fairchild, whose expansive upper body eloquently conveys ardor and abandon, while his feet manage no end of smart stuff. Later, M. Fairchild and Stafford perform a frighteningly fast side-by-side duet, embroidering the floor with the tips of their toes.

What else? Lots. Women reclining on the floor like denizens of a harem. Ringer doing her "Valse de la Cigarette" (joined by other female addicts), getting sick, and being lugged in by the guys and deposited onstage (she's OK, but not the one our hero wants). *Namouna* is so long, and there's so much fascinating dancing, that you need to see it more than once to take everything in. Fairchild searches among a group of identical beauties. At some point, he's rocked by a cluster of women and wakes up puzzled. Ulbricht bounds through the air, beating his legs together like a reincarnation of *Sleeping Beauty*'s Bluebird. The women in yellow return, re-costumed in white wigs and propeller-blade tutus like those of the stars. The eight corps men skip and prance and display manly camaraderie. It's a good thing the danceable music changes mood and tempo every few minutes. Whelan and Fairchild perform a fine grand pas de deux, complete with her making running dives into his arms, after which he and Ulbricht chase each other around for a while without apparent animosity. Then all bow to the happy couple and leave them alone onstage to kiss while the curtain falls.

Take your grandmother, take your five-year-old to this delicious, maddening slumgullion of a ballet, the playground of a very, very gifted choreographer. Just tell them not to ask you what it means. Or maybe ask *them* to tell *you*.

May 4, 2010

Elizabeth Kendall (1947–)

ONE OF the most striking things about Elizabeth Kendall's books is the wide range of her interests and subjects. Her eccentric upbringing in St. Louis, her education at Harvard, her early years in New York journalism, her passion for dance and for classic movies, her ideas about clothes, her intense involvement in things Russian (including the language) have determined the course of her writing. Her first book, *Where She Danced* (1979), explored the roots of American modern dance; her second, *The Runaway Bride* (1992), is an engaging exploration of Hollywood romantic comedy. *American Daughter* (2000) and *Autobiography of a Wardrobe* (2008) are two very different kinds of memoir. Her latest book, *Balanchine & the Lost Muse* (2013), is the result of intense research in Russian archives about the lives of the great choreographer-in-the-making and his friend and classmate, the brilliantly talented young ballerina Lidia Ivanova, who was mysteriously murdered just days before she was to join Balanchine and Alexandra Danilova in the small group who, in 1924, made their escape from St. Petersburg to the West. Kendall, who has received Guggenheim, Ford, and Rockefeller grants, has for many years been an associate professor of literary studies at The New School.

Ragtime

A DEADLY blow to "classic" dancing was struck by ragtime music and dance when they arrived in the teens. Some rag music had been in the air since the minstrel shows of the 1890s, some cakewalking had been tried out by the general public, but then rag dancing had returned to the dance halls and brothels of the red-light, "tenderloin" districts of Chicago, St. Louis, Sedalia, Kansas City, Memphis.

In San Francisco it emerged again. After the 1906 earthquake had destroyed much of that city, in the rubble grew up a shantytown which was so violent, so chaotic, and so unabashedly sinful that it drew tourists in droves. It was called the Barbary Coast. Here in vast palaces of gilt and tinsel the dregs of humanity danced "to the savage beat of tom-tom, cymbal, horn and banjo"—inspiring the onlookers, especially entertainers in the West on tour. In 1910 Anna Pavlova went anonymously to a Coast dance palace, coaxed her partner Mikhail Mordkin onto the floor, and began to dance to a ragtime beat, whereon the tawdry crowd grew silent and retreated to give them room. Pavlova on her own stage had shown the public a wild and abandoned kind of dancing, and so had Isadora Duncan, but in them it was called Dionysian; now the same impulse reached the masses via the syncopated music and the raunchy ambiance. New York producers grabbed onto the whole idea of ragtime: in 1910 the *Ziegfeld Follies* featured a "Barbary Coast Bear Café"; Lew Fields's 1911 show *The Henpecks* imported a Barbary Coast "coon shouter," Blossom Seeley, who ragged across the stage, singing "Toddlin' the Todolo"; at the Beaux Arts club, Barbary Coast dancers taught the customers a jaunty walk in close embrace and the craze was on for turkey trots, grizzly bears, bunny hugs, humpback rags. Shock was expressed, and some private amusement. A few young people who "trotted" or ragged at unseemly moments were tried in court; but then the defense lawyer sang "The Grizzly Bear" and the whole courtroom joined in on the chorus, "Everybody's Doin' It."

However, by 1912 these wild dances had vanished, "victims of gracelessness," said *Vanity Fair*. Instead appeared the smoother one-steps, hesitation waltzes, South American tangos, and maxixes—called the "glides." In them, a ragtime exuberance was contained, smoothed out, and subtly dramatized. The couple's positions were formalized—in fact, because of their formality, these dances were closer in spirit to Carnegie Hall "classic" concerts than to Barbary Coast ragging. They involved a conscious acting-out of the musical mood—the one-steps and "walks" were quick, light, and sunny, the Latinate "glides" dark and smoldering. To do any of them took a dramatic imagination and a loss of embarrassment, connected with a lithe body and a daredevil sense of timing.

It was the character of the music that invited this dancing wit.

Written ragtime was the creation of several virtuoso musicians—Scott Joplin, Louis Chauvin, Ben Harney—who synthesized romantic piano music and Afro-American folk sounds. They put the chromatic ardors of Chopin and Liszt inside robust rhythmic phrases, and so changed that European melancholy into something more playful, elusive, and devil-may-care, but still lyrical. Ragtime was constantly shifting moods over its springy beat—from bombastic to sweet, from pompous to tender. And just as quintessential ragtime was a humorous comment on romantic music, so the ragtime couple dances also quoted from romantic "classic" dancing—they took over not only graceful poses but whole steps: skips and kicks and skittering runs. Ragtime dancing used the same tug and pull at the music's momentum that Isadora Duncan had incorporated into her style. However, the serious origins of ragtime music and dancing were soon obscured by their rapid popularization. Around 1912, urban culture began to manufacture something like a ragtime universe.

With the dancing fad, all the dinner orchestras in restaurants and clubs demanded new and novel tunes—so Tin Pan Alley came to the rescue. Composers like the young Irving Berlin made pseudo-rags with self-advertising lyrics, "Alexander's Ragtime Band," "The International Rag," "Everything in America Is Ragtime." Berlin had an ear for slang; he matched it with his tunes, and soon most rags had catchy semi-nonsense lyrics—"He Had to Get Under, Get Out and Get Under," "Hello Frisco, Hello," "Who Paid the Rent for Mrs. Rip Van Winkle Rag," "Très Moutarde," "De la Fumée (Some Smoke)." Songs made mockeries of sacred concepts—inventions, legends, affectations, and anything that claimed to be Art. The poor devitalized "classic" dance came under attack when Irving Berlin ragged the "Greek" Spring Song ("That Mesmerizin' Mendelssohn Tune") and Yiddishized vaudeville Oriental ("Sadie Salome"). In fact, ragtime's mischief put a temporary stop to America's complaining about its own artistic inferiority. "Some people rave about Wagnerian airs / Some think the Spring Song is divine / Talk like that is out of season / What I like is something pleasin'," declared Joe Snyder's lyrics to Scott Joplin's "Pineapple Rag." The songs and their dances presented American irreverence in such clever fashion that Paris, London, Berlin, and the whole Continent caught the fever. Ragtime became a major cultural export, one of our first.

Meanwhile, in American cities, a kind of high life emerged. It was lavishly modern, featuring electricity, loud music, fancy décor, but was so unfamiliar it seemed fantastical. Critic James Huneker called the night-time New York of the teens a new Babylon, a lost Atlantis raised from the sea, with all its hotels, theaters, clubs "rising tier upon tier, starry with illumination." Most of them contained spots for dancing. The Beaux Arts was the first to remove its dinner tables from the floor, Bustanoby's followed, then Reisenweber's, the Café de Ninive, Rector's, Sherry's, and then the tea parlors, theater rooftops, hotels—the Astor, the Vanderbilt, the top of the Strand, the Biltmore, the McAlpin, the New Amsterdam, the Ritz, Claridge's, Healey's, Madison Square Tower—these hosted daily and nightly crowds of people who came for the brassy music, the dancing, and a few drinks or bites of food in between. Electric lights and mirrors illuminated the vast salles, and painted flowers, winged bulls, slaves, nymphs, satyrs, and mermaids adorned the walls—a hallucination of the exotic taste Stanford White and the gentlemen connoisseurs had wished on New York.

An orchestra, or sometimes two—one for ragtime and one for tangos—dominated the room in raised palmy enclaves, and so did an array of statuary; at the Biltmore it was the plaster Neptune and his surround that gave the name to the operation, "Les Cascades." On the floor thousands of little wicker or grille chairs and tables were strewn outside the low railings that marked the dancing space. And here people of all ages and classes—society ladies with feather aigrettes, businessmen in black dinnerwear, lounge lizards, chorines, and in the more democratic spots, shopgirls and clerks—rubbed elbows while tangoing and one-stepping and polkaing. Dancing was praised and decried as the great equalizer. Indeed, it seemed that coordination and stamina were the only useful attributes in this dancing society—the older virtues, a good name or an education, were momentarily superfluous. The suddenness with which new fortunes were made at this time, the overwhelming mix-up of the social order, created something like chaos in the ballroom. Ragtimers themselves were bewildered at why they, ordinary upstanding citizens, would submit themselves night after night to an atmosphere of haste, jostling, and barbarism worse than that of a political convention.

Discussion of the dancing went beyond simple good and evil. Of course there were still ministers who believed dance halls were the

Gates of Hell, temperance orators who said dance halls helped the liquor interest, social workers who declared they corrupted young working girls. But ragtime had risen in the world, as high as select clubs and ballrooms in private homes, and that put the dancing in another light. It stood for the social chaos that characterized the American teens. There was a helplessness about the anti-dance rhetoric in those years. How could dancing be evil when the sons and daughters and wives of leading citizens were dancing along with everyone else? Who was left to set an example to the uncultured classes? Those were the fears of all Americans who were comfortable with the old order. But the old order was vanishing with America's great "success" in world commerce. This ragtime melee established the conditions necessary for change; in it the "best people" were indistinguishable from everyone else. Cities were growing, and city life had dispensed with small-town values. Social configurations had to become blurred, especially in New York, since waves of newly rich from the Midwest— Edith Wharton called them "the invaders"—were arriving to live in the great over-stuffed hotels and dance in the tea parlors and on the theater rooftops.

The old urban elite and the few serious art, theater, and music critics who had embraced modern European art were ironically forced into a conservative position. They feared that the already fragile American culture would disintegrate in the mad whirl of ragtime. James Huneker, critic for the New York *Sun* (1902–1917), ruefully remembered all the abuse heaped on the vaudeville Salomés of several years back; now when all women were Salomés there was nothing left to say. It wasn't the carnality of the dancing that bothered him, the "knee to knee" positions of the couples, it was the exhibitionism—young people flaunting themselves as on a stage. The social drift toward this tendency had shown itself even before the dancing appeared: first there had been late supper orgies after a play, then cafés with some sensational singer or dancer in the aisles; now that respectable café patrons themselves were "performing," where could it end but with those same patrons "mounting the vaudeville stage and doing flip-flops and splits and such things before a hired audience of reformed ballet girls"? This is what the high-society youths in Rupert Hughes's 1914 novel *What Will People Say?* fantasized for themselves—and they were sincerely alarmed at their own recklessness. Everyone was alarmed somewhat.

Those who defended the modern ragtime dances nervously reminded the public of their sportive nature—at least dancing got the men out of their stuffy offices and the women away from their interminable bridge games. Inactivity, they claimed, was the ultimate American sin—worse than exhibitionism. Even some hygiene, dress-reform, and open-air fanatics conceded that ragtime, while low-down and "inartistic," had physically awakened a number of people. But this was no real comfort for the astonishing transgressions implied in ragtime dances.

The country's real ambivalence about social dances might have kept people from seeing what was in them—just as it had with "classic" dancing—except that a number of chic young couples appeared: they danced on Broadway, presided in the late-night cafés and palaces, and conveniently embodied the whole dancing mania. The ragtime industry created them partly to be imitated—they posed on song covers, modeled clothes, wrote dance instruction manuals. But their main function was to demonstrate, which the best ones did with a daring and inventiveness that finally no one was ashamed to copy. The most prominent of these couples paired an American girl with an exotic, Latin-looking young man: Florence Walton and Maurice Mouvet, Joan Sawyer and Carlo Sebastian, Bonnie Glass and Rudolfo di Valentino, Mae Murray and Clifton Webb. The men had a reticent physical ease with women that their American counterparts couldn't quite attain. On the dance floor they not only partnered the girls but furnished a sort of environment to show them off: they blended in with the décor and lent a mystery to the routines. And of all the couples, the most beloved was an Englishman, Vernon Castle, and his American wife, Irene.

The Castles, because of their origins, were considered the most scrubbed and wholesome of dancers: Vernon was an engineering student who had stumbled onto theater as a hobby and then wooed Irene, a New Rochelle debutante, away from genteel life and onto the stage. Vernon was thin, his blond hair was receding, but his perfect manners elicited an air of mischief in his dark, slender, gaminlike wife. They had the distinction of "arriving" in New York with some Parisian renown; while stranded in that city they had invented a dancing act for the Café de Paris—and what they had invented, out of Vernon's incomplete recall of "coon-shouter" Blossom Seeley's "Grizzly Bear" from *The Henpecks*, 1911 (Vernon had played a bit part in that Broadway show), became the international dancing style of the next few years. In Paris the young and winsome Castles were the first entertainers to sit down with the guests and then rise from their center table to start the entertainment; back in New York they continued to attract both friends and patrons among the wealthy. In 1912 they played on Broadway in *The Sunshine Girl* and soon, with the backing of shrewd theatrical agent Elisabeth Marbury, they opened a select dancing club, Castle House, on West 46th Street, then a late-night café, Sans Souci, right off Times Square, and then an ultra-tasteful dance palace on Long Island, Castles by the Sea. Every few months they left their country estate and went out on the road in a series of exhibition-contests with themselves as soloists and judges. These events gave them a means to tour the country outside of the vaudeville circuits, and, unsullied by vaudeville, Vernon and Irene were a living advertisement for the handsomeness, the sunniness, and the slight piquancy of the "modern" dances.

The Castles' real contribution to dancing came not from their reputation but from their performing aplomb. Their every routine was choreographed and rehearsed minutely until they moved together in continuous and surprising harmony. They skimmed down the long polished floors, decorating their path with little kicksteps, hesitations, and lightning zig-zags that never interrupted the natural sweep of motion. At crescendos and stoptimes they had showier tricks: he flipped her up and around his body; he lifted her forward in the air as she showed a dainty foot; he held her at the waist as she bent back, rolled around his arm and then up—but always they continued to move, their little steps propelling them in one clear direction at a time. He was immaculately turned out in black tails; she wore white or diaphanous pastel with one or two tunic layers that belled out as he spun her. Their very coolness and lightness increased the excitement of the show; they seemed to be riding the wave of ragtime through no effort of their own.

What Vernon had done was to take a simple social amusement, couple dancing, and make it a highly expressive genre. First of all he gave a dance a shape on the floor. From the high, light, tandem stepping of the one-step he made the Castle walk, in which the gentleman propelled the lady backward to the other end of the room, then kept steering her in ever smaller circles until they had to stop, unwind, and start back in the opposite direction. The step was addicting and pleasing to think about, since its end was its new beginning. For their exhibition routines Vernon not only set floor patterns, he made steps that fused several earlier dancing styles—minuets, polkas, and drawing room waltzes, the little tap and soft-shoe steps from the music hall, discreet high kicks from the cakewalk, and the spirit of partnering from the modern Russian ballet. In that kind of ballet the man's task was to show off the woman's line, and in the Castles' dancing, no matter how complicated the steps, their purpose was Vernon's presentation of Irene. Her "line" was what people saw when the Castles danced, and it was the line of Isadora's and Pavlova's "classic" dancing observed by Vernon. Irene's fluid back, her gracious bends forward over pointed foot, her decorative over-the-shoulder glances, her pointed foot raised in a little arabesque in back—all those were positions adopted from the "classic" stage. Irene was one of the truer professional heirs of Isadora Duncan. She was coolly and proudly "Greek," though not with any of Isadora's grand heroic resonances. She was an Amazonette, a Duncan reduced, streamlined, made portable by a partner.

In the realm of popular fads, of which "modern" dancing was a part, Irene Castle not only mirrored a new age, she improvised some of its features—calf-length dresses, low-heeled dancing pumps, little Dutch caps—and she was probably the first American woman whose ideas had such an impact on fashion. When she had her hair cut short (before an appendectomy), a host of women copied her; she put a seed-pearl band around her brow to hold her short hair back, and so did thousands: these were more faint allusions to the antique, or to an aesthetic-hygienic style now diluted into high fashion. A newspaper said the Castle hair looked like "a cross between an ancient Greek runner and a child's bob." The country forgot, in its preoccupation with Castlemania, that these clothing and dancing experiments had begun with the "classic" dancers, Duncan and St. Denis: they were the ones who had stood the ridicule of their own time, only to see their queer dress and unhampered bodies become a fashionable conceit.

Every smart dress was now a dancing dress. Simply to talk about the cut of clothes, said fashion experts, was to describe dancing. Even women who never braved the dance floor sought the effect invented by Loïe Fuller, Isadora Duncan, and Ruth St. Denis and fixed by Paul Poiret—light stuffs wrapped around the body, with additional trailers that moved and caught the light. The dresses dramatized the connection between a moving body and the space around it. After the long nineteenth-century debate on women's natural forms versus corsetting, the now triumphant looseness in the torsos of gowns, the draped softness at the necks, prompted a whole new range of twisting motions. Women were encouraged by their clothes to spiral up from the waist, to look over their shoulders, to look up, to open their necks to the air. Asymmetrical curves and faintly Dionysian poses were crucial to sitting, walking, and dancing. The tangos and one-steps travelled fast but still required full expressive use of women's upper bodies, and full use of the arms with a partner, to give the bodies room to shift direction. All these ways of moving were reminiscent of the "artistic" poses taught in Delsarte recitation classes in girls' schools, with their stress on opposition motions and oblique lines. And the gowns indicated even more theatricality—they were costumes. They made reference to the artistic but jumbled realm of the Antique, of harems and woodland glades, nymphs and satyrs, and Paris and Oriental slave girls.

Vanity Fair, February 1914, picked out two gowns from among the crowd at the opening of the Castles' Sans Souci to epitomize the flights of fancy women permitted themselves when dressing up. One was "Oriental,"

> a concoction of white satin, seemingly with Turkish trousers. No one would have believed six months ago that any dressmaker would dare put so much material into a skirt as this one had. The plaits at the waist were allowed to flare into extraordinary fullness over the knee and were turned under and gathered to the shorter lining of chiffon cloth. It was slashed in front almost to the knees and filled in with ruffles of white tulle which fell over flesh pink stockings. The slippers were of black velvet with small buckles of brilliants.

The other, worn by a slim blonde, was "Greek,"

. . . a gown of tulle, a tunic with an irregular edge, bodice a Greek surplice affair, caught with a sprig of apple blossoms on each shoulder. The colors are lavender, pink, faint blue and white, one shade overlapped the other, producing a lovely opalescent effect. The origin of the gown was evidently the gown Mlle Pavlova wears when she dances to the strains of Mendelssohn's "Spring Song."

The ragtime craze mixed a vague artificial idea of Art (Pavlova never danced the "Spring Song") with the restless vitality of American life, and the figure of the American girl exemplified the mixture; she was a half-fanciful creation, more a cultural myth than a real person; but she dominated the era—in magazines, in books, in a string of Broadway plays that celebrated her escapades and her costumes: *Poor Little Rich Girl, Oh! Oh! Delphine!, The Lady of the Slipper, The Sunshine Girl, The Girl from Utah.* She was not the patrician and humorless 1890s Gibson Girl but a much more impish creature with delightful, if untrustworthy, whims—and she was useful for defining the contradictions of the age.

She was not independent, for husbands and fathers still chivalrously supported her, yet she was modern because she was a dancing addict and the sign of a future when no one would bother with social conventions and ceremonies. Self-expression, a suspicious concept, was born with her. Then, it didn't mean cultivating the personality; it meant crudely ignoring the proprieties and acting instantly on one's desires. Again and again, writers connected this girl to the aborted pace of modern life. *Vanity Fair* called her "the princess of an age that has turned the home into the hotel, the painting into the photograph, the book into the review, the letter into the telegram"—and, they might have said, the human encounter into a dash on the dance floor. But dancing, like this fond image of a girl, also kept hold of something old-fashioned. There was repose in it, the repose of the mesmerizing, broad-swinging tempi of ragtime. There were fanciful costumes and surroundings and a set of gestures that made clear to anyone who watched just how to move, to pose, to arrange oneself in relation to others in a fast-moving world. These rag dances were a teacher. For aspiring women who hadn't been to finishing school or for girls who were waiting to grow up, they gave an instant comprehension of just what airs and graces to put on. For all its reputedly obsessive pace, ragtime dancing maintained in the end that there was still gracefulness in human society.

1979

ALLEGRA KENT (1937–)

ALLEGRA KENT began to study ballet when she was eleven, in California, with Bronislava Nijinska and Carmelita Maracci, and she continued her training in New York, at the School of American Ballet. At fifteen, she was invited by Balanchine to join New York City Ballet. Soon he was choreographing for her—first the luminous "Unanswered Question" section of *Ivesiana*, then the (innocent) embodiment of the Kurt Weill/Bertolt Brecht *The Seven Deadly Sins*. (Lotte Lenya was their far-from-innocent embodiment.) Perhaps her most famous role was as The Sleepwalker in *La Somnambula*, which Balanchine revived for her in 1960. Originally titled *Night Shadow*, it had been the first ballet Kent ever saw, back when she was eleven.

Apart from assuming many of the great Balanchine roles—Terpsichore in *Apollo*, the Second Movement of *Symphony in C*, the lead in *Agon*, among others—she was crucial to a number of new Balanchine works: in *Brahms-Schoenberg Quartet* and in the stylized eroticism of *Bugaku*, both with Edward Villella; with Jacques d'Amboise in the exquisite divertissement pas de deux in the film of *A Midsummer Night's Dream*. And she was one of the original cast of ten in Jerome Robbins's *Dances at a Gathering*.

Kent danced for thirty years with City Ballet. After her retirement she began to write. (She's a lifelong avid reader.) Her *Water Beauty Book* was both visionary and practical—like Kent herself. Her book for children, *Ballerina Swan*, was widely applauded. And her autobiography, *Once a Dancer . . .* , has been acclaimed as one of the finest dancers' memoirs of our time. She has also written frequently for *Dance Magazine*. She teaches ballet at Barnard College.

Memories of Madame Karinska

I N THE realm of costume creation and execution, Barbara Karinska was the quintessential artist and George Balanchine's choice collaborator. She was uncannily attuned to Mr. B's deepest thoughts and feelings about ballets and ballerinas and translated them from passion into peau de soie. Whatever communication transpired between them must have been a mixture of language and extrasensory perception, and the results were a stunning materialization—his great choreographic vision enhanced and fulfilled in fabric.

Karinska made legions of glorious garments for ballerinas, premier danseurs, the corps de ballet, divas, and actors portraying all sorts of characters—mice, men, queens, goddesses, and bumpkins for the movies, theater, musicals, opera, and ballet. I was lucky that a few of her woven wonders were made for me.

I first saw Madame Karinska backstage one evening at the City Center while she was directing a last-minute costume delivery. A trim woman in a navy-blue suit, with a short crop of lavender hair, was pointing in various directions to her staff. A team of men and women with costumes folded over their arms was bustling about, searching for the dressing areas. The costumes were for immediate use. And for the most part, the seams would be sewn, not merely pinned, in place. I learned that there was never time to get everything done. This was in 1953, and I was a brand-new member of the New York City Ballet—a wide-eyed 15-year-old who had never witnessed such a spectacle before. Yet what made the biggest impression on me was Karinska's lavender hair. I wondered if the beauty parlor had made a mistake. I was soon to learn that there were no mistakes with this extraordinary woman.

Later that year I was sent down to Karinska's shop for a fitting. Up to that time I had worn other girls' costumes, but now I was in the corps of a new work by Lew Christensen called Con Amore. After I had stripped to tights and leotard, my measurements were taken and recorded in a black notebook; not only waist, hips, and bust, but also inseam, head girth, and wrist. Then a long, tulle, yellow-ocher skirt was pinned at my waist and a bodice was positioned over it with little tugs, adjusting the center of me to the center of it. All of this was done by a kindly Russian woman. When Karinska appeared at the doorway, her assistant announced, "This is Kent." Karinska nodded nonchalantly and walked over to inspect me, wearing her usual navy-blue suit and sensible shoes, her lavender hair adding a touch of wit. Her eye had detected an imperfection on my costume. Scrunching up a bit of fabric with her fingertips, she fiddled and twisted, giving instructions in rapid Russian. I perceived that I was more object than subject. The subject was "tutu." But just as she left the room, she gave me a small encouraging smile.

Ten years later—when I went in for my *Bugaku* fitting—Karinska and I were old friends. She had made many costumes for me, including those I wore in *The Seven Deadly Sins* and *Stars and Stripes* and even a "secret" white tutu for *Swan Lake* to pack for our Australian tour, just in case I had to dance Odette. Now, for this Asian occasion, Balanchine came with me to the shop. As the waistband of my tutu was secured, I looked down and gasped at the beauty of the details. The skirt formed a giant fuchsia chrysanthemum. At the tip of each pointed petal was a dewy rhinestone. The paler pink bodice had a few thin gold stripes and kimono sleeves. Karinska gleamed an exultant smile as Balanchine said, "A triumph!" The wig that I was to wear throughout the ballet was a sculpted sweep of shiny black horsehair with two little nests of jeweled ornaments. It was practically weightless. Edward Villella's wig, which I saw resting on a wooden head form, resembled a samurai warrior's hairstyle and mine a geisha's.

But there was more. Over white tights, I tried on a white bikini with appliqués made of fabric flowers. And then a white silk organza kimono was brought into the room. All its edges were finished with a roll of white horsehair tubing and it had a long train. Dipping my arms through the sleeves, I secured it in place with one snap hidden under a small flower. The gown had fluidity and transparency but no weight. Dancing in it, I would feel like a flying fish riding over the waves. Bending down, Karinska picked up the long tail and flung it into the air. "Ah," said Mr. B as he watched the fabric floating to the floor. Choreography and costume had merged with gauzy grace.

In 1970, at another of my fittings at Karinska's shop, Madame was crocheting a green woolen chain, pulling loop through loop with her crochet hook. The new costumes for *The Firebird* were in production.

Working from drawings by the original designer, Marc Chagall—vivid, bold, impressionistic—Karinska had to fill in what was missing. She explained that she was making stems for the flowers to be attached to the maidens' dresses. There was something charming about seeing Karinska working on a stem. Maybe, like me, she had learned to crochet as a child. Maybe her grandmother had taught her. Maybe they spoke together about fairy tales and the mythical Firebird. Certainly Karinska's work for this ballet was of the long ago and far away, springing from her cultural heritage. *Firebird*, with its magnificent purples and crimsons, was another one of her monumental achievements.

Once, while I was visiting her at home, Karinska led me to her closet to see one of her dresses from the 1920s, a navy-blue sheath encrusted with beads. "Take it down," she requested.

I almost couldn't; it must have weighed twenty pounds or more. I gave her a strange look.

"Yes, I wore it."

Onstage Karinska had created weightless confections for her subjects, yet she had worn heavy clothes in everyday life. For the stage, garments had to be etherealized for effortless motion.

I lived an important part of my life in Karinska's creations. Night after night during many seasons over the course of thirty years, I pursued my childhood dream of dancing, and I did so for the most part in her costumes. I explored some of the greatest choreography ever invented while hooked or snapped up in her sumptuous creations.

And I wasn't the only one in my family to wear a Karinska original. One day in 1962 when I went to the shop for a fitting, Karinska had a surprise for me—a little puff of pink on a tiny hanger. "For your daughter," she said. A tender tutu for Trista. Karinska understood that side of me. And it fit my daughter perfectly without a single fitting.

Thank you forever, Madame.

October 2003

LINCOLN KIRSTEIN (1907–1996)

SURELY the greatest cultural impresario America has ever had, Lincoln Kirstein embraced art, film, photography, criticism, and, above all, dance. The rich son of a Boston merchant (Filene's department store), he went to Harvard where he founded the brilliant magazine *Hound & Horn*. He was involved in the founding of the Museum of Modern Art and later inspired the creation of MoMA's film department. He was instrumental in building the great dance collection at the New York Public Library, was perpetually acting as patron and guide to talented artists, and had a deep interest in the art of photography. He founded and edited the essential scholarly journal *Dance Index*.

And, of course, it was he who, in 1933, went to Europe to locate a choreographer who could come to America and create a classical ballet company, and style. It was George Balanchine whom he settled on, and, in October of that year, Balanchine arrived in New York, first to cofound, with Kirstein, the School of American Ballet (which would more or less become Kirstein's personal fiefdom) and then, the following year, to create *Serenade*, Balanchine's first work choreographed in America. Through the 1930s, Balanchine and Kirstein collaborated on several dance companies designed to showcase Balanchine's work, and after Kirstein returned from a wartime stint overseas, much of it spent recovering looted art throughout Europe, they created Ballet Society, which, in 1948, morphed into New York City Ballet. Kirstein remained its general director until 1989.

In writing about the widest range of dance, he combined a profound knowledge of dance history and aesthetics with a deadly polemical style. Among the most important of his more than thirty-five books are *Movement & Metaphor*, *The New York City Ballet*, and *Nijinsky Dancing*. His private life was, to say the least, complicated, made more so by a lifelong struggle with bipolarism. Yet no one achieved more in so many fields and left behind so crucial a cultural legacy. Along the way, he was presented with countless honors, including the Presidential Medal of Freedom, the National Medal of the Arts, and New York's Handel Medallion. Not that he cared.

The Music Hall, Revues, the Movies

THERE ARE so many varieties of popular dancing in America that they are better categorized by the place in which they are danced, or by the people who dance them, than by the quality of the dancing itself. The quality of the dancing as form, as movement, even as an indication of a national expression has only one facet which is shared by nearly every sort of performer—its virtuosity.

For example, take the Radio City Music Hall. On that enormous half-shell what has ever been presented as handsome or as theatrical as its auditorium? It is practically impossible for one person to prevail as an artist alone on the stage, since the human scale is wholly destroyed by the height of the proscenium. The voice is well amplified throughout the hall, but unfortunately there are no glasses to swell the apparition of a minute performer for the distant back rows. The dance, however, is hardly neglected at Radio City. There is a ballet corps under the direction of the house choreographer, Florence Rogge. Her task of turning out a different routine every week, with her girls dancing four shows a day and rehearsing the new one in between, is not a very thankful one. She does what anyone would do—invents what she has the energy to think out and, for the rest, repeats what has been done before. The main problem is to keep the big stage filled with nervous action in the varying conceits of peacock's tails, harems, galleons, or motor shows that the sign-painters in the studios bat out.

The Roxyettes, those fifty-two tested automata, can always be counted on by the grateful management to magnetize applause. These girls, trained not to any music but to a metronome, have the gift of insensate repetition down to the last kick. It is nerve-racking to consider what there is about a dancer repeating a turn on the stage which finally beats the watchers into clapping, or about the line of Roxyettes clipping their hoofs with a one, two, three which gives such a sense of relief to so many people—the relief of recognition, of mechanized motion, of precise inertia, of realizing how long it must have taken them to get that way. Yet the Roxyettes, fifty-two of them dancing what would be insupportable for one to dance alone, have in their subhuman geometry the only moments of theatrical effectiveness of all that monstrous scene.

The problem of a really good dancer on the Music Hall stage is much more serious. When one long accusing spotlight assails him from somewhere in the arena's night and pins him, tiny in front of the contour-curtain or a Roxy set, his arms and legs have to fly out in such spiral spokes from his trunk that only the most active can survive it. A few weeks ago two serpentine virtuosi almost belied this. Barry and Coe in white pants and mess jackets executed a series of slow-motion passages—snakes writhing from the sand, rubber torsos and octopoid legs—that were thrilling. If they had been in a house of reasonable size they would have had not only claps but cheers. Buck and Bubbles, perhaps the best team of colored dancers in America today, went through a combination apache-tango that was no less beautiful in its perfect timing than Moss and Fontana's miracle waltzes, but almost insupportably funnier.

Virtuosity is of course, in vaudeville, its own reward, but even excellent dancers, who often appear at the Music Hall, have not the added power of annihilating the crippling lights and the general gigantism of the mise-en-scène. Virtuosi need a friendlier space. Their stuff both merits and demands it. What could be done with the Music Hall as far as spectacle goes is a perennial subject of pleasant, fruitless speculation. A herd of elephants (not one baby elephant as in its *Schéhérazade*), a school of whales, even Reinhardt using the material of the circus for a melodrama, or Meierhold bringing up massed armies on the three double-revolving and interlocking elevator stages, would meet difficulties.

The present *Ziegfeld Follies* brings up several disturbing problems in American dancing. In the first place, Patricia Bowman, the delicate and able technician who has left her post as first dancer at the Music Hall for the occasion, is seen to better advantage than in years. Those who have had the good fortune to watch Miss Bowman in class realize how gracious her exquisite gifts can be. She is too fine for the crassness of Broadway, and yet there has been, until now, nowhere else for her to go. Compared with the visiting Russians of the Monte Carlo

Ballet, she has as much schooling or more, but not the background to dance against—which in her case is so important. Also in the *Follies* are those two very young eccentric tap dancers Vilma and Buddy (as Walter Winchell says, Ebsens makes the heart grow fonder). That was surely true a year ago. Their gaiety, their frank diffidence and ingenuity were entirely charming. But now, no matter what the music or costume or set, their dance is the same. Buddy is in the awkward position of a juvenile growing up. The first youthful flush is mannered and semi-permanent. The exploitation of the essence of youth by a dancer is tiring both to him and his audience. As on the dramatic stage, a persistent juvenile never grows up; he fades away. Then the question of the great American contribution—tap dancing. This essentially aural technique, which polishes the eardrums of the listeners with its soothing, subtle, and braided staccatos, rarely delights the eye. The arms and shoulders of a tap dancer are too often dead. Though Snake Hips and Bill Robinson are entirely released, nevertheless it seems nearly impossible for whites to tap with their whole body.

Fred Astaire is perhaps the one white tap dancer who maintains his ingenuousness into his thirties. But then, he has more than his taps to support him; he has above all his delivery, his engaging extreme professionalism which gives him the air of an aristocratic and, on occasion, a tragic amateur.

The dancing in *As Thousands Cheer* is mainly interesting on account of Charles Weidman's arrangement of several of the song hits. He has conceived a very effective plastic dance for Letitia Ide, who has fine looks and moves with sympathy and force. American group dancers are more and more employed as decorative interludes in good revues. It almost seems a solution for the "group," since it is so hard for them to construct a full evening's program for more than two or three concerts a year, and the heterogeneous composition of an "intimate" or an intelligent musical show offers a frame without too many vulgarizing limitations.

Choreography in moving pictures has recently approached an imperial lavishness. Busby Berkeley, working for Warner Brothers, has conceived the sumptuous sequences for the *Gold Diggers of 1933*, *Footlight Parade*, and *Fashions of 1934* series. His formula for socking moving-picture audiences is a combination of geometry, mass pulchritude, and water. The camera can be mounted under glass, hung from above, or placed at any of the possible 180 angles, receiving the kaleidoscopic symmetry of countless blondes whose legs and arms develop into points of stars, links in a necklace, or caryatids of Babylonian fountains, the spouts of which, drenching them with water, they hold between their breasts. There is not a great deal of dancing, but enough to give movement to the close-ups. The long shots, owing to the number of persons used in precision work, might be photographs of anything but chorus girls. Good dancing somehow doesn't get across on the screen. The warmth of Fred Astaire's stage presence is ineffective in his pictures. In *I Am Suzanne!* there was a nice idea of contrasting a live dancer with large marionettes, but all the delicate heroine was given to do, in her role as the greatest dancer in wherever, was some very rough trick adagio. The camera can amplify eyes, nose, and teeth to apocalyptic dimensions and emphasis. Somehow dancing, more than acting, requires the actual miracle of the human body in action. The present exhilaration, the rising blood, the sweeping color are nearly as moving as what is danced, and the shadows can't take it.

Just as popular American music seems increasingly more valid, more emotionally effective, than the work of our conscious and synthetic composers, so more satisfaction in dancing can be derived from vaudeville and revues than from the various group recitalists. We await the day when a fusion will be realized, when a directing intelligence with a sense of lyric style can utilize all of the natural virtuosity at hand.

March 14, 1934

Martha Graham

PERHAPS a skillful draughtsman could do it, or a painter. Someone with an evocative connection between their memory, their present eye, and a sharp hand that could put it down for someone else to see. Otherwise it is impossible to give another person any idea of the difference between what Martha Graham looked like to me when I first began to see her and what she seems to me now. I cannot assume that the change is entirely with me or entirely with her. But there is a very great change and I submit my analysis of it because I think it is not an uncommon experience for some of the people who have watched her for the last seven years.

Even then she seemed strong, so strong in fact that I could only with the greatest difficulty look at her at all. I saw her as a sort of rigid embodiment of a principle I did not wish to understand. I felt her as an arrogant and blind assertion of gesture and movement which were both repellent in themselves, and based on some substructure as capricious as it was sterile. What I considered to be her brand of stark hysteria antagonized my sympathy, and her exhaustingly arbitrary invention angered my eyes. I left her concerts, to which I could not but continue to go, irritated to the point of exasperation and physically worn out. I told this to one of her earliest and most powerful admirers. He nodded his head like a diagnostician, and said "Exactly," as if it was sure proof of some toxin working. I was suspicious of it just as I would be suspicious of some active and inexplicable energy which was not an immediate personal threat but which might be the demonstration of some power I had best beware of since I could not be sure how it would next affect me. It worried me like a headache. Her wiry concentration, her awkward, jarring idiosyncrasies and stammering activity repelled me so strongly that I was continually drawn back to see her almost to exorcise myself of curiosity, or to lay the ghost of all the irritating questions which raised themselves when I watched her.

Why was all this so violent? I was very accustomed to dancing, and it had long been my first interest. Perhaps that was just the reason. I was brought up on the Russian Ballet, and I had an exclusive and obsessive passion for it. I had not seen enough dancing to know that not only were there other kinds of dancing, but that the Russian Ballet at that time was a dilute replica of an original intention, and that its later developments were decorative survivals depending on shocks from many extraneous sources other than dancing, to keep it alive. I had not seen the original Russian Ballet of 1909 to 1919. My first experience of it was the post-war period of 1923 when the School of Paris had displaced the original Russian collaborators, and when Diaghilev was in the full throes of the cubist revolution. It was all extremely theatrical, physically stimulating and violently opposed to the accepted exotic complacencies of *Schéhérazade*, *Cléopâtra*, or *Prince Igor*. It made no difference that the dancing was only a little less important than the music, and that the painters' portion—the dresses and the decor, were the real excuse for the whole show, which was, in essence, anti-theatrical and anti-choreographic.

So, when I first saw Graham, I mistook her attitude, confused her approach, and decided it was all very old-fashioned, provincial, unresourceful and ultimately uninteresting in comparison to the urbane sights and sounds, the perverse, acid disharmonies and nervous excitement then active in the disintegration of the classic tradition of the ballet. I went to Graham expecting to be shocked further than by the collaborations of Picasso, Cocteau and Massine. I was unequipped for her simplicity and self-blinded to her genuinely primitive expression. For me the primitive was the primitivistic, the Stravinsky of *Sacre* and *Noces*, with all their attendant resources of complex colour, historic reference and elaborate orchestration. The archaic was the archaistic of the *Afternoon of a Faun;* the contemporary was the chic of *Parade* or *Les Biches.* This solitary dancer, not even a girl, with her Spartan band of girls seeming to me to press themselves into replicas of the steel woman she was, appeared either naive or pretentious, which, I could never fully decide. But the force of the personality of the woman magnetized me continually.

It is the theatrical aspect of dancing that attracts me most, and it was her specifically conceived work for the theatre that first overcame my blanket resistance to her. After seeing the dances in Katherine Cornell's *Romeo and Juliet*, and after watching rehearsals for the living choral frieze in John Houseman's production of MacLeish's *Panic*, I felt I had a nucleus of comprehension, or at least satisfaction in her work which might, in time, absolve me from further hate. By that time my long love affair with the Russian Ballet had resolved itself in something less than an affectionate friendship, and my dissatisfaction with the heirs of Diaghilev opened my mind, of necessity, to other possibilities for dancing. Seeing Wigman as a soloist, and later as a composer, however, further momentarily confused me. Somehow I expected a corroboration of my original opinion of Graham in watching Wigman. What I actually felt was her enormous difference from the American, and chiefly that assertion of blind, vague, quasi-mystical self-expressionism which is the unfortunate universal heritage of the descent from Wagner. Yet my own acumen was insufficiently skilled to reconcile the difference between Graham and Wigman. Certain

superficial similarities, such as the use of percussion, furthered a confusion already aggravated by an instinctive concept of their genuine
opposition.

The rest of the history of my larger comprehension of Graham is too
subjective to be of much interest and would involve autobiographical
rationalization, half-truth and accident which is interesting only to the
writer. To admit the element of a gradual revelation by unfrightened
eyes would be nearer the truth and just as logical. Yet I cannot pretend
that where once I thought was all blackness has become in a flash, all
light. I believe that in Graham's work of five and six years ago there
were still elements of her own unachieved revolt, unassimilated and
inorganic, which coincided with those insecure and immature philos-
ophies of Spenglerian decay and European snobbery with which I was
then equipped and which colored my opinion of her art. The lack of
necessity for a continuation of that particular energy imperative in an
artist's first personal revolt brings a breadth and freedom impossible
and even undesirable in earlier stages. The concentration demanded
to cleanse inertia from any tradition or form is seldom attractive and
often as repulsive as the dead growth for which it is the specific antidote. But this concentration remains nervous, and after it has won its
fight can exert itself into a calmer and more expansive activity.

To write descriptions of dancing is even more aimless than to paint
pictures of music. One can at least quote musical phrases or point to
a handy phonograph. Most photographs are intrinsically as subjective
and unsatisfactory as dance criticism, and the so-called "candid" camera is the greatest trickster of all. So far the films have given us no hint
of the record for which we hope with some confidence. So to write
about Martha Graham's dances would be only interesting if the writer
was the equivalent of his subject. It is a pity that the public is so prone
to take what they are given from the daily unequipped and undigested
press, yet one cannot flatly decide there is no valid place for writing about dancing. One is much struck by reading William Butler
Yeats' vindication of his drastic editing of Wilde's *Ballad of Reading
Gaol*: He simply said his own position as a poet permitted it. This
proud statement is irrefutable. We are interested in seeing Dunoyer de
Segonzac's or even Bourdelle's drawings of Isadora Duncan, but who
takes the trouble to read the "Appreciation" of even such genial critics
as Huneker or H. T. Parker? They seem like the quaint testimonials

of lovers. Even a great poet's opinion, like Gauthier's rhapsodies to Fanny Elssler or Taglioni only serve to cause a lifetime's vain work for scholars. What were they *really* like? The most one can do about Graham is to see her. The seeing is at once the supreme satisfaction and the principal praise. The quality so powerful in the visionary realm of space is dilute in speech and faint in print. When Ruth St. Denis or Shankar or Kreutzberg speak of Graham, one can listen with respect. What Isadora would think of her would be fascinating. That Toumanova admires her is interesting, and yet . . .

And yet one must say something, not exactly for the record, not even for one's children who are doomed to the same questions we share about the last generation, but rather as one leaves the theatre saying to people we don't even know—"Wasn't it wonderful?"

The dance and the dramatic stage are pre-eminently the fields of creative art in which women have equalled and can surpass men on their own terms. Three American women have meant more to contemporary dancing than any other three women of any nation, and one can almost say as much as any three other men. Ruth St. Denis showed a new conglomerate nation the dance idioms of all its component peoples in a form which they could credit with intensity and dignity, and she laid the foundation for an interest in the possibility of theatrical dancing on a continent which had suffered from the blasts of puritan hatred for a frank and fluent physicality. Isadora, by the large assertion of her personal vision, gave the idea, if not the form, of dance as an unassailable position for serious endeavor, in terms of an immediate necessity. Martha Graham, in developing a usable technique and a powerful presence, has employed not merely the exotic cultures of the world, nor the vision of a past perfection, but she has, on their foundation, erected a personal classicism and a contemporary expression suitable and equal to her place and time.

Graham's whole achievement is forcefully apparent over the last year. Her technical usages seem as well forged as the group of dancers who have been trained to demonstrate them. The story of her heroic struggle against all sorts of resentments and inertia is very fragmentarily echoed in such opposition as my own. As proof of her arrival, of that arrival free of the necessity to attack further the immediate sources from which she has sprung, and free to create works in the scope of a serene maturity, are two large facts, increasingly obvious.

The first is the least important, but it has its interest. Graham is considered almost an academy by certain dancers and dance enthusiasts who, appreciating her present work, have forgotten the fifteen years of varied experiment, rejection and influence which have gone into smelting her ore into its present ingot. They forget the years of theatrical experience, the time with Denishawn, the investigation of Greece, Mexico, and our own Southwest, the French Gothic, the Far East, and every technical device or innovation available to a dancer. And so when Graham emerges with a new direction or even an accentuation, an extension of an old one, they sometimes accuse her of a change which seems to them a betrayal. They have decided what kind of movement they will expect from her, and if this tendency is not demonstrated as orthodox, she is declared her own first heretic. It was not the most comforting of cynics who said that he loved his friends but he adored his enemies. Every strong artist can resist the head-on attack of their convinced opponents, but the impatient solicitude and insinuating pressure of admirers is even harder to take, particularly when they personally identify one aspect only in the admired artist with the entirety of their admiration.

The other and far more important testimonial of Graham's immediate situation is the work she has presented in the last two years. The pieces for her group are longer, more varied and grow more as dramas danced than as fragmentary dramatic dances. She is the protagonist against a background of her group that is sometimes choral, and sometimes a group that collectively complements her as a balancing soloist. Her use of decor even when it is not completely successful, as with the "Mobiles" of Calder, or Noguchi's forms, shows her intention of presenting a synthesis refusing none of the responsibilities that the theatre offers. The two straight lines that point herself against the segment of the fence-rails in *Frontier* are at once cleanly suggestive and helpful to her dance, enlarging the perspective and at the same time centering her on the stage which is broad plains and a sector of the globe.

It is distressing and confusing to invoke nationalistic qualities as a pre-eminent value in an artist's essence today, particularly when every praise of nationalism seems an affront and a threat to a wider understanding of the peoples of the earth who are fighting to keep their integrity as human beings against the pressure of Fascism. But Martha

Graham has a specifically American quality which cannot be ignored and which must be apparent to everyone. It is not a red, white and blue patriotic exuberance, nor even the naive free-blown boundlessly hopeful openness of the young continent which Europeans always professed to see in Isadora. America has become middle-aged, if not mature in the last twenty years. Graham's connection with our continent is less racial than essential and geographical. She has in *Frontier* much of the courage of Whitman's unachieved dream, but she has also a more realistic and present spirit. By now she has presupposed the ferocious, bland, hysterical puritanism of "Act of Piety" and "Act of Judgment" which Hawthorne would have so completely recognized. She has created a kind of candid, sweeping and wind-worn liberty for her individual expression at once beautiful and useful, like a piece of exquisitely realized Shaker furniture or homespun clothing.

Artists working today are not ignorant of the scope of times through which they live. There have been few occasions in modern history when, due to recent advances in communications and the scientific interpretation of history, artists have been so conscious of their position in relation to the large events smashing around them. But there are very few of these artists, however sincere, who either from lack of skill, talent or concentration, have been equal to the material with which their times provide them. When Martha Graham presented *Immediate Tragedy* she made a keystone masterpiece of the same powerful wave-length as the concatenation of energies operating throughout the world today. The news from Spain in daily cables alternately frightens and thrills us. The battle of Spain is *the* immediate tragedy of our lives, far more so than the Great War. In her dance we do not think of Graham as an exponent of the "modern" dance, or even of dancing at all. But only by the dance can such an intense, clear and sweeping vision be inscribed. In it she is an artist who can presuppose not only a technical mastery which is now as triumphantly universal as it was once aggressively personal, but she is also a conscious creator who has resolved the atmosphere of Spanish history from the Inquisition to Guernica, the temperature of violence and pride, that staggering human pride in which she has erased the means of her art to give us a positive declaration, a revelation of catastrophe and ultimate control.

1937

Popular Style in American Dancing

PROBABLY most people in America acquainted with dancing entirely through films have no preconceived notion of what a dancer should be like. In Europe, however, and in those American capitals where Continental theatrical habits have been imposed, there is a specialized public which expects a certain type of theatrical dancer. Many ballet audiences eagerly expect the stereotype imposed by the Russians of twenty years ago and their present imitators, and any variation of the pattern is rejected as inadmissible not merely in the general line of ballet but in the category of dancing at all. The international-Russian type clothes itself with alien glamor, an atmosphere of charming magnificence, a sex appeal that is consciously formulated and has something to do with the idea that these dancers are more than human, that they have gifts bordering on the divine, and that the audience is privileged to see them at all. That they are incomparable is accepted without question, and the accidental fact of their Slav birth or association brings forgiveness for all their faults, which are frequently serious.

This has had various sad effects. Many talented young American students have consecrated themselves to imitating the inimitable Pavlova and Nijinsky, whom most of them have never seen. When the failure of the imitation has become too apparent for further self-delusion, they have subsided into a patient imitation of third-rate Russian corps de ballet. Worse than this, audiences which have been drugged into believing there is only one pattern, the Slav, have distrusted any variant, and hence made it practically impossible for an earnest American to develop with any integrity in a serious form of the art.

A serious form of the dance is one in which the dancer is presented as of the first importance. You don't get this in movies. What you do get in movies is the presence of a considerable body of American dancers who perform in their unique, indigenous, and creative style. Each one of them has a different and specific quality, yet one can generalize from the group. Instead of setting a stereotype of remoteness, spectral grandeur, and visionary brilliance, the Americans are volatile, intimate, frank, and they have an added theatrical flavor of close proximity to their public. The most important thing about American dancers is the retention of their amateur status and their nearness to the audience. No Russian dancers were ever supposed to be amateurs. We all have heard how their professional life started at the age of nine. In America our national academy has been the dancing-school recital, gymnasiums decorated for proms, night-club floors, and vaudeville stages. The frontier spirit of spontaneous collective entertainment where everybody got up and danced as they could still persists. But with a difference. Our dancing artists have selected and amplified all that is most useful in the amateur spirit to make of it a conscious and brilliant frame for their individual theatrical projection.

Even now it seems as if Fred Astaire had not been out of college very long, and Hal Le Roy is still cutting up at Sigma Chi dances. Eleanor Powell is a triumph of the girl-scout ideal. The college angle cuts across the ballroom slant in Ginger Rogers. Paul Draper's elegance and musicality stem from the tradition of Vernon Castle and the Crystal Room at the Ritz. None of them seem in any way alien or strange to us. Buddy Ebsen is the incarnation of the foot-loose hick or the dancing sailor, a variation on Buster West's neater, more stylized, but less dramatic work of some years ago. Ray Bolger reverses Walt Disney's formula by being a dancer for whom there must first have been a drawing like Dopey or Donald Duck, with his kindly, insane personality and accomplished eccentricity. There are many others.

The time will come when their strong technique and intense charm will be used in other than a fragmentary, incidental, or merely diverting way. But it is up to the audience to recognize it for what it is worth, to make the just comparisons with other dancers in other forms, and to take the Russians side by side with our own artists for what they are worth. The Americans will not suffer by it.

April 16, 1938

Balanchine and the Waltz

BALANCHINE'S present canonization of the Viennese waltz has been anticipated by many exercises in the form over fifty years. A student, first in the former Russian, then the Soviet State School, he was taught the waltz both as a social and theatrical dance. Marius Petipa and other ballet-masters of the nineteenth century had seen what was once a specifically German country-dance evolving into the dominant ballroom specialty of the Viennese, theatricalized into the splendid compositions of Delibes and Tschaikovsky.

For Les Ballets 1933, a small but elegant company appearing at the Théâtre des Champs-Elysées, under the aegis of Edward James, Balanchine composed for Tilly Losch, the Viennese mime and dancer (and wife of James) *Les Valses de Beethoven*, a series of brilliant short pieces in which the waltz was projected past the "German" dances of Mozart, toward the full orchestral development of Weber and the Strauss family. Emilio Terry, a Cuban architect allied to the then innovative school of Surrealism, invented a monochromatic decor in the manner of a baroque architectural rendering with an anthropomorphic fireplace. Balanchine's perverse and provocative dances had a strange charm, but at the time, the revival of so unfamiliar a score seemed deliberately arrogant to Parisian critics who recalled that Diaghilev had rejected Ravel's *La Valse* as undanceable, and which even La Nijinska had failed to bring to a triumph for Ida Rubinstein at the Grand Opera.

In the year following came Balanchine's American debut, and for fledgling students of his newly-founded School of American Ballet, he composed a work, still notable in the repertory, and for many years, one identified as the "signature" ballet for his companies. Tschaikovsky's *Serenade for Strings* pursued the extension of waltz themes through a series of inter-related variations, *pas de deux* (and *trois*). This was a Russian ballet built for American dancers: save in solo portions, the girls were unpartnered. This was a theatrical abstraction with no relation to the social dance of Viennese ballrooms. However, a swinging fluidity and graciousness, combined with its poignant melancholy and sense of lyric purity, has kept it on stage for forty years, and it has joined the body of works performed all over the world.

When Balanchine's original American Ballet Company came to serve the Metropolitan Opera Association on 39th Street for three years commencing in 1935, his first new work was a sprightly popular piece to music from *Die Fledermaus* and other Johann Strauss, Jr., polkas, mazurkas and waltzes. It was memorable for the personification of the eponymous "Bat" itself, made up of a girl and boy entwined, each supporting one huge barbed and spangled bat's wing of black silk, hovering over the ballroom, separating and reuniting the dancers. Later, in 1941, with Robert Stolz, composer of the popular *Zwei Herzen in Drei Viertel Takt* (Two Hearts in Three-quarter Time), as conductor, Balanchine staged *Die Fledermaus* as a whole (renamed *Rosalinda*), which had a considerable run in repertory with *The Merry Widow*, which he also produced for the New Opera Company. He used his own dancers trained at his School. The boys wore balletic versions of formal ballroom frock-coats, the girls were on point. The dances had the special lightness and effervescence of the genre, which was something fresher than the commercial theater ordinarily offered at the time, for the classic idiom was pronounced and the ballets were interwoven into the dramatic action.

In 1944, when his own company was in wartime abeyance, Balanchine staged for Ballet Theatre *Waltz Academy* to music by his friend Vittorio Rieti, in a handsome architectural setting by Oliver Smith, suggesting the domed attic practice-room of a French opera house. The formal exposition of a variety of waltzes seemed somewhat professorial or didactic in Rieti's pastiche of Rossini, despite its considerable sophistication and wit. It might have done better a decade later. The waltz, however, was never remote from Balanchine's practice and he invented a number of disparate pieces by Glinka (1953) and Glazounov (1960) alongside the annual ceremonial of the *Valse des Fleurs* (Waltz of the Flowers) (1954), which remains the ensemble climax of Act II of *The Nutcracker.*

In 1951, in the face of Diaghilev's unforgotten disapproval, Balanchine produced Ravel's *La Valse*, which the composer had imagined more as a vision of the glories of the Tuileries and Compiègne, the world of the second Napoleonic empire, than the Vienna of Franz Joseph. This was a Frenchified Austria and its intensely melodramatic treatment had a sinister atmosphere of foreboding which was prefaced by the orchestration of Ravel's earlier suite, *Valses Nobles et Sentimentales. La Valse* remains one of the choreographer's most admired ballets, and its debut was distinguished by the exquisite dancing of Tanaquil Le Clercq, the powerful miming of Francisco Moncion and the delicate and generous partnering of the late, deeply-lamented Nicholas Magallanes. *La Valse* is danced, a quarter of a century after its inception, alongside Balanchine's latest recension of the waltz.

In 1960, at the considerable insistence of the late Morton Baum, who had a special attachment to the score, Balanchine set the twin series of Brahms' *Liebeslieder Walzer* (which this very spring he is mounting for the Vienna Staatsoper Ballet). This was a domesticated, intimate, yet operatic presentation of an elegant variety of partner-ings, duets, trios, quartets and their inversions, a girl and boy, a boy and two girls, with all the changes rung on their entrances and exits. It was the dance enshrined in a private house, rather than in the splen-dor of ballroom or court, and the combination of voices supporting and balancing the dances gave yet another example of Balanchine's continual rehabilitation of the commonplace.

The etymology of the word waltz is obscure, but the German *walz-ender tänze* seems to involve the root *vel*, to turn, and *welle*, wave, possible roots of the English "wheel"; the movement infers slide rather than hop. The transformation of the waltz from rude country-dance of folk-gatherings, with its thumping triple beat, to the taffeta flow of an easy high-society in the dusk of the Austro-Hungarian empire, forms a magical gloss on the history of social dance-music. The shift from village green to ballroom, from bounce and lift to the seam-less fluency launched from polished floors, from village bands to the supremacy of the great Viennese band-masters, marks chapters from feudal peasantry through the industrial revolution, and the rise of a middle class through the decline of imperialism through two world wars. At the hands of Joseph Lanner and the family Strauss (father and sons), primitive forms developed into an extended metric, character-ized by one chord, plus one real pulse in the bar which appears as a base-note with chord groups on the second and third quarter-notes. The second quarter-note of the accompaniment is slightly anticipated in the playing, and there are further marked variants, in which a bal-ance of the onward flow of movement hesitates as an accent. The waltz is fast, slow, moderate, capable of endless ornamentation, with a dis-tinctive prosody of its own, ranging from the elegiac to the hectic or near-hysterical. In his autobiography, Richard Wagner wrote of the younger Strauss' conducting:

> I shall never forget the extraordinary playing of Johann Strauss, who put equal enthusiasm into everything he played and very often made the audience almost frantic with delight.
> At the beginning of a new waltz this demon of the Viennese musical spirit shook like a Pythian priestess on her tripod,

and veritable groans of ecstasy raised their worship of the magic violinist to almost bewildering heights of frenzy.

Balanchine's new large-scale ballet, *Vienna Waltzes*, owes something to familiarity, over a long period, with the inspired conducting of Herbert von Karajan, whose commitment to the classic traditions of Viennese lyricism has been the criterion of his epoch. While both Mozart and Beethoven contributed to the full breadth of the form, and while there are wonderful pieces for dancing by Lanner, Waldteufel, Leo Fall and Oskar Strauss, Balanchine has limited himself to but three archetypal composers, representing the ballroom dance at its peak, the theatricalized social dance tailored for light opera, and the apotheosis of the dance by the last of the great Viennese operatic masters.

Johann Strauss, the younger, may be almost imagined as the Franz Joseph of the waltz, the king-emperor who saw himself as an epitome of the high-bourgeoisie, a king-incognito, whose private dinners at Sacher's were the talk of the town, and yet who presided over the ballrooms of the Hofburg and Schönbrunn in all his imperial dignity as the nation's paterfamilias. Franz Lehár discovered a magical world of Central European princelings and glamorous widows. His light operas became the source of dance music for the whole world before they were supplanted by the concertizing jazz-band. Finally, the *Rosenkavalier* waltzes of Richard Strauss are one of the most fascinating and bewildering of stylistic anachronisms. Ostensibly set in the epoch of Maria Theresa in the mid-eighteenth century, his waltzes derive from Joseph, Johann Strauss' gifted brother, and recapitulate the atmospheric development of the form from its birth through its final efflorescence and decadence. These are lovesongs, to dance itself, to the city which danced them into being, and to a civilization whose ancient vitality and splendor had passed, but whose very decline was a celebration of heartbreak transcended.

In New York's Museum of Modern Art, there is a landscape of the Vienna woods by the great Austrian painter Gustav Klimt. Only very recently has his unique vision come to typify the whole epoch of the city at the end of the last century and the start of our own. Now it is recognized as equally powerful as the *fin de siècle* of Toulouse-Lautrec in Paris or Aubrey Beardsley in London. Klimt decorated the

Burgtheater with splendid murals of singers and dancers; the magical patchwork mosaic of his Byzantine backgrounds form an extraordinary frame for psychological portraits which are resonant of a capital town in its Alexandrian decline, a city which was the seed-bed of Freud, and von Hofmannsthal, Berg, Webern, Schönberg, and Schiele. Rouben Ter-Arutunian has steeped himself in the linear patterns and brushwork of Klimt and in the geometric intricacies of the Wienerwerkstätte. In this Vienna the baroque of Fischer von Erlach and the Kaiserstadt had gone with the long-abandoned minuet. Buda and Pesht were vestigial memories. The colors of the Rose Cavalier, a soprano in satin breeches, the last heir of Mozart's Cherubino, were white, black and silver, reflected in mirrors. Balanchine has filled Ter-Arutunian's tall ballroom with a maelstrom of couples, whose movements are echoed in reflected light off shimmering glazed surfaces.

Balanchine's choreography is almost a mathematical exposition of the metric of the waltz and its plastic motion. The patterns proliferate as if by cell-division. The forward lift of the dance, its *vorheit*, its one-two *and* three, the elasticity of anticipated accents, prompts the initiative of the man supporting the swing, glide and turn of his receptive partner. The design not only embraces couples, but couples who, as doubled partners, turn into variants of quartets and sextets, with single figures threading through the waves of action. The units redistribute themselves in a ceaseless swing and flow, the movement echoing itself on the floor as it is reflected in the mirrors. In critical moments, Balanchine has used the *atempause*, the "breathing pause," an infinitesimal break on a marked beat which gives vastly greater impulse to the beat which follows. Amplified into the monumental, the final waltz fragments itself before the end, into a tremendous recapitulation, fusing memories and melodies of earlier forms. Before this, Balanchine had analyzed the spiky fragments of Webern *(Episodes*, 1959) and Schönberg (*Opus 34*, 1954). The acid clarity, harshness and absence of conventional lyricism, the triumph of neurosis and obsession were the logical consequence of defeat and disaster. Now, Balanchine has jumped backwards in time, and has made from the almost over-familiar melodies of the ballroom a strong and novel statement of the waltz, its structure and ambiance.

1977

Anna Kisselgoff (1938–)

A RECIPIENT of Denmark's Order of the Dannebrog, France's Order of Arts and Letters, and Iceland's Order of the Falcon for her writing on dance, Anna Kisselgoff was born in Paris and grew up in New York, where she studied ballet with Valentina Belova and Jean (Ivan) Yazvinsky, a dancer in Diaghilev's Ballets Russes. After first reporting on dance in Paris, she joined *The New York Times* in 1968, becoming its staff dance critic in 1977, a post she held until 2005. During her years on staff, she filed in-depth interviews on every dancer, choreographer, and company director of substance in the Western Hemisphere, Russia, and Western Europe, among them Boris Kochno, Galina Ulanova, Maya Plisetskaya, and Ninette de Valois. Outside the *Times*, her writings on George Balanchine appeared in publications in Europe and America, and her writings on other dance subjects appeared in anthologies from New York to Beijing. A graduate of Bryn Mawr College, she holds an M.A. in European history and an M.S. in journalism, both from Columbia University.

Introduction to *Bronislava Nijinska: Early Memoirs*

IT IS hardly an exaggeration to suggest that this is the book about Vaslav Nijinsky for which the world has waited for more than half a century. Written by the person closest to Nijinsky in his formative years, Bronislava Nijinska's early memoirs provide an unprecedented insight into the personality and creative development of this great dancer and choreographer.

As his sister, she writes totally and most revealingly from the inside—from the heart of the Nijinsky family as it has never been revealed before. At the same time, she speaks as an internationally known creative figure in her own right, opening up new aspects in the history of Russia's Imperial Maryinsky Ballet and Serge Diaghilev's Ballets Russes. It is important to remember that the young dancer in this volume became one of Diaghilev's choreographers, sealing her distinguished reputation with *Les Noces* in 1923 and *Les Biches* in 1924.

A loving sister and a major artist with a firm aesthetic viewpoint, Bronislava Nijinska might be expected to approach her subject with no more objectivity than Nijinsky's other biographers. His contemporaries and colleagues, with few exceptions, have left self-servingly inaccurate accounts, colored by the vested interests of their own reputations. Others who did not know him—recent historians, chiefly—have been prone to concern themselves with illustrating artistic or psychological theses.

Nijinska's own account is certainly subjective. Its very value rests precisely upon its highly personal nature. No secondhand narrative could match the intimacy of her detailed eyewitness recollections. In human terms, this is a profoundly moving book. Its emotional range has the breadth of a Russian novel.

The enormous amount of information that Nijinska conveys at so many levels also turns this book into a prime historical source. One of its important disclosures is embodied in the actual descriptions of Nijinsky's dancing. For the first time, this technical information has survived into print. Nijinska names not only the steps in his performances but also describes how they were executed. Coached and taught by her brother in private classes, Nijinska is uniquely qualified to analyze the physical basis of his extraordinary technique. Those who ascribe to mere legend the report that Nijinsky could perform the rare virtuoso feat of *entrechat-dix* need only refer to the many occasions when Nijinska saw him execute these multiple leg beats in the studio.

Nijinska is capable of explaining the previously unexplainable—the special training and anatomical features that enabled her brother to acquire his exceptional jump. She is always concerned, however, with communicating the artistic intent and imagery of her brother's dancing.

If there is an overriding theme in this book, it is Nijinska's insistence upon the aesthetic creed of the Nijinskys—namely, that artistry and creativity must not be sacrificed to technique.

This was the emblem as well of the great artistic enterprise known as Diaghilev's Ballets Russes. Yet an important leitmotiv of Nijinska's story is her belief that she and Vaslav instinctively sought an artistic direction before either ever encountered Diaghilev.

This complex assertion rests upon four major aspects of these memoirs. The first is the picture of Vaslav Nijinsky himself. The second is Nijinska's portrait of Diaghilev, involving eyewitness accounts that flesh out this other legendary figure's character. Another major element of this story is the insider's view of a crucial period in the history of ballet—the transition from the nineteenth-century academicism of Marius Petipa to the expressiveness of Mikhail Fokine and the modernism of Nijinsky's choreography. Although this ground has been well trod, Nijinska freshly records the atmosphere in the Imperial Theatres and in the Ballets Russes, directing attention to the personalities and ballets supplying that atmosphere. Finally, these are the memoirs of Bronislava Nijinska, documenting her own growth as an artist, and replete with personal revelations.

There are also two special aspects to this volume that reach beyond its focus on the Nijinsky family. The first is contained in new information about ballet in provincial pre-Revolutionary Russia, and the second is its picture of life in Russia at the turn of the century.

In chronicling her parents' careers as itinerant dancers in the Russian Empire, Nijinska fills an important gap in ballet history unfamiliar to the West. English-language biographies of Italian dancers such as Virginia Zucchi and Enrico Cecchetti, who appeared in Russia's private theatres, have already demonstrated that a degree of ballet activity existed outside the Imperial Theatres. Yet the common image of nineteenth-century Russian ballet is that of the Imperial Ballet, restricted to two official government ballet academies attached to two ranking companies—the Maryinsky in St. Petersburg and the Bolshoi in Moscow—and all supported by the Imperial household. The idea that Russian ballet was an aristocratic entertainment stems from this administrative network. But it does not take into account the kinds of ballet to which Russians of other classes were exposed.

In vivid descriptions of the ballets and ballet pantomimes choreographed and performed by her parents, Nijinska reveals the wide-ranging state of the art form within Russia. It was common to find ballet in the municipal opera houses of major provincial cities such as Kiev and Odessa; in resort towns with their summer theatres; and even, as her father's career amply demonstrated, in the circuses.

It is doubtful that the level of dancing and choreography in these private companies met the highest standards of the Imperial Theatres, yet such conclusions must be tempered by Nijinska's own esteem for these performances. As she points out, such touring companies were often headed by the same Italian ballerinas who appeared at the Imperial Theatres. Her mother had danced in a troupe with Carlotta Brianza, the first Aurora in *The Sleeping Beauty*, and had absorbed a degree of Italian training. Nijinska's appraisal of her father—from the viewpoint of adoring daughter but also, perhaps, of an artist—ranks him as a great character dancer who chose not to enter the Imperial Theatres. It should also be remembered that the Warsaw Great (Wielki) Theatre, which supplied these private touring companies with their *corps de ballet*, would later provide Diaghilev with many of his own dancers.

The repertory on this touring circuit was on a popular level, but the classics could filter down in different versions. This was the period when the Imperial Ballet was going into decline. Nijinska's enthusiasm for her father's choreography is thus understandable beyond the context of filial attachment. Thomas Nijinsky knew how to hold an audience. His ballets were not classical, but the variety of idioms he incorporated into his presentations left its imprint upon his children.

Indeed, another significant discovery of this book is its proof of the amazing extent to which Bronislava and Vaslav Nijinsky were exposed at a young age to nonclassical forms of dance. It is not so surprising that they learned Ukrainian and Polish dances, social dances, and a variety of character dances from their parents. But an unexpected encounter is their exposure to a black American tap-dancing team named Jackson and Johnson, complete with cane and tails, in the same theatre in which their father worked. And circus life, as Nijinska notes, provided a valuable store of idiosyncratic movement that she could utilize creatively much later in her ballets for Diaghilev.

It would be wrong, then, to think of the sheltered life of the Maryinsky School as the only dance world the Nijinsky children had experienced. Unlike their classmates, they had seen more open horizons. In view of the modernist choreographers they became—in view of their break with academic forms—we can now take into account their early awareness of a multitude of movement possibilities.

Although of Polish descent, Nijinska writes as a Russian. She has a typical love for the Russian countryside, whose beauty she captures in vivid nature descriptions. St. Petersburg is her beloved city, and her picture of everyday urban existence is a kaleidoscope of carefully observed detail. Her view of Russian life is panoramic: the colorfulness of a summer spent next door to gypsies and Cossacks is juxtaposed with the splendor of a princely mansion belonging to Vaslav's benefactor.

Although these memoirs constitute the first part of Nijinska's autobiography, they serve largely as a new biography of Vaslav Nijinsky. The usual depiction of a slow-witted youth, silent or sullen, molded artistically by Diaghilev, is at odds with Bronislava's portrait. The Vaslav in this book is a child filled with excess energy, deeply marked—like his sister—by the emotional trauma of his parents' separation and, later, by his elder brother's mental illness.

Vaslav's development cannot be separated from the family background here provided for the first time in anything close to such depth. Nor should one overlook the insights Nijinska offers into her brother's personality. His early aloofness in the Maryinsky, she asserts, was actually an attempt to avoid putting on airs. He is shown to have grown up well-read and with a perfect ear for music. There is no doubt in Bronislava's view that he was as creatively inclined in his dancing as in his choreography. His reinterpretation of the Blue Bird *pas de deux*, involving his adoption of a new costume, showed his independence even within the fossilized traditions of the Imperial Ballet.

Among the most valuable pages in this volume are those concerned with Nijinsky's work on his first three ballets, *L'Après-Midi d'un Faune, Jeux*, and *Le Sacre du Printemps*. It is Nijinska's brilliant insight that this was the first time a choreographer had demanded total exactitude from his dancers, requiring that every part of the body be aligned to gain maximum expressiveness. Her image here is of a sophisticated creative artist, knowing exactly what he wished to accomplish.

Nijinska presents new versions of certain episodes crucial to Nijinsky's life. Her account of his dismissal from the Imperial Theatres, with its implication that Mathilda Kshessinska's entourage was involved,

differs from earlier narratives. The disclosure that Nijinsky was classified as a deserter because he could not gain exemption from military
service explains why he could not return to Russia. Of further illumination is Diaghilev's inactivity on her brother's behalf on this issue.

While Nijinska was not a member of Diaghilev's inner circle, her
personal account contributes new and valid information, particularly
with respect to the artistic impetus of the Ballets Russes' first years,
and its director's later treatment of her brother. In this regard, Diaghilev's avant-garde reputation emerges as less adventuresome than
usual. This is the Diaghilev uneasy about Nijinsky's choreographic
innovations and all too ready to listen to advice that Nijinsky's ballets
are bad box office and should be withdrawn.

Yet in her comparison of the lack of artistic ambience in the Imperial Theatres and the stimulation of the Ballets Russes, Nijinska recognizes her generation's debt to Diaghilev. These are pages replete
with information about the Petipa ballets and the genesis of works
that became part of the Diaghilev repertory. It was Bronislava, for
example, who suggested to Fokine that the Street Dancer's solo in
Petrouchka be a parody of Kshessinska.

Among the book's personal revelations, Nijinska's relationship with
Feodor Chaliapin emerges as a motif to her development as an artist
during the first years of the Ballets Russes. The full autobiographical
story of her own career, however, is contained in another set of her
memoirs, continuing from the 1914 close of this book.

Despite her attraction to Diaghilev's modernism, Nijinska's choreography proved her eventually to be a pioneer of twentieth-century
neoclassicism. Many of her theatrical concepts were taken over by
others. She did the original ballet versions of Ravel's *Bolero* and *La
Valse*, also Stravinsky's *Le Baiser de la Fée*, and she danced the role of
the Faune in her brother's ballet after the period described here. In
1934, she portrayed Hamlet in her own ballet of the same name.

After leaving Diaghilev, she worked in a variety of ballet companies in South America, Europe and the United States. She headed her
own company, the Théâtre de la Danse, in Paris in 1932–34 but she
did not, in the end, attach herself to a permanent institution whose
artistic profile would be identified with her own. Nonetheless, if the
public could not always be sure to find her ballets in the same place,
her influence was keenly felt by the key figures of contemporary bal-

let. Among them was Frederick Ashton, who was a young dancer in Ida Rubinstein's company in 1928 when Nijinska was its choreographer. Today, as one great neoclassical choreographer paying tribute to another, he reaffirms the unwavering opinion of Nijinska he has held since that initial encounter: "She was a genius, one of the very few."

1981

LAURA LEIVICK (1950–)

OHIO NATIVE Laura Leivick studied classical ballet with Frederic Franklin at the National Ballet School, in Washington, D.C., and English literature at the University of California, Berkeley. In 1981, she designed and presented public ballet history programs as part of Nancy van Norman Baer's landmark "Pavlova" exhibition at the Fine Arts Museums of San Francisco in the California Palace of the Legion of Honor, which celebrated the centenary of Pavlova's birth. The essay here dates from the era of that exhibition. Since the mid-1980s, Leivick has lived in New York, where she has worked as an editor for magazines and published essays and reviews on dance, literature, and related cultural subjects in *The New York Times*, *The Wall Street Journal*, and other leading periodicals.

Miss Brodie's Swan

IN A public television serialization of Muriel Spark's *The Prime of Miss Jean Brodie*, Miss Brodie's select pupils at the Marcia Blaine School for Girls are accused of lacking team spirit. It is the eve of a local performance by the ballerina Anna Pavlova's touring troupe. On Miss Brodie's classroom wall hangs the most appetizing photograph ever made of the great dancer in costume for her *Dying Swan* solo, arms entwined *en couronne*, head cocked, face dipping languorously into deep shadow, expression almost shrewd. The cut of Pavlova's features and limbs repeats a tapering hypnotic curve, like half a heart. Flanked by this icon of her heroine, the subversive Miss Brodie tells the little girls the truth: team spirit is for the *corps de ballet*.

Team spirit was not Pavlova's strong suit; she was in general no subscriber to schoolgirl ethics. She was born in 1881 an outsider, the illegitimate daughter of a laundress and a Jewish nobleman. She dissembled about her age and parentage, professed Russian Orthodox Christianity, and practiced a personal inventory of superstition. She was an early partisan of the upstart choreographer Fokine, and with him a leading figure in the notorious 1905 ballet strike in St. Petersburg. Her nastiest biographer, Oleg Kerensky, matches the successful progress of her career at the Maryinsky to a succession of liaisons with powerful men: the Maryinsky director's nephew, a ballet critic, a general, and a prince. She settled at last on Victor Dandré, a wealthy member of the St. Petersburg Duma.

Pavlova enlisted in two foreign tours before dancing Fokine's works in the legendary 1909 Paris season of Diaghilev's Ballets Russes. A Valentin Serov painting of her in motion was on the poster; Levinson wrote rhapsodically of her Jewish, almost Oriental ardor and her Russian lyricism. In each area, the Ballets Russes presented her competition: the exotic Ida Rubenstein, the grave and gentle young Tamara Karsavina. Pavlova reportedly fainted when the audience shouted more enthusiastically for her partner Nijinsky during their curtain calls. She backed out of the title role in Fokine's *Firebird*, designed as her vehicle for the 1910 season, pronouncing Stravinsky's music horrid. She assembled a touring company of her own, alternating between it, the Maryinsky, and Diaghilev's company. The Maryinsky fined her for her prolonged absences. In London, she booked an engagement in direct competition with Diaghilev's season. In 1911, Victor Dandré, who had apparently taken to embezzlement of municipal funds to support Pavlova and her enterprises, was accused of so doing. Pavlova severed her connections with Diaghilev, bailed out Dandré, and installed him as her manager. In an interview published in the twenties, Diaghilev compared Pavlova to his ballerina Spessivtseva at the former's expense. Introduced to the British critic Arnold Haskell, Pavlova asked him point-blank, "Are you on my side or Diaghilev's?" Haskell said the issue was "the triumph of the individual" versus the spirit of cooperation.

In 1916, Pavlova acted the title role in Universal Pictures' feature *The Dumb Girl of Portici*, which, at $250,000, was hyped by the studio as the most expensive production ever. Pavlova's fee was $50,000. She said film could not even properly record her costumes; however, she continued to have films of her dancing made privately. Serge Lifar, later ousted from the Paris Opera for his alleged collaboration with the Nazis, said Pavlova acted as a Russian spy while on tour during the First World War. Two of the rare articles published under Pavlova's name in the twenties were ghost-written by Vera Caspary, later known for writing murder mysteries and screenplays. Many of the famous full-length photographs of Pavlova *en pointe* were extensively retouched about the feet. Her colleague Madame Felia Doubrovska said the ballerina would not let anyone examine her toe shoes. She was a mysterious and domineering figure to her *corps de ballet* girls, some of whom she had selected and trained from childhood at her home in their native England. She gave them Russian stage names and billed them as "Pavlova's Incomparable Ballet Russe." Kerensky says they referred to her as "X"; it is said that the best of them were occasionally, without notice, substituted for Pavlova in performances.

Victor Dandré lived with and managed Pavlova from 1911 until her death on tour in The Hague in 1931. They claimed to have married; as yet no marriage certificate has surfaced. The missing document deprived Dandré of any portion of her estate. Dandré wrote a reverential biography of Pavlova, and pieced together film clips into a short feature used to raise money for a Pavlova memorial.

Miss Brodie, who shared with the dancer a demimondaine sense of personal honor somewhat exaggerated by her detractors, was probably unfamiliar with these gritty items from the Pavlova dossier. No matter how research amends it, the original received picture is significant in its pleasing pungency. This complex, vivid, selfish Pavlova seems to have developed in the business while her pious civilian fans were promoting a pallid Immortal Swan.

This tender fowl was the legitimate child of Pavlova's repertory and popular culture. In the aesthetics of her self-presentation, the ballerina approached an insipid schoolgirl ideal. Her dances, all specially tailored or choreographed vehicles, traded on morbid pathos, sentimentality, coquetry, folk charm, and pretty exoticism. She impersonated a Fairy Doll, a Snowflake, a Fading Rose, a Poppy at sundown, a nineteenth-century ingénue at a ball, poor duped Giselle, Columbine, La Peri (Servant of the Pure), the forsaken Gypsy Esmeralda, a Dragonfly, the goddess Flora, a Chrysanthemum discarded by a Poet, a Spanish innkeeper's daughter, a Greek maiden in figured draperies, a Russian peasant, an eighteenth-century lady at a ball, and so on.

That her repertory and company were not first-rate is a matter of record. Haskell uses the passive voice to mitigate Pavlova's responsibility for the situation: "She was all her life associated with mediocrity—in music, décor, and by comparison in the company in which she danced—but she herself was never anything but great." Agnes de Mille holds Pavlova responsible:

"She rough-housed and savaged the music for any effect she wanted. And the choreography—oh God! the choreography! Her own inventions, *California Poppy, Autumn Leaves, Blue Danube Waltz*, were probably the silliest and most tasteless items I have ever seen. She was incapable of creative imagination. And in the dances tailored for her, the Gavotte, *Coquetries of Columbine, Don Quixote, Dragonfly*, she made use over and over again of a barren string of five ballet steps."

Some say Pavlova willfully chose this mediocre presentation in order to enhance her own dancing by contrast; others, that Dandré put her up to it. It is clear instead that she was absolutely sincere in taste that was execrable according to the standards of art as opposed to popular culture. Yet every arbiter of the standards of art came to worship at her feet. Few had de Mille's courage; most could not resist patronizing or excusing the ballerina's métier and mythos, and so distinguishing themselves from her common audiences.

Pavlova was a ladies' favorite, a conservatives' darling. She danced at Red Cross benefits and operated a home for displaced Russian girls. She and her ballet master Ivan Clustine did three how-to ballroom dances for 1915 *Ladies Home Journals*. These dances were to have been designed by the fashionably insouciant Castles, but the *Journal* readership objected. Pavlova's dances included a ladylike waltz and a decorative gavotte; the editors described the numbers as "suitable for home use." An Australian hostess invented the Pavlova, a passion fruit and meringue dessert, in honor of the visiting ballerina; ladies' magazines ran the recipe. Pavlova posed for publicity stills in chic modest fashions, in meditative poses with lilies, riding a camel, playing with dogs, elephants, swans. In mid-praise for Pavlova's fierce personal loyalty, generosity, and indomitable will to dance, her protégée Muriel Stuart complained that "the books (only) talk about her love of flowers and puppy dogs and things like that."

Pavlova did not intimidate the innocent. Her matinees drew mothers and tots in droves. As she bourréed out to die the death of the Swan in London, a child exclaimed, "O Mummy! See the dear little white duck!" The child Ninette de Valois impersonated Pavlova's Swan at dancing school recitals; the child Alicia Markova (Lilian Alicia Marks) was coolly presented by her mother as "The Miniature Pavlova."

The ballerina's looks were an asset in this context. She was slim, exquisite, interesting, elegant rather than grand. "Men like ballerinas who are beautiful and more *'belle femme,'*" she explained. "Women (look at me and) say, 'Look how thin and tender she is. She probably has a good heart and is very nice.'" Lincoln Kirstein dryly describes the Pavlova of Legat's caricature as "thin to a degree." Frederick Ashton thought her flat-out "ugly" when she was not performing. Dr. Nadine Payot, moved by the pathetic offstage contrast between the dancer's aging face and youthful body, developed a line of preservative cosmetics.

Pavlova's dancing was eccentric and personal; she predated the Apollonian ideal for female technique that took hold in post-Revolutionary Russia, and the Western ethic of subordinating self to choreography. Yet she was the first to open, clarify, and elongate the classical body line; as Mme. Doubrovska said, "she appeared very tall . . . she was *allongée.*" This expansiveness replaced "womanly charms." On the many films of her that survive, her *pointe* work appears utterly delicate and natural: she alights on one *pointe* without registering impact and takes flight again without effort. She invented a few *pointe* maneuvers, among them a transfiguration of a child on a scooter: revolutions on one fixed *pointe*, subtly propelled by touches of the other to the floor close by. She was insufficiently turned out. She tended to not quite straighten her knees; this flaw gave her work an odd informality and bounce. Her turns were sudden, impetuous, and few. Yet she realized ballet's ideal of unnatural motion, movement not under the jurisdiction of the laws of physics: the slow-motion film of her *Rondino* is equally exquisite run forward or backward. Costumes and props she brilliantly manipulated to color and extend a dance, never allowing them to become interesting in themselves or to seem mere embellishments.

With her middlebrow repertory, her pretty wedding-cake costumes, her acceptable mystique, and her missionary zeal in touring, Pavlova made herself the first and indelible ballet dancer in the experience of many thousands worldwide. She did not seek the subtle appreciation of connoisseurs, although she graciously accepted it as her due. Her programs generated a world, and her will drew audiences inside. Her stated aim was "to help them forget for one hour the sadness of life": it was hard to object. Once seated in the theater, audiences were faced with an aesthetic spectrum, not a hierarchy. Her loony Dragonfly was beautiful, the Swan's shudders were beautiful. Her eager gaiety was nearly Dionysian. Carl Van Vechten tells how, at the Metropolitan, the end of the Bacchanale *pas de deux*, "in which Pavlova was finally swept to the earth, held the audience in tense silence for a moment after it was over." Agnes de Mille scoffs, "Corn? Thunder and fire." In the *Dying Swan*, Pavlova dared be grotesque: Tobi Tobias writes of the "almost incantatory arms," of an overall impression at once "savage and pathetic." Her mad scene regularly overpowered productions of *Giselle*. The great dancer was not an object of intelligible desire; she traded in inspiration and she bore witness.

After the class attends Pavlova's matinee, Miss Brodie has her young pupils over for tea. They sit stricken. The teacher has been prodding one of these credulous girls to dream of being a ballerina. Now that she has seen Pavlova, Miss Brodie suggests, the girl may be inspired to dance for them. The other children clamor in agreement. The object of Miss Brodie's ambition declines firmly, without explanation. Miss Brodie smiles like a cat: Pavlova has given a little girl courage, if only the courage to stand firm against the spirit of cooperation.

1981

José Limón (1908–1972)

BORN IN Mexico, the eldest of twelve children, José Arcadio Limón moved with his family to the southwestern United States, ultimately landing in Los Angeles, in 1915. He had expected to become a painter, first attending UCLA as an art major and then, in 1928, traveling to New York to study at the New York School of Design. The next year, he was taken by a girlfriend to a dance performance of the German duo Harald Kreutzberg and Yvonne Georgi. Kreutzberg was especially impressive, and, overnight, it was Goodbye painting! Hello dance! After less than a year as a student in New York's Doris Humphrey–Charles Weidman school, Limón was dancing on Broadway and choreographing his first work, a duet with Letitia Ide. By the time he was drafted into the United States Army, in 1943, he had been chosen as one of the first fellows in the Bennington Festival, at Mills College; performed in Humphrey–Weidman concerts and shows; and danced in two Broadway productions choreographed by George Balanchine (*Keep Off the Grass* and *Rosalinda*, where he performed with the outstanding ballerina Mary Ellen Moylan). This man was born to dance!

In 1946, Limón finally became a United States citizen and founded his own modern dance company, with Doris Humphrey as artistic director. (By 1968, with considerable foresight, he added a companion foundation and institute to oversee the licensing of his dances—the first such instrument established by one of the major moderns.) Known for his intense and vigorous dance-dramas, which spring from an encompassing empathy, often labelled humanism—notably his 1949 quartet *The Moor's Pavane* (a distillation of Shakespeare's *Othello*)—Limón also mastered the art of what dancers today call "dancey-dances" for both groups (*Mazurkas, There Is a Time*) and soloists (*Dances for Isadora, Chaconne*). The beguiling cameo of Martha Graham and large, sensitive word-portrait of Humphrey's work in the writing below come from Limón's *Unfinished Memoir*, edited by Lynn Garafola.

(from) *An Unfinished Memoir*

ONE NIGHT after the performance I came face to face for the first time with a legend. I had accompanied Doris and Charles to a restaurant for supper and found that Martha Graham and Louis Horst were to join us. Remembering my first encounter with Graham, I was terrified and tried to find some pretext for escaping. To no avail. I had to sit in the presence of this strange woman who, over the years, was to frighten and fascinate me. On this occasion I listened to the conversation tongue-tied. I remember her commenting on the opera and on the dances. "Your dancing, Doris, I was moved to tears by it." It took years for me to treat this great artist as human, to see her as a warm, loving, fellow being. I had watched her repeatedly in *Primitive Mysteries*. Her performance had a gemlike, diamond-hard perfection. Costumed in stiff, immaculate white organdy, she moved among her dancers as an infinitely remote planet moves in its orbit. The dance, a masterpiece of the American dance, was also evocative of astronomical perfections. It was cold, so cold, and distant.

Doris called her new work, when it was finished, *New Dance*. It was the product of a mind that other times would have designated as "masculine." In those times women were deemed the inferior sex and denied the challenge of education. Oxford, Salamanca, and the Sorbonne were closed to them, and science and art were the exclusive prerogative of the male. On rare occasions a female would miraculously break the fetters that bound her sex and astound an incredulous world. Thus, Sappho, Joan of Arc, St. Theresa of Avila, Queen Isabella, Queen Elizabeth, Catherine the Great, and any number of others. Our times have inured us to looking at women with new eyes. Ability, comparable to and sometimes greater than that of men, has manifested itself in all human pursuits, with one laudable exception: there has been no female Bonaparte.

In the dance of our day there is no question as to the preponderant genius of women. Men are hard put to match the historic achievements of Anna Pavlova, Isadora Duncan, Ruth St. Denis, Martha Graham, and Doris Humphrey. This is not to deny the stature of such male luminaries as Nijinsky, Fokine, and Kreutzberg.

The American dance, as we know it, in the second half of the twentieth century is largely the product of two titanic artists, both women and both completely feminine women. There is no justification whatever for the old bromide of a masculine mentality in the body of a female. For fifteen years the Graham company was composed entirely of women. With these young, superbly trained girls, Graham created a miraculously expressive, technical vocabulary. This vocabulary was intensely, completely female, deeply rooted in the entrails, organs, and psyche of the female. It was used to compose a body of works unequaled in revelatory power, primordial rituals of mystical intensity celebrating an ancient, but consciously remembered matriarchy. The male of the species, during this period, was not even remotely alluded to. He simply did not exist.

Doris, on the other hand, worked with men. She cast *New Dance* for herself, her ensemble of twelve women, Charles, and four other men, William Matons, George Bockman, Kenneth Bostock, and myself. *New Dance* was a work of symphonic dimension. Its theme—the relation of man to his fellows—would unite it with two subsequently composed works, *Theatre Piece* and *With My Red Fires. New Dance* was a poetic vision of an ideal state, where order, grace, and beauty reigned.

The curtain rose to reveal pyramidal arrangements of blocks at the four corners of the stage. Standing or seated on these were spectators at an arena where a heroic spectacle was to take place. Doris and Charles stood dead center stage, poised to begin. After a sonorous overture of percussion and cymbals, the two began a magnificent duet, full-bodied and affirmative, that evoked the strength and assurance that is man's, and the grace and beauty that is woman's, and the heroic nobility of their joint destiny. A summons and a credo, this duet was also a preamble to the fifty minutes that followed. The quality of the movements, the beautiful off-balance turns, the leaps that exploded into the air with no visible preparation, the asymmetrical, contrapuntal rhythms, the intricate, dazzling patterns of bodies and limbs intoxicated with space, always more space—all this would permeate the fabric of the work.

There was a sudden pause. The women descended to the arena. The men retired. In the passage that followed a myriad asteroids described a spacious orbit. Doris was the central planet, whirling endlessly. Around her the women encircled her circles. Centripetal. Implosive.

The swiftly whirling movement created an irresistible centrifugality, and suddenly the stage was empty.

The men took over. Darting diagonals pierced the arena. There were careening runs that climaxed in bounding horizontals and bodies bent double backwards in the air; jagged, stamping rhythms; arms and legs projected outward from an inner explosion; leaps that ended in long strides on the knees. Here was all the dynamism and force of the male nature unleashed.

And, again, the arena, pulsating with unbounded energy and anticipation, emptied.

The women entered in a slow and majestic procession, with long slides, suspended balances on one foot, backs arched, faces raised, and arms spread wide—like a celebratory and jubilant anthem. The men joined them, and the procession became more exultant, until the *lento maestoso* overflowed into a fugal *allegro con brio*.

This fugue was one of those superb, contrapuntal edifices that Doris, master choreographer that she was, liked to place in the climactic portions of her works. It was a summation, a zenith, a dramatic cessation of all movement and sound. The dancers pushed the constructions from the four corners of the stage to the center, fitting them together to form a large pyramid. Now, the "Variations and Conclusion" that were the coda of the work began.

Order, clarity: these have been mentioned often as the twin goals of artists, scientists, and philosophers. Ultimately, the cosmos is the supreme manifestation of these concepts. The organization of the entire universe from the gigantic stars to the minutest components of all matter is a work of choreography, awesome in its structure and precision. All of sentient life, as we know it, is subject to its pattern and rhythm. Only man, capricious, perverse, and fallible, seems intent on violating this order, creating darkness where there is light. But architects, philosophers, poets, and musicians compensate for this propensity to nihilism in man's nature.

The choreographic genius of Doris Humphrey was an affirmation of order and clarity. In this coda she created a dance that evoked the ordered congress of planets. It was most ingeniously wrought in its details, as elaborately simple as a snowflake or a many-petaled flower. From each corner of the stage, in ordered succession, a soloist would be projected diagonally to the central pyramid, and from there cover the stage with a choreographic variation, while the others progressed in a contrapuntal design to the next corner. The mathematical beauty and precision upon which the coda was built was a miracle of order and clarity. The work came to a climax in a centripetal gathering of energies into the central pyramid.

These are only words. Lightning is swift and dazzling. Thunder is sonorous. Only those who have been momentarily blinded by the one and deafened by the other can know what is meant by a verbal description of the phenomenon of an electric discharge from the heavens.

There is no cinematographic record of *New Dance*. There are only a few photographs and the recollections of those who witnessed the flash of its lightning and the roar of its thunder. For that is how *New Dance* was perceived by audiences, and that is what it was to me, who was shaped, molded, and tempered by it. I have not seen or heard its like since.

1998

Alastair Macaulay (1955–)

Born to a farming family in Essex, England, Alastair Macaulay read Classics at Cambridge. A passionate correspondent, his letters from 1976 to 1978 about dance prompted friends to urge him to try criticism. Once he began to review the performing arts, in 1978, he found he was in his element. He taught dance history beginning in 1980, and in 1983 he was founding editor of the quarterly *Dance Theatre Journal*; between 1987 and 2002, he served as chief examiner in dance history to the Imperial Society of Teachers of Dancing. In 1988 and 1992 he spent periods in New York as a guest dance critic of *The New Yorker*.

Macaulay served as chief theater critic of the *Financial Times* between 1994 and 2007 and as chief dance critic for the *Times Literary Supplement* between 1996 and 2006. His short biography, *Margot Fonteyn*, was published in 1998, and his extensive book of interviews with Matthew Bourne, in 2000; a considerably expanded second edition, *Matthew Bourne and His Adventures in Dance*, followed in 2011.

In 2007, he was appointed chief dance critic of *The New York Times* and moved to New York that year. As the *Times* dance critic, he has covered dance genres from ballet and modern dance to tango, hip-hop, flamenco, and Asian dance. He has reviewed dance in over twenty states in the United States, in several European countries, and in India, where he has spent two four-week periods. In late 2010, he undertook a coast-to-coast "*Nutcracker* Marathon," reviewing twenty-eight different productions of the ballet. Since 2012, he has organized annual research seminars and presentations on individual ballets (*The Sleeping Beauty*, *Swan Lake*, Balanchine's *Serenade*, *Giselle*, Nijinsky's *L'Après-midi d'un faune*, and Robbins's *Afternoon of a Faun*) at the New York Public Library for the Performing Arts. High among his passions as a dance critic is the choreography of Frederick Ashton, George Balanchine, and Merce Cunningham, of whom he is completing a critical biography.

His Moves Expressed as Much as His Music

MICHAEL JACKSON will be remembered as a great and widely imitated mover. Other things about him will be remembered too, but it is amazing how many of them are apparent in his dancing. The sweet boy, the angry dissident and the weirdly glamorous star are all there; and so is the androgyne who gives off conflicting male/female signals in the course of a single number. You can see what he has learned from the urban tensions of "West Side Story," the disco craze of "Saturday Night Fever," the jazz-based choreography of Bob Fosse and from a line of divas from Judy Garland to Diana Ross. (There's even a little Audrey Hepburn there.)

Among the vast array offered by YouTube of clips of his performances, "Michael Jackson's Best Dance Moves" strikes me as fairly gruesome. It is what it implies: a collage of separate moves arranged to break Mr. Jackson's work up into tricks and special effects, all fitted to a single song. Even in his best work, Mr. Jackson relied too often on known stunts: the crotch-grabbing and moonwalking are just the most famous of these, and on too many occasions the audience seems to be waiting for him to do them.

It's no secret that Fred Astaire—who during the 20th century was widely revered among all dance artists as its greatest dancer—singled out the young Jackson for praise. But Astaire died in 1987, and it's hard to believe that he would have applauded the later Mr. Jackson without extensive reservations. Watch Mr. Jackson live at the Super Bowl halftime show in 1993, wearing his trademark dark glasses and ponytail with loose locks falling forward over the brow, starting out in quasi-military uniform, and you see he does everything the audience wants with skill, energy and almost no spontaneity. Even the anger seems synthetic now.

But to watch "Don't Stop 'Til You Get Enough" (1979) is to be amazed at just how much charm the 20-year-old Mr. Jackson had, and the charm gets more infectious as the dancing proceeds. You begin by noticing the pelvis, doing its characteristic pulsation, and you recognize how close you are to the world of John Travolta in "Saturday Night Fever." Fairly soon, you take in the heels, or rather the action of the insteps that keeps rhythmically lifting the heels off the floor, and then, in various ways, you see the ripple of motion between feet and those very slender hips.

But Mr. Jackson was an upper-body dancer too: there's a marvelous moment here when he tilts back and stays there. Now go to "Billie Jean" in Motown's 25th-anniversary celebration (1983). You can see that already everything is much more choreographed, both in the bad sense of unspontaneous and the good sense of dance structure. Most of the time his dancing is so aflame you don't feel any lack of freshness, and he's so alert that you hardly have time to laugh—though I think you ought, happily—at the way his busy pelvis keeps hoisting his pants up and revealing his off-white socks. (The changing expanse of socks becomes part of the rhythm.)

You don't have time because he gives you so much to look at. There are few popular dancers today who keep drawing your attention to footwork: He was always one of them. Here in "Billie Jean" he turns the feet in and out; he raises right and left feet in alternation; he isolates the action of one leg and then the other; he goes rhythmically knock-kneed: It's riveting. Later, when he jumps and stamps, those moves are dance effects, always part of the rhythm. And meanwhile, until late in the song, he never stops mouthing the lyrics. He's always intense, and still occasionally vulnerable. The spring he can get out of those feet is very exciting: you can see how much impetus he gets out of them—turning in and out, they sometimes propel him backward—which is just a foretaste of what's to follow.

Mr. Jackson was just 24 in 1983, and the androgyny was already evident. When he shows us the debonair angle at which he can wear a hat, he's much more like Garland than anyone else; when he splays his hands and bends his knees in jazz effects, he recalls the chic archness of Hepburn in "Funny Face," and toward the end those feet of his go right up onto point. And in between he gives us some early hints of his later macho crotch-grabbing.

Yet all this is not to mention the moment in the "Billie Jean" Motown show when he stops singing and sends the audience, justifiably, wild: the moonwalking, whereby he slides briskly backward while giving the impression of walking emphatically forward. He doesn't overdo it—about five paces, on two separate occasions—and it's a thrill, both times. By the end, you're amazed at this marvelous young mass of contradictions.

There are several other Jackson clips worth rewatching. In "The Way You Make Me Feel"—a number perched right on the edge of absurdity in the way Jacko half-menaces a girl in the need to prove his sexual desire—one transfer of weight from one foot to the other is razor-sharp and breathtakingly fast, and there are other pure-dance moments that keep wiping any laughter off your face. Here and in several numbers—actually, this is still true at the Super Bowl halftime show in 1993—Mr. Jackson is one of those rare dancers with whom you feel you'd pay just to watch him walk. He can do it with all kinds of different dynamics, and sometimes with a rushing impetus that's irresistible.

The later Jackson didn't lose all those dance gifts. But he diluted them, and he hid them beneath his increasing need to hide the vulnerable-boy aspect in him. It is easy to dislike many of the later videos: even as early as the late '80s, the kind of drama he puts onto screen often looks fakey, and isn't always rescued by his skill as a performer. But the gifts were sensational, and the way he honed them was, at first, superb. Astaire's praise was more than deserved.

June 26, 2009

Notice the Feet in That Body of Work

W HAT constitutes dance? We've known for at least a century that dance can happen with the dancer sitting, reclining or kneeling. In the first three decades of the 20th century Isadora Duncan turned such movements into legend. In recent decades dance has only become harder to distinguish from other forms of physical activity.

Here, however, I honor the importance of feet and footwork in dancing. Every part of the body—arms, fingers, thighs, eyes, waist, pelvis, neck—can make an irresistible contribution to this art. But the effect of the foot is disproportionate. Make a complex rhythm with your hands (like drumming), and in visual terms it's just a local phenomenon. Make even a simple rhythm with your feet—slow, slow, quick, quick, slow—and your whole body is engaged.

The foot is at the root of poetry. Lines of verse are divided into feet, and that's because words, music and dance were once intimately connected. And in terms of physical complexity, the foot is among the most miraculous mechanisms of the body. (Dancers with broken or fractured bones in their feet have given great performances.) The instep, the toes, the heels and the soles can be used together in multiple ways. Whether in shoes with heels (as in flamenco, tango or ballroom); sheathed in ballet slippers and poised on point (as with women in ballet); or bare (as in much modern dance, in most African dance and, often with bells round the ankles, in Indian dance), the foot is what gives human movement much of its texture and meter.

Two of the most remarkable visiting dancers to New York in 2009 made footwork a matter of sensational importance: the Russian ballerina Natalia Osipova (dancing two roles with American Ballet Theatre at the Metropolitan Opera House in July) and the Argentine tango dancer Gabriel Missé (dancing in September in two milongas and in two Fall for Dance performances at City Center). Both these dancers left an impression of blaze behind them, and, though they're compelling through to their fingertips, much of that incandescence came, in contrasting ways, from beneath the ankle.

With Ms. Osipova the exceptional thrill came from the liftoff provided by her feet; in more than 30 years of watching ballet I've never seen that degree of spring. Many of Mr. Missé's steps came in percussive clusters too dense to decipher, some bombarding a single spot of floor with rapid-fire insistence, others suddenly pouncing like a cat.

I don't mean to suggest that either of these artists relies on footwork as a stunt. Ms. Osipova is remarkable to watch just standing on point. She is one of those ballerinas (the Russians seem to have a preponderance of them, but they're rare anywhere) whose weight seems to contradict reality and to flow not down to the toe but up through the body and into the air. Mr. Missé is a beguiling spectacle simply when gliding cheek to cheek with his partner (Natalia Hills) in a tranquil current; his feet are always central to the flow and drama of his dancing.

No dances make more splendid use of the sole of the foot and its contact with the floor than those of India. (The best-known genres in New York are Odissi, Kathak and Bharatanatyam; I wish we saw more of each.) I especially love the way a dancer will lift a flexed foot, hold it parallel to the floor and then bring it down so that its sole slaps the ground like a cymbal. (Whereas most dancers like to perform on sprung floors, Indian dancers often prefer the solidity of stone.) This effect is just one among many; each Indian dance form makes vivid uses of the foot's ball and heel, often deploying the instep with terrific speed and intricacy.

Whatever the dance idiom, good choreography shows how many different moves this relatively small part of the anatomy can make. Watching George Balanchine's "Nutcracker" the other day at New York City Ballet, I was struck again by the many ways he deploys the feet. The Soldier doll in Act I does much with his feet flexed and on his heels. The Coffee dancer keeps crossing one knee in front of another and gliding on her slippered soles. The male Tea dancer's feet keep exploding sideways like firecrackers. The Marzipan soloist hops on one point while slowly revolving full circle, then performs jumps in which each foot writes rings in the air (known as gargouillades).

Duncan (1877–1927) generally danced barefoot, which, like her abandonment of the corset, struck some as distasteful. Grandly rapturous in manner, she defended her style by saying, "I believe in the religion of the beauty of the human foot." This religion's vocabulary began with what used to be called natural footwork—walking, running, hopping and skipping—and she taught children, in their earliest lessons, to make compound rhythms with their feet. Inspired by the sculptures of ancient Greece, she noted when one foot should stay flat on the floor while the other leg lifts, or when the dancer should rise onto the ball of one foot.

Without Duncan's heroism, such a style started to seem quaint. Yet in 1988 Mark Morris, without claiming to reproduce Duncan's style literally, made a tremendous impression while reviving its essence in his full-evening "L'Allegro, Il Penseroso ed il Moderato." Strongly marked by the rapturously Grecian flavor that had been part of Duncan's notion of the natural in dance, this work rightly became the most enthusiastically greeted work of Mr. Morris's career to date. Here again was the beauty that Duncan revealed in walking, running, hopping and skipping.

Other great choreographers of American modern dance have rediscovered natural footwork in quite other ways. Paul Taylor's 1975 "Esplanade"—a yet more exceptional classic—is also made up of walking, running, skidding, sliding, falling; its particular secret is the way it makes these movements heart-stoppingly spontaneous. None of its steps quite looks like a classroom exercise, and yet they are, evidently, steps.

I have been writing to celebrate feet and footwork, but I also wish to issue an alarm. Other than Mr. Taylor, Mr. Morris and Twyla Tharp, how many of today's choreographers—in ballet, modern dance or other genres—take much interest in how much the foot can do? In ballet, footwork reached peaks of coloratura accomplishment in the choreography of Frederick Ashton (witness his "Rhapsody," 1980) and George Balanchine (see his "Ballo Della Regina," 1977) that no subsequent dance maker seems interested in rivaling.

Too many modern-dance choreographers today like to use the flat foot as an anchor, with the dancing happening from the ankle up; they seem reluctant to ask their dancers to use their insteps or even their heels. Footwork is where ballroom dancing begins, yet few ballroom exponents today seem remotely as interested in steps as they are in high kicks, acrobatics and displays of overwrought sexiness. I have sat through an all-tango evening in which Mr. Missé and Ms. Hills were the exceptions in making footwork a serious part of the music and the drama.

So when I get the blues about the future of dance, I foresee a world without footwork. But there is reason to hope that such a world may be avoided. The feet of David Hallberg, Mr. Missé and Ms. Osipova are exceptional by any historical standard, and there are other feet to anticipate. Soledad Barrio appears this Christmas in New York with Noche Flamenca (Lucille Lortel Theater, Dec. 24 to Jan. 16), and Rocío Molina will dance as part of the city's 2010 Flamenco Festival (City Center, Feb. 12): I know of no dancers today who better show—below the ankle in particular—the brilliance and color of flamenco rhythm.

The choreographer Alexei Ratmansky keeps growing as a dance poet; his poetry is often at its most subtle and various when showing what the foot can do, and several new Ratmansky creations are coming in 2010. The British modern-dance choreographer Richard Alston brings his dance company to the Joyce Theater next month (Jan. 12 to 17); at his variable best he is the most musically revealing choreographer today and the one who makes the most virtuoso use of footwork (and shows how the two skills are connected).

Daft as this may sound to nondancers, the foot has sometimes been considered the most divine part of the body. When the Romantic ballerina Marie Taglioni appeared in Russia in the late 1830s, a cartoonist depicted her single point descending from a cloud, as if heaven sent. Mr. Alston's first work as a dancer, in the 1960s, was in baroque dance, with the teacher-choreographer Belinda Quirey. As she used to say, "The good Lord may have had an off day when he made the knee, but he surely was in marvelous form when he made the foot."

December 9, 2009

Where Light Replaces Sound, and Movement Offers Comfort

At one moment in the hourlong "Necessary Weather," Sara Rudner and Dana Reitz are dancing simultaneous solos, each in a separate pool of light created by Jennifer Tipton. Even if you disliked dance, the show—a revival of a 1994 collaboration by these three women at the Baryshnikov Arts Center—would be worth seeing for Ms. Tipton's astounding contribution; and even if you already knew from many other productions that Ms. Tipton has long been the world's most remarkable creator of lighting for dance, you haven't seen her most miraculous ideas until you've seen "Necessary Weather." But this particular moment is memorable because of the quite different ways the two dancers react to the light.

Ms. Reitz—like Ms. Rudner barefoot and dressed in a white pajama-like outfit—does a soft shimmying step on the spot, as if taking pleasure in the light but not addressing it. Ms. Rudner, however, turns her face to it. There have been other moments when each woman has done so, sometimes like a sunbather; but here the uncanny effect is that, at once, the rest of Ms. Rudner starts to crumble. She sags at the knees; her shoulders decline; her spine yields. She seems to disintegrate before our eyes, and soon she has collapsed to the floor, while Ms. Reitz dances on. It seems connected to how Ms. Rudner turned her face: she has come too close to the sun or has given too much of herself to it.

Both dancers are in their 60s, both are looking good, and it is still easy to believe Ms. Rudner is the greatest dancer in the world. You want to be nowhere else while she's dancing. Every part of her contributes to the most simple movement. The rich bend of her knees, the easy ripple of her spine, the broad planes of her face, and her wonderful mane of graying grapevine curls all play their part, as does the luscious texture of her insteps. When she and Ms. Reitz shimmy together, it's hard to look at Ms. Reitz just because Ms. Rudner's motion, though not larger, is so much fuller.

Never mind the deities of the ballet: the embodiment of Terpsichore today is Sara Rudner. And that decline-and-fall moment is the more amazing because it's atypical: Ms. Rudner's dance character tends toward the robust, the sensuous, the twinkling and the outgoing. When she's still—and there are episodes here when she appears tranquil, as if in moonlight or sunlight—she somehow suggests an invisible inner motion that never ceases, so that you feel aware of the dreams and impulses passing through her mind even while she closes her eyes and moves no muscle.

The dance occurs in silence, and it is one of a handful of the greatest and most successful examples of dancing without sound accompaniment that I have ever encountered. Usually silence—like long pauses in a modernist play—makes an audience start to cough nervously but industriously; not so here. We're spellbound, largely thanks to Ms. Tipton. Sometimes the floor seems to vanish and the two women float around as if suspended. In one episode, they're lighted a glowing pale green, like will-o'-the-wisps, and in another they and the air they move through are a dim but charged red.

At other moments, circles of light on the floor become the brightest points onstage. Ms. Reitz's most wonderful scene comes when she lies down on the floor beside one such point of light as if it were the face of her beloved; she cradles it with her hand, lies close to it, and then suddenly turns onto her side to face it, as if they were in bed together.

Often the back wall seems not to be there at all, but sometimes it suddenly looms into quite different kinds of view, as when Ms. Reitz stands and plays with the large changing shadows she casts at the back, which make it shimmer and vibrate like a softly shaken veil.

Many meanings flow readily from those dances in which one woman is in the light while the other passes nearby in the darkness: the dead and the living, the undead and the angelically blessed, the ego and alter ego, the options of parallel universes. But these women keep things light. A straw hat they carry shines like the Holy Grail at one point: it's magical, but it's also just a hat, and they stay playful.

Of the many marvels here, perhaps nothing enchants more than when the two women break together into the barefoot equivalent of a soft-shoe routine, so juicy as they walk their bouncy way through a few old steps. Did we actually hear them sing "Tea for Two"? Members of the audience burst rightly into gleeful laughter: it was that simple, that happy, that infectious.

May 14, 2010

LÉONIDE MASSINE (1896–1979)

WHEN BIOGRAPHERS and critics talk about the great choreographers, they naturally focus on the great works. But great choreographers have to eat, and so they may take on all kinds of extracurricular projects. Balanchine's Broadway and Hollywood efforts are well known (including *On Your Toes*, *The Goldwyn Follies*, and *Cabin in the Sky*), but who knew that Michel Fokine did the dances for a 1918 Broadway extravaganza called *Mecca*? (Dorothy Parker, reviewing it for *Vanity Fair*, called Fokine the best thing in the show.) Or that Léonide Massine, Diaghilev's discovery and "protégé" who, for twenty or more years, was the world's dominant ballet choreographer—*La Boutique Fantasque*, *Parade*, *Gaîté Parisienne*, *Le Beau Danube*, *The Three-Cornered Hat*, *Les Présages*—worked (slaved?) for three years as the choreographer and lead dancer at the famous Roxy Theater in Manhattan, the chief rival to Radio City Music Hall? Massine tells us all about it in his highly readable autobiography, *My Life in Ballet*. And we can watch him today at work (and with fascination) in those two famous over-the-top movies by Michael Powell and Emeric Pressburger, *The Red Shoes* and *The Tales of Hoffmann*.

(from) *My Life in Ballet*

ONCE *Ode* had opened at the Théâtre Sarah Bernhardt my work for Diaghilev was finished. Now that Balanchine was doing so much of his choreography, I felt there would not be enough work for the two of us, and when I discussed the position with Eugenia, whom I had been seeing as often as possible during our season in Paris, I found that she thoroughly understood and approved of my desire to do more choreographic work on my own. She herself was anxious to do something more challenging than her work at the Folies-Bergère.

We had heard that there were excellent opportunities at that time for dancers in America, and we discussed the idea of going there together. We were married in Paris in the summer of 1928 and sailed for New York a few days later.

New York can be a cruel city, especially for young out-of-work foreigners. In Europe I had made something of a reputation, but in America I was just another dancer who had been vaguely associated with the Ballets-Russes. It did not take long for me to discover that American interest in ballet was no greater than it had been when I made my first visit ten years earlier. I presented all my introductions, and when the theatre proved of no help I tried the films. I soon found that they were interested only in musical comedy and had hardly even heard of Diaghilev. Eugenia, who through all those grim months when I went from office to office, from agent to agent, was encouraging and optimistic, urged me to try just once again, and summoning up all my courage I went to see S. L. Rothafel. I liked him as soon as we met. He was a man of great natural charm, and very responsive to new ideas. He had just begun staging live shows between the films shown at his cinema, the Roxy, and he offered me a contract to choreograph some ballets for them. It was the first offer I had had since I arrived in New York—and the last—and I accepted it immediately. The productions at the Roxy, I discovered, were vaudeville-type spectacles performed on a vast raked stage. I was amazed at the way the director, Léon Leonidov, managed to manoeuvre the interminable rows of sequined and high-kicking chorus girls on and off stage. When I was introduced to Leonidov he told me that I would be expected to provide a new ballet every week, with occasional solos and *divertissements*. There was a large orchestra and a well-trained company of about thirty dancers, with an excellent *prima ballerina* named Patricia Bowman; and so I set to work.

It was a staggering responsibility to have to create every week a ballet which would appeal to the enormous Roxy audience, particularly as my productions had to be co-ordinated with the weekly theme of the rest of the spectacle and in keeping with the season of the year. I composed Spring Ballets, Easter Ballets, Christmas Ballets, and ballets for such festivals as St. Valentine's Day, Hallowe'en and Thanksgiving. The music was mostly Victor Herbert, Sigmond Romberg and Franz Lehár. As well as rehearsing the new ballet, which had to be ready by Thursday in each week, I also danced four times a day, and five times on Saturday. I did not see much of New York. When I was not at the Roxy I was in my bed, asleep. Eugenia was in the *corps de ballet*, and she too danced four times a day and five on Saturday. It was a miserable life for her, but she realized we had no choice, and never complained.

Fokine was living and teaching in New York at this time, and occasionally doing choreography for musical comedies. One Sunday Eugenia and I went to call on him, and found him still distant and withdrawn, though he gave us a cordial welcome. I asked him to come and see us at the Roxy, and the following week he arrived in my dressing-room just after I had been dancing in the Blue Bird *pas de deux* from *The Sleeping Beauty*. He was as formal and polite as ever, but he told me—and I believe he was sincere—that he had never seen a better performance of it, not even at the Maryinsky.

Towards the end of my first season at the Roxy I was invited by Ida Rubinstein to go to Paris and choreograph two productions for her company there. Rothafel granted me temporary leave of absence, and Eugenia and I sailed for Europe, feeling as if we had suddenly been let out of prison. It was wonderful to walk about Paris again with Eugenia. We went back to the studio where we first met, and spent our free time shopping and visiting picture galleries. The sight of the Châtelet, and the Opéra, with Carpeaux's statue of 'La Danse' outside, brought back a host of memories. Ida Rubinstein's company, which included Anna Ludmilla, Alexis Dolinoff, and Nijinska, who did most of the choreography, was appearing at the Académie Nationale de Musique et de Danse. One of the ballets she had engaged me to do was based on the story of David and Goliath (the other was *Alcine*). The libretto was by Doderet, the music by Sauguet. It was an opulent affair, with costumes by Benois, but it was not a success. Rubinstein, who was really more of an actress than a dancer, was beautiful and statuesque, but though she had a striking stage presence it was difficult to get her to move gracefully. As she was dancing the part of David, and the whole ballet was centred on her, I had very little opportunity for original choreography. *David* had its first production on 16 May 1929, and Eugenia and I returned to the Roxy where our contract had another year to run. In August we were having a much-needed holiday at Virginia Beach. While walking along the sea-front I bought a newspaper and read that Diaghilev had died in Venice on the 19th. I sat down on a bench and thought of all the years I had spent with him, all the ballets we had collaborated on, all the times I had danced for him. I could not believe he was dead. I felt as if I had lost someone from my own family. Although I had twice left his company, I had the deepest affection and admiration for him, and knew too how much I owed him. He had been the outstanding influence on my artistic career. There never was anyone with quite his genius for recognizing and encouraging talent, and more than anyone else of his generation he understood the importance of bringing to the service of the ballet painting, music, and poetry at the highest level. His irreproachable taste and judgement often led him to make harsh criticsms, but they were always beneficial to the artists concerned. I myself always accepted his criticisms without question. Having been so closely connected with him for so many years, I think I must have felt his loss more than anyone.

Some months later, when we were back at the Roxy, I had a telephone call from Cole Porter, asking me to his flat for a drink. I had always admired his work and was anxious to meet him. When I arrived he told me how grieved he had been at the news of Diaghilev's death, and how unfortunate it was that the company had been disbanded. He then introduced me to Ray Goetz, a Broadway producer, and soon they were telling me of their plan to form an American Ballets-Russes company to perform all the Diaghilev ballets in New York and on tour. They asked me if I would take over the artistic direction of it. Needless to say, I was thrilled at the idea, and was sure that Goetz, with his enthusiasm and intelligence, would be the ideal business manager of such a company. The great problem was how to get hold of the original Ballets-Russes costumes and properties. I wrote to Diaghilev's lawyer, Maître Aaron, who told me that everything was in store in a warehouse on the outskirts of Paris. He also told me that as Diaghilev had left no will, there was no one to pay the storage charges, and everything had been seized by the French government. With the help of Maître Aaron, I managed to buy everything belonging to fifty-five ballets—backcloths, front curtains, costumes, properties, and all scenic accessories. Just as I thought our venture was really under way, there came the Wall Street crash. America was plunged into a financial depression, and Goetz was no longer able to sponsor the new company. My contract was cancelled, and I found myself the owner of all the Diaghilev material, stored far away in Paris, with no means of using it.

The only bright spot in the next year was that as soon as my contract at the Roxy expired I was asked by the New York League of Composers to choreograph a new version of *Le Sacre du Printemps* for a charity performance at the Metropolitan Opera House. Although this was an exciting assignment, I found it very difficult to go back to this early work after so many years. However, I was given a large cast of excellent dancers, and found that the facilities at the 'Met' were as good as those in any theatre in Europe. As rehearsals progressed I found the ballet again taking shape in my mind. Martha Graham's powerful performance as the Chosen Maiden added considerable strength to the production. I found her a most subtle and responsive dancer to work with, and her small stature and delicate movements gave the role an added poignancy. We were all very relieved when *Le Sacre du Printemps* was enthusiastically received, and hoped it was a sign that New York was beginning to take ballet seriously.

1968

Johnny Mercer (1909–1976)

Savannah born and bred, son of a well-to-do family who owned the first car in town, surrounded by African American music from early childhood, and determined to break away from the South he loved, Johnny Mercer was in Hollywood by 1935 and broke into the big leagues of lyric writing while still in his mid-twenties with huge hits like "Lazybones," "I'm an Old Cowhand," and "Goody Goody." The list is endless—"Blues in the Night," "That Old Black Magic," "Too Marvelous for Words," "Skylark," "Laura," "One for My Baby," "Hooray for Hollywood," "Moon River," "Days of Wine and Roses," "Autumn Leaves," "Come Rain or Come Shine," "On the Atchison, Topeka and the Santa Fe" (for his great love, Judy Garland), "Ac-Cent-Tchu-Ate the Positive," and hundreds more—it's estimated that he wrote up to 1,500 songs in all. Nineteen of them were nominated for Oscars, four of them won. Among those was *not* the hilarious "Arthur Murray Taught Me Dancing in a Hurry," written for the 1942 movie *The Fleet's In* and sung by Betty Hutton. (You can watch her over-the-top-of-the-top performance on YouTube.) Is it autobiographical? When he was college age he really did take dancing lessons from Arthur Murray himself. In his spare time he was one of the three founders of Capitol Records, and a highly successful singer—with fourteen top-ten hits, four of them at number one.

"Arthur Murray Taught Me Dancing in a Hurry"

> Life was so peaceful at the laundry,
> Life was so calm and serene,
> Life was tres gay

Till that unlucky day
I happened to read that magazine!

Why did I read that advertisement,
Where it says, "Since I rumba, Jim thinks I'm sublime!"?
Why, oh why
Did I ever try
When I didn't have the talent,
I didn't have the money,
And teacher did not have the time? Boy!

Arthur Murray
Taught me dancin' in a hurry;
I had a week to spare,
He showed me the ground work,
The walkin' around work,
And told me take it from there!

Arthur Murray
Then advised me not to worry;
It would come out all right!
To my way of thinkin'
My dance is stinkin',
I don't know my left from my right!

The people around me can all sing,
"A-one and a-two and a-three,"
But any resemblance to waltzing
Is just coincidental with me!

'Cause Arthur Murray
Taught me dancin' in a hurry;
And so I take a chance.
To me it resembles
The nine day trembles,
But he guarantees it's a dance!

My tango resembles a two-step,
My rumba makes people turn pale,
My conga goes into a goose-step,
Till the FBI is doggin' my trail!

'Cause Arthur Murray
Taught me dancin' in a hurry;
Maybe the stars were wrong,
If I ain't a menace
To Ruth St. Denis,
I'll do until one comes along!

Turkey trot
Or gavotte?
Don't know which,
Don't know what.
Jitterbug?
Bunny hug?
Long as you
Cut a rug!

Walk the dog,
Do the frog,
Lindy hop
Till you drop!
Ball the jack
Back to back,
Cheek to cheek
Till you're weak.
You've heard of Pavlova?
Well Jack, move over!
Make way for the queen of the dance!

1942

MARK MORRIS (1956–)

MARK MORRIS was born in Seattle. His father taught him to read music, and his mother encouraged him to take lessons in dancing. As a teenager, he wanted to be a flamenco dancer, but a trip to study flamenco in Spain, still under the rule of Francisco Franco, exposed him to the regime's homophobia and he returned to the U.S. with different dance dreams.

In the 1970s, when he was dancing in New York with the companies of Hannah Kahn, Lar Lubovitch, Eliot Feld, and Laura Dean, he displayed personal beauty, kinesthetic imagination, and an electrifying effect on the space around him; his dancing reminded some observers of photographs of the young Isadora Duncan. Paradoxically, he looked like no one else yet seemed to be channeling the origins of modern dance. When, in 1980, he founded the Mark Morris Dance Group (MMDG), he chose dancers not only for their strength and commitment to his work but also for their individual personalities and physiques—and, perhaps most important of all, for their disciplined responsiveness to music. Morris's dancers are essentially physical musicians. He reads orchestral scores and sometimes conducts the live music he insists on for all performances of his dances, apart from those few that are set to particular recordings. He also sometimes conducts his stagings for opera. The idea in Morris's declaration that "I love it when sound and sight are saying the same irreducible thing" leads some observers to find links between his artmaking and that of choreographer Doris Humphrey and, before her, to some of the Denishawn School's repertory. His approach has also attracted charges that he "Mickey Mouses" the music—an issue Morris touches on below in both his 2010 commencement address for the Longy School of Music and his comments on Walt Disney's Silly Symphonies of the 1930s.

From 1988 to 1991 he and his MMDG dancers from New York

were appointed the national dance company of Belgium as the Monnaie Dance Group Mark Morris at the Théâtre Royal de la Monnaie, in Brussels. (It was for this historic opera house that he choreographed two of his most acclaimed full-evening dances: the 1988 *L'Allegro, il Penseroso, ed il Moderato*, to Handel, and the 1991 *The Hard Nut*, Morris's version of Tchaikovsky's *Nutcracker*. While in Brussels, for the Théâtre Varia, he also choreographed the 1989 hour-long danced opera *Dido and Aeneas*, to Purcell.) In 1990, Morris cofounded—with Mikhail Baryshnikov—the White Oak Dance Project.

"I make it up and you watch it. End of philosophy," is how Mark Morris has summed up his art.

Where I Come From

I AM OFTEN asked for a list of choreographers who have most influenced me in my own work. Along with George Balanchine, Merce Cunningham, and Busby Berkeley, I invariably mention Walt Disney.

And in naming Disney, I mean the teams of directors, animators, composers, reference models, and background artists involved.

For my entire career, I have been accused of the dreaded sin of "Mickey Mousing" the music (as if music itself contained an embedded dance that needed only a cryptographer to release it to the world). I figure that somebody brilliant taught us all how to watch dancing and music and to recognize the bond between the two. I love it when sound and sight are saying the same irreducible thing. The inevitable. That's what Disney does. From the very early Silly Symphonies (my favorites) through *Cinderella* and *The Jungle Book* (not my favorites) via the great *Fantasia*, I marvel at the variety of choreographic invention and aptness. What a remarkable resource of whimsy, fantasy, art!

What a trip! Take *Water Babies* (1935): I first saw *Water Babies* when I was young enough to think that it was some kind of documentary. It is a strange, amazing pastoral fantasy that features naked babies (distinctly male and female although they have no genitals) who sleep in water lilies, harness the power of birds and bugs, and can pray in English. There's even a bullfight with a bullfrog. Seeing it again as an adult gave me a kind of melancholy. That's when I realized that I actually believed in that world. It is where I come from.

It is not just a place where I first heard Rossini and Mendelssohn and Schubert, where I first encountered W. C. Fields and ZaSu Pitts and Cab Calloway. It is also the place where I came to believe, without question, that everything—people, the moon, spiders, animals, trees, clocks, even fire—had a spirit. And usually a personality and a face. Flowers can not only walk, they also prance and mince and swagger. Hens can gather up their skirts daintily to escape a fox attack. Skeletons play xylophone on each other's ribs using femurs for mallets. How do they do it?

Everything is alive. Everything is animated.

In my own work as a choreographer, I happily and purposely observe a direct, symbiotic relationship of music and action. I call it dance.

It is where I come from.

2008

Commencement Speech, Longy School of Music

"Music is a song and a dance."—Lou Harrison

Hello—and thank you.

I want to begin with a quote from a review I read recently, that really laid everything bare for me about what we're all doing:

> Our experience of music, more than any other art form, except perhaps dance, draws on our awareness of the living moment, of the here and the now. This is perhaps why music seems so often to retain its links to the performance of ritual, to the sacredness of places and why, in a world where technological change—not least in the music recording industry—gnaws away at the force and meaning of physical presence, live contemporary music remains important. [Guy Dammann, in the *Times Literary Supplement*, in a review of the Huddersfield Contemporary Music Festival]

To me, this says it all. It's a rallying cry, a caution sign—it's what we need to know and understand about what's happening to us, and the realm we call The Arts.

I was in the fifth or sixth grade in Seattle when I saw the Koleda Balkan Dance Ensemble. It was the first time I had seen people singing and dancing at the same time, and I wanted to be part of it. It was welcoming, everybody was invited, and I actually felt like I could do it.

Later, I joined the group and it changed my life. It set me on the path which has brought me here, speaking to you.

And I'm here because I want to tell you how important it is what you do, what we do. It's hard. Conditions are worsening. As usual, classical music is dead. Live performance is being pushed farther and farther to the fringes. But it's necessary, and it's vital that you know how necessary.

I want to offer you the following points:

First, on being alive and your civic duty as musical persons: Here's my suggestion: Don't just play the trumpet and do the crossword puzzle. Read and participate. Be active and know what's going on. Engage in the world as it is now—read everything Alex Ross writes; read the weblogs of Jeremy Denk, Kyle Gann, Parterre Box, Barihunks. Read John Cage, George Bernard Shaw, Virgil Thomson.

Listen to music, always—and listen to music for instruments other than the one you play. Read full scores for fun. Learn the words, if there are words, especially if you're not singing them yourself. The words are why the piece is happening—why the composer wrote that particular music—and it's why you're there.

I used to listen to music every waking second. I thought I would perish if there wasn't something playing. I had a constant dramatic soundtrack playing behind my life. And now because it's my job to work with music all day long, in various irritating forms and repetitions, and because I'm fortunate enough to work with musicians constantly, in my studio or on the road, I don't really listen to music anymore the way I used to—recreationally. Now it's mostly study and research. But that's our work—and because I have access to live music every day—it's different now.

Make it your duty to hear everything you can, as often as you can stand it. I'm not talking just about recorded concert music—I mean listen in the largest sense of the word. Hear. Notice. Be aware. Take notes and make notes. Find interest everywhere.

The great poet Frank O'Hara wrote this statement:

> I am mainly preoccupied with the world as I experience it, and at times when I would rather be dead the thought that I could never write another poem has so far stopped me. I think this is an ignoble attitude. I would rather die for love, but I haven't.
>
> I don't think of fame or posterity (as Keats so grandly and genuinely did), nor do I care about clarifying experiences for anyone or bettering (other than accidentally) anyone's state or social relation, nor am I for any particular technical development in the American language simply because I find it necessary. What is happening to me, allowing for lies and exaggerations which I try to avoid, goes into my poems. I don't think my experiences are clarified or made beautiful for myself or anyone else; they are just there in whatever form I can find them. What is clear to me in my work is probably obscure to others, and vice versa. My formal "stance" is found at the crossroads where what I know and can't get meets what is left of what I know and can bear without hatred. I dislike a great deal of contemporary poetry—all of the past you read is usually quite great—but it is a useful thorn to have in one's side.
>
> It may be that poetry makes life's nebulous events tangible to me and restores their detail; or conversely, that poetry brings forth the intangible quality of incidents which are all too concrete and circumstantial. Or each on specific occasions, or both all the time. [An essay by Frank O'Hara for *The New American Poetry* (1959)]

Second, cultivate contradiction. Think for yourself. Trust your instincts. Doubt them, too. Question everything. Know that equal temperament is a big cheat. It's a paradox. And so, too, may be your conferred degree. Here's my experience: It took me about twenty-five years of listening to classical Indian music to really hear it on its own terms. And I'm no dilettante. I traveled extensively in India, stayed for a while over and over, and really participated with the classical forms. And here's what I've learned: #1. It's so hard!! And #2. No one is ever off the beat or out of tune in India.

Pau Casals said: "Do not be afraid to be out of tune with the piano. It is the piano that is out of tune." [Pau Casals, *The Way They Play*]

R.H.M. Bosanquet said: "The rationale is that if people who are taught music are taught that this one is right and another wrong, they will come to believe it. If they are taught the other systems of interest as well as the equal temperament, they would appreciate the excellences of all." [R.H.M. Bosanquet, *An Elementary Treatise on Musical Intervals and Temperament* (1876)]

Third—be aware of the implications and consequences of technology. Don't just use it because it's there—or because everyone else is using it. It would be a grave mistake to forego the millennia of music created and performed before the digital empire.

John Philip Sousa, in 1906, said: "The time is coming when no one will be ready to submit himself to the ennobling discipline of learning music. Everyone will have their ready made or ready pirated music in their cupboards. Something is irretrievably lost when we are no longer in the presence of bodies making music. The nightingale's song is delightful because the nightingale herself gives it forth." [John Philip Sousa, *The Menace of Mechanical Music* (1906), as quoted in Alex Ross's forthcoming *Listen to This*]

It's a lot of work to put on a show. Everyone here knows that. And it's a lot of work to go to a show. And, of course, it costs money.

It's taking more and more work to go to a performance, because it's easier and easier to stay at home. The electronic pull which keeps us isolated in our homes becomes greater every day. Why work only to get stuck in a show you may not like when there are 820 channels at home? Why chance a messy run-in with a friend who you could easily and discreetly text? Why see a performer who you know couldn't possibly measure up to the agreed-upon-by-experts, best-ever, historical recordings you've amassed in your collection, illegally?

Because we need to. Because performing is living. Representation is metaphor. Art is divine.

Video is a lie. The CD is a lie. The internet is a lie. Television is a lie. I love them all. All are the past masquerading as the present. All are dead, electronically feigning life. They fool us into thinking that they are contemporaneous with our lives, that they are entertaining us and connecting us, right now, all together.

But they're not. Electronic media separate us, isolate us, make us live in the past. Strip the electronic gloss from your iPod and you realize you're staring at the equivalent of crumbling parchment. I have a vision for the apocalypse—after all is said and done, the surviving few will emerge from the rubble, amidst the cockroaches, only to find themselves back where we all began—beating out rhythms. Banging two iPods together will be the percussive noise of the Brave New World.

Live performance is uncomfortable. Whether sitting on a hard bench or the plushest, velvet cushion, being in the presence of a performing human is somewhat uncomfortable. It is focused confrontation, not easy co-existence. You can't talk, have a snack, go to the bathroom, applaud, or perform any of the myriad acts which make television such a soothing, regressive experience. Immobilized, trapped in the darkness, oppressed by the messiness of possibility, there is unease created by the implicit realization that anything can happen.

It takes work. But that work pays off. The effort of engagement admits you to worlds of experience which are unique, corporeal and true. Difficult but essential, in corporeality is truth. Music live is radically different from music recorded. And the difference is this: Live music is music. A recording is a simulacrum, an aide-mémoire, maybe a guide or learning tool. But music is in the flesh and in the moment, and it joins together those who hear it in a way that's both ancient and inexplicable. Individuals listening together and feeling less alone. All art aspires to the condition of music, according to Walter Pater.

The danger of corporeality, the body, however, is that it can be overutilized in an effort to project "Truth." It is up to us to know the limits—where to take the experience of the body, and how much is too much.

That's something I loved so much about the philosophy of the late, great choreographer Merce Cunningham. He was basically making up the same dance his entire life, but it was because he just couldn't get enough of this concept: the body in space and time. That's it. An entire life of curiosity, spent asking this question, and coming up with beautiful solutions.

All music is made with the body. It is a human, alive form. And it's your responsibility to be aware of this, and be in control of it. You aren't just the negative space around your instrument—you are the instrument. If you spend your whole life holding a violin, and you take the violin away, who are you? Are you missing that extension of yourself, or are you an open body in space and time? That's a choice you can make every day. Sit up straight—think about what kind of body you want to embody—and how that is going to make a difference in your music making. The body is the music. Don't name your instrument—it's a thing. Singers, don't call it "the voice". It's your voice. And, everybody, breathe—you have to anyway, you might as well enjoy it.

Here's another thing: music is expression, not self-expression. A lot of people don't understand that controlling emotion is an essential part of any performer's bag of tricks. Here's a beautiful example of what I mean. I was once in Tokyo and we were bumped from the plane and forced to spend the night near a mall at the outskirts of the city. One shop had a display of about 1,000 TVs for sale. On every one was the same image: a geisha crying with a handkerchief. I watched this picture for several minutes. I couldn't believe how moving it was, this camera came in for a close-up, and I realized that the crying geisha was a puppet. It was a chunk of wood that a seventy-five-year-old guy was manipulating. It made such an impression on me that I have never forgotten it. When it comes to emotion, you see, mastery—and not indulgence—is everything.

Finally, and this goes for lots and lots of things, not just music, but you need to know the original forms of your essential art. Whatever it is you choose to do, making music, cooking, kickboxing, gardening, breeding—know that it's not an original idea, you're not the first person to do it. Know the past and how it got us here. A waltz is not just three beats; it's a dance! Know what it was about, the waltz, don't just play one TWO THREE, one TWO THREE. It was a hugely popular dance in various forms over many years. Everyone knew it. So don't play the Bach Cello Suites until you know what a Sarabande, a Gavotte, and a Bourrée is. Music isn't reiteration of notation—it is alive, and has a point. Know the purpose, and have a purpose.

Music is my raison d'être. Really, it's that simple. It's why I choreograph dances, it's why I love Walt Disney, it's why I whistle constantly, it's why I started a company and built a building and established a school in Brooklyn dedicated to the form and function of music and dance. It's why teenagers and I anticipate new episodes of *Glee*.

Music is useless. It's Muzak, theme song, easy listening, mass production. It's Radiohead and Bob Marley reinterpreted for xylophone to lull babies to sleep. It's esoteric, experimental, sound art, and the like. Music is silence. No matter its significance, relevance or efficacy, it's everywhere. It's a lullaby sung by a father to his newborn. It's the commercial jingle that you hate but immediately know. It's that annoying ringtone. Music is personal.

Music is universal. Music is national, the anthems played at the Olympic Games, emotionally charged with history and circumstance and freedom fights and revolutions. Music is a disease—ever had an earworm? Music is an antidote—ever read Oliver Sacks? Music is brand new, happening all the time, in new ways and forms. To some it is regressive, to some it is the essence of our times. Music is old, perhaps as old as our species—I imagine percussive, rhythmic noise was one of the first inventions of the world of humans. Music is soundtrack, background, daily. It is stand alone, falling apart, ephemeral.

I have no advice for you. Music is you. Share the wealth.

2010

H. T. (Henry Taylor) Parker (1867–1934)

The formidable H. T. Parker was probably the most authoritative (and admired) theater critic of the first part of the twentieth century, writing from his prominent situation as both theater and music critic for *The Boston Evening Transcript*. As music critic, he frequently reviewed dance, but unlike most such non-specialists, he was highly knowledgeable, and he observed dance deeply, feelingly, and with great acuity. He wrote tellingly about Isadora Duncan, who "widened the expressive scope and vividness of the dance . . . and increased its humanity," and he interviewed Vaslav Nijinsky with understanding and sympathy when Diaghilev's Ballets Russes (sans Diaghilev) appeared in Boston, in 1916. Parker always signed his articles "H.T.P.," which initials, joked *Time* magazine, were often taken to stand for "Hard-to-Please" and/or "Hell-to-Pay." Actually, he was a generous and thoughtful writer, not a slasher. In her *New York Times* review of *Motion Arrested*, Parker's collected dance writings edited by Olive Holmes, Anna Kisselgoff singles him out on the young Martha Graham, "whose face is that of a woman who visions, reflects, then wills and accomplishes," and whose works were "the promise of an American dance" and "for the while, they are also its fulfillment."

A Dancer Whose Art Is All Her Own

The charm of Miss Isadora Duncan's dancing, as she disclosed it last night on the stage of Jordan Hall, is its exquisite innocence, its exquisite lightness and its exquisite plasticity. Youths, in the pauses between her dances, sold pamphlets up and down the aisles and called it the dancing of the future—which, of course, is pure conjecture. The preliminary advertisements in turn called Miss Duncan's dancing "a revival of Greek—or was it classic?—art." That designation was no less

482

conjectural. If the archaeologists may be trusted, scanty indeed are the accounts of Hellenic dancing or even allusions to it that have come down to us. Dancing figures are plentiful on vases and reliefs, wall paintings of imitative Romans. Miss Duncan has obviously studied such figures. As clearly she has meditated upon the pictures of the early Italian painters—Botticelli and Fra Angelico for example. Quite as sedulously, seemingly she has observed the rhythmic movements of natural objects, like the leaves of the forest or growing grain swept by the wind, and of children and other spontaneous and natural folk. Out of all these strands she has woven the form, the manner, and the artistry of her dancing. No one of them may fairly name the whole fabric. Most of all, she has woven it out of her own imagination, skill, and ambition, of intuitions, experiment, and trials. It is fairest and clearest to name it Miss Duncan's dancing and rest content.

It is the more truly Miss Duncan's dancing because it relies almost wholly upon itself. The stage of Jordan Hall was roofed and draped with green hangings that, under the lights that were turned upon the dancer, became of more neutral hue. They hung in full soft folds to a floor covering of like neutral tint. A small orchestra—say twenty or thirty men—sat beneath the stage. It sufficed for the music to which Miss Duncan danced last night, chosen from Gluck's opera of "Iphigenia in Aulis." A part of it followed the dance tunes of the opera. The rest was delicately rhythmed airs from it used as music for the dance. Miss Duncan made no effort to translate into motion and miming the whole legend of Iphigenia, slain by her own father, Agamemnon, on the altars of Artemis to appease the angry goddess and speed the Argive fleet to Troy. She made no more effort to follow the dramatic narrative of the opera. Still less, seemingly, did she try to individualize herself as Iphigenia, with her tale and her fate written upon her face and her moving body. Rather Miss Duncan chose certain episodes from the legend, or from the opera, or from both, that suited the purpose and the manner of her dancing. Less concretely, she danced as often for the dancing's sake to fragments of Gluck's music in the opera, as she did later in the evening to the music of Schubert or Johann Strauss. The plasticity of Gluck's music, its undulating line, its clear soft poignancy, its fineness of rhythm and a remoteness and detachment in it, when it is played for such dancing, made it the more serviceable and becoming to her purposes. Miss Duncan finally wore no distinctively Greek dress except in a single episode. Hers were rather a succession of dancing tunics, of very bright, diaphanous, clinging stuff, sensitive to the slightest motion and oftenest of neutral colors. They made a dress that had invariable charm of flowing fold and changeful line. Many a dancer has been more heavily and fully clad and given much more suggestion of nakedness. For though Miss Duncan be bare of feet and legs, of arms and shoulders, there is in her and in all that she does a pervading suggestion of chastity and of a singular and virginal innocence. There is no thought whether she has beauty of face or body or limb. There is thought only of beautiful motion.

The captivating quality of that motion is its innocence. No doubt behind Miss Duncan's dancing, since she schools pupils in it, is some sort of technical system, and the suggestions of picture and relief and the movements of nature that have helped to fashion it are often clear. There is, however, no visible technique, no evolution from the six "classic positions" to the fullness of virtuosity that displays itself and is its own emotion and its own satisfaction. Bravura enters not into Miss Duncan's dancing. Rather it seems to spring spontaneously into being, to be the instinctive translation of the rhythm and the mood of the music, or of some vaguely indicated episode, in wholly natural and seemingly unfettered movement. From the shore the Greek maidens see the approaching fleet; the joy of the sight wells in them and quickens their spirit. Their natural impulse is to dance. Miss Duncan is seemingly one of them. Her joy speaks in every motion of her body, in the play of her arms, in the carriage of her head, in the responsive flow and swirl of her draperies. The joy and the dance are as innocent, as free from self-consciousness as though there were no one to see. The buoyancy of her movement seems spontaneous and from within. The music merely points the dance rather than persuades it. So, again, when Miss Duncan would dance of the joys of the spring and of the moods that it awakens, she is exquisitely virginal of aspect and motion. At the end of the evening, she turned Bacchante to Strauss's waltz of the Blue Danube, and never was there more innocently sensuous Bacchante imparting the joy, the zest and the warmth of life that the music stirs within her. Her means were her body and its motions, and yet the impression was of disembodied and idealized sensuousness. So, again, with the sterner physical zest, the suggestion of the young barbarian, in her Scythian dance out of Gluck's opera. Each motion idealized the impulse that it would impart. It is this innocence, this spontaneity, this idealized and disembodied quality in her dancing and in her posing that make Miss Duncan less persuasive when she resorts, as she did last night in one dance upon a partially darkened stage, to pantomime. It was not clear; it was not significant; it was a succession of beautiful, plastic, intent, but otherwise innocent poses.

The fascination of Miss Duncan's dancing lies no less in its beauty. She moves often in long and lovely sinuous lines across the whole breadth, or down the whole depth, of the stage. Or she circles it in curves of no less jointless beauty. As she moves, her body is steadily and delicately undulating. One motion flows or ripples, or sweeps, into another, and the two are edgeless. No deliberate crescendo and climax ordered her movements, rather they come and go in endless flow as though each were creating the next. And those movements have no less plastic beauty. They change, they fall together, so to say, like the colored glasses in the kaleidoscope, and Miss Duncan seems a figure off a Greek vase. They flow and fall again, and she is like to a dancing figure upon a Roman wall. Again, and she plays at ball like Nausicaa by the sea in the Odyssey, and each movement turns the game—an imaginary game in which there is only one player—into an idealizing beauty. She plays at knucklebones—the ancient jackstones—upon the shore at Colchis with Iphigenia's train, and it is as though she were the lovely essence of their sport. This pervading beauty springs, most of all perhaps, from the exquisite lightness of Miss Duncan's movements. A dancer could hardly be less free from the grosser bonds of flesh and muscles and nerves, from all physical and material conditions that would bind her to the earth. Miss Duncan treads the stage as though it were the air; she moves through the air as though it were the finer ether; the impression, though the eyes do see, is that she is as incorporeal as the sylphs, as fairy footed as the elves. Her dancing is as intangible, as un-material, as fluid as are sound or light. There is spirit-like quality in it.

This beauty springs no less from the delicate modulation of Miss Duncan's dancing. It does not indicate a large mood. It rather distills and concentrates the pure and delicate essence of each mood. It very seldom rose last night to passionate expression. Rather it idealized and disembodied the mood that it would suggest. It was not graphic, either of suggested character or of suggested emotion. It was only beauty and with a beauty that was full of delicate harmonies and captivating subtleties. Else would its range have seemed narrow. Out from a corner of the hangings came Miss Duncan. Perhaps flowers decked her hair and tunic. Oftener she was unadorned. The dance began. There was no impression of physical beauty or of physical charm. Eye and fancy saw only beautiful motion, exquisitely adjusted to the line of the music, animated to its rhythm, attuned to its harmonies. The music ran in arabesques of sound. The dancer moved likewise in as lovely arabesques of motion. Came a point of rest, and the lines of her body flowed into soft, clear pose. There were seconds or moments of luminous pause, and the motion began again. Sometimes it carried the dancer gliding across the stage. Sometimes it sent her in swifter motion. Again the movement was slow and languorous. Oftenest it was the motion of the whole body; but again it was the motion of arms in adroit modulation and suggestion, or of legs that were still more sensitive and significant.

It is the custom to speak of absolute music—of music that exists in itself and by itself, that imparts nothing but itself, and that makes its own beauty and emotion and thereby persuades and stirs its hearers. Of such, for example, is a symphony by Mozart. Miss Duncan's dancing is absolute dancing in a still fuller sense. It is peculiar to itself; it knows no rule, and it has no customs except those that she imposes. It has no purpose but to achieve its own beauty and to make responsive emotion to itself. Everywhere it cultivates fineness—in its rhythm, in its harmonies, its shading and suggestions. Everywhere it cultivates a chastity of motion and expression that give it a spiritual quality, a disembodied and poetic sensuousness—the sensuousness of Shelley's poetry. Like it, too, it has its lyrical quality, and its movement to the eye is often like the fall of delicate and rhythmically sensitive verse upon the ear. It is for connoisseurs of the eye as poetry is for the connoisseurs of the ear—granted the equal imagination behind. It goes and comes as of some animate and evanescent figure of the air. It accomplishes its ends in seeming spontaneity and innocence, as though it were of childhood. It really achieves them—it is easy to suspect—by calculated, practised and reflective artistry.

November 28, 1908

Miss St. Denis Dances

NEARLY AT the end of a long entertainment at Keith's yesterday, in which such ambitious or energetic film-makers as the familiar Charles Evans or the unfamilar Felix Adler gave much pleasure to the audience, Ruth St. Denis, the dancer, reappeared in Boston for the first time in several years and for the first time also in this town trod a vaudeville stage. In New York and in Philadelphia, she has lately danced anew in an entertainment of her own. From it she has now taken the five best-liked and most adaptable numbers to try her fortunes with a new public in a new environment. In New York that public was interested and cordial; in Boston, yesterday afternoon, it was not less so. It could, moreover, watch and applaud with a good conscience. Our august board of censors, being occupied with winter vacations and other seasonable pastimes of the great and good, did not condescend to scrutinize with their own eyes the costumes and the posturings of Miss St. Denis and her company, but despatched their favorite emissary to New York to spy upon them. He found no more than bare shoulders and bare feet to interest him and, after a pleasant excursion to the capital at the charge of the municipal treasury, reported in the dialect of his kind that Miss St. Denis was "unobjectionable."

Accordingly that fortunate young woman; a comely youth, Mr. Shawn, whose stalwart and supple figure recalled not a little that of Mr. Mordkin; and six or seven girls, slight, lithe, fresh and seemly, danced their dances before unpolluted Bostonian eyes. Two were merely intermezzi, continuing for a few minutes before an ordinary "drop" while the stage behind was set for a scene of India or Egypt. In one Miss Dotillo danced what the programme called a "tragic dance"; in fact it had no other character or illusion than her own youthful figure in more or less rhythmic motion gave to it. In the other, a Javanese dance, Miss Forman's profile under a curious head-gear that emphasized it; her slender body; her skirts now clinging and now parting; and the angular or undulating motion of her arms and hands did summon a little of the illusion that stirred Catulle Mendès and Hugo Hofmannsthal to fervid prose when such dancers descended of old upon Paris and Vienna. Now and again, Miss Forman's small sharp features, her intent glance, her rigid and distended body and the fine angles of her arms—and hands—all in profile upon the air rather than against a "drop" that had no kin with them—did carry the exotic suggestion of a gentle and dreamy dancing in relief rather than in the round. At the least it was unusual to see and it bore out what little to Western imaginations the designation suggested.

It was such dancing in relief that made one of Miss St. Denis's own numbers the most pictorial and interesting of the series. The dull blue hangings of the stage disclosed a low façade—say of a tomb or monument—in ancient Egypt. Against it in Egyptian dress were posed girlish figures that beat, tambourine-wise, upon thin rectangular Egyptian drums. In the doorway into the monument, Miss St. Denis and Mr. Shawn stood posed in the rigid and angular fashion of Egyptian mural painting. The orchestra accented more and more sharply a rhythm that was like the accelerating beat of a drum. Forth from the doorway came the two dancers and danced to it, but always with their arms, their hands, their legs and their bodies moving in straight sharp lines or arrested for an instant and even longer in cleanly-cut angles. The impression was of figures, stretching before the eye an Egyptian frieze, painted as it were upon the air, always in unity with itself yet of no little variety. It was a novel illusion of the dance; it was the dancing by straight line and sharp accent in a primitive fashion that Mr. Nijinsky cultivated—and indeed invented—in his last days with the Russian Ballet. Miss St. Denis, it now appears, has tried her hand at it, too, and with interesting result.

Of course, one of Miss St. Denis's numbers was a mimed and danced Hindu scene like those in which she first won her vogue. Yesterday, according to a note on the programme, it was a "legend," wherein an over-vain and luxurious Indian princess was transformed at death into a peacock that ever afterwards preened itself in the glaring sunshine before the white marble of her tomb. The mimed and—it was easy to suspect—the somewhat abbreviated action did not make the course of the legend clear; but it gave Miss St. Denis opportunity to wear the feathered panoply of a peacock's blues, greens and gold and to keep the expanding lines and the glinting colors in slowly rhythmed motion. It gave opportunity also for her to dance as the princess untransformed in the long undulations that she makes delicately modulated and beautiful linear movement: it brought Mr. Shawn to the stage in the costume of an Indian youth that well displayed his well-muscled and supple body; and it left room for an agreeable dance of Hindu women in which, at last, the moving lines were all curve. They were so also in the half-mimed and the half-danced "episode" with which the eclectic Miss St. Denis began. "The Spirit of the Sea" the programme named it and against a sea-green background, the stage revealed her as a wide-eyed, wondering, very slight and very fair-haired sprite of the waters cast upon a beach. On the sands by the rock, she danced her wonder and her nature in long, drooping, sea-green veils that she moved rhythmically about her as in wave-like motion until the billowing of them filled the air and hid all but her halo of sea-washed hair. If Miss St. Denis can go forward with the dance after the manner of Mr. Nijinsky, she can also go backward with it after the manner of Miss Loïe Fuller of ancient memory.

February 15, 1916

Manifold Nijinsky

SEEN ON the stage in the illusion of personation, costume, action, Mr. Nijinsky seems a tall, even substantial figure. Seen in his own person in the quiet of his rooms or across a dinner table, he is actually of no more than medium height and of slender contours. A Slav unmistakable in the smallness of his head, the fineness of his features, the brightness of his narrow eyes, the mobility of sensitive mouth and chin. A dancer or at least a personage of the theatre in a flowing ease of carriage that has become a second nature. A man of the cultivated world not only in the intonations of his speech which is French when it is not Russian but also in the plasticity of his mind and manner—all three mirrors as it were of a quick sensibility to many varied interests. (Mr. Nijinsky may dwell and work apart except when he is before his audiences, but he follows none the less the ways and the concerns of the immediate mankind about him, even to the conditions that make slow the counting of the vote of California and Minnesota.) A man, finally, who is no mere dancer and mime by natural aptitudes, arduous training, assiduous application and the general applause, but who kindles his artistries, faiths and ambitions out of a keen and meditative mind and a finely touched and unquenchable spirit.

For Mr. Nijinsky is no contented technician of the dance, super-latively as he may exemplify the older virtuosity in such a piece for the display of it as "The Enchanted Princess" or, in a measure the quasi-idyllic "Phantom of the Rose." He was schooled in it for nine years, as is every Russian dancer; he practised it for years afterward in the imperial theatres of Petrograd and Moscow before a public more expert and insistent with these technical felicities and feats than any other in the world. He still makes use of them daily in mimed imper-sonation and graphic suggestion, remote indeed from the ends for which the elder French and Italian ballet-masters designed them. They conceived the art of the dance as self-contained, self-sufficient, absolute, reward enough in its own agilities, graces, subtleties for those that practised and those that watched and applauded it.

Obviously it asked little of the mind; it gave as little room for the play of the spirit. Yet for the dancer and the mime of these later and newer days who would ply his intellect and set free his fancy and feel-ing in all that he undertakes, this old virtuosity provides often the apt and ready means—a shading here, a happy stroke there, a luminous point upon an implication that might otherwise be dark, a persuasive suavity that ingratiates and kindly disposes the spectator. The alert-ness, the patience, the dexterity, the endless quest for exactitude of the older virtuosity have their uses in the new freedoms. In itself it may be no more than a relatively paltry goal; yet, without it the dancer and the mime of these days lacks his tested tools.

So Mr. Nijinsky in amiable wisdom, retrospective and present, clear-minded and exactly phrased always, about the art of the dance. As lucidly and with a like gentle confidence and conviction, he is ready to link the present with the future. He recalls the repertory of the Russian Ballet: on the one side the pieces that exemplify the dance, pure but hardly simple—"The Sylphs," "The Enchanted Princess," "The Phantom of the Rose," "Butterflies," "Carnaval"— ballets of atmospheric and poetic suggestion as well as of the skill that they exact; on the other side, the mimodramas—"Cleopatra," "Schéhérazade," "Thamar," seeking illusion by acting that should be only the more graphic because it is wordless and using the dance in itself, as a means and aid to dramatic impersonation and narrative. It was possible for him, for Mr. Fokine, for the ballet, to continue to multiply either species, deriving a "Butterflies" from a "Carnaval," for example, making the dance serve new fancies, transfiguring as in "Armida's Pavilion" that upon which it had exercised itself of old. Similarly, mimodrama could go on with mimodrama—of agonized passion, of Oriental scene.

But the outcome would be—to make a kind of paradox—a monotony diversified within itself, content with pretty terpsichorean fantasias or with mimed and excited action. Stravinsky's "Firebird" did little more than blend these fantasias of the dance with quasi-dramatic fable out of old folk-lore. Even "Petrouchka" widened the field only by the setting of a fantastic and ironic tale within the busy and realistic action of the booth and the fair.

Yet in "Petrouchka"—as Mr. Nijinsky proceeded with brightening eyes and nervously graphic fingers, intent now upon that which kindles his mind, warms his heart, and is to him faith, work, ambition— yet in "Petrouchka" was the germ of the idea that first persuaded and finally conquered him. Stravinsky and Benois bid the spectators look into the half-human puppet's piteous little soul. He is more interesting, more touching for what he is than for what he does. The interest and the illusion of the fantasias were dynamic, upspringing from the grace, the charm, the beauty of motion. The interest and the illusion of the mimodramas sprang from visualized and intensified action. But the appeal of Petrouchka, the puppet, was, in a measure, in what he half-humanly was in his reactions to his fantastic fortunes. He touched his audience by what it felt about him rather than by what it merely saw him do. Why not, then, go forward to a ballet that should depend much more upon this static suggestion, a ballet that should not be full of dynamic emphasis, a ballet almost—to put an extreme case—without movement?

In "The Afternoon of a Faun" Mr. Nijinsky first worked out his idea of a ballet that should be intrinsically static, impersonal so to say, of spiritualized atmosphere and illusion, of reticent means and of means newly devised or employed. Studious always of pictures and sculptures, the old Greek bas-reliefs suggested the simplicity, the directness, the sparingness, even the rigidity of line in pose and gesture that he sought. From the actors on the stage of the spoken word, when they add to their abilities intuition, inspiration and what in short is called genius, emanate, though they speak not and stir not, the sensations, the emotions, the traits of the personage that they are assuming in the circumstances of the play. May not a dancer and mime of the speech-less theatre so receive, intensify and transmit, so bear to his audience the sensations and the illusions that Debussy's music and Mallarmé's verses bear? May not he and others beside into whom he has infused his intent weave out of pose and gesture and graphic impression, from within outward, an atmosphere like that which Debussy weaves in tones?

So Mr. Nijinsky designed and accomplished his version of "The Afternoon of a Faun." So, he went forward to Debussy's "Jeux," to Stravinsky's "Le Sacre du Printemps," to the present "Till Eulenspiegel" and the future "Mephisto Waltz." In "Jeux" he sought to simplify and spiritualize light fancy until the audience should forget that it was looking upon youth that might be on their way to or from tennis, yesterday, today, tomorrow and feel only the play of ever-renewed young moods, caprice, pastime and affections. He purposed a distilled illusion, he used as distilled and concentrated means. So far as he could accomplish his end, the piece—half-mimed, half-danced and sometimes merely a still projection—characterized. In "Le Sacre du Printemps"—spring rites of a primitive and pagan Russia—he returned to static suggestion, to rigid, sparing but always clearly rhythmed pose, gesture, movement, to this intensified projection by subtler and keener means than action, of the beliefs, the emotions, the ceremonies of primitive folk and faith. Already he had persuaded Stravinsky to his experiments and they worked upon "Le Sacre" in a common courage and loyalty.

Then for a year or two pause for the nursing of new ideas, for the shaping of new designs, for the fresh opportunity. It came with "Till," and therein Mr. Nijinsky would have the choreographic theatre flower in the denotement of character in this Eulenspiegel, in the graphic concentration of a place, a time, a folk, their moods and their manners, in hint withal at a social philosophy. The stage of the mime may thus match, may outdo, the austerer stage of the spoken word. Who shall say that he has not succeeded? So Mr. Nijinsky ended, but not until he had lifted once more the expository, the graphic finger: "Mais, souvenez-vous bien! C'est pour le Beau en maintes, formes, aspects, visages, que je travaille."

Thus ran an hour or two of rambling and stimulating theorizing; a vision, as it were, into the designing and directing mind and the prompting and inventing spirit of the artist, whose work the world sees in result but not in process. Not long before in a crowded theatre, Mr. Nijinsky had exemplified at one extreme his command of that elder virtuosity which is the means of the dancer and the mime and at the other the developments of those means into revelation of character and idea. For the first time he danced here the little scene, technically a pas de deux, that, isolated from Tchaikovsky's ballet of "The Sleeping Beauty," bears for title "The Enchanted Princess." In it, arrayed in the jewelled cap and broidered doublet of some seeming prince of the Indies, he had displayed the airiness, the fleetness, the lightness which are the perfect flower, by the Russian standards, of this technical skill and technical imagination. His light bounds into the air were impeccably swift, agile, exact: the play of hand, arm, head and body were in perfect symmetry, each little stroke of detail—the end or the beginning of a pirouette, for example—was flawless and fluid; each flowing movement, each momentary pose exhaled ease, grace, elegance, fancy. If the connoisseur rejoiced in method and style, the layman saw with equal, if more careless, pleasure.

Here was the Nijinsky of old beginnings; in "Till," in contrast, was Nijinsky of the present end. Perhaps the course of the performance was clearer than it had been on Monday; perhaps, the frequenters of the ballet, more familiar with the piece, were now able to distinguish the illusion of Mr. Nijinsky as Till from the illusion of the whole. So seen, he fulfilled his own faith in the characterizing arts of the dancer and the mime. In the prank upon apple-stall and bread-basket was the sportive Till—yet with a more serious intent or two underneath—and the litheness, the swiftness of his rhythmed pillaging had its beauty of the dance. This Till grimaced with his foot, with his whole body, when he mocked the pious pretence of the monks; wove the arabesques of the dance yet in and through them; was derisive courtier when he pretended to woo the rich and high-placed dames; put a kind of counterpoint into his miming when he made a mock of pedantic learning.

Then, the Till, all the mantles of disguise thrown aside who danced in long, swift lines in great arcs about the square, the elation of his power and victory, the happiness of a free spirit. Out of the face, the arms, the whole being of this Till spoke the jest that was more than half earnest when the rabble lifted him to deserved kingship. The miming of Till before the inquisitors was more within the ordinary scope of mimodrama with the twinges and twitches of dread in exact accord with the checked and tremulous leaps of Strauss's music. Then, resurrection and glorification with the outshining from Till of that inner illumination which Mr. Nijinsky believes the mime no less than the actor can compass—the triumph of an idea and a temperament in perpetual symbol, the "apotheosis" of the ancient ballet made a thing of simplicity, significance and beauty. In practice no less than in faith Mr. Nijinsky does not flag.

Mr. Nijinsky's theory and practice are his own but the reflex of them upon the ballet that he now directs and that he would fashion as much may be in his own image, ran clear in two instances, as they seemed, in the performance of the afternoon. Again young Mr. Gavrilov took the part of Petrouchka in Stravinsky's like-named piece. Again also he painted his face in the quest of puppet-illusion until it was too stiff to be expressive; but as though conscious of this self-imposed limitation, and with a like touch of originality to that which ran through his slave in "Schéhérazade," he sought characterization in another and singular way. He stressed the black mittened hands of little Petrouchka; made them twitch in the scene before the booth not only with all puppet strings and wires but also his human impulse toward the ballerina and the blackamoor. Again in his box, the restless, tireless, black hands shuffled up and down and over the wall as though to thrust through them, and find a way out of confinement and for Petrouchka out of himself. Or they beat upon the air in his impotence, humiliation, burning desire to express his passion and pain as a man and not as a doll. And it was with these clutching black hands, almost, that Petrouchka breathed his last breath. Mimed characterization, mimed state of soul that might have contented Mr. Nijinsky himself.

So, too, and even more subtly with Mr. Bolm's Pierrot of "Butterflies." His eyes aside, his face is rigid in the white mask. Oftener than not his hands are hidden in his long and waving sleeves. Yet tremor after tremor of emotion plays through Pierrot when he has caught his butterfly-maid. He wonders at her; he loves her; he fears her; he aches for her and for himself when she is spent, faints and plays, maybe, at death itself. Happy is he when she revives, elated at her smallest favor, wistful over her slightest caprice, piteous with disillusion when she does not even fly away but departs in the very earthly and prosaic state of father and mother, attendant swain and attendant footman.

Graphic, even touching, were these sensations of Pierrot as his audience watched and felt them, but they came less from any means of miming visibly plied by Mr. Bolm than by that magic telepathy of personation that Mr. Nijinsky would exalt.

November 9, 1916

CLAUDIA ROTH PIERPONT (1952–)

CLAUDIA ROTH PIERPONT began contributing to *The New Yorker* in 1990 and has been a staff writer for the magazine since 2004. She is the author of three books: *Passionate Minds* (2000), a collection of essays about women writers ranging from Hannah Arendt to Mae West; *Roth Unbound: A Writer and His Books* (2013), an exploration of the life and work of Philip Roth; and *American Rhapsody* (2016), a collection of essays on American subjects including George Gershwin, Nina Simone, and the Chrysler Building.

Pierpont's writings on theatrical dance and design have appeared in periodicals for the general reader and in specialized dance publications. The essay here, commissioned for this volume, was developed from remarks that the writer made on a panel as part of "Celebrating George Balanchine's *The Four Temperaments*," a public, daylong seminar put on by the Dance Critics Association, in 1985. A portion of the contents was previously published in *Ballet Review*.

Balanchine's Temperaments

AFTER TWO or three days of choreographing *The Four Tempera-ments*, in the fall of 1946, Balanchine asked the dancers what sort of creatures they thought they were meant to be. None of them knew, but some ventured the idea that they might be worms, or insects. Gisella Caccialanza, who was dancing the Third Theme, recalled that Balanchine replied in the negative and then told them, grandly, "You're temperaments." She said that he promised to explain this statement later, but of course he never did. Explanations were not part of Balanchine's system. If his ballets contained meanings beyond the juxtaposition of music and movement—or meanings that arose from the juxtaposition of music and movement—he was the last to talk about them. Words were confining, ideas were limiting, and interpretations were generally ridiculous. "Everybody thinks that 'Sanguinic' means you cut yourself," he remarked decades later, "or somewhere else you cry." Ballet was not capturable in words: music and dance, Balanchine insisted, belonged to "the world where there are no names for anything."

The Four Temperaments was a new development in Balanchine's work. Rigorously classical yet expressively shaped and bent, it appeared emphatically modern in a way that foretold a long and famous line of "black and white" ballets: *Agon* (1957), *Episodes* (1959), *Movements for Piano and Orchestra* (1963), *Violin Concerto* (1972), *Symphony in Three Movements* (1972). Balanchine had been choreographing for more than twenty years when, on November 20, 1946, the ballet appeared on the opening program of Lincoln Kirstein's new and belligerently anti-commercial company, Ballet Society, performing on the barely adequate stage of New York's Central High School of Needle Trades. It was difficult even to make out the choreography, at first. The costumes, by the Surrealist painter Kurt Seligmann, so obscured the dancers' bodies and so hampered their ability to move—with enormous headdresses, mittens, breastplates—that Balanchine went around with a pair of scissors shortly before the opening, snipping away. By 1951, there were no costumes at all, only the tights and leotards that signified the end of the Diaghilevan concept of the almighty scenic designer, and put the black and white into the "black and white" ballet.

But, despite its clear place in this development, there is no other work quite like *The Four Temperaments*. A sense of meaning embodied in abstract movement, glancing and mysterious, is not uncommon in Balanchine's ballets; it is, indeed, the openness to metaphor and suggestion that makes his works so imaginatively rich. Yet the idea of a hidden language presses upon us with peculiar intensity in this ballet, and is bound to an ineffable dramatic power. The signs of this language are specific, repeated, insistent: the "Egyptian" gestures of the Second Theme, two dancers moving as in a frieze with semaphorically flashing arms, up and down, up and down; the deep backbends in the role of Melancholic (how does a standard gymnastic move become a tragedy of character?); the flight of the Sanguinic couple in a circuit of lifts that seem to circumnavigate the earth. What, if anything, do these movements and gestures "mean"? Is the question a pointless attempt to name the passing illusions whose power lies in the very fact that they cannot be named—and that they are illusions? *The Four Temperaments* is also unique, however, in that such questions can be viewed in terms of the goals of a composer who, unlike Balanchine, was not averse to words.

The ballet's title was the idea of Paul Hindemith, the German composer from whom Balanchine commissioned a score, sometime in early 1940. Balanchine had no ballet company at the time, but he was flush with money from his work on Broadway, and he wanted something new for his musician friends to play at the gatherings he held regularly in his apartment. His only request was that the instrumental forces be small enough to fit in his living room, and include a piano and strings. Hindemith's early and best-known music, from the twenties, was harshly experimental, and had put him at odds with the Nazi regime almost from the start. (Non-musical matters added to the friction: Hindemith, whose wife was half-Jewish, refused to conceal his contempt for Nazi policies.) In 1938, his work had been included in the Nazis' "Degenerate Music" exhibition, and the Hindemiths had moved to Switzerland. In 1940, they emigrated to the United States, where, that fall, he took up a teaching post at Yale. It was in New Haven, in October, that Hindemith composed *Theme with Four Variations (According to the Four Temperaments) for String Orchestra and Piano*, with each variation "corresponding to one of the temperaments," as he told his publisher: "one melancholy, one sanguine, one phlegmatic, and one choleric."

The subject was not a surprising choice for Hindemith, although such extra-musical subjects were generally outside the modernist norm. But so was much of his post-twenties work. In recent years, his defense of the tonal and the traditional had placed him in opposition to the musical vanguard. He was a passionate musical historian, and his work of the thirties reflected influences ranging from Renaissance and Baroque to classical symphonic styles. An opera about the German sixteenth-century painter Matthias Grünewald was his major opus to date; the libretto, which Hindemith wrote himself, was filled with scenes based on the painter's work, including a *Concert of the*

Angels that he had set to a beautiful German folk tune. He had composed a ballet for Léonide Massine based on Giotto's frescoes of St. Francis, and he was working on another score for Massine, based on works by Breughel, when he broke off relations with the choreographer, in April 1940, for what he called "artistic reasons." Some musicologists believe that parts of the Breughel score were used in his next ballet, *The Four Temperaments*, the following fall.

But there was more to Hindemith's unorthodoxy than immersion in Renaissance and Baroque art, or a refusal to relinquish melody. Inspired by his historical explorations, he believed that the principles of music reflect a larger universal order. In his introduction to *The Craft of Musical Composition*, a book that he completed before his emigration, he announced his agreement with ancient theorists who held that "tonal materials" were among the "building stones of the universe," and that the universe itself was constructed in the "same proportions as the overtone series, so that measure, music, and the cosmos inseparably merged." He hoped that his book would rekindle something of this mystic spirit. And he pursued the spirit himself in the central composition of his later life, an opera about the seventeenth-century German astronomer Johannes Kepler, in which he sought to dramatize both Kepler's life and his convictions about the music of the spheres. The opera is titled, after Kepler's own treatise, *The Harmony of the World*.

Stravinsky famously said that music cannot express anything but music, a statement that reflects a basic tenet of modern aesthetics. Paintings about painting; poems about words. Hindemith's attitude seemed by contrast retrogressive, even sentimental. In *The Four Temperaments*, he found another subject that blended history, art, and mysticism: an antique medical system dividing the human race into four essential types, which combine or predominate to form our individual selves. From Hippocrates to Dürer, from Kant to Jung, the temperaments were credited with either physiological or psychological truth. We can't know how seriously Balanchine (presumably a Stravinskyan) considered the subject when he received the score, toward the end of 1940. His first attempt to choreograph the music, for a South American tour in 1941, was derailed when Kirstein entrusted the designs to the Russian Surrealist painter Pavel Tchelitchev, who threatened to hijack the production—retitled *The Cave of Sleep*—until Hindemith objected to the departure from his concept, and the project (too expensive in any case) was called off.

Five years later, with the creation of Ballet Society, Balanchine took on the score again. This time, Hindemith's concept was retained; as Balanchine told the dancers, they were temperaments. Balanchine was not given to statements, but he could inhabit a great diversity of musical styles and intentions. Could it be that the insistent language of *The Four Temperaments*, its pervasive sense of larger meanings, reflects Balanchine's response to Hindemith's transcendent goals? Is it possible that Balanchine may even have had a few such goals of his own?

Melancholic, sanguinic, phlegmatic, choleric: the four absolutes of human nature were associated in early philosophical systems with the great "fours" of everything else—the seasons, the winds, the times of day, the elements. Balanchine, discussing *The Four Temperaments* in *Stories of the Great Ballets*, referred only to the elements as historical analogues. Earth, air, water, fire: one can understand how the elements suggested a physical territory for dancers to inhabit. A floor to stand on, forces that support and resist and contain and threaten—not a program, certainly, but a start on making Hindemith's music visible.

Three sequential themes announce the basic musical material. The simple melodies that build these themes continually reappear, familiar but radically changed in rhythm or tempo or orchestral texture, and take on radically different emotional colors. This is the nature of the variation form, but the clarity of the original components and the marked personality of each variation keep the listener exceptionally aware of links between formal development and expressive impact, as when a flowing melody played by a solo violin at the beginning of the Third Theme—a Siciliano, a kind of pastorale akin to lullabies and shepherd's pipes—becomes, in the Melancholic variation, a driving march. The three pas de deux that Balanchine set to these themes also display suggestively "thematic" movements—severe profile poses, supported splits, those semaphoring "Egyptian" arms—which reappear, physically multiplied and emotionally amplified, in the finale. The movement throughout these themes imparts a sense of highly conscious human drama, building from the simple joining of hands to the Third Theme's hieroglyphically precise if mysterious images: a woman clinging to a man's back as he walks, searching, his arm extended toward an unseen horizon; the two dancers fused into a single scarab-like creature out of dream or myth.

The figure of Melancholic rushes on and rises into a stretched-up arabesque, on half-toe, and then drops limply downward. Identification with the earth is strong in the relation of this single male dancer to the floor, and in the sense that gravity is continually working on him. He tries to jump and to run but he is always pulled low, before rising to begin the ever-defeating process again. For a long time he simply crouches at the center of the stage. But his most defining movements are those that crash almost violently from up to down: an arabesque that suddenly reverses into a forward kick and strains upward, before the dancer falls to the side in a crumpled heap; a bounding jump that collapses into a deep backbend, again and again, suggesting continually broken aspiration. With nothing in the surrounding space to impede him, it seems to be, rather, something within—as history and legend have it—that cripples this powerfully muscled figure.

The most famous *Melancholia* in the history of art is Dürer's engraving of a great winged creature sitting heavily in a corner, earthbound, eyes fixed in concentration. The tragedy of the figure is in its useless wings: here is a being meant for flight—something like a dancer—paralyzed by a failure of will. As Hindemith surely knew, the Melancholic was believed to be the artistic temperament: reaching beyond his limits, brooding at his failures, prone to madness.

The spiritual tragedy of the ballet's Melancholic is dramatized by the entrance of a small group of women. First, a pair of protectors arrive, like inspiration—to the full company of strings—when he is at his lowest, crouched at center stage; their light leaping about stirs him to rise and join them. There is a playfulness to their dancing together, not unlike the muses with Apollo—a sense of encouragement, of coaxing—but these moments are only the prelude to a trial. Four more women enter as a phalanx with great lancing kicks, in a gust that sends Melancholic and his helpmeets spinning. This furious entrance is set to the brutal march that Hindemith created out of the earlier pastorale, just as the women's threatening kicks and stabbing pointes come out of the swinging battements and carefully placed pointes of the themes. The four women form a small gauntlet, which Melancholic enters alone; but whatever he feels there is too much for him. He runs to the two protectors waiting outside, holds out his hands, and, in a passage that involves kneeling and turning and harnessing their power to him, takes them back with him into the dangerously charged space. There was a telling detail at this moment in Mikhail Baryshnikov's performance: he threw his hands out to the two women—this is the choreography, but the hands can be placed rather than thrown—with a wild desperation, an open plea for help. He made explicit what is present even when the role is played more abstractly; the drama cannot be kept out.

The climax of the variation occurs when Melancholic repeatedly runs up and down the stage, stopping only at its farthest ends—the back wall, the edge of the orchestra pit—where he drops to one knee, then arches into the deepest possible backbend. When he comes to the front of the stage and drops down, his arms stretch behind him and his head hangs back, so that his face all but disappears. Rising and turning to reverse his path, he inexorably drops down again: this time, as he arches back, his extended arms come straight out toward us and his face hangs before us, upside down, in the air. The effect is of tremendous anguish and direct appeal.

In the great revival of *The Four Temperaments* in 1975, after the ballet had been out of repertory for a few years, Bart Cook made this role his own. Cook's remarkable pliancy, and his propensity for high expressiveness within smoothly rounded forms, prompted Balanchine to choreograph, the following year, a new male solo for a revival of the fifties ballet *Square Dance*, a solo that stands in clear relation to Melancholic. Danced to a Corelli sarabande (the rest of *Square Dance* is set to Vivaldi), the solo is extremely formal yet has a passionately emotive tone, with courtier-like bows addressed to no one—this is a figure deep in fantasy—and one heartstopping moment in which the dancer reaches out directly to the audience. But the essence of this soliloquy is a passage that contrasts the dancer's fixed position, his feet nearly pinioned in tight little turns that go nowhere, with a yearningly stretched upper body that suggests a longing beyond bounds.

With Sanguinic, the second variation of *The Four Temperaments*, the operative element is air. This is the only pas de deux among the variations, and the use of two dancers, male and female, makes it possible for the woman to stay aloft. But the ballerina is also an allegro virtuoso—the role was created by Mary Ellen Moylan, and reincarnated in 1975 by Merrill Ashley—and she is perfectly capable of being airbound on her own. By definition, Sanguinic is everything Melancholic is not. Balanchine was joking about cutting yourself, but ancient medical systems did credit the Sanguinic's character to blood. (Phlegm and different forms of bile were believed to be responsible for the others.) As a result, this temperament is healthy, thriving, joyous, and very rare.

In the theme and variations form—that is, in a work of art about transformation—one element mysteriously becomes another and similar things acquire different meanings. A startling example of Balanchine's physical alchemy occurs when the Sanguinic ballerina performs a sequence of steps that is a variant of one of Melancholic's. Making an entrance as her partner completes a solo and falls to his knee, she runs past him and kicks up into the air as she throws her torso back from the waist. The combination is nearly simultaneous, and difficult: "He wants you falling backwards and flying forwards through the air" is how Merrill Ashley put it. Melancholic, in his version, kicks up into a big turning jump, one leg thrown out before him as he lingers a moment in the air, then breaks into a backbend that follows so naturally it seems a consequence of the jump—literally a backlash. His movements are sequential and full-blown, while the Sanguinic ballerina has to perform all the essentials at once—kick up, fall back—and do it fast. Her momentum is never broken, despite the contradictory impulses; she lands on her feet and keeps on moving into the next kick, three times in all. ("I feel like I'm going to rip every ligament in the landing leg," Ashley added, "your weight's so far behind you.") At first, the ballerina tends to look stiff in the upper body, because we have been prepared for the upward drive to be joined to Melancholic's deep backward curve. But, with Sanguinic, the emphasis shifts to the kick up—to the legs. And with the ballerina's head and shoulders thrown back, the sequence becomes an unharnessed image of high spirits, although it is made of the same materials as Melancholic's despair.

The quintessential image of the Sanguinic variation is the circuit of lifts done twice around the stage, early in the pas de deux and again at its end. These are low lifts, with the ballerina held just at the level of her partner's chest, but they evoke a tremendous sense of altitude and distance. Mary Ellen Moylan described this pas de deux as taking place "in another atmosphere." Arlene Croce, in her landmark essay on *The Four Temperaments*, wrote that the Sanguinic variation "takes us to the top of the world, and twice we ride around its crest, its polar summit." I have been put in mind, while watching these lifts, of a line from Robert Fitzgerald's translation of the *Iliad*, about the goddess Athena, who "rears her head through heaven as she walks the earth." All of this derives from a few motions made by the ballerina while she is borne along: steadily extending one leg, rudder-like, and making a clearing gesture with her hands, she parts the currents of an oncoming wind and disperses the clouds.

At the end of the first circuit of lifts, the dancers, in response to the ebbing energy of the music, sink into a pair of tight revolutions in place, as the man lowers the ballerina to the floor and the little corps de ballet rushes on. Later, as the end of the movement approaches and the music begins again to swell, the pair repeat the same tight revolutions but with the energy in reverse, steadily building, a preparation for takeoff into the final lifts. This time, however, when they complete two full polar circuits, they continue on beyond the point where they wound down before; it seems that a trigger point is passed, as the music keeps building and they keep going. And there is a release of energy like an explosion: as the dancers reach the wings, a final lift vaults the ballerina straight and very high into the air, and she flies off.

Or she did. In a rehearsal of the Sanguinic variation that I saw Balanchine conduct with Anthony Blum and Merrill Ashley, on the very day of the revival's première—November 11, 1975—he was insistent that the final lift sail up and out at full height, straight off the stage, as it did that evening and for some time afterward. But this exclamatory exit has been changed. Now, after a single high lift, the man puts the ballerina down when they near the wings, and the pair run off together. It seems possible that the change was made when the ballet was televised, to create a clear frame and to prevent the dancers from seeming to disappear off the side of the screen. Or perhaps it was an act of mercy for a new partner's back. (The PBS tape, made in 1977 with Ashley and Daniel Duell, does indeed show him putting her down.) But the brilliance of that final soaring trajectory is missed.

This exit also sharpened the contrast with the slow, uncertain entrance of a solitary figure from a corner of the stage. Lethargic,

CLAUDIA ROTH PIERPONT 505

limited in reach, and comically solemn as he passes his variation's simplest tests—climbing through a crossing web of girls' legs, holding up his own foot—the Phlegmatic soloist is psychologically unmistakable. He can make himself very small: at times, crouching behind a corps of four, he completely disappears. The dancer who originated the role, Todd Bolender, stamped it not only with his physical qualities but with his theatrical persona: known for his rubbery body and his wit, Bolender brought a *commedia dell'arte* quality to the movement even in 1997, when, at the age of eighty-three, he coached Albert Evans for the Balanchine Foundation's Video Archives. No one except Bolender had danced the role as long as he was active in the company, into the early 1960s—no one even learned it. On the single occasion when he was too sick to dance, Balanchine said that he would go on himself, although he ultimately talked Bolender into performing, with a fever of one hundred and two. To judge from Bolender's account on the video record, Phlegmatic is ideally light, stealthy, cat-like; and his comedy has a dead-pan Buster Keaton undertone of fear and pain.

The entrance is simple, a man just walking along with one arm raised before him, in search of something, very like the man seen earlier in the Third Theme. (This kind of searching figure had already appeared in Balanchine's *Serenade* (1934), and one might say that Bolender's later role in "The Unanswered Question" (*Ivesiana*, 1954) is Balanchine's boldest characterization of man's hopeless search for an ideal.) According to Bolender, a "quality of search" defines the entire variation. Jean-Pierre Bonnefous, who danced the role in 1975, felt that he had arrived at this entrance "from far away," and was on "a long, long trip." Yet what we see of the trip is abbreviated. The figure walks a few steps; he stops; he starts again; then suddenly his hand droops, his head falls, his arm collapses, his knees fold, and he undergoes an oddly Charleston-like seizure—knees in, knees out—that stops him in his tracks. The softly questioning music keeps this collapse from seeming a tragedy; so does his quick recovery of equilibrium. Phlegmatic is indecisive and easily spooked, but he is never down for long.

The ballet's vocabulary is subject to further revision. Here, backbends are merely acrobatic, or curiously experimental; clearing gestures are made with hands that clear nothing at all. But there are also uniquely Phlegmatic effects: a small repertoire of hand-on-hip gestures and fashion-model poses that bespeak insouciance and fatal distraction. (Wasn't he on his way somewhere?) Bolender, working with Evans, cleaned decades of change from well-known passages to reveal their startling original intent. A mannered retraction of the figure's hands toward his chest, teasingly effete, turns out to have been a plain expression of fear: a sudden snatching back of the hands to protect the chest on a single quick breath. A mechanical crumpling of the entire figure, one notch per note, was once a searing passage of pure anguish: "Balanchine wanted this to be as though you were in some sort of terrible pain," Bolender instructed, and added that the choreographer had trusted him to devise a series of tortured poses. After demonstrating something of what he had done, Bolender asked Evans to make up poses of his own, and for a moment this young dancer, who had seemed too athletic and generically classical for the role, looked like one of Michelangelo's slaves.

Jean-Pierre Bonnefous was a very different dancer from Bolender— heavily muscled, tense, electric—but he had the interiority that Bolender stressed as essential to the role, a sense of dancing only for himself that Bolender felt had disappeared from modern perfor- mances. It is true that the variation has lost piquancy over the years, but whether that is because Bolender was out of the country when Balanchine reset the ballet in 1975, as Bolender maintained, or because Balanchine developed different ideas, or simply because Phlegmatic is the most ineffable and easily effaced of the temperaments, we cannot know. Here, too, the final moment of the variation has been altered, and in a way contrary to its original intent. In the familiar ending, Phlegmatic, accompanied by his corps of girls, rises onto half-toe and sweeps his arms high in the air, and the group rushes offstage together. This exit is theatrical—a flourish, the end of an act. Originally, how- ever, the girls rushed off without him, and Phlegmatic was left to raise one arm and walk offstage alone, just as he'd entered, resuming the journey that will presumably never end.

Lincoln Kirstein described Phlegmatic as "fluidly sluggish," and Arthur Mitchell—who learned the role from Bolender—said that the real difficulty is "to get the accents with the feet and retain fluidity in the body." But that is about all the fluidity there is: nothing more in the variation suggests the element of water. Just as well. The essence of *The Four Temperaments* is its elusiveness, and suggestions about the elements are meant to highlight an artistic heritage that Balanchine may have drawn on, at will. This viewer's sense that he had drawn on it at all arises not from any desire to discover a system or (God forbid) an explanation for the ballet's mysteries, but from a strong visceral impression made by a sequence in the last of the variations, Choleric.

Erupting onto the stage at her first entrance, all discord and flashing limbs—she is best played by a leggy dancer, like the role's originator, Tanaquil Le Clercq—the Choleric ballerina is one very angry, disruptive force. After her first solo, the man from the Sanguinic pair comes on and attempts to partner her, but he no sooner puts his hands to her waist than he throws them violently up into the air, as she bursts away in arabesque—it's as though she were truly too hot to handle, scalding to the touch. This incident can be played with varying degrees of sharpness and drama, of course. Karin von Aroldingen used to make one want to shout "Fire!" in the crowded theater—an unexpected and bewildering impulse that led me to wonder about connections with the elements. Von Aroldingen also created a shimmery little fire dance out of Choleric's rise from the floor after four men emerge and tap her to life, sizzling and hissing. It should be said that this imagery is largely absent from Colleen Neary's performance in the ballet's televised version, although in the 1980s Maria Calegari rose like a shower of sparks (being a redhead did not hurt). Make of it what you will, Balanchine did, in fact, choreograph a Fire variation, in Ravel's opera *The Spellbound Child*, which was presented on the same Ballet Society program, in 1946, as *The Four Temperaments*.

In order for the dramatic forces to coalesce in the ballet's climax, the disruptive energy of Choleric must be quelled. This requires more than a single effort. In the final section of the ballet, she is penned within a square marked by four couples—the three Themes and the Sanguinic—and crouches down, with her arms over her head. The four surrounding women rise into supported penchées and swing their extended legs over her; she rises and pushes through these legs as though through a gate, and spins off to the side of the stage. With Choleric removed, each of the women is lifted, in turn, in low arabesque, and her pointe is lightly touched down in the empty space where Choleric stood; then she is lifted and lowered again, in arabesque, onto the other pointe. But Choleric has not yet been dispelled. She returns to the center of the group, and the ritual is repeated: the penchées swing in, and she pushes through them as before, but this time she spins all the way to the wings and, with a final exiting arabesque, is gone. The sequential lifting in arabesque recurs, with a single pointe lowered each time into the emptied space. It seems that a cleansing is being performed: that each ballerina's pointe is being used to purify the ground where Choleric stood.

In medieval legend, the horn of the unicorn was dipped into contaminated pools to draw out the poison. One of the great Unicorn tapestries at the Cloisters, in New York, shows just such an image of the unicorn lowering his head to place the tip of his horn in the water. Can this image possibly have influenced *The Four Temperaments*? The tapestries went on view at the Cloisters at its opening, to tremendous fanfare, in 1938. And Seligmann's original design for Choleric's costume included an ummistakably large (and unwieldy) unicorn's horn. Certainly Balanchine knew the legends: Suzanne Farrell has spoken of his dream of making a *Dame à la licorne* ballet for her, based on the related set of tapestries in the Musée de Cluny. The subject accords with the four temperaments in period and spirit, and confirms the impression of those who have seen a "bestiary" in the ballet. Just eight months after making *The Four Temperaments*, Balanchine included a version of this passage in the adagio of *Symphony in C*: the ballerina is lifted by her partner in arabesque and lowered so that her pointe pierces a space framed against the floor by the arms of two corps dancers; she is lifted out and the sequence is repeated to the other side. The abstract poetry of this passage hardly yields to thought, yet it clearly had its genesis in *The Four Temperaments*, and in Balanchine's belief in the transforming magic—as metaphorically potent as a unicorn's horn—of the ballerina's pointe.

We know that Balanchine experimented with different endings. A rehearsal film from 1946 shows us what he called his "Radio City Music Hall number": a tightly revolving mass of figures, crouching and writhing as they circle around—heads dropping forward and back as when Melancholic is caged among his phalanx of women—with figures tossed straight up into the air from the center of the melee. Kirstein described this ending as "a volcanic fountain or atomic disruption of bodies." Informally, people around the company called it "the atom bomb ending." In November, 1946, that image must have seemed obvious, even insistent; the ending was "Radio City" in its use of the technique of a stageful of figures merging into one enormous living simulacrum, in this case of the brand-new shape of apocalypse.

The ending didn't work. Balanchine, throughout his career, sought effects larger than the stage could hold—the flood he wanted for *Davidsbündlertänze*, in 1980, might have been realizable only at Radio City—and in changing the ending he may have acquiesced to the gap between a desired image and the results obtainable with a group of dancers. Or he may have felt that this ending wasn't musically appropriate. The rehearsal film is silent. How did the curtain come down? Probably as in *Cotillon* (1932) or *La Valse* (1951), with the stage still spinning full tilt. But Hindemith's final rhythms are stately and measured, marked *maestoso*. And the music mounts not to chaos but to triumph: the melody-bearing strings rise over the discordant opposition of the piano, drawing it toward their harmonic path like a magnet until, in the final moments, the piano begins to peal around the melody like church bells, and the two lines converge and fall away.

For the ballet's next performances, in February 1947, at New York's City Center, Balanchine made the completely different ending we know today: the "runway" or "lane," as it has been called, composed of two parallel lines of dancers—marching forward into place with high battements and stabbing feet, turning, bending, reaching as they stretch across the stage—travelled by pairs of dancers in high lifts. The music's qualities of flight and ecstatic release are embodied in this extraordinary image. But this runway (which retains some slight adjustments made for the 1977 television version) may be no less a stage picture than Balanchine's first ending, with a given shape and associations that do not explain the music but serve it.

In the finale of his opera *The Harmony of the World*, Hindemith constructed a grand-scale physical allegory, with planets and stars shown whirling through space. Even more remarkable, these heavenly bodies are heard. In his faith in the correspondences between music and the cosmos, the composer determined to invent the kinds of harmony that his equally visionary astronomer-hero claimed to have discovered: the sounds of planetary motion, or the music of the spheres. This was an impossibly bold idea, probably doomed from the start. (The musical substance of the climax is a huge chorus, with orchestra, punctuated by *Four Temperaments*-like pealing chimes.) Hindemith began the libretto in 1939, the year before he composed *The Four*

Temperaments; the colossal work was finished and performed only in 1957, and has been largely forgotten. Still, the composer's goals may have survived elsewhere. Without a hint of a story or of astronomical intent, but with a genius for making the spirit of music visible, Balanchine seems to have found and conveyed Hindemith's vision of cosmic exaltation.

Balanchine achieved this vision in the same way that, historically, men first tracked the heavens: by building an architectural structure, in the form of standing columns that frame and gauge the passing planets in their flight. Thus, when the double ranks of dancers march to the center of the stage, a great peristyle comes into place. Balanchine is building a temple, and it is worth noting—for the historian, if not the dancer—that early temples were seen as runways for celestial traffic, the rows of columns intended to "open the road to the world of the gods," in the words of Mircea Eliade.

It is possible, too, if one is so inclined, to see Balanchine's architecture in a less archaic, more classical light. In that view, the soaring, sharply peaked lifts traced by the principal couples above the ranks describe a monumental triangular pediment that vaults into place overhead. The flying figures seem at once to shape the architecture and to suggest the famous images carved on the great classical pediments: the windswept messenger gods and the chariots rising from the corners of the earth to draw the sun and moon across the sky.

This interpretation, to adapt a Balanchine locution, may seem dreadfully fancy. But consider, finally, Lincoln Kirstein's description of a hypothetical ballet, which began with his and Balanchine's idea for a work that would follow *Apollo* and *Orpheus*, and be called *Apollo Architectons*. Kirstein described the subject to be set to music in a letter to Stravinsky, in 1953: "Balanchine sees a marvelous theatricalized cosmic space in an architectural frame, more like Palladio than the baroque." But hadn't Balanchine already made just such a ballet? What else could they go on to do but *Agon*?

2017

Megan Pugh (1982–)

A NATIVE of Memphis, Tennessee, and daughter of Dorothy Gunther Pugh, founding artistic director of Ballet Memphis, poet and scholar Megan Pugh earned a B.A. in American Studies from Yale and a doctorate in English from the University of California at Berkeley. Her essays have appeared in *The New Republic*, *Boston Review*, and *The Village Voice*. She lives in Portland, Oregon, where she teaches at Lewis & Clark College of Arts & Sciences. The entry below is the introduction to her first book, *America Dancing: From the Cakewalk to the Moon Walk*, published in 2015.

(from) Introduction: An American Style

WHAT MAKES a dance American? People have been asking that question for at least a hundred years. Their answers betray a longing for wholeness, as if the country and its art could be distilled to some core set of values. American dance, critics have maintained, should embody freedom, democracy, individualism, and community. It should be welcoming, strong, beautiful, and free. It should spring from the soil, reflect history, give form to present-day feelings, and prophesy a collective future. None of those descriptions deals with the question of how dancers might hold their heads, move their hips, or educate their feet. Instead, they offer impressionistic attitudes, attempts to make a coherent whole out of the national experience. But national experience is too varied, and too vexed, to pin down. America keeps shifting beneath Americans' feet.[1]

Still, the effort to define the nation by means of its art has had perpetual appeal. For the author and educator Constance Rourke, who took up the challenge in 1931, performance was at the heart of the process. Here's Rourke in *American Humor*, her pivotal study of the national identity, on the Yankee peddler, who swapped his way through stories and almanacs to the center of the popular stage: "The American stepped full-length into the public glare, and steadily heightened the early yellow light. He gazed at himself in the Yankee plays as in a bright mirror, and developed the habit of self-scrutiny, which may have its dangers for the infant or youth, whether the creature be national or human."[2] Rourke's pronouns are as shifty as the Yankee peddler's salesmanship. In her first sentence, the American is an actor, ushering in a new dawn. One period later, the American is a member of the audience, looking up at himself. In a feat of syntactical wizardry, Rourke gets at the give-and-take between what is performed and what is absorbed, the way art both shapes the world and is shaped by it.

Today, the assertion at the heart of Rourke's book—that there is such a thing as an "Americanness" waiting to be discovered—might sound dated. National archetypes seem like the stuff of smug exceptionalism, the belief that the country is elevated, and separate, from the rest of the world. They can also seem oppressively essentialist, erasing the differences among diverse populations. Performance both skirts and takes up those problems. Performing the country means turning it into an imaginative creation. In the hands of artists, or the bodies of dancers, America becomes an idea, something to bring citizens together as they test out who they are, and who they'd like to become.[3]

Americanness may be an impossible conceit, but as the stories in this book make clear, people keep trying to define it. It's a way for Americans to make sense of their home. It's a mantle American artists have been eager to claim for themselves, and a quality that American audiences have been eager to find in dance, where they seek to discover—or perhaps invent—truths that emerge, bare and essential, from bodies in motion. How we move, the thinking goes, should show us who we are.

Some of the dancers whose stories follow took pains to present their creations as quintessentially American. At the height of World War II, Agnes de Mille set her ballet *Rodeo* in the Old West, site of so many of the nation's fundamental myths. When Bill Robinson and Shirley Temple dance together in *The Littlest Rebel* and *The Little Colonel*, which take place during and after the Civil War, they charm both

Yankees and Confederates, symbolically unifying a nation torn asunder. Paul Taylor, who has choreographed over a dozen dances set in various American pasts, says he prefers modern dance to ballet, in part, because it's homegrown.

But a sense of what makes the country itself often reverberates on lower frequencies, in the movements. Fred Astaire syncopates his way into ballet's entrechat-trois, a series of hummingbird-like beats of the leg, and inflects European tradition with the rhythms of black America. The dancers in Paul Taylor's *Company B* combine modern movements with Lindy Hop lifts and military marches, the angst of war bubbling up through the pep of popular culture. When Michael Jackson moonwalks, he follows in the steps of both 1970s California street dancers and nineteenth-century blackface minstrels. Histories that run so deep may not be consciously tapped into, or even recognizable. But they remind us that dance is not always as spontaneous as it might appear. Whether intentionally or not, dancers pick up, pass down, and repurpose other people's movements.

Dance is a notoriously slippery art. Unlike books, paintings, and recorded music, which can all be apprehended as discrete objects, dances don't exist without bodies to do them. Move a certain way, and the movement becomes you. But the movement is never yours—at least, not in the sense that a poem or a piece of Tupperware might be yours—because someone else can come along and imitate your steps. That slipperiness is one of the reasons dance can help us think about national identity: Americans have discovered themselves, in part, by pretending to be other people. What can we make of these imitations? They tell us that the history of American dance is composed not just of self-invention, but of love, mockery, and a longing for a mobility that can come from assuming someone else's character, imaginatively inhabiting that person's body, and making another's steps your own.[4]

Sometimes the borrowing is explicit. Fred Astaire and his co-choreographer Hermes Pan talked frankly about learning from black dancers, including both Bill Robinson and Pan's family's chauffeur. In the video for "Smooth Criminal," Michael Jackson pays open homage to Fred Astaire, wearing the same outfit as his idol in *The Band Wagon*'s "Girl Hunt" routine. When Agnes de Mille used square dancing in *Rodeo* to call up an old form of community, she plopped it smack in the middle of the piece. You can't miss it.

But at other times, histories are submerged. Watching *Rodeo*, you might not guess that de Mille imagined the leading cowboy's most climactic solo—as her choreographic notes make clear—as both jazzy and black, or that in the same scene he was supposed to take cues from the Italian-American comic Jimmy Durante. Yet those influences are part of why audiences and critics described *Rodeo* as a quintessentially American ballet, imbuing it with what Ralph Ellison calls "the homeness of home."[5]

Blending, masking, and mockery have been central to much of the art that has made Americans feel at home. "Everyone played the appropriation game," Ellison writes, and that "everyone" implicates the entire nation from its beginnings: Boston Tea Partiers donning feathered headdresses and caking their faces with war paint; white southerners adopting black speech patterns; Duke Ellington quoting from Chopin's funeral march; Elvis Presley singing like Arthur Crudup; Shirley Temple learning to tap from Bill Robinson; Fred Astaire and Ginger Rogers yoking vaudeville gags with ballet; Paul Taylor swiping steps from his employer Martha Graham and from strangers he watched on the street. Whether consciously or not, we are forever recombining vernacular forms, creating—as Ellison puts it—"a consciousness of who and what we have come to be." The vernacular can thus be a "gesture toward perfection," as the many coalesce into the one, *e pluribus unum*. But that ideal unified one is impossible to reach. Culture both coalesces and falls apart.[6]

Hybridity is not unique to the United States. That is how culture works. In the sixteenth century, enslaved African Americans in the Spanish colonies created the sensuous, percussive zarabanda, a dance that sailed across the Atlantic and eventually found its way into the French courts as the slower, statelier sarabande. In nineteenth-century Denmark, August Bournonville injected classical ballet with national folk dances, while Marius Petipa did the same in Russia. And in nineteenth-century Rio, Afro-Brazilians combined the polka with local lundu dancing to create the maxixe, which became an international ballroom sensation. Yet just as these histories depend upon particular places and times in which particular people forge new steps and styles, the histories of American dance reflect a country, and its people, on the move. Place matters.[7]

The artists who are the subjects of this book all combined dance forms and styles to conjure up the spirit of a nation, a spirit that their audiences recognized as the homeness of home. But digging up the sources of homeness can change that home. This is because of another dynamic, to which Ralph Ellison is equally attuned: histories do not simply become detached; they are repressed. "By pushing significant details of our experience into the underground of unwritten history, we not only overlook much which is positive, but we blur our conceptions of where and who we are," he writes. "It is as though we dread to acknowledge the complex, pluralistic nature of our society, and as a result we find ourselves stumbling upon our true national identity under circumstances in which we least expect to do so." This book is an attempt to make readers stumble.[8]

These days, when concert dance can seem to be the most elite of all art forms, and when social dancing appears to be more visible on reality-TV competitions than in everyday life, it can be hard to remember that dance has been central not just to American art but to American life, as artists shaped national identity in public movement. That identity was first embodied in the cakewalk, when in the same decade that "separate but equal" became law Americans from all walks of life rejoiced in a step that antebellum slaves had invented to mock their masters. It later took shape in the virtuosic tapping of Bill Robinson, who danced debonairly up the stairs to play an emperor and whom Hollywood forced to play second fiddle to a white toddler. It found a form in the blending of tap, ballet, ballroom, and social dance that Fred Astaire and Ginger Rogers presented as a homegrown vernacular, the many forming a one, even as, outside the movie houses, an economically depressed nation struggled with class and racial conflicts. It rested in the square dances that Henry Ford hoped would teach a mixed-race America to revere purer, whiter times, and that Agnes de Mille wished could restore hope to the nervous youth of the Atomic Age. It burst forth from the acrobatics of the Lindy Hop and made its way onto the country's toniest stages, as Agnes de Mille, George Balanchine, Jerome Robbins, Lew Christensen, and a host of other choreographers loosened the mores of ballet. It emerged in the damning commentary and pedestrian grace of Paul Taylor's choreography, and spread across the globe when Michael Jackson turned the moonwalk into a sign of technological domination and human ingenuity.

All these artists danced as part of a broader, public conversation about what America was and what it might become. For all of them, the country was haunted by histories, both acknowledged and unacknowledged, excised from their dances or buried somewhere deep inside them. The tapping of a foot can be the rapping of a séance table, Morse code from a forgotten past. These are stories of national creation, and of national haunting.

Notes

1 My thinking on these issues owes a good deal to Ralph Ellison's description of "Adamic wordplay," which attempts, "in the interest of a futuristic dream, to impose unity upon an experience that changes too rapidly for linguistic or political exactitude." Ralph Ellison, "The Little Man at Chehaw Station," *The Collected Essays of Ralph Ellison* (New York: Random House, 1995), 511–12. See also Benedict Anderson, *Imagined Communities: Reflections on the Origin and Spread of Nationalism* (New York: Verso, 1991).
2 Constance Rourke, *American Humor: A Study of the National Character* (1931; repr., New York: New York Review of Books, 2004), 26.
3 While American Studies, as a field, tends to regard Rourke as something of a pioneer, her work has little traction in theater studies. For a good exploration of her scholarly afterlife, see Jennifer Schlueter, A "Theatrical Race: American Identity and Popular Performance in the Writings of Constance M. Rourke," *Theatre Journal* 60, no. 4 (December 2008): 529–43.
4 Anderson, Rourke, and Ellison are central to my thinking on these subjects, but I would be remiss not to mention some of the reams of other fine criticism devoted to performance and identity, both national and racial, within the past few years. See, for example, Daphne Brooks, *Bodies in Dissent: Spectacular Performances of Race and Freedom, 1850–1910* (Durham, N.C.: Duke University Press, 2006); Jayna Brown, *Babylon Girls: Black Women Performers and the Shaping of the Modern* (Durham, N.C.: Duke University Press, 2008); Shannon Jackson, *Lines of Activity: Performance, Historiography, Hull-House Domesticity* (Ann Arbor: University of Michigan Press, 2000); and Philip J. Deloria, *Playing Indian* (New Haven: Yale University Press, 1998).
5 Ellison, "Going to the Territory," in *Collected Essays*, 611.
6 Ellison, "Little Man at Chehaw Station," 511; Ellison, "Going to the Territory," 612, 608. Ellison may seem to be supporting a doctrine of American essentialism, but as Hortense Spillers has pointed out, he argues that culture is "dynamic, even restless, over and against closed or poised." See Spillers, "'The Little Man At Chehaw Station' Today," *boundary* 2 30, no. 2 (2003): 15. My thinking diverges from Ellison's regarding the "gesture toward perfection," though; the vernacular can also fight the move from many to one with both individual and collective force.
7 See John Charles Chasteen, "The Prehistory of Samba: Carnival Dancing in Rio de Janeiro, 1840–1917," *Journal of Latin American Studies* 28, no. 1 (February 1986): 29–47; Nancy Goldner, "The Guards of Amager," *Nation*, June 26, 1976, reprinted in *Reading Dance*, ed. Robert Gottlieb, 286–89 (New York: Random House, 2008).
8 Ellison, "Going to the Territory," 595–96.

Nancy Reynolds (1938–)

At the age of eleven, Nancy Reynolds had the good luck to begin her ballet studies with the young Balanchine ballerina Tanaquil LeClercq. Later, she attended the School of American Ballet, and, in 1957, joined New York City Ballet, with which she danced for five years.

After studying art history at Columbia, she became an editor at Praeger Publishers, to which her outstanding contribution was the commissioning and editing of Lincoln Kirstein's magisterial *Movement and Metaphor*. Her lifelong absorption in City Ballet led to her *own* magisterial—and absolutely essential—book, *Repertory in Review: 40 Years of the New York City Ballet,* which, ballet by ballet, traces the history of the Kirstein-Balanchine enterprise up to the book's publication, in 1977. No critic or student can be without it. Reynolds served as one of the chief editors of the *International Encyclopedia of Dance*, and she oversaw the publication of *Choreography by George Balanchine: A Catalogue of Works*. Her extensive career as a dance writer led to *No Fixed Points: Dance in the Twentieth Century*, a massive and highly esteemed work of history written with Malcolm McCormick. In 1994, reflecting her role as research director of the George Balanchine Foundation, and through an inheritance from her father, she established the Balanchine Video Archives, which consist of extensive films—organized and directed by her—that record Balanchine principal dancers transmitting their knowledge of ballets he created on them to current dancers: priceless documentation! The piece below was presented as a speech in a program at the New York Public Library for the Performing Arts.

Tribute to Maria Tallchief

I CONSIDER MYSELF a lucky person. I saw Maria Tallchief dance when she was in her prime, indeed if I may say so, in the prime of her prime—those years in the 1950s when she was burning up the floor in *Firebird, Pas de Dix*, and *Allegro Brillante*. The flashing, speedy, technically daring feats Balanchine choreographed on her created her reputation, but Maria herself would be the first to remind us that in those same years Balanchine made for her a lyrical *Swan Lake*, a Romantic pas de deux in *Scotch Symphony*, a brilliant yet delicate French-styled *Sylvia* variation, a *Nutcracker* pas de deux in the grand manner. Less well remembered is her tender, searching pas de deux in the "Prélude" of *Bourrée Fantasque*. While *she* was commanding the stage, *I* was sitting in the second balcony of City Center, looking down. Later, I remember being in class with her. She danced neatly and correctly but without any flair; clearly, she saved that for performance. Then one fine day I was no longer in the balcony but on the stage of City Center myself, dancing behind (far behind) the great Maria Tallchief.

Praise for her performances in those years was lavish; in one of my favorites, a reviewer wrote, "She dances *Firebird* like a flame." In another, her frequent partner, André Eglevsky, marveled at her "series of relevé turns in attitude en avant at unbelievable speed—unbelievable—and clean, clean, clean." (This was in the coda from *Sylvia*.) A great deal was written about her leg and footwork, about the way she slashed through space; her speed; and the timing and phrasing of her movements to create the greatest tension and suspense. And I'd like to mention something else, which was less often remarked on: her particularly lovely port de bras and indeed her expressive use of the upper body. She achieved her effects with a remarkable directness: her arms, always in concert with one another, traced paths from position to position without embellishments or elaborations or curlicues or fussy pieces of business along the way. (And broken wrists were out of the question!) This simplicity of port de bras, in combination with her generous use of épaulement, could impart to her entire upper body a French flavor, a folk flavor, a "Bolshoi" flavor, a classical flavor, a Romantic flavor. (Of épaulement she said, "We do everything we can not to face straight forward.") Her arm movements, even the most apparently gossamer, were supported by a steely strength. She once challenged me to move her arms as she held them in position. I couldn't budge them. "Arms should always be strong," she said, an idea that in all my years in dance had never occurred to me. (And she placed them exactly where she wanted them—arms never flew off into the wild blue yonder.)

"Musicality" can be difficult to describe. But whatever it is, Maria had it. When dancing, she seemed to have an instinctual feeling as to where the music was going and to be THERE, at that place. I was not surprised to learn that she had perfect pitch; she said, "I never counted. The notes told me when to move." But I have observed her in the studio, counting when teaching others. Her counting of Stravinsky revealed the structure, and particularly the rhythm, of the music. She could also count one rhythm while she danced another. In that way, both the music and the dance were illuminated. We are all aware of Balanchine's reverence for the music. It seems clear that Maria gave him something that he valued enormously.

It's well known that, so far as teaching goes, Balanchine was Tallchief's greatest influence, but not her only one. (Since I am presuming that many in this audience know something about Balanchine's profound remolding of her technique, I will not dwell on that at the moment.) Tallchief studied during her formative years with Nijinska. Referencing Balanchine, she later remarked, "you know, Nijinska had beautiful feet, great jumps, stupendous batterie. She concentrated on balancing, jumping, and turning, but was not so interested in the elegant and refined presentation of the foot that Balanchine espoused (by the hour)." Anyone who remembers Tallchief's thrilling, edge-of-the-cliff balance at the end of the *Nutcracker* pas de deux will know she learned Nijinska's lesson well, and the speed and dynamism of her pirouettes were surely aided by a whipping motion of the arms taught in Nijinska's classroom. She also knew ballet's history—in the studio she was coached in the classics by Balanchine—in *Swan Lake*, *Giselle*, *Beauty*. It is perhaps forgotten that she performed Bluebird and the Grand Pas de Deux from *Aurora's Wedding*, as well as Black Swan, with Ballet Theatre in the 1940s.

As you may know, I am in charge of the George Balanchine Foundation Video Archives program. In our main video series, the originators of Balanchine's great roles—those on whom he choreo-graphed his masterpieces—teach and coach those roles to dancers of today, thus passing on Balanchine's ideas (and their own) at the time of creation. On the very night of the party celebrating the Endowment that made the series possible, Tallchief offered to participate—the first to do so. Because of her belief in the project, we now have twelve tapes of Tallchief coaching and commenting on her roles in *Allegro Brillante, Pas de Dix, Orpheus, Firebird, Four Temperaments, Sylvia, Symphony in C, Nutcracker, Swan Lake, Apollo,* and the original *Baiser de la Fée.* A cornucopia.

As a coach, quite frankly I expected her to be a prima, interested only in herself. (As we know, many great performers are not great teachers.) This was not so at all. She was very caring. She had a great eye for detail. She sized up instantly what a dancer could and could not accomplish in a few hours of taping, and concentrated on where progress could be made. She made corrections to faults I hadn't even noticed. When I ran the tape later, I was amazed at the things I had not caught on the run. But sure enough, she had been right.

Among many other things, precision was what Maria's dancing was about. In first arabesque positions, she called for "eyes one foot above the wrist . . . always." In coaching, hers *always* were. And I am betting you could have measured that foot of space between eyes and wrist and found it to be exactly twelve inches every time.

Another directive she quoted Balanchine as saying was, "Look over the balustrade, into the lake." "It will give your face a very poetic expression," she would add. At least once she then wondered aloud, "Now why didn't Balanchine say 'river'? Or 'ocean'? He said 'lake.'"

At the height of her career critics consulted their lexicons and found a special word for Maria's dancing: "brio." She danced with "brio," they wrote again and again, meaning that she brought vigor and vivacity to her performances. I don't recall their using this word for any other dancer.

Today it seems to have fallen into disuse as far as dance is con-cerned. Perhaps like the number 3 on Babe Ruth's Yankees uniform, the word was retired when Maria no longer danced. Perhaps she "owned" it. Perhaps it was reserved for her alone.

2014

Jerome Robbins (1918–1998)

Choreographer, dancer, theater and film director, producer, show doctor, founder of the American Theatre Lab (devoted to the development of experimental productions) and of his own ballet company, Jerome Robbins straddled the worlds of ballet and theater, of Broadway and Hollywood, of New York City Ballet (where George Balanchine made him a ballet master for life) and Ballet Theatre (where Robbins started). In 1987, at the New York Public Library for the Performing Arts, he established the Jerome Robbins Archive of the Recorded Moving Image; two years earlier, he had arranged to give the Library a continuing gift of a portion of his royalties from *Fiddler on the Roof*. Today, the Library's entire dance holdings are called the Jerome Robbins Dance Division.

Although not often cited for his writing, Robbins was a prolific composer of unpublished works: journals, letters, notes, and materials related to his choreography. The letter below to the figurative painter Bernard Perlin (1918–2014)—a uniquely expansive statement by Robbins of his perspective on his own dancemaking—is somewhat mysterious. The full text seems only to exist as Robbins's dictated recording, whose existence was recently discovered, via the NYPL catalog, and was transcribed in its entirety for the first time for this anthology by Christopher Pennington of the Jerome Robbins Foundation and Trust. As Pennington explains, it's not yet known if the letter was ever sent. Evidently, though, Robbins took time over it. Each word is considered. And, in a mere four paragraphs, the choreographer manages to anatomize and to sum up his views on dance technique and style, on the relationship of a dancemaker to his dancers in the moment of creation, on the difference between his own choreographic process and George Balanchine's, and on the idea that a ballet is a total world, "with its own morality and behavior peculiar only to it"—a literary achievement on its own terms.

Moves, his 1959 silent ballet to which he refers below, was choreographed for his short-lived company, Ballets: U.S.A. (1958–1962). It is still performed by New York City Ballet.

On Choreographing

Dear Bernard,

I've been thinking about some of the questions you asked me and thought maybe I could make them a little clearer. Regarding the kind of movement that is in my jazz ballet (and I guess for that matter that's in *Fancy Free* and all my ballets), the basic technique that I depend on and insist upon from all dancers is a ballet technique. I don't think that jazz dancers could do it without ballet training (I occasionally use completely balletic movements), nor do I think that dancers trained strictly and preventively in only ballet technique could do it (as I use references and movement derived from contemporary dancing as well as influence of the freedom of the body as used in the modern dance). I don't consider it "personal" in the sense that I criticize a lot of the jazz dancers—their classes and technique as being a representation of the only way that they can move.

As to having to show the movements, this is not an individual thing. Every choreographer has to do this, even if he's working in a strictly classic ballet, because, unless there is invention within it—and the invention must come out of the choreographer—it is lifeless and dull. Balanchine always showed me what he wanted when he choreographed for me *Till Eulenspiegel* or *Bourrée Fantasque* or when he revived *Prodigal Son* for me. Even Fokine had to show movements. Every choreographer *has* to do this; and although the movements may be closer or further from the strictly classic ballet technique, the vocabulary of the strictly classic ballet technique can be used as a frame of reference, which I think you found even at my audition. When Balanchine showed Maria Tallchief the role of Swan Queen in his version of *Swan Lake*, Maria is to have said, "If only I could do the port de bras and dance it the way that you do."

I think that all choreography has to be shown to a dancer and the dancer eventually picks up the "style" that the choreographer is aiming at. Of course, unconsciously, every dancer picks up a lot of personal stylistic approaches of the choreographer. A Graham dancer will use her hands and head in a certain way. The same with a Tudor dancer, a Balanchine dancer, a de Mille dancer, and I suppose even a Robbins dancer. I'm the least aware and worst person to understand or realize what if any influence my dancing has had here in America. People always come to me and say, "Oh, so much of television is *yours*"; or, "Everyone is kind of a poor imitation of *you*," etc. etc. I never know exactly what they mean by that. I don't think I have a school of dance as much as an approach to theater and the presence on stage and what it is I want to evoke on the stage and in the audience. I know a lot of people feel I am a jack-of-all-trades, what with my success on Broadway, in ballet, in television and (I hope) in movies. But George ran the whole gamut also and at one point was the reigning choreographer of Broadway, knocked off a couple of films—one of which, *Goldwyn Follies,* is still a classic as far as ballet is concerned—and now happens to be settled more or less strictly in the ballet field. I would think that not only is this because of his growth as an artist and his need for that specific outlet but, from my own experience, I have found that the less money involved and at stake in a project, the more freedom there is. Consequently, a list ranging from the most amount of interference and lack of freedom going toward the least amount of interference and most amount of freedom would range from television to movies to stage to ballet, and I can only fully understand and agree with him in his present goals. For myself, I know that my ballet *Moves, A Ballet in Silence*, must have in some way come out of the stuss and storm [sic] of *Gypsy*. I did *Moves* immediately after *Gypsy*. In that show, I was involved with an author, a composer, a lyricist, two producers, a scene designer, a costume designer, a star, and the horde of hanger-on-ers and would-be helpers and advisers. And, as a matter of fact, even before the show came into town, I was already starting to work on *Moves*, where I worked with just the dancers and myself and space. What a pleasure it was and how quickly the work evolved, faster than any other ballet I'd done before, and I finished almost thirty minutes of it in three weeks. My usual rate of speed is about five minutes a week. George's, I imagine, about a ballet every ten days or two weeks. I'm not as fast as he is and I realize this, which is always somewhat inhibiting when I start to work with the New York City Ballet group.

His craft, skill, and facility make the dancer used to his particular kind of speed, and, in comparison, everybody else seems rather a blunderer and fumbler. George seems to go directly toward what he wants either through intuition, skill, or what-have-you. I have to work through many layers of what I don't want until I start to get toward what I do want. Once I hit that vein or key, I work rather rapidly. But generally I would say for most every ballet that I've done, I must have at least a half of one left over that I haven't used. Occasionally, this is not the case, as in the "Passage for Two" section of the jazz ballet, which I choreographed in about a half hour. But that quickness, that knowledge and that ability, at that time, of being able to go directly to what I want, happened after I had completed all the rest of the ballet and knew completely the key, mood, color, atmosphere, quality, etc., etc. of the ballet. I was living in it and therefore it was fairly easy for me to allow uninhibited and direct communication with that part of me that can create freshly.

I don't think it's terribly hard just to do "choreography." I have never felt it's been difficult to fill up a certain amount of time with a certain amount of music. What I find is the challenge and what I strive for constantly is to say what I have to say as freshly as possible in a way that possibly hasn't been said before with an attempt to communicate what I am trying to say to the audience so they have the same emotional response to it as I feel to the subject. Sometimes when I start a ballet, I'm not always sure what the subject is, although I have a feeling toward it. It's rather like searching in the fog for something you know is there or modeling with clay and only by work and stripping off layer after layer do I finally get to the key and essence of what it's about. What I've just described is one way of work. Another way (and that which is most common to Broadway and occasionally to ballet) is to know specifically the character's situation, atmosphere, story, the moment of what is about to happen on stage and to tell what you have to tell as succinctly and directly but always inventively as possible. *Fancy Free*, my first ballet, had a very detailed scenario and the final ballet hardly varied from it at all. I don't write scenarios out anymore for a number of reasons. One, I don't have to in order to convince people that I've got a story. But, more importantly, I feel that what I am striving for in ballets has altered and that the "story" ballet is not quite as interesting and fascinating to me as is the nuance, ritual, and saying something in movement which evokes a whole atmosphere, life and relationship, which cannot be said in words but which is understood through movement and gesture by the audience.

Of course, all of this is theory; and no one has said it better than Stravinsky, who, when asked what theory was, said, "usually hindsight." I never like to put down in words or commit myself to working theories because I find they change, so that exactly the opposite is what I will head toward at one time or another. But I will say, the foregoing is, in a general way, what my thinking is at this time. If you take the program of Ballets: USA, as performed in our long tour in Europe in '59, you'll find the first ballet was *Moves*, an enormously provocative and abstract ballet, which, to me, was about relationships. The second ballet was *Faun*, which told a story directly but with, to me, an enormous amount of nuance and subtlety. The third ballet, *Opus Jazz*, again was jazz dancing on the surface but striving to tell a much more profound and important aspect of the teenagers' attitude toward life today, particularly in cities. The fourth ballet, *The Concert*, had definite characters who, although they started logically in a realistic situation, allowed their fantasies to carry the ballet away and evoked recognizable human foibles, successes, and disasters that the audience could identify with. I do believe in the ballet as a ritual. Most ballets celebrate something or another. The most fascinating part to me is that each ballet creates a total world of its own with a morality and behavior particular only to it. Good choreographers convince the audience of this world and its behavior and its relationships immediately. The audience feels safe and secure that what they are seeing on stage is fact and they can believe in it. Poor choreographers fumble, twist, are embarrassed or struggle bombastically to convince you. Hardly ever do you see a Balanchine ballet or a Graham ballet without knowing that a master hand has been behind this and that one feels absolutely secure and can believe what is happening on stage.

All best wishes as always.
Sincerely, . . .

February 1961

Marcia B. Siegel (1932–)

RESPECTED WRITER and teacher Marcia B. Siegel is a contributing editor for *The Hudson Review* and a senior contributor to *The Arts Fuse* (ArtsFuse.org) in Boston. At one time a dance critic in New York for *The Soho Weekly News*, she covered dance for sixteen years at *The Boston Phoenix*.

From 1983 to 1999, Siegel was a member of the resident faculty at the Tisch School of the Arts, New York University. She has taught at Boston Conservatory, Sarah Lawrence, and Mount Holyoke and has held teaching residencies at The Ohio State University, Arizona State University, the Hong Kong Academy for Performing Arts, the Vienna Dance Festival, and the Walker Art Center in Minneapolis.

Siegel was a founder of the Dance Critics Association, and, in 2004, she was the Association's senior critic honoree. In 2005, she received the Congress on Research in Dance (CORD) award for her contributions to dance research.

The latest of Siegel's four collections of reviews and essays, *Mirrors & Scrims: The Life and Afterlife of Ballet*, won the 2010 Selma Jeanne Cohen Prize from the American Society for Aesthetics. Her other books include *Howling Near Heaven: Twyla Tharp and the Reinvention of Modern Dance*, *Days on Earth: The Dance of Doris Humphrey*, and *The Shapes of Change: Images of American Dance*.

Dance Theatre of Harlem's Nijinska

BRONISLAVA NIJINSKA's choreographic reputation is based on two splendid works, made within a year of each other for Diaghilev's Ballets Russes. Because *Les Noces* (1923) and *Les Biches* (1924) are virtually the only ballets of hers that survive, critics and historians continue to wonder whether they were the fortuitously preserved vestiges of a closetful of treasures, or if they're just the trinkets from an otherwise dowdy wardrobe.

Dance Theatre of Harlem, celebrating its twentieth-anniversary season at City Center, presented both ballets, plus another Nijinska work, the ballet spoof *Rondo Capriccioso* (1952), which has never been seen in this country. The choreographer's daughter, Irina Nijinska, staged all three works for DTH, assisted by Howard Sayette for *Les Noces* and Rosella Hightower for *Rondo*.

Set to music of Camille Saint-Saëns, *Rondo Capriccioso* is basically a pas de deux in an all-purpose exotic style, for a Bird of Paradise and a Prince, Stephanie Dabney and Ronald Perry, framed by Two Hunters, Dean Anderson and Marck Waymmann. The Prince, dressed in shocking pink, stalks the ballerina, who wears a lavender bodice and a tutu and bathing cap made of white feathers. She leaps slowly away from him while checking to see he's not too far behind. Eventually he catches her, of course, and arranges her in a variety of lifts, the hardest of which are delegated to the Hunters. The higher she's hoisted, the more surprised she looks and the faster she flutters her hands. When the Hunters aren't otherwise occupied, they ripple a long orange cloth to float over and behind the couple's most decorative effects, and in one deft maneuver they drape it over the ballerina's extended leg in the final lift, just as the Prince throws her completely upside down over his shoulder.

From the initial moments of the piece, when the Prince spies on the Bird of Paradise by sticking his head out between the two Hunters as if they were bushes, *Rondo* is a collection of clichés and decadent devices cribbed from the late nineteenth-, early twentieth-century showpieces that filled up the idle moments in every ballet company's repertory for all the years of Nijinska's career. The audience at DTH's first performance, however, didn't emit a giggle, even though Dabney intermittently signaled that it was supposed to. Maybe this was because Dabney and Perry play the same roles straight in *Firebird*, elsewhere in the repertory, but that should have made the double entendre funnier.

Dance humor is an intriguing subject. With Bronislava Nijinska it's even more elusive than usual, because she had a subtle wit, often characterized as "feminine" in the male-dominated world of Diaghilev, and because she could count on her sophisticated audience to recognize her sly allusions with very little prompting from the dancers. *Les Biches* (Poulenc) is the most mysterious ballet I've ever seen—a strange cocktail party where the women outnumber the men five to one, where the three male guests are brawny types dressed as if they've come straight from the gym, and where the guests play boisterous games with a large, moveable sofa.

There are some halfhearted flirtations, and some more serious, offbeat ones. Two girls in gray (Kellye Gordon and Erika Lambe) do a close-harmony duet that culminates in a surprised kiss. One of the athletes (Eddie J. Shellman) is attracted to an androgynous creature (Virginia Johnson) in a blue velvet tunic and white gloves. The Hostess, draped in pearls, commandeers both of the other two men.

One of the most remarkable things about *Les Biches* is that it's all dancing, no miming or trademark gestures to build characters or plot. The DTH corps looked wonderfully vain and sensuous promenading on their pointes, shoulders swaying with their arms straight down and hands angling out at the hips. Francesca Harper was terrific in the Hostess's allegro variation; for some reason she doesn't make an appearance till late in the party, and her bubbling solo gives the whole ballet a second wind. Virginia Johnson was opaque, remote, as the Girl in Blue, bourréeing sideways and shielding her face with one flat hand. But Shellman and his cohorts, Marck Waymmann and Robert Garland, continually muffed the multiple air turns that are supposed to make the athletes so irresistible.

Les Noces is a masterpiece of massed designs and rhythms, a theatricalized version of a Russian peasant wedding. What Stravinsky and Nijinska celebrate is a ritual of continuance and community that supercedes individual, romantic choice. The company looked a bit unsure of the music's fiendish meters at first but then locked into its massive, implacable logic.

July 28, 1989

Prince of Lightness: Merce Cunningham (1919–2009)

MERCE CUNNINGHAM'S early admirers singled out two things about him that are seldom remarked on now: his light touch and his latent dramatic qualities. After his first independent concerts, in the mid-1940s, critic Edwin Denby noted that he didn't create "different objective characters, but rather lyric variations of his own character." In 1957 James Waring, a leading teacher-choreographer during the countercultural tidal wave that was rising in Downtown New York, described Cunningham's dances as being like the after-effects of stories that took place offstage, "not the event itself in explicit flesh. The art is one of feeling, not of meaning." And a few years later, when his choreographic approach and his company had taken shape, *Village Voice* dance critic Jill Johnston said that in his dance, "emotion is created by motion rather than the reverse." It wasn't until the '70s that Cunningham, along with the young Turks eventually called postmodern dancers, began to be talked about in the austere rhetoric of formalism.

Emotion, feelings, drama were modern dance's meat and potatoes at mid-century. By then the choreographic pioneers, Martha Graham, Doris Humphrey and their followers, had made their breakthroughs and become established—dried up in the eyes of younger observers. Cunningham was filling "the vacuum left by exhausted forms," said Johnston in 1960. Modern dance had set out to embody personal styles, thoughts, feelings, and moralities. Whether framed as character study, music visualization, or plotless metaphor, the dances represented the individual choreographer's drives and visions. To some, this was the great strength of modern dance; to avatars of ballet, like Lincoln Kirstein, it was a fatal limitation.

As essentialized in later histories, modern dance was based on storytelling and personal anguish. This construct overlooks what really set modern dance apart from ballet in the postwar period. Modern dancers took themselves seriously as artists. They were concerned with humanist ideals and dedicated to resisting the escapist temptations of popular dancing and ballet. They were determined to clean up the decadent reputation of the female dancer, to portray male dancers as unthreateningly heterosexual, and to create an art dance that middle class audiences could recognize. These long-internalized aspirations for ennobling the profession cast an aura of high-mindedness over the entire modern dance enterprise in the '50s. After decades of parsimonious production values, tragic but sympathetic archetypes, stern portraits of social ills, and militant calls to action, the altruism was subsiding but the weightiness persisted. The centers of artistic power and resistance were shifting. As Americans settled into a postwar culture of complacent acquisitiveness and nebulous political anxiety, the modern dancers were losing ground, shoved aside by a resurgent interest in ballet.

Unlike other offspring of the modern dance companies, Merce Cunningham was a dissident, not a disciple. He gave his first solo concerts while he was still dancing with Martha Graham, but whatever Graham and the rest of the modern dancers were doing, he was going to be different. He *was* different. Like John Cage, with whom he shared these first of a lifetime's adventures, he was making a kind of anti-dance, as Cage was making anti-music. Not something that dismissed dance altogether but something that pulled the garment inside out and found it wearable. As he was trying out things, gradually divesting himself of modern dance's imprint, his personal style and attitudes came through. He later acknowledged the thematic presence of fear, satire, humor, tranquility, and Eros in his early dances.

They certainly looked odd, even challenging, to the modern dance constituency. He had a hard time getting started and was rejected for years by the festivals and New York presenters who sustained the field. It was Cunningham's lightness that shocked them. Modern dancers didn't jump a lot in those days; his physicality favored the airborne, the frictionless. His distorted, eccentric moves might mean he was making fun of something; his air of impassivity might be covering for derision. But he wasn't leveling criticism so much as encouraging lightness of thought, thereby lifting the burden of conscience from the viewer's shoulders. Those who were receptive saw with a kind of relief that he wasn't trying to prove anything or project any social agenda. He was asking the audience to concentrate on nothing more than dancing.

Cunningham's dancing had always been extraordinary. Even those who disapproved could agree on that. But how was he to keep going without repealing and eventually stereotyping himself? By 1951, as he began to collect a small cadre of other dancers, he was searching for ways to avoid imprinting them with his own mannerisms and preferences. John Cage had already started exploring alternatives to the egocentric rules of Western music composition. The notion of chance liberated both of them from traditional rules and expectations.

Cage's first book of lectures and anecdotes, *Silence*, was published in 1961, and I read it with astonishment for the first time around 1964. I was new to dance and a little daunted by Cunningham's powerful, cryptic pieces. He was doing *Night Wandering* then, a mysterious duet with Carolyn Brown where they wore tunics made of animal skins and moved like a pair of big cats. *Winterbranch* infuriated the audience with aggressively loud sound, and lighting that jolted from glare to obscurity, and dancers in black who fell and rolled on the floor and vanished in the gloom. There was *Story*, where dancers came and went, wearing regular clothes in outlandish ways. And *Antic Meet*, a comedy in the zany spirit of the silent movies. *Aeon*, which I only knew from its intimidating reputation, was a very long company piece that gave no clues or tracking information.

Silence explained a lot of this for me without going into specifics, but far more important, it taught me a whole new way to think about art. Published during a brief period of experimental bookmaking, it was designed so that every chapter was laid out differently, the entries set in different typefaces and sizes, sometimes three or four fonts to a single page. At first you couldn't make sense of the text; then you'd see that the design imposed a visual logic onto the words. I didn't know anything about Apollinaire or the Dadaists, collage or Cubism. What Cage had to say was provocative, aphoristic, often amusing, and, it seemed to me, totally original.

What struck me first, of course, was the assumption that art did not have to depend on the artist's intuition or await the arrival of some benevolent Muse. Composing by chance was a more workaday activity. Music could be thought of as a group of sounds to which you assigned variables like duration, pitch, and sequence. For each sound you tossed a coin or drew a card to give a value to each variable. The dense, quasi-mathematical diagram that resulted became the score. In return for handing over control of decision-making to an impartial process, you gained resources beyond your own imagination. You'd have to extricate yourself from your own habits and from what you'd been taught about the rules and the history of your art form, because, as Cage says, learning to play Bach wouldn't make you a composer, only an imitator of Bach.

Letting go, a Zen-inspired discipline that Cage advocated, has enormous implications for the artist and the audience. Once the compositional process is shorn of its old dependence on things like form, memory, and mimesis, everyone's engagement with the work becomes more immediate. The audience experiences a continuum of events of equal value that leads us onward through the piece, rather than drawing us back into previous related parts of the piece. There's no clinging to familiar themes, no splurging on special embellishments, no flattering invitation to reflect on our own experience. Everything will be unfamiliar; everything will be remarkable.

For Cunningham, the uses of chance were probably less philosophical and more pragmatic than for Cage. He was convinced that turning some of the choreographic work over to disinterested forces would give him a much broader scope than anything his personal choices or limitations would allow. According to Carolyn Brown, whose 1968 Ballet Review article "On Chance" is still the most lucid account of the subject, "If the artist's impulse is to search for truth, then he was not coming close, he felt, by concerning himself only with the known." Instead of inventing, composing, editing, and directing all the movement himself, he subjected certain aspects of a dance to random selection procedures. This could involve consulting the I Ching (the Chinese Book of Changes) to devise a complex charting system. Implementation could be as simple as rolling dice to determine how many times a phrase is repeated, or as playful as using the defects in a sheet of paper to determine locations on the stage.

Cunningham was a riveting performer and a consistent adventurer in creative work, but he understood the value of giving himself limits. James Waring once observed that his dancing revealed a "fierce vitality held in restraint." The only time I remember seeing him dancing in a rage was at the end of his 1966 work Place. Frenzied, manic, he writhed and thrashed along the floor until he disappeared from view. But even this moment of excess was contained by an enormous plastic bag that he was either pulling up around himself or trying to slither out of, or both.

Chance was a way of damping down personal revelation, defeating the interfering ego, enlisting powerful but disinterested collaborators to drive the creative engine, and cultivating a stance of neutrality. Musicians and designers worked separately, with only sketchy outlines of the dance under construction to guide them. The completed work would incorporate whatever they contributed. Sometimes things meshed beautifully, like the airy, unpredictable dancing speeds; the open, almost incidental sounds (Morton Feldman); and the overall pointillist backdrop and costumes (Robert Rauschenberg) in *Summerspace* (1958). Sometimes the other elements threatened to drown out the dance, like the barrage of mixed media and electronics in *Variations V* (1965). Sometimes they demanded a share of the dancing space, like Neil Jenney's rakish, wheeled aluminum structures for *Objects* (1970) or Andy Warhol's floating silver pillows for *Rain-Forest* (1968). Cunningham and the dancers simply got on with their performance.

Sometimes the chance-based operations came up with a dance so hard to perform they couldn't have imposed any drama if they tried. Yet the dances were often thrilling. The technically rigorous choreography was made doubly difficult because the parts of the body could be plotted non-sequentially, or aimed in opposing directions, or working in several counter-rhythms at a time. Their performing gave off a high-intensity charge. "What makes a performer interesting," Cunningham says during *Mondays with Merce*, an online series of videos inaugurated in the past year, "is that he or she knows exactly what they're doing, and at the same time they're free. Zen again, the concept of freedom within discipline.

Some of this sense of freedom also came from the built-in element of indeterminacy. When John Cage spoke of the expanded possibilities that become available when one rids oneself of preconceptions, he also recognized and even encouraged the accident, as a potential element of an artwork. His scores often incorporated natural sounds (*musique concrète*), ambient sounds (the building's air conditioning system, the approaching and receding wail of a fire truck outside), and specific time intervals to be filled in ad lib by the members of the orchestra.

The idea of indeterminacy fueled decades of open-form dances based on game structures, tasks, environments, and experimental predicaments, but Cunningham's dances were never improvised. Some choices might be turned over to the dancers, or he'd build in elements guaranteed to take them by surprise. Dances were set and rehearsed, but he might change the order of the sections before each performance. The music and scenery might not materialize until the final rehearsal. In any case, he feared that if his dancers rehearsed by putting the movement together with a piece of music, their performance would become automatic. Cage's antipathy to musical tradition led him from his early prepared piano pieces to experiments with amplified natural sounds, electronic distortion, radio static, sampling, and other digitized manipulations of pre-taped material. All of these sonic maneuvers took place during performances; neither the musicians nor the dancers could know in advance exactly what they would hear. Dancing in this milieu of both rehearsed and unexpected demands required alertness, high concentration, and an exceptional sensitivity to everyone else on the stage as well as oneself.

The chance procedures became more and more elaborate, even mechanical. Cunningham published *Changes*, a book of notes and notations, in 1968. A kind of scrapbook in the form of a palimpsest, it layered fragments of information, photographs, programs, and complicated choreographic charts in seemingly random order. Once you studied it, though, you realized that the information gathered on any given page applied to the same dance, and usually somewhere on the page you'd even find the title of the dance. (I immediately wrote in page numbers and indexed the whole book.) Besides the plotting and charting of every move in a dance—I suspect he enjoyed this task a little bit, even before he stopped dancing—he spent many hours working in the studio to adapt the steps he'd produced by chance, to make them physically possible to execute.

In the 1970s, spurred by his never-quenched curiosity about new ways to make dances, he investigated film for the first time, and with a succession of film- and video-makers, principally Charles Atlas and Elliot Caplan, he made dance film into a new adventure, countering the long-held belief that dance on screen could never be more than a pathetic token of itself. Though he probably did document the stage repertory with in-house videotape, for public and television release he abandoned the standard practice of filming a dance straight on, beginning to end, as a record of the choreography. What the camera could do became part of the choreography. He danced in gravityless space against assorted backgrounds produced by television's Chroma-key process (*Blue Studio*, 1975). He used moving cameras to track the dancers (*Locale*, 1980), cut and pasted shots of the same dance being done in different environments and even different eras (*Changing Steps*, 1989), and transformed the dancers into giant animated trace-forms via Motion-Capture software (*BIPED*, 1999). Some of these films were translated from existing stage dances. Others were cho-reographed for the screen and later adapted as stage dances. Around the beginning of the 1990s, his own movement limited by age and arthritis, the computer program Life Forms allowed him to create movement on screen.

One of the great mysteries about Cunningham to me has always been what it was, for him, that made one dance different from another. By the time he died on July 26, he'd choreographed about 175 works. He may have had as much invested, creatively, in the chance-work as he did in mounting the results on the dancers. When he had to describe a dance, he spoke enthusiastically and in great detail about the chance procedures by which he'd arrived at it, and barely hinted at what it might mean or how it should look.

If I try to remember a work of his, I realize that often what has stayed with me is a scenic or auditory image, or a memory of how the dancers coped with some imposed awkwardness, but not very much about the actual dancing. I can visualize the way Cunningham dancers dance, but not the dancing in a given Cunningham piece. I see them creating moving minimalist paintings by pushing around Frank Stella's frames with the brightly colored banners stretched across them (*Scramble*, 1967). I remember John Cage, sometimes with David Vaughan, drinking champagne and reading droll stories at the side of the stage (*How to Pass, Kick, Fall and Run*, 1965). I remember how different the 1975 *Sounddance* felt after Mark Lancaster replaced his original bulky tentlike set in 1994 with an extravagant panel of silky draperies. Aside from props and incidents, I wonder, what is a Cunningham dance?

To get past your initial reaction, you really have to look at a dance a few times, especially a Cunningham dance, which asks you to set aside the mind's instinctive longing for coherence. Paradox is a favorite device of Cagean discourse, and maybe we should be able to entertain both the idea that a dance is no more than a momentary experience and the idea that the same dance is a product of immense, collective creativity and hard work. The Cunningham company has kept a small selection of old dances in repertory, but in recent years my dance-going has largely been confined to Boston and Jacob's Pillow. Cunningham hasn't played Boston since 1978. So except for the few dances that have been filmed in their entirety and are available for study, I can't fully explore what distinguishes one from another choreographically.

This is probably my preservationist temperament, still arguing with his determination to move on. The dissolving of one dance into another in memory speaks for the success of his determination to make each dance experience a new one, to make sure we looked forward to new works and didn't miss the old ones. But now there will be no new ones. Last June, after he had celebrated his 90th birthday with a new dance, the Cunningham company announced a plan for the future, anticipating the time when the leader would no longer be present. The organization wanted to avoid the years of litigation and the long-unsettled condition that encumbered Martha Graham's company after her death in 1991. Historically, independent choreographer-directors have been careless or merely casual about the succession of their work. If they have led their own companies, they've either disbanded them when their creative energies waned or their interests led them elsewhere, or they assumed that the remaining dancers would figure out how to go on. Only the Alvin Ailey and José Limón companies have outlived their founders for any length of time and remained artistically viable.

There are two big issues to consider here—the fate of the dance company itself with its related activities, and the future of the repertory. The Cunningham company will book a two-year schedule and then disband, according to the plan. Initially no one was named as artistic director to run the company during what will inevitably be seen as a "farewell tour." Performing and the rest of the company activities are expected to continue much as before, under Trevor Carlson, executive director of the Cunningham Foundation, and Cunningham's assistant, Robert Swinston. The Cunningham Trust will manage licensing of the dances under a plan that seems based on a model established a few years ago by Twyla Tharp. Dances that have been documented in various ways—film, notation, teaching tapes, designs—will be set on other dance companies by former dancers who are familiar with the work. In Cunningham's case, the dancers Robert Swinston and Patricia Lent will share Trust responsibilities with Carlson, attorney Allan Sperling, and Laura Kuhn, who also runs the John Cage Trust. In the initial announcements, no provision was made for the Cunningham School, which runs an extensive program of public and company classes at its New York studio.

Understandably, operating details of the plan still needed to be worked out as the summer was ending. Although Cunningham was said to endorse this scheme, if his energies had permitted he might have preferred a more open-ended option. His dances were more than usually ephemeral. They depended so much on the dancers who performed them, and on the mutable nature of the scores, sets, and lighting, that even when being given night after night they weren't meant to become fixed. Cunningham dancers were trained specifically for his choreography and its unique world-view. When the company is no longer in existence, even if the Cunningham technique continues to be taught, something else will be missing: that nexus of information exchange, correction, practice, and discovery that takes place among company dancers in the studio. This is where the real creation and preservation of dances takes place.

Much of Merce Cunningham's approach depended on instilling an attitude in the dancers: letting go, paying attention to the moment, hearing the movement's phrasing, being able to call on any part of the body to move independently of the other parts. "To train you repeat, but you don't think of it that way," he told the dancers. "You can always do something of what it is," and, "Instead of saying no, you say yes." It's hard to see how the Cunningham repertory will evolve now, as it's bound to do. If it's not fixed choreography and it's not a cultivated style, will it be subsumed into conventional ballet? Much as I loved the dances and want to see them survive, they may lose their character as balleticized novelties. It's possible they'll eventually become more like templates on which people will build new dances, or objects that get recycled by way of new chance procedures. Maybe dancers will form new companies to choreograph in their own ways, using his invigorating ideas.

Merce Cunningham, when you met him, was a very quiet, calm,

and private person. He gave hundreds of interviews, answering questions graciously and dodging them adroitly. He never gossiped or passed judgment; he never interpreted dances in any but the most objective terms. For a dancer of such gifted and absorbing physical energies, his words could also be gripping, momentous. A whole shelf of books and articles preserves his thought. He wasn't dictatorial or dogmatic, but what he said left you with a challenge or a new way to look at yourself. Someone reported to me what may have been his last words. After looking at a new video of one of his dances, he was asked what he thought of it. He said: "I would like to change some things."

2009

SALLY R. SOMMER (1939–)

THE PRESENTATION to Sally Sommer of the 2013 Tap Preservation Award by the American Tap Dance Foundation reflects the standing she has achieved in the world of social dancing, popular dancing, and, of course, tap dancing. By the 1970s, when she came to New York, she was writing about tap for *The Village Voice*, and since then she has become one of our leading chroniclers of vernacular American dance, revealing it to the general public as well as to generations of students— since 2001 in her position as a full professor at Florida State University. (Earlier, she taught at Duke and at New York's City College.) She has written extensively, given lecture demonstrations, spoken on National Public Radio, appeared on public television, and is the creator of the acclaimed documentary *Check Your Body at the Door*, about New York's legendary underground House dancing in the 1990s.

Below, she eulogizes one of the crucial figures in the history of American tap, Gregory Hines.

An Appreciation: Gregory Hines

GREGORY HINES was admired as a gracious and charming performer onstage, in film and in television. But he was also a dance revolutionary who took the upright tap tradition, bent it over and slammed it to the ground. Hines would have been the last to call himself radical. He simply said: "I am a tap-dancer. That's how I express myself." As a tap-dancer from the age of two he expressed the idiosyncrasies of his imagination most easily in his dancing.

In the 1980's Hines recast the image of the black male tap-dancer and roughed up the rhythms. He added new stylistic dimensions and volume to tap, and helped to shift perceptions of the tap-dancer from an entertainer to a serious dance artist. It was Hines who provided the building blocks of a new tap style, which, in the late 1990's, would be copied and expanded by his protégé Savion Glover into the next generation's styles. Positioned between the older tap masters he loved and the up-and-coming hard-core youngsters who loved him, Hines was the bridge, interpreting the past and pushing it toward the future.

The older tap masters Hines admired, like Honi Coles, Leon Collins, Eddie Brown, Chuck Green, Harold Nicholas and Charles Cook, possessed old-school elegance and polished skills. They dressed sharply and danced in an easy, swinging upright style. No matter how funny— how "down"—they might get, they were always pre-1950's gentlemen. And they kept good time.

Then Hines broke the codes. By his national dance tour in 1986, he had perfected the new image. Suddenly the tapper was sexy, muscled, new-school and macho. Hines worked out at the gym so the T-shirt was tight, the body had substance, the line was strong. Hunkered over like a prizefighter, unsmiling, he cocked his head and stared at the floor as if looking for answers.

Hines danced hard and messy, sometimes slurring his sounds angrily. He threw in African dance moves that revealed deeper, older connections. He designed a miked portable stage to amplify the taps and put the tap-dancer on equal footing with the loud music. He played his floor like a drum, testing the surface until he found "the spot," sounding the wood for melodies, pitches and thunks.

Certainly he had a hip, cool presence. But with Hines the cool always slipped. If the T-shirt and slacks were reminiscent of Gene Kelly, it was blunted by bad tailoring. When Hines danced hard, a gap of skin always showed between the bottom of his pants and the top of his socks. His shoelaces seemed too long. Or in the middle of a phrase, he would suddenly stop, wipe his brow, take a swig from a water bottle and start chatting to the audience.

But the biggest break Hines made was in the rhythms. He shattered the neat foursquare tempos. In a 1986 interview he told me, "I just wanted to get out of that time box."

So he purposely obliterated the tempos, throwing down a cascade of taps like pebbles tossed across the floor. In that moment he aligned tap with the latest free-form experiments in jazz and new music and postmodern dance. Since rhythm is perceived only as a regular pulse, any rhythmic break knocks the breath out of the listener because it is so unexpected—so visceral.

Hines's break with the sacred tap traditions was monumental. It jerked tap out of a pre-1950's aesthetic and pushed it into the 1990's and beyond. He renewed tap by roughing it up and giving it emotional weight.

Tap-dancers have always improvised. But Hines brought the audience in even closer, refining an insight by the legendary Bubbles, John Sublett: "Listen to my feet, and I will tell you the story of my life."

August 14, 2003

Susan Sontag (1933–2004)

Novelist by ambition, essayist by temperament, filmmaker and playwright by will, public intellectual by circumstance, political activist by moral imperative, bisexual by nature, high-school graduate at fifteen, wife at seventeen, college grad (Phi Beta Kappa) at eighteen, mother at nineteen, acclaimed for her courage, damned for her arrogance: Susan Sontag's life was so full, and her friendships and love affairs around the world were so plentiful, that one wouldn't think she'd have enjoyed much leisure to follow a demanding art form such as theatrical dance. As Margalit Fox wrote of her in *The New York Times*, "she was a master synthesist who tackled broad, difficult, and elusive subjects: the nature of art, the nature of consciousness, and, above all, the nature of the modern condition." A gourmet of world literature and film, she was omnivorous in her interests, regardless of whether they concerned high or popular art.

And yet, her devotion to aspects of ballet and of modern and postmodern dance was intense and ongoing. A few years before the untimely end of her life, owing to complications from leukemia, she was in a serious car accident, which put her in a wheelchair, her head swathed in bandages. And that is how she demanded to be taken to the Brooklyn Academy of Music, oblivious to the jaws dropping throughout the lobby. As she explained to an acquaintance, no car crash was going to cause her to miss an important world premiere by Mark Morris.

In the early talk on dance criticism, below, given at a conference, Sontag observed that she didn't herself write about dance and didn't then plan to. But her fervor occasionally overcame those reservations. Among her subsequent dance writings are a long essay extolling the genius of Mikhail Baryshnikov, and (in the words of Jill Johnston) "a prose meditation in ten short numbered segments" that Sontag contributed to the 1990 exhibition catalogue *Cage. Cunningham. Johns: Dancers on a Plane*. Her greatest enthusiasms in dance included

Cunningham himself, Balanchine, Baryshnikov, Suzanne Farrell, and Lucinda Childs, with whom she had a long personal relationship.

On Dance and Dance Writing*

I'M SPEAKING at the close of a week's dialogue on dance criticism among dance professionals. Being a stubbornly unspecialized writer who is interested in almost everything, I have written about several of the arts and about art in general (I am sometimes, mistakenly, called a critic)—but never about dance; and I'm not planning to. I am, however, a passionate member of the audience for dance and a tireless reader of writing about dance. I don't know what the desirable new ways of thinking or writing about dance might be, or if there are any. My hunch is that there can be a new, better idea about dance writing only when there is new, better dance. My own view is that what is needed is for more people to write well, not for some people to write differently. All this is to suggest that I think dance criticism is in rather good shape; that is, that the prevailing assumptions about dance are more right than wrong. I would like to consider why dance seems to me such an imperative art and why the best writing about dance seems to me so profound, so peculiarly profound.

When I travel, as I often do, and fall into conversation about American arts, as often happens, I generally find that people abroad vastly overestimate us. A number of interviews, in which I'm asked to speak about this art and that, have turned into a stream of nay-saying. I explain to people in Warsaw or Tokyo or Mexico City or Paris or Munich that American movies are lousy; I insist that there is good painting that is not American (no, Virginia, painting did not move from Paris to New York in 1945, thereby deserting the rest of the planet); I point out that we do not (since the departure of Nabokov) have one great, international-class writer—of the stature of Calvino, Beckett, Borges—in this country. And so on and so on. Yet it is my perverse, rather than patriotic, pleasure to end up pointing out that

---

*An edited version of an informal talk, followed by questions.

there is one art at which we really are better than anyone else. There is one and there is only one and it is dance. Dance is the one art where Americans are, have been for some time, doing the best work in the world. The greatest dance in the world is here. It has more diversity, more imagination, more experiment—and better classicism. (We have the best Russian ballet.) It was largely in this country that modern dance was created, for the most part the work of women dancers; and it's here that we have the culminating version of the Italo-Gallic-Russian tradition that we call the classical dance, namely Balanchine's New York City Ballet.

I'm not going to make any Whitmanesque declarations about why dance should inevitably have found its place *here*, in this encyclopedic country. I want simply to note our good fortune. And to evoke the dimensions of the triumph of dance, more exactly of the versions of artistic modernism represented in the various dance traditions, which seems so obvious now.

It is hard for us to realize the impact, the centrality of dance developments in the early decades of this century—what dance meant for the audiences of the period. (Here it should be noted that though we've had or ended up with the best dance, the best audiences were first in Western Europe, in London, Paris, Berlin, and elsewhere.) The tumultuous reception before and after the First World War of Loïe Fuller, of Isadora Duncan, of the Ballet Russe, was different in kind from that accorded any other performances of the period, and rightly so, for these were the most exciting events seen on a stage since Wagner. That is to say a great deal, for the advent of the Wagnerian aesthetic was the single most challenging and important artistic event of the nineteenth century, one that had an incalculable influence on all the arts: theatre arts, literature, and painting as well as music. (Wagner's ideas, the Wagnerian model, directly influenced, to speak only of writers, those as different as Shaw, Proust, Woolf, Lawrence, Joyce, Mann.) As Wagner's music dramas had done in the 1860's and 1870's, the new dance operated a veritable seduction of the public, and seemed to require a comparable commitment. Seduction is not too strong a word to explain the fervor of early dance audiences. And, as we can see from the adherence of two great poet-intellectuals of the period, Eliot and Valéry, these dance events were viewed as something about which one *had* to have an opinion. (A comparable testimony would be Baudelaire's championing of Wagner.) There was a dance-shock, as there had been a Wagner-shock; there was—and still is—dance-zealotry among audiences, as there had been Wagnerolatry.

A hundred years after Wagner, three-quarters of a century after the advent of modern dance and the Ballet Russe, we tend to house these events in static notions of a long-established art form. "Opera." "The dance." But to speak of the origins of modern dance—both the revival and transformation of the classical ballet (first seen as an alternative to the ballet) is to speak of an event which reflected changed ideas about art in general, not just dance in particular.

We need to look at the history of dance in terms of larger genealogies that pertain to all the arts of the modern era. Two genealogies explain our Janus-faced modernism. One starts with the German and English Romantics in the early nineteenth century and proceeds through Wagner to the Symbolists. This tradition is defined by the search for an ideal form of art—an art which is free, pure, total. It can take two forms: either it will be totally inclusive (of ideas, of art forms) or it will be totally stripped down. The other, as it were complementary, tradition central to modernist practice denies that an ideal form of art is attainable, or desirable. Rather, it proposes art as a form of creative destruction: the destruction of art in the name of art. This second tradition can be followed in the genealogy that goes from Symbolism to Dada and Surrealism to the conventions of aleatoric calculation and non-calculation, dissolving music into sound and dance into movement: anti-art "gestures"—anti-theatre, anti-dance, anti-painting, anti-poetry—all in the name of art: a glorious, instructive suicide. These two traditions are both lavishly represented in the spectrum of contemporary dance.

The early modern dance figures—mainly heirs to the Wagnerian and Symbolist notions of a new, free, ideal, total art—were bold from the beginning. Loïe Fuller, an exemplary figure in this sense, is one prototype of modern dance ideas, including the most radical of all: eliminating the dancer. As Frank Kermode describes in his essay "Poet and Dancer Before Diaghilev," Fuller lent her work more and more to the idea that a dance performance consisted essentially of light and fabric, different kinds of materials being moved, and that ideally one does not need to have the dancer on stage at all. That is pure Wagnerianism. In the ideal theatre that Wagner had constructed for the first performance of the Ring tetralogy, a curved black wooden shell covers the distracting sight of the orchestra. (Another innovation: he started each performance with the theatre in total darkness.) Afterwards, Wagner quipped that, having invented the invisible orchestra, he would like to invent the invisible stage.

My thesis is that all of the principal modernist alternatives are summed up in the variety of modern dance. This is of great significance when we come to consider the question of what writing about dance could or should be. All dance writing involves some hypothesis, some definite and explicit expectation about dance. If, as I think, dance writing has changed essentially in the last decades, this has come about because of the emergence of a new notion of what dance itself is.

The dance that we are connected with, the Euro-American neoclassical form at least, goes back roughly four centuries, and it has always been encapsulated in other forms: in public festivals in which there was spectacle, costume, music, ritualized enactments, and even discourse; in elaborate court entertainments; in larger theatrical forms such as opera, in which a ballet was for a long time an obligatory element. It is only in the twentieth century that dance emerged as an autonomous art independent of its connection with other theatre events. Lincoln Kirstein has pointed out that Balanchine, Diaghilev's last choreographer and the heir to much of Diaghilev's tradition, nonetheless differs from him in one crucial respect: Diaghilev, good Wagnerian that he was, thought of the dance performances he produced as total art-works fusing the skills of composers, designers, painters and writers with those of choreographers and dancers. In the Ballet Russe dance became the center of a prodigious, all-embracing theatre event. Balanchine has dispensed with virtually all of the outward shape of the classical ballet tradition. As the contribution of the painter or the set designer and the role of the story has been steadily whittled down, the work of the choreographer as a conception and of the dancers becomes important in a way it never was before. Even when Balanchine attempts to use some of the more traditional theatrical elements, he doesn't seem to be able to stick with them. He may start out, as he did in his new Schumann ballet, with chandeliers, trees, curtains, murals, furniture. But at each succeeding performance one or two elements of the set are missing. I saw it again last night, and can report that he's done away with the chandelier. If in two years there is no set left at all, this should come as no surprise, really, for that is the direction in which most of us in this country are convinced that dance should go. We understand dance as dance, and dancers as dancers (not actors). We have many different versions of dance and many ideas about what it could be, but we know that it should not be on the same footing as the visual element—or even as the music. (Balanchine says that the music is the floor on which the dancers walk or the water in which they swim. Cunningham develops his choreography without the music, or sound environment, that will eventually be paired with the dance movements in public performance.) This is a radical transformation and one that shows that the neo-classical dance and modern dance, which originally arose as a repudiation of ballet, have something in common. Dance as such has now achieved an irrefutable primacy, and this is clear to most of us whatever our particular predilection, taste or prejudice may be. We now know something about what dance is that the most sophisticated members of the nineteenth and early twentieth century audiences could not understand.

The articulation of this transformed view of dance has, therefore, been a project for the writing done on dance in the modern period. The great achievements of dance writing in the last thirty or forty years have come about because of the redefinition or, rather, the re-creation of the form itself. I eagerly read dance writing from and about the past, from Gautier forward; I am enthralled by everything written about the Ballet Russe, especially the eloquent articles of Adrian Stokes. But I don't recognize dance writing as something I can say yes to, not from a historical point of view but as something that accords with my own experience, until I get to Edwin Denby. His is the first writing that I take seriously as an account of dance, as opposed to an account of someone's pleasure in dance. Denby describes what bodies are actually doing on the stage. That might seem a remarkably obvious necessity, but it was not recognized as such until relatively recently. Read the contemporary descriptions of the Diaghilev performances. What you find are effusive declarations about how "magical," "marvelous," "overwhelming," "exciting," the performers were, how gorgeous or witty the sets, how thrilling the music, how brilliant the costumers, et cetera; but little mention of the knees or feet or elbows or shoulders. The quality of dance writing changed dramatically—came of age, in my view—when people began to write eloquently and precisely about the body. That is the glory of dance writing and that (as far as I know) began in the 1930's and 1940's, the period of Denby's early reviews and in which Lincoln Kirstein, whom I consider a major American essayist and superb writer, began to publish writing on dance.

We know, of course, what exalted Lincoln Kirstein. But I consider it no accident that both Denby and, later Arlene Croce, who have in my view set the standard for dance writing, are people whose formative aesthetic experience was Balanchine. The new standards for dance set by Balanchine made it clear to them what dance was, and how to talk about it. The knowledge has, of course, been generalized. Jill Johnston (an able dance writer in her early incarnation) and Deborah Jowitt had Cunningham and the Judson dancers, not Balanchine, as their formative experience. And yet the way in which they wrote was set by Denby. He opened up the territory, and others moved out from there. It was the way of writing developed by certain people whose allegiance was above all to Balanchine that made it possible for others to write about very different kinds of dance having nothing to do with transformations—fulfillments—of ballet.

I count my reading of an essay by Denby called "Forms in Motion and in Thought" as a turning point in my life. It changed my sensorium. I see myself, other people, movement, the arts, the world differently for having read it. That seems to be what we perennially, appropriately hope that art and writing about art may do. I think of dance as a theatre of the ideal: of ideal bodies, of ideal movements and forms, of ideal exactness. And I sometimes find ideal prose when I read about dance. The sort of eloquence people are sometimes inspired to when writing about dance has a peculiarly apt relation to its subject. In reading dance writing I experience in an immediate way the vindication of art as a source of pleasure and art as a construction of form, notions which seem wonderfully self-evident when writing about dance. All sorts of ideas are at stake when one writes about dance: ideas of pleasure, of sensuality, of civility, and of order, for dance is the locus of an extremely complex relation between tradition and innovation. (One wants it to be exactly as it was. One wants it to be better than ever.) And wonderful reconciliations take place in dance and in dance writing. What we experience in our lives, and even more so in our reflection, as quite opposite sometimes seem to be united in dance: a feeling for physical work as a way of life, a feeling for refinement, a feeling for the nobility of the body and an intimation of what spiritual life is, and the transcendence of personality. All these things seem concretely, coherently, convincingly incarnated in dance—and in the best writing about it.

Q: What would you say the role of the dance critic is?

A: The role of the dance critic is no different from that of anyone who writes about the arts: to set and defend standards, to help create a discriminating audience. Criticism should give us a model for an intelligent, inspiriting way to talk about the arts. It must disparage the bad and help people to enjoy and love the good, even if, or especially when, the best work is somewhat difficult of access. I think of the critic as a kind of public defender—of the art *against* the public when necessary, and a defender on behalf of the public for the art.

There are also more particular obligations for the dance critic, as I have tried to suggest. An important project in dance writing in the last three decades has been teaching people how to look and what to see. Real dance criticism, properly speaking, began when writers introduced an accurate description of what the bodies are actually doing on the stage. It was, I have suggested, when the modern movement on the one hand and Balanchine on the other showed that dance is dance—not theatre—that people began to write well about dance.

Q: The dance as dance that you're speaking about is really only one part of a much larger spectrum. Jazz dance, folk dance, and the many varieties of popular or social dance are equally valid and, some would say, healthier specimens of the form. Dance as dance seems to have emerged at the same time that science as science appeared, namely with the development of the atom bomb. They both seem to derive from the separation of technique and feeling.

A: Well, that is the opposite of what I think. Your argument is one used by many people to attack Balanchine or Cunningham or other modernists. Sterile formalism, and so forth. A familiar, insidious charge. But I can think of nothing more moving, in the most old-fashioned sense, than the so-called abstract ballets of Balanchine—"Agon" and

"The Four Temperaments," for example. When I use the phrase dance as dance I mean something of a quite different order than science as science. I don't believe that they derive from similar sources or that they appeared at the same time. It wasn't Hiroshima that revealed to us the triumph of a technological rationality disassociated from moral or humane restraints; that had been clear long before the construction of those ultimate horror weapons. And I do not believe that dance as dance is the result of the atrophying or the abstraction of some "real" or more humane dance. It is true that certain references of an anecdotal kind have been eliminated—at least, that has been the effort. But there are all sorts of elements that appear in the dance vocabulary of any given period which link in imperceptible ways the most varied genres. When these elements are recognized, what at first seemed abstract is no longer so.

Arlene Croce recently wrote about the way that ballets which have been in repertory for decades are transformed. We are astonished when we see films or tapes of these "same" ballets as they were danced in 1945 or 1955 because the style of movement, the way the body is used, is so much tied to the period. In fact, all of the dance forms of any period have something recognizably in common. Now we can see stylistic similarities in the ballet, Broadway show dancing, and popular dancing of thirty years ago, as say, twenty years from now people will see relationships among the different dance forms of today. So nothing is really that abstract. Abstraction is itself a fiction.

Recall how the idea of dance as dance developed.

The neo-classical ballet vocabulary of today is, as everyone knows, ultimately derived from French and Italian court dancing of the seventeenth century. This dancing was done not by professionals but by confident, devoted amateurs. (Louis XIV himself was an extremely active dancer. Between the ages of 13 and 31 he took leading roles in twenty-seven ballets at Versailles.) What happens in the succeeding centuries is a gradually increasing professionalization of performance. Dancing is no longer performed as a variety of sport, competing with any number of other aristocratic diversions; it is a full-time activity. With that shift comes a change in the level of the performer's skill. The professional has the time, as the noble dilettante does not, to develop a highly refined technique; and that is indeed what occurred. By the nineteenth century the ballet vocabulary had become a vocabulary of physical virtuosity.

With the twentieth century we enter fully into the democratic modern era. Dancing is still professional, but there is a significant pull away from this kind of technical virtuosity because it is experienced—to use a horrid word of recent currency—as "elitist." That is, it is seen as sterile, unnecessary, limiting, and above all undemocratic. The desire of the early modern dancers for a return to more so-called natural movement had a moral, even a political impulse. And that same impulse was at work in the (only slightly) later emergence of the desire for abstraction—or, to put it more accurately, for ridding work of anecdote, something that all the modern arts have tended to do. These converge most didactically in certain dance works of the 1960's in which untrained performers enact the most commonplace, everyday actions in what are entirely abstract structures.

So the notion of dance as dance is not the exhausted finale of a once vigorous form, as you seem to feel, but rather its fulfillment. The evolution I have just outlined is one part of a complicated story, in which many different kinds of aesthetic and ethical considerations come into play. But virtually everyone in this story—this is the basic point—understands dance as dance. Both the Soho choreographer picking performers among people on the street and the most exactingly old-fashioned ballet master share the new idea—to us, self-evident—that there is such a thing as an ideal treatment of movement. Dance as dance.

Q: You've said that dance is central to different but complementary traditions of modernism: the quest for an ideal form and the pursuit of art as creative destruction. You suggested that the Ballet Russe and Balanchine are manifestations of different aspects of the aspiration for the ideal. But what about the other? Is there a major figure or style which expresses the second tradition, the destruction of art in the name of art?

A: The figure who matters most to me, whom I most admire, is Merce Cunningham. He is also one of my favorite dance writers. Cunningham's view—that everything has its place, that we can not but do what we are doing and that it can not but be right—is, in effect, a repudiation of the very notion of the ideal, the whole point of which is that there is one way of making art which is better than any other way. Cunningham suggests that to say things are not all right is pretentious and ultimately indefensible or, worse, that it causes pain and suffering. In practice, of course, there is enormous discrimination—as well as playfulness and tranquility—in what Cunningham does. I take his views as a recipe for freeing our imaginations.

Q: But if Cunningham and his ideological colleague John Cage were really to practice what they preach, they would have to give up concert situations altogether. A concert situation by definition creates a frame for looking which is separate from what we call life.

A: But all of the great modernist gestures of this tradition, if carried to their logical conclusion, abolish themselves. The great coquetry of the modernist movement has been to move as close to the edge as possible without plunging over. Of course, some do. Yvonne Rainer stopped dancing and started making films. But Cage and Cunningham deal in a nihilism which is so elegant, so playful, and—above all—so appetitive that it won't be contained. "Of course, we shouldn't be doing this," they seem to say, "but then, why should we even say we shouldn't be doing this? Let's do it." The brilliance of their work is that they don't fall over the edge. They extend it, beautifully. They're doing just fine.

Q: There seems to me to be a third part to the model of modernism which you've described, which has to do with a social vision. A good deal of modernist work has been propelled by a desire not just to destroy art but to destroy what is perceived as fundamentally oppressive in modern society, to effect social transformation. It is my view that this impulse has been selectively ignored by a critical establishment intent on defining what is allowable abstraction. There is a notorious anecdote about Nelson Rockefeller going down to the Museum of Modern Art after a dinner party with a bunch of his friends, some of whom felt that what they saw on the walls there was subversive and dangerous and should not be allowed. Nelson turned to them and said, "It's all right as long as we control the critical appreciation of this art." I think that he got what he wanted.

I'm not proposing that there was ever an active conspiracy, but I think it's obvious that the selective appreciation of a certain kind of minimalist abstraction has ripped that abstraction out of its social context. Criticism, and I include dance criticism, has become a kind of technical rationale unconsciously in lockstep with some of the most abusive aspects of modern society.

A: I don't think that the Rockefellers or any of their plutocrat peers *need* to control, either in a direct or indirect way, the critical reception of contemporary art. They just have to leave it alone and it will take its natural place as decoration, as entertainment, as solace, as pleasure. It is the great stupidity of the Soviet government to think that there is any kind of inherent critical potential in abstract art. They make it so, by defining it as dissident. If they would just let their painters be, the art would take its place in the reception halls of the Kremlin just as it has taken its place in the corporate board rooms of America. Art becomes radical or subversive only in a context—a repressive context of which we have, for all practical purposes, no experience. In a society which grants the artists virtually complete license, what could constitute a significant social challenge? Of course, a specific work produced at a given historical time and place may indeed reveal injustices or name taboo subjects. Think of Goya. But I am not convinced that art is capable of any long-lasting, consequential challenge to political systems. To insist that it perform this function is to misunderstand its real value, to place expectations on art that cannot be fulfilled. Art, real art and not propaganda, is not the kind of weapon you suggest. But I do agree that attitudes toward art are important, and often reinforce oppressive power. However, the danger is quite different, I think. It is the danger that, in the name of some demagogic ideal masking as justice, the right to diversity in art and thought, to seriousness, to fecklessness, to subtlety, to pessimism, and, yes, to what is called "elitism" will be taken away from us; and we will be able—or want—only to produce art that "everybody" (that is, the state) approves of.

1980

PAUL TAYLOR (1930–2018)

PAUL TAYLOR didn't begin college (Syracuse University) studying dance, where his main interests were swimming and art. But when he saw some dance pictures in the college library he transferred to Juilliard, where he got a degree in dance history. This was in 1953. By 1954 he was making dances. By 1955 he had joined Martha Graham as a soloist, and he stayed with her for seven years. He was her "naughty boy," but she supported him and encouraged him every step of the way. Taylor was almost the exact opposite of the other great dancer/choreographer who emerged from under Martha's wing, Merce Cunningham. Whereas Cunningham's work grew more and more abstract, Taylor—despite such superb nondramatic works as *Aureole* and *Esplanade*—was profoundly invested in observing the human condition: sometimes at its most brutal, as in *Big Bertha* and *Last Look* and *Speaking in Tongues*; sometimes joyously, as in *Orbs*; sometimes plangently, as in the masterpiece *Sunset*; sometimes wryly; sometimes oracularly; sometimes mystically; often comically. Through the more than fifty years his dance company has existed he chose, trained, and developed an endless parade of superb dancers and built a formidable institution to showcase them—and himself: until his retirement from the stage, he was one of the strongest and most exciting dancers in the world.

Paul Taylor's autobiography, *Private Domain* (excerpted below), is powerful, jaunty, revelatory, armored—as contradictory as the man himself. But you can tell from it how much writing for him was a labor of love.

Black Mountain, Hell's Kitchen, and Broadway

SOON AFTER leaving Juilliard I stuffed practice clothes, Ace bandages, Infrarub, and a few other less important items into a laundry
bag and headed south to Black Mountain. I had been invited by Merce
to spend the summer with him and his other five company members at an artists' colony in North Carolina, where after two months
of classes and rehearsals we were to perform a concert of his works
which would include *Septet*, *Dime a Dance*, *Banjo*, and *Collage*.

At rehearsals Merce wasted no time on theories or verbal explanations of what his dances meant. He simply showed us their steps
and, except for telling us their counts, said nothing about how we, as
performers, should interpret them. Presumably, the dances were not
about anything, and as performers, we were to execute rather than
interpret. This puzzled me, because the dances seemed to have subjects, or at least emotional climates, and because Merce danced his
own roles dramatically. Each of his movements, be they sharp or soft,
shouted or whispered, startled or stealthy, clearly meant something to
him. For instance, at the end of *Septet*, instead of merely tiptoeing in a
line with the rest of us, he seemed to be deeply involved in some kind
of religious procession, perhaps one that related to the Catholic altar
boy he had once been; in *Untitled Solo*, an obviously psychological
study, he was communicating personal but unspecific conflicts. Yet, to
his dancers, he wasn't letting any cats out of the bag. We never knew
if he chose not to tell us the meanings behind his dances because it
might make us over-emote in our own performances, or because such
tipoffs would give glimpses into a personal life that he preferred to
keep private. At any rate, undramatized steps and performances were
what seemed to be expected from the rest of us.

We all adored Merce and rehearsed beaverishly to learn his dances.
The two months were filled with uninterrupted work and more work,
and the only one of us who did anything other than dance was Anita,
who caught the mumps.

At the end of the summer, soon after we left, Black Mountain folded
due to financial difficulties. Unfortunately, I may have contributed
slightly to the collapse. Although I had been led to think that the

summer would be expense free, the head administrator, poet Charles Olson, presented me with a bill for room and board, which I was unable to pay.

Back in New York, and sporting a beard which in '53 was far out, and needing a place to live, I went around knocking on tenement doors. Landlords were unimpressed with the beard, my occupation, and especially the fact that I had no source of income. With help from Graham classmate Murray Gitlin, I was finally able to convince one of the landlords to let me rent his fifteen-and-a-half-dollar-a-month railroad flat in Hell's Kitchen. Even in '53 the apartment wasn't much of a bargain. It was called a railroad flat because of its three lined-up closet-sized rooms, the caboose being the communal john out in the hall, I guess; and it had no heat, though for mild warmth in winter-time, a cast-iron gas stove could be illegally lit. There seemed to be a strong possibility of setting off an explosion from the neighborhood's abundant garbage and cat-urine fumes.

Later on, when subletting to Joe Layton, who was soon to become an affluent Broadway and Hollywood director, I would have earned myself three dollars a month profit had he not been so hard to collect from.

After furnishing the flat with "objets trouvés," most of which were local street gleanings, I sat down on a pseudo–art deco chair to survey the results of my decorating efforts. There on the newly enameled black floor and matching black walls, scuttling industriously, were communities of water bugs and various types of roaches. Most were dull brown, a color that went poorly with my color scheme, and none were nearly as attractive as the bugs that I'd been chums with at Edge-water Beach. Possibly I was losing my zest for insect life, or else these New York ones had lost their charisma. I then noticed a brave little mouse scaling the leg of my brand-new packing-crate table. On mak-ing it to the top, it brazenly sat there expecting a handout. Being no longer sheltered by institutions, and hungry myself, in fact getting hungrier all the time, I was unable to drum up much compassion.

Up to then I had received scholarship handouts from Syracuse, the American Dance Festival, and Juilliard. Classes at Martha's school and Merce's were also gratis, and the ones from Tudor and Miss Craske at the Metropolitan Opera Ballet School, cut rate. Rehearsals with Martha, Merce and, later, Pearl Lang I did for love, as did their other dancers; and so, the subject of food being foremost on my mind, I began to leaf through *Variety* and *Show Business* to find out who was holding auditions for what. Although show dancing was not what I had come to New York for, any kind of performing experience was bound to be worthwhile. I started making the rounds regardless of what the auditions were for, as long as the job would pay.

After other hopefuls and I had lined up like so many hunks of ham or slices of cheese, we were asked to tap dance, sing, act, and do acrobatics. Just because I could do none of these didn't keep me from wasting everyone's time. Instead of tapping, I flapped ineptly, then got a "Next"; instead of a circular series of Russian cartwheels, I used my hands and barely managed a single, which of course got me another "Next"; instead of singing a current show tune, I mumbled "Happy Birthday" and earned myself the rarely heard "Get out of here and don't you ever come back!" It was slightly discouraging that no one could recognize a star when they saw one.

Continuing the rounds, I eventually came upon the perfect audition, one where I was the only applicant. The producers of a TV commercial needed someone who could be a gorilla and fit into the costume, size medium, that they had already rented. After squeezing into it (I hardly popped the seams at all), and after assuring the director that I ate bananas well, I was hired.

It was to be my professional debut, one that would have been more auspicious if I had been allowed to dance, or at least waddle a bit. Too bad only vine swinging was required.

On rushing straight from Merce's rehearsal, I arrived for the taping late and was quickly sewn into the costume; and then, the eye holes being too high, someone had to lead me in front of the camera, where I was handed something that felt and smelled like a bunch of wax bananas. The director or someone else said, "Go, guy, swing your heart out!" No one seemed to care when I complained that I was being jabbed by a coat hanger that had been left inside the costume.

I began to get other commercial work, at the same time dancing with various modern dance companies and taking two classes daily. Just remembering my schedule and getting to the rehearsals and classes on time was an accomplishment in itself. Merce had been rehearsing us all fall for a midwinter week-long season at the small and inadequate Theatre de Lys in the Village. He had his own scheduling demands, and so, though nothing was said, it was a safe assumption that he was not pleased by my being late to one or two of his rehearsals. On my part, I was beginning to indulge in a dangerous thing. I'd started to look at his dances with a critical eye and picture how I would make them if I were he. When a dancer does that too often, there's only one thing to do—make your own.

Things came to a point of no return over *Dime a Dance*, a suite of short solos, duets, and trios. Each company member had learned all the parts of all the sections, but we were not to know which part to perform until after the curtain went up. From a basket onstage different objects were to be drawn which would denote who would perform what. Unfortunately for me, the object that signified what I would dance was never drawn. Several weeks later, disappointed at not dancing in *Dime a Dance*, I asked Merce if future opportunities to dance were also to be decided by chance. He did not answer my question, or could not, but said that if I disapproved of chance methods, he thought it sensible for me to leave the company. I had gained a lot from Merce, was very fond of him, and admired the steadfastness of his beliefs. Had he indicated a preference for me to stay, and if I could have forced myself to agree with chance methods, I might've flipped a coin to decide about leaving. (A dime would've been appropriate.) As things stood, I chose to give Merce my notice. Since then we have remained friendly and I still admire his strength of belief and the clarity and lack of sentimentality of his dances.

When working with the American dance pioneer Charles Weidman, and although under his direction, I saw very little of him. He had already contributed much to the field but was now past his prime. His *Lysistrata* was to be presented in tandem with Robinson Jeffers's play *The Cretan Woman* at the President Theater on Broadway. I auditioned, was selected, and then rehearsed at an Eighth Avenue ex–funeral parlor where Mr. Weidman lived. Since he was rarely well enough to attend rehearsals, his two assistants and some of the cast set most of the dance. Just before we opened, the costumes were taken back by the costume makers, who believed that the producers were crooks and not likely to pay for them. Without sets, however, and wearing our own practice clothes, we went on anyway and performed the dance twice before closing.

One day in '54, while trudging from one rehearsal to another, I stopped off at the Stable Gallery near Columbus Circle to see what was up in the painting world. After giving the main floor a quick once-over, I went downstairs to see what was in the basement and found a copper-haired guy of about my own age sweeping dirt into a pile. He introduced himself as Bob Rauschenberg, said that he was a painter and that he supered the gallery for its director, Eleanor Ward, in return for being allowed a basement show of his own. The basement was featuring his latest work, something that he called dirt paintings. One of them had just fallen off the wall. Charmingly, he went on to say that he had made them by planting birdseed in earth-filled frames and that after grass had sprouted, and although he had sprayed fixative by the quart, it had been hard to get the frames to hang on the wall without everything falling out. Nevertheless, in spite of a minor gravitational problem, he believed his work to be an embodiment of the concept of art being nature, and vice versa. In addition to the dirt paintings, his show included some enigmatic stones and a few small boxes filled with curiosities that he had scavenged from beaches and streets. To me these all seemed very beautiful, mysterious, darkly comical, and somehow atavistic. Bob had at least two gifts—imagination and gab—and I immediately complimented him on his work, although it crossed my mind that he might be more of an idea man than a technician. While he talked I became convinced that, like me, he was bound to become important, but for the time being he was struggling and flat broke.

He lived in a ramshackle loft on Pearl Street down at the densely packed skyscraper tip of Manhattan, where he had been daubing an enormous white canvas with white oil paint—no painted shapes, just the real ones from the thick daubs. Since he kept running out of paint and having delays until he could afford more, the canvas was taking a long time for him to complete. By the time it was done it had yellowed with age because of the cheap paint, but that and other of life's picayune impediments didn't seem to bother him.

In '78, twenty-four years after he and I first met, both of us were awarded life achievement medals from Brandeis University. Others receiving similar awards were Saul Bellow, Grace Paley, Jessica Tandy, and Hume Cronyn. The ceremony was held at the auditorium of the Guggenheim Museum, and my old ballet teacher Antony Tudor was in the audience. Bob, by then a multimillionaire, was print-making at his portion of Captiva Island in Florida, and so a friend of his, Tanya Grossman, was accepting his award for him. My off-the-cuff acceptance speech was taped by her and later sent to me:

"There's a sort of coincidence going on here tonight, and it's about Bob and me. You see, we—uh—well, we both came to New York at the same time and we met, and he was one of the first people I ever met in New York, except he wasn't a New Yorker. He was from Texas, I think, and—ah—that we should be getting these same awards at the same time here seems like—umm—[*something garbled*], and I wish he was able to be here because, well, uh, I did very much want for him to see me get my award. Well, I guess maybe I'll have to tell him I got mine first.

"Anyway, when we met Bob said something to me that—I don't know why, but it's stuck in my mind all these years. He said . . . let's see . . . well, it was so stupid that it's no wonder I've forgotten [*awkward silence here*]. Oh yeah, now it comes back. Ahem. Bob said, 'All hot water is, is cold water heated.' You see? It was sort of dopey, right? But not really, because where I lived there wasn't any heat or hot water, and in the wintertime the whole place would freeze solid, and you had to wear hats and gloves inside to rehearse in and you had to write home with a pencil because of the ink freezing and cracking the bottle, and all, you know? So when I mentioned the cold to Bob he knew that I had a hot plate, so that's when he said, All hot water is, is [*rumble from passing bus here*] . . .'

"Anyway, what Bob said showed a kind of optimistic attitude—I mean, that anything, anything at all you wanted, was possible. And I think I must've caught a little of Bob's attitude and it's helped my company and me over some bumps. Sure, I remember what he said, and I sure hope he knows that I . . . Tanya, will you tell him that I remember what he said? And so these awards prove Bob right, that anything's possible, and this award is very [*more mumbles*] umm—and I appreciate it, and—uh, thank you."

After leaving Merce's company in '54, I began to work fairly regularly with five or six acquaintances and classmates. This loosely formed fly-by-night group was the original of the one in my name that exists today and was created mainly for the purpose of gaining performing experience rather than as an outlet for my choreography. Three or four times a year we shared programs with other fledgling dancers and dance makers at small stages such as at the Henry Street Settlement House, or Master's Institute, an Upper West Side residential hotel. Most of these shared programs were under the aegis of Dance Associates, a conglomeration of groups that were selected and encouraged by James Waring. Besides dancing and making dances, Jimmy generously arranged the dates, sent out fliers, and in general organized the concerts. He could have been called business manager except that we were not a business—that is, little or no money changed hands. The concerts were given without backing, usually went unannounced in the newspapers, and were performed practically in secret. There were few production costs. Costumes were made out of dime-store wares and refurbished hand-me-downs. We improvised with whatever could be begged or borrowed in the way of rehearsal space. Although the management of International House had not given permission, some of us used the gravelly, railingless, and risky roof there to rehearse on.

Some of the dance associates whose work later became better known were choreographers Richard Englund, Benjamin Harkarvy, Marvin Gordon, Paul Sanasardo, and Lee Theodore; composer John Herbert McDowell, who wrote dance scores for us and others by the hundreds; painters Bob Rauschenberg and Jasper Johns; dancer/costume designer Ruth Sobotka; and two dancers who danced mainly with Waring—David Gordon and Toby Armour. As far as I know, all of these people donated their time and talent. Two or three dance critics usually reviewed us, but probably only because there was much less dance then going on in New York.

Jack and the Beanstalk was the first dance that I made while connected with Dance Associates. It had original music by a young composer Jimmy had recommended. Bob did the costumes and props, which included a self-illuminating golden egg and a beanstalk that was merely a long string held up by gas-filled balloons. The dancers were Viola Farber, who was in Merce's company, Alec Rubin, Leslie Snow, Don Boiteau, Anita, and, of course, myself. The dance was supposed to be a nonnarrative fairy tale—that is, its six sections had no story or character delineation, but were separated one from another by still poses meant to resemble story-book illustrations and which were intended to get the narration over with in a hurry. Any hint of

Jungian psychology as typified by Martha's interior landscapes was carefully avoided, as well as anything of a heroic or weighty nature. The dance was neo-old-hat-ism; I was taking a stand for brainlessness and physical fluff.

At the dress rehearsal the score's barely completed orchestration was heard for the first time. It did not sound right to me, so I asked the musicians to play it at low volume in a back room behind the stage, explaining to them that the dance would then be improved by an atmosphere of mystery and remoteness. Even keeping the door closed didn't help much.

After the dance was performed the audience just sat there. No boos, no clapping, nothing. This was not surprising to me, as I had assumed that the dance was neither good nor bad. It was never performed again, and its transitoriness was celebrated by a small ritual which Bob and I conducted. Taking the beanstalk and its balloons out into the alley behind the theater, we released them and watched them disappear into the sky. "Isn't it just great, the way dances are so easy to erase?" said Bob, and I wholeheartedly agreed. We were not the least interested in leaving monuments to the future—in fact, we saw a kind of glamour in impermanence. Bob had lately gotten hold of a valuable de Kooning drawing, erased it, and hung it in his own show. As I understood it, the main idea was to flush a painting or a dance out of your system and then go on to the next one. (In the distant future I was to change my mind.)

After a summer spent dancing in Pearl Lang's company at Jacob's Pillow in Massachusetts, I return to the city and again make the rounds. There's an interesting rumor on the dancer's grapevine—Jerome Robbins, Broadway's top choreographer, is directing Mary Martin's *Peter Pan* and needs an acrobat who can dance a little. There has been no casting call in the trade sheets, but the show has already been performed on the West Coast and is to open in three days at the Winter Garden. Naturally, I rush right over as fast as I can. Unquestionably, working for Robbins would be a valuable experience.

At the Winter Garden a stage doorman tells me that there's no audition being held, but after telling him that I have an urgent message for Mr. Robbins, I'm allowed in. My eyes being slow to adjust to the dark, when stepping onto the stage I trip and almost fall. From out front someone yells, "Hey, what the hell are you doing in here?" The voice is deep and I assume it to be Robbins's.

"I'm the dancing acrobat, sir, the one everybody says you need," I reply, swelling my stomach and hunching a little, since I've heard that most acrobats are short and stocky.

"Bub, what's needed around here isn't a dancing acrobat but more cleaners. This goddamn place is filthy."

My eyes now adjusted, I can see that a cleaning woman has been speaking. She runs her vacuum up and down the aisles for a while, and then the real Robbins and his dance captain come in and I repeat what I said to the cleaning woman.

I'm then asked to do back flipflops, but not having any idea what they are, I say, "Don't you want to see me do some ballet first?"

"Later, maybe. Your flipflops, please."

"How about if I sing something?"

I'm told that my singing isn't especially needed and am again asked to flipflop. There seems no point in giving myself away, so I explain that mine are a little rusty and ask to show them later, intending to take a tumbling lesson somewhere as soon as possible.

Robbins says I can have ten minutes to brush up and gestures to the front lobby. There I find a group of little boys, the show's lost children, who are jostling each other around on thick carpeting. When I ask one of them if he can tell me what a flipflop is, he looks pleased, vaults into the air, arches backwards, comes down on both hands, and pops back onto his little feet as if shot from a toaster. The stunt seems to be on the risky side—a scary direction to take—but the show is apt to run, and a job is a job. After several attempts to copy the kid—each time landing on my head—the ten minutes are up, so I return to the stage, where I announce that my flipflops are perfection, then ask Robbins if there is anything else that he'd like to see. But he insists.

This is the moment of truth. Adrenaline courses through my veins. Eyes shut, I heave upwards and, after an endless moment of panicky disorientation, come crashing down on my feet. They sting like blazes, but I'm grateful not to have broken my neck.

"Umm . . ." he says doubtfully. "Now do them fast, one after the other, and make sure to travel in a straight line."

There's a limit to what adrenaline can do, and the straight line turns out to be a slow zigzag. However, perhaps because he has no time to find anyone better, Mr. Robbins hires me.

I'm quickly taught the part of one of Captain Hook's dancing, singing, brawling, slightly simian pirates. At rehearsals Robbins seems like an enthusiastic camp counselor explaining the rules of an enjoyable rainy-day indoor game. The dancers, several of whom have worked with him before, are terrific and do the show's charming and beautifully crafted song-and-dance numbers with pizzazz.

The flipflops are needed during a fight aboard designer Peter Larkin's red velour pirate ship, part of which, at Robbins's insistence, has been junked in order to leave more space for the action. Dancer Don Lurio, soon to star in his own TV series in Rome, is dancing the role of a boxing-gloved kangaroo. He is to beat me up, and as a result of a final punch, I'm to exit backwards through an opening downstage right which is disturbingly close to the cement proscenium. Don says for me not to fret, that I'll be able to aim myself in the right direction by lining up on him. To gain more control and less panic, after rehearsals I take a couple of flipflop lessons at a gym.

On opening night I line up as planned, pull off a fairly decent line of flipflops, but veer a bit too far right and crash into the proscenium, breaking my nose and squashing it flat to the left. After crawling offstage, I see Mary Martin's maid passing by with a load of clean towels. "Hey, may I use one of those to wipe blood with?" I ask.

"'Deed, no chorus boy ain't gonna soil up my Miss Martin's towel," she said.

"Well, that's all right," I say back, snatching the top one. "I'm sure she won't mind. You see, I'm going to be a big star myself soon."

After the opening kangaroo bit Don helps me to an emergency ward, where an intern tells me that though my septum has been deviated, he can do nothing for me, since noses aren't really his bag. But I persuade him to push while I pull, and between us we're able to shove it back into place.

Several days later I still can't breathe through it, so I go to a surgeon, who agrees to repair it, and since this is to be his first operation ever, he agrees to a reduced rate. Some weeks later, after removing the bandages and looking in a mirror, I'm sorry to see that the nose, never very long to begin with, has gotten even shorter; but when I mention it, the surgeon sets me at ease with assurances that all noses lengthen with age. "Just be patient," he says. "It will eventually grow back to its original length." (These days, over three decades later, I'm still patiently waiting.)

There being no understudy for me in *Peter Pan*, it never occurs to me to miss a performance. Heavy landings out of the flipflops keep jarring the tender nose and sometimes cause me to bite my tongue. And, though continuing my lessons, I never learn to land gently. I partially solve the tongue-biting problem, however, by having a dentist file down the two sharp points of my incisors. And then, after about two months of performances, my wrists begin to go and I sprain one of them. When I ask the dance captain if the flipflops might be replaced with back somersaults, I'm told that since I'm hardly seen because of everything else that's going on in the fight scene, I can leave them out until my wrist gets better.

Robbins has long since stopped coming to see the show, but that night he or someone else notices the flipflops missing, and I get a pink slip the next day. There's nothing much to complain about—understandably, performance standards have to be maintained.

It's possible to find another job, one more within my range. Cyril Ritchard, the show's elegant Captain Hook, generously recommends me for a nonspeaking part in a TV production of *Mysterious Island*, which stars Rita Gam. Big silent types are needed to leer and lurk around in a plastic jungle.

In a few years my company receives the first of several grants from the Robbins Foundation. Jerry has always been interested in what new dance makers are up to and, having seen or read about my concerts, is not only helping but showing me that he thinks my work worthwhile. Later on, in '84, he again aids my company, this time with a twenty-five-thousand-dollar grant, for which, should I ever work for him again, I'd gladly flipflop as often as possible.

Instead of lessening with familiarity, fear of flipflops and concern for the hardness of the proscenium increased with each performance. Show biz demanded a lot more fortitude than I thought, and, in a way, it's a relief not to have to go back to the Winter Garden anymore. In spite of what I told Mary Martin's maid, I'm not at all sure about ever starring in anything, for, since I left Juilliard, the preordained future has begun to seem less rosy. Taking a cue from old Dr. Tacet, I've begun to ask myself, "Have you the heart of a lion, the soul of a saint? Or even, dear boy, the fecundity of a hare?" Comparing myself with other dancers causes reassessments to be made. Living economically makes my stomach rumble. When funds run out, I resort to eating canned dog food, sometimes swiping it from supermarkets. To restore dignity, however, I make up for such moral lapses by snitching caviar from Bloomingdale's.

As always, the cloistered world of Miss Craske's ballet classes has smoothed the difficulties of city life. While they last, her classes are sheltering isles of order—something like my old barred and bubble-decaled haven of a crib back at the Brighton Hotel—and it's tempting to think of her classroom as protective insulation rather than as something that builds technique. The unequivocal Cecchetti system which she teaches is comfortingly symmetrical, and she herself radiates perfect calm. Having studied with the Italian master, even teaching for him in her native London, she had then met a guru, Baba, and followed him across German U-boat-infested waters to India, where she'd proven her devotion to him and his teachings by living an impoverished life of servitude and, it's said, by hanging with other Babaites from the ledge of a cliff. After that, she returned to teaching ballet, Tudor being one of her students.

Though her classes sometimes seem tedious, and are not what I consider dancey dancing, for the hour and a half that they last, just being there gives me an illusion of well-being. She is admired by all, and her wisdom and peaceable manner are those of a woman who's passed an ordeal by fire with flying colors. Although I never mentioned it to her in so many words, the perilous bouts with the kangaroo probably wouldn't have been possible for me without the fortitude that she'd inspired.

Not employed often enough to collect unemployment insurance, I've been earning enough to scrape by and continue concert work. Paid to be a dragonfly in the Jones Beach Marine Theater's *Arabian Nights*, for which Rod Alexander choreographs an insect dance, I back up Nirska the Butterfly Lady (bugs always my leitmotif). Madam Nirska sports twenty-six-foot China silk wings and platform shoes—an impressive sight to behold, especially in a wind storm. Tenor Lauritz Melchior makes his entrance on a portly elephant—a well-matched pair—but the elephant isn't housebroken and leaves the stage unsanitary for those of us who have to follow in bare feet. Also included is a water ballet, the swimmers having their own problems, with sea nettles. My favorite sight of the two-month run is when a fellow chorus boy foolishly mistakes depilatory for hair bleach, then molts.

Rehired by Jerry Robbins for his TV version of *Peter Pan*, I managed one last flipflop, this time merely crashing into the key grip.

In modern concerts I've partnered Natanya Newman, an extraordinary dancer who's been in Martha's company, also in Merce's *Sixteen Dances*. Beautiful Pearl Lang begins to give me solo roles, including some of Glen Tetley's old ones. Some of these are performed at the ANTA in a Broadway season advertised as "three weeks of the greatest in contemporary dance." (Through a printer's error, my name in the *Playbill* comes out five times the size of Pearl's.) Bethsabée de Rothschild presents this season twenty repertoire pieces and eighteen premieres performed by seven companies and six independent soloists. The notices are less than raves. Winthrop Sargeant, music critic for *The New Yorker* and Martha's sister Geordie's ex-husband, writes that "for those who attend the theater for uplift, a lot of the season has been lugubrious." John Martin of the *Times* thinks that the mixed programs, which seem to be trying to offer something for every taste, also automatically have something against every taste. The *Herald Tribune*'s Walter Terry, a nice guy who can be counted on to like almost everything, says he does, but probably nobody believes him. The thumbs-down on this panoramic view of modern dance is likely discouraging for Bethsabée—also annoying, in that she's had to put up with many of the choreographers' complaints over unequal allotments of performances, stage rehearsal time, billing, and other ticklish matters. After the season is over, for whatever reasons, she limits her backing solely to her friend Martha for a while, then moves to Israel, where she founds the Batsheva company.

When not dancing, I work for my painter pals, Bob Rauschenberg and Jasper Johns. Their careers haven't yet quite gotten off the ground, and so they're bolstering their meager incomes by designing and making department-store window displays, paying me by the hour to help at their loft on Pearl Street. Some of the displays are commissioned by Gene Moore of Tiffany's, a man known for his taste and discrimination as well as for aiding many rising artists by hiring them. At present he's still doing it, and I'm proud to be included as one of his artists, whom, in my case, he aids by donating the set and costume designs that he often creates for my dances.

Bob and Jap's loft is so small that in order to make room for the display work, Bob sometimes throws out a few of his old paintings. Once, when I find his last remaining dirt painting in the trash, I ask him for it and he signs the back "To Pete." This early work, like all the paintings of both artists, is soon to be coveted by major museums around the world. For reasons of sentiment I've never sold it—not that I couldn't have used the cash.

While working on the displays, Bob and Jap often talk about art. As far as I can make out, their main intent is to glorify, or at least present in a new way, ordinary objects. These things—Coke bottles, coat hangers, light bulbs, etc.—aren't supposed to be symbols. The idea is to appreciate them for their own beauty. If there's a message, it seems to be a recommendation for everybody to expand their vision, to get a kick out of stuff that's usually considered homely, corny, or even unsightly. Neither paints pictures of anything, exactly—they recycle the thing itself. Both disapprove of likening things to other things. Both have a fondness for the same objects, but Jap can get more wrapped up in American flags than Bob can, judging by his large numbers of them. And Jap likes numbers better, large numbers of numbers done in wax. Bob sometimes slips into exoticism, such as a stuffed angora goat with a tire around its middle. Jap is a fine draftsman. Bob can't draw at all, even if he wanted to. Bob's works, mirroring his own nature, have a high gloss of humor and are collages of enthusiastic charm and dark mayhem underlined by strong commitment. Jap's works, in my inexpert opinion, are less charming, almost frighteningly spartan, and so strong that I find them hard to relate to. Bob's I can laugh with; Jap's, for all their virtue, laugh at me. Both painters seem to look askance at most contemporary realists, as well as at the expressionists and impressionists, preferring Man Ray and some of the other dadaists. Monet's water lilies and Whistler's portrait of his mother are two of the exceptions. The window-display work bore a certain kinship to the two future greats' own painting. For instance, one set of Tiffany windows, a job that didn't take long, had plain ordinary dirt dumped in them, over which were strewn cut diamonds. Much of what I absorbed from the two artists strongly affected my early dances—one of the most useful things learned from Bob being that sometimes the quick, easy way is best.

1987

WALTER TERRY (1913–1982)

A DANCE critic for almost fifty years, Walter Terry, born in Brooklyn and raised in Connecticut, was not only an acute and influential reviewer but a large presence in the world of dance as a tireless propagandist for the art. A superb lecturer, a writer (of twenty-two books), an ardent supporter of the new, he was a great friend to a host of figures ranging from Ruth St. Denis to Alicia Markova: a man as convivial and enthusiastic as he was knowledgeable. After graduating from the University of North Carolina, Terry began his career in 1936 at the *Boston Herald*, and, by 1939, he had become the leading dance critic of the *New York Herald Tribune*, his passionate interests ranging from regional dance companies to the art of the Royal Danish Ballet. He reigned at the *Tribune* until 1966, with a three-year time-out during World War II while he served in the Army overseas (temporarily replaced at the paper by Edwin Denby). After the demise of the *Tribune*, he spent the rest of his career as dance critic for *The Saturday Review*. A generous collection of his reviews—*I Was There*, published in 1979—remains fresh and immediate, because he *was* there, and excited to be.

Ballet on Ice

S WAN LAKE is about to freeze over, and the swans themselves are getting ready for it. The old Tchaikovsky favorite has long given sanctuary to swan maidens and their queen, but Catherine Littlefield has taken away their toe slippers and put them on skates. If any one has a right to surprise swan lassies with a change of climate, that one is Catherine Littlefield, for Miss Littlefield is a classic ballerina in her own right, she has directed her own companies in successful appearances here and abroad, she put dancers on bicycles in *American*

Jubilee and she is a choreographer of recognized ability. Now she is trying to unite spread eagles with arabesques in *It Happens on Ice*, the new extravaganza coming to the Center Theater on the tenth of this month.

Fairly quivering with ideas on the possibilities of ballet on skates, Miss Littlefield dashed into her first rehearsal and threw most of her young athletes on their faces with the intricacies of her skating steps. Soon she discovered that skates have a double edge and that an attractive arm movement could throw the skaters' balance from one edge to the other so suddenly that disaster was the only possible result. A little study cleared up matters, and before long she had her skaters conscious of ballet line, group composition, able to adapt their spins into ballet turns, their jumps into long ballet leaps. Until he came under the Littlefield direction, one young man had supposed that music was only to keep the audience's ears busy, but he soon learned that ballet on skates meant that music and motion were destined to pay close attention to each other.

At rehearsal the other day I saw some of the new works. Little, blonde Catherine Littlefield kept warm with coat, mittens, a blanket, and coffee while she shouted directions to her skaters. There was *Swan Lake*, with its swan maidens, its queen, its prince, its hunters, and the evil magician. Hedy Stenuf, the "prima skaterina" for the company, glided, soared, and swirled in breathtaking fashion, while Gene Berg, as the magician, pursued her more fleetly than man ever pursued fair lady. These two dancing skaters, along with Skippy Baxter as the prince, are certain to win stellar positions for themselves in the great field of ballet.

Before anti-classicists get worried, I want to assure them that Littlefield has more tricks up her sleeve. A ballroom polonaise replete with elegance, etiquette, and élan is on the schedule, and a Currier & Ives glimpse of a day on the old skating pond is in production. This latter work is a gentle but hilarious satire on the naughty boys who trip every one up, the bevies of girls being taught to skate by patient swains, the governess and her elite charges, the young lovers and the show-off skater who builds up to near-decipherable figure eight to the tune of ardent applause. A jazz number, *So What Goes*, splices pep with all the appurtenances of love: a huge ring, a rose, angels, the lovers' knot, and the necessary lovers. A swing ballet and an iced version of a Negro spiritual will complete the Littlefield contributions.

I have always maintained that the American dance should and must partake of athleticism, for the simple reason that a nation's dance should honestly reflect the character of its people, and Americans are decidedly sports-minded. Great dancers have contributed richly to this union of sports with dance, but here at last is an actual fusion of the two, for ballet on ice possesses the rhythm, the patterns, the drama, and the characterizations of dance while it partakes of the skill, the speed, and the muscular prowess of the sport of skating.

The character of the rehearsal was typically American. No foreign yells, no posturing in front of mirrors marked the proceedings. Miss Littlefield issued terse, vernacular commands in a loud, firm voice. The skaters called her Catherine, the boys winked as they sailed by, but Miss Littlefield was boss, and the skaters snapped to attention when a reprimand was launched at them. The girls and boys have quickly learned the group spirit necessary to good sports of good dancing, and the men have managed to assume the grace of ballet without submitting to the effeminate gestures which curse so many males in the ballet.

It Happens on Ice should do several things for the American theater. It should help to carry those who profess disinterest in dance over the hurdle which separates athletics from dancing. It should influence American dancers who have failed to see the tie between dance and sports. It should, of course, open up a new field of entertainment, for the possibilities of ballets on skates are limitless. For the sake of upholding the supremacy of dance, I would like to mention in passing that skate dancing does possess certain limitations in the matter of movement: small gestures, subtle mime, and slow movements are practically out, detracting somewhat from the range and diversity of expression. But take skating, dancing, or theater entertainment in any form of motion as your criterion, and you will be convinced, I think, that Catherine Littlefield is becoming a theater figure of the first rank, a girl who is leaving her mark in the revue, in the ballet, and on ice.

October 6, 1940

Fantasia's Dances

MADEMOISELLE UPANOVA is the perfect ballerina. She has long legs that give scope to her movements, she has a willowy neck and her little white ballet skirt is an inseparable part of her anatomy, for she was born wearing it. Of course, Mlle. Upanova is an ostrich, but she can execute an entrechat or an arabesque with the best of her dancing sisters. Currently appearing in *The Dance of the Hours* from *Fantasia*, this tripping ostrich exudes fake eye-lash glamour and displays the virtuosity of ballet technique in a performance which is a riotous, satiric reflection of the real thing.

Walt Disney is a great choreographer. Moments of beauty, human tenderness and humor are conceived in terms of dance, and the sequences of pure fantasy are projected through rhythm, pattern and motion. Donald Duck in his most thwarted and irate episodes would blow up and bust if he didn't dance out his frenzy; the pallid Snow White had real moments of loveliness when she danced in the cottage with the dwarfs; and who can ever forget the first Silly Symphony when the skeletons danced to the macabre accompaniment of their rattling bones. In *Fantasia* Walt Disney has assembled the richest qualities of his choreography: humans, animals and flowers dance in ballets which poke fun at dancing and in ballets which exalt it.

A Slam at Ballet   During the production of *Dance of the Hours*, the Disney staff turned into balletomanes. Artists followed the Ballet Russe on its tour of California, making performance and back-stage sketches of Paul Petroff, Irina Baronova and others. A group of ballet dancers were taken to the Disney studio where they danced over and over again the traditional passages of *Dance of the Hours*. Repetition caused exaggeration to creep into their movements, and at this point the sketchers managed to capture on paper a suggestion of ballet to its silliest. The final result in *Fantasia* is an immortalization of ballet's pet foibles. You see the ostrich ballerina looking archly at the audience while her frenzied feet writhe through a complicated pattern; you see Ben Ali Gator, the premier danseur, giving his partner, Hyacinth Hippo, extra impetus in her pirouette by pulling her tail, and you see pretentious coyness in the attitude of every animal performer. These are kind-hearted and honest cracks at the worst aspects of ballet.

In the *Nutcracker Suite*, Disney turned to the sheer visual beauty of dancing. Flower petals falling upon water were swept into the gliding measures of a waltz, bits of milkweed-down were tossed by the breezes into the lightest of ballerinas, dewdrops slid down blades of grass and quivered from leaf to leaf in a fairy dance, frost designs spun an ice ballet and a cluster of mushrooms turned into a gamboling gang of midget mandarins.

Dances of Nature   The person who dares to express his belief in a system of nature which is rhythmic and patterned is branded a mystic, yet Disney has done just that in *Nutcracker Suite* and in *Rites of Spring*. He has succeeded, I think, because he has not relied upon the inadequacy of words to express this theme but has shown us through his great and visible art that such a system does exist. Both of these sequences are purely fantasy, yet a fantasy which gives significance and drama to reality. In *Rites of Spring* we are shown the surging, rhythmic and planned growth of microscopic life carried to its ultimate in the gigantic beasts of pre-historic days. Seeking food and water, the titanic animals make their final trek across the desert wastes, their weary movements resembling a great processional of death. *Nutcracker Suite* is based upon the nature of our own times, a slow-moving nature whose rhythms and patterns are lost to our eyes; but with the speed and clarity of Disney's discerning brand of fantasy, these rhythms and patterns become clear and credible for the first time. With man pretty impressed with his own importance, it's a good thing to show him that other forms of life are also possessed of beauty, growth and a valid place in the schemes of things.

Beethoven's *Pastoral Symphony* has many moments of beauty and humor, and they are due to the dancing and the capering of the animals rather than to any of the bloodless activities of the human characters. *Night on Bald Mountain* is an excellent ballet in the grotesque. The spirits of evil and of death race throughout as the lesser furies dance wildly on the brink of Hell and the unfortunate captives dance their last halting measures on the palm of Satan before he crushes them to death. Dance lovers will find much of *Fantasia* rewarding in its choreographic scope, stimulating in its brilliant use of a great art. Others, I think, will be led to an understanding of dance, an excitement in it, for Walt Disney, through the medium of motion pictures, is bringing great dance and simple dance to every one.

November 24, 1940

TWYLA THARP (1941–)

BORN IN Indiana, raised in California, Twyla Tharp is an all-American girl. No wonder her work looks so American! Or is that backwards? Does American dance now look Tharpian? She's certainly done enough to reconfigure it. Starting out as a choreographer, in 1965, with a solo called *Tank Dive*, at first—like so many brilliant young talents— she was a kind of provocateur, but her talents and ambitions were too large for such an ultimately limiting approach. She was, instead, a revolutionary, and her goal, even if she didn't immediately proclaim it, was to end the ballet-vs.-modern wars by marrying our two great strands of dance, partly through infusing both with the vernacular. By 1976 she had succeeded so well that Arlene Croce would refer to her "amalgamation of high and popular art which no other choreographer except Balanchine has achieved in this country." It didn't take her long. She had studied with Martha Graham and Merce Cunningham before joining Paul Taylor's company, which she soon left to start her own.

In 1973 came *Deuce Coupe* (to the Beach Boys—ballet to rock!) for the Joffrey, her breakout popular hit. Which led fairly quickly to *the* hit: *Push Comes to Shove* (1976), for American Ballet Theatre and Baryshnikov. There have been many other popular successes and critically acclaimed masterpieces, from *Eight Jelly Rolls* and *The Bix Pieces* to *Nine Sinatra Songs* and *In the Upper Room*. There has been Broadway: her wonderful Billy Joel show, *Movin' Out*, rang up 1,331 performances and won her a Tony. There have been movies: with Milos Forman alone, *Hair*, *Ragtime*, and *Amadeus*. There have been the Kennedy Center Honors, the National Medal of the Arts, Guggenheims, MacArthurs. There has been family—a son and a grandson. And there have been books: her autobiography, *Push Comes to Shove*, excerpted below; *The Creative Habit*; *The Collaborative Habit*. She's done it all, but for her, living means doing more. She's made something like 160 works, and she's making new ones still. Twyla Tharp never stops—and she never *will* stop.

(from) *Push Comes to Shove*

AT A time like this, the only thing to do is call Jerry. Jerome Robbins and I had met fifteen years before. One day I had simply phoned him. "It's been long enough that I haven't met you. Come to dinner," I said—an act of chutzpah for which I've always been grateful. That night at dinner, in talking about his new ballet, *The Goldberg Variations*, my tough-guy persona was out in force. I suggested to Jerry that he should have given me every third variation; this would have given *him* the theme but *me* the last word. Jerry, who had been seeing my work since *Medley* in 1969, took that in stride, saying he really didn't want to do the ballet over again, but maybe I would work with him on some other set of variations. That called my bluff, and instantly I got cold feet. A moment of horseplay at the door, when he waltzed me to the right and I switched roles and took him to the left, suggested potential confusion in such a collaboration. I promised to think about it, but then the reality hit home. How could I create with the Broadway legend who had made the focused violence of the knife fight in *West Side Story*, the Uncle Tom's Cabin sequence in *The King and I*, to say nothing of his many classic ballets at the New York City Ballet, from *Afternoon of a Faun* and *The Cage* to *Dances at a Gathering*? I said no. But Jerry is relentless. A befriender of strays, he prefers mutts with mostly terrier in them. Finally I gave in. We decided to use Brahms' "Variations and Fugue on a Theme by Handel," and Jerry submitted the proposal to Balanchine. Jerry's talent is prodigious and his reputation awesome, but this was something else. When Balanchine approved the project, this was God speaking.

For all my adoration, or precisely because of my adoration, I saw Balanchine only three times over the years. For a long time I had steadfastly refused to take advantage of offers to be introduced, fearing I would simply burst instantly into tears. However, when I was in Nashville with Misha for the taping of *The Prodigal Son*, it had happened. I had watched as Balanchine demonstrated to the dancer performing the father's role how he wanted the very last moment of the ballet done for the camera—the moment when the father takes the repentant son into his arms. As Balanchine reached for Misha, the whole set tensed because Balanchine was not a large man and he was just recovering from a bypass operation. But Balanchine had insisted, and finally Misha pulled up his feet. Balanchine literally held all his weight.

Later that day, at lunch, Misha ate quickly and left to rest for the afternoon; I was alone and went back for seconds. The assistant director, Emile Ardolino, was standing by me and suddenly called my name. I turned around and there was Balanchine. I had no time to think; I simply bowed and Emile introduced us. Then Balanchine bowed, saying he was a great admirer, and I bowed, saying, No I was a great admirer . . . and back and forth it went a couple of stammering seconds for me until Balanchine asked if I would like to go back onto the floor because he needed to think a moment.

We went into the darkened studio and he talked about how much easier it was, how much quicker, to move dancers, altering formations if necessary, than to move cameras. Then he took a large velvet-bound book from a leather case. Inside were several Russian icons enameled with semiprecious stones. He told me that the makeup people could not get the effect right on the Siren in *Prodigal Son*. He wanted her to have the richness of these saints' golden inlays.

In truth, that is all I remember of the meeting, except his appearance, which was, as always, perfect—black slacks, white shirt, his Western string tie. However, I was left with the feeling that all along I had been right: Balanchine was responsible for every detail.

Several years later, Balanchine was in the hospital. I went twice, wearing stockings with seams and being sure they were absolutely straight, and putting on a perfume that I hoped would please him. (On premiere nights, Balanchine always gave his principals fragrance, different for each girl.) The first time I went, his assistant, Barbara Horgan, brought me in. Balanchine nodded but did not speak. I showed him a Japanese cutout template I had brought as a gift. It puzzled him, but when I taped it to the window, causing the light passing through to cast patterns about the room, he smiled. The second time, he was very sick, and frightened, too, because a stranger had come into the room and the attendant was making quite a fuss getting him out. So I just left what I had brought for him—a Walkman with a favorite cassette of mine, one of Mozart's last works, the Adagio and Rondo in C for

Glass Harmonica. After that, I got together with a friend and we made sure that every day from then on there would be a small, but different, flower brought to his room.

I read of Balanchine's death when I was flying back from a film location, in a *New York Times* that had been left on an empty plane seat. For the next year, every morning I went into the studio to work, I could not keep myself from crying. I missed Balanchine terribly—the thought that he would not be making any more dances, that he would not be springing into an incredible late blossoming as Matisse had, that I was now completely alone in the studio. I imagined making a dance to his memory, but the thought was ludicrous. He was embedded in every step I did.

By the time Jerry and I finally began to work on our ballet, Balanchine was gone. The New York City Ballet was struggling valiantly to go on, determined to keep his legacy alive. Jerry all along had worked in tandem with Balanchine, the two of them making their work with the company about dancing, not careers. When Balanchine was incapacitated, Jerry kept things going with *Dances at a Gathering*. We both knew the ballet we were beginning could not just be about respecting the past; it would also have to provide a challenge in order to keep things going. The New York City Ballet dancers had always been a part of my standard, the living evidence of Balanchine's discipline. Now I would be working with his dancers in his studio, even having the key to his dressing room, which Jerry and I shared. I wondered what it must have been like for Jerry to live in the shadow of Balanchine at the City Ballet for so many years, the intimidation Jerry must have felt as he contributed his own talents to this great company, helping to develop the very best in dancing. I had a dream in which Jerry and I ran into each other in a rickety old bus—the one that has chickens on top, is packed with natives who don't bathe, and has tires whose patches blow out regularly—sightseeing down in the Yucatán. When there was a stop for everyone to get out and visit the Loch Ness monster, Jerry and I declined, staying on the bus. But we knew the monster, a huge, dinosaurlike snake, lived in a filthy sewage-ridden murk partially covered by some of the oldest floorboards in theatrical history. You stood on these to visit with him. After I told this dream to Jerry over dinner one night, I asked him if he knew who the monster was. "Sure," Jerry said. "George."

Standing in Balanchine's traditional down-right corner of the stage at the State Theatre—the spot where he always stood to watch the performances—I felt woefully inadequate. However, Maria Calegari and Bart Cook, my principal couple, worked unstintingly to make both simple and complex material crystal clear. Rosemary Dunleavy, Balanchine's ballet mistress, entered each day asking if I would want to change anything and then set about doing it, never once suggesting in her attitude that tomorrow this too might be gone. The entire company was still committed, with a deep faith, to dancing, not to product. One day, when I'd come up with a good idea (one of the few Balanchine had not already had), asking Merrill Ashley to jump down into catches rather than up, and then used that momentum to propel huge tosses in the chorus, everyone in the room caught their breath because invention was what this institution had been bred for.

While Jerry and Balanchine had worked together on several occasions, I began without any idea of how to collaborate on a ballet. Jerry had the notion of dividing the company into two camps, the blues and the greens. He wanted the blues. "Of course, Jerry, you know green is a lousy color," I said. We began by alternating variations, although each of us could add anything or bring our group through the other's sections at any time so no one would know for sure who had done what. We worked off one another; sometimes we'd choreograph simultaneously in the studio, sometimes I'd take a theme of his and elaborate on it in a later variation. Sometimes I would see opportunities for a choral background in a figure he'd put down. He'd see a bit of movement he liked and he'd extend it—a swoop reversed, dipped, and lifted. We'd do a little partner-swapping, remating our principal couples (he'd taken Merrill Ashley and Ib Andersen), or I'd make a variation for Ib and he'd borrow Maria for a gloss on one of my sections, a brief satire. There actually never were any harsh moments between us. Jerry went out of his way to be encouraging as he passed through a rehearsal, and he remembers that one day, when he was boggled, I came into our dressing room and told him to take a big bite out of whatever was bothering him the most. We each tried to watch videotape to keep up with all the rehearsals and be as organized as possible, but the opportunities in this kind of situation are endless, and we were running out of time. One day Jerry and I both decided we could not have the ballet ready for its premiere—one of the problems with collaborations is that there is someone to bitch to—and Jerry went off to tell Lincoln Kirstein. Who sent him right back with: "George never cared what the critics would say on opening night. Just get it up." And we did. Best of all, Jerry and I remained friends.

Jerry has a reputation for being difficult. He drives himself crazy with his work, questioning everything over and over, trying this and that until everyone else is ready to go crazy too—but only because he believes there is a right way and a wrong way, not just a possible way. Jerry is one of the most complex people I have ever known, capable of every human response in the book: wise, generous, pragmatic, accepting, unreasonable are just a few. It has been watching Jerry work that I have best felt some of the possibilities of dance—whether listening to him extolling his dancers in rehearsal to forget they are dancers and "just start to move," or standing at the back of the orchestra with him during a revival of *The King and I*, waiting in that suspended, breathless pause just before the king sweeps off to the thunderous downbeat of "Shall We Dance?" or joining with him and a synagogue congregation in midtown Manhattan as everyone clasped hands and went dancing out into the streets, a scene in real life right out of *Fiddler*.

But even Jerry—always generous to me creatively, and financially through his foundation—couldn't help me now. "What the hell are you doing that for?" he said when I told him about *Singin' in the Rain*.

Jerry's instinct was right. *Singin' in the Rain* was about to become my worst nightmare.

1992

Tobi Tobias (1938–)

BROOKLYN NATIVE and self-motivated writer of highly crafted prose from the time she was a small child, Tobi Bernstein learned about the existence of ballet as a "pre-adolescent," from a photograph she saw in *Life* magazine of, in her words, "a woman in an extraordinary pose—strange and beautiful." It was the Balanchine ballerina Diana Adams, and a future dance critic was born. Bernstein studied modern dance at the Alwin Nikolais studio and majored in English at Barnard, with a concentration in writing. After graduating, she married Irwin Tobias (who would become a professor of theoretical chemistry at Rutgers University); "hand-raised" (Tobias's term) their two children; and began to publish what would become some two dozen children's books, among them biographies of New York City Ballet stars Maria Tallchief and Arthur Mitchell.

In the 1970s, she initiated her career as a dance journalist with a story for *Barnard* magazine on Twyla Tharp, writing many features and reviews for *Dance Magazine, The Village Voice, The New York Times*, and *The Soho News*, and going on to serve for twenty-two years as the dance critic of *New York Magazine*. In addition, between 1976 and 1990, she served as a consultant and writer for the *Dance in America* television series on PBS. In 1979—having learned that no company record of Bournonville training and practice existed— she was led on her own to put together an astounding oral history, "The Royal Danish Ballet and Its Bournonville Tradition," speaking with several generations of Bournonville-trained dancers across the world. Deposited at the Harvard Theatre Collection, it brought Tobias a knighthood from Denmark's Queen Margrethe II, in 1992. *Obsessed by Dress*, Tobias's 2001 book, for all ages, of literary quotations about fashion is still in print.

In 2012, Tobias became the first online dance critic to be singled out as a finalist for the Pulitzer Prize in Criticism. As the Pulitzer board wrote, she was honored "for work appearing on ArtsJournal.com that reveals passion as well as deep historical knowledge of dance, her well-expressed arguments coming from the heart as well as the head."

Mining the Past

TRISHA BROWN has been choreographing for half a century; from today's vantage point her development can safely be termed evolutionary. Examining the path of her career, it's easy to trace the innate logic that led her from simple (nevertheless ingenious) pedestrian ideas, actions, and gear to complex creations, rich in theatrical artifice, that somehow remained pure. Perhaps the most remarkable aspect of this journey is the interest aficionados of the arts still take in Brown's works of long ago.

As part of its *On Line: Drawing Through the Twentieth Century* exhibition, the Museum of Modern Art scheduled performances on January 12th, 15th, and 16th (at 2:00 and 5:00 each day) of Brown's *Sticks* (1973), *Locus Solo* (1975), *Scallops* (1973), and *Roof Piece Re-Layed* (a version of the 1971 *Roof Piece*).

Brown's works of the early Seventies—the period in which it became clear that she was a leading figure in what would be called postmodern choreography—were as fresh as lemonade made from scratch, as I remember it from my first visit to Paris. When you ordered *un citron pressé* in a modest to downright humble café, you were brought a pitcher of cool water, an empty glass tumbler, a lemon, a small serrated knife, and a downsized reamer (used in old-fashion kitchens to squeeze the juice out of citrus fruits). As I recall, there was a basin of sugar already on the table; ice was unheard of. The lemonade you produced with this simple equipment was the very essence of the drink—just as Brown's early pieces offered the salutary shock of dancing that's been reduced to its essentials.

Today, four decades after Brown created them, those dances still look new.

The choreography is divinely matter-of-fact. Though most of the action requires extraordinary skill, the tone with which it's executed is unemphatic—gentle and calm, full of reticent grace. Should anyone ask you what's going on in these dances, you might even say that each performer simply executes the task she/he has been given.

Simply executing the tasks one has been given. Isn't that a possible prescription for a satisfying life? Those who think not must rest content with the dancers' echoes of the incomparable fluidity Brown displayed in her performing days and the constant evidence in her choreography of a singular intelligence and a wit expressed in swift, tiny flashes, like the lights of fireflies in a darkening sky.

The MoMA program took place in the museum's Atrium, from which you could gaze down on the expansive street-level lobby and up to look-out points on four floors of gallery space. The venue itself is alive with architectural possibility. The audience, standing or sitting on the Atrium floor, bordered a huge square marked off for performance, the onlookers becoming a living frame for the dancing.

The program opened with the 1973 *Sticks* in which four dancers in snug long-sleeved white jerseys and loose white pants partnered with wooden beams maybe two inches square and ten feet tall. Working in unison, the performers seemed to be the puppeteers and the sticks their puppets, as they executed extraordinary feats of balance so that the sticks could lean at precarious angles or meld, ends touching, into a single line that floated, wavering just a little, a couple of feet above the ground.

Locus Solo (from 1975) was performed by Diane Madden, who has worked—and bonded—with Brown for some three decades. Today, she's the company's rehearsal director. A small, strikingly lithe woman with a blond ponytail and a visible delight in dancing, she took possession of a small square marked off dead center in the larger space. Her movements, themselves straight-edged and scrupulously within the indicated boundaries, looked as if she were exploring the parameters of her domain—and its possibilities, rather than its restrictions. After a time, the addition of some leaning, almost falling moves to the strictly vertical ones allowed Madden to suggest a lyrical vein in her activity, though she took scrupulous care not to overemphasize it. Finally Brown's and Madden's combined alchemy revealed that the small dancing ground was larger than we'd first imagined. It had a third dimension—height; it was really a cube. What more could anyone want?

The program's most complex piece was *Roof Piece Re-Layed*, an ingenious adaptation of the 1971 *Roof Piece* that must have had pavement-bound spectators tilting their heads backward to ogle the tops of buildings stretching downtown and then westward from a starting point in SoHo. The original piece—which I'm sorry to say I know only by hearsay—had fifteen dancers, clad in red for visibility, positioned at least a block apart on the route's rooftops, transmitting a string of gestures down the line to one another as they stood in the sky. None of the dancers could see more than a few of the others. The starter, Brown herself, improvised the initial material. Once the wordless scmaphored "message" reached the end of the line, it traveled back again to the beginning, modified as is a verbal message in the children's game of Telephone. Among the participants were Liz Thompson, Valda Setterfield, David Gordon, Douglas Dunn, and Sara Rudner.

In the re-imagined (as they say these days) version for MoMA, the dancers—eight of them this time—were again in red. Six appeared at various levels of the Atrium's walls behind rectangular glass panes of different sizes. Two were unshielded; you could have reached out and touched them, if you dared. One of these, a man, was down in the lobby that the Atrium overhangs. Standing on a low block near the Sculpture Garden, he looked like another statue that had simply added motion to its traits. Madden stood out on the Atrium floor looking like—well, Madden, who, once seen, can't be forgotten.

As in the original version of the piece, any one dancer could see only a few of the others. It seemed impossible to decipher which of them was the "starter." To me the material for all eight rooted-in-place bodies looked memorized, not improvised, because it seemed to be accurately copied as it traveled. I could have asked about this afterward but I didn't. I didn't really want to know. In an era like ours, which has made privacy extinct, art at least should be allowed to keep some of the mysteries that are part of its (al)lure.

January 14, 2011

John Updike (1932–2009)

ONE OF America's finest twentieth-century novelists (the "Rabbit" tetralogy, the "Bech" cycle, the notorious *Couples*, etc.), one of the greatest of its short-story writers, and a fluent poet, John Updike was also an amazingly prolific critic, writing countless book reviews for his home base, *The New Yorker*, as well as a wealth of art reviews for *The New York Review of Books*. He was not, however, a dance writer— he was far more interested in golf than in ballet. Yet he was always interested in specifically American phenomena, and here he captures the essence of that quintessentially American dancer, Gene Kelly.

Genial, Kinetic Gene Kelly

HE HAD plenty of Ginger but no Ginger: although he danced affectingly with Leslie Caron, amusingly with Debbie Reynolds, snappily with Judy Garland, bouncily with Rita Hayworth, broodily with Vera-Ellen, and respectfully with statuesque, stony-faced Cyd Charisse, we think of Gene Kelly as a guy in loafers and a tight T-shirt tap-dancing up a storm all by his lonesome. His torso and his profile were beautiful, and he had a touching little scar on the left side of his mouth, and the musical comedies in which he starred never failed to deliver his dream girl into his embrace; yet somehow his image left no space around it into which a moviegoing housewife could project herself. Even boneless, balding, big-eared Bing Crosby was more of a heartthrob. In the masculine romp of *On the Town*—for this viewer the very best of all Kelly's musicals—Frank Sinatra is cast as a sex-shy nerd, yet in this secondary and comic role he conveys that mysterious attraction, that shadowy depth of contradictory possibilities, which Kelly rarely manifests amid the outpouring of his glittering, genial gifts.

In contrast—in the inevitable contrast, white socks versus white tie—millions of moviegoing housewives imagined themselves dancing with Fred Astaire. The two dancers, though similar in the intelligence and ardor of their dedication to their art, were differently conditioned. Astaire began his career on the vaudeville stage as his sister Adele's dance partner, and it is as a consummate ballroom dancer, weightlessly swirling his partner through a polished and heavenly space, that he lives in our pantheon. Kelly, thirteen years younger, came too late for the ballroom tradition. As related in *The Films of Gene Kelly*, by Tony Thomas, Kelly's first stage partner was his brother Fred, and he trained his body on high-school athletics in his native Pittsburgh. In the 1958 television documentary *Dancing—A Man's Game*, Kelly said, "I played ice hockey as a boy and some of my steps come right out of that game—wide open and close to the ground." His Canadian-born father flooded their back yard and gave him hockey lessons; his mother loved the theatre and saw to it that he and his two brothers attended dancing school. At fifteen, Eugene Curran Kelly was working out with a semipro ice-hockey team; while attending Penn State, he was a gymnastics instructor for the YMCA. After college, he founded a dancing school with his mother, and then went to Chicago to take ballet lessons from Bernice Holmes. He came to New York in 1937, at the age of twenty-four, and got his first break as the dancing character in William Saroyan's *The Time of Your Life*, in 1939; his big break came as the star of *Pal Joey* (1940), a musical based upon his fellow-Irishman John O'Hara's epistolary sketches of a nightclub singer, loner, and heel.

Hollywood welcomed him in 1942. His dancing was more athletic and balletic than Astaire's—one cannot imagine Astaire doing the dizzying number on a high building framework that Kelly performs in *Living in a Big Way* (1947); the aerial acrobatics of *The Pirate* (1948); the swooping roller-skate tap dance of *It's Always Fair Weather* (1955); or the sidewise scuffle on hands and feet that Kelly agilely lowers himself to in several films—and his screen persona was less partnerable. Some of his most memorable numbers, such as the duet with his own reflection in *Cover Girl* (1944), come in the lonely trough between love at first sight and eventual reunion with the heroine. In another technical tour de force, *Anchors Aweigh* (1945) had him dancing with animated cartoons, as did the "Sinbad the Sailor" episode of *Invitation to the Dance* (1956). In the latter sequence, as in many live numbers throughout his films, Kelly—the third of five children, and

the middle son—is in the middle of three dancing men. Male partners seem to free him up to be his most cheerfully spectacular and
inventive self—for instance, a creditably dancing Sinatra in their two
sailor musicals; Donald O'Connor in *Singin' in the Rain* (1952), beginning with the marvellous throwaway vaudeville bits in the opening
flashback; Michael Kidd and Dan Dailey in the celebrated trashcan-
lid dance from *It's Always Fair Weather*; and Astaire himself in the
introductory segments of *That's Entertainment Part II* (1976). Astaire
at the time was seventy-seven years old, yet noticeably the looser of
the two—especially in his arm movements—as he and Kelly perform
some charmingly low-key dance patter.

Of course, Kelly can glide through the steps with a woman, and can
execute a tap routine in perfect synchronization beside her, but up
close he lacks a certain ineffable touch. In Kelly's first Hollywood film,
For Me and My Gal (1942), there is an incidental moment in which
George Murphy, in the role of the ousted suitor, does a brief turn with
Judy Garland that is consummate in its courtly ease of motion; we see,
through a chink of the main romantic plot, just how a woman should
be danced with—with a feathery lightness, and a feather-stiff spine.

Yet it is in *For Me and My Gal* that we are most fully persuaded that
the Kelly character is loved by the heroine. Garland, only twenty in
1942 but a vaudeville trooper since the age of four and for six years a
Hollywood presence, had wanted Kelly for the part, instead of Murphy, who had originally been cast as the guy who gets the gal. She
tutored Kelly in acting for the camera. "It was Judy who pulled me
through," Kelly later said. "She was very kind and helpful, and more
helpful than she even realized because I watched her to find out what
I had to do." An intensity of mutual regard does burn through when
they gaze each into the other's shining black eyes or crisply tap-dance
side by side. Kelly, fresh from his brash Broadway role, is still swaggering, and his reedy intonation suggests a gentler younger brother
of James Cagney's sassy, defiant George M. Cohan. Kelly and Garland
both have a slightly troubled, orphaned air, which lends believability
when the film—with the hero's decision to beat the First World War
draft by mangling his own hand on a trunk lid—takes *a film-noir*ish
turn, and which sees them through the musical's timely metamorphosis into a rousing war movie, complete with dead Germans and
smoky battlefields. It is Garland's nervous energy, clarion voice, and

still-girlish looks that carry the picture; confronted with so volatile and compelling an expressiveness, Kelly's relatively immobile face yields traces of a sulky city waif, with something of Bogart's or John Garfield's bruised appeal. He was subsequently cast, in the freewheeling manner of studio-run Hollywood, in a number of non-dancing roles—in one film, *Christmas Holiday* (1944), as the would-be killer of Deanna Durbin. He dies in her arms, begging forgiveness.

The chemistry between him and Garland had faded when they were paired again, in 1948, in *The Pirate*. This fanciful action-farce, situated on a level of unreality that might be called arty, is Kelly's movie, though the rights to the stage play had been purchased by M-G-M's Arthur Freed as a vehicle for Garland, to be directed by her then husband, Vincente Minnelli. Garland has aged beyond her years, and the zany plot has her and Kelly mostly at odds; at one point, she unloads nearly all the breakable furniture of a colonial palace in his direction, in one of filmdom's great exhibitions of throwing by a left-handed female. Kelly's personality is so encased in his flamboyant parody of John Barrymore and Douglas Fairbanks as to be impenetrable, and the concluding number, "Be a Clown," appears to have jumped in from some other musical. Garland sings her best number supposedly in a hypnotic trance and her whole performance seems a bit dazed— gamely she makes her moves and hits her marks without really getting what is going on. Kelly's most with-it partners are a pair of black dancers, the Nicholas Brothers, whom he insisted on including in spite of warnings that even such mild miscegenation would cost the film some Southern bookings.

Their third pairing, in *Summer Stock* (1950), revives the chemistry, but with the current reversed. Kelly, as a dance-happy city slicker, is in top form; Garland, who would not work for M-G-M again, looks overweight and considerably older than Kelly. Her addictions and inner travail were on their way to cutting short her precocious career; it is his physical electricity, along with the droll byplay of Gloria De Haven and Eddie Bracken, that lifts this lame bucolic romance halfway off the ground.

No one in the post-war era worked harder to expand musical comedy's boundaries than Kelly. Making his debut as a co-director with *On the Town* (1949), he persuaded the management of M-G-M, which in those days hated to leave its Culver City sound stages, to let him shoot on location in New York; in three hurried days, he and a crew captured all the various shots of New York scenery that, sprinkled among the sound-stage footage, give the film an unprecedented spaciousness. Brought in quickly on a forty-six-day schedule, on a budget of merely $1,500,000, *On the Town* remained a proud favorite of Kelly's; he said, "After *On the Town* musicals opened up." Watching a number of Kelly films on video, I found myself continually smiling throughout this one; there is almost nothing stale about it, and nothing painful, such as the overblown ballet in *An American in Paris* (1951) or the grating voice Jean Hagen was obliged to put on in *Singin' in the Rain*. The opening shots of the enchanted Manhattan skyline at dawn, the unprefaced arrival of song in the voice of a sleepy dockworker, and the perennial theatricality of sailor suits instantly transports the action to a plane of buoyant make-believe where singing and dancing are the norm. Besides the Statue of Liberty and the Rockefeller Center Prometheus, *On the Town* has the terrific tapping of Ann Miller and some postmodern dialogue: Betty Garrett, as the amorous taxi-driver Brunhilde Esterhazy, says to Sinatra, "I like your face. It's open, you know what I mean? Nothing in it. The kind of a face I could fall into. Kiss me." Alice Pearce, in the now unthinkable role of a laughably ugly girl, says, after a brief date with Kelly, "At last I have something to write in my diary. I've been using it for laundry lists." Not quite Congreve or Shaw, but flip, sharp, and sweet. *On the Town* is that happy occasion, an ambitious film not spoiled by any sign of ambitiousness.

Two years later, Kelly, as star and choreographer, presented an overtly ambitious display of what dance meant to him and could mean to the movies, *An American in Paris*. His love of France gives warmth to a number of episodes, and rather paternally enfolds the gamine heroine he chose for his leading lady, the eighteen-year-old ballet dancer Leslie Caron. But Oscar Levant is a dour presence, there isn't enough for the French performer Georges Guétary to do, and Kelly's artist-hero's murkily dubious affair with Nina Foch's rich patroness strikes an off-note that doesn't go away. The climactic ballet to the music of Gershwin's *American in Paris* now appears, with its French-painter sets and eclectic busyness, pretty heavy kitsch, while the dancing episodes of the corny Thirties farces of Astaire and Rogers feel ever more precious and pure.

That ineluctable invidious comparison dogs Kelly's renown. In the years when Hollywood musicals were still a popular genre being churned out in abundance, Kelly's ebullient performing prowess and venturesome spirit put him at the head of the pack; now he tends to be remembered as the Astaire-not, a chesty hoofer with a slant smile who danced the Hollywood musical into its coffin. Astaire's Thirties movies played to a giant captive audience, an America stuck in the Depression, with little else but the radio to amuse it. Kelly's post-war movies were competing with a rising television that was keeping more and more of the adult middle class at home. The furious energy of *Singin' in the Rain* has something desperate about it; it is, like Cinerama and the Fifties Biblical epics, trying to outshout and outdazzle the little home screen. O'Connor's frantic gymnastics to "Make 'Em Laugh" and Kelly's delirious[1] splashing in the famous title number have an attention-getting excessiveness. The most relaxed and old-fashioned number—the peppy furniture-hopping of O'Connor, Kelly, and Debbie Reynolds to "Good Mornin'"—is the most pleasing. (One wonders how much American furniture was broken by adolescents trying to emulate the smoothly controlled sofa-topple that the three dancers ride toward the camera.) Even the film's nostalgic topic, the critical moment when sound came to the motion pictures, has a pleading undercurrent—*Love us*, the movies are saying, *like you used to*. But no brilliance of performance, no breadth of screen, no new suavity of color (the early-Fifties movies all look blue, with everybody wearing powder-blue suits and even blue fedoras) could bring the crowds back. John Springer, in his 1966 history of the Hollywood musicals *All Talking! All Singing! All Dancing!*, names *Singin' in the Rain* "the best movie musical ever made" and yet writes:

> By the mid-Fifties, the "Golden Era" of movie musicals indeed seemed over. Many of the brightest originals . . . were making disappointing showings at the box office. As the world market became an ever more important factor in final box office grosses, it became evident that in many foreign coun-

---

1. He was sick, it turns out, in the drenching day and a half it took to film this ebullient number. "In addition to being constantly wet, I had a bad cold and a fever," he later said.

tries musicals were not being shown at all. Or occasionally
they would be shown with song numbers neatly snipped out.

There was something artificial about the movie musical which audiences came to resist—even to the point of wanting the songs snipped
out! It has almost always been a tense and potentially awkward
moment when the background music swells and the hero or heroine
takes a breath to project a melody into his or her significant other's
face. But we put up with it for decades, pleasurably, as a rendering, on
film, of stage magic. Song and dance go back to the very beginnings
of theatrical performance. The Greek tragedies were partly chanted;
Shakespeare thinks nothing of interjecting a song. By assembling in a
theatre we license the performers to do whatever they can to entertain
us: sing, dance, juggle, cavort. The live presence of performers makes
theatre a social event, in which the gala dress of the audience echoes
the costumes onstage. But the cinema, once past the primitive phase
when a stationary camera filmed a stage complete with proscenium
arch and footlights, became more interior—a kind of seen novel, con-
sumed in a private darkness and ever more skillfully imitating, with
its camerawork, the shifts of consciousness. As the movie audiences
forgot the live performances of vaudeville, travelling opera companies, and small-town theatricals, and the upright piano lost its pride
of place in the American home, the conventions of musical comedy
came to seem incongruous. These conventions were always somewhat incongruous; the majority of musicals concerned show business,
whose professionals would naturally demonstrate singing and dancing skills and might plausibly use them to enact their private lives.
But actors and actresses make up a tiny fraction of humanity, and
backstage is a narrow world. It wore thin. Real people don't sing and
dance, and it is a rare musical—*On the Town*, *Oklahoma!*, *West Side
Story*—that convinces us they do.

Also, noting the particular European and foreign resistance to
Hollywood musicals, one might speculate that there was something
specifically American about these films—a brassy optimism and a
galvanizing work ethic. From the muscularity of the performers to
the dizzily wheeling multitudes of choral dancers and swimmers, the
atmosphere is cheerfully industrial. The style of the images may be
insouciant—*Look, Ma, I'm tap-dancing!*—but their message is power,

American power, the power released from Everyman by the emancipations of democracy. In this factory of American self-celebration, Kelly, who rose from the assembly line to the managerial level of choreographer and director, was ideally electric yet chaste. The musicals were about sex, but sex puritanically streamlined. They demonstrated to their public how to make love in the old sense of the phrase (as when William Dean Howells writes in *Venetian Life* of an "idle maiden" who "balanced herself half over the balcony-rail in perusal of the people under her, and I suspect made love at that distance, and in that constrained position, to some one in the crowd"). Making love is finding the way to the fadeout kiss, not what comes after it. To the question "How can I get a guy/girl?" the Hollywood musicals answered, "Dance with/sing to him/her." Again and again, after their spoken spats, they musically melt, Rogers and Astaire, Howard Keel and Kathryn Grayson, Kelly and whoever, into each other's arms. Around 1955, they begin to melt away. The profitable movie musicals to follow will tend to feature Elvis Presley. The tune changed—rockand-roll (its very name gutsy and lewd) made the elaborate sublimations of the musical comedy seem arcane, if not silly. Another language had become academic. Few spoke the language when it was a live one with more fluency than Gene Kelly, and none more gamely embodied American élan.

March 21, 1994

Carl Van Vechten (1880–1964)

THE MAN whom some have called the white godfather of the Harlem Renaissance was born in Cedar Rapids, Iowa, and it wasn't until 1906, when he was twenty-six and had graduated from the University of Chicago, that Carl Van Vechten moved to New York. He was hired as an assistant music critic for *The New York Times* but soon was writing dance criticism—one of the very first writers to discuss American modern dance. (His subjects ran from Maud Allan to Alvin Ailey.) He had seven novels published by Knopf, including *The Tattooed Countess* and the controversial *Nigger Heaven*, but in 1930, when he was fifty, he stopped writing almost completely in order to devote himself to photography, concentrating on performers and writers: from Karen Blixen to Theda Bara, from Norman Mailer to Alicia Markova. He knew everybody, and he and his second wife, the actress Fania Marinoff, *entertained* everybody. (Marinoff was a worldly and intelligent actress; Van Vechten's main erotic life, however, was with men.) His connection to the African American cultural life of his time was strong and deep. He helped forward the careers of Langston Hughes, Zora Neale Hurston, Richard Wright, and many other black writers. He was a good friend of Paul Robeson's. And he was the only white person the great singer Ethel Waters trusted.

Maud Allan in Greek Dances

More Beautiful In Face and Figure Than Some
of Her Predecessors.

MISS MAUD ALLAN, an American girl, who has won no inconsiderable amount of fame in Europe and in England with her dances, made her initial appearance before a New York audience yesterday afternoon in Carnegie Hall. A large and very fashionable gathering greeted the dancer. In fact it has been a long time since so many automobiles have been lined up in front of this staid concert hall. Apparently all of the seats were filled and many were standing at the back. It was an enthusiastic audience, too, and Miss Allan was forced to repeat several of the dances which particularly caught the public fancy.

Most of Miss Allan's European reputation rests on a dance which she has called "A Vision of Salomé," which introduces light and scenic effects, and which was one of the earliest features of the later Salomé craze which swept rapidly down from Germany across the Atlantic to New York, where it is just beginning to be brushed away.

It was not in this dance, however, that Miss Allan chose to make her first American appearance. Instead she elected to appear in another sort of dance with which New York is at present very familiar, thanks to Miss Isadora Duncan, the group of dancers which Miss Loïe Fuller brought over, and finally to the ballet in Gluck's "Orfeo" as it is danced at present on the Metropolitan Opera House stage.

These dances, accomplished to music written by the great composers—it will be remembered that Miss Duncan even went so far as to use Beethoven's Seventh Symphony—show the dancer in poses presumably inspired by a study of Greek vases. Bare-limbed and scantily draped in filmy gauzes, diaphanous in texture and unvivid in color, she floats from one pose to the next, emphasizing the plastic transitions with waving arms and raised legs and sundry poses of the head.

Miss Allan in spirit and in the nature of her dances resembles her predecessors. However, she is more beautiful in face and figure than some of them, and she has a grace, a picturesque personal quality, which is all her own. Yesterday the stage of Carnegie Hall was hung in green draperies and the lights but dimly indicated pale colors. The orchestra was the Russian Symphony Society, under the direction of Modest Altschuler.

It has sometimes been complained of in these columns that dancers take great liberties in dancing to music which was never intended for that purpose. However, Miss Allan in her programme yesterday scarcely transcended the bounds of good taste in this direction. She danced to Rubinstein's Melody in F, Mendelssohn's "Spring Song," two mazurkas, and a valse of Chopin, Grieg's "Peer Gynt" suite, the

Funeral March from Chopin's B flat minor sonata, and Rubinstein's "Valse Caprice."

Between these dances the Russian Symphony Orchestra was heard in the "Andante Cantabile" from one of Tschaikowsky's string quartets, Saint-Saëns's tone poem "Le Rouet d'Omphale," the overture to "The Merry Wives of Windsor," and the Oppolitew-Ivanow "Caucasian Sketches."

January 21, 1910

The Lindy Hop

EVERY DECADE or so some Negro creates or discovers or stumbles upon a new dance step which so completely strikes the fancy of his race that it spreads like water poured on blotting paper. Such dances are usually performed at first inside and outside of lowly cabins, on levees, or, in big cities, on street corners. Presently, quite automatically, they invade the more modest night-clubs where they are observed with interest by visiting entertainers, who, sometimes with important modifications, carry them to a higher low world. This process may require a period of two years or longer for its development. At just about this point the director of a Broadway revue in rehearsal, a hoofer, or even a Negro who puts on "routines" in the big musical shows, deciding that the dance is ready for white consumption, introduces it, frequently with the announcement that he has invented it. Nearly all the dancing now to be seen in our musical shows is of Negro origin, but both critics and public are so ignorant of this fact that the production of a new Negro revue is an excuse for the revival of the hoary old lament that it is a pity the Negro can't create anything for himself, that he is obliged to imitate the white man's revues. This, in brief, has been the history of the Cake-Walk, the Bunny Hug, the Turkey Trot, the Charleston, and the Black Bottom. It will probably be the history of the Lindy Hop.

The Lindy Hop made its first official appearance in Harlem at a Negro Dance Marathon staged at Manhattan Casino some time in 1928. Executed with brilliant virtuosity by a pair of competitors in this exhibition, it was considered at the time a little too difficult to stand much chance of achieving popular success. The dance grew rapidly in favor, however, until a year later it was possible to observe an entire ballroom filled with couples devoting themselves to its celebration.

The Lindy Hop consists in a certain dislocation of the rhythm of the Fox Trot, followed by leaps and quivers, hops and jumps, eccentric flinging about of arms and legs, and contortions of the torso only fittingly to be described by the word epileptic. After the fundamental steps of the dance have been published, the performers may consider themselves at liberty to improvise, embroidering the traditional measures with startling variations, as a coloratura singer of the early nineteenth century would embellish the score of a Bellini opera with roulades, runs, and shakes.

To observe the Lindy Hop being performed at first induces gooseflesh, and second, intense excitement, akin to religious mania, for the dance is not of sexual derivation, nor does it incline its hierophants towards pleasures of the flesh. Rather it is the celebration of a rite in which glorification of self plays the principal part, a kind of terpsichorean megalomania. It is danced, to be sure, by couples, but the individuals who compose these couples barely touch each other, bodily speaking, during its performance, and each may dance alone, if he feels the urge or is impelled to by his partner. It is Dionysian, if you like, a dance to do honor to wine-drinking, but it is not erotic. Of all the dances originated by the American Negro, this the most nearly approaches the sensation of religious ecstasy. It could be danced, quite reasonably, and without alteration of tempo, to many passages in the *Sacre du Printemps* of Stravinsky, and the Lindy Hop would be as appropriate for the music, which depicts in tone the representation of certain pagan rites, as the music would be appropriate for the Lindy Hop.

1930

Eloquent Alvin Ailey

THE FIRST important Negro dancing that I remember is George Walker's extravagantly elegant performance of the cakewalk, pranced with his equally talented wife, Aida Overton Walker, as partner, a performance derived from spectacular muscular control that, by comparison, makes other, more recent, exhibitions of this back-straining folk dance seem weak-jointed and flabby. George Walker could strut to the Queen's taste, and eventually, with his celebrated vis-à-vis, Bert Williams, he did just that at a command performance at Windsor Castle before the noble eyes of her Royal Majesty Queen Victoria, Empress of the Indies.

The next great Negro dancer I recall is Bill Robinson, the superb Bojangles, one of the few executors of any race who employed his entire body in his act. He tapped not only with his nimble feet, but also enlisted, with electrifying results, the aid of both hands, both expressive eyes, his mobile torso, and even his hat, which appeared to have a life of its own, in his brilliant exhibition.

After these major interpreters, Negro dancers arrived in profusion: Katherine Dunham, more a creator than a performer; Pearl Primus, who first developed a fine style all her own, moving expertly, with great precision to Negro folk tunes, and who later became adept in authentic African gyrations; Janet Collins, one of the earliest to create viable emotional movement for the spirituals, later enjoyed ending a program with a vivid impression of a tipsy New Orleans belle in red calico ruffles, returning from a Mardi Gras ball, and who eventually transformed—through her transcendent grace and magnetic person-ality—the ballet in the second act of *Aida* into a work of art on the vast stage of the Metropolitan Opera House. Avon Long was irresistible in his own sharply-etched, unique manner; Asadata Dafora was prob-ably the first to introduce his native African dance to America; Jose-phine Baker, in her fantastic and capricious performances, aroused the jaded French to the highest degree of enthusiasm they had shown to any foreigner since the retirement of Mary Garden.

Arthur Mitchell has become an important artist with the New York City Ballet, and his partners are the most beloved of the white bal-lerinas. Mary Hinkson and Matt Turney are two of the most highly regarded dancers of the Martha Graham Company. Mary Hinkson has also danced with Arthur Mitchell and the New York City Ballet in *The Figure In The Carpet* and with Alvin Ailey in Harry Belafonte's *Sing, Man, Sing.*

I have seen the béguine danced to perfection at the Bal Colonial in Paris, and I have witnessed spectacular calypso dancing on the quai of Port of Spain, Trinidad, where Geoffrey Holder became acquainted with mystical voodoo rituals and the natural beauty of the West Indian folk dance.

Into the midst of this luxuriant medley, Alvin Ailey, with his beautiful partner, Carmen de Lavallade (herself an unusually gifted dancer), plunged into *House of Flowers* like two young animals. The effect was like that of a happy explosion. Such really desperate energy has rarely been evoked before in a light musical.

Alvin Ailey has all the attributes of a great dancer: he is young, beautiful, strong, with a perfect body and with the technique of dance well welded into his system. He knows how to approach practically all dance problems, except perhaps those of the classical ballet, and I dare say he could easily learn to perform these—given desire, time, and a period of study with the professional experience of George Balanchine. He can lift, leap, crawl and slide, even glide, to make your heart beat faster. His prodigious strength makes it possible for him to execute consecutive movements without pause in perfect rhythm. Great strength is the basis of all great dancing, for a dancer must be tireless in face of any difficulty. Ailey is a gifted actor, too, with real atmosphere in any costume he may assume.

Since her first appearance with him, Carmen de Lavallade has danced with him on many occasions, and they were seen together in their unforgettable brilliance in his low-down *Roots of the Blues*, an experience—almost a career—for any beholder in its compelling realization of John Sellers' wailing melodies, illuminated by towering ladders in the background.

Alvin Ailey choreographs all the numbers he dances with skill, invention, a good deal of imagination, and variety. In the *Hermit Songs* of Samuel Barber, he employs a deeper, more passionate emotion than he used in *Roots of the Blues* in his spontaneous and eloquent movement. He should further be inspected in *Revelations*, a dramatic setting of some familiar spirituals, and in *Gillespiana*, danced to music by the celebrated cornetist.

Some of us remember, many of us will never forget, a tender, introspective piece of Ailey's called *Ode and Homage*, in which he danced with a kind of solemn mournfulness. This was a tribute to his teacher, Lester Horton, also the instructor of Janet Collins and Carmen de Lavallade. It was performed to music by Peggy Glanville-Hicks and was given only once in March of 1958. It can be said truthfully that it deserves a revival.

Alvin Ailey danced in Jamaica with Lena Horne's company, at Jacob's Pillow, at the Lewisohm Stadium, and in the picture version of *Carmen Jones*. He has also acted successfully in plays. As a matter of fact, he is usually successful in whatever he attempts to do.

1962

David Vaughan (1924–2017)

A DUAL citizen of his adopted United States and of his native England, David Vaughan had a considerable impact on both countries as a dance historian, a dance critic, and the archivist and key staff member for the Merce Cunningham Dance Company during nearly its entire existence. Following attendance at Oxford and four and a half years in the British army during and after World War II, he worked onstage as a chorus boy in London, an actor both on and Off-Off Broadway, an occasional narrator for Cunningham, and, for decades, a singer in cabaret. In his nineties, he performed in Canada and the United States. with his friend Pepper Fajans in the intimate and touching show *Co. Venture*, presented by the Brooklyn Touring Outfit.

Vaughan started ballet late, at the age of twenty-three, "puny and underweight," with Audrey de Vos, a London teacher whose anatomical analysis helped him to build up his body and made it possible for him to become a professional dancer. He came to New York in 1950 to accept Lincoln Kirstein's invitation to enroll in the School of American Ballet, where Vaughan met Cunningham and studied with Anatole Obukhov, the subject of the memoir here. Vaughan went on to choreograph for film (Stanley Kubrick's *Killer's Kiss*, 1955) and for Dance Associates, the dancers' cooperative he cofounded in New York with the choreographer, designer, and poet James Waring.

Revered for his critical biographies *Frederick Ashton and His Ballets* and *Merce Cunningham: 50 Years*, in 2012 he was appointed Resident Dance Historian at the New York Public Library for the Performing Arts. Several months before his death, he completed Waring's biography.

(from) Beautifully Dance: Anatole Obukhov

I FIRST CAME to the United States in the fall of 1950, with a scholarship at the School of American Ballet, then still in the great studios at 575 Madison Avenue where the school had opened in 1934. My teachers were Felia Doubrovska, Muriel Stuart, Pierre Vladimiroff, and Anatole Obukhov. Obukhov was, simply, terrifying. He came into the studio preceded by a roar of "Pah-see-shun num-berr one," and continued to shout throughout the class. The class was unbelievably hard. In form, it was unvaried. There were three more or less equal parts: a barre of about twenty-five minutes, very fast and exhausting, followed by a long adagio that took three-and-a-half minutes on each side; both groups did it to the right and to the left, twice, so that the whole thing took roughly half an hour; the last half-hour was devoted to grand allegro—in Obukhovian English, "fasterr possibly" (i. e., as fast as possible).

He was, at first sight, a funny little man with a clown's face, and an absolute dynamo of energy. He had several disconcerting habits (they were meant to be), of which the worst perhaps was that of standing immediately in front of you and snapping his fingers in rhythm right under your nose. (I realized after a while that he was probably looking at the person behind you.) His command of English was not extensive, but he could wither you with his expressive scowl and a snarl of "tairrible!" Once, when I was standing with my arms in an imperfect fifth position en haut, he got me to lower my shoulders by the very direct method of hitting me hard on each of them. I was quite frightened of him, and did not look forward to his classes.

But as I continued to take them, I found that I loved them more and more. I got stronger, and could more or less get through them, and as I got used to him, he got used to me. He hated to see new faces in class, I think, and this may have been why he tried to frighten new students. Once he asked me if I were going "at home" (to England) in the summer, and when I said no, he said, "In School of American Ballet in summer is tairrible situation: all new people." As time went on I grew to learn that the only really fierce thing about him was the passion with which he cared for classical dancing; throughout his classes, from the very first plié, he would repeat, like a mantra, "Dance, dance, dance," and sometimes "Beautifully dance." Anyone who studied with him would remember these phrases, along with other idiosyncratic locutions such as "Company numberr first," and the subdivisions "Big miss," "Small miss," and "Gentlemeness." (This was more polite than Miss Stuart, who once said, "We'll have the tall ladies, the short ladies—and the bearded ladies.")

Some teachers instruct through analysis, with a basis of anatomical knowledge; others by example. Obukhov was, par excellence, an example of the classical style at its most graceful, precise, and elegant. In himself he was elegant to the point of fastidiousness: for class, he was always dressed in a fine white shirt with a white handkerchief in the pocket, blue trousers, and gray or black kid shoes, and he wore a cologne scented with lily of the valley. (Once, at the end of class, he presented his devoted pianist, Mrs. Ouroumoff, with a little bouquet of these flowers that I think came from his own garden in the country.) In American schools the pupils habitually applaud the teacher at the end of class (something I had never heard in England); Obukhov hated this and always silenced any attempt at it.

His personal grace and delicacy were reflected in his enchaînements, which were characterized by the most exquisite fantasy. Those long adagios were like passages from an old Petipa ballet, and many doubtless were; he was very fond, for example, of a series of pirouettes en dehors from fourth position ending first with the right arm overhead and the left to the side, next with the left arm overhead and the right to the side, finally with both arms overhead—as in Aurora's variation in Act One of *The Sleeping Beauty*.

The adagios themselves were subdivided into three parts: first a series of battements tendus of one kind or another, then the adage proper, and finally a short petit allegro coda. (This form also roughly corresponds, of course, to that of the adagio in the classical pas de deux.) They were so rich and beautiful that I used to write them down every day when I got home. He would sometimes say that he was going to repeat the adagio the next day, and command us to remember it. Needless to say I made sure that I knew it by heart when I came to class next day. Then he would demonstrate an adagio that was a perfect variation of the previous one, and at the end say, "Same exactly, yes?" "Well, not exactly," I was bold enough to say. "I change."

There was not much in the way of individual correction in his classes, though once to my astonishment he got down on his knees in front of me to correct the way I closed my foot into fifth position from battement tendu. I had developed the fault (often seen but seldom corrected nowadays) of closing the toe first and then bringing the heel down, and he carefully pushed my foot back so that heel and toe closed together in the proper way. He would not have countenanced the practice, also often seen today, of embellishing an exercise. "Why you change step?" he would have asked, or "Why you mistake?"

He was a great clown—as great as, say, Stan Laurel. His imitations of inept pupils were hilarious, if sometimes a little cruel. Talking one day before class about a dancer who was appearing with New York City Ballet, he said, "He is so fat," and puffed out his cheeks and grew fat before our eyes. One evening after class I was sitting with some other dancers at a window table in the Automat around the corner from SAB, and he passed by with Madame Nemchinova. Seeing us, he stopped and did a little scene in perfect classical mime: "If you eat too much, you will grow fat—look at me, I never eat too much, and see how slender I am." It was in the finest tradition of the Imperial Ballet.

I never saw him dance, to my sorrow—not on the stage, that is. I could never understand why Balanchine did not have him appear as Drosselmeyer in *The Nutcracker*. Outside the classroom, one knew little of him. Muriel Stuart once took me to a party for Russian Easter at the Obukhovs' apartment, in the building next door to the school, but he was in another room playing cards with the other Russian men most of the evening. However, Nemchinova showed me an album of photographs of them both in the great days.

As I have said, he had a limited command of English, though I am sure it was not as limited as he pretended. Certainly he was capable of expressing himself vividly in class. But conversation was not easy: the longest conversation I ever had with him was when I returned from England after seeing the Bolshoi in 1956; he wanted to know all about them. Otherwise, his conversation tended to be somewhat cryptic: once I was standing outside the big studio; he came up to the door, looked up at the clock, sniffed, and said to me before going in to teach his next class, "Well, Imperial School, yes?" I suppose I had some idea of what he meant—I felt all too inadequate myself to come up to the high standards he set for us, but I always hoped he knew how much

I *wanted* to be as good as he wanted us to be. For all of us who had the great good fortune to study with him, he was a link with the great tradition at its purest.

1996

Edmund Wilson (1895–1972)

AMERICA'S most influential literary critic, Edmund Wilson was also a novelist, a polemicist, and a journalist. Before he had published his magisterial *Axel's Castle* and *The Wound and the Bow*, he had written reviews and personal impressions for *The New Republic*, including the piece below—yes, he was highbrow, but he could also be low-down. He certainly enjoyed popular entertainments like Minsky's burlesque shows and, as we see below, *The Follies*.

Wilson's personal life was complicated: four wives, including the brilliant and opinionated Mary McCarthy, who gave as good as she got. He had previously (and unsuccessfully) carried the torch—for years—for poet Edna St. Vincent Millay. But nothing could interfere with his prodigious torrent of work. Among his most famous and important books are *To the Finland Station*, *The Scrolls from the Dead Sea*, and *Patriotic Gore* (about the literature of the Civil War). His journals, published posthumously, are fascinating and revelatory.

Wilson had been a close friend of F. Scott Fitzgerald's at Princeton, and, after Fitzgerald's death, he completed and saw through publication both *The Last Tycoon* and *The Crack-Up*. For many years he was the leading book critic of *The New Yorker*. And—crucial to *this* book—he laid the groundwork for what would become The Library of America.

The Finale at *The Follies*
Dress Rehearsal

IN THE dusk of the darkened house, the Tiller girls link in a swinging line, practicing their steps and humming their refrain: alone in the dark, without orchestra, their voices sound girlish and soft. *Finale!* They troop to the back. The little waitresses in lavender come off—the pale green and lavender set folds away with large leisure and ease. An incisive New York voice—Florenz Ziegfeld, who is standing at the front of the house: *You've got to get those stockings right!* Their garters are out of alignment. *There's nothing to the costume but the stockings!* A rustle of laughter. *Darn right!* A Spanish mission has been unfolded—behind it, a backdrop of bright orange sandstone and bright purple cactus. A tall girl with a flopping sombrero mounts a pedestal and begins to pose. *All right: let's go!* The Tenor takes the stage: *Although I stand here singing, A rope I should be swinging, But I've really got to get it off my chest!* The show girls—white, green, white, white, black, orange; purple, green, orange, black, white, green. *You've got two white ones together! Put somebody between them. You go over on the end, Gladys. Now, begin again!* The girl who is doing the Circassian slave in the number *The Pearl of the East*, soft-molded in a fawn-colored robe under which she is almost nude, pale hair smoothed close to her calm little head to accommodate the flooding yellow wig, moves softly down the house toward a friend. The show girls come in again: one is missing. *Who died?* She appears. *Now do that over.* In the wide space behind the backdrop, a great long-legged loose-legged girl is throwing herself about like a colt; a man holds up his gray hat for her; smiling, amiable, superb, she kicks it; then he sets out to sketch her. *Now, what's the matter with the light? Keep the light off the scenery!* The electrical lighting apparatus with military urgency is rushed to the wings. *Look out!* the smart nasal voice of the liveliest girl in a small town, *You'll get killed like that some day! I suppose you've come to make some more sketches. Yes? Well, you can't sketch them when they're leaping around like that!—I want to look before they leap.* She is gone. *I don't think she got that.—Say, do they ever get anything?* The lighting uncomfortably wavers from a warm orange to a cold pink. *Say: the girls are all right. It's the lights!—I know it: I'm explaining to the girls about the lights!*

The ponies are trooping downstairs with the pink legs and arms of the South Seas. *Come on, dumbbell!*—one reaches back for the hand of the girl behind her. A toe dancer sits rubbing her feet, strapping on her silk shoes. Another stands on one white leg, lifting the other straight up before her—hugging it, she leans against the scenery; with young intent eyes she watches the show. *You'll find it rough but gentle, Romantic, sentimental, Though I'm not a butter and egg man from the West! I would LIKE to corRAL*—The Tiller girls burst in, in a line—

orange leggings and orange sombreros. *No: they don't come in yet.* The music of the orchestra stops: their voices sound girlish and foolish. *You don't come in on the beginning of the refrain: you come in on the second half of the refrain.* He sings the verse and half the refrain. *You come in on the second half of the refrain. Now do it over!* The girl on the pedestal, bored, breaks her pose and performs a shimmy step. The toe dancer drops her upright leg and lifts the other leg up, nursing it as she watches. *No brains! no beauty! no personality! Can't sing—can't dance—can't act!—stand 'em on their heads and they're all alike—you know!—Who's fucking her?—I don't know—but she's got a built-in radio in her apartment—so she says.—You still here? Still sketching, eh? Say: the doorman has orders not to let in any more synthetic men—what I call synthetic men. I've got to go on again! So long!* Will Rogers mounts the block, about which the Tiller girls are wheeling. *Say: he's going to whirl the lasso around the whole thing. Yeah: he's clever!* They crowd the wings. Behind them waits the Negro wardrobe woman, patient with a shade of sullenness—knowing herself handsome in another kind, she bides there, blinking at all that white beauty, those open-eyed confident white girls in their paradise of bright dresses: turquoise skirts and canary cloaks, pink bodies hung with dark green leaves, tall white flowerlike stalks that burst into purple and orange—all of them excited by the costumes and the music, proud to have been picked by Ziegfeld, happy to look like the covers of popular magazines—brown-eyed, clear-skinned, straight-browed, straight-backed.—A touch of the hand in passing: *Tomorrow at 11 o'clock?* The thin girl comic, a little strained: *How long has this been going on?* The curtains close. *No: listen here! The second time you close in—the second time! The curtains close: you're turning. They open: you're still turning. They close again: you close in and you stop! Now, go through it again from the beginning!*

The Tenor takes the stage: *Although I stand here singing, A rope I should be swinging, But I've really got to get it off my chest!* The towering shapes of the show girls, blooming in their enormous sombreros: black, white, green, white, orange, white; purple, green, orange, black, white, green. *You'll find it rough but gentle, Romantic, sentimental, Though I'm not a butter and egg man from the West!* The show girls droop away. *I would LIKE to corRAL, A very merry necessary little gal!* At the signal, the Tiller girls enter: white with orange leggings and sombreros, white with purple leggings and sombreros. They make a swinging line: all together, with the strong urgent beats of their kicking they send home the strong beats of the music. *I would LIKE to corRAL!* They crack their whips all together. Will Rogers mounts the pedestal: the tall girl drops to a sitting pose, hugging one knee, hanging the other. The Tiller girls circle about the pedestal, two rings, one inside the other and turning in opposite directions. He drops his lariat down about them, making it whirl in the opposite direction to the outer circle of girls. *I would LIKE to corRAL!* The beat has mastered everything; it pounds fast in a crash of orange. For two minutes, in wheeling speed, focused in the green-gilt proscenium frame, they concentrate the pulse of the city. The bronze gilded curtains close on the girls and the turning lariat. They open: the rings are still turning. They close, as the circles draw in and halt.

March 25, 1925

Editor's Note and Acknowledgments

THE MORE than thirteen hundred pages in Robert Gottlieb's anthology *Reading Dance: A Gathering of Memoirs, Reportage, Criticism, Profiles, Interviews, and Some Uncategorizable Extras* contain almost 240 entries. The contents of this anthology overlap with three of them. Among other previous anthologies of dance writing that I admire and have learned from without raiding them are *Dance as a Theatre Art: Source Readings in Dance History from 1581 to the Present* (2nd edition, 1992), edited by Selma Jeanne Cohen and Katy Matheson; *What Is Dance? Readings in Theory and Criticism* (1983), edited by Roger Copeland and Marshall Cohen; *The Dance Experience: Readings in Dance Appreciation* (1978), edited by Myron Nadel and Constance Nadel Miller; and *The Dance Has Many Faces* (1951), edited by Walter Sorell. Among anthologies of even more specialized writing, I'd like to mention two: *Stravinsky in the Theatre* (1949; begun as a 1947 issue of *Dance Index*), edited by Minna Lederman (1896–1995), a cofounder of the League of Composers and the founding editor of the League's influential magazine *Modern Music*, which ran from 1924 to 1946 and where she edited Edwin Denby's first professional dance writings in America; and *Tributes: Celebrating Fifty Years of the New York City Ballet* (1999), edited by Christopher Ramsey, which contains many inspiring—and unexpected—literary contributions.

I learned to read with total enjoyment, thanks in large part to my father, who voiced each word aloud—including the syndication and copyright boilerplates—of every funny in both of Philadelphia's daily papers. His best performances were reserved for the artful Sunday comics, printed in glowing colors with a rotogravure process on huge, slippery sheets of special paper. My first "real" book to read to myself, inscribed to me by my mom when I was about three, was an anthology of British and American writings, offering excerpts from late nineteenth-century classics mixed up, higgledy-piggledy, with poems and songs and the Pledge of Allegiance, and I have never loved a book more. Every aspect of it was transporting: the gold-on-plum illustrated endpapers, the covers bearing characters from some of the stories inside, the aristocratic serif font, the alternation of matte paper and coated stock, the exquisite two-color and four-color pictures, the musical words and actual music on staves, the characters human and animal and fantastical. Even with the amazements of today's paper engineering, I've yet to find an anthology more magical.

There were moments when, in assembling the contents of this anthology, I was moved to remember that childhood talisman, and I tender thanks to the many collaborators who have both eased and enriched the process. Bob Gottlieb's help simply has been indispensable in every aspect of the anthology; if you like something, it's likely to be the realization of one of his enthusiasms or suggestions. The staff at Library of America has proven both eager to help and sensitive in offering their considerable skills, among them Reggie Hui (Contracts and Permissions), Trish Hoard (Managing Editor), and Brian McCarthy (Associate Publisher). Hilma Rosa, Office Manager, was a most gracious morale-builder. Geoffrey O'Brien, retiring as Editor-in-Chief, suggested a number of sterling entries. And, of course, my thanks to Max Rudin, head honcho.

Insofar as I could, I've resisted the impulse to impose a homogenous style of punctuation and other copyediting issues on these essays and poems: In keeping with Library of America's editorial ideals, in most instances the writings are published here as they appear in the sources where I found them. For example, Emily Dickinson is given her spelling of "opon" for the word most English-speaking readers know as "upon." There were some other changes. In places where the absence of a comma changes the meaning of a passage, and I'm aware of the intended meaning, I've put in the comma. In one contribution, where a dead author had a disfiguring mistake of fact in the original, I removed the phrase; and in one case where the living author had a mistake of fact in an essay, I consulted with the person about correcting the mistake and then did so, as I'd want an editor to do on my behalf. In several essays, the respective authors requested individual word changes or very brief revisions, and I made those changes for them.

The informed and devoted staffs of several libraries made it possible for me to consider nearly four centuries of writing on American dance: the Library of Congress; the Jerome Robbins Dance Division of the New York Public Library for the Performing Arts at Lincoln Center (my thanks most especially to Linda Murray, Jan Schmidt, Arlene Yu, Alice Standin, Daisy Pommer, Tanisha Jones, and Charles Perrier); the Butler Library of Columbia University (thanks especially to Mary Cargill); the Barnard College Library; the Manuscripts and Archives Division of the Stephen A. Schwarzman Building of the New York Public Library, Astor, Lenox and Tilden Foundations; and the Margaret Herrick Library of the Academy of Motion Picture Arts and Sciences (thanks especially to Kristine Krueger). Leslie Getz and Don McDonagh generously opened their extensive personal dance library to me. Suzannah Friscia, Rhitu Risal, and Ariel Rivkin, all Barnard undergraduates at the time, provided much-appreciated volunteer secretarial help.

I also am deeply grateful for and to all the friends and colleagues with whom I've discussed this over the years and who contributed general ideas, fact-checking assistance, encouragement, and/or nominations of works for consideration. Among them are Miriam Arsham, Ansie Silverman Baird, the late Jean-Claude Baker, Lynn Matlock Brooks, Peter Canby, John Canemaker, the late Mary Cochran, Martin Steven Cohen, Bonnie Costello, Nancy Vreeland Dalva, Renee E. D'Aoust, George Dorris, Jennifer Dunning, Juan José Escalante of the José Limón Foundation, Irving Feldman, Lynn Garafola, Beth Genné, Mary Meeker Gesek, Mildred Goldczer, Gail and Zvi Golod, Robert Greskovic, the late Dennis Grunes, Sally Hess, Emily Hite, Marvin Hoshino, Jock Ireland, Peter Kayafas, Yuriko Kikuchi, Richard Kostelanetz, Russell Lee, Patricia Lent and Jennifer Goggans of the Merce Cunningham Trust, Wendy Lesser, Laura Leivick, Yaël Tamar Lewin, Janet and Irwin Light, Phillip Lopate, Alastair Macaulay, Elizabeth Macklin, Sara Swan Miller and Marty Miller, Margaret Morrison, the late Patrick O'Connor, Erin Overbye, Claudia Roth Pierpont, Alexander Rannie, Susan Reiter, Marta Renzi, Nancy Reynolds, Janice Ross, Sharon Skeel, Elizabeth Spires, Evert Sprinchorn, John Szwed, Peter Townsend, Sandra Velasquez, Barbara Muhs Walker, Martha Ullman West, Dee and Richard Wilson, and Mary Jane Fukushima Yagi and Robert Yagi. I have no thank-you sufficiently encompassing to acknowledge the limitless support of Ariel Nikiya Cohen.

Merci beaucoup to William Ausman for alerting us to Balanchine's remarks, from 1952, in Serge Lido's French-and-English album.

A garden of gratitude to individuals who personally gave or helped secure permissions to include some of the texts: Barbara Horgan (George Balanchine), Christopher Pennington (Jerome Robbins), William Murray and Nancy Umanoff (Mark Morris), Robert Cornfield (Edwin Denby), Nicholas Jenkins (W. H. Auden, Lincoln Kirstein), Valerie Barnes (Clive Barnes), Irwin Tobias (Tobi Tobias), Ingrid Nyeboe (Jill Johnston), and Nancy Balliett (Whitney Balliett).

I apologize if anyone who should have been remembered here has escaped mention.

—Mindy Aloff

Acknowledgments for Assistance with Photos

FIRST, OF COURSE, to the New York Public Library for the Performing Arts at Lincoln Center, under the adorable autocracy of Jacqueline Davis. Then to Linda Murray, the extraordinarily capable and benign chief of the library's Jerome Robbins Dance Division, the prime source for all dance-related scholarship: we dance critics, historians, and scholars could not proceed without it. And within the Dance Division, to Phil Karg, who gets things done not only effectively but amiably, as if we weren't driving him crazy. And to Jeremy Megraw in the Billy Rose Theater Division, who's both patient and fun.

Thanks to Photofest (and Derek Davidson), as always responsive and professional beyond the call of duty. Thanks to Graydon Carter for a crucial intervention, and to Ivan Shaw, Courtney Ercolino, and Allison Ingram at Condé Nast for their cooperation and generosity. Heartfelt gratitude to Annie Leibovitz for her superb portrait of Michael Jackson.

Thanks to Sothebys' Joanna Ling for her cooperation over the Cecil Beaton portrait of the Ballet Theatre artistic committee. Thanks to Ellen Sorrin and the New York City Ballet archive for helping with the Tanaquil Le Clercq portrait of George Balanchine and Lincoln Kirstein. Thanks to Tom Patrick at the Paul Taylor Dance Company and Christopher Zunner at Alvin Ailey, and to Craig Highberger and the Jack Mitchell estate. Warm thanks to Twyla Tharp for cutting to the quick and making things painless, and to James Klosty for his unique shot of Merce Cunningham, Carolyn Brown, and John Cage. Thanks to Richard Overstreet and Gul Duzyol for untangling our dealings with the SIPA agency in Paris over Lido's beautiful picture of Martha Graham, Stuart Hodes, and Matt Turney. And thanks to whoever else pitched in along the way. Dealing with permissions takes a village!

—Robert Gottlieb

Sources and Permissions

ber 12, 1922, reprinted in *O My Land, My Friends: The Selected Letters of Hart Crane*, eds. Langdon Hammer and Brom Weber (New York: Four Walls Eight Windows, 1997). Copyright © 1997 by the Estate of Hart Crane.

Arlene Croce, "Dance in Film," *Afterimages* (New York: Alfred A. Knopf, 1977). Copyright © 1977 by Arlene Croce. "Adagio and Allegro," *Writing in the Dark, Dancing in* The New Yorker: *An Arlene Croce Reader* (New York: Farrar, Straus and Giroux, 2000), originally published in different versions in *The New Yorker*, January 30, 1978, and in *Going to the Dance* (New York: Alfred A. Knopf, 1982). Copyright © 2000 by Arlene Croce. "Edwin Denby," *Sight Lines* (New York: Alfred A. Knopf, 1987); Part 1 combines portions of articles originally published in *Dance Magazine* and *Harper's* with the text of a tribute delivered at the New York Public Library for the Performing Arts at Lincoln Center. Copyright © 1987 by Arlene Croce. Used by permission of the author.

Merce Cunningham, "The Function of a Technique for Dance," *The Dance Has Many Faces*, ed. Walter Sorell (New York: World Publishing Co., 1951). Copyright © 1951 by Merce Cunningham. Used by permission of the Merce Cunningham Trust.

Nancy Dalva, "Letter from Manhattan," *The Brooklyn Rail*, June 3, 2011. Used by permission of the author.

Agnes de Mille, "La Argentina," *Dance to the Piper* (Boston: Atlantic Little, Brown, 1952). Copyright © 1952, 1980 by Agnes de Mille. "Rhythm In My Blood," *And Promenade Home* (Boston: Atlantic Little, Brown, 1956). Copyright © 1956, 1984 by Agnes de Mille. Used by permission of Harold Ober Associates Incorporated.

Edwin Denby, "Flight of the Dancer," *Mademoiselle*, October 1943, reprinted in *Dance Writings and Poetry*, ed. Robert Cornfield (New Haven, CT: Yale University Press, 1998). Copyright © 1998 by Rudolph and Yvonne Burckhardt. "A Briefing in American Ballet," *Kenyon Review*, Autumn 1948, reprinted in *Dance Writings*, eds. Robert Cornfield and William MacKay (New York: Alfred A. Knopf, 1986). Copyright © 1986 by Rudolph and Yvonne Burckhardt. "Against Meaning in Ballet," *Ballet*, March 1949, reprinted in *Dance Writings and Poetry*, ed. Robert Cornfield (New Haven, CT: Yale University Press, 1998). Copyright © 1998 by Rudolph and Yvonne Burckhardt. Used by permission of the Estate of Edwin Denby.

Charles Dickens, "Dancing at Five Points," *American Notes for General Circulation* (London: Chapman & Hall, 1842).

Emily Dickinson, "I cannot dance upon my Toes," *The Poems of Emily Dickinson: Reading Edition*, ed. R. W. Franklin (Cambridge, MA: The Belknap Press of Harvard University Press, 2005). Copyright © 1951, 1955, 1998, 1999 by the President and Fellows of Harvard College, renewed 1979, 1983 by the President and Fellows of Harvard College. Copyright © 1914, 1918, 1919, 1924, 1929, 1930, 1932, 1935, 1937, 1942 by Martha Dickinson Bianchi. Copyright © 1952, 1957, 1958, 1963, 1965 by Mary L. Hampson. Used by permission.

Isadora Duncan, "The Dance of the Future," *The Dance of the Future* (Leipzig: Eugen Diederichs, 1903).

Katherine Dunham, "Thesis Turned Broadway," *California Arts and Architecture*, August 1941, reprinted in *Kaiso!: Writings by and about Katherine Dunham*, eds. VèVè A. Clark and Sara E. Johnson (Madison: University of Wisconsin Press, 2005). Copyright © 2005 by Katherine Dunham. Used by permission of the Estate of Katherine Dunham.

John Durang, "The Greatest Dancer in America," *The Memoir of John Durang: American Actor 1785–1816*, ed. Alan S. Downer (Pittsburgh: University of Pittsburgh Press, 1966). Copyright © 1966 by the University of Pittsburgh Press. Used by permission of the University of Pittsburgh Press.

Ralph Waldo Emerson, "On Fanny Elssler," October 16, 1841, *Selected Journals 1841–1877*, ed. Lawrence Rosenwald (New York: Library of America, 2010), www.loa.org. Copyright © 2010 by Literary Classics of the United States, Inc.

Barbara Milberg Fisher, "Nightmare in Copenhagen," *In Balanchine's Company: A Dancer's Memoir* (Middletown, CT: Wesleyan University

Jill Johnston, "Lucidly Defined," *The Village Voice*, October 14, 1965, reprinted in *Marmalade Me* (New York: Dutton, 1971). Copyright © 1971 by Jill Johnston. Used by permission of Dutton, an imprint of Penguin Publishing Group, a division of Penguin Random House LLC.

Deborah Jowitt, "On *Afternoon of a Faun*," *Jerome Robbins: His Life, His Theater, His Dance* (New York: Simon & Schuster, 2004). Copyright © 2004 by Deborah Jowitt. "Two New Ballets at NYCB Glance Backward with Trick Glasses," *The Village Voice*, May 4, 2010. Copyright © 2010 by Deborah Jowitt. Used by permission of the author.

Elizabeth Kendall, "Ragtime," *Where She Danced* (New York: Alfred A. Knopf, 1979). Copyright © 1979 by Elizabeth Kendall. Used by permission of the author.

Allegra Kent, "Memories of Madame Karinska," *Dance Magazine*, October 2003. Copyright © 2003 by Allegra Kent. Used by permission of the author.

Lincoln Kirstein, "The Music Hall, Revues, the Movies," *The Nation*, March 14, 1934. "Martha Graham," *Ballet: Bias and Belief: Three Pamphlets Collected and Other Dance Writings of Lincoln Kirstein* (New York: Dance Horizons, 1983), originally published in *Martha Graham*, ed. Merle Armitage (Los Angeles: M. Armitage, 1937). "Popular Style in American Dancing," *The Nation*, April 16, 1938. "Balanchine and the Waltz," *Vienna Waltzes*, Gala Preview Program, 1977. Writings by Lincoln Kirstein are copyright © The New York Public Library (Astor, Lenox and Tilden Foundations). Used by permission.

Anna Kisselgoff, "Introduction to *Bronislava Nijinska: Early Memoirs*," *Bronislava Nijinska: Early Memoirs* (New York: Holt, Rinehart and Winston, 1981). Copyright © 1981 by Anna Kisselgoff. Used by permission of the author.

Laura Leivick, "Miss Brodie's Swan," *The Threepenny Review*, no. 4, Winter 1981. Copyright © 1981 by Laura Leivick. Used by permission of the author.

Paul Taylor, "Black Mountain, Hell's Kitchen, and Broadway," *Private Domain: An Autobiography* (New York: Alfred A. Knopf, 1987). Copyright © 1987 by Paul Taylor. Used by permission of the author.

Walter Terry, "Ballet on Ice," *New York Herald Tribune*, October 6, 1940. "*Fantasia's* Dances," *New York Herald Tribune*, November 24, 1940, reprinted in *I Was There: Selected Dance Reviews* (New York: Marcel Dekker, 1979).

Twyla Tharp, "(from) *Push Comes to Shove*," *Push Comes to Shove* (New York: Bantam, 1992). Copyright © 1992 by Twyla Tharp. Used by permission of the author.

Tobi Tobias, "Mining the Past," *Arts Journal*, January 14, 2011. Copyright © 2011 by Tobi Tobias. Used by permission.

John Updike, "Genial, Kinetic Gene Kelly," *The New Yorker*, March 21, 1994, reprinted in *More Matter: Essays and Criticism* (New York: Alfred A. Knopf, 1999). Copyright © 1999 by John Updike. Used by permission of Alfred A. Knopf, an imprint of the Knopf Doubleday Publishing Group, a division of Penguin Random House LLC, and Penguin Books Ltd. All rights reserved.

Carl Van Vechten, "Maud Allan in Greek Dances," *The New York Times*, January 21, 1910. "The Lindy Hop," *Parties* (New York: Alfred A. Knopf, 1930), reprinted in *The Dance Writings of Carl Van Vechten*, ed. Paul Padgette (New York: Dance Horizons, 1974). "Eloquent Alvin Ailey," *Dance 62*, 1962, reprinted in *The Dance Writings of Carl Van Vechten*, ed. Paul Padgette (New York: Dance Horizons, 1974). Writings by Carl Van Vechten © by The Van Vechten Trust. Used by permission.

David Vaughan, "(from) Beautifully Dance: Anatole Obukhov," *Ballet Review*, vol. 24, no. 4, Winter 1996. Copyright © 1996 by David Vaughan. Used by permission of the author.

Edmund Wilson, "The Finale at the Follies: *Dress Rehearsal*," *The New Republic*, March 25, 1925, reprinted in *The Shores of Light: A Liter-*

ary Chronicle of the Twenties and Thirties (New York: Farrar, Straus & Young, 1952) and in *The American Earthquake* (New York: Farrar, Straus and Giroux, 1958). Copyright © 1958 by Edmund Wilson, renewed 1986 by Helen Miranda Wilson. Used by permission of Farrar, Straus and Giroux, and The Wylie Agency LLC.

Photographs

Isadora Duncan: Jerome Robbins Dance Division, the New York Public Library for the Performing Arts.

Bill Robinson: George Hurrell/Vanity Fair © Condé Nast.

Ginger Rogers and Fred Astaire: © RKO/Photofest.

Merce Cunningham and Carolyn Brown: © James Klosty.

Martha Graham, Matt Turney, and Stuart Hodes: From *Ballet: Serge Lido IV.* © Serge Lido/SIPA Press. Jerome Robbins Dance Division, the New York Public Library for the Performing Arts.

Members of the Artistic Committee of Ballet Theatre: © Cecil Beaton Studio Archive. Jerome Robbins Dance Division, the New York Public Library for the Performing Arts.

George Balanchine and Lincoln Kirstein: Courtesy of New York City Ballet Archives, the Tanaquil Le Clercq Collection. BALANCHINE is a Trademark of The George Balanchine Trust. Jerome Robbins Dance Division, the New York Public Library for the Performing Arts.

Alvin Ailey: © Alvin Ailey Dance Foundation, Inc. and the Smithsonian Institution. Collection of the Smithsonian National Museum of African American History and Culture. Photography by Jack Mitchell. All rights reserved.

Paul Taylor: © Jack Mitchell.

Twyla Tharp: © Greg Gorman.

Suzanne Farrell: © Billy Rose Theatre Division, the New York Public Library for the Performing Arts.

Michael Jackson: © Annie Leibovitz.

Index

Fokine, 151–55; jazz, 522–25; Jerome Robbins's *Afternoon of a Faun*, 394–99; Jerome Robbins's *Watermill*, 278–80; leaps in, 219–23; by Les Ballets Trockadero, 12–15; Maria Tallchief dancing, 517–20; meaning in, 235–40; Mikhail Baryshnikov's tribute to George Balanchine, 83–87; New York City Ballet in Copenhagen, 270–77; performed by Fanny Elssler, 268–69; performed by Patricia McBride, 7–9; psychological, 137–40, 143; at Radio City Music Hall, 106–12; at Roxy Theater, 466–69; Royal Ballet's *Sleeping Beauty*, 113–24; Ruthanna Boris's memories of George Balanchine, 99–103; at School of American Ballet, 600–604; Vaslav Nijinsky dancing, 489–95; W. H. Auden on *The Nutcracker*, 27–31; women in, 48–49

Ballet (magazine), 189
Ballet Imperial (ballet), 18–19, 86
Ballet International, 227
Ballet Memphis, 511
Ballet National du Sénégal, 339
Ballet Review, 159, 181–82, 308, 496, 532
Ballet Russe de Monte Carlo, 16, 99–100, 151–56, 204, 224–29, 231, 234, 361, 396, 421–23, 437–39, 442, 445–46, 466, 468, 482, 488, 490, 526, 544–47, 551, 572
Ballets 1933, Les, 190, 432
Ballet Society, 86, 231, 233–34, 270, 284, 294, 419, 497, 500, 507
Ballets Trockadero de Monte Carlo, Les, 12–15, 25
Ballets: U.S.A., 270, 522, 525
Ballet Theatre, 433, 519, 521
Ballet Today, 16
Balliett, Whitney, 50–52
Balling-the-Jack, 372, 376
Ballo della Regina (ballet), 178–79, 461
Ballroom dancing, 60, 72, 162, 320–32, 407–12, 431, 435, 459, 461, 514–15
Bal Nègre (revue), 258
Balustrade (ballet), 307
Bamboula, 129–32
Bando Tamasaburo V, 11
Band Wagon, The (film), 169–70, 513

Band Wagon, The (musical), 78–79
Banjo (dance), 555
Barbe-bleu, La (spectacle), xxiii
Barber, Samuel, 341, 598; *Adagio for Strings*, 334
Barkleys of Broadway, The (film), 169
Barnes, Clive, xxiii, 53–65, 343
Barnett, Lincoln, 66–82
Baronova, Irina, 186, 226, 572
Barrett, Maude, 194
Barrio, Soledad, 461
Barry and Coe, 421
Barrymore, John, 173, 588
Barthelmess, Richard, 163
Barton, Jim, 75
Baryshnikov, Mikhail, 83–87, 278, 288, 294, 308, 339, 474, 502, 542–43, 575–77
Baryshnikov Arts Center, 83, 203, 462
Basie, Count, 50–51
Bassae, Antony, 13
Batsheva Dance Company, 567
Baum, Morton, 433–34
Baxter, Skippy, 570
Bayadère, La (ballet), 24, 282
Beard, Dick, 234
Beatty, Talley, 258
Beau Danube, Le (ballet), 465
Beaumont, Cyril, 30, 136, 143
Beaux (ballet), 336–37
Beaux Arts Club, 405, 407
Bebop, 4, 6, 376–77
Beck, Hans, 23
Bedini, Jean, 329
Beethoven, Ludwig van, 64, 157, 213, 248, 297, 435, 573, 594
Beggar's Dance (dance), 353–54
Begging Dance, 146
Belafonte, Harry, 597
Bell, Isaiah, 344–45
Belova, Valentina, 437
Bennington Festival, 450
Benny, Jack, 161, 290
Benoît, Robert, 467, 491
Beregi, Oszkár, 296
Berg, Alban, 436
Berg, Gene, 570
Berkeley, Busby, 111, 165–67, 176, 422, 474
Berlin, Irving, 406
Berman, Eugene, 101, 230–31
Berman, Pandro, 79–80